The Laws of the Roman People

The Laws of the Roman People

PUBLIC LAW IN THE EXPANSION AND DECLINE OF THE ROMAN REPUBLIC

Callie Williamson

UNIVERSITY OF MICHIGAN PRESS
Ann Arbor

First paperback edition 2016

Published in the United States of America by
The University of Michigan Press
Manufactured in the United States of America
♾ Printed on acid-free paper

2019 2018 2017 2016 7 6 5 4

A CIP catalog record for this book is available from the British Library.

Library of Congress Cataloging-in-Publication Data

Williamson, Callie.
The laws of the Roman people : public law in the expansion and decline of the Roman Republic / Callie Williamson.
p. cm.
Includes index.
ISBN 0-472-11053-5 (cloth : alk. paper)
1. Public law (Roman law)
2. Rome—Politics and government. I. Title.
KJA2850.W55 2004 2004008128
342.45'632—dc22

ISBN13 978-0-472-11053-7 (cloth)
ISBN13 978-0-472-02542-8 (electronic)
ISBN 978-0-472-03661-5 (pbk. : acid-free paper)

THIS BOOK IS FOR

Olwen Callie Blessing

Preface

IN 91, THE Italian allies of Rome broke away and formed a federation they named Italia.[1] The basis for the most serious revolt ever to shake the Roman state was the strident desire on the part of the allies, who now made up the bulk of the Roman army, for equal standing with the Romans or the destruction of Rome.[2] Led by the Samnites and Marsi, the Italian federation included most of the Oscan-speaking peoples of central and southern Italy. While other allies did not join them—including most Latins and Etruscans, the two largest groups in Italy after the Romans, as well as the Umbrians, Greeks, and Bruttians—their loyalties were nonetheless equivocal.[3] At the Paelignian town of Corfinium, situated high in the central Apennines, the allies established a federal center, called Italica, on the model of Rome.[4] Corfinium became the site of a federal mint, the central meeting place of a Senate drawn from elite members of the different tribal states, and the muster point for the Italian legions called up to fight the Romans. A brief and bloody war ensued that ended formally for most participants only after the Romans, in 90, called together in a voting assembly to consider a proposal of law, agreed as a people to a major redirection of their goals on granting citizenship. Loyal allies would henceforth be brought into the Roman state as full citizens. By the end of 89, Italia was dissolved.

Together the revolt by Rome's Italian allies and the outcome of the Roman people's prompt decision to accept all the allies as Romans tell us much about the remarkable cohesion the Romans had achieved throughout Italy by the first century. In terms of lost lives and property, the war, known to contemporaries as the Italian War or the Social War (*bellum Italicum, bellum sociorum*), was the most devastating ever experienced in Italy.[5] It was in fact a civil war, despite essential cultural, political, and linguistic differences separating many of the participants, in particular the Oscan-speaking peoples, from the Romans. Such differences notwithstanding, it was a war for inclusion.[6] The ferocity of all the combatants reveals firm agreement among the peoples of Italy about the common way of life they had come to share in the course of conquering the lands rimming the Mediterranean Sea. How such a single imperial system was made possible and how the collective voice of the Roman people expressed in a public lawmaking assembly came to have sufficient force across Italy to help bring to an end a bitter war forms the quest of this book.

The story of the expansion of Rome from a small cluster of settlements on the Tiber River in central Italy to a vast empire covering most of the known Mediterranean world has long fascinated historians. Beginning with the subjugation of Italy in the fourth century, the Romans by the end of the first century had conquered an empire stretching from the Sahara Desert to the North Sea, from Spain to Syria. Facilitating this unprecedented territorial expansion was the gradual amalgamation of Romans and Italians as they adjusted to each other in the process of creating a Roman state in Italy and fighting shoulder-to-shoulder as world conquerors.

An integral part of Roman expansion is the momentous changes it brought in the traditional structures and customary patterns of life for Romans and Italians alike over the period between the fourth and first centuries. Initially forced to accommodate themselves to the conditions of Roman rule in Italy, Romans and Italians soon faced the consequences of successful overseas conquests as well. An influx of capital from successful trade and war promoted the urban development of Italy. The access to land resources in Italy was, for many people, reduced over time because of the growing number of wealthy Romans and Italians investing in land. The concentration of land in relatively few hands was accompanied by agricultural changes and the transformation of the labor force, with thousands of imported slaves working on capital-generating plantations and ranches, replacing the free herders and farmers of subsistence operations. Roman and Italian men became more extensively involved in military service. Between 200 and 44, the beginning of Rome's expansion into the Greek East and the end of the "free" Republic marked by the assassination of C. Julius Caesar, at least 10 percent and sometimes as high as 60 percent of the male population of Italy, ages seventeen to forty-five, was regularly engaged in military service for increasingly long periods of service.[7] As a result primarily of extending citizenship to Italians, Rome experienced a general citizen population increase over the period of greatest expansion, from an estimated half a million Roman inhabitants in 340 to 13.5 million Romans by 28.[8] The accumulated impact of these developments was overwhelming and resulted finally in the emergence of a Roman emperor. But time and again during the course of expansion the Romans surmounted crises and upheaval to create a Roman state in Italy at the core of one of the largest and most stable empires in the ancient world.

Few explanations for Roman expansion to date address the unity underlying Rome's initial successful expansion and consolidation throughout Italy, especially in the most dynamic period of growth between roughly 350 and 44. In expanding across Italy, the Romans encountered and eventually absorbed a much larger population of Italian peoples with distinctive languages and customs.[9] For all involved, Roman conquest must have entailed considerable disruption for individuals and communities. How did Romans resolve the inevitable conflicts accompanying the conquest of Italy in order both to survive and to expand further? Why did the vast population of Italy so readily lend its support and agreement to the wrenching social changes brought about by this expansion? What enabled Rome, alone among ancient Mediterranean societies, to expand to such unprecedented size and yet to maintain for so long the stability of its small-scale origins?

More than one hundred years after the Romans had first embarked on their world conquest, the Greek Polybius identified institutional features of a unique Roman character—namely, the Roman political and military systems—as crucial factors in Roman success. Polybius was the first historian to seriously examine the bases of Roman expansion but by no means was the last. In the present century, scholars have sometimes assumed that Roman success rested on overwhelming force, turned against the peoples of Italy, who were then bound to contribute troops to conquering Roman armies. By force of Roman arms, Italy became a Roman state from which the Romans, joined now by reluctant Italian allies, launched external campaigns of military conquest.[10] Scholars have also assumed that the comradeship of arms provided a unifying bond of shared self-interest among the Roman and Italian fighting men of Italy, ensuring their willing cooperation in successful wars of conquest.[11] Or the hierarchic ties of dependency believed to be characteristic of a Roman patronage system linked Roman political leaders, that is, elected officeholders and senators, and the soldiers and citizens of Rome in common political and military endeavors. Or again, the Greek presence in Italy introduced a set of unique

Greek ideas about urban life and community at the top levels of society that, taken up by the Romans and disseminated throughout Italy in a process of Hellenization, provided the cohesive force drawing together all the peoples of Italy. This Roman "civilizing mission," as Michael Rostovtseff called it, fueled by Greek ideas, eventually brought a common cultural veneer to the entire world empire the Romans created. While these notions are clearly part of any adequate explanation of Roman achievements, they assume rather than explain the resolution of conflict essential for the emergence of the level of accommodation achieved by the Romans throughout Italy. If we accept them as explanations for the remarkable success of the Romans we are left with the question as to why any or all of them did not work in a similar fashion for other Mediterranean societies. What was unique about Roman expansion?

This study examines the role of public law in enabling the Romans to confront the otherwise insurmountable challenges of expansion across Italy, especially the absorption of conquered peoples, during the period from roughly 350 to 44. For centuries, the Romans developed a community consensus on the passage of law relating to the most critical aspects of their society in a public process concluded in the voting assemblies of Rome. The results of these decisions were the *leges* and *plebiscita*—called variously in English statutes, enactments, positive laws, or public laws—that formed a part of the larger body of decisions generated by all of Rome's governing institutions (the assemblies, the Roman Senate, and elected officials) and also included Senate decrees (*senatus consulta*) and magistrates' edicts (*edicta*). Although the larger body of decisions can be described collectively as "public law," in this study I use the term "public law" to refer specifically to leges and plebiscita. In contrast to the decrees of the Roman Senate, decided and formulated following discussions open only to members of that select body, and in contrast to the pronouncements of magistrates, made after consultation with the Senate or an informal council of senatorial advisors, the leges and plebiscita required the formal participation of the Roman people in an elaborate public event launched by the formal announcement (*promulgatio*) of a public law proposal or query (*rogatio*) and concluded weeks later by the voting assembly's decision to accept or reject the proposal as law. And in contrast to the citizen events, which were part of a regular calendar of public occurrences falling on fixed days in fixed months (the regular annual festivals; the electoral assemblies every July, after the Games of Apollo, when the people met to elect all high- and low-ranking officials in the centuriate and tribal assemblies; the formal military levies in January; and the quinquennial census), Rome's lawmaking meetings and assemblies were initiated irregularly by tribunes, consuls, praetors, and sometimes other officials whenever they had bills to promulgate requiring the approval of the Roman people at large. In theory this could happen anytime throughout the year on days when such meetings were legally and religiously permissible. In practice the assemblies met to enact law on what appears to the modern eye to be a random basis.[12]

While the issues addressed in public law proposals touched almost every aspect of Roman life, and some issues appear inconsequential to modern eyes, many were obviously of utmost importance in facilitating Roman growth and expansion. In 367, Roman voters accepted the "Licinian-Sextian Rogations" as law, which broadened access to the political leadership on the part of members of wealthy plebeian clans and increased access to land resources for all members of the majority population. With this decision, the threatened dissolution of the Roman citizen body was averted. During the Second Punic War, between 218 and 201, the Roman people considered an unprecedented number of proposals modifying the rules pertaining to political and military leadership to facilitate Rome's survival during her most serious military crisis to date. In 133, when access to land resources on the part of the majority population of Italy was severely reduced, Romans, Latins, and Italians converged on Rome to ensure the voters' acceptance of the land redistribution proposal of Ti. Sempronius Gracchus. In 90, the decision of the Roman people, convened in a lawmaking assembly, to grant Roman citizenship to all the inhabitants of Italy brought an effective end to the Italian War between Rome and her Italian allies, a conflict that threatened the existence of the Roman state even more than the Second Punic War. The study of public law as a process to discern the collective voice of Romans, critical to the expansion and survival of Roman society as we know it, has much to recommend it.

To date, however, the diversity of the issues presented to Roman assemblies over the entire period of the Republic have proven an almost impenetrable hedge to any broad interpretation of the achievements of public law.[13] Modern studies that offer the most profound insights into Roman public law generally focus on the regulatory or normative outcome of specific laws at the expense of the nuances of the public lawmaking process through which all public laws passed. As a consequence, they ignore the extent to which this process was linked to society and its significance in its contemporary Roman setting. Such is the case with *Roman Statutes*, a collaborative effort by Roman historians, epigraphers, and Roman legal specialists.[14] But the social historian wonders also why the Romans resorted to public lawmaking assemblies on the occasions identified previously and what role public law played in Roman society to explain why political leaders and Roman voters turned to lawmaking assemblies at critical junctures in Roman history. My goal is to put the meticulous array of ancient testimony collected in such essential works as *Roman Statutes* into context in an endeavor to explain what kind of society would produce law in the particular way that the Romans did in public assemblies.

Similarly, the complicated political nature of the lawmaking process in the Late Republic obscures many of its customary functions, as well as its social and cultural underpinnings. Public lawmaking in the years between 91 and 44 was highly politicized, the lawmaking arena increasingly used by individual politicians to reach goals set by personal ambitions. Unfortunately, key aspects of public lawmaking, such as tribal voting units and voter participation, are commonly interpreted, in this and other periods, solely in light of this reality. Exploiting such ready-to-hand organizations as collegia and sodalitates, with the aid of bribery or patronage, political leaders mobilized voters by appealing to their self-interest to support their own proposals or to defeat the proposals of political opponents. The discerning Lily Ross Taylor, for instance, whose *Party Politics in the Age of Caesar* provides the classic statement of the politicized nature of lawmaking, also provides in *The Voting Districts of the Roman Republic* an interpretation of voting units that is shaped by this understanding.[15] Missing is a sense of the importance of public law and the lawmaking process to the group ultimately responsible for its generation, the Roman people.

The thesis of this study, very simply, is that public lawmaking was a central process in facilitating the development of Roman society. For almost two hundred years after the beginnings of Roman expansion in Italy, the Romans and conquered Italian peoples labored to develop a tolerable accommodation to each other. In this mutual accommodation, public lawmaking played a pivotal role. Overall, throughout the course of development of a pan-Italian imperial system, from roughly the fourth century to the early first century, innumerable conflicts were resolved, most often by the Roman Senate or a wide variety of elite officeholders. But throughout the course of the expansion as well, Roman political leaders also involved the entire citizenry in resolving critical issues by proposing binding remedies to public lawmaking assemblies. Underlying the effectiveness of this public process was a certain level of required knowledge about Roman social structures and the complicated relationships among them, about Roman social and political groupings and their reciprocal responsibilities, and about the role of oratory in allowing political leaders to reflect the will and manage the emotions of the Roman people. Likewise, participants in the lawmaking process had to know the religious meaning of the events unfolding in lawmaking assemblies. The result was the creation of a Roman state in Italy that successfully incorporated a large and diverse population.

Any effort to deal with public lawmaking must also deal with a number of perplexing paradoxes. Public lawmaking assemblies were convened only in Rome even after the Romans had expanded across Italy and established citizen settlements at great distances from the city. The growth in scale of the Roman citizen population over my period of interest, from roughly 150,000 voting males in 338 to perhaps one million by 44, deepens the mystery. Public lawmaking assemblies required the participation and approval of the Roman people, yet the most stringent restrictions were associated with the process of public approval. Public lawmaking assemblies lasted for more than half a millennium, yet the significance of the lawmaking process changed almost overnight during the reign of the first emperor, Augustus. In brief, any effort to focus on public lawmaking assemblies is complicated by the very nature of the phenomenon. Public law emerged out of an extraordinarily complex structure of decision making on which much work remains to be done if we are to understand the context within which the phenomenon took place. The present effort represents a first step.

An effective history of Rome's most fundamental institutions appears to demand a total history of all of Rome, precisely because of the degree to which they were embedded in Roman society. While such a history has yet to be written, and an historian concentrating on a specific topic must set some limits on his or her investigation, it is essential to travel a certain distance into the Roman historical underbrush to understand the emergence and functions of any basic institution. This is particularly true in the case of public lawmaking assemblies that appear to be associated with the resolution of the most important of the innumerable conflicts that the drive across Italy and the Mediterranean region must of necessity have involved. A corollary to the central position of assemblies in Roman society is the extent to which their end products were so widely accepted and the extent to which all Romans, new and old, participated in the process of public lawmaking for so many centuries. The depth of involvement in public lawmaking by individuals from across all of Italy, presumed by the level of participation visible in many reported lawmaking assemblies, stands as one of the best indices of the successful Roman absorption of conquered lands and their peoples. An understanding of public lawmaking assemblies, therefore, requires that we examine the Roman expansion across Italy, paying particular attention to the manner in which great numbers of newcomers acquired Roman ways.

The book is divided into three parts. Part 1 explores the complexity of the public lawmaking process and its uses in an effort to identify what needs to be explained about the practice. Chapter 1 presents the function and meaning of lawmaking, based on a compilation of all reported public law proposals and enacted laws and a detailed case study of public lawmaking during the period of the Second Punic War, and provides an essential framework for the entire study. Chapter 2 examines the inner workings of public lawmaking sessions in the mid-first century, when we best know them, and the public presentation of the law by Rome's political leaders. An analysis of a set of public orations, *De Lege Agraria*, by M. Tullius Cicero addressing the merits of a public law proposal underscores the importance of the public arena of lawmaking to aspiring and ascendant politicians. Equally important, Cicero's concern for substance and process shows that the masses of voters still displayed the traditional respect for public lawmaking that gave the process its universal authority, even when the Republic was on the wane. The degree to which lawmaking assemblies were embedded in Roman life becomes obvious in chapter 3 in an analysis of the central role of the Roman people in making legitimate law. In view of the size and wide scattering of the citizen population as well as the intricate procedural and factual knowledge required to vote, an explanation of the participation by Roman voters in lawmaking assemblies is vital. Romans voted in lawmaking assemblies not as individuals but as members of a group, most frequently a tribe. A majority of tribes, therefore, not citizens, gave voice to the sovereign will of the Roman people. The expression of consensus through group action was a given. But the legitimization of a proposal of law was the result not merely of receiving a certain number of votes but of observing various rituals and procedures during the assembly at which the law had been accepted by the majority of Roman tribes. Only when everything was done correctly did the proposal become law, validated by its passage through the lawmaking assembly and enforced throughout Roman lands by virtue of the authority of that process. The viability of the process rested at all times on the deeply held expectations about ritual and procedure, which permeated all levels of society. These expectations helped create a resilient system that diffused potential lawmaking authority among hundreds of members of the Roman elite and involved the Roman people, through their tribes, in a complicated expression of the fundamental power of the entire society.

Part 2 focuses on society at large to identify the conditions that encouraged the widespread acceptance of public lawmaking as the Romans conquered Italy. Only infrequently in this initial investigation is there direct evidence of the intervention of public lawmaking assemblies during the Roman expansion across Italy. But when we do find such evidence, the kind of proposals that were debated in public lawmaking sessions and the results of such sessions in developing a community consensus in resolving problems often appear pivotal in making the expansion possible—the conquest of Italian peoples, the absorption of new citizens, and the growth and development of the city of Rome. Lawmaking assemblies stood within a complicated structure of Roman crisis resolution that made possible the historically unprecedented absorption of conquered peoples during the creation of the Roman state in Italy. Part 2 thus establishes the essential preconditions for the acceptance of public lawmaking and the role played by the process itself in facilitating the amalgamation of Romans and Italians and the growth of Rome. The quest begins in chapter 4 by exploring the conditions underlying the Italy-wide acceptance of Roman ways, among them public lawmaking. The cornerstone on which the Romans built their unique state in Italy during the initial and most critical course of their expansion can be traced to the veneer of understandings shared by all inhabitants of Italy that grew out of common reactions to the geography of the peninsula. As the Romans conquered other Italians and imposed a new legal, administrative, and economic organization on confiscated lands, Italians were forced to accommodate themselves to the changed conditions. The Romans in turn fastened on courses of action that channeled patterns of life in Italy, characterized by a high level of mobility and interaction, in directions amenable to the acceptance of Roman order and organization. Roman success can be measured by the extent to which non-Roman inhabitants accepted the mediating authority of the Roman Senate, magistrates, and also public lawmaking assemblies—to the point, at times, where they agitated for the passage of public laws in Rome.

To understand this general acceptance of public lawmaking events throughout conquered Italy we turn, in chapter 5, to an exploration of the incorporation of noncitizens into the Roman system through grants of citizenship and the continual reintegration of citizens through military service. Of particular importance in integrating new members in the Roman system was the innovative use made of the Roman tribes. Likewise from the fourth century, Italians assimilated to Roman ways through military service with the Roman army. Thus, as expansion progressed, a steady stream of newcomers strengthened Rome by becoming, or aspiring to become, full members of the society with full rights to engage in the rituals and events that accompanied citizenship. Among the most meaningful of these were voting assemblies, where Romans expressed their power as citizens. In the changing social and economic relationships that evolved out of the gradual incorporation of Italians into the Roman imperial system, at all levels of society, lies the key to the widespread acceptance of the public lawmaking process as a mechanism for resolving conflict and maintaining social stability among a traditionally highly mobile population now centered on the city of Rome.

This process of establishing a Roman structure of order across Italy was on all levels also a process of strengthening the vital links to the city of Rome, which comes under investigation in chapter 6. Once Roman expansion across Italy commenced, the regular movement of Romans and non-Romans to and from the city intensified. Initial Roman efforts to organize conquered lands along the lines of traditional structures of control developed in the city of Rome could not have anticipated the difficulties of dealing with the wide variety of outsiders now migrating to the city on a temporary or permanent basis. Yet the Romans succeeded in imposing themselves on local networks, creating a society that increasingly and resolutely centered civic, ritual, and economic functions on Rome. As the focus of Roman life throughout Roman Italy, the city of Rome was the sole venue for public lawmaking sessions. The unique Roman talent for mediating challenges in light of Roman custom and Roman traditions was augmented by the use of public lawmaking assemblies in Rome to create the conditions believed necessary for the growth of the city. By narrowing our focus on the exceptional degree of internal order that characterized Rome in spite of its exceptionally large population and the continual movement into and out of the city, we locate public lawmaking assemblies in the structure of order that underlay the Roman achievement.

Part 3 concludes the study with an increasingly detailed analysis of lawmaking activity in the critical last stage in the declining Roman Republic, from the late second century to the assassination of C. Julius Caesar in 44. The consequences of assimilation profoundly changed the composition of the Roman leadership and the traditional relationships between political leaders and people. Chapter 7 considers how the determination to maintain a traditional Roman balance in the system underlay the efforts by elite Romans to restore the perceived, fading integrity of the traditional public lawmaking system in the face of the challenges of absorbing new citizens in the third and second centuries. In spite of critical tensions among old and new citizens during the course of Roman expansion, Roman efforts at preserving what they believed were the essential and basic preconditions for the effective functioning of the public lawmaking process resulted in the continued endurance of a cohesive, expanding, and complex Roman society.

Chapters 8 and 9 utilize earlier findings in a detailed analysis of the politicization of lawmaking activity during the critical last stage in the declining Roman Republic, from the Italian War beginning in 91 to the assassination of C. Julius Caesar in 44. The solution to the Italian War, namely, the granting of citizenship to all Italians, signaled an end and a beginning: the end of a Rome that could develop agreement on the societywide resolution of apparently intractable problems through the use of public lawmaking and the beginning of an unprecedented shift in the social and political foundations of the Roman Republic that continued to run its course until the demise of the Republic in 44. The attenuation of social networks that followed the Italian War was reflected in changes in the traditional balances among the various elements at lawmaking assemblies, a development best seen in the increased efforts by elite Romans to use the lawmaking process in a new, more direct and more self-interested way than ever before. By his invention of the office of "Dictator for Writing the Laws and Restoring the State," L. Cornelius Sulla unwittingly took a major step in sowing the seeds of the demise of a unique lawmaking process that had played a major role in the expansion of Rome. By granting such power to one man, Romans had lost a vital element of the public lawmaking process. Paradoxically, both the final demise of the traditional lawmaking process and the culmination of the changes that led up to it were signaled by the passage of laws in 44, found in the assassinated Caesar's notebooks. The compelling authority of a dead man to legitimize law sets the stage for the final adjustment leading to the end of public lawmaking assemblies, the institution of a Roman emperor. No longer would the Roman leadership unequivocally accept the decision of the Roman people assembled in a lawmaking assembly as the Roman people's will. From here on out the Roman leadership would tolerate only the right sort of lawmaker and the right sort of law. Public lawmaking became a victim of its own success. An epilogue summarizes the findings of this study about the role of public lawmaking in Roman society and places them in a wider, comparative historical context.

METHOD: A COMPILATION OF LAWS AND PROPOSALS

Among the most important sources of information for public lawmaking are reports of public law proposals and enacted laws found scattered throughout nearly the entire corpus of ancient Roman authors and Roman documents. This book makes original use of these reports, which involve both the drafts (rogationes) and end products (leges and plebiscita) of Rome's public lawmaking assemblies and convey details ranging from the substance of the law to the public law sponsor to the mundane details of the lawmaking occasion. The information derived from the reports was assembled using basic procedures for handling such data, presented in appendix A. The initial effort of assembling pertinent details about all known and surmised laws and proposals produced a base list of 781 laws between 509 BCE and 23 CE. Taking away all hypothetical or unreliably reported laws, using criteria set out in appendix A, reduced the list to 559 reliably reported laws and proposals between 350 and 25 BCE, listed in appendix C, and 541 laws and proposals between 350 and 44 BCE, my period of interest in this study. Based on information provided in the ancient record about these laws and proposals, I produced a variety of tables used throughout the text as appropriate to provide the basic framework for my discussion.

Although my compilation of laws is not all-inclusive in that it does not represent the entire body of public law proposals ever considered in ancient Rome, it does consist of the entire corpus of available proposals of law and enacted laws recorded by ancient sources. Although there was obviously a great deal of agreement between our ancient sources, particularly ancient authors, as to which laws ought to be remembered over the period, the surviving body of proposals of law suggests that none of them gave us a comprehensive listing. (A full discussion is provided in appendix B.) Through either the accident of survival or deliberation, all of the ancient authors were selective.

Like all historians, therefore, I am to some degree a prisoner of my sources as I seek to systematically bridge the gap between the impossible task of finding and processing every public law or proposal of law and the insights gleaned from detailed case studies of issues, participants, and procedures at single events selected from different time periods. To those who would insist on assuming that beneath the body of surviving laws on which this study is based there lies a "true" body of laws that remains to be discovered, I would make two responses. One, whatever their biases, our ancient authors, among the most observant minds in Roman society, believed that the great majority of laws on my listing deserved to be remembered. And two, since it is the only such body of information in existence, it is by definition the best. In sum, it seems reasonable to suppose that we have the most complete "database" that can presently be assembled for examining the functions of lawmaking assemblies. It seems reasonable also to conclude that the discovery of any significant number of new laws in the future would strengthen my emphasis on the central importance of public lawmaking in the Roman Republic.

I have benefited from the comments of anonymous readers and others who read the manuscript at an early stage, especially Fergus Millar and Leah Shopkow. I also thank Keith Bradley, Donald Engels, Hartmut Galsterer, Michael Maas, and John North. Tom Elliott, director of the Ancient World Mapping Center at the University of North Carolina in Chapel Hill, has provided invaluable assistance in producing maps for the book. I am especially grateful to David Potter for his thoughtful reading and suggestions and to Ellen

Bauerle for providing encouragement and support. My greatest debt I owe to Patrick J. Blessing. I am most grateful to Mary Hashman and the rest of the professional staff at the University of Michigan Presss.

Notes

1. All dates are BCE unless otherwise noted.

2. *Consortium imperii:* Justin 38.4.13. Italian aims: E. Gabba, "Rome and Italy: The Social War," in *CAH* 9, 2d ed. (Cambridge, 1994), 104–28; P. Brunt, "Italian Aims at the Time of the Social War," in *The Fall of the Roman Republic and Related Essays* (Oxford, 1988), 93–143; A. N. Sherwin-White, *The Roman Citizenship*, 2d ed. (Oxford, 1973), 134–49; and E. Badian, "Roman Politics and the Italians (133–91 BC)," *Dial. di Arch.* 4–5 (1971): 373–409.

3. P. Brunt, *Italian Manpower, 225 BC–AD 14* (Oxford, 1971), 89.

4. M. Pallottino, *A History of Earliest Italy* (Ann Arbor, 1994), 155.

5. *Bellum Italicum* is used by Cicero (e.g., *Font.* 41) and Velleius Paterculus.

6. Some scholars believe that the Italian "self-assertion," i.e., surgent Italian identity and consciousness, in the years leading up to the war is incompatible with a desire for inclusion in the Roman system: M. Crawford, "Italy and Rome," *JRS* 71 (1981): 159; Pallottino 1994. The trend is itself testimony to the Romans' success in forging a state whose institutions were compatible with ethnic diversity.

7. Numbers of Romans and Italians in military service: Brunt 1971, 416–512; see chapter 4.

8. The number of inhabitants in 340 is based on the census figures for that year, estimating the adult men at 31 percent of the total population: Brunt 1971, 53 (with reference to the year 225). On the number in 28 see E. Lo Cascio, "The Size of the Roman Population: Beloch and the Meaning of the Augustan Census Figures," *JRS* 84 (1994): 23–40, and E. Lo Cascio, "The Population of Roman Italy in Town and Country," in *Reconstructing Past Population Trends in Mediterranean Europe*, ed. J. Bintliff and K. Sbonias (Oxford, 1999), 164. Brunt estimates five million people of citizen status (excluding infants) in 28: Brunt 1971, 121. See also chapter 7, note 1.

9. It would be impossible here to survey all the scholarship on the topic, which falls under the broad rubric of "Romanization." Suffice to say that the focus has shifted from the cultural impact of an ascendant Rome to independent developments among Italy's diverse groups and reciprocal interchange. A good overview is provided by J.-P. Vallat, "The Romanization of Italy: Conclusions," in *Italy and the West: Comparative issues in romanization*, ed. S. Keay and N. Terrenato (Oxford, 2001), 102–10.

10. H. Mouritsen, *Italian unification: A study in ancient and modern historiography* (London, 1998), presents a more informed variation of this view, arguing that the ancient account of unification is a construction after the fact and that the Italians did not want unification.

11. Brunt 1988, 117; A. Keaveney, *Rome and the unification of Italy* (London, 1987), 28; J. Göhler, *Rom und Italien* (Breslau, 1939).

12. The various assemblies that made law are addressed in chapter 1.

13. The exception is J. Bleicken, *Lex Publica: Gesetz und Recht in der römischen Republik* (Berlin and New York, 1975), especially 100–513. Bleicken adheres to the political perspective of the ancient recorders.

14. M. H. Crawford, ed. *Roman Statutes*, 2 vols., Bulletin of the Institute of Classical Studies. Supplement 64 (London, 1996).

15. Lily Ross Taylor, *Party Politics in the Age of Caesar* (Berkeley, Los Angeles, and London, 1949); Lily Ross Taylor, *The Voting Districts of the Roman Republic* (Rome, 1960).

Contents

Tables

Maps

Maps by Callie Williamson, Tom Elliott, Rachel Barckhaus, and Andrew Hull.

Digital versions of maps in this book are freely available for nonprofit educational use as part of the Maps for Students Program of the Ancient World Mapping Center at the University of North Carolina in Chapel Hill. Please visit the Center's Web site for more details: <http://www.unc.edu/awmc>.

Abbreviations

ANRW	H. Temporini, ed., *Aufstieg und Niedergang Der Römische Welt*. Berlin and New York, 1972–.
Bruns[7]	K. G. Bruns, *Fontes Iuris Romani Antiqui*, ed. O. Gradenwitz. 7th ed. Tübingen, 1909. Reprint, 1969.
CAH	*Cambridge Ancient History*. 2d ed. London, 1970–2000.
CIL	*Corpus Inscriptionum Latinarum*. Berlin, 1863–.
FIRA	S. Riccobono, *Fontes Iuris Romani Anteiustinianae*. 3 vols. Florence, 1941.
ILLRP	A. Degrassi, ed., *Inscriptiones Latinae Liberae Rei Publicae*. Vol. 1 (2d ed., Florence, 1965). Vol. 2 (Florence, 1963).
ILS	H. Dessau, *Inscriptiones Latinae Selectae*. Berlin, 1892–1916. Reprint, 1962.
LPPR	G. Rotondi, *Leges Publicae Populi Romani*. Milan. 1912. Reprint, Hildesheim, 1966.
MRR	T. R. S. Broughton, *The Magistrates of the Roman Republic*. 3 vols. Chico, CA and Atlanta, GA, 1984–86. (Vols. 1 and 2 originally published by the American Philological Association, New York, 1951–52.)
PCIA	*Popoli e Civiltà dell'Italia Antica*. A cura del'ente per la diffusione a l'educazione storica. 9 vols. Rome, 1974–.

PW	A. Pauly, G. Wissowa, and W. Kroll, *Real-Encyclopädie der klassischen Altertumswissenschaft*. Munich, 1894–1972.
RS	M. H. Crawford, ed., *Roman Statutes*. 2 vols. London, 1996.
Mommsen, *R.St.*	T. Mommsen, *Römisches Staatsrecht*. 3 vols. Leipzig, 1887–88.

Abbreviations of journals follow the abbreviations listed in *The Oxford Classical Dictionary*, edited by S. Hornblower and A. Spawforth, xxix–liv, 3d ed. (Oxford and New York, 1996) (*OCD*^{3}), or the *American Journal of Archaeology* at <http://www.ajaonline.org/shared/s_info_contrib_7.html>. Abbreviations of the names of ancient authors and documents also follow *OCD*^{3}.

PART ONE

PATTERNS AND PROCESS

CHAPTER ONE

Public Law in Rome

IN 81, AT THE conclusion of a bloody civil war, the Roman people approved a bill sponsored by L. Valerius Flaccus, as interrex, making L. Cornelius Sulla "Dictator for Writing the Laws and Restoring the State" (*dictator legibus scribendis et rei publicae constituendae*).[1] Sulla's first act as dictator was an innovation. By the authority of dictator granted him by the lex Valeria, Sulla posted the names of forty senators and sixteen hundred equestrians in the Forum with the directive that anyone who wished might kill with impunity the men whose names appeared there. Later more senators were added to the list. Eventually, a total of forty-seven hundred wealthy men of all ranks were proscribed and their property confiscated and sold or reassigned. The restoration of the Roman state had begun. Over the next eighteen months Sulla continued his campaign to restore order, sometimes on his own authority as dictator but often by the full process of public law requiring the sanction of the Roman people. The dictator promulgated at least twenty proposals, which the Roman people, when the scheduled day of voting arrived, in public accord embraced as law. Sulla stepped down as dictator in 80, his task completed.[2] Thirty-four years later, in 46, C. Julius Caesar in his turn was created "Dictator for Writing the Laws and Restoring the State" during a bigger and more costly civil war.[3] Over the next two years Caesar presented at least twelve public law proposals. Not since the Romans created a board of "ten men for writing the laws" (*decemviri legibus scribendis*) at the end of the fifth century had there been such intensive lawmaking efforts in Rome.[4] But never before the dictatorships of Sulla and Caesar had public law been used so extensively and so directly to resolve specific political and social crises.

For centuries the Romans reached decisions about law relating to the most critical aspects of their society in a public process concluded in the voting assemblies of Rome. The first reported public lawmaking occasion fell in the first year of the Republic, 509, when the first consul M. Iunius Brutus, in accordance with a Senate decree, carried a measure to exile all members of the Tarquin clan. The last reported occasion of certain date occurred during the reign of the emperor Nerva, CE 96–98, when the emperor himself presented a bill assigning land to poor Romans. In between lay roughly six hundred years and 750 unevenly reported public law proposals or enacted public laws.

Over the many centuries of public lawmaking activity, the historical circumstances surrounding the production of public law are haphazardly recorded. It is paradoxical that the most famous public laws with the profoundest consequences are sometimes puzzlingly detached from precise historical circumstances. A plebiscite commonly known as the lex Aquilia de damno, for instance, dating perhaps to the early third century, between 287 (the date of the lex Hortensia making plebiscites binding on the entire Roman community) and 133–12 (the period of the Gracchi) provided the foundations for the fundamental Roman delict, or tort, dealing with wrongful damage to property, *damnum iniuria datum*. Roman jurists commented extensively on the meaning and application of relevant provisions of the lex Aquilia, much of their commentary surviving in the Digests, where it provides a clear measure of the importance of the lex Aquilia in the development of Roman private law. Yet we know next to nothing of the contemporary issues prompting a lawmaker possibly named Aquilius to draft and promulgate such a public law proposal and prompting the Roman plebs at some time reportedly in the first half of the third century to accept it as law.[5] Why was this issue addressed in a public law at all, rather than by the praetor in his edict?

Another famous public law, the lex Agraria of 111, owes its celebrity primarily to the accidents of survival facing a bronze tablet on which the law was engraved in the late second century, possibly in the Roman town of Forum Sempronia (Fossombrone) in Umbria.[6] Ceremonially displayed in a town center or temple precinct, bronze tablets engraved with laws provided a monumental record of the enactments of Rome's assemblies. Since very few such tablets have survived to the modern period, chance alone has given us a record of this single most instrumental public law in the development of Roman land tenure, the lex Agraria, that instituted momentous changes in the legal status of Roman public property (*ager publicus*). While the historical circumstances of the law are broadly known, precise details are lacking.[7] The identification and content of the lex Agraria have been at issue since discovery of the bronze fragments on which it was engraved near Urbino, in north Italy, in the fifteenth century CE.[8] In particular, scholars have been at pains to determine what precisely the lex Agraria enacted and where this law fits in the scheme of agrarian legislation of the period reported by ancient narrative sources.[9] Who was the lawmaker? Why was such a law or indeed any of the land laws between 133 and 111 presented to the people? Why did not the Roman censors, or consuls, or indeed the Senate decide about the legal status of ager publicus in this instance as they had in other instances?

No less fundamental questions haunt even those public law sessions that are recorded in some detail, as for instance when the tribune Ti. Sempronius Gracchus in 133 promulgated a proposal to recover ager publicus in private possession and redistribute the land to poor Romans—the epochal, initial proposal in the hotly debated series culminating in the lex Agraria. The draft of his proposal had been carefully prepared by Gracchus and a council of advisors that included friends and family members, among them some of the highest-ranking senators of Rome. Gracchus's public speeches on the measure, as reported by the later historian Appian, touched on burning issues of the day: access to land resources, military manpower needs, and a slave labor force.[10] Crowds of people came to Rome, both supporters and opponents, to be on hand when the day of the voting assembly arrived: rich men who stood to lose some of their holdings on ager publicus, long in their possession even if irregularly held; men of military age, soldiers, and ex-soldiers without land; Roman and Latin colonists and restricted-citizen inhabitants (*cives sine suffragio*) of *municipia;* and Italians interested in the disposition of such land.[11] Inns and private accommodations could not hold all the Romans, Latins, and Italians who descended on Rome, bent on attending the outcome of the vote. Our ancient informants go on to report a complicated shuffle before Gracchus's proposal was eventually enacted. Another tribune, Octavius, vetoed the measure just as Gracchus ordered the herald to read it for the last time before calling the plebeian tribal assembly to vote; and a Senate discussion of the proposal failed to produce a formal sanction by that body. Gracchus nonetheless convened a second voting assembly at which the people first agreed, by the unanimous vote of the first eighteen tribes (*tribus*) declaring their decision, a majority of the thirty-five tribes present, to remove Octavius from office for his failure to support the people's interests. The people then voted to accept Gracchus's land redistribution measure, now somewhat modified, as law. The expressed will of the Roman people prevailed, recognized by Gracchus, if not by Octavius or the Roman Senate.

Despite this relatively detailed picture of the circumstances of the lex Sempronia agraria, one of the best known lawmaking events of the Roman Republic, our knowledge of the context of those circumstances is nonetheless as incomplete in several important respects as it is in the case of the lex Agraria. Attendance at Gracchus's public lawmaking sessions provides a case in point. Not only did vast numbers of people travel sometimes great distances to Rome to attend Gracchus's assembly, but they did so in some cases knowing they could not vote—in 133 the general grant of citizenship to all Italians was nearly fifty years in the future. Only citizens could enact law or elect Rome's political and military leaders in legitimately convened assemblies. Nonetheless, noncitizens as well as citizens converged on Rome in 133 to participate in the public lawmaking event sponsored by Gracchus. The participation by so large and diverse a group serves as a significant measure not only of the importance of the issues but also of the mechanism used to address those issues—a public lawmaking event. The general involvement of Romans from throughout Italy from all levels—from that of the elite Roman, a man of wealth and status if not a senator or elected official, to that of the ordinary citizen—in the public lawmaking process, especially in the years before all Italy became officially Roman at the conclusion of the Italian War, is striking. Yet, given the complexity of the rituals and procedures involved in public lawmaking assemblies, it is not axiomatic that all Romans should have a sufficiently sophisticated level of knowledge to participate effectively in public lawmaking assemblies. And it is certainly not axiomatic that newer citizens from throughout the conquered lands should participate as effectively as Romans, which they did. Such widespread involvement of participants from all levels of society throughout Italy in a complicated public lawmaking session requiring a deep knowledge of the Roman way of life has yet to be explained by historians.

THE DIMENSIONS OF LAWMAKING ACTIVITY

This book thus seeks to join public law to life in the Roman Republic throughout Italy during the years of greatest expansion, ca. 350 to 44. In this chapter my main project is to use my compilation of evidence about public law and lawmaking to focus as precisely as possible on what needs to be explained. What does the surviving evidence show about public lawmaking activity during the period in Roman history within which it was most extensively used, that is, the years from ca. 350 to 44? To begin, over the entire period of Roman public lawmaking, from roughly 509 BCE to 96 CE, reports on about 669 proposals or laws are known. But the main focus of my investigation is on our main period of interest, rather arbitrarily extended for ease of comparison by a few years at one end and divided into twenty-five-year blocks of time, as shown in table 1.1.[12] Although cutting across the conventional periodization used by Roman historians, the table reveals some striking variations over time in the Romans' resort to public law, which are unrelated to changes in the volume of reportage.[13] Over the quarter century from 249 to 225, for instance, Romans gathered to consider proposals of law about once every six years on average, for a total of only four occasions. Over the quarter century from 74 to 50, however, law sponsors called Romans together on 118 occasions, on average just over five times yearly. These are the extremes of Roman lawmaking activity.

The most intense lawmaking activity over our period of interest obviously falls in times of reported historical crises. The Second Punic War is fought between 218 and 201, and concurrently the number (43) of public laws for the quarter century within which it lies more than doubles any similar earlier period. Support for the thesis that the Romans existed in a constant state of crisis after 133, the beginning of the "century of revolution," is provided by a climb in the incidence of public law proposals at around that time. Lawmakers offered 68 bills, a new record, for public scrutiny over the quarter century from 124 to 100. In turn this total is almost matched by the 67 laws proposed over the following quarter century, 99 to 75, years that include the critical events of 91 to 81 and the temporary abeyance of the office of tribune. Roman law sponsors presented a record-breaking 118 laws to the Roman people from 74 to 50, a time span that brackets the slave revolt led by Spartacus between 73 and 71 and the Catilinarian conspiracy of 63. Our era of interest concludes with the third highest incidence of laws for any quarter century in Roman history, 67 laws between 49 and 25. This quarter century witnessed the first round of civil wars involving Julius Caesar and Pompey and the second round of civil wars involving Octavian and M. Antonius, that is, 44 to 31.

But what does all this mean for public lawmaking on a year-to-year basis? What could a Roman citizen expect in the way of public lawmaking events during a typical year? Arranging the incidence of lawmaking assemblies, or the absence thereof, on the basis of individual years within our selected periods, as in table 1.2, confirms the tendency toward a high rate of lawmaking during times of crises and the increasing frequency of lawmaking sessions as we approach the emergence of the Empire. Overall, as column 2 in table 1.2 indicates, for almost half (144) of all years over our period no public lawmaking sessions held the Romans' attention. For each of 79 years (column 3) the Romans participated on a single occasion in the public consideration of a law proposal, followed by two occasions per year for each of 32 years (column 4), three per year for each of 19 years (column 5), and four occasions per year for each of 11 years (column 6). In 5 years across the period Romans participated in five lawmaking sessions (column 7), and in 23 years they participated in six such sessions (column 8). Overall, in those years in which the Romans considered public law proposals (181), an average of about two and a half (2.6) laws per year were presented. All quarter-century divisions have a number of years with no lawmaking activity and a peak year in which lawmaking activity occurred many times. During the quietest quarter century, that is, 249 to 225, for 21 out of the 25 years not a single public law was proposed; at the other extreme, however, from 74 to 50, in 24 years out of 25 years, Romans participated in the public consideration of at least one law.

After 225, the patterns of public lawmaking shift significantly, as noted in table 1.2. In contrast to earlier times when Romans could expect state heralds to summon them to at most one meeting a year to hear arguments on the merits of a law proposal, now they found themselves enduring the rigorous public lawmaking process three or four times during a single year. The finer calibration in table 1.2 confirms the findings in our previous table of a relationship between crises and the incidence of public lawmaking as the Romans extend their control across Italy and the Mediterranean. Although public lawmaking follows no simple discernible pattern, the general trend is in the direction of more laws in more years for each quarter century and more laws during times of crises, as we approach the end of the Republic, by which time Romans were engaged in about five public lawmaking assemblies in a typical year. After 125, the years in which the number of law proposals climbs to six or higher are also far more frequent than earlier. Over the same period, the highest rate of law proposals in any single year ranges from thirteen in 123 to a high of nineteen laws in 44, the most we see in one year (column 9, table 1.2). Within each quarter century, except 199–175 and 174–150, there is a year of intensive lawmaking activity: 217 with six laws or proposals, 133 with seven, 123 with thirteen, 81 with eighteen, 58 with sixteen, and 44 with the historically unprecedented nineteen laws (column 9). All were years of turmoil. The years of the 50s, in which Romans participated in a remarkable seventy-two lawmaking events, and the 11 years from 91 to 80, in which lawmakers promulgated fifty-five bills, were the busiest in Roman history. Given the customary requirements for the public display and recitation of law proposals and the religious and political rituals accompanying the public passage of law, such a grueling schedule of lawmaking meetings and assemblies meant that throughout the century preceding the demise of the Republic the Roman people spent much, if not most, of their year involved in one way or another with the public lawmaking process.

ISSUES IN LAWMAKING

What issues inspired proposals of law? This is a complicated question, for many of the law proposals as reported are exceedingly difficult to label. After rejecting accepted categories as too imprecise, I devised a more refined labeling system that allowed me to examine, with some degree of confidence, the subject matter of 559 public laws—the entire body of reliably reported laws for the period between 350 and 25 (table 1.1). Altogether these proposals and enacted laws address 254 subjects or issues. Of these, 74 subjects appear more than once, as listed in table 1.3. By far the most important issues inspiring Roman lawmakers to resort to the public lawmaking process, listed in table 1.3, are repeated law proposals dealing in some way with senators or elected officeholders, Rome's political leaders: chief among such issues, at twenty-one occurrences, are proposals to appoint special commissions of investigation, that is, to establish courts of inquiry to collect information and take decisive action on an important matter most often involving elite Romans. Other popular issues also involved political leaders and other elite Romans: the suspension or circumvention of law, usually (though not always) to bend the rules of office holding to the advantage of any individual; selection of commanders; creation of extraordinary boards; assignment of provinces; abrogation or prorogation of command (*imperium*); triumphs; and the removal of a tribune from office. A total of 44 separate issues involving the political and social leadership spurred Romans to participate in 205 specific lawmaking meetings. A total of 30 other issues involved the wider population—often including the political leadership it should be noted; the categories are somewhat loose. Among these other issues, citizen grants to individuals and groups, 19 in number, were most frequently aired. Reflecting the exigencies of expansion, I note that declarations of war, of which 16 were passed, and the foundation of colonies vie for second place among other issues in table 1.3, followed in third place by the distribution and assignment of land (15). Also prominent in the listing are repeated proposals dealing with grain distributions, peace, voting, crimes, the settlement of debts, and individual civil or citizen liberties (*provocatio*).

Of the remaining 254 subjects, 180 appear only once during the period, as in table1.4, where the listing of issues is divided into those involving the political leadership and others. As with the repeated issues in table 1.3, these individual issues overwhelmingly involve matters relating to political leaders and other elite Romans, with a total of 98 lawmaking sessions covering individual issues pertaining to their activities. Although some issues here seem frivolous to modern eyes (importing wild beasts from Africa is one of the more obvious examples), the great majority of all the proposals appear in no way less important than the repeated issues listed in table1.3, as we might expect given that they moved Roman lawmakers to initiate the public lawmaking process. Through the presentation of these individual bills, Romans tried to remove a consul from office, they first deprived of power and then reinvigorated the office of tribune, they defined the voting rights of freedmen, they regulated the election of military tribunes, and they fixed the length of tenure of provincial governors, to point at some of the more obviously important listed issues that were covered in a one-time public law proposal. The variety and extent of issues in tables 1.3 and 1.4 over the period reveal the wide reach of decisions made by public lawmaking assemblies into every conceivable nook and cranny of Rome's social, political, economic, and religious system, no matter how inconsequential or how vital. More important, the variety and extent of issues underscore the importance to the Roman people of the public lawmaking process in maintaining their society as they expanded across Italy and incorporated other Italians into the Roman state.

But to what extent did these patterns of issues inspiring Roman lawmakers to initiate the lawmaking process change over time? To examine this question I listed issues that inspired public lawmaking events for five selected critical periods in Roman history: 350 to 219; 218 to 201; 200 to134; 133 to 92; and, finally, 91 to 44, as noted in table 1.5. These periods encompass significant historical developments: the initial stage of Roman expansion in Italy to the Second Punic War (350–219); the Second Punic War itself, the first major crisis faced by the Roman state (218–201) and worthy of separate consideration both for that reason and because of the first-time, strikingly high incidence of lawmaking throughout the crisis; the beginnings of Roman expansion into the eastern Mediterranean and the years following, when the social problems consequent on expansion were first recognized in a serious way (200–134); the tribunate of Ti. Gracchus to the Italian War, when building social problems came to a head in the war of the Italian allies for inclusion in the Roman state (133 to 92); and the Italian War to the assassination of Julius Caesar, the period of the precipitate decline of the Republic (91–44). Although our selected spans are uneven in length, they allow us to focus on the relationship between broad developments and the issues presented to Roman voters in public law proposals to a far greater degree than the arbitrary quarter-century divisions of tables 1.1 and 1.2. It is immediately clear, for instance, from table 1.5 that changes occurring in the topic and frequency of the repeated issues presented to the Roman people from one of our selected periods to the next are, as we might expect, best explained by the historical circumstances of each period.

Over our earliest time span in table 1.5, that is, the 131-year period from 350 to 219, Romans participated in a lawmaking session about once every three years for a total of fifty-three such public sessions. When we list all proposals of law for this period, as in table 1.6, we find that these irregularly held sessions covered thirty-seven topics, of which thirty were raised only once, and the remaining twenty-three covered seven topics repeated anywhere from two to ten times. By far the most recurrent overarching topic of concern to Romans in the public law proposals presented to them is the behavior of political leaders and other elite Romans, which forms 40 percent of the total listing in table 1.6. As they expanded across Italy, the Romans were compelled, time after time, to come together in lawmaking assemblies to develop a consensus on questions of leadership and the behavior of elite Romans, including efforts to open office holding at all levels to the widest possible field, action in the case of a commander's surrender, the announcement of the Senate's opinion about the matter at hand prior to assemblies, the suspension or circumvention of law, and extension of a commander's imperium. Next in importance is declaring war, which accounts for ten public lawmaking sessions during the period, as noted in table 1.6. Taken together with the repeated and individual sessions to pass laws to send requested military assistance (to the Mamertines), to establish a board to arrange the outfitting and repair of the Roman fleet, to approve treaties, to confirm peace, or to fix the punishment of a place or of rebellious troops, we can see a concern with matters bearing on the progress of Roman expansion. Similarly as shown in table 1.6, both repeated and single issues also address the vigor of the Roman people, including three public law sessions on the granting of citizenship to groups, two on the general force of plebiscites, and one each on the assignment of land, the end of debt bondage, and civil liberties. Finally, efforts to regularize market conditions, or protect property throughout Roman territory, make up an additional important block of six public law sessions, including public legislation to establish state oversight over the weights and measures used in markets, to set legal business on market days, and to address the payment of debts.

The perceived importance of public lawmaking assemblies to Romans in dealing with perceived structural limitations in periods of stress is suggested by the extent to which Rome's elected officials called such sessions over the seventeen years of the Second Punic War, 218 to 201, as shown in table 1.7. Almost twice per year on average Romans considered public law proposals, participating in thirty-eight lawmaking sessions over seventeen years, a sixfold increase over earlier years in the frequency with which Romans debated public law proposals. As in the earlier years, however, the Romans used the public lawmaking process to resolve issues of leadership and the behavior of political leaders as well as other elite Romans. More than half (sixteen) of the twenty-nine different topics presented to the Romans as proposals of law (table 1.7) address these concerns. But there were differences of focus compared to previous times in the leading, repeated concerns: leadership was most prominent in the creation of extraordinary administrative boards, the selection or election of commanders and dictators, and abrogation or extension of imperium. Likewise, the confirmation of peace and the granting of citizenship inspired public lawmaking on more than one occasion. Similarly, the earlier concern with regularizing market conditions seems now to be conditioned by war, as reflected in the fairly prominent cluster of proposals that attempted to regularize currency and regulate personal expenditures. Overall, the suspicion that Romans were trying to deal with unsettled conditions across a broad front, suggested by the unprecedented frequency of the public law sessions, is strengthened by the focus of topics of this period.

The conclusion of the Punic Wars coincided with a dramatic drop in the Romans' resort to public lawmaking—albeit the frequency of public law proposals is not as low as the level of the 131 years before the war—as shown in table 1.8, which covers our next selected period, 200 to 134. With sixty-one proposals of law over these sixty-six years, Roman involvement in the public law process is on average slightly less than one proposal per year. Of this overall total, eleven issues are presented anywhere from two to six times to account for a total of thirty-three sessions: the remaining twenty-eight issues are brought to public lawmaking events one time. Of the overall sixty-one topics, matters involving the political and social leadership, at thirty-three, more than half, again dominate as the inspiration for public law. Next in importance are issues relating to the Roman expansion across Italy, in particular to the perennial concern with regularizing market conditions. Together the laws regulating personal expenditure, women's capacity to inherit, money lending, the lease of ager Campanus, and two laws extending certain Roman laws to Latin and Italian allies account for a significant block of seven proposals, as noted in table 1.8. An intersecting set of concerns are the proposals relating to the distribution or assignment of land, the foundation of colonies, Roman civil liberties (provocatio), the citizen status of former slaves and their sons, privileges and honors for individuals, the grant of citizenship to an outside group, and efforts to expel Latin and Italian immigrants from Rome. Prominent also as providing the inspiration for multiple sessions are the appointment of special commissions of investigation, the suspension or circumvention of law, confirmation of peace, declarations of war, and a new concern, presented twice to the Roman people, voting by written ballot.

Over our next selected time span, the almost half century from 133 to 92, that is, the period marked off by the tribunates of Ti. Gracchus and M. Livius Drusus, Roman lawmakers called the Roman people to consider about two and a half public law proposals per year, more than in the preceding years, although still less than the average frequency over the Second Punic War. While matters involving the political and social leadership again form a large cluster among issues that inspired such sessions, at thirty-eight proposals, for the first time other issues, involving the majority population, as well as senators, elected officeholders and other Romans of wealth and status, are more prominent at forty-nine proposals, or almost half of the total number of proposals over the period (table 1.9). Legislation dealing with the founding of colonies heads the listing of repeated issues, followed by the appointment of special commissions of investigation, the distribution or assignment of land, the grant of citizenship, and the distribution of grain to citizens. Among other issues addressed more than once in public law proposals presented to the Roman people are bills to set the term of military service, to vote by written ballot, to extend Roman civil liberties, and to fix the composition of juries. A large number of repeated and single issues addressed in public law proposals involve the conditions facilitating trade and expansion within Italy but also beyond its borders. These include using the bequest of King Attalus to finance a land commission; leasing state contracts in Asia; regulating port duties; building new roads in Italy; the status of landholdings; regulating boundaries; and extending an existing action-at-law, the remedy of *manus iniectio*, against money lenders (*faeneratores*). An issue never before presented to the people, namely, the outright abrogation of an enacted public law, also inspired two public lawmaking sessions. We shall return to this in chapter 9. The extent to which the issues brought to the people touch on more diverse facets of political, social, and economic order hints at a more commonplace recourse to public lawmaking assemblies in this period.

This trend toward a more commonplace and diverse use of the public lawmaking process intensifies as we approach the crucial final years of the "free" Republic, 91 to 44, shown in table 1.10. Now Romans attended anywhere from one to twenty public lawmaking sessions in a single year, the average number reaching the unprecedented level of five per year, the busiest sustained period of lawmaking in Roman history. Whether or not the lawmaking process was observed in its entirety by the dictators, Sulla and Caesar, the point nonetheless holds: Romans were involved with public lawmaking throughout much of the year.[14] Not only did the number of issues broached at lawmaking sessions, during the period from 91 to 44, exceed that of earlier periods, but many (37) of these same issues were far more likely to be presented to the Roman public at lawmaking events on more than one occasion. Of the total 139 issues over that time span, most (93) appeared only once in the record. But other issues were aired more often: 18 appear twice; 13 appear three to five times; and 6 appear between six and eleven times. Clearly, the issues were becoming more complicated and conditions were changing so fast that the Romans were often forced to reconsider them. The variety and tenacity of the issues provide more evidence of the growing political and social turmoil of the period.

Of the various topics inspiring action by key Roman lawmakers and the Roman people between 91 and 44, issues relating to political leaders and other elite Romans became even more dominant as inspirations for proposals of law, as shown in table 1.10. More than half of the lawmaking sessions over the entire period were devoted to such legislation, for an unprecedented total of 141 separate sessions out of 234, on eighty separate subjects. The presentation of so many public law proposals relating to elite Romans suggests a certain degree of social turmoil, especially at the upper levels of society. Particularly expressive of disruption are proposals calling for the recall of exiles, which led to 11 events, no fewer than 7 special commissions of investigation, as well as a large cluster of laws (29) relating to more precisely defined criminal matters, involving for the most part political leaders, from the juries of criminal courts to particular crimes, another cluster (15) making innovative changes in the Roman structure of political office and Senate membership, and finally an unprecedented number of proposals (6) granting privileges and honors to individuals. That all levels of Roman society and all regions of Italy were experiencing a certain amount of turmoil is indicated by the high number of proposals for granting or defining citizenship (11), distributing land (9), and assigning new citizens to tribes or creating new tribes (3). At the same time, the group of proposals (19) designed to regularize communications and trade suggests a continuing society-wide concern with the necessity of maintaining trade and commerce over a much larger area. Among these are proposals dictating interest payments on debts, port duties, the settlement of contracts on land, the supervision of roads, and the metal content of coins. We shall return to the complexity of the issues presented to the Roman people between 91 and 44 in some detail in part 3.

Finally, it should be noted that across the entire period from 350 to 44, the changing variety of issues addressed in public law proposals are in many respects indistinguishable from issues addressed by the Roman Senate. While a detailed comparison of Senate decrees and public laws is beyond the scope of this study, my compilation assembles some rough indicators of similarity. A small number of public laws confirmed or overturned previous Senate decrees. A larger number of laws reflect Senate involvement in the lawmaking process, by which I mean the Senate's more direct intervention in the process rather than the earlier, formal expression of its opinion about a law proposal. Law sponsors customarily presented projected proposals to the Senate before promulgation, and the Senate's official opinion (*patrum auctoritas*) about a public law proposal, believed to relate to possible religious flaws in a proposal, was broadcast before the Roman people voted on a public law proposal (in accordance with a public law of the fourth century). But the Senate also at times involved itself directly in the lawmaking process to the extent that it initiated a law by passing a decree that instructed a consul or some other magistrate to present a particular matter to the people in a public law proposal. The Senate's concurrence with a lawmaker's proposal might also be so resounding as to justify the comment of ancient authors. A rough count of such laws in the period from 350 to 219 shows that the Senate intervened in the lawmaking process on 14 occasions out of 53, either giving its public approval of a proposal or formally advising that a proposal be brought to the people in matters involving war, treaties, gifts to Roman senators received from foreign rulers, and grants of citizenship, that is, in matters involving external affairs, thus underscoring the value of the public lawmaking process in facilitating Roman expansion. Similarly, from 218 to 201, Senate intervention came in a different range of 15 issues out of 38 involving questions of leadership, wartime penalties, use of confiscated land, and state cult. The apparent concurrence between Senate and lawmakers in this time of crisis is exceptional. Between 200 and 134, issues concerning the suspension of existing law (3), war (2), the foundation of colonies, the extension of Roman debt law to all Italy, personal expenditures, relations between candidates and voters during electoral campaigns, Italian residents of Rome, leadership, and peace invited Senate involvement on 14 occasions out of 61. Thereafter, the number of such occasions appears to diminish drastically. Between 133 and 92, the Senate intervened on a single lawmaking occasion (out of 98) involving the grant of citizenship to an individual. Between 90 and 44, the Senate intervened 11 times (out of 234) in matters relating to exiles (6), the grant of autonomy to a foreign city, electoral bribery, a citizenship grant, and the city of Rome grain supply. Overall, both the external affairs of the Roman state and internal matters invited the Roman Senate's intervention in the public lawmaking process. Intervention, however, was a far more likely occurrence in the years before 133 than after. Finally, while issues of concern to the Roman people and the Roman Senate appear to be to a large degree intertwined (so much so that the total count of proposals over the period includes about ten reported laws that modern scholars think are more likely to be Senate decrees), the topics of proposals in whose generation the Senate was involved suggest that presenting a bill served as an important accepted mechanism in each period for resolving especially vexing matters. We shall pursue this avenue in later chapters.

SPONSORS OF PUBLIC LAW

Of the men elected each year to office between 350 and 25, no fewer than thirteen, and eventually as many as twenty, magistrates had the authority to convene assemblies (*ius agendi cum populo* or *cum plebe*) and thus the capability of sponsoring proposals of law. The number includes Rome's ten tribunes, two consuls, and from one to eight praetors.[15] These then were Rome's potential lawmakers. Considering that the only regularly elected high officials who did not convene the people for this purpose were the four aediles and the eight (eventually twenty, after 81) quaestors, potential lawmakers comprised roughly half the total number of annually elected magistrates: a striking measure of the diffusion of power among high officeholders in Rome in the most formative years. Although the potential lawmakers were a formidable group in numbers alone, however, not every member of the group availed himself of the privilege of proposing laws to public assemblies.

Public law proposals were in fact unevenly presented by officeholders during the years when the Republic expanded and grew in complexity, as we can see when we organize patterns of sponsorship of public laws for our five selected critical periods over our period of interest, as shown in table 1.11. Although extraordinary magistrates did occasionally present bills to the assembled people (and once, perhaps, a priest and another time an aedile), the common practice more typically involved the tribunes, consuls, or praetors, holding the annually revolving high offices filled by vote of the people in the plebeian tribal assembly (tribunes) and the centuriate assembly (praetors and consuls). Although our evidence is somewhat incomplete for our earliest selected time span, 350 to 219, it seems that tribunes, with 32 percent of all proposals of public law, led the list, followed by dictators, consuls, and praetors, roughly in that order. For the remaining, selected historical periods of interest, as noted in table 1.11, more reliable information reveals that tribunes had doubled their performance to 61 percent over the seventeen years of the Second Punic War, a four-to-one lead over consuls and praetors, which they managed to maintain down to the last century of the Republic. The involvement of consuls in lawmaking dropped from 18 percent of the total for the period between 200 and 134, as noted in table 1.11, to 7 percent for the following period, 133 to 91.

Out of the total number of 234 laws or proposals over the years from 91 to 44 as shown in table 1.11, almost one-half (44 percent) were sponsored by tribunes, one-quarter (25 percent) by consuls, and 5 percent by praetors. Although tribunes still lead all others as sponsors of public laws during this most recent period, their representation had dropped significantly from the 66 percent figure of the earlier half century to 44 percent, as shown in table 1.11. On the other hand, the 25 percent of public laws proposed by consuls between 91 and 44 represented a significant expansion from the 7 percent representation over the years from 133 to 92. A striking feature of this most recent period is the lawmaking activity of the singular office of dictator legibus scribendis et rei publicae constituendae: the two men who held this office, Sulla and Caesar, sponsored a remarkable thirty-three laws between them, 14 percent of the unusually large number of public law proposals during this golden age of public lawmaking.

But to what extent were the various political leaders who proposed laws associated with the most powerful Roman clans (*gentes*), that relatively small handful of families in any generation that, in the analysis of Ronald Syme, ruled Rome?[16] I attempted first to determine the number of lawmakers produced by the various Roman clans that provided Rome's political leadership, over our five selected periods, on the basis of 154 public law "titles" or clan names on which information has survived (these furnish the tag naming individual laws: lex Cornelia, lex Aurelia, and so on), as shown in table 1.12. With a total of sixteen clans recorded and the titles of thirty-three laws unreported, relatively few clans appear in our earliest period, 350–219, in proportion to the total number of laws, fifty-three. Almost as many clans, twelve, appear in the next column covering the far shorter span of the Second Punic War. During the same time period the titles of twenty-three proposals or laws are unreported and the frequency of lawmaking across the period is 38. With our third period, 200–134, the number of clans more than doubles to thirty-six, the titles of only sixteen proposals or laws are unreported, and the frequency of lawmaking across the period is 61. While the number increases only slightly in the years between 133 and 92, to forty, when the titles of twenty proposals or laws have gone unreported and the frequency of lawmaking across the period is 98, it climbs higher in our final period to fifty-four clans. In this last period, the titles of thirty proposals or laws are unreported and the frequency of lawmaking across the period is 234. Despite the incompleteness of table 1.12, it is clear that no one clan, or even handful of clans, monopolized Roman public lawmaking.[17] Rather, from the Second Punic War onward, there was a substantial increase in the number of clans whose involvement in lawmaking was manifest. At the same time, within each period some clans show a greater degree of involvement than others—whether the numbers reflect the activities of a single individual or several from different branches of one clan.

A further attempt to more precisely identify individual law sponsors and the relationship between lawmaking activity and political careers entailed matching the names of individual law sponsors, when known, and their offices in our five selected periods. The names of known sponsors of public law in the years between 225 and 44 for three selected periods in Roman history–225 to 134, 133 to 91, and 90 to 44—are listed in tables 1.13–15. In the ninety-one-year period between 225 and 134, out of a total number of 101 laws or proposals, 13 to 17 laws or proposals were sponsored singly or jointly by consuls, 4 to 8 by a praetor, and 65 by tribunes.[18] Of the sixty-four individuals we can identify by name, thirteen are consuls, four are praetors, forty-nine are tribunes, and one holds an unknown office, M. Iunius Brutus, perhaps a praetorship. More than one-third (38) of all reported laws and proposals across the period between 225 and 134 fall within the relatively brief span of the Second Punic War years, when lawmaking activity was greatly intensified, and almost one-quarter (fourteen) of the named sponsors fall within the same years. We have more comprehensive information for the forty-two-year period between 133 and 91, which shows that out of a total number of 98 laws or proposals, 7 laws or proposals were sponsored by consuls, 1 by a praetor, and 65 by tribunes.[19] Between 133 and 91, as well, the names of forty-seven sponsors are known, including twelve consuls sponsoring bills either singly or jointly, one praetor, and thirty-six tribunes.[20] Among these named sponsors are ten "new men" (*novi homines*), including nine tribunes, and one consul.[21] Of the new men who sponsored bills as tribunes, three held further office, one as praetor, and two advanced to the consulate as well.[22] Out of the total number of 234 laws or proposals throughout the forty-six-year period from 90 to 44, 102 were sponsored by tribunes, 59 by consuls, 12 by praetors, and 35 by the dictators Sulla and Caesar.[23] The names of twenty-seven consuls who sponsored bills, either singly or jointly, are recorded, as well as nine praetors and forty-nine tribunes (table 1.15). One consul, M. Tullius Cicero, was a new man. Among the named tribunes, almost half, eighteen in number, were new men. To our knowledge, many of the named tribunes (including eight new men) advanced to higher office: nine to the praetorship, and eight more to the consulship. Of these tribunes with further political careers, four also sponsored laws as praetors or consuls. One of the named sponsors in the period between 91 and 44, Q. Pompeius Rufus, consul in 88, had also sponsored a bill at an earlier stage of his career before 91, as tribune in 99. The patterns of clans and offices confirm the idea of an extensive and expanding diffusion of power among Roman political leaders and elite families as we approach the end of the Republic.

The exercise of matching named sponsors and offices greatly refines the patterns in table 1.12. The most striking findings are the lawmaking activity of an increasing number of political newcomers—new men—whose fathers or grandfathers had never held high office in Rome, as we move toward the Empire, and equally the unusually intense lawmaking activity of a small number of individuals either in a single office or over the course of a longer political career and several offices: C. Sempronius Gracchus, L. Appuleius Saturninus, L. Cornelius Sulla, Cn. Pompeius Magnus, C. Iulius Caesar, P. Clodius Pulcher, A. Gabinius, P. Vatinius, and M. Antonius all sponsor anywhere from six to thirty-one laws. These are exceptionally high numbers for any one individual.

Overall, more political leaders begin to take the risk of advancing public law proposals as we approach the first century. As always, tribunes perform most of the lawmaking activity across the period, followed by consuls. Praetors lag far behind. Tribunes had always been the most active lawmakers. Now, more tribunes propose public laws, notwithstanding the ten-year suspension of the office between 81 and 70. Similarly, more consuls and more praetors sponsor public law proposals than in any earlier period. Over the same time a broader range of families appear to be involved in lawmaking in crisis years, in particular more new men are involved after 133. Among the individuals who sponsor public law a few stand out as exceptional lawmakers—nearly all tribunes. The two dictatores legibus scribendis et rei publicae constituendae of the first century, Sulla and Caesar, form a unique pair of lawmakers. In sum, the period between 90 and 44 appears to be one in which not only more families and more new men but also more offices were involved in the promulgation of more laws than throughout the earlier periods.

Summary speculations are possible. The involvement of those political leaders who had the authority to convene the Roman people in presenting proposals of law to the Roman people underscores the unique role of public lawmaking assemblies within Roman society. Lawmaking was a critically important arena for elite Romans, one in which they exercised the personal dimension of their leadership to the fullest by displaying their ability to discern the will of the people through public orating.[24] Notwithstanding the increasing number of risk takers, lawmaking remained a relatively rare act for individual officeholders even in the first century. The well-known careers of the majority of the most active sponsors of public law between 133 and 44 suggest that public law sponsors tended to be men with exceptionally high political aspirations.

In fact, as the Republic wore on, a clear and strong connection was emerging between effective leadership and public lawmaking. This is most evident in the lawmaking activity and career paths of tribunes and new men. When the Romans turned more frequently to public lawmaking in crisis years, the laws were most often fielded by tribunes. We should not be surprised since tribunes, because of their functions as officers of the plebs, were closer to the people than consuls or praetors. Tribunes, moreover, stayed in Rome.[25] The clustering of laws in crisis periods suggests that tribunes, in particular, mediated changes that met with the concurrence of the Roman people in critical times. But we might suspect that the political aspirations of individual tribunes—especially tribunes who were new members of the political elite, often from newly admitted families—were crucial to their participation in public lawmaking. The office of tribune was instrumental in further political advancement—thus the extent to which changes in the origins of men involved in public law sponsorship reflect the transformation of the Republic. The extraordinary dictatorships of Sulla and Caesar provide further confirmation of the relationship between the sponsorship of public law and effective leadership in the period between 90 and 44. But throughout the period between 225 and 44, the political dimension of public lawmaking, especially participation in the public debate, was of some consequence to officeholders with the authority to convene the people.

ASSEMBLIES

Tables 1.16 and 1.17 display the volume of lawmaking activity in each of Rome's three popular assemblies, the *comitia centuriata* (centuriate assembly), in which the Roman people (*populus Romanus*) voted in centuries (*centuriae*); the *concilium plebis* (plebeian tribal assembly), in which a portion of the Roman people, the plebs, voted in tribes (*tribus*); and finally the *comitia tributa* (tribal assembly), in which the Roman people again voted in tribes. I have listed them here in probable order of generation. It should be noted that neither is the comitia tributa directly attested nor are the circumstances of its creation known.[26] Rather, it is the widely accepted modern formulation of Theodor Mommsen, who postulated the existence of a voting assembly in which patricians as well as plebeians voted in their tribes, on the model of the concilium plebis.[27] The presumptive comitia tributa is enmeshed in the overall scheme (as understood today) of lawmaking in Rome's firmly attested assemblies, the comitia centuriata and the concilium plebis, in spite of efforts to cast doubt on the resiliency of the constitutional arguments on which it rests. Suffice to say that the evidence attesting the involvement of three distinct voting assemblies in the enactment of public law is overwhelming (I shall return to this). Accordingly, table 1.16 collects the different volumes of lawmaking activity in the comitia centuriata, concilium plebis, and comitia tributa.

In line with our findings in the previous section, the largest number of public laws were presented to or were intended for presentation to the concilium plebis. As shown in table 1.16, between 350 and 219, 32 percent of all proposed and enacted laws involved this assembly; between 218 and 201, 60 percent; between 200 and 134, 54 percent; between 133 and 91, 66 percent; and between 91 and 44, 44 percent.[28] Visible across the entire period are fluctuating levels of lawmaking activity in the plebeian tribal assembly, which plainly match the patterns of sponsorship by the elected officials of the Roman plebs, the tribunes, who had the authority to convene this assembly. Over much of the Middle and Late Republic, from the Second Punic War to the dictatorship of Sulla, half or more of recorded laws for the period passed through Rome's concilium plebis.

Notably smaller and more uncertain is the volume of lawmaking activity involving both the comitia tributa and the comitia centuriata, assemblies convened by consuls, dictators, and praetors. More precisely, our sources seldom record the form of the popular assembly to which these curule sponsors of law presented or intended to present their bills during our period of interest, 350–44. As shown in table 1.17, where the information is collected by quarter centuries, the information accompanies only 8 percent of laws over our period of interest—a rather small number, given that consuls or praetors presented roughly half the reported proposals and enacted laws in table 1.17 to the Roman people, presumably in one or the other assembly. Evidently, the office held by a curule law sponsor is more likely to appear in the record than is the assembly over which he presided. Of course, the same holds true for tribunician law sponsors; however, the involvement of the concilium plebis is rightly assumed because it was the only assembly tribunes convened. Did ancient reporters take the assemblies of curule law sponsors for granted in the same way? Was there an understood relationship, with respect to the enactment of law, between curule sponsors of law and either the tribe-based or century-based assembly of the Roman people?[29] Given that ours is a patently modern question, the likelihood of a comprehensive explanation secured by explicit testimony seems remote.[30] Still, it is worth the attempt to render somewhat more intelligible the respective levels of lawmaking activity in the comitia tributa and the comitia centuriata.

The prevailing interpretation posits well-defined constitutional areas of responsibility for the centuriate assembly, implicitly leaving others for the full tribal assembly.[31] To the former assembly, accordingly, consuls brought matters relating to imperium or the election of curule magistrates, to include declarations of war and the creation of curule offices. Moreover, only consuls and dictators convened the centuriate assembly, whereas praetors (as well as curule aediles, in the case of *iudicia populi*) convened only the comitia tributa, the full tribal assembly. Similarly, urban praetors tend to be identified as sponsors of laws relating to civil law issues, who presented bills to the comitia tributa (unless the sponsor is identified specifically as a tribune or the law as a plebiscitum). By the same token, a public law as well as the responsible assembly might be hypothesized because the circumstances, if they fall into determined categories—the creation of an office, declaration of war, or citizenship grant—appear to require one.[32] The assignment of laws sponsored by consuls, praetors, and dictators to the comitia tributa or the comitia centuriata as well as the assignment of responsibility between the two assemblies on a legal basis are now taken for granted. It should be stressed, however, that the prevailing interpretation is an integral facet of that monumental achievement of late nineteenth and early twentieth century scholars, the Roman constitution.

For this reason, the interpretation is not unconditional, as the reservations of some scholars about the presumptive comitia tributa confirm. Another view, first introduced at the beginning of the century and revived in 1975, rules out entirely the possibility of a distinct comitia tributa and posits instead that the concilium plebis became a comitia tributa when convened by curule magistrates.[33] In effect, there was no lawmaking by the populus Romanus in tribes because the comitia tributa was an assembly of the *plebs Romana*. In 1986, however, Farrell established a clear distinction between the terms *concilium* and *comitia*, as used by Livy and Cicero, thus ruling out any possibility of viewing the concilium plebis and comitia tributa as one and the same assembly of the plebs Romana.[34] Whether Rome's comitia tributa and concilium plebis were two distinct assemblies of the populus Romanus and the plebs Romanus, respectively, as Mommsen supposed, or one and the same assembly of the plebs Romana convened by different magistrates has been settled conclusively on the side of Mommsen. Nevertheless, a related explanation of the lawmaking activity in Rome's assemblies persists that posits that all laws were made in the concilium plebis and that no laws were presented to the centuriate assembly (except declarations of war).[35] This is in part a second resurrection of the previous hypothesis and a further attempt to reject or redefine the comitia tributa. In either case our sources uniformly attest that the populus Romanus at times voted in tribes as well as in centuries.

Caution nonetheless applies to the prevailing interpretation of the two lawmaking assemblies of the populus Romanus. Specifically, a number of scholars, in more recent years, have convincingly argued that the ancient sources cannot support a strictly constitutional interpretation of the purview of Rome's legislative voting assemblies, particularly in regard to the centuriate assembly, either in specific instances or even overall.[36] Indeed, the terms that Livy and Cicero, our most important sources, regularly use to say "the consul carried a law" or "the praetor presented a bill to the people" apply to either assembly. Only when the voting units, tribus or centuriae, are named can we be more or less confident about identifying an assembly as comitia tributa or centuriata.

Tables 1.16 and 1.17 display the limitations both of the ancient record and of our understanding of the circumstances determining an elected official's choice of assemblies to make law. There is no consistent and obvious relationship between the lawmaking activity in the comitia tributa or the comitia centuriata and the sponsors of law who had the authority to convene these assemblies, namely, the consuls, dictators, and praetors. Some laws, including declarations of war, were presented to or intended for presentation to the comitia tributa, some to the comitia centuriata. In turn, at one time, a consul, a dictator, or a praetor involved both assemblies in lawmaking. In brief, when presented in tables, the evidence suggests even more clearly a changing and ad hoc use of both assemblies, in particular, the centuriate assembly.[37]

THE SECOND PUNIC WAR, 218–201

To fill out the framework so far established through processing my compilation of public laws let us next examine the first major crisis of the expanding Republic, the Second Punic War from 218 to 201, with a view specifically to narrowing the focus on the relationship between Roman law and life in a time of crisis. The most unprecedented and most intensive period of lawmaking activity in Roman history began in 218 when Hannibal, the young Carthaginian commander of Spain, unexpectedly crossed the Alps into Italy at the head of an army of foreign troops fighting in the service of Carthage for pay. The Romans mustered quickly to deal with Hannibal's invasion. Quickly the consul, P. Cornelius Scipio, who was already en route to take command of an anticipated campaign against the Carthaginians in his assigned province, Spain, turned back at Massilia in order to confront Hannibal in northern Italy. He was defeated at the Ticinus River by the invaders, the first of a series of sometimes desperate reverses faced by the Roman state over the next few years. At successive battles, Roman armies were again and again stunningly defeated by Hannibal's mercenary army as it traversed Italy gathering support from Gauls and certain of the Italians, culminating in the calamitous rout at Cannae in southern Italy in 216, where almost forty-eight thousand soldiers fell, about half of them

Roman—among them the consul and two quaestors; twenty-nine military tribunes, some of consular and praetorian rank; as well as eighty senators—and forty-five hundred were taken prisoner.[38] Never before had Romans seen utter ruin so close at hand.

Responses to the crisis of the Second Punic War were societywide in variety and scope. Alliances in Italy, formed by Rome over the previous 150 years with Italians and Latins, faltered. Towns hastily threw up walls for defense in anticipation of Hannibal or Rome. Men, women, and children in the regions through which armies marched abandoned their farms, migrating temporarily for safety to nearby towns and to Rome. Across Italy, businessmen, the class of contractors known as *publicani*, quickly entered the field of army supply and profited. Cash supplies dwindled as Roman state outlays for supply mounted, and individuals fearful of plunder buried valuable belongings for later recovery. Of all cities in Italy, Rome especially, the clearinghouse of formal response, was abuzz. Cash resources had to be secured through a variety of stratagems embracing the civilian population. As army after army was routed, the regular Roman leadership had to be augmented. Manpower to replenish depleted legions had to be found from new sources, including men without sufficient property rating for military service, underage youths, and even slaves. As was customary, clear decisions were made swiftly and confidently by commanders with imperium in the field, by elected officials with the power of edict, and by the Roman Senate.[39] But at such a time of pervasive crisis the Romans turned also to lawmaking assemblies.

For the first time the future of the Roman state was seriously threatened, and from then until the resolution of the threat in 201 the Romans reacted with the most intensive period of lawmaking activity in history before the surges in such activity of the first century.[40] Across this seventeen-year period an unusually large number of bills, listed in table 1.18, required attention by Roman voters in public lawmaking assemblies. In 218, two measures were carried, including the declaration of war against Carthage, not long before Hannibal's lightning descent into Italy. But in the year following, in 217, the Roman people assembled to consider six measures, the highest number ever presented to the people in a single year since the beginning of Roman expansion in Italy. The tribunes carried a measure releasing former consuls from an earlier plebiscite of 342 that prohibited them from standing again for the consulate before ten years had passed. The urgent need for experienced commanders was patent. Also in 217, shortly before his death in battle at Lake Trasimene, the consul C. Flaminius tried to remedy a desperate wartime need for cash by carrying a law depreciating the value of Rome's bronze coinage, the as, relative to the silver sestertius.[41] After the death of the consul Flaminius, and in the absence of the surviving consul, Cn. Servilius Geminus, who would ordinarily have made the appointment, again in 217 the Roman people elected a *dictator rei gerundae causa*, Q. Fabius Maximus, and a *magister equitum*, M. Minucius Rufus, to take charge of the war in northern Italy.[42] Following the alarming defeat at Lake Trasimene, the Romans turned sharply to their gods. On the counsel of the *pontifex maximus*, who advised that societywide authorization was required, a proposal was put to the Roman people to endorse the ritual dedication called *ver sacrum* recommended by the priests (*pontifices*) of Rome to expiate the disaster.[43] The outcome is unrecorded. Later in the year, responding to public discontent and the dissatisfaction of the magister equitum with the stratagem of Q. Fabius Maximus to avoid direct engagement with Hannibal in battle, the tribune M. Metilius proposed to remove Maximus from his office. When the bill failed he proposed another to make the magister equitum co-dictator. And in the years following 217, down to the end of the war in 201, as noted in table 1.18, anywhere from one to five laws or proposals addressing the crisis are recorded in all but four years, for a total of thirty-eight spanning the war years.[44] Such intense communitywide effort to pass public laws over such a short time span is not recorded again until the two years spanning the tribunates of C. Sempronius Gracchus, 123–121, and the disruption of the first century.

Most of this activity understandably focused on the conduct of war. Leadership was the primary issue throughout the period, as we can see from table 1.18. Not only in 217, but again in 210, the Roman people elected a dictator to conduct military operations in Italy. In a novel step in 215, the Roman people gave the authority of a consular commander to M. Claudius Marcellus so that he could direct the war against Carthage in Sicily; in 211 they allowed Marcellus to keep his imperium when he entered Rome in an ovation; and in 209 the tribune C. Publicius Bibulus proposed unsuccessfully that Marcellus's imperium be abrogated. In 211 the people unanimously approved the selection of the underage P. Cornelius Scipio (Africanus), son of the consul of 218, to direct the war in Spain with proconsular imperium, and in 204 they prorogued the command of the two proconsular commanders who were already there, L. Cornelius Lentulus and L. Manlius Acidinus.[45] In 208 the people accorded imperium to C. Aurunculeius, praetor in 209, so that he could command a province regularly handled by a praetor.[46] In 202 P. Cornelius Scipio was chosen unanimously by a plebeian tribal assembly to conduct the war in Africa, contrary to the recommendations of the Senate. In 201 the plebs selected C. Cornelius Cethegus to command in Spain.

Other issues dealt with in lawmaking assemblies also pertained directly to war. In 215, the year following the disaster at Cannae, tribunes proposed the purchase of slaves for military service and made arrangement also for the special board to make the purchases. Similarly, in 212 tribunes carried a bill enabling the conscription of underage youths by the fiction of requiring them to swear the military oath as though they were seventeen.[47] Both measures followed serious depletion of Roman manpower. In another direction we see rewards to groups and individuals for their role in the war effort—a grant of citizenship to three hundred Campanian cavalrymen for service in Sicily in 215; to three foreigners, a Spaniard, and a Syracusan in 211; and to a Carthaginian in 210. M. Claudius Marcellus in 210 was given the right to keep his imperium when he came into Rome to celebrate his ovation for his victories in Sicily.[48] Penalties were also levied. Cn. Fulvius Flaccus, praetor in 212 who had been tried and convicted of treason (*perduellio*) before a popular assembly for the defeat of his army by Hannibal, was exiled by decision of a plebeian assembly after he left Rome.[49] The tribunes Sp. Carvilius and L. Carvilius carried a measure exiling the war contractor M. Postumius of Pyrgi after he failed to appear to answer capital charges for swindling the Roman state.[50] The scam involved deliberately scuttling empty ships purportedly carrying army supplies for which the state had contracted and collecting compensation for the imaginary cargo. Public outrage was so high that the tribunes set his fine at two hundred thousand asses, despite protest by other contractors, and proposed exile when Postumius fled. Penalties against allies who broke their treaties with Rome were also considered in lawmaking assemblies. After Rome captured Capua in 210, the tribune L. Atilius carried a measure instructing the Senate to determine appropriate punishment.[51]

Still other issues addressed in lawmaking assemblies involved war funds and the division of spoils, again as we see in table 1.19. These include the measure restricting the carrying weight of ships owned by Roman senators, brought to the people by the tribune Q. Claudius shortly before the onset of war in 218 and supported by C. Flaminius—an effort to protect Rome's "war chest" for the anticipated struggle with Carthage—and the measure by C. Flaminius in 217 depreciating the value of Rome's bronze coinage—an effort, as noted, to increase cash resources.[52] The bill carried by the tribune C. Oppius in 215 limiting the value of clothing and jewelry a woman could wear was another effort to increase cash resources and, similarly, two carried in 209 and 204 limiting gifts and remunerations receivable by Roman patrons, legal advocates, and others.[53] A measure in 210 authorizing the Roman censors to lease lands in the newly confiscated ager Campanus dealt in a timely fashion with the division of spoils in one of the most fertile regions of Italy. This was the first but by no means the only time that the highly desirable land in Campania was the subject of a lawmaking assembly.

Who was responsible for this lawmaking activity? Throughout the years of the Second Punic War, we see a total of thirty-eight laws or proposals whose sponsors in fifteen cases are known by name, as shown in table 1.19. These include two consuls (C. Flaminius, consul in 217, and P. Cornelius Scipio, consul in 205), one praetor (P. Licinius Varus, praetor urbanus in 208) and twelve tribunes. The political standing of these sponsors of law between 218 and 200 was fairly consistent. One, M'. Acilius Glabrio, a tribune in 201 who enacted jointly with a colleague, Q. Minucius Thermus, that the Senate should make peace with Carthage and that Scipio should bring the army home, was a new man—a man with no political antecedents of the rank of consul or praetor.[54] He later became praetor in 196 and consul in 191.[55] Of the rest, three (P. Cornelius Scipio, P. Licinius Varus, and Q. Minucius Thermus) belonged to noble families and eight (Q. Claudius, M. Metilius, M. Minucius, L. and Sp. Carvilius, M. Cincius Alimentus, L. Atilius, and C. Publicius Bibulus) belonged to families that, although containing some noble branches, were at the time not included among the ranks of the most illustrious clans of Rome.[56] If not political newcomers, they were nonetheless men on the outside of the inner circle of ascendant clans.[57] Some of them were more obviously successful than others in their later careers. M. Metilius, tribune in 217, was next reported as legate and envoy in 212.[58] C. Publicius Bibulus, tribune in 209, was plebeian aedile perhaps in 195.[59] M. Cincius Alimentus, tribune in 204, was prefect in 193.[60] Q. Minucius Thermus, tribune in 201, had been military tribune in 202 and was curule aedile in 198, praetor in 196, and consul in 193.[61] No further career is reported for M. Minucius, tribune in 216; C. Oppius, tribune in 215; L. and Sp. Carvilius, tribunes in 212; L. Atilius, tribune in 210; and M. Lucretius, tribune in 210.

In view of the range of possible avenues available to the Romans for responding to crisis, specifically the decisions of elected officials and of the Senate, we must question why the Romans resorted so often to public lawmaking during the Second Punic War. What in particular made public lawmaking such an appropriate avenue of response to crisis that more proposals passed in review during the most critical war to date than in any previous period?[62] Since this question will engage us throughout this study, here let us look more closely at what these public laws achieved in the circumstances. We begin with the Roman leadership, the primary issue across the period of the Second Punic War. Time and again we see the Romans making adjustments in the regular patterns of leadership due to the exigencies of war. In particular, the Romans supplemented the number of commanders by presenting bills to lawmaking assemblies that adjusted or reinterpreted the rules for holding the office of consul, for instance, or adapted the power of command (imperium) to unanticipated circumstances, or selected dictators, or even modified the dictatorship. In all such instances involving leadership, the Romans resorted to lawmaking assemblies in order to put the most publicly recognized, most competent men in charge of the war through the modification to a greater or lesser extent of regular institutions or ordinary practices. The legitimization of leaders by society at large in a public lawmaking assembly ensured the strongest response in a time of war. Leadership was the archetypal issue touching all members of society, especially in time of war.

While military command was the first concern in this regard, areas of domestic leadership also necessitated a turn toward lawmaking assemblies. Across the period of the war a number of reported measures addressed the need to perform some specific, irregular administrative function, geared toward strengthening the society for war. Extraordinary commissions were created by vote of the people in three years to perform a wide range of tasks: the dedication of a temple to Venus Erycina (215) and the resolution of a shortage of silver (216), the purchase of twenty-four thousand slaves for military service (215), the restoration of city walls and towers, the inventory of temple goods, and the restoration of the temples of Fortuna and Mater Matuta (all three in 212 by a single plebiscite). In less troubled times at least some of these tasks, we might imagine, would fall perfunctorily to a regular official such as the aedile or to a senatorial task force created by Senate decree. But in wartime, particularly such an unprecedented war that produced uncommonly high casualties among Rome's senators and elected officials, the ordinary routes were blocked and the usual sources of funds were constrained. It was also vital that a communitywide consensus be established on many issues. The Romans therefore resorted to lawmaking assemblies to create special boards to handle specific tasks.

But in the remedy inspired by immediate concerns we sometimes discern deeper issues troubling the Roman state. Although the obvious focus of lawmaking events in the period from 218 to 201 is war, it is equally apparent that other more fundamental issues intersect with this overarching concern. Particularly visible are the strains of an expanding number of Romans of wealth and status. Consider again the issue of leadership, primary throughout the war. In 217, as noted, tribunes carried a bill exempting former consuls from the ten-year gap between one consulate and the next prescribed by law. In 203, tribunes carried a measure clearing the consul of C. Servilius Geminus of criminal intent to deceive the people (*fraus*) when in the recent past he held plebeian offices—the tribunate sometime before 209 and the plebeian aedileship in 209—unaware that his father, a former praetor who was thought to have died when serving as a land commissioner in northern Italy, was in fact alive and prisoner of the Gauls.[63] An earlier enactment prohibited sons of curule magistrates from holding plebeian office in their fathers' lifetimes.[64] Roman adaptability, even to the point of circumventing existing law, significantly through a societywide measure, is very much in evidence. But in the case of these enactments we are clearly also dealing with measures adjusting existing law that had widely diffused power among eligible Romans. Such a diffusion of power could doubtless serve as a hindrance to quick decision making under the conditions faced by Rome during the Second Punic War, when the state desperately needed a rapid source of competent commanders to replace commanders who fell in battle. Even so, issues of leadership are barely submerged and from time to time—the failed proposal to abrogate the imperium of M. Claudius Marcellus provides a case in point—resurface, even in wartime.

Other enactments similarly address the strain of an expanding number of elite Romans very directly—even in wartime. These are the enactments setting restrictions on the display and outlay of wealth, especially by elite Romans. Extravagant displays of wealth or large outlays of cash by individual Romans made Romans uneasy at the best of times; such behavior was especially unpopular in Rome in wartime given the cash demands of the war as well as the sacrifices of a great many people. The concern is reflected in the lex Metilia of 220, two years before the war, which set limits on extravagant dress. It was followed up by the controversial lex Claudia of 218, carried by the tribune Q. Claudius a few months before the outbreak of war. This enactment—presented shortly after the consular elections of June, supported by the consul designate C. Flaminius, and fiercely opposed by the Senate—prohibited senators and senators' sons from owning seagoing boats larger than the carrying weight of thirty amphorae. Livy, writing two hundred years after the event, states that the motivation behind the measure was to restrict the commercial activities of senators by enabling them to transport crops, but no more, from their farms because money making was considered undignified for senators.[65] Modern historians believe that deeper concerns were involved. Cargo lost at sea set up a chain of events: the senator's financial ruin; his reduction to a lower property rating; his removal from the Senate list by the censor at the next census; and his replacement in the Senate by a new senator through adlection. Thus the statute attempted to prevent senators from engaging in risky trading ventures in order to maintain the current Senate membership. John D'Armes has described the lex Claudia as an attempt to preserve the old order, necessitated by the heavy involvement of wealthy men in trading ventures accompanied by the new membership in the Senate.[66] But given the immediate circumstances, namely, the anticipated approaching war with Carthage, a more likely explanation for the tribune Claudius's sponsorship of the lex Claudia is a concern on the part of some Romans to preserve the wealth of elite Romans so that they could invest their capital in the coming war. When war did come, Romans in the highest property classes were assessed to contribute fixed amounts to the state to pay the sailors.[67] The Roman people approved related measures throughout the war: the lex Publicia of probably 209, restricting gifts that clients could give to their patrons at Saturnalia to the small human figures shaped from wax used in the ceremonies of that holiday, and the lex Cincia of 204, restricting the amount of remuneration legal advocates received for legal defenses and regulating the degree of relationship permissible in giving and receiving gifts.[68] Finally, the sheer size of the group of lawmakers known by name during the period, their families and political careers, is itself testimony to circumstances facilitating risk taking in the lawmaking arena by men from newer or less powerful clans.

Whence such a variety of concerns? The necessity of securing cash resources in wartime in a limited cash economy, a development from the exigencies of war specific to the wartime period from 218 to 201, clearly plays a role in the lawmaking activity of that period. But several other developments intersect, devolving primarily from Roman expansion in Italy over the previous 150 years. Chief among them are the admission of new members to the Roman equestrian class and the new business interests of Romans and Italians in an expanding, monetized economy. Throughout the Second Punic War we see Romans turning to public lawmaking assemblies to resolve matters arising from these longer-term developments as well as from the circumstances of the war itself.

FUNCTIONS AND MEANING OF PUBLIC LAWMAKING

What can we say so far about the functions and meaning of public lawmaking? Let me begin with the most obvious feature of Roman public law: the extraordinary persistence of the phenomenon. For half a millennium the Roman people displayed an enduring commitment to public lawmaking assemblies, especially in times of crisis. Despite the extraordinary range of issues addressed in such public assemblies, certain patterns emerge from the palimpsest. Across the more than three hundred years of our period of interest Romans voted in public lawmaking assemblies on fundamental matters, most often involving military and civilian leadership and ranging from the rules for elite officeholders, disposition of state land, the constitution of courts, questions of war and peace, citizenship and civil rights, the abrogation of existing statues, to the establishment of special commissions to investigate previously unknown conditions. With each successive period, however, the Romans mooted different issues in public lawmaking sessions unique to the circumstances at hand. That Romans could abstain from lawmaking activity for many years and yet retain both an appreciation of the functions of lawmaking and a detailed knowledge of the necessary procedures for enacting legitimate law suggests that the process rested on many of the beliefs and assumptions of everyday Roman life. On the other hand, throughout the first century, the Romans resorted to lawmaking activity with such frequency as to radically change its character.

Overall, most of the issues involved in lawmaking assemblies seem also in some way to deal with some vital aspect of community life. Nevertheless, it is obvious that it was a rare issue that was taken to these rather irregularly held assemblies. They dealt at times with issues that the Roman Senate at the same time also addressed in its decrees. Or the Senate sometimes recommended that certain matters be presented to the people in a public law proposal. Thus, an issue addressed at one time in a lawmaking assembly could at another time be resolved in other ways, by the Roman Senate or by magistrates with imperium. There are no consistently obvious reasons to the modern eye why such was the case. Only close scrutiny of the circumstances of each issue sheds light on why matters were handled as they were. While modern scholars accept broad principles about the sovereign role of the Roman people in resolving matters pertinent to the Roman people, the specific instances do not always conform to the principle, as we shall see in later chapters.[69]

In identifying specific issues for public adjudication and in convening the Roman people for public sessions to handle such issues, a number of magistrates had the authority to take action, although overall relatively few political leaders with the authority to do so ever sponsored public law proposals. Initially, the tribunes played a key role, convening twice as many lawmaking sessions as their nearest rivals, the consuls. After the Second Punic War, however, the pattern becomes more complicated as the incidence of lawmaking gathers speed. Although they are joined by more consuls, praetors, and an occasional extraordinary magistrate or dictator in convening public lawmaking assemblies, tribunes remain most important in proposing public lawmaking assemblies up to the end of our period of interest, 44. Again, there are no consistently obvious reasons to the modern eye why one officeholder rather than another convened the people in a lawmaking assembly. The most persistent modern rationale assumes some formal, constitutional basis and pursues the question from another angle, namely, why the Romans met to enact law most frequently in a plebeian tribal assembly, less frequently in a full tribal assembly, and only rarely in a centuriate assembly.

However, more immediate factors can be adduced to explain the patterns of sponsorship, and at times therefore the type of assembly, in certain periods. For instance, consuls were seldom in Rome for any length of time during the Second Punic War, 218–201. At all times, the nature of their office kept tribunes in Rome. Moreover, after 133, aspiring political leaders used the office of tribune more aggressively in furthering their political careers. The clustering of laws in crisis periods combined with the high level of involvement of tribunes in such periods suggests that tribunes in particular mediated changes that met with the concurrence of the Roman people in critical times. The overall lawmaking activity by consuls, praetors, and tribunes is skewed by the unique activity of a small group of individual lawmakers, specifically the tribune C. Gracchus, and the sometimes consuls, sometimes dictators Sulla and Caesar. While no one clan ever held a monopoly on proposing law, a greater number of clans appear to be involved in lawmaking in crisis years, such as the period of the Second Punic War, and in particular more new men are involved after 133. Over the first century, the elite sponsors of public law came from at least fifty different clans. Additionally, the period between 90 and 44 appears to be one in which not only more families but more offices were involved in the promulgation of more laws than throughout the earlier periods. Tribunes in this period are still by far the most active lawmakers as in earlier periods, notwithstanding the ten-year hiatus in the office of tribune imposed by a public law of the dictator Sulla. Most new men are involved in lawmaking at this level as well. At the same time, the lawmaking activity of consuls and praetors was boosted after 81 by other public laws of Sulla, which had the effect of keeping consuls and praetors in Rome until after their year of office.[70] Now, consuls and praetors are more involved in lawmaking than before. Both the pattern of sponsorship and the incidence of lawmaking activity in relation to the total body of officials with the authority to enact laws with the people confirm that not every man with the required authority took it upon himself to enact law. These patterns, however, also confirm the idea of an appreciable diffusion of power among elite Romans throughout the period, which expands as we approach the end of the Republic. In turn, the creation of the office of dictator legibus scribendis et rei publicae constituendae suggests that some Roman leaders viewed the public lawmaking capacity of office as a way of legitimizing political position.

Finally, our exploration permits a few general observations about the achievements of public lawmaking activity in Roman society. In 325 years of public lawmaking activity, between 350 and 25, the most apparently intractable issues in Roman history, as well as what appear today as some of the most frivolous, were addressed in public law proposals and decided by the people. Whether in times of crisis or times of relative peace the Romans resorted to public lawmaking assemblies to resolve what we regard as some of the most vital issues in their history, for example, laws to settle questions on the distribution and ownership of lands throughout conquered territory. At other times the Romans turned to public lawmaking assemblies to decide far less weighty matters, at least from a modern perspective, for instance, when the assembly convened in 241 to exempt the senator L. Caecilius Metellus from the public law prohibiting senators from entering the Senate house carried on a litter or the many public lawmaking sessions between the third and the first centuries convened to regulate the cost of dinner parties.[71] Thus, across this 325-year period the issues addressed in public lawmaking assemblies could be both urgently important and seemingly unimportant; they could be both communitywide in scope and narrowly focused on an individual or group. Public lawmaking assemblies dealt with issues involving the survival of the Roman state and also covered what to modern eyes appear to be the most trivial matters. Despite the importance of many of the issues with which public lawmaking assemblies dealt, their activation appears infrequent and random.

Something of the special importance and resiliency of Roman lawmaking emerges from the arrangements achieved through laws enacted in public assemblies during the Second Punic War, especially involving the Roman leadership. It would seem that when existing offices and the regular leadership were insufficient to the situation at hand, public lawmaking gave the Romans wide latitude to move beyond customary limits to remedy deficiencies in a process that involved individuals on all levels of society in the decision. At that time, the risk of presenting such remedies as public law proposals to the Roman people was taken by tribunes, who were junior-level officials and often men from politically obscure families. In the circumstances of the Second Punic War, a great many of the issues involved suggest that the public lawmaking process served as a flexible instrument for developing consensus on issues that might otherwise have proven disruptive. In all periods the range of topics considered in public lawmaking sessions suggests that the Romans used the process as a means of addressing issues that could not be resolved in another, more usual, traditional manner by the Roman Senate or by elite officeholders serving in a wide variety of official offices. The issues Roman lawmakers presented to the Roman people further suggest a continuing societywide concern with the necessity of adapting to the conditions and consequences of Roman expansion across Italy and the Mediterranean. Thus, whatever the focus and scope of the particular public law proposal or public law, they have little meaning outside of a full understanding of their surrounding circumstances.

Our quest for such an understanding continues in the remainder of part 1 with an examination of the lawmaking process itself, whose distinctive features make it a singularly important object of study. Public law was generated by the Roman people when convened in a voting assembly by one of their elected officials and subject to the approval or disapproval of the Roman people. The elaborate ritualized procedures at public lawmaking sessions provided a microcosm of the social and political functioning of the Roman world and involved a wider range of participants in a more elaborate series of customary behaviors than almost any other public process. Every stage of public lawmaking provides clues to the complex interaction between different groups in Roman society and to beliefs and assumptions underlying their behavior. In the next chapter we turn to the presentation of public law and in particular to the role of oratory in allowing political leaders to reflect the will and manage the emotions of the Roman people.

Information for Tables in Chapter One

Note that tables 1.3 and 1.4, which organize information by subject only, not date, utilize all 559 laws, because all 559 are lodged securely within the 325 years between 350 and 25 BCE. Tables organizing the information by quarter centuries between 350 and 25 (tables 1.1, 1.2, and 1.17), for purposes of analysis, are based on 494 laws and proposals because no more than 495 (out of 559) can be precisely or approximately assigned to a fixed, twenty-five-year span of time. Tables that organize the information by conventional, historical period between 350 and 44 (tables 1.5–1.12, 1.16, 1.18, and 1.19), for purposes of analysis, are based on 484 laws and proposals (out of 541) because it is possible to assign some laws of uncertain date, though not all, to these broader, more easily defined periods. These variations are the unavoidable outcome of periodization.

The overall patterns remain the same, notwithstanding. Among the 559 laws reliably falling between 350 and 25 BCE, 64 (11.4 percent) cannot be positively dated to any twenty-five-year block within the larger period. Of these, 17 (3 percent) are of unknown date altogether; seven (1 percent) fall between 350 and 219; nine (2 percent) between 200 and 134; 27 (5 percent) fall between 133 and 44; and five (less than 1 percent) are dated after the end of the Republic. In brief, there are still more laws or proposals in the last century of the Republic, even though they are uncertain in date. Furthermore, among the 541 laws reliably falling between 350 and 44 BCE, 57 (10.5 percent) cannot be positively dated to one of the conventional historical periods. Of these, 26 (4.8 percent) are of unknown date altogether; two (less than one-half of 1 percent) are dated before 200; 10 (2 percent) are dated before 149; 15 (3 percent) are dated before 80; one (less than one-quarter of 1 percent) is dated after 390; one (less than one-quarter of 1 percent) is dated after 253; and two (less than one-half of 1 percent) are dated after 241. Hence, the volume of absolute uncertainty is relatively small (4.8 percent), and the remaining 7 percent does not contradict the overall impression from the tables organizing information by conventional, historical period that more laws were proposed or presented to assemblies after the mid-second century.

TABLE 1.1 Frequency of Lawmaking Activity by Quarter Century, 350–25

Period	Frequency (by number and percentage)[a]
350–325	14 (2.5)
324–300	13 (2.3)
299–275	10 (1.8)
274–250	9 (1.6)
249–225	4 (0.7)
224–200	43 (7.7)
199–175	30 (5.4)
174–150	19 (3.4)
149–125	33 (5.9)
124–100	68 (12.2)
99–75	67 (12.0)
74–50	118 (21.1)
49–25	67 (11.9)
Unknown	64 (11.4)
Total	559 (100)

Source: See appendixes A and C.
[a]Percentages do not always add to 100 because of rounding

TABLE 1.2 Patterns of Lawmaking Activity for Selected Periods, 350–25

(1) Period	(2) Years without Laws	(3) Years with One Law	(4) Years with Two Laws	(5) Years with Three Laws	(6) Years with Four Laws	(7) Years with Five Laws	(8) Years with Six or More Laws	(9) Highest Number in One Year (year in parentheses)
350–325	15	5	3	1				3 (339)
324–300	16	5	2		1			4 (300)
299–275	18	4	1		1			4 (287)
274–250	16	7	1					2 (264)
249–225	21	2	1					2 (241)
224–200	7	6	3	4	2	1	1	6 (217)
199–175	7	9	6	2				3 (189)[a]
174–150	14	6	2	2				3 (167)[a]
149–125	7	12	2	2			1	7 (133)
124–100	6	5	5	2	2	1	3	13 (123)
99–75	6	9	2	2	1		4	18 (81)
74–50	1	4	4	3	1	3	8	16 (58)
49–25	10	5		1	3		6	19 (44)
Total	144	79	32	19	11	5	23	

Source: See appendixes A and C.
[a]More than one year in quarter century with this total.

TABLE 1.3 Repeated Public Laws by Category and Subject, 350–25

Issues Involving Leader

No.	Subject
21	Special commission of investigation
14	Recall of exile(s)
14	Privileges for individual(s)
11	Suspension or circumvention of law
11	The crime of repetundae
8	Jury composition
8	The crime of ambitus
7	Creation of extraordinary board
7	Assigning a province
6	Selecting a commander
5	Abrogation of a commander's imperium
5	Prorogation of imperium
5	Abrogation of an existing law
5	Exile of individual(s)
4	Triumph for a commander
4	Removal of tribune(s) from office
4	Restoration of citizen rights to individual(s)
3	Censors' authority to review Senate members
3	Election of a dictator
3	Reassigning provinces
3	Food and guests at dinner parties
3	Election of priests
3	Cost of food at dinner parties
3	The crime of maiestas
3	Selection of a dictator
3	The crime of vis
3	Assignment of consular provinces
3	Assignment of oversight of weights and measures
3	Local jurisdiction in Italy
2	Addition of members (equestrians) to Senate
2	Announcement of auctoritas patrum before assemblies
2	Selection of two commanders
2	Ages for holding office
2	Necessary conditions for a triumph
2	Obnuntiatio in assemblies
2	Law sponsor's election to post created by his law
2	Restrictions on tribunes
2	Removal of consul from office
2	Expanding the number of quaestors
2	The power to give exemptions from the law
2	Assignment of oversight over grain supply
2	Grant of tribunician powers to Caesar
2	Creation of new patrician families
2	Ratification of Caesar's acta

Subtotal: 205
Percentage: 54

Other Issues

No.	Subject
16	Declaration of war
16	The foundation of colonies
15	Distribution or assignment of land
15	Group grant of citizenship
10	Distribution of grain to citizens
7	Confirmation of peace
7	Civil liberties (*provocatio*)
5	Settlement of debts
5	Modification/extension of legis actio procedure
4	Regulation of suretyship (*sponsio*)
4	Individual grant of citizenship
4	Citizen status of ex-slaves and others
4	Voting by written ballot
4	Status of landholdings
3	Port duties
3	Permissible gambling
2	Lease of ager Campanus
2	Punishment of a town
2	Assignment of guardians
2	Expelling Latin and Italian immigrants from Rome
2	Term of military service
2	The ruler of Egypt
2	Enrollment of new citizens in all the tribes
2	Confirmation of grants of citizenship by commander
2	Remission of rents in Rome
2	Restoration of power to King Deiotarus
2	Judicial organization of Cisalpine Gaul
2	General validity of plebiscites
2	Consecration of buildings, areas, and altars
2	Administrative organization of municipia

Subtotal: 150
Percentage: 40

(continued)

Table 1.3 (*continued*)

Unknown: 24
Percentage: 6
Total laws: 379

Source: See appendixes A and C.

TABLE 1.4 One-Time Public Laws by Category and Subject, 350–25

Issues Involving Leaders

Opening censorship to plebs
Interval between offices, consecutive offices, plebeian consuls
Two-man board for outfitting and repairing fleet
Number and qualifications of augurs and priests
Election of IIIviri coloniae deducendae
Gifts of Ptolemy to ambassadors
Surrender of a commander
Iteration of the censorship
Selection of military tribunes by the consul
Stipend of censured equites
Expanding the number of praetors
Jurisdictio of urban praetor
Carrying weight of boats owned by senators
Abrogation of a dictator's imperium
Equalizing imperium of dictator and magister equitum
Expensive clothing
Proconsular imperium for a praetor
Women's clothing/jewelry/horse-drawn carriages
Extension of proconsul's imperium until ovation
Election of the military tribunes of legions 1–4
Exculpating C. Servilius from breaking the law
Authorization to make peace with Carthage and recall army
Creation of three-man priesthood (*epulones*)
Authorization to negotiate a peace
Provincial governor's power of requisition
Assignment of responsibility for intercalation
Number of guests at dinner parties
Number of praetors in alternate years
Return of M. Popillius Laenas to appear before court
Annulment of state leases and contracts made by censors
Extension of commander's imperium until his triumph
Reelection to the office of consul
Theater seats for equites
Rejection of peace and surrender of commander
Jurisdictio of land commissioners
Iteration of office by tribunes
The public horse of senators
Reelection to office of previous year's tribunes
Magistrates who have been deposed by the people
Ages for election as military tribune
Allotment of consular provinces by the Senate
Election and responsibilities of the IIIviri capitales
Use of bequest of King Attalus
Liability for trial of Romans on state business abroad
Authorization for praetor to escort Jugurtha to Rome
Expulsion from Senate of individuals losing imperium
Importation of wild animals from Africa
Membership of tribunes in the Senate
Trinundinum and unrelated measures in one proposal
Addition of equestrians to Senate and jury composition
Election of jurors by the tribes
A ceiling on senators' debts
Replacement of a commander
Order, interval, and age limits for holding office
Establishment of standing courts and jury composition
Number of priests and restoration of co-optation
Restrictions on provincial governors
Restoration of the office of tribune
Right of tribunes to seek other office

(*continued*)

TABLE 1.4 *(continued)*

Issues Involving Leadership

Responsibility for letting state contracts
Praetor's observance of his edict
Loans to foreign states
Creation of a command against pirates
Senate audiences with foreign embassies
Loans to foreign envoys
Selection of Vestals
Assignment of Egypt as a province
A candidate's entourage
Standing for office when absent from Rome
Recall of a commander from his province
Depositing the law in the archives
Transfer to a plebeian clan
Reassignment of oversight over temple reconstruction
Ratification of a commander's acts
The staff of a provincial governor
Magistrates who put citizens to death without trial
Comitial days and their interruption
The voting order of jurors
Senate and comitial meeting days
Responsibility for restoring King Ptolemy
Personal expenditures by senators
Proconsular imperium and assignment of province
Interval between office and promagistracy
Cost of travel equipment
Supervision of roads
Capacity of Pompey's men to stand for office
Eligibility for selection to priesthood
Length of provincial governorships
Travel outside Italy by citizens, ages 20–40
Abolition of the office of dictator
Attendants for plebeian aediles
A commission to examine Caesar's acta
Repeal of decrees of Antony and Lepidus
Lictors for Vestal Virgins
Placement of statues of divus Iulius
Reprieve of two proscribed individuals
The appointment of municipal prefects
Assignment of a judex after 30 days

Subtotal: 98
Percentage: 54

Other Issues

Water supply of Rome
Mutiny by soldiers
A day when the ludi Romani are repeated
Renewal of treaty with Samnites
Treaty with Lucani
Legal business on market days
Action among co-owners for division of common property
Punishment of legio Campana
Damage to property
Damage done by a dog
Military aid to the Mamertines
Treaty with Hiero of Syracuse
Value of bronze coinage
Public vow of a sacred spring
Punishment of Campanian rebels by the Senate
Gift giving by clients on the Saturnalia
Wrongful ownership of citizen/slave of citizen
Celebration of the ludi Apollinares
Games of chance
Gift giving by defendants in law cases
Extension of Roman laws on debt to allies and Latins
Children in will
Fraud perpetrated against minors
Moneylending
Size of legacies
Capacity of women to inherit
Ownership of stolen property
Return of a widow's dowry
Sexual offenses against freeborn people
Extension of the lex Fannia to all Italy
Amount of sponsio before centumviral court
Expulsion of foreigners from Rome
The formulary procedure
Conditions of military service
Lease of state contracts in Asia
Interest payment on principal of debts
The crime of sicarii and venefici
Confirmation of heirs
Construction of new roads

(continued)

TABLE 1.4 (*continued*)

Order of voting in the centuriate assembly
Foreign participation in the cult of Jupiter Capitolinus
Stopping a colony foundation
Voting bridges (*pontes*)
Victory on a coinage issue
Addition of bronze to silver coinage
Creation of new tribes
Introduction of the semiuncial as (coin)
Proscription of citizens
Enactment of law in the centuriate assembly
Removal of citizenship from towns
The crime of falsa
Interest rates

The crime of iniuria
The crime of peculatus
Limitations on suretyship
Malicious prosecutions
Confirmation of citizenship
Remittance of purchase price of proscribed property
Autonomy for a foreign city
Voting rights of freedmen
Expulsion of foreigners from Rome
Debt and land distribution
Land boundaries
Contracts of the publicani of Asia
Roman relations with foreign cities and states
Authorization to dedicate a statue on Capitolium
Restoration of collegia
King Deiotarus and Pessinus

Annexation of Cyprus as a province
Involvement of quaestorian scribae in trade
The crime of parricidium
The crime of sodalicia
Annexation of Numidia as province
Acquisition of servitudes through usucapio
Immunity for Delos
Hire of sheperds of free status
List of eligible grain recipients
Extending the pomerium
Tax burden and provincial status of Crete
Appeals to the people
Minimum portion allowable to heir under a will
Remission of rents in Rome and Italy

Subtotal: 82
Percentage: 46

Total: 180

Source: See appendixes A and C.

TABLE 1.5 Repeated Public Laws by Selected Periods, 350–44 (frequency in parentheses)

350–219

Declaration of war (10)
Grant of citizenship to group (3)
Suspension or circumvention of law (2)
Announcement of auctoritas patrum (2)
Punishment of a community (2)
Prorogation of imperium (2)
The general validity of plebiscites (2)

Single issues: 30
Subtotal laws: 53

218–201

Creation of extraordinary board (4)
The selection of a commander (3)
Suspension or circumvention of law (2)
Confirmation of peace (2)
Election of a dictator (2)
Grant of citizenship to individual (2)

Single issues: 23
Subtotal laws: 38

200–134

Special commission of investigation (6)
Suspension or circumvention of law (4)
Declaration of war (4)
Confirmation of peace (4)
The foundation of colonies (3)
Abrogation of an existing statute (2)
Distribution or assignment of land (2)
Privileges and honors for individuals (2)
The crime of ambitus (2)
Obnuntiatio in assemblies (2)
Voting by written ballot (2)

Single issues: 28
Subtotal laws: 61

(*continued*)

TABLE 1.5 *(continued)*

133–92

Uncertain or conjectural (11)
The foundation of colonies (6)
Distribution or assignment of land (4)
Crime of repetundae (3)
Grant of citizenship to outside group (3)
Civil liberties (3)
Jury composition (3)
Recall of exile(s) (3)
Selection of a commander (2)
Abrogation of an existing statute (2)
Sponsor's election to post his law created (2)
Voting by written ballot (2)
Term of military service (2)

Single issues: 38
Subtotal laws: 98

91–44

Recall of exile(s) (11)
Distribution or assignment of land (9)
Uncertain or conjectural (8)
Special commission of investigation (7)
Grant of citizenship to outside group (7)
Privileges for individuals (6)
The crime of ambitus (6)
Settlement of debts (5)
Jury composition (5)
The crime of repetundae (5)
The foundation of colonies (5)
The distribution of grain to citizens (5)
The assignment of a province (4)
Restoration of civil liberties (4)
Suspension or circumvention of law (3)
A triumph for a commander (3)
Selection of dictator (3)
The crime of vis (3)
Assignment of consular provinces (3)
Local jurisdiction in Italy (3)
Censor's authority to review Senate (2)
Abrogation of a commander's imperium (2)
Prorogation of imperium (2)
Reassignment of provinces (2)
Citizen status of ex-slaves and their sons (2)
Food and guests at dinner parties (2)
Removal of tribune(s) from office (2)
Port duties (2)
The crime of maiestas (2)
Exile of individual(s) (2)
Restrictions on tribunes (2)
Enrollment of new citizens in all the tribes (2)
Removal of a consul from office (2)
Confirmation of commander's grants of citizenship (2)
The power to give exemptions from the law (2)
Assignment of oversight over grain supply (2)
Remission of rents in Rome (2)
Interest payments on the principal of debts (2)

Single issues: 93
Subtotal laws: 234

Unknown: 57

Total laws: 541

Source: See appendixes A and C.

TABLE 1.6 Public Laws by Subject and Category, 350–219 (frequency in parentheses)

Issues Involving Leaders	Other Issues
Suspension or circumvention of law (2)	Declaration of war (10)
Prorogation of imperium (2)	Citizenship grant to group (3)
Announcement of auctoritas patrum in assemblies (2)	Punishment of community (2)
Stipend of censured equites	General validity of plebiscites (2)
A triumph for a commander	Dissolution of debt bondage
Censors' authority to review Senate membership	Civil liberties
Election of the military tribunes of legions 1–4	Confirmation of peace
Special commission of investigation	Distribution or assignment of land
Expanding the number of quaestors	Expensive clothing
Interval between consecutive offices, plebeian consuls	Settlement of debts
Opening censorship to plebs	Mutiny by soldiers
Creation of two-man board for outfitting and repairing fleet	Repetition of ludi Romani
Number and qualifications of augurs and priests	Renewal of treaty with Samnites
Election of IIIviri coloniae deducendae	Consecration of buildings, areas, and altars
Gifts of Ptolemy to ambassadors	Treaty with Lucani
The surrender of a commander	Legal business on market days
Iteration of the censorship	Punishment of legio Campana
Oversight of weights and measures by aediles	Military aid to the Mamertines
	Treaty with Hiero of Syracuse
Subtotal laws: 21	Subtotal laws: 32
Percentage: 40	Percentage: 60
Total laws: 53	

Source: See appendixes A and C.

TABLE 1.7 Public Laws by Subject and Category, 218–201 (frequency in parentheses)

Issues Involving Leadership	Other Issues
Creation of extraordinary board (4)	Confirmation of peace (2)
Selection of a commander (3)	Grant of citizenship to individual (2)
Suspension or circumvention of law (2)	Declaration of war
Election of a dictator (2)	The value of bronze coinage
Carrying weight of boats owned by senators	Public vow of a ver sacrum
Abrogation of a dictator's imperium	Grant of citizenship to group
Equalizing the imperium of the dictator and magister equitum	Women's clothing and accoutrements
Proconsular imperium for a praetor	The absent M. Postumus Pyrgensis
Extension of proconsul's imperium	Punishment of Campanian rebels by the Senate
Abrogation of a commander's imperium	Lease of ager Campanus
Prorogation of imperium	Gift giving by clients on the Saturnalia
The assignment of a province	Celebration of the ludi Apollinares
The selection of two commanders	Gift giving by defendants in law cases and value of gifts
Exculpating C. Servilius from knowingly breaking the law	
Authorization to make peace with Carthage	Subtotal laws: 15
The exile of individual(s)	Percentage: 39
Subtotal laws: 23	
Percentage: 61	
Total laws: 38	

Source: See appendixes A and C.

TABLE 1.8 Public Laws by Subject and Category, 200–134 (frequency in parentheses)

Issues Involving Leadership	Other Issues
Special commission of investigation (6)	Declaration of war (4)
Suspension or circumvention of law (4)	Confirmation of peace (4)
Abrogation of an existing statute (2)	The foundation of colonies (3)
The crime of ambitus (2)	Distribution or assignment of land (2)
Obnuntiatio in assemblies (2)	Privileges for individuals (2)
The ages for holding office	Voting by written ballot (2)
Abrogation of a commander's imperium	Grant of citizenship to group
The assignment of a province	Civil liberties
The selection of two commanders	Lease of ager Campanus
Creation of a three-man priesthood (*epulones*)	Extension of Roman laws on debt to allies and Latins
Authorization to negotiate a peace	Moneylending
Reassignment of provinces	Citizen status of former slaves and their sons
Assignment of responsibility for intercalation	Number of guests at dinner parties
Number of praetors elected in alternate years	Expulsion of Latin and Italian immigrants from Rome
The return of M. Popillius Laenas	The capacity of women to inherit
Annulment of state leases and contracts made by censors	Food and guests at dinner parties
Extension of commander's imperium until he triumphs	Extension of the lex Fannia to all Italy
The crime of repetundae	
The election of priests	
Rejection of peace and surrender of commander	
The importation of wild animals from Africa	
Membership of tribunes in the Senate	
Subtotal laws: 33	Subtotal laws: 28
Percentage: 54	Percentage: 46
Total laws: 61	

Source: See appendixes A and C.

TABLE 1.9 Public Laws by Subject and Category, 133–92 (frequency in parentheses)

Issues Involving Leadership		
Special commission of investigation (5)	Assignment of a province	Ages for election as military tribune
The crime of repetundae (3)	Election of priests	Allotment of consular provinces by Senate
Jury composition (4)	Jurisdictio of three men for granting and assigning land	Authorization for praetor to escort Jugurtha to Rome
Recall of exile(s) (3)	Removal of tribune(s) from office	Expulsion from Senate of individuals losing imperium
Selection of a commander (2)	Iteration of office by tribunes	The crime of maiestas
Abrogation of an existing statute (2)	The public horse of senators	Exile of individual(s)
Law sponsor's election to post he created (2)	Addition of members to Senate from equestrian class	Trinundinum and unrelated measures
Abrogation of commander's imperium	Magistrates deposed by the people	Selection of military tribunes
		Jury matters
Subtotal laws: 38		
Percentage: 38.7		

Other Issues		
The foundation of colonies (6)	Declaration of war	Lease of state contracts in Asia
The distribution of grain to citizens (5)	Cost of food at dinner parties	Port duties
Distribution or assignment of land (4)	Regulation of suretyship	Construction of new roads
Status of landholdings (4)	Grant of citizenship to individual	Order of voting in centuriate assembly
Grant of citizenship to group (3)	Wrongful ownership of a citizen or citizen's ex-slave	Foreign participation in the cult of Capitoline Jupiter
Citizen liberties (3)	Expulsion of Latin and Italian immigrants from Rome	Stopping a colony foundation
Voting by written ballot (2)	Use of bequest of King Attalus	Voting bridges (*pontes*)
Term of military service (2)	The ruler of Egypt	Victory on a coinage issue
	Expelling foreigners from Rome	Modification or extension of legis actiones
	Conditions of military service	Land boundaries
Subtotal laws: 49		
Percentage: 50		
Unknown: 11		
Percentage: 11.2		
Total laws: 98		

Source: See appendixes A and C.

TABLE 1.10 Public Laws by Subject and Category, 91–44 (frequency in parentheses)

Issues Involving Leadership

Recall of exile(s) (11)
Special commission of investigation (7)
Privileges for individuals (6)
The crime of ambitus (6)
Jury composition (5)
The crime of repetundae (5)
The assignment of a province (4)
Restoration of civil liberties (4)
Suspension or circumvention of law (3)
A triumph for a commander (3)
Selection of dictator (3)
The crime of vis (3)
Assignment of consular provinces (3)
Censors' authority to review Senate membership (2)
Abrogation of a commander's imperium (2)
Prorogation of imperium (2)
Reassignment of provinces (2)
Removal of tribune(s) from office (2)
The crime of maiestas (2)
The exile of individual(s) (2)
Restrictions on tribunes (2)
Removal of a consul from office (2)
The power to give exemptions from the law (2)
Assignment of oversight over grain supply (2)
Assignment of oversight over weights and measures
Expanding the number of praetors
Election of a dictator
Creation of extraordinary commission
Abrogation of an existing statute
The necessary conditions for a triumph
Theater seats for equites
The election of priests
Addition of equestrians to Senate
Addition of equestrians to Senate/jury composition
The election of jurors by the tribes
A ceiling on senators' debts
The order, interval, and age limits for holding office
Establishment of standing courts/jury composition
The number of priests and restoration of co-optation
Restrictions on provincial governors
Expanding the number of quaestors
The crime of peculatus
Restoration of the office of tribune
Right of tribunes to seek other office
Responsibility for letting state contracts
The praetor's observance of his edict
Loans to foreign states
Creation of a command against pirates
Senate audiences with foreign embassies
Loans to foreign envoys
Selection of Vestals
Assignment of Egypt as a province
A candidate's entourage
Standing for office when absent from Rome
Recall of a commander from his province
Depositing of law in the archives
Reassignment of oversight over temple reconstruction
Transfer to a plebeian clan
Ratification of a commander's acts
The staff of a provincial governor
Magistrates who put citizens to death without trial
Comitial days and their interruption
The voting order of jurors
Senate and comitial meeting days
Assignment of responsibility for restoring King Ptolemy
Personal expenditures by senators
Proconsular imperium and assignment of province
Interval between office and promagistracy
Cost of travel equipment
Supervision of roads
Grant of tribunician powers to Caesar
Capacity of Pompey's men to stand for office
Length of provincial governorships
Eligibility for selection to priesthood
Travel outside Italy
Creation of new patrician families
Ratification of Caesar's acta
Abolition of the office of dictator
A commission to examine Caesar's acta
Appeals to the people

Subtotal laws: 141
Percentage: 60.2

(*continued*)

TABLE 1.10 *(continued)*

Other Issues

Distribution or assignment of land (9)
Grant of citizenship to outside group (7)
The foundation of colonies (5)
The distribution of grain to citizens (5)
Settlement of debts (5)
Local jurisdiction in Italy (3)
Citizen status of ex-slaves and their sons (2)
Food and guests at dinner parties (2)
Port duties (2)
Enrollment of new citizens in all the tribes (2)
Confirmation of commander's citizenship grants (2)
Remission of rents in Rome (2)
Interest payments on the principal of debts (2)
Confirmation of heirs
Interest rates
Judicial organization of Cisalpine Gaul
The ruler of Egypt
The crime of sicarii and venefici
Cost of food at dinner parties
Addition of bronze to silver coinage
Creation of new tribes
Introduction of the semiuncial as (coin)
Enacting law in the centuriate assembly
Proscription of citizens
The removal of citizenship from towns
The crime of falsa
The crime of iniuria
Limitations on suretyship
Permissible gambling
Remittance of purchase price for property of proscribed
Autonomy for a foreign city
The voting rights of freedmen
Expulsion of foreigners from Rome
Debt and land distribution
Contracts of the publicani of Asia
Roman relations with foreign states
Authorization to dedicate a statue on Capitolium
The restoration of collegia
King Deiotarus and Pessinus
The annexation of Cyprus as a province
The involvement of quaestorian scribae in trade
The crime of parricidium
The crime of sodalicia
Annexation of Numidia as province
Acquiring servitudes through usucapio
The hire of shepherds of free status
List of eligible grain recipients
Extending the pomerium of the city
Tax burden and provincial status of Crete
Restoration of power to King Deiotarus
Immunity for Delos

Subtotal laws: 85
Percentage: 36.3
Unknown: 8
Percentage: 3.4

Total laws: 234

Source: See appendixes A and C.

TABLE 1.11 Public Law Sponsors for Selected Periods by Number and Percentage[a]

	350–219	218–201	200–134	133–92	91–44
Consul	2 (4)	3 (8)	11 (18)	7 (7)	59 (25)
Tribune	17 (32)	23 (61)	33 (54)	65 (66)	104 (44)
Praetor	1 (2)	3 (8)	1 (2)	1 (1)	12 (5)
Dictator	6 (11)				33 (14)
Consul or praetor	10 (19)	5 (13)	1 (2)	2 (2)	
Other					1[b]
Unknown	17 (32)	4 (11)	15 (25)	23 (23)	25 (11)
Total	53	38	61	98	234

Source: See appendixes A and C.

[a]Percentages do not always add to 100 because of rounding.

[b]Less than 1%.

TABLE 1.12 Clan Membership of Law Sponsors by Selected Periods (numbers of laws sponsored by clan members in parentheses)[a]

350–219
Antistia
Atilia
Decia
Flaminia
Flavia
Hortensia (2)
Maenia (2)
Marcia
Metilia
Ogulnia
Ovinia
Papiria (2)
Poetilia
Publilia (3)
Silia
Valeria (2)

Clans: 16
Unknown: 33
Laws: 53

218–201
Acilia
Atilia (2)
Carvilia
Cincia
Claudia
Cornelia
Flaminia
Licinia
Metilia (2)
Minucia (3)
Oppia (2)
Publicia

Clans: 12
Unknown: 23
Laws: 38

200–134
Acilia
Aelia (2)
Atilia
Atinia (3)
Aufidia
Baebia (3)
Caecilia
Calpurnia
Cassia (3)
Claudia
Cornelia (2)
Didia
Fannia
Fufia
Fundania
Furia
Gabinia
Iunia
Iuventia
Laelia
Licinia (5)
Livia
Lucretia
Marcia (3)
Minucia (2)
Mucia
Orchia
Papiria
Petilia
Porcia
Rutilia
Scribonia
Terentia
Valeria (2)
Villia
Voconia

Clans: 36
Unknown: 16
Laws: 61

133–92
Acilia
Aebutia
Aemilia (2)
Appuleia (7)
Aufeia
Caecilia (2)
Calidia
Calpurnia
Cassia
Cicereia
Clodia
Coelia
Didia (2)
Domitia
Duronia
Fabia
Fulvia
Gabinia
Iunia (2)
Licinia
Livia (4)
Mamilia (2)
Manlia
Marcia (3)
Maria
Memmia
Minucia (2+)
Norbana
Octavia
Papiria (2)
Peducaea
Pompeia
Porcia (2)
Rubria
Rutilia
Sempronia (23)
Servilia (2)
Thoria
Titia (2)
Valeria

Clans: 40
Unknown: 20
Laws: 98

91–44
Aemilia (2)
Alliena
Ampia
Antia
Antonia (14)
Atia (2)
Aufidia
Aurelia (6)
Caecilia (8)
Caelia (4)
Calpurnia (4)
Caninia
Cassia (2)
Clodia (13)
Cornelia (35)
Fabia
Fabricia
Flavia
Fufia (2)
Gabinia (7)
Gellia
Helvia (2)
Herennia
Hirtia
Iulia (26)
Iunia (2)
Licinia (4)
Livia (6)
Lucilia
Mamilia
Manilia (3)
Marcia
Messia (2)
Minicia
Ninnia
Papia (2)
Papiria (2)
Peducaea
Plautia (5)
Pompeia (12)
Porcia (3)
Pupia (2)
Roscia (2)
Saufeia
Scribonia (6)
Servilia
Sulpicia (4)
Terentia
Trebonia
Tullia
Valeria (3)
Varia
Vatinia (6)
Visellia

Clans: 54
Unknown: 30
Laws: 234

Total laws: 484

Source: See appendixes A and C.

[a]Because consular laws usually carry the names of both consuls, there is no one-to-one correspondence between clans and laws.

TABLE 1.13 Sponsors of Public Law by Office, 225–134

Name[a]	Office Held when Sponsoring Law	Year
?M.? Metilius[b]	tribune	220
?Maenius	tribune	219
Q. Claudius	tribune	218
M. Metilius	tribune	217
M. Minucius	tribune	216
C. Oppius	tribune	215
L. Carvilius	tribune	212
Sp. Carvilius	tribune	212
L. Atilius, praetor 197?[c]	tribune	210
M. Lucretius	tribune	210
C. Publicius Bibulus	tribune	209
P. Licinius Varus, praetor 208	praetor	208
P. Cornelius Scipio Africanus, consul 194	consul	194
M. Cincius Alimentus	tribune	204
?P. Silius	tribune	204
M'. Acilius Glabrio, consul 191	tribune	201
	consul	191
Q. Minucius Thermus, consul 193	tribune	201
P. Porcius Laeca, praetor 195	tribune	199
C. Atinius Labeo, praetor 195	tribune	196
	praetor	195
C. Licinius Lucullus	tribune	196
M. Fundanius	tribune	195
L. Valerius Tappo, praetor 192	tribune	195
?M. Baebius Tamphilius, consul 181	tribune	194
	consul	181
Q. Aelius Tubero	tribune	193
M. Sempronius Tuditanus, consul 185	tribune	193
M. Iunius Brutus, consul 178	praetor	191
(Q.) Terentius Culleo, praetor 187[d]	tribune	189
C. Valerius Tappo	tribune	188
Q. Petillius	tribune	187
Q. Petillius Spurinus, consul 176	tribune	187
C. Orchius	tribune	182
P. Cornelius Cethegus, consul 181	consul	181
L. Villius Annalis, praetor 171	tribune	180
C. Claudius Pulcher, consul 177	consul	177
A. (or C.) Licinius Nerva	tribune	177
C. Papirius Turdus	tribune	177
M. Lucretius	tribune	172
Q. Marcius Scilla	tribune	172
M. Marcius Sermo	tribune	172
P. Licinius Crassus, consul 171	consul	171
C. Cassius Longinus, consul 171	consul	171

(continued)

TABLE 1.13 *(continued)*

Name[a]	Office Held when Sponsoring Law	Year
Q. Voconius Saxa	tribune	169
P. Rutilius	tribune	169
T. Sempronius	tribune	167
M'. Iuventius Thalna, consul 163	praetor	167
C. Fannius Strabo, consul 161	consul	161
P. Cornelius Dolabella, consul 159	consul	159
M. Fulvius Nobilior, consul 159	consul	159
?Q. Caecilius Metellus Macedonicus, consul 143	consul	143
?Aelius	tribune	153
?Fufius	tribune	153
?Atinius	tribune	149
L. Scribonius Libo	tribune	149
L. Calpurnius Piso Frugi, consul 133	tribune	149
M. Scantius or Scantinius	tribune	149
Livius	tribune	146
C. Licinius Crassus	tribune	145
T.? Didius	tribune	143
P. Mucius Scaevola, consul 133	tribune	141
C. Laelius Sapiens, consul 140	consul	140
A. Gabinius	tribune	139
L. Cassius Longinus Ravilla, consul 127	tribune	137
L. Furius Philus, consul 136	consul	136
Sex. Atilius Serranus, consul 136	consul	136

Source: *MRR*; *PW*; Scullard 1973; Wiseman 1971.

[a]Underlining indicates "new man." The highest office (other than tribune) attested for the lawmaker follows his name.

[b]Question mark preceding name indicates that year of office as law sponsor is uncertain. Question mark following praenomen indicates that praenomen is uncertain.

[c]Question mark with year indicates that date is uncertain.

[d]Parentheses with name or portion of name indicate that the identification of the lawmaker is uncertain.

TABLE 1.14 Sponsors of Public Law by Office, 133–91

Name[a]	Office Held when Sponsoring Law	Year
Ti. Sempronius Gracchus	tribune	133
C. Atinius Labeo Macerio	tribune	131
?C.[b] Papirius Carbo, consul 120	tribune	130
M. Iunius Pennus	tribune	126
M. Fulvius Flaccus, consul 125	consul	125
??Aebutius, praetor 125	praetor	125
?Aufeius	tribune	123
?M. Iunius Silanus, consul 109	consul	109
C. Sempronius Gracchus	tribune	123
	tribune	122
?M. Acilius Glabrio	tribune	122
M. Livius Drusus, consul 112	tribune	122
?Cn. Marcius Censorinus	tribune	122
C.? Rubrius	tribune	122
M.? Minucius Rufus, consul 110	tribune	121
?L. Calpurnius Bestia, consul 111	tribune	120
C. Marius, consul 107, 104–100, 86	tribune	119
Q. Marcius Rex, consul 118	consul	118
M. Aemilius Scaurus, consul 115	consul	115
Sex. Peducaeus	tribune	113
C. Memmius, praetor 104?	tribune	111
?Sp. Thorius	tribune	111
M. Iunius Silanus, consul 109	consul	109
C. Mamilius Limetanus	tribune	109
C. Coelius Caldus, consul 94	tribune	107
T. Manlius Mancinus	tribune	107
Q. Servilius Caepio, consul 106	consul	106
P. Rutilius Rufus, consul 105	consul	105
L. Cassius Longinus	tribune	104
Cn. Domitius Ahenobarbus, consul 96	tribune	104
L. Marcius Philippus, consul 91	tribune	104
?Clodius	tribune	104
L. Appuleius Saturninus	tribune	103
	tribune	100
?C. Servilius Glaucia, praetor 100	tribune	101
P. Furius	tribune	99
Q. Pompeius Rufus, consul 88	tribune	99
	consul	88
M. Porcius Cato	tribune	99
Sex. Titius	tribune	99
Q. Caecilius Metellus Nepos, consul 98	consul	98
T. Didius, consul 98	consul	98
Q. Calidius, praetor 79	tribune	98
?M. Duronius	tribune	97
?C. Valerius Flaccus, consul 93	praetor	96

(*continued*)

TABLE 1.14 *(continued)*

Name[a]	Office Held when Sponsoring Law	Year
L. Licinius Crassus, consul 95	consul	95
Q. Mucius Scaevola, consul 95	consul	95
M. Livius Drusus	tribune	91
?Minicius	tribune	91
Saufeius	tribune	91

Source: *MRR*; *PW*; Scullard 1973; Wiseman 1971.

[a]Underlining indicates "new man." The highest office (other than tribune) attested for the lawmaker follows his name.

[b]Single question mark preceding name indicates that year of office when sponsoring law is uncertain. Two question marks preceding name indicate that year when sponsoring law and office held when sponsoring law are uncertain. Question mark following praenomen indicates that praenomen is uncertain.

TABLE 1.15 Sponsors of Public Law by Office, 90–44

Name[a]	Office Held when Sponsoring Law	Year
L. Iulius Caesar, consul 90	consul	90
Q. Varius Severus Hibrida	tribune	90
Cn. Pompeius Strabo, consul 89	consul	89
L. Calpurnius Piso (Frugi), praetor 74[b]	tribune	89
C. Papirius Carbo, praetor 81	tribune	89
M. Plautius Silvanus	tribune	89
L. Cornelius Sulla, dictator 81	consul	88
	dictator	81
Q. Pompeius Rufus, consul 88	consul	88
P. Sulpicius	tribune	88
L. Cornelius Cinna, consul 87, 86, 85	consul	86
L. Valerius Flaccus, consul suffectus 86	consul	86
M. Iunius Brutus	tribune	83
L. Valerius Flaccus, consul 100	interrex	82
M. Aemilius Lepidus, consul 78	consul	78
Cn. Sicinius	tribune	76
C. Aurelius Cotta, consul 75	consul	75
M. Aurelius Cotta, consul 74	consul	74
M. Terentius Varro Lucullus, consul 73	consul	73
C. Cassius Longinus, consul 73	consul	73
L. Gellius Publicola, consul 72	consul	72
Cn. Cornelius Lentulus Clodianus, consul 72	consul	72
Cn. Pompeius Magnus, consul 70, 55, 52	consul	70
	consul	55
	consul	52
M. Licinius Crassus, consul 70, 55	consul	70
	consul	55

(continued)

TABLE 1.15 *(continued)*

Name[a]	Office Held when Sponsoring Law	Year
L. Aurelius Cotta, consul 65	praetor	70
Plautius	tribune	70
C. Visellius Varro	tribune	69?[c]
C. Antius (Restio)	tribune	68
C. Calpurnius Piso, consul 67	consul	67
C. Cornelius	tribune	67
A. Gabinius, consul 58	consul	58
L. Roscius Otho	tribune	67
C. Manilius (Crispus)	tribune	66
C. Papius	tribune	65
?Fabius[d]	tribune	64
M. Tullius Cicero, consul 63	consul	63
C. Antonius Hibrida, consul 63	consul	63
T. Ampius Balbus, praetor 58	tribune	63
	praetor	58
L. Caecilius Rufus, praetor 57	tribune	63
T. Labienus, praetor before 59	tribune	63
P. Servilius Rullus	tribune	63
D. Iunius Silanus, consul 62	consul	62
L. Licinius Murena, consul 62	consul	62
Q. Caecilius Metellus Nepos, consul 57	tribune	62
	praetor	60
	consul	57
L. Marius	tribune	62
M. Porcius Cato, praetor 54	tribune	62
M. Pupius Piso Frugi Calpurnianus, consul 61	consul	61
(M. Aufidius) Lurco	tribune	61
Q. Fufius Calenus, consul 47	tribune	61
	praetor	59
L. Flavius, praetor 58	tribune	60
C. Herennius	tribune	60
C. Iulius Caesar, dictator 48, 46–44	praetor	62
	consul	59
	dictator	46–45
P. Vatinius, consul 47	tribune	59
L. Domitius Ahenobarbus, consul 54	praetor	58
P. Clodius Pulcher	tribune	58
L. Ninnius Quadratus	tribune	58
L. Caecilius Rufus, praetor 57	praetor	57
P. Cornelius Lentulus Spinther, consul 57	consul	57
Q. Fabricus	tribune	57
C. Messius	tribune	57
L. Caninius Gallus	tribune	56
C. Porcius Cato	tribune	56
C. Trebonius, consul 45	tribune	55

(continued)

TABLE 1.15 *(continued)*

Name[a]	Office Held when Sponsoring Law	Year
?Mamilius[e]	tribune	55
?L. Roscius Fabatus, praetor 49[e]	tribune	55
?A. Allienus, praetor 49[e]	tribune	55
?Sex. Peducaeus[e]	tribune	55
?C. Fabius[e]	tribune	55
Ser. Sulpicius Galba, praetor 54	praetor	54
M. Coelius Vinicianus, praetor 48?	tribune	53
L. Lucilius Hirrus	tribune	53
Q. Caecilius Metellus Pius, consul 52 Scipio Nasica	consul	52
C. Scribonius Curio	tribune	50
M. Aemilius Lepidus, consul 46, 42	tribune	49
M. Antonius, consul 44, 34, 31	tribune	49
consul designatus 31	consul	44
?Rubrius	tribune	49
M. Caelius Rufus, praetor peregrinus 48	praetor	48
A. Hirtius, consul 43	tribune	48
P. Cornelius Dolabella, consul suffectus 44	tribune	47
L. Antonius, consul 41	tribune	44
L. Cassius Longinus	tribune	44
C. Helvius Cinna	tribune	44

Source: *MRR*; *PW*; Scullard 1973; Wiseman 1971.

[a]Underlining indicates "new man." The highest office (other than tribune) attested for the lawmaker follows his name.

[b]Parentheses with name or portion of name indicate that the identification of the lawmaker is uncertain.

[c]Question mark with year indicates that date is uncertain.

[d]Question mark preceding name indicates that year of office as law sponsor is uncertain.

[e]See note 17 on page 58.

TABLE 1.16 Public Law Assemblies for Selected Periods by Number and Percentage[a]

	350–219	218–201	200–134	133–92	91–44
comitia centuriata	1 (2)		2 (3)		2 (1)
concilium plebis	17 (32)	23 (60)	33 (54)	65 (66)	104 (44)
comitia tributa		3 (8)		1 (1)	6 (3)
Not plebeian	20 (38)	6 (16)	15 (25)	9 (9)	96 (41)
Unknown	15 (28)	6 (16)	11 (18)	23 (24)	26 (11)
Total	53 (100)	38 (99)	61 (100)	98 (100)	234 (100)

Source: See appendixes A and C.

[a]Percentages do not always add to 100 because of rounding.

TABLE 1.17 Public Law Assemblies by Quarter Century by Number and Percentage[a]

Period	comitia centuriata	concilium plebis	comitia tributa	Not Plebeian	Unknown	Total
350–325	1 (7)	2 (14)		9 (64)	2 (14)	14 (99)
324–300		6 (46)		3 (23)	4 (31)	13 (100)
299–275		4 (40)		4 (40)	2 (20)	10 (100)
274–250		1 (11)		2 (22)	6 (67)	9 (100)
249–225		1 (25)		2 (50)	1(25)	4 (100)
224–200	1 (2)	27 (63)	3 (7)	6 (14)	6 (14)	43 (100)
199–175		15 (50)		8 (27)	7 (23)	30 (100)
174–150	1 (5)	9 (47)		4 (21)	5 (26)	19 (100)
149–125		20 (60)	1 (3)	5 (15)	7 (21)	33 (100)
124–100		50 (74)		5 (7)	13 (19)	68 (100)
99–75	1 (1)	25 (37)	1 (2)	38 (57)	2 (3)	67 (100)
74–50	1 (1)	69 (59)	4 (3)	34 (29)	10 (9)	118 (100)
49–25		14 (21)	1 (1)	27 (40)	25 (37)	67 (99)
Unknown		9 (14)			55 (86)	64 (100)
Total	5 (1)	252 (45)	10 (2)	147 (26)	145 (26)	559 (100)

Source: See appendixes A and C.

[a]Percentages do not always add to 100 because of rounding.

TABLE 1.18 Public Law Issues, 218–201

Year	Issue
218	Carrying weight of senators' boats[a]
218	Declaration of war
217	Suspension or circumvention of law[a]
217	Value of bronze coins
217	Public vow of a ver sacrum (sacred spring)
217	Election of a dictator[a]
217	Abrogation of a dictator's imperium[a]
217	Equalizing imperium of dictator and magister equitum[a]
216	Creation of extraordinary commission[a]
215	Proconsular imperium for a praetor[a]
215	Creation of extraordinary commission[a]
215	Grant of citizenship to individuals
215	Creation of extraordinary commission[a]
215	Women's clothing and accoutrements
212	Exiling the absent M. Postumus Pyrgensis
212	Suspension or circumvention of law[a]
212	Creation of extraordinary commission[a]
211	Selection of a commander[a]
211	Exile of individuals[a]
211	Grant of citizenship to individuals
211	Proconsul's imperium—extension[a]
210	Grant of citizenship to individuals
210	Punishment of Campanian rebels
210	Election of a dictator[a]
210	Lease of ager Campanus
209	Abrogation of a commander's imperium[a]
209	Gift giving by clients on the Saturnalia
208	Prorogation of imperium[a]
208	Celebration of ludi Apollinares
205	The assignment of a province[a]
204	Gift giving by defendants in law cases
204	Confirmation of peace
204	Selection of two commanders[a]
203	Exculpating C. Servilius[a]
202	Selection of a commander[a]
201	Selection of a commander[a]
201	Authorization to make peace with Carthage
201	Confirmation of peace

Source: See appendixes A and C.

[a]Leadership issues.

TABLE 1.19 Named Sponsors by Year and Office, 218–201

Year	Office	Name
218	tribune	Q. Claudius
217	tribune	M. Metilius, possibly same as tribune 220
217	consul	C. Flaminius, consul 223
216	tribune	M. Minucius
215	tribune	C. Oppius
212	tribune	L. Carvilius
212	tribune	Sp. Carvilius[a]
210	tribune	L. Atilius
210	tribune	M. Lucretius
209	tribune	C. Publicius Bibulus
208	praetor urbanus	P. Licinius Varus
205	consul	P. Cornelius Scipio Africanus, consul II 194
204	tribune	M. Cincius Alimentus
201	tribune	M'. Acilius Glabrio, consul 191
201	tribune	Q. Minucius Thermus,[a] consul 193

Laws of unknown sponsor: 23

Total laws: 38

Source: See appendix C and *MRR*.
[a]Jointly sponsored a law with the preceding individual.

Notes

1. On the title, reported by Appian, *B.C.* 1.99 but not in the *fasti Capitolini*, see Mommsen, *R.St.* 2.703, and F. Hurlet, *La dictature de Sylla: Monarchie ou magistrature républicaine? Essai d'histoire constitutionnelle*, vol. 30, Institut Historique Belge de Rome. Études de Philologie, d'Archéologie et d'Histoire Anciennes (Brussels and Rome, 1993), 95 with n. 5.

2. On Sulla's abdication in 80 see *MRR* 3.74–75.

3. For a comparison of Caesar's position with that of Sulla see Hurlet 1993, 172–75, and chapter 9.

4. The comparison has been drawn before, e.g., R. Seager, "Sulla," *CAH* 9, 2d ed. (Cambridge, 1994), 199.

5. For the latest edition of the text see *RS* 2 No. 41.

6. For the latest edition of the text see *RS* 1 No. 2.

7. Date and identity of the lex Agraria: *RS* 1.53–60 No. 2; A. Lintott, *Judicial reform and land reform in the Roman republic* (Cambridge, 1992), 282–86, cf. 48–49. The ancient debate is recorded in Appian, *B.C.* 1.7–27. See further chapter 4.

8. Discovery and earliest interpretations of the fragments: A. Lintott, "The so-called *tabula bembina* and the humanists," *Ath.* 61 (1983): 201–14.

9. Cf. Appian, *B.C.* 1.7–27 with commentary of E. Gabba, *Appiani bellorum civilium liber primus* (Florence, 1958); and K. Johannsen, "Die lex agraria des Jahres 111" (Ph.D. diss. Munich, 1971).

10. Appian, *B.C.* 1.11.

11. Italians: Gabba 1958, 29, and Gabba, "Rome and Italy in the second century *B.C.*," (*CAH*, vol. 8, *Rome and the Mediterranean to* 133 *B.C.*, ed. A. E. Astin, F. W. Walbank, M. W. Frederiksen, and R. M. Ogilvie, 2d ed. (Cambridge, 1989), 240. While the term *Italiotai* sometimes includes Roman inhabitants of Italian land, it is surely to be understood in its broader application in the context of the occasion reported by Appian, in view of the involvement of allies in the later difficulties confronted by the commission when trying to determine boundaries and possession. See Brunt 1988, 131, with reference to the observations of Gelzer on Appian's tendency to translate Roman *agrestes* as *Italiotai*. Mouritsen 1998, 15–16, with n. 39, agreeing that agrestes means rural Romans, provides a useful discussion.

12. See "Information for Tables in Chapter 1."

13. See appendix B.

14. Called leges Corneliae and Iuliae, the laws of the dictators were sometimes enacted on the sole authority of the dictator and sometimes in assemblies. See chapters 8 and 9.

15. In principle all praetors could convene the people. In practice it appears that only the urban or peregrine praetor did so: *LPPR*, 120. Lawmaking by praetors: T. C. Brennan, *The praetorship in the Roman republic* (Oxford, 2000), 1.119–120.

16. R. Syme, *The Roman revolution* (Oxford, 1939), 18.

17. Table 1.12 measures only clan involvement; it does not provide a one-to-one correspondence between clans and individual laws. For instance, some laws were sponsored by two (or more) officials, both of whose clan names provided the title for the resulting law. These are most often consular laws although a few tribunician laws are also known by the names of more than one sponsor, notoriously the lex Mamilia Roscia Peducaea Alliena Fabia—now identified as the lex Iulia agraria of 59 (*RS* 2 No. 54). In such a case table 1.12 credits the respective clans with the sponsorship of one law—without recognizing that it is the same law. As a result, the numbers following each clan name indicating the number of laws that a member of that clan was involved in sponsoring do not add up to the frequency of laws for the period. Additionally table 1.12 does not distinguish either among the various branches of a particular clan or among the nameless and named members of particular clans. Thus the lawmaking activity of individual law sponsors is invisible in table 1.12.

18. The sponsor of four proposals is believed to be either a consul or a praetor. The offices of the sponsors of twelve laws or proposals are unknown.

19. The sponsors of two laws are unknown.

20. Q. Marcius Rex sponsored a bill either as praetor by 121 or consul in 118 (*MRR* 1.521, 527).

21. Aedile: Remmius; consul: T. Didius.

22. Praetor: Q. Calidius; consuls: C. Marius and C. Coelius Caldus.

23. Only nine laws or proposals were sponsored by men whose offices are unknown.

24. See chapter 2.

25. E. S. Staveley, *Greek and Roman voting and elections* (London, 1972), 132.

26. Lintott notes a reference in Livy to the comitia tributa: A. Lintott, *The constitution of the Roman republic* (Oxford, 1999).

27. And so, coming into existence after the concilium plebis: Mommsen, *R.St.* 3.322–24. He called it the comitia tributa. Mommsen conjectured that the comitia tributa was separate from the concilium plebis because it incorporated both patricians and plebeians but that this tribal assembly was modeled on the concilium plebis insofar as citizens voted in their tribes.

28. Between 349 and 287, when the lex Hortensia made plebiscita binding on the entire Roman people, eleven, or 32 percent (since 350), of all recorded laws (thirty-four) were presented by tribunes. On the effectiveness of tribunician laws before 287 see M. Humbert, "La normativité des plébiscites selon la tradition annalistique," in *Mélanges de droit romain et d'historie ancienne: Hommage à la mémoire de André Magdelain*, ed. M. Humbert and Y. Thomas ([Paris], 1998), 211–38.

29. Not so in the case of elections: consuls convened the centuriate assembly for the election of curule magistrates.

30. On the respective roles of these assemblies in generating public law see most recently U. Paananen, "Legislation in the Comitia Centuriata," in *Senatus populusque romanus: Studies in Roman republican legislation*, ed. J. Vaahtera (Helsinki, 1993), 9–73.

31. E.g., Staveley 1972, 122–32.

32. See appendix B.

33. R. Develin, "Comitia tributa plebis," *Ath.* 53 (1975): 302–37, and R. Develin, "Comitia Tributa Again," *Ath.* 55 (1977): 423–25.

34. J. Farrell, "The distinction between comitia and concilium," *Ath.* 74 (n.s. 64, 1986): 407–38. Farrell's arguments rest specifically on a comprehensive analysis of the uses of the terms *comitia* and *concilium* used by Livy and Cicero. Cf. Lintott 1999, 53–54.

35. R. E. Mitchell, *Patricians and plebeians: The origins of the Roman state* (Ithaca, NY, 1990); and K. Sandberg, "The concilium plebis as a legislative body," in Vaahtera 1993, 74–96. These efforts to give the concilium plebis sole responsibility for lawmaking in the early and Middle Republic are unpersuasive.

36. Paananen 1993. Cf. Farrell 1986, 411 n. 24.

37. Only twice, for certain, in the Late Republic, in 81 (lex Cornelia de civitate Volaterranis adimenda) and 57 (lex Cornelia Caecilia de revocando Cicerone).

38. Losses: Livy 22.49.15–18. Brunt 1971, 419, holds that losses perhaps amounted to thirty-five thousand, half of them Roman.

39. Independent decisions of commanders: A. Lintott, *Imperium romanum: Politics and administration* (London and New York, 1993), 43–46; and A. Eckstein, *Senate and general: Individual decision-making and Roman foreign relations, 264–194* (Berkeley, Los Angeles, and London, 1987). A different view is taken by K.-J. Hölkeskamp, *Die Entstehung der Nobilität* (Stuttgart, 1987), 170–203; cf. Hölkeskamp, "Conquest, competition and consensus," *Hist.* 42 (1993): 34.

40. The lawmaking activity of the period has also been addressed by R. Feig-Vishnia, *State, society and popular leaders in Mid-Republican Rome, 241–167* (London and New York, 1996).

41. The name of the sponsor is owed to an uncertain restoration of Festus p. 347 M: see P. Willems, *Le sénat de la république romaine* (Louvain, Paris, and Berlin, 1885),

2.438, n. 3, and 449. According to Livy 21.53 and 22.6, C. Flaminius spent only one day in Rome during his consulate. On the depreciation in this year see M. H. Crawford, *Coinage and money under the Roman republic* (London, 1985), 55.

42. Polyb. 3.87–88, Livy 22.8.6. See discussion in *MRR* 1.243.

43. Livy 22.10.2.

44. As noted in table 1.18, the highest number of laws or proposals in any one year is six, in 217, the year after the war began; the lowest is one, in four years (216, 205, 203, 202). In three years, two lawmaking occasions are reported (218, 209, 208); in four years, three lawmaking occasions are reported (212, 204, 201, 200); in two years, four lawmaking occasions are reported (211, 210); and in one year five lawmaking occasions are reported (215).

45. 211: Livy 26.2.5; 204: Livy 29.13.7.

46. According to Mommsen the people did this because he was given Sardinia and Sicily as his province, normally assigned to praetors: Mommsen, *R.St.* 2.211 n. 1. The presumption is that the people make such decisions only when the rules have to be bent.

47. Val. Max. 7.6.1 (slaves); Livy 25.5.8 (underage youths).

48. Livy 26.21.4.

49. Livy 26.3.12; Val. Max. 2.8.3; see *MRR* 1.271 n.2.

50. Livy 25.4.9.

51. Livy 26.33.12.

52. The lex Claudia is dated between 223 and 218, depending on whether scholars believe the tribune Claudius presented his bill in C. Flaminius's first (223) or second (218) consulate. On the "war party" in Rome see Scullard, *Roman politics* (Oxford, 1973), 39–55.

53. The lex Publicia and the lex Cincia (= *RS* 2 No. 47).

54. Both tribunes are described by Scullard 1973, 81, as "staunch supporters of Scipio later."

55. *PW* 35.

56. P. Licinius Varus, P. Cornelius Scipio belong to the "Aemilian-Scipionic group": Scullard 1973, 39–55.

57. The classic views on the evolving Roman "nobility" in relation to the offices of consul and praetor and the impediments to political advancement facing men outside this nobility, presented in M. Gelzer, *The Roman nobility* (Oxford, 1969), and Scullard 1973, have been refined by P. Brunt, "Nobilitas and novitas," *JRS* 72 (1982): 1–17.

58. *PW* 1, 9; *MRR* 2.591.

59. *MRR* 2.609.

60. *MRR* 2.544.

61. *MRR* 2.592.

62. For a constitutional explanation of the tribunes' functions see J. Bleicken, *Das Volkstribunat der klassischen Republik* (Munich, 1955); cf. Feig-Vishnia 1996.

63. Date of his tribunate: *MRR* 1.271 n. 5.

64. Summary of debate about the legal issues: Scullard 1973, 276–77.

65. Livy 21.63.2; cf. Cic., *Verr.* 2.5.18.45.

66. J. D'Armes, *Commerce and social standing in ancient Rome* (Cambridge, MA, 1981), 31–34; F. Cassola, *I gruppi politici romani nel III secolo a.c.* (Trieste, 1962), 216–17. On the new nobility see Hölkeskamp 1987.

67. Livy 24.11.7–9. Crawford 1985, 60–61, postulates that metal was initially available, then around 215 the Romans went to credit and subvention of sailors' pay by the wealthy.

68. Lex Cincia: *RS* 2 No. 47.

69. Broad principles: Lintott 1999.

70. See T. Hantos *Res publica constituta: Die Verfassung des Dictators Sulla* (Stuttgart, 1988), 73–74, who believes that the six new praetors as well as the previous praetor urbanus and praetor peregrinus presented laws to tribal assemblies.

71. 241: Polyb. 6.16.3; Plin. *N.H.* 7.43 (45), 141.

CHAPTER TWO

Presentation: Oratory and Law Drafts

IN JANUARY OF 63, M. Tullius Cicero seized the opportunity of his inaugural speech as consul, a formal occasion shared with other newly elected officials, to denounce a recent land bill sponsored by the tribune P. Servilius Rullus and his colleagues. Over the next few weeks three more public speeches followed, two later published among the triad called *De Lege Agraria,* in which Cicero aired in eloquent detail the faults of the lawmaker and his bill.[1] In high relief throughout these public orations is the essentially open and civic character of lawmaking: a crowd of Romans assembled purposefully from Rome's thirty-five tribes; the elected officeholder, flanked by other senators, addressing them from the Rostra; in view of everyone a posted text of the bill under debate; and, above all, the oratory.

Sitting at the heart of the lawmaking process in the public meeting (*contio*), Cicero's orations against Rullus's proposed land scheme furnish the richest source we have for exploring the presentation of law to the Roman people by their political leaders, our focus in this chapter. *De Lege Agraria* 2 and 3, together with the *Pro Lege Manilia* of 66, form the longest and most complete set of public speeches addressing the merits of public law proposals among the many small fragments of such speeches by Roman orators preserved by ancient recorders.[2] Furthermore, they are the only extant speeches that address a long and complex law draft.[3] Cicero's public denunciation of the rogatio Servilia serves to remind us of the degree to which tradition, power, social position, personal characteristics, and oratorical skills underlay the functioning of the lawmaking process as late as 63, nearly the end of our period of interest. It underscores also the singularly complex understanding of the various facets of lawmaking common among the participants on all levels and articulated by political leaders in their presentation of the law. Given the well-honed skills needed to draft and promulgate a public law proposal, to orate at length about the proposal, and to engage a Roman audience in the give-and-take accompanying the public lawmaking process, it is understandable that not all eligible officeholders chose to propose law. That a significant number of officeholders did nonetheless propose public laws and that a significant number of other senators and elected officeholders plunged eagerly and effectively into the public debate raises questions about the purposes served by such a high level of face-to-face interaction.

Throughout the entire lawmaking process—from generating and drafting a proposal to displaying the draft to going before the people to support or undermine the proposal and finally to convening the people in the appropriate assembly to vote—all political leaders tried to do the same thing: get the approval of the Roman people as measured in the majority vote of the assembled tribes. Oratory like Cicero's public speeches on the Rullan land proposal focused intently on the crucial role of the Roman voter and indeed on the role of everyone present on the particular occasion of the speech. Some in the audience came as prospective voters, others as vitally interested listeners; some hoped for guidance from the speaker, others hoped to influence the eventual outcome by the weight of their collective desires. Clearly, as conveyed in public orations and law drafts, the presentation of law required not only a high level of knowledge and involvement from Rome's political leaders but an ability to stir the hearts and minds of the Roman people.

ROGATIO SERVILIA AGRARIA

At the end of 64, the tribune P. Servilius Rullus and several colleagues promulgated a proposal of law instituting a colonization scheme involving land purchase and distribution in Italy and the provinces. The prospective colonists, numbering in the many thousands (five thousand in the colony at Capua alone), would be drawn initially from citizens without land and later from the discharged soldiers of the legions under Pompey's command, still under arms in Syria in late 64. The land to be colonized and distributed included privately owned land in Italy as well as the small amount of remaining public property (ager publicus) in Italy, the ager Campanus and ager Stellas, the only public property of the Roman people left in Italy, and land in the provinces that was Roman by right of bequest or conquest.[4] The complex arrangements for the selection and purchase of lands to be distributed and the maintenance of a fund to finance the program were to be handled by an elected commission. Such in brief was the scope of the rogatio Servilia agraria.

The motivations of the bill's sponsors as presented by contemporaries were complex. As often presented by modern historians, the bill reflects the antagonisms and imbalance between Rome's powerful men in the mid-60s: Pompey on the one hand, Caesar and Crassus on the other.[5] Purportedly Caesar, not Rullus, was the real draftsman, and his aim, in the careful formulation of a complex piece of legal drafting, was to diplomatically restore the political balance between himself and Pompey, shattered by Pompey's victories in the East, through a program of land distribution. Land grants would undoubtedly win for Caesar the gratitude of the city population, the primary beneficiaries of the bill, scholars believe.[6] However, the rogatio Servilia agraria also addressed critical tensions in Roman society whose antecedents lay in events of a generation before, long before the immediate political situation in Rome in late 64. Economic and social crisis had been building since the Italian War of 91–89 and the civil war of 83–81. At the end of that war, as part of his "restoration" of the Roman state, L. Cornelius Sulla had confiscated and redistributed many hectares of arable land in Italy. Roughly 120,000 men, mostly veterans of Sulla's legions, benefited from the distribution, nearly one in ten of the male citizen population.[7] The number of men who lost their property is unrecorded, but it includes the 4,700 or more men who had been proscribed by Sulla and whose holdings were seized, as well as private landowners or landholders of land belonging to rebellious communities in Italy, whose territory was taken by way of reparations.[8] Nearly twenty years later men throughout the regions affected were still embittered. In 78 and 72, there had been unsuccessful attempts in lawmaking assemblies to reinstate the proscribed or to exact the payment for confiscated lands from the buyers that had been remitted in 81. The college of tribunes in 63 proposed several bills along similar lines, including Rullus's proposed land redistribution scheme.

With hindsight, Rullus's bill offered real hope for resolving severe economic and social crisis, whose causes went beyond the circumstances of 83–81. In particular, the bill addressed the problem of access to land resources facing rural Italians in an innovative way. Rather than repossess and redistribute existing holdings on ager publicus in Italy, little of which was left anyway, the measure ordained the purchase of land not only in Italy but in the provinces from people willing to sell. The measure also ordained the redistribution of provincial ager publicus. Providing for an expeditious and effective implementation, the bill created a much larger commission of men (ten in number) than the usual *IIIviri agris dandis adsignatis*, who since 133 ordinarily had *iurisdictio*, and gave them praetorian rank, which carried with it both imperium and iurisdictio so the commissioners could do their work effectively in Italy and the provinces. Underscoring the widespread popular appeal of the directness of this scheme was the swift resistance the bill met from leading senators, particularly from Rome's newly elected consul, Cicero.

DE LEGE AGRARIA 2

Cicero's contribution to the public debate on the rogatio Servilia agraria provides a rare opportunity to evaluate the broad scope of lawmaking sessions in creating and maintaining community agreement in a world of increasingly diverse peoples.[9] Oratory, as an essential aspect of the much larger and complex process of public lawmaking, involved far more than rhetorical conventions, although these to be sure were important. We can imagine that the crowd facing Cicero that day in January clearly anticipated the occasion of his speech with no small amount of excitement. They were drawn by the circumstances and also by the speaker, Cicero, who had been elected consul several months earlier to the wide acclaim of the people. A new man from Arpinum, a Volscian town given partial citizenship in 303 and full citizenship in 188, Cicero had political successes and misfortunes that seem to have embodied the aspirations of new citizens, registered finally in the census of 70. Cicero's own emphasis on his "newness," at the beginning of his address, confirms its importance to him and his listeners. He was a speaker of great skill, Rome's most famous orator, known for his compelling and intricate style of delivery. We can imagine the crowd in the Forum, gathered to hear the new consul address them for the first time: purposeful, interested, passionate.

Regardless of the motives drawing such an audience, Cicero's initial public oration, *De Lege Agraria* 2, is many things. It is one side of a dialogue between a high Roman official and the Roman people. It is an exercise in the persuasion of those among them who would cast a vote. The speech also suggests those features of a public law proposal that would render the law appealing to the Roman people.[10] The arguments used by Cicero to persuade voters to reject the bill obviously attempt to play on the interests of the crowd assembled to listen to what he had to say. The arguments suggest, too, the traditional procedures for handling a valid law and so provide a valuable index of the beliefs that informed Roman behavior in their effort to regulate their society. Hence the oration belongs to the specific occasion of a meeting used by Cicero to address the recent proposal of the tribunes and cannot be separated from the circumstances in which that proposal was formulated, promulgated, and debated.[11] *De Lege Agraria* 2 is also a literary text intended for an audience of elite Roman readers. The oration was published after the fact by Cicero in a collection of his consular speeches intended to broadcast the achievements of his year in Rome's highest office.[12] Hence the speech conveys the shared understandings of elite Romans about the expected tone and content of the interaction between political leaders and the Roman people. Whether approached as a snapshot of a real meeting or as a polished literary text, the speech offers a unique and valuable opportunity for gaining insights into the Roman world. While the speech offers only the consul's side of the dialogue between himself and his audience, what the Roman people thought, opined, or hoped for on the occasion of the exchange can be surmised from Cicero's expression of his own thoughts, opinions, or expectations about it. When framed in the language of argument, these are a revealing barometer of voter interest and popular aspirations.

Among the many arguments, one theme predominates: the sovereign power of the Roman people. A commonplace theme in Roman oratory, popular sovereignty figures prominently in Cicero's characterization of the Roman people, specifically in the language he uses in talking about the people. Language is politicized. The adjective "your" (*vester*) firmly attaches the recurrent words *honos, beneficium, otium, libertas, vectigalia, commodum,* and *imperium* to the Roman people.[13] *Vestra libertas* and *vestra vectigalia* occur most frequently.[14] *Vester* is an important signpost to the kind of image of the Roman people Cicero wanted to convey in his speech. Most of the abstract nouns so modified are significant words in the political vocabulary of the Romans, as identified by modern scholars on the basis of usage in speeches and political monographs: "freedom" (libertas), "leisure" (otium), "authority" (auctoritas), and "empire" (imperium).[15] The others are made so in the context of the speech. That the consul, one of Rome's most compelling speakers, spoke to them repeatedly from the Rostra about "their authority, their empire, their revenues, their money, their gain" suggests that the crowd reacted intently and favorably.

All of these terms emphasize the Roman people's dominion over a large portion of the known world. But one term emerges as a particularly compelling theme, namely, "revenues" (vectigalia). The law, Cicero charges, will diminish the revenues of the Roman state if not lose them altogether. At issue especially are lands that generated revenue: the ager Campanus, an exceptionally fertile plain to the south of Rome in Italy; public property of the Roman people (ager publicus), whose possessors paid rent to the state treasury; and conquered or inherited lands in the provinces. Cicero's concern with the loss in revenues that would result from Rullus's land redistribution scheme is emphatic. Indeed, for dramatic effect, no passage in *De Lege Agraria* 2 surpasses the moment when Cicero called on the herald to read aloud the list of lands to be sold from the text of the draft:

> Now read to me in order the list of the property of the Roman people to be sold at auction according to the text of the law; and by Hercules! I think that the announcement of it will bring grief and bitterness to the [herald] himself. You have gone through the property in Italy; go on into Sicily. There is nothing in this province, of all that our ancestors left us as our own . . . which Rullus does not order to be sold.
>
> (*Leg. Agr.* 2.18.47–48; Loeb trans.)

Skillfully here Cicero created an emotional context for the herald's performance, leading up to the moment by talking about other sales that would be detrimental to the interests of the Roman people and describing how the herald himself would respond to hearing the list he was about to read. The herald's voice, reading aloud from the draft, is not preserved in the literary version of the speech; his performance is instead an interruption in Cicero's flow of words as he instructs the herald to read (after "herald himself" and "go on into Sicily"). We can see in Cicero's technique a logical progression from the sale of private and foreign lands to the public land of the Roman people, whose sale would enjoin the loss of the people's birthright, their revenues (vectigalia), snatched away by Rullus. The list must have been delivered with great effect. In this way, Cicero aimed to influence the Roman people in their capacity as voters.

I draw attention to the theme of revenues lost because it rests on the assumption that the people share in what I shall loosely call the profits of empire. Why not? They are, in Cicero's words, the masters of the world (*domini omnium gentium*). The theme is worth noting also because it appears to hide another, deeper premise, namely, that the people want access to resources, in particular land. The premise surfaces in several arguments. Cicero condemns the purchase arrangements for privately owned land, or land held in good title as though it were privately owned, because these arrangements would make available only lands that were poor quality for farming. He observes that men would emigrate to Egypt in droves because of the fertility of the land and the bounty of the region.[16] Some arguments reveal a senator's reading of what the Roman people value, for instance, Cicero's comparison of the division of the ager Campanus into allotments with a similar division of the Field of Mars (Campus Martius) or his exhortation to the city plebs not to give up the valued perquisites that accrue with city life in exchange for land allotments: their influence, their votes, their dignity, and the city itself with its Forum, games, and festivals. These are red herrings. Much more concrete is the universal desire to have land and more generally to have access to the resources of empire. These arguments form the basis of Cicero's appeal to the voters in *De Lege Agraria* 2, and in a dramatic way they reveal Cicero's assumptions about the interests and aspirations of the Roman people.

RHETORIC

Cicero used conventions of public speaking that reveal something of the shared presumptions of magistrates and people about the business of preliminary lawmaking meetings and the skills political leaders needed to articulate the will of the Roman people. Let me begin with the conventions of rhetoric, shaped by the exigencies of argument and persuasion and drawn from the rhetorical craft of the Greeks.

The conventions of rhetoric are obvious in *De Lege Agraria* 2, where arguments combine to produce a flurry of charges against the tribunes and their proposed bill. The bill benefits opprobrious men, it makes kings of the commissioners, it attacks Pompey, it serves the interests of the lawmakers, and it is not in the interests of the Roman people, which as all Romans knew were paramount. Cicero presents his case skillfully. Much of the detail included in the speech and its presentation follows Cicero's charge that the law would give some men unlimited and arbitrary power. Even though the Roman people thought that the land scheme would bring them something beneficial, namely, access to land, they were mistaken.[17] Instead, as Cicero carefully explains, the law was designed to bring Rullus and the other ten commissioners (decemviri), who were men motivated by greed and lust for power, the means to do what they wanted to do without hindrance:

> [T]here has never been an instance of royal power which was not restrained, if not by some law, at least by certain limits. But in this case there are no limits; all the kingdoms, all your dominion in its widest extent, all the countries some of which are free from your rule and others with which you are not yet even acquainted, are included by permission of the law.
> (*Leg. Agr.* 2.14.35; Loeb trans.)

Cicero's insistent gloom about the future commissioners' aims informs his analysis of the draft statute again and again.

Thus, on the heels of the passage quoted previously, Cicero directs the people's attention to a clause that allowed the commissioners to sell "anything" whose sale was authorized in Senate decrees from 87 or later.[18] Criticizing the obscure language, Cicero charges that the drafters of the law were deliberately obscure, anticipating that imprecision of statement would enable the commissioners to do what they liked. Cicero takes the same approach to the next clause as well. He analyzes it, focusing again on vague wording, which he explains as follows:

> He thought it was a lengthy list and was afraid of passing over anything; and so he added "or anything else," that is, as you see, saying briefly that nothing is excepted. By this article I assert that all nations, peoples, provinces and kingdoms are handed over and made a free gift of to the sway, jurisdiction, and authority of the decemvirs.
>
> (*Leg. Agr.* 2.15.38–39; Loeb trans.)

Again Cicero centers his discussion of the clause on the commissioners' self-interest. He comments cynically on phrases from the proposal, showing how far "or anything else" (*aliudve quid*), instead of a more precise phrase, could be taken in its interpretation. In all fairness to the drafters of this bill, it should be stressed that Cicero's analysis of such clauses aimed to present them in a certain way.

Without a doubt, Cicero was always very deliberate. He carefully selected features of the proposal for discussion. He created an effect, he made a point, and he aimed to seduce his audience to his point of view. In the example just given, he presented this clause as dangerous, because the commissioners would be allowed to sell anything they pleased. To demonstrate the self-interest of the bill's sponsors and the potentially arbitrary authority of the decemviri under the law, Cicero used details from the proposal that could support the point. In service of persuasive ends, he was selective in the proofs he constructed to support his arguments. Cicero's skill at selecting detail for effect can best be seen at the moment, roughly midway through the speech, when he calls on the herald to proclaim the list of lands to be sold (2.18.47–48). Careful selection for the sake of effect was the design of deliberative speaking, whose ends are reflected in the very terms the Romans used for orating about public law proposals: *suasio* (speaking for) and *dissuasio* (speaking against).

The personal dimension of Cicero's attack is also clear. Before embarking on his analysis of the law, Cicero carefully built up a model of the good lawmaker, which incorporates all the lawmaker's responsibilities and how he should carry them out (2.1.1–3.6). In brief, the good lawmaker should enact statutes in the people's interest, he should be knowledgeable about Rome's laws, and he should be direct and conscientious in bringing his knowledge and expertise to the public argument about law. The model set, Cicero then systematically attacked Rullus in his capacity as lawmaker. Rullus had deviated from the accepted procedures for formulating and promulgating a proposal of law, Cicero claimed, and had compounded his failure by an inarticulate public delivery at the opening session announcing the proposal. At that meeting Rullus had ignored the conventions of language used on such important occasions. Thus he was not forthright in communicating his proposal of law to the people. Instead he promulgated the proposal furtively. Characteristically he acted out of self-interest and not in the best interests of the Roman people. He maneuvered to keep the Roman people ill-informed. He was hostile to the Roman people. Moreover, he dissimulated. Demonstrating the point, Cicero tells the people that Rullus, out of their hearing, made slighting remarks about them—he refers to Rullus's speech to the Senate on 1 January—and he tells them what he said, evidently paraphrasing (at 2.26.70 and 2.29.79) what Rullus did say to the Senate. Basically Rullus was a bad magistrate.

Cicero sets up a contrast between elected officials who belong to an elite among such officials and others who do not. What distinguishes them is their command of the conventions of lawmaking, derived from knowledge and experience and dependent on family standing. Cicero uses the theme of *nobilitas* as a base. The tradition of consuls is recounted, men who were *nobiles*, whose families kept the death masks of their ancestors. Cicero emphasizes his own place in this tradition although he entered office as a new man (2.1.1–3). The elite group naturally has the people's interests at heart. Its members in office act on behalf of the people, as Cicero says he will in his consulship (2.4.9). Naming a few other members of the elite group at various points in his speech, among them Ti. and C. Gracchus, *clarissimi* (2.5.10), Cicero emphasizes their nobilitas.

And then there was P. Servilius Rullus. "See the difference," exclaims Cicero in his first public speech, "between Gnaeus Domitius, tribune of the people, a noble of nobles, and Publius Rullus, who in my opinion wanted to test your patience by calling himself noble" (2.7.19). Elsewhere Cn. Domitius is pointedly described as vir clarissimus (2.7.18), a "noble" member of Cicero's elite group, unlike Rullus. In fact, Rullus was probably not from an illustrious branch of the Servilii. His father is thought to be one of the *tresviri* who supervised the mint in 100; no other office is known for him.[19] Twice Cicero alludes to the father as an auctioneer (2.20.53 and 2.25.67), a description arising in the context of the speech from the provisions in the land law concerned with selling land. The Roman people, for whom Cicero was building up his portrayal, would certainly have known what Rullus's background was; and remarks of this nature are probably versions of the truth. The truth was that Rullus was not a nobilis. He did not, therefore, belong to Cicero's elite group.

In a passage that portrays vividly this maladroit officer of the Roman plebs, Cicero makes plain the meaning of Rullus's exclusion from this hypothetical group:

> [W]hen I was informed . . . that the [tribunes] were drawing up a land law, I felt a desire to learn their intentions. . . . I was kept in the dark. . . . I accordingly withdrew my offers of assistance. . . . In the meantime they continued to assemble privately, . . . to summon darkness and solitude to their aid in their secret meetings. . . . At last the tribunes enter upon office; the speech of Rullus in particular is expected. . . . I waited for the man's expected law and speech. At first no law is posted. He orders a meeting for December 12. A crowd gathers round on tiptoe of expectation. He unrolls a very long speech in very fine language. The only fault I could find was that . . . [no one] could be found who was able to understand what he said. . . . At last, however, as soon as I was elected, the law was publicly posted. By my instructions, a number of copyists came running up all together, and bring an exact transcript of it to me.
> (*Leg. Agr.* 2.5.12–13; Loeb trans.)

The elite group observed certain conventions about lawmaking. There was a free exchange of information among them. So Cicero scores a point by charging Rullus with not consulting Cicero, the consul-elect, about the law he was drafting or even making the text available to him. Cicero offered his help to the tribunes in drafting the agrarian law; they turned him down. They met in secret, at night. In the end, Cicero did not even see the text of their proposed law until Rullus had promulgated it and posted the written notice. He was forced to the extreme step of making his own copy of the proposal before he could come to the people with his opinion of it. Cicero contrasts this implicitly with the accepted state of affairs in which, by the time the law was promulgated, he would have known what the law said. Cicero presents these facts as proof of Rullus's exclusion from the elite group. This is more apparent to us in the light of the circumstantial information Cicero gives elsewhere about the exchange of information among political leaders and their peers and associates about laws in draft that were freely and regularly circulated before promulgation. The widely held convention of a free exchange of information is emphasized by the charges of secrecy Cicero raises against Rullus and his fellow tribunes.

Elected officials were also expected to know their job. A tribune who did not know the order of vote of the thirty-five tribes was an affront to the Roman people. In more ways than this, though, Cicero claims in *De Lege Agraria* 2, Rullus was ignorant of the laws and customs of Rome. Specifically, Cicero criticized Rullus indirectly for not knowing, or not taking proper account of, the arrangements of several existing laws: the provisions in Ti. Gracchus's agrarian law for electing commissioners (2.6.16–7.17); those on priests in Domitius's law of 104 (2.7.18–8.20); and provisions from the Aebutian and Licinian laws. Cicero makes a significant point about expected knowledge: "But how is that lawful? For old laws are in existence—not consular laws, if you think this of any importance—but laws made by tribunes, which were very acceptable to you and your ancestors" (2.8.21). Rullus's efforts to win election as decemvir under his own law contravened the two laws here named, Cicero tells his audience, which made explicit provision against such a possibility. In delivering this detail Cicero stresses that both laws were tribunician laws, not consular laws. Conceivably a tribune might be forgiven for proposing a law that would annul the latter; but it was something remarkable (or Cicero makes it so) not to be aware of laws of his own predecessors in office. It was left for the consul to bring them to public notice.

Again, Cicero makes the charge directly, saying that Rullus has forgotten in one clause the arrangements made in the previous one: "And is such a man to fetter the world with new laws [*leges novae*], a man who in the third article forgets what has been laid down in the second?" (2.10.26). A *lex nova*, which made a new arrangement, still had to take account of existing laws. Here Cicero charges Rullus with not even knowing what was in his own law. Bringing the details of previous laws into his discussion in the way he does, Cicero subtly makes the point that Rullus does not know what Cicero and others of the elite group know and builds up the impression that Rullus lacks the right knowledge of Rome's laws. We can see here how important Roman senators thought it was for a magistrate who sponsored laws to know the laws of Rome. And it was not always the case that he did.

With such ad hominem criticisms Cicero was undermining Rullus's credibility as a lawmaker and at the same time reinforcing his own credibility. Cicero presents himself, compared to Rullus, as a magistrate of a completely opposite caliber. He emphasizes his own haste in sending his copyists (*librarii*) to transcribe a copy of the draft statute, so that he could study it and bring the people his expert analysis (2.6.14). Cicero, unlike Rullus, held the people's interests uppermost and fulfilled his responsibilities toward them. We can imagine the occasion of Cicero's speech and how unfavorably Rullus, the undependable tribune, contrasted with Cicero, whose forthright account of his own remarks to the Senate in which he declared he was going to be the people's consul prefaced his subtle attack on Rullus: "I declared in the Senate that, as long as I held this office, I would be the people's consul [*popularem consulem*]" (2.4.9). The contrast between Rullus and Cicero forms the foundation that Cicero publicly lays for his profound objection to Rullus's draft statute. The previous passage portrays vividly this maladroit officer of the Roman plebs.

From the venom of the attack scholars have been justified in wondering how accurately *De Lege Agraria* 2 conveys the substance of Rullus's proposed law. Calling the speech "perverse," some scholars believe that Cicero deliberately misrepresented the law and that we must be wary of any detail Cicero provides about the bill because it is most likely tendentious. While exaggeration is a common feature of public oratory, and notwithstanding the obvious merits of the proposal, there is nonetheless an underlying reality to Cicero's criticisms as well. A conspicuous example is Cicero's charge that Rullus's proposed manner of electing the ten-man commission was a dangerous innovation. Of course, such commissions are common throughout the period of the Republic: among the public law proposals across our period of interest many involved the appointment or election of extraordinary commissions for purposes ranging from land distribution, as here, to the repair of city walls. And, beginning with the land law of Ti. Gracchus, some land commissions were given the power of adjudication by vote of the people. Rarely, however, did commissions have the authority of praetor. More important, Rullus veered from common Roman practice when he proposed that the vote of seventeen rather than eighteen tribes would determine the membership of the commission, as was done in the election of pontifex maximus. Thus Cicero properly, from the perspective of his own day, censures P. Servilius Rullus for undermining the unencumbered expression of the Roman will through the collective voice of a majority of the tribes. Why Rullus would deviate from custom in this way is unknown to us: Cicero offers no explanation other than the one he gives. But why should he? The explanation Cicero gives allows him to give vent to outrage that a tribune would commit such a flagrant blunder.

Rullus's shortcomings as a lawmaker constitute such a prominent line of argument in *De Lege Agraria* 2 that we may reasonably extrapolate from the immediate to the broader context. If he is to persuade his audience, a speaker must be attentive to the concerns that move them, and Cicero was an expert in the art of persuasion. In this case we may be sure he gauged what the people wanted and expected from their political leaders: the people did notice how elected officeholders carried out their responsibilities, and they did value the effective and proper communication of information of concern to them. Without the full disclosure of information in public meetings, a community consensus regarding public law was impossible in Rome. In his chronicle of Rullus's failings, then, Cicero gives us a unique glimpse of the people's expectations about lawmakers and political leaders on lawmaking occasions and indirectly about their own involvement in the process. In the case of P. Servilius Rullus, the particular flaws that Cicero identified in his bill were multiple, ranging from imprecision of language to dangerous innovation. But the most devastating charge that Cicero leveled publicly against him was his inability as a lawmaker to discern the will of the Roman people.

In the picture he draws of Rullus as an incompetent tribune, Cicero also hints at the complexities of the relationship between Roman political leaders and the people. He tacitly recognizes that what he has to say about the rogatio Servilia agraria will be weighed against what Rullus and other political leaders have to say. To a large extent the success or failure of any bill therefore depended on the effectiveness of a law sponsor's ability when interacting with the crowd assembled at a public lawmaking session to articulately and aptly reflect the will of the Roman people.

To the reader of the published speech, it is evident that Cicero went to the meeting knowing the proposal had popular support; for he disparages the basis of this support, describing the proposal as a bill that gave the people a handout (*largitio*), using the common term for the perquisites dispensed to tribesmen by tribal leaders or to soldiers by commanders. Subsequently Cicero introduced his disapproval of this popular bill carefully and adroitly, subordinating it to the expression of his gratitude and debt to the voters for giving him their highest office and their favor and of his intention to be the people's consul. He threw in a few words, too, on what the Roman people treasured most, namely, their peace, their liberty, and their leisure. This initial rhetoric aimed to win the crowd. Only then, abruptly, did the consul introduce his attack on the proposal. Given the skillful and understated way Cicero shifts from his gratitude, his merits, his program, and the people's wishes to the tribunes and their proposal, it is doubtful if the severity of his disapprobation was known in advance to the crowd. At the end of his speech with a rhetorical flourish Cicero notes the approbation with which the crowd received his dissuasio, and at the beginning of his next public speech, *De Lege Agraria* 3, he notes their hostile attitude. His public acknowledgment of the change in attitude, probably because his position surprised and disappointed them, points to the importance of the orator's skill in sensing the mood of his audience at such events and, in turn, in using that recognition to manage their emotions.

When orating to a crowd played such an important part in a magistrate's political career, possessing the means of organizing thought and speech in order to successfully move a crowd and persuade voters was crucial. The emotional content of a moving oration is largely intuitive and personal. Yet there were techniques that made the exercise easier. The study of rhetoric provided these. All surviving speeches and fragments of speeches about law were persuasive in character, delivered by elected officeholders and senators in the hopes of influencing one section or another of the Roman people to cast their votes in a particular way. Their persuasive arguments used the commonplace themes of a developed rhetorical discipline, which by the first century was fully a part of the intellectual baggage of members of the Roman elite. Interest, self-interest, gain, and favor were common themes, attested in rhetorical handbooks like the *Rhetorica ad Herennium*, published in the 80s. It was part of the rhetorical training of members of the political elite to know how to construct a deliberative speech around them. Predictably, the charges of *De Lege Agraria* 2 reflect commonplace tactics and themes of the art of rhetoric. But the argument was based solidly on political realities as Cicero saw them.

CONVENTIONS OF THE PUBLIC DEBATE

Rhetoric did not provide the only tool Cicero had at his disposal in constructing *De Lege Agraria* 2. Another convention, involving the proper way to debate the pros and cons of a public law proposal, is also evident. Throughout the speech Cicero is remarkably organized and precise in his criticisms of the public law proposal. He tells his audience that to form those criticisms, occupying most of both *De Lege Agraria* 2 and 3, he focused closely on the draft statute. Cicero claims he studied the statute carefully from first clause (*caput*) to last (2.6.15) in order to present his findings to the Roman people. In delivering these findings, Cicero proceeds as the order of ideas and clauses in the text of the draft dictated, dealing with concrete issues of substance. By way of preliminary organization, he first situates each point precisely within the text of the law by clause; thereafter he takes up individual points in order. So at 2.7.17 he starts on the first clause (*primum caput est legis agrariae*), and at 2.7.18 he moves on to the second (*item, inquit, eodemque modo capite altero*). While Cicero does not tackle every clause in his critique—since there were at least forty, we might expect that would have been a rather long task—we nonetheless have the strong impression that he preserves the sequence of chapters he does tackle. This is one kind of sale, he comments at one point, "but listen to those which follow" (*sed attendite animos ad ea quae consecuntur*, 2.14.38). Similar signposts are visible elsewhere: *hoc capite* (2.15.39) and *sequitur enim caput quo capite* (2.18.47).

Cicero's discussion of the proposal of law is also remarkably detailed. He prefaces his individual arguments with direct and indirect quotes from the text, and during the elaboration of his arguments he appears to quote freely from, or paraphrase, the draft. One passage previously quoted will illustrate (2.14.35–36); there are others (e.g., 3.2.6–7 and 2.18.47–48). While much of the detail Cicero includes is derived from the draft statute, much also comes from other sources, mainly legal documents. In his analysis of the arrangements instituted in Rullus's draft statute Cicero frequently introduces information about arrangements already instituted in other statutes or Senate decrees. The pattern in his method of producing extraneous detail is simple: he informs the people about a particular statute or Senate decree and he tells them what it says.

> These are the Licinian and second Aebutian laws which not only prohibit anyone who has proposed a law concerning any commission or power from being appointed to any such commission or power but even excludes his colleagues, kinsfolk, and relatives by marriage.
>
> (*Leg. Agr.* 2.8.21; Loeb trans.)

In this instance, Cicero delivers precise detail, not generalities, to confirm that Rullus's intention to become a commissioner under the terms of his own statute was contrary to law.

Two features of a style of speaking about law emerge from the organization and detail of Cicero's speech. First, the draft statute was analyzed in considerable detail. Cicero looks at features of the style and language of the draft; he discusses lack of precision in drafting or simply the choice of words. Second, Cicero did not presume prior knowledge about the draft statute. Instead, he himself supplied any relevant details the people might need to follow his objections: he tells the Roman people about legal precedents; he paraphrases, quotes, or reads large sections of clauses from the law (e.g., 2.8.21; 2.18.47–48). So, the formation of the argument did not depend on what the people could be expected to know already. The combination of fairly complex material and careful articulation is striking and suggests that the composition of speeches supporting and opposing proposed law reflects distinctly Roman conventions of talking about law. Rhetoric was not the only body of technique and learning drawn on by Roman speakers.

Since such a convention is nowhere articulated by the Romans, it might be objected that the conclusion is unsound. Indeed, the *De Lege Agraria* 2 and 3 are atypical among the mostly minute fragments of public orations addressing public law proposals. Moreover, Cicero's own manner of handling a public suasio, in the *pro lege Manilia*, is quite different. Instead of systematically analyzing the draft statute Cicero concerns himself with the nature of command. Instead of focusing on precise issues raised by the text he sweeps through the current political situation in Rome. But the rogatio Manilia was much more limited in scope than the rogatio Servilia—it extended the extraordinary command against the pirates given to Pompey by the lex Gabinia to include Syria and the War with Mithridates—and this probably explains the difference. Since the lex Manilia dealt with a specific appointment to command and was not nearly as complex as Rullus's proposed law on land distribution, Cicero reasonably tailored his argument and its presentation to fit. Not all decisions made by the Roman people involved drafts the length of Rullus's proposed law.

But when political leaders critiqued drafts as long and detailed as this, their suasiones and dissuasiones probably were crafted around a close review of the substance and language of the draft. We find some corroboration in circumstantial descriptions of the public debate about law. Cassius Dio's reports of meetings in 59 and 55, for instance (discussed later), show magistrates who are expected to or who do in fact pick through the draft of a proposed law. Presumably, when they did so, they proceeded through the clauses consecutively, from beginning to end of the draft, in much the same way that Cicero worked through Rullus's proposal in 63. That a conventional way of structuring and organizing a speech was at work seems clear. Undoubtedly, an orator of Cicero's talents would show himself to be a master of all conventions, legal as well as rhetorical, in constructing his speech opposing Rullus's public law proposal. In turn the most devastating of the criticisms Cicero leveled against Rullus was that he was master of none.

ORATORY AND POLITICAL SUCCESS

In 43, M. Antonius nailed the severed head and hand of Cicero to the speaker's platform in the Forum, trophies of his murder of Rome's most famous orator. The violence and location of the display, recalling Cicero's vehement orations denouncing Antonius the previous year, provide an emphatic measure of the importance of public speaking in an oral society. From the speaker's platform Cicero and other political leaders harangued, cajoled, and roused Roman voters; they praised and reviled their colleagues and their colleagues' proposals of law; they condemned and exonerated Rome's policies, her plans, her friends, and her enemies. All matters of concern to the entire Roman community were aired in full view of the Roman people in such oratorical sessions. But Roman oratory in public lawmaking sessions involved far more than the presence of a Roman leader haranguing a crowd. At all times public speaking was a lively exchange between the speaker and his crowd of listeners. The crowd shouted approval, or it heckled, or it might even prevent a man from speaking altogether. The crowd demanded substance, skill, and presence from public speakers. Appearing before a crowd therefore could be a daunting experience; the celebrated military man, C. Marius, was famous also for his fear of addressing the crowd in the Forum. But those political leaders who had the courage to face the crowd found themselves engaged in an intimate dialogue with their listeners, the Roman people.

Public oratory was vitally important to the political leaders of Rome. When orating to a crowd, an officeholder, or would-be officeholder, or senator made direct contact with the Roman people. On display were not only his powers of marshaling words and arguments but his emotional connection to the people and their needs. In public lawmaking sessions the urgency of the issues that compelled a certain group to form the crowd gave the orator's delivery for or against a proposal a commensurate urgency, if the speaker had talent enough and a sense of drama. Orating was a physical exercise employing the speaker's entire body in addition to his emotions and intellect. Cicero's severed hand was nailed to the Rostra alongside his head in 43 because the orator's hands, in particular his right hand, contributed to his powers of swaying a crowd. But there was give-and-take in the exercise, as Cicero acknowledged in his speeches *De Lege Agraria* twenty years before his murder. The mutual interaction between political leaders and people on the occasions of lawmaking is revealed in efforts, on the part of both groups, to sway one another. Formally, orating for or against a proposal served this purpose for political leaders while voting yes or no served a similar purpose for the Roman people. There was more leeway in public oratory. Oratory was essential in maintaining the personal dimension of leadership.

In order to garner support effectively, a political leader had to participate in the public debate. Participation was not always guaranteed, however, in the highly competitive atmosphere of late Republican Rome. The opportunity of speaking, which by convention all officeholders and senators had, came over time to be subject to restriction. At least one extortion law deprived the senator duly convicted of his right to orate before the people in a meeting: *infamia* was incompatible with public oratory and with political leadership.[20] Lawmakers also began to refuse some men permission to speak on some occasions. The consul Caesar's well-known refusal to let his colleague Bibulus address a meeting in 59 prompted the latter to stay home for the remainder of his year in office, periodically dispatching ominous notices from behind the closed doors of his house aimed at disrupting all public business. Others were less direct than Caesar. In order to avoid refusing a senator the opportunity to speak, magistrates employed various ruses: physically barring a man from the speaker's platform or the Forum itself was usually effective. The final meeting before the assembly convened to vote on a proposal of the tribune C. Trebonius, in 55, regarding the assignment of commands, is instructive. One senator, M. Porcius Cato, was allotted two hours to speak but devoted the time to political matters peripheral to the proposal without once addressing himself directly to the proposal. Yet at the end of two hours Cato would not stop speaking because he wanted an excuse to charge that Trebonius had not allowed him to discuss the proposal.[21] In the end Trebonius had him pulled from the tribunal, and when Cato climbed back up he finally had him hauled off to prison. When the meeting was resumed on the following day, Trebonius prevented another senator, Gallus, from speaking against the proposal by locking him in the Senate House, where Gallus had spent the night in order to avoid being kept forcibly from the Forum in the morning.[22] More extreme (and employed only twice according to the record, by Ti. Gracchus in 133 and that same C. Trebonius in 55) was the threat to remove a man from office. Gracchus not only threatened his colleague Octavius but carried out his threat, successfully. Senators later regarded his move as an uncustomary restriction on participation in a public debate. One senator objected that Tiberius might let him speak but would penalize him for it later.[23] Thus, refusals were at one and the same time common occurrences, in the last century of the Republic, and occurrences contrary to convention. In incidents of this kind we can see the value magistrates and senators attached to the opportunity of speaking. Oratory enabled them to sway their peers as well as the people.[24] The importance of oratory in Roman political life is clear in such lawmaking episodes.

In view of the gradual increase in the membership of their class over the third and second centuries, Rome's leaders not surprisingly developed a strong sense of the right kind of oratory that allowed full scope to the common though unspoken markers of membership in Rome's entrenched elite. The right kind of oratory was characterized by a certain style, wit, and pronunciation that identified the orator as the "right sort" of man—urbane, that is Rome-bred, a man whose family was of long-time standing. The qualities of *urbanitas* distinguished the right kind of oratory. Newer members of the Roman elite from Italian towns mostly lacked these "unspoken social markers."[25] Instead, when such men began to orate to the people in Rome, following election to the office of tribune and the opportunity to address public law courts (*iudicia publica*), granted in the late second century, their oratory characteristically relied on directness and emotion.

Such differences in the style of public orating favored by members of the city elite on the one hand and by Italian aspirants to Rome's leadership on the other point to some of the different resources utilized by old and new members of the political leadership.[26] Their approach to elected office was through military service and law courts. Unlike Roman nobility, they must rely on patronage or on their own merits—and the limitations of patronage are obvious in the experiences of C. Marius, small-town protégé of the Metelli, whose patron not only discouraged Marius's political ambitions but publicly humiliated him in the process. In the circumstances, oratory became essential for political newcomers in breaching the ranks of Rome's political leadership. Equally important was the development of a style of their own, known as *eloquentia popularis*. We can imagine that the directness and emotional content of their style of public oratory mirrored the face-to-face camaraderie of the military environment where most may well have had their start, serving as military tribunes in the legions. The exigencies of operating in an arena dominated by the great clans of Rome made it imperative for such men to make the most of their own personalities and strengths. Good oratory gave a man an advantage.

LAW DRAFTS

Some Roman statutes were remarkably long and complicated legal documents. The Rullan proposal of 63, the object of Cicero's public speeches *De Lege Agraria*, contained at least forty provisions, all lost. But we may instructively compare this ghost bill with the fragments of another, the lex Agraria of 111, whose fifty-eight surviving clauses, amounting to one-third of the original, require eleven modern pages in very small print (*RS* 1 No. 2). This statute is not only long, it is also meticulously precise in its language, its definition of categories, and its attention to detail. Consider the passage opening the first five clauses:

> Quei ager poplicus populi Romani in terram Italiam P. Muucio L. Calpurnio cos. fuit, extra eum agrum. . . exceptum cavitumve est nei divideretur . . .
>
> [Whatever public land of the Roman people there was in the land of Italy during the consulship of P. Mucius and L. Calpurnius, apart from that land, whose division was excluded or forbidden . . .]
>
> (*RS* 1 No. 2, trans.)

The stage set precisely not once but five times, each clause then continues to define specifically a category or condition of land, once public, which is hereafter to be private. That the land shall be private is not finally stated until the beginning of the sixth clause:

> ager locus aedificium omnis quei supra scriptus est extra eum agrum. . . locum de quo supra exceptum cavitum est. . . nei divideretur, privatus esto. . .
>
> [Let all the land, place and building which is written above . . . be private, except for the land and place concerning which an exception and stipulation is made above.]
>
> (*RS* 1 No. 2, trans.)

Fifty-two more clauses follow of similar complexity. There would be at least 150 if the law survived in full.

As we can see clearly in such surviving texts of law, the issues presented at public lawmaking sessions could be highly technical, demanding considerable resources of knowledge. The lex Agraria required knowledge of the status of land in Italy as determined by statute and custom, likewise the status of conquered land in Africa and Corinth, the kinds of lease, and conditions of tenure. Even beyond their content, the composition of law texts themselves was quite a production, in an age that relied on papyrus rolls and wax-covered wooden tablets for such tasks.

It is hard to imagine the hours-long performance of the lex Agraria by the herald in a public lawmaking session, after an even longer public debate about the measure, without thinking of a restive crowd of dry-throated Romans wishing they were anywhere else but there. It is hard, too, to imagine how the immediacy of a public lawmaking meeting served Roman public law sponsors in the production of such long-winded texts. But this is projection: in the modern Western world, legalese is the jargon of legal specialists and the production of legal documents is remote from the decision-making process itself, a job for specialists in compartments surrounded by codes, precedents, and legal decisions. In Republican Rome, the production of law unfolded in an environment barely touched by a nascent bureaucracy of professional clerks (*scribae*). Hence, we must look first for the men who drafted documents of such technical complexity in the ranks of Rome's political leaders, among the same men who directed the public argument about law.[27] Who among these men drafted law and their method of producing law drafts form our subject here.

Senate and public discussions about law, exhibiting a level of technical detail as striking as the complexity of the laws themselves, indicate where to begin looking for the drafters of public law. In a revealing letter Cicero wrote to Atticus on 15 March in 60, three years after condemning the Rullan proposal, we read about his contributions to the public debate on a similar measure, the rogatio Flavia agraria:

> With the approval of [the people in a meeting] I advocated the deletion from the bill all provisions detrimental to private interest. I was for releasing from its operation such land as was in state ownership in the Consulship of P. Mucius and L. Calpurnius, for confirming the Sullan settlers in their holdings, and for leaving the people of Volaterrae and Arretium, whose land Sulla confiscated but did not distribute, in possession. One proposal I did not reject, that land should be purchased out of the additional funds accruing during a period of five years from the new tributary revenues.
>
> (*Att.* 1.19.4; Shackleton Bailey trans.)

Here we see an ex-consul attending closely to the content of a proposed bill, arguing that some provisions should be taken out and others left alone, while the crowd roared its approval (*secunda contionis voluntate*). The conclusion that senators were deeply involved in the production of law on a very basic level and in a very public setting is unavoidable. More can be added to this simple idea.

Writing anxiously to Atticus during his exile in late 58 and 57 or orating with grand self-assurance in the Senate and Forum on his safe return in 56, Cicero charted the uncertain waters of legal drafting for modern historians.[28] His subject, in some detail, was the flurry of draft statutes generated in the attempt of friends and associates to bring him back from the Greek desolation of Thessaloniki. Six were actually promulgated and two more might have been by tribunes, a praetor, and a consul; another two were drafted but never proposed.[29] Thus, ten proposals at least were mooted formally or informally, making the episode to exile and recall Cicero the most intensively disputed lawmaking effort in Roman history, a strong measure of the importance of the issues in 63 as well as of Cicero's charisma as a mesmerizing orator and a successful new man. As we shall see, too, in part 3, the episode also is indicative of changes in public lawmaking. In any event, the interest Cicero displayed in his own recall produced a remarkably detailed picture of the earlier stages in the production of law.

A plaintive commentary to Atticus (*Att.* 3.23) about three of the drafts produced in these earlier stages is worth quoting at some length:

> The bill of the [tribunes of 58] had three clauses, the first concerning my return. This was carelessly drafted, for it restores nothing except my citizenship and rank . . . The second clause . . . is common form. . . . As for the third clause . . . do ask yourself why it was put in and by whom. . . . [It] makes one all the more suspicious of some malicious intention when one finds them including a provision which did not affect themselves but was contrary to my interest. . . . Nor did that escape Clodius. At a meeting on 3 November he remarked that this clause laid down for the Tribunes-Designate how far they might go. And yet you must be aware that no law contains such a clause. . . . I should be grateful if you would inquire how it was that Ninnius and others failed to see this, and who brought the clause in. . . . But if there is anything left to hope for, take a look at the law which Visellius drafted for T. Fadius. It seems admirable to me. Sestius's draft which you say you approve of, I don't like.
>
> (*Att.* 3.23.4; Shackleton Bailey trans.)

The letter, dated 29 November, in response to several letters from Atticus concerning the status of legal efforts in Rome to recall Cicero, addresses specifically a proposal that the tribunes of 58 promulgated on 29 October, the anticipated proposal from the tribunes of 57 and two drafts of this.[30] It is obvious from the letter that promulgation swayed public opinion even if the proposal was not expected to pass muster: What the proposal said mattered. Informally here (compared to his comments about other laws cited earlier) but far more insistently because his own future was at stake, Cicero again picks unhesitatingly and deftly at the technical knots of draft statutes.

Incidentally he provides concrete information about the men directly involved in their production—the tribunes, first of all, as Cicero's comments on the third clause of the first proposal make clear. Cicero was afraid that the tribunes of 57 would be influenced by the third clause from the proposal promulgated on 29 October in drafting theirs. It had the potential to make future laws null and void. In the statute exiling Cicero, Clodius had included a sanction that set heavy penalties on anyone who even so much as brought up for discussion the subject of Cicero's return. He had posted it at the Curia. The other tribunes of the same year then drafted a clause in their proposal not to avoid making themselves liable under Clodius's statute, because they would not be anyway, but to hamper future proposals. Whether the tribunes of 57 did adopt the clause in their proposal is not known. As Rotondi pieced the details together, the tribunes of 57 promulgated two proposals. The first was proposed by C. Messius alone. The second was proposed by other tribunes. What happened to either is not known: Were they perhaps never promulgated? Were they withdrawn or did they fail to pass the assembly? In any event the texts of these two proposals were not the drafts of Sestius and Fadius. It appears that the proposal promulgated by most of the college jointly was a collaborative draft that drew on the proposal drafted by the previous college of tribunes and so may also have incorporated individual contributions. Clearly, Cicero held the tribunes jointly responsible for the contents of their promulgated statutes.

But men who did not hold office were also involved. Cicero in exile, a senator of consular rank, obviously took a deep interest in the language of the statute: his property and political future were at stake. Atticus, a wealthy equestrian and Cicero's intimate friend, was also obviously interested—he to some extent acted as Cicero's go-between. The involvement of others was more direct. Two drafts intended for the tribunes of 57 were drafted by men who neither would sponsor their proposals nor indeed were even elected officeholders. One was written by Sestius, tribune-elect for 57, and the other by Visellius, a senator who held no office (*privatus*), for T. Fadius, another tribune-elect.[31] Cicero referred to Sestius's draft in an earlier letter, written on 5 October (*Att.* 3.20), criticizing its wording. Thus Sestius had drafted his proposal before entering office and before the tribunes of 58 promulgated their proposal on 29 October.

It should be stressed that copies of these drafts produced by Sestius and Visellius had not been promulgated but were in circulation. Cicero in faraway Greece had copies; Atticus could get them. Drafts were circulated freely before promulgation. During Cicero's exile in 57, it is evident that the men working on the mechanics of recalling him to Rome sent him copies to keep him informed and also to allow him to have a say in the drafting processes. It is not immediately clear how Cicero got the copies, but presumably from friends. Elite Romans had a highly personal style of interaction. In the case of the statute promulgated on 29 October, Cicero knew the date of promulgation from other sources than Atticus; Atticus had written Cicero on the day the statute was posted.[32] The tenor of Cicero's response does not suggest that Atticus had sent him a copy of that proposal then. Cicero already knew what it contained, and by the time he answered Atticus's letter he already knew it had been rejected by the assembly.[33] Nor could Atticus have sent Fadius's draft, because Cicero wrote him to "have a look at it." In another letter, in January of 45, Cicero wrote Q. Lepta that he had contacted Balbus to ask for details about the content of a statute.[34] It cannot be determined whether it was a statute already approved by a voting assembly, a proposal still in the advertising stage, or a proposal not yet promulgated. What matters is that Cicero found the information Lepta wanted about a particular detail in the statute not from a public source—that is, a written notice that advertised the proposal, or a copy deposited in the Aerarium, or the engraved bronze tablet—but from a private source: Balbus. Similarly, in 58, Cicero does not appear to have received a copy of the tribunes' proposal from the written notice of it. It is clear that political leaders and other elite Romans circulated the drafts of proposals among themselves, in an informal and private way. In a society that drew a blurred line between state and private initiative, such informality is hardly surprising.

Cicero's comments on these drafts show how closely elite Romans were involved in piecing together a statute. On one side we see tribunes collaborating on a proposal. On the other we see contributions on a different level in the shape of criticism and suggestion by the senator, Cicero, and the Roman equestrian, Atticus. Some of the texts were drafted by the tribunes themselves, some by tribunes-elect, and one by a low-ranking senator who did not hold any office at the time. He might be the kind of specialist Cicero elsewhere calls a *scriptor legum*. But there was a definite method of procedure involving members of Rome's political leadership directly: elected officeholders consulted with other officeholders and senators, and even equestrians, about the laws they intended to bring to the people.

Contributors to the public debate give us further insights into the formulation and drafting of law.[35] Meetings were convened by the proposal's sponsor or by other magistrates, and at these meetings the magistrate alone or a crowd of speakers harangued the people. By long-standing convention, a law's sponsor gave other officeholders and senators without office every opportunity to voice their support. Thus, in 58, P. Clodius convened several meetings in order to enable the consular senators Pompey, Crassus, Caesar, and Piso and the praetorian Gabinius to lend their support to his proposal to send Cicero into exile. He even called one meeting in the Campus Martius so that Caesar, who had already taken up a military command at the time, could speak.[36] Anyone who wanted to should have been allowed to speak, opponents as well as supporters of a proposed statute. Indeed, the initiative to speak sometimes came from the speakers themselves, who by convention could not be refused. Loudly condemning the tribunes for their failure to invite him to speak about the Rullan land bill in an earlier meeting of their own, Cicero publicly voiced his opposition to that proposal in his own inaugural meeting as consul, in January of

63.[37] But sponsors understandably tended to call on men who would speak in support of their law and to ignore men who would not. Needless to say, there are many examples of sponsors who even refused permission to speak on some occasions to some men, depending on their point of view, their rank, and consequently their experience and expertise, and their influence. Refusals of this sort were at one and the same time common occurrences in the first century and occurrences contrary to convention. This tension makes them useful to the modern historian in recovering the meaning of the choreography of the public debate.

Whether one speaker alone or a crowd of speakers harangued the people in their public meetings about proposed law, the lineup of contributors to this public debate was by no means haphazard. The rank and reputation of individual elected officeholders and senators loomed large in the public debate about law.[38] Each speaker wielded his influence (*auctoritas*) in aid of, in defense of, or in opposition to the lawmaker and his proposal. The role of influence began even before a sponsor promulgated a proposal of law, when he sought the advice of other political leaders in drafting it. After promulgation, the formal announcement, and presentation of the proposal, he sought their approval publicly. Specifically, a sponsor sought the public support of influential men, inviting elected officeholders and senators to contribute to the public discussion precisely because they were influential. The tribune Clodius in 58, as noted earlier, ensured that the people heard what all the leading men of the day had to say about his proposal to banish Roman leaders responsible for the deaths of Romans without trial in 63. When Caesar, Pompey, and Crassus, the three most influential men in Rome by virtue of their individual auctoritas, failed to support Cicero publicly, he left Rome even before the people made their decision.[39] When orating to a Roman crowd, even more important than what a man said was the influence he carried in saying it.

To understand the basis of this influence as well as its import for the drafting process, it is worth examining the involvement of senators without office (privati) in the public debate.[40] While ancient explanations for their involvement are sometimes misleading, writers nonetheless provide the framework of attitudes and conventions underpinning the events they describe. Writing at a time when the Roman people still met in lawmaking assemblies, Livy comments on the involvement of privati in the public debate when describing an unprecedented incident during a lawmaking event. In 167, the praetor peregrinus, M'. Iuventius Thalna, promulgated a proposal to declare war on Rhodes.[41] Two tribunes vetoed his proposal, even pulling the praetor from his tribunal.[42] The actions of all three officeholders were unprecedented according to Livy. It was irregular for a praetor to propose a war declaration without first consulting the Senate and consuls. Similarly, tribunes did not veto proposals before senators without office had spoken about them, because, Livy writes, it was customary to let senators have their say about proposals before any vetoes were brought in order to give any magistrate who had not stated his intention to veto the chance to change his mind on hearing the faults of the statute pointed out.[43] Moreover, any who had come with the intention of vetoing might be influenced by the authority of those who spoke in support of it.[44]

The key elements in this account are the phrases "the faults of the statute" (*vitia legis*) and the "influence of a man of status and experience" (auctoritas). The faults of the law were evidently better known to experienced senators, men with auctoritas, than to junior magistrates, in particular tribunes. Vitia in the context of a public lawmaking session usually meant irregularities such as religious obstructions, recognizable to men who have experience with omens. Thunder, birds in wrong places, and other ominous sights and sounds all could potentially vitiate the proceedings. Their announcement by a political leader qualified to obstruct the proceedings, called *obnuntiatio*, was regulated by statute beginning in the second century, because the gods' disposition on lawmaking events was such a vital element in the legitimate decision reached by an assembly. Significantly, as Pina Polo has pointed out, most privati invited to address the people in a contio were also members of priestly colleges.[45]

But does the term "faults" have reference only to religious obstruction? Livy presupposes that senators without office would bring more knowledge and expertise to lawmaking than magistrates, in any area. Accordingly, the faults of the statute should include any objection to a proposal raised in the public discussion or in the Senate discussion, consisting in technical or general points. Cicero's criticisms of Rullus's public law proposal provide a cogent example. About 40 years earlier, the Senate issued a blanket condemnation when it decreed in 100 that Saturninus's proposed grain law was not in the people's best interests. Saturninus had not taken his statute to the Senate first; it was discussed there nonetheless on the motion of Servilius Caepio.[46] A proposal could be flawed in various ways: the draft statute could be clumsily drafted, it could be inaccurate in its reference to existing statute, or it could be simply out of sync with existing law, with Roman custom, or with the accepted values and intent of the Roman community.[47] All of these issues were raised at one time or another in the speeches about laws or in reported debates. There were always reasons for vetoing laws, because it was expected that reasons should be given. When in 122 the tribune Livius Drusus vetoed C. Gracchus's proposal, Appian notes that the Senate advised him not to give a reason.[48]

Influence (auctoritas) also enters into Livy's explanation. He juxtaposes it against the preceding faults of the law. Like the other, this, too, causes magistrates to change their minds. He is talking specifically of the influence of senators on tribunes and not necessarily on praetors and consuls. Even so, in this incidental remark, Livy tells us that senators brought two contributions to the discussion: their ability to spot faults of the law, that is, technical exper-tise, and their influence or authority. In this mid-second-century episode, as recounted by a late-first-century historian, the contributions of privati to the public debate were clearly significant.

In like manner the imperial historian Cassius Dio saw them. Commenting on the public meeting convened by the tribune Trebonius in 55, Dio reasons that citizens in a private capacity spoke before magistrates so that their views would not be influenced by the authority of the latter and their comments therefore less freely contributed.[49] The explanation oversimplifies the more complex reality underlying the interactions among senators and elected officials of different ranks. Writing some two hundred years after the end of the Republic, Dio could hardly be expected to understand Republican conventions.

The same historian comes closer to late Republican realities when describing the public meeting called in 59 by the consul Julius Caesar, in which Caesar invited the senators Pompey and Crassus to discuss his proposed land law. The invitation was odd, observed Dio, because neither man held office in that year—they were privati. Dio goes on to explain Caesar's choice of interlocutors by noting that although they held no office they were the leading men in Rome and, where the people were concerned, the most influential.[50] Here we see, from the perspective of an imperial historian, the network of influence linking political leaders and people. More important, Dio has grasped the native power of both Pompey and Crassus in 59, surpassing even the collective voice of the Roman Senate.

At this time the maverick potential of individual senators was firmly in place if not willingly recognized by the "right people," still absorbed in the traditional importance of their collective front. In this regard Caesar's meeting in 59 was in one very important respect exceptional: it was convened for the explicit purpose of circumventing the Senate's refusal to give their affirmation to Caesar's proposal.[51] Caesar promulgated his proposal of law without it. But then he sought the affirmation of individual, high-ranking senators. In his colleague Bibulus, as noted, Caesar met with another refusal. It was then, in the public meeting, that he asked Pompey and Crassus for their public support. Pointedly, Caesar replaced the recommendations of the Senate and of his colleague in the consulate with that of his foremost political associates, two privati. Power usually always prevails. Yet in this incident there is no question of the abuse of power or indeed of the subversion of convention. Caesar followed the rules: if the Senate could not articulate the will of the people, Caesar, Pompey, and Crassus would. Cassius Dio's misunderstanding of Caesar's invitation emphasizes the new political reality in the late Republic, namely, that the personal authority and consequently the influence of a Roman senator in a private capacity supersedes both the authority of the Senate and the authority of an elected officeholder in matters of public law.[52]

In any event, commentators were always elected officeholders and senators and typically were officeholders beyond the office of quaestor, namely tribunes, praetors, and consuls, or senators who had held these offices. When Cicero spoke against the Rullan proposal in 63 he was consul; his first public delivery on a proposed statute—in support of the tribune Manilius's proposal to give a military command to Pompey (*pro lege Manilia*)—was delivered only four years before, in 66, when he was praetor. M. Porcius Cato, in contrast, was praetor-elect when he spoke against the proposed statute of C. Trebonius in 55—he had been quaestor in 64, perhaps, and tribune in 62. Caius Gracchus was quaestor when in 126 he spoke against the proposal of the tribune M. Junius Pennus to prohibit non-Romans from residing in Roman towns.[53] Personal style and security of position may explain the difference: diffidence was typical for Cicero, a new man unready to make waves. Men with noble antecedents or self-assurance tried the waters sooner. Gracchus was addressing an issue he was patently absorbed in throughout his career. Cato had exercised a command pro praetore in Cyprus and Byzantium between 58 and 56. It was a man's standing and authority that counted in the public debate, and these normally accrued with office. A law sponsor regularly sought the support of authoritative men for his proposal, inviting consuls and praetors to join in the public debate and high-ranking senators as well, regardless of whether they held office, precisely because their words carried weight. The public debate pitted members of the political leadership against one another in a contest of public reputation and authority. Understandably, when these depended to a large extent on rank derived from office, the men of highest rank, consulars and praetorians, had the edge.

The kind of edge some men had over others offers an explanation for the depth of the discussion and debate about law. For rank was no empty measure in Rome, but a mark of experience. Senators who had held one or two or especially all three of the lawmaking magistracies, the offices of tribune, praetor, and consul, were likely experts in the production of law. Not only did they have experience. They had, or should have had, knowledge and expertise, too, which in the best of circumstances are acquired by experience. But there were gradations in their expertise and wide ranges of knowledge: consuls and praetors and consular and praetorian senators of high rank were bound to be more experienced in lawmaking than tribunes or quaestorian or aedilician senators. Thus, high-ranking senators and officeholders were regarded as sources of knowledge and expertise. Men of experience who had themselves sponsored law contributed their knowledge and expertise to the discussion about law. In sum, the varying levels of knowledge found among the political leaders conditioned their contributions to the public debate.

A system in the production of law rises to view from this elaborate choreography. Statutes were formulated in a process of collaboration, consultation, and discussion. The participants in the process depended in part on the sponsor. If a college of tribunes sponsored a statute, all or some were routinely involved in the process, working together in the fashion shown by Cicero's report of the laws drafted by the tribunes of 57. But they did not rely on their own efforts alone. Instead they consulted higher magistrates and senators. When drawing up his agrarian law in 133, Ti. Gracchus had, as advisors, P. Crassus, the pontifex maximus, a leading lawyer and ex-praetor (he was consul in 131); his brother, P. Mucius Scaevola, consul in 133 and also an eminent jurist; Ap. Claudius Pulcher, ex-consul and princeps senatus; and others (Plutarch, *Ti. Gracch.* 9.1). In 63 Cicero claimed to have offered advice, as consul-elect, to Rullus and his fellow tribunes on the land law they were drafting. They turned him down. The hierarchic tendency of consultation during the earliest stages of drafting was pronounced: junior officeholders consulted senior officeholders and senators. It never went the other way. Similarly, in the public debate, sponsors availed themselves of the expertise of other men.

Accordingly, elected officials and senators directly addressed the language, phrasing, antecedents, and implications of proposed law on many occasions and in widely different arenas. Before promulgation a proposal was mooted among colleagues and advisors in a magistrate's circle (*consilium*), in personal discussions, and in correspondence. Still before promulgation, the lawmaker typically took his draft proposal to the Senate for discussion, as Rullus did in 63. After promulgation, proposals were mooted in public lawmaking meetings. On all these occasions the nature of the discussions, whenever attested, appears similar, but it is worthwhile to examine the possible outcome of debate in the various arenas.

Chronologically, in the career of a proposal the Senate discussion usually came first. The nature of the discussion in the Senate on a law before it was promulgated is illustrated by few direct examples. But where we have reports of prolonged discussion, it was directed to technical details of drafting and content as well as to general points of law.[54] Dio gives us a description of the points covered in the Senate's discussion of a statute in connection with that same law of Caesar's in 59 described earlier.[55] Criticism of the text, leading to changes or deletion, was one point of discussion. The value or legality of the proposed statute was another. During this meeting, Cato urged the senators not to give their approval to any new laws; likewise Caesar's colleague Bibulus had said, when Caesar asked him for his opinion, that he would not agree to any new laws in his consulship. The point at issue is the proposed law's relation to, or contribution to, the body of existing statute law. Thus Senate discussions of proposals addressed the technical, legal, and procedural features of law. The language of statutes, their content, and purport, as well as the procedures of legislative assemblies and the whole lawmaking process, came under scrutiny.

These matters also came under scrutiny in the public debate about law. Comparison of Cicero's public speeches *De Lege Agraria* 2 and 3 with the speech *De Lege Agraria* 1, delivered in the closed session of the Roman Senate, reveals that the level of discussion about law in public meetings was no less technical than the level of discussion in the Senate. The arrangements of the proposal were examined; legal precedent, language, as well as legal and political consequences entered into the commentary. In the matter of substance there is no difference between *De Lege Agraria* 1 on the one hand and 2 and 3 on the other. On a superficial level the Roman voters' knowledge about the technicalities of lawmaking ranged over the same ground as that of commentators.[56] The level of detail and the nature of the arguments employed are another matter. Nonetheless, the existence of a shared universe of knowledge about public law is obvious in public lawmaking sessions like the one Cicero conducted in January of 63.

But while discussions in the Senate and in public lawmaking meetings ranged over similar issues, they differed in their impact on the law draft. In either venue, discussions aimed to correct, delete, or uphold clauses in proposals or the entire proposal. We can see this most clearly in the case of Senate discussions before proposals were promulgated. While the same aim emerges from descriptions of public meetings, the law draft at this point had already been promulgated. Any changes in the draft hereafter required the sponsor to withdraw the proposal, change it, and advertise the draft again for a period of three Roman weeks. Consider again the public career of the rogatio Flavia agraria, in 60, where in at least one public meeting a consular senator proposed changes in the bill, obviously viewing the meeting with its public debate as a viable occasion for suggesting changes and the people's support as affirmation of the changes.[57] And, since the proposal was formally mooted for well over the minimum advertising interval of three market days (*nundinae*)—Cicero first mentions it in a letter to Atticus dated 2 January and in the letter of 15 March cited previously—scholars have assumed it must have been withdrawn and amended.[58] Thereafter Flavius promulgated the bill anew in accordance with the lex Licinia Iunia of 62, scholars believe, which prohibited the alteration of proposals already promulgated. In any case, one difference between discussions in the Senate and in public lawmaking meetings was precisely the impact the discussion could have, before and after promulgation, on a proposal of law. How the contributions of privati affected the production of a draft statute directly is uncertain in some respects. In the case of the praetor's proposal for war in 167, Livy presents the achievements of the public discussion in terms of the veto and nothing more. But influence in relation to a possible veto enters into the forefront of Livy's comments because that was the point on which he introduced this explanation. He is giving here only one side of the reception, given the contributions of senators: how it is received by magistrates in relation to their decision, already made, to veto or not to veto. He was not saying that what the senators had to say was directed only to, or heard only by, magistrates who intended (or not) to veto. Sponsors of law, especially tribunes, sought or avoided their opinions publicly for this reason: what high-ranking senators had to say about proposed laws conveyed information about various technical points that the drafters were unaware of or did not want known.

Let me return to the involvement of political leaders and other elite Romans in the production of law and the significance of their contributions. Several purposes were served in the collaborative system of formulating and drafting law described earlier. Personal interest and attachment were clearly served in the contributions of experienced senators in the earliest stages of drafting, as Cicero's involvement in the laws to recall him shows. Contributions brought a consensus of opinion to the statute that was finally drafted. Even more, they brought consistency, regulating as it were the standard of laws. The collaborative method imposed the quality control that accounts for the continuity of style and legal usage that shows through in the surviving statutes, notwithstanding frequent awkwardness. There were in effect two points at which the standard of proposals was controlled. While a statute was in process of formulation, the sponsor or sponsors, if it was a college of tribunes, sought the technical expertise and experience of senior elected officials, senators or others. We see something of this in Cicero's correspondence with Atticus about the laws being drafted and proposed to end his exile in 57. There are no examples of a law sponsor with his advisors, holding a discussion over the text in process of formulation. Cicero suggests in his speech on the tribunes' agrarian proposal in 63 that consuls looked into laws in the works; it was part of their job. Consultation with more experienced elected officeholders and senators, discussion by the Senate of the drafted text, and discussion in public meetings both provided the technical advisors tribunes needed in order to formulate and draft bills and served as checks on the technical quality of laws brought to the people.

The hierarchic tendency in this system of collaboration and consultation reveals its purposes. In part the tendency was a natural reflection of the essentially hierarchic character of the Roman leadership. In part, too, it was a reflection of the hierarchy of experience: Consuls and praetors knew more than tribunes. But arguably inexperience was only relative: a tribune after all was still a member of the political leadership, a very narrow band. On examination men who became tribunes were successful because they had several qualifications: they were equestrians and they had reputations as military men, legal experts, or speakers. Our evidence is imprecise, but we have the strong impression that these qualifications were always expected on the part of other elite Romans and Roman voters. So, relative to other Romans in the top ranks, tribunes were experienced. Yet even among men of the same rank, some were considered experts. M. Marcellus was elected consul for 51 because of his knowledge of Rome's statutes (*nomoi*), knowledge that he then directed toward efforts to remove Caesar from his command.[59] Why the wide range of abilities? The hierarchic tendency in the system arises in part, too, from the increasingly complex social reality of the late Republic.[60] Inexperience was not a matter of ability but familiarity with the traditional resources of legal knowledge and traditional training of elite Romans. Rank and status remained real qualifications, carrying with them the baggage of required performance even in the absence of hard knowledge.

Cicero was aware of this. Cicero indeed was a well-placed witness both to the presumptions shared by members of his class about a traditional standard of knowledge and expertise held by an elite group and to the growing detachment of those presumptions from the realities of the group as it had then become. From his public speeches against the Rullan proposal, for instance, we form a strong impression of the conventions of lawmaking observed by political leaders that rested on two foundations: the free exchange of information among elected officeholders and senators and knowledge of Rome's laws and customs. But Cicero himself insisted that some magistrates—specifically Rullus—were unfamiliar with the conventions. For Cicero the breakdown occurred because some magistrates—specifically Rullus—came from obscure backgrounds; for Cicero nobility made a man reliably privy to the conventions. Yet as modern historians have demonstrated, mobility and obscure background were the norm rather than the exception, especially among tribunes in Cicero's day, a phenomenon to which we shall return in later chapters.[61] Cicero's insistence on a long-entrenched inner circle of more elite members among Rome's rulers resonated with self-image, not reality.

However, where Rullus is concerned, we are left after reading Cicero's public denunciation with the image of a man whose secrecy, in the way he promulgated his proposal, and whose lack of knowledge about the laws of Rome were at variance with an accepted standard. Whether the image is accurate or not, we can see the importance that Rome's political leaders attached to a process in which sponsors consulted and collaborated with other (higher) elected officeholders and senators in the production of law and came equipped with a certain standard of legal and procedural knowledge. Yet it was not always the case that they did. Paradoxically, we are also left with the sense that the success or failure of a lawmaker depended on more than the merits of a particular public law proposal. In spite of wide support, Rullus apparently withdrew his bill in the wake of Cicero's blistering attack rather than face the veto threatened by one of his colleagues.[62] Rullus and his advisors may indeed have drafted a flawed public law. But Rullus's failure of will and Cicero's success in presenting Rullus as a lawmaker who failed to discern the will of the people are owed at least in part to Cicero's recognized powers as a public speaker.

CONCLUSION

Visible in the details Cicero records of Rullus's proposal is the template that guided Roman legal draftsmen in the last two centuries in dealing with one of the principle issues exercised in Rome's public assemblies—namely, access to land resources. The speeches *De Lege Agraria* also tell us how such laws should be processed: they should not be privately developed; they should be written so that they are understandable; and they should be explained by the right people, namely, the informed elite. In the arguments of *De Lege Agraria*, we have an example of the public endorsements of a bill and of the assumptions and expectations that formed them. Given that we know the events of 63 relatively well, in Cicero's public orations we can see clearly how an officeholder interacted with the people about a proposed law during the public stages in the production of law, transpiring in public meetings. The reciprocal bond between the Roman people and their political leaders can be seen in Cicero's complicated oratorical choreography, a sequence expected and understood by his audience, and by the extent to which he is accepted as an authority by Romans on the details of the proposed law. The reliance by the Roman people on their leaders to publicly convey proposed laws to them gave enormous power to those with effective speaking skills.

The entire career and literary output of M. Tullius Cicero underscore the political importance of public oratory in Rome. A new man who attained the office of consul in 63, Cicero built his reputation and his attachments through his performances in the law courts. But as Cicero's public oration *De Lege Agraria* 2 makes clear, public meetings convened by officeholders to discuss the merits of public law proposals provided Roman leaders with one of the most critical opportunities for public orating in which they tested their leadership to the fullest. When orating to a crowd, an officeholder, a would-be officeholder, or a senator made direct contact with the Roman people. On display were not only his powers of marshaling words and arguments but also his emotional connection to the people and their needs. In public lawmaking meetings the urgency of the issues that compelled various groups to flock to the session gave the orator's delivery for or against a proposal a commensurate urgency—if the speaker had talent enough and a sense of drama. That there was give-and-take in the exercise, a mutual interaction between leaders and people, is revealed in efforts on the part of both groups to sway one another. Oratory was vitally important to the political leaders of Rome.

Since only a small fraction of all elected Roman officeholders who had the authority to convene lawmaking assemblies actually exercised the privilege, it appears that for most political leaders the mere occupation of an office and the exercising of whatever authority came with it seem to have satisfied the desire to engage in public service. Others, however, went beyond such a limited view of their situation and took it on themselves to interact with the Roman people in order to discern their sovereign will, to publicly define issues of law, and to risk the rewards or penalties that came with pursuing such a course. A proposer of public law thus took a calculated risk. Could he sell his public law proposal, carefully drafted to appeal to at least eighteen of the thirty-five tribes? Had he discerned the will of the majority of Roman tribes correctly in his presentation of the issues?

The general sophisticated political acumen suggested by the exchange between a political leader and the Roman people on such occasions underscores the depth of the bond that united all Romans. While the extent to which these same Romans depended on Cicero and other elected officeholders and senators to convey the precise details of the law to them suggests a wide gap in levels of knowledge between citizens on different levels of the social structure, attention nonetheless also had to be paid to issues of form and substance. How well a public law proposal was drafted mattered as much as the public argument about it. Accordingly, a certain high level of knowledge about the issues and their presentation was required from the law sponsor and every other orator involved in the public debate about law. In particular, political leaders who proposed law were expected to have the right tools for the job. The customary process of drafting laws rested on the wide base of knowledge found among elite Romans who worked together with their clerical assistants to produce the texts of laws presented to the people. The diligent involvement of elected officeholders and senators in the task of lawmaking reinforces the central importance of lawmaking in maintaining unity in the Roman community across the period.

Hence Cicero's opposition to P. Servilius Rullus's popular attempt to draft a land law called forth all of his considerable oratorical skills. Proceeding in the formal manner customary on such occasions, Cicero became engaged in an intense dialogue with his audience, thus providing us with an unprecedented opportunity to uncover the most fundamental assumptions held by the Roman people. "Masters of the world," the Romans deserve the resources of empire, Cicero tells them, thus allowing us to gauge the arguments that moved Romans in 63 as well as the conventions of speaking to which they were attuned. Cicero's selection of themes to attack the proposal alerts us to the common sense of how their society ought to be ordered, shared by political leaders and the Roman people. Cicero's concern for substance and process shows that the masses of voters still displayed the traditional respect for public lawmaking that gave the process its universal authority, even at a period of acute disruption, in 63, when the event took place.

Cicero's skillful attack on Rullus in *De Lege Agraria* 2 serves to remind us of the degree to which social position, personal characteristics, oratorical skills, and tradition underlay the functioning of the lawmaking process as late as 63, nearly the end of our period of interest. It underscores also the singularly complex understanding of the various facets of lawmaking common among the participants on all levels and articulated by political leaders in their presentation of the law. The whole project for the leaders was to garner support by reflecting most accurately the desires of the Roman people in Rome's institutions and by confirming shared attitudes on the uses of power in Roman society. But for the people, the project was to confer public sanction on a proposed course of action through the collective, assenting voice of the Roman people. The guiding if unspoken principle of the public debate as shown in *De Lege Agraria* 2 was clearly understood by all participants in public lawmaking, namely, the sovereign power of the Roman people and the importance of their opinions when expressed as a group while observing the proper procedures in a public lawmaking assembly. We shall see next the extent to which these notions of reciprocity and the central role of the Roman people underlie the process by which the Romans agree to the legitimacy of public law.

Notes

I am grateful to the University of Chicago Press for permission to reprint the sections of this chapter that first appeared in their journal *Classical Philology* as "The Roman Aristocracy and Positive Law," *CP* 85 (1990): 266–76.

1. Cicero delivered three speeches publicly about Rullus's proposal (*Att.* 2.1.3) and one to a closed session of the Senate.

2. The fragments of speeches are collected in H. Malcovati, *Oratorum romanorum fragmenta*, 3d ed. (Turin, 1967).

3. The Rullan proposal had at least forty clauses. Since we know of the proposal only through Cicero's speeches, the text in its entirety and the arrangement of all its clauses are lost.

4. Ager publicus in Italy: E. G. Hardy, "The agrarian proposal of Rullus in 63," in *Some problems in Roman history: Ten essays bearing on the administrations and legislative work of Julius Caesar* (Oxford, 1924), 72; D. Rathbone, "The development of agriculture in the 'ager Cosanus' during the Roman republic: Problems of evidence and interpretation," *JRS* 71 (1981): 10–23. Provincial land (perhaps Egypt, Bithynia, Cyprus, Achaia, and Macedonia): Hardy 1924, 74–77.

5. For an analysis of the political and social context of the proposal see especially T. P. Wiseman, "The senate and the *populares*, 69–60," *CAH* 9, 2d ed. (1994), 327–67; see also E. Gruen, *The last generation of the Roman republic* (Berkeley and Los Angeles, 1974), 389–96; C. Meier, *Res publica amissa*, 2d ed. (Wiesbaden, 1980), 267–80. Useful for its focus on resources and expenses is H. Schneider, *Wirtschaft und Politik: Untersuchungen zur Geschichte der späten römischen Republik* (Erlangen, 1974), 328–44.

6. Wiseman 1994, 349–51.

7. Chapter 8, note 28.

8. Chapter 8, note 26.

9. For a different kind of evaluation see A. J. E. Bell, "Cicero and the Spectacle of Power," *JRS* 87 (1997): 1–22.

10. J.-L. Ferrary, "Rogatio Servilia agraria," *Ath.* 66 (1988): 141–64, provides an analysis of actual words and phrases in the statute (*ipsissima verba*) preserved in Cicero's speech. Cf. Hardy 1924, 68–98.

11. On the easy redaction and dissemination of public orations see F. Pina Polo, *Contra arma verbis: Der redner vor dem Volk in der späten römischen Republik* (Stuttgart, 1996), 26–29. Some believe Cicero's public speeches probably do not represent the speech as delivered, because they were heavily edited before publication, e.g., F. G. B. Millar, *The crowd in Rome in the late republic* (Ann Arbor, MI, 1998), 9–10, who nonetheless uses them as evidence of what was spoken in public meetings.

12. Publication: W. C. McDermott, "Cicero's publication of his consular orations," *Philol.* 116 (1972): 277–84; see also previous note.

13. The same emphasis on "your empire," etc., appears in Cicero, *pro lege Manilia*, on which see Wiseman 1994, 339.

14. Terms appearing once modified by *vester* are *auctoritas*, *ius*, *potestas*, *fructus*, *diligentia*, *pecunia*, and *vis*.

15. J. Hellegouarc'h, *Le vocabulaire latin des relations et des partis politiques sous le république* (Paris, 1963).

16. *Leg. Agr.* 2.16.42.

17. *Leg. Agr.* 2.4.10.

18. *Leg. Agr.* 2.14.35–36.

19. On the elder Rullus and his remote connection with *nobilitas* see M. H. Crawford, *Roman republican coinage* (Cambridge, 1974), 1. 329; R. Syme, "The Historian Servilius Nonianus," *Hermes* 92 (1964): 410.

20. See chapter 7; cf. *Rhet. Her.* 1.12.20.

21. Cass. Dio 39.34.3.

22. E.g., Cass. Dio 39.35.

23. Plut., *Ti. Gracch.* 14.5–6.

24. The point is made again and again in the ancient testimony. This was the significance, too, of the consul Bibulus's refusal to comment on Caesar's agrarian proposal in 59. Like the Senate he did not lend his influence; his only remark was that he would approve no new legislation that year (Cass. Dio 38.4.3).

25. J.-M. David, "Les orateurs des municipes à Rome," in *Les "bourgeoisies" Municipales italiennes aux IIe et Ier siècles av. J.C.* (Paris and Naples, 1983), 309–23.

26. See J.-M. David, *Le patronat judiciaire au dernier siècle de la république romaine* (Rome, 1992); and Pina Polo 1996, 65–93.

27. C. Williamson, "Lawmaking in the comitia of republican Rome: The processes of drafting and disseminating, recording and retrieving laws and plebiscites" (Ph.D. diss., University of London, 1984), 81–102; cf. *RS* 1.7.

28. *Att.* 3 and *Dom.* in particular.

29. *LPPR*, 400–402.

30. The law draft of the eight tribunes is now *RS* 2 No. 57. See P. Moreau, "La rogatio des huit tribuns de 58 av. J.C. et les clauses de sanctio réglementant l'abrogation des lois," *Ath.* 77 (n.s. 67) (1989): 151–78.

31. Visellius's career: *MRR* 2.635 and *MRR* 3.222. A tribuneship in 69 is proposed, because a Republican inscription attests to a lex Visellia (*CIL* 1^2.2.744). If the suggestion is correct, he would have had lawmaking experience. See *MRR* 2.132. G. V. Sumner, *The orators in Cicero's Brutus* (Toronto, 1973), 139, disagrees with Shackleton Bailey's identification on the grounds that C. Visellius Varro was dead in 58. Instead, he suggests that the Visellius of Cicero's letter was someone else, "perhaps the real author of the lex Visellia," i.e., another member of the ruling elite.

32. *Att.* 3.23.1.

33. *Att.* 3.23.3.

34. *Fam.* 6.18.1.

35. Pina Polo 1996, 178–92, provides lists of the known political leaders, privati and elected officials, who orated in public meetings of all kinds, including lawmaking meetings.

36. Cass. Dio 38.16.5–17.3.

37. *Leg. Agr.* 3.1.1

38. Significance of rank: Williamson 1984, 30, 38–45, 91–96; Pina Polo 1996, 34–65.

39. Cass. Dio 38.16.5–17.3.

40. This is covered in detail by Pina Polo 1996, 34–38; cf. Williamson 1984, 41–45.

41. Livy 45.21.6–7.

42. Livy 30.4.6.

43. Livy 45.21.4–6.

44. Livy 45.21.5–7.

45. Pina Polo 1996, 35.

46. *Rhet. Her.* 1.12.21.

47. Called *Formfehlern* in Mommsen, *R.St.* 3.364.

48. Appian, *B.C.* 1.23. Appian goes on to say that tribunes were not required to give a reason for their vetoes, but the implication is that it was customary for them to do so.

49. Cass. Dio 39.35.1–2.

50. Cass. Dio 38.4.5–6.

51. On the lawmaking of 59 see chapter 9.

52. Cass. Dio 38.2.1–3.

53. Sources in *MRR* 1.508.

54. Cass. Dio 39, 1 ff. (Caesar's land law in 59); Cic., *Sest.* 34.73–74 (Clodius's law exiling Cicero in 58); Cic., *Leg. Agr.* 1 passim.

55. Cass. Dio 38.2.1–3.3.

56. Cf. Pina Polo 1996, 123.

57. It is not certain that Cicero's suggestion was actually implemented or that Flavius even took note of it. At some point before the day of the assembly, Flavius altered the text of the statute himself, adding a provision making land grants to all citizens, not only to Pompey's soldiers (Cass. Dio 37.50.1).

58. *Att.* 1.18 and 1.19.4. On the latter see D. R. Shackleton Bailey, *Cicero's letters to Atticus* (Cambridge, 1965), 1.336. He must have promulgated it and called the final meeting before the voting assembly, because of the events of the meeting Cass. Dio describes: the consul, Metellus, criticized each clause in the law and prevented Flavius from going ahead with it; Flavius threw the consul in prison, threatening to keep him there until the law could be presented to the people.

59. Cass. Dio 40.58.3–59.1.

60. See further part 3.

61. See in particular P. J. J. Vanderbroeck, *Popular leadership and collective behavior in late Roman republic, ca. 80–50 BC* (Amsterdam, 1987), 23–66.

62. Cicero claims a tribune had promised to veto the bill; much later Pliny reported that the tribes rejected it: Pliny, *N.H.* 7.117.

CHAPTER THREE

Legitimization: Participants and Procedures

PICTURE A RESOLUTE P. Servilius Rullus in the spring of 63, unmoved by Cicero's persuasive eloquence some weeks earlier and primed to take his bill to the Roman people. The tribune's call to assemble on the scheduled day would set in motion a rush of complicated maneuvers intended to satisfy a range of practical, as well as procedural and ceremonial, requirements.[1] Baskets (*cistae*) brimming with voting tokens (*tabellae*) and empty baskets to hold the votes of each tribe stood ready near the temporary voting platform (*pons*), surrounded by a guard of reputable observers (*custodes*) from each tribe, drawn from the jury lists.[2] Enumerators (*diribitores*) from the tribes stood by to count the votes. Now the herald (*praeco*) intoned the controversial bill for the last time, without (let us imagine) obstruction. And when Rullus finally proclaimed, "The law has been read. Form your voting units and let the ballots be distributed" (*Lex recitata est. Discedere et tabellam iubebo dari*), thousands of voters stepped out of the expectant crowd and into their respective tribes. The pitcher (*sitella*) was carried in, and lots were cast to determine which tribe would vote first, the *principium*. A tribesman from the principium, selected by Rullus to cast the first ballot, approached the platform, where he accepted two tokens from the observer, each marked with a letter ("U" for *uti rogas* [yes] or "A" for *antiquo* [no]), cast his ballot in the jar, discarded the other token, and returned to the crowd to make way for the next man. The voting was now under way. Tribe by tribe, in regular sequence, the voters individually approached the platforms and cast their ballots. Tribe by tribe the enumerators tallied and declared each tribal vote. Just as soon as a majority of tribes had voted the same way (eighteen out of thirty-five), the issue was decided. Tribes that had not yet voted would not do so; the process was now over. Of the assembled voters, at least as many might never cast their ballots as did. In such (or similar) fashion was the sovereign will of the Roman people (*iussa populi*) decided, not only in Rullus's day but three generations before, not only in tribal assemblies but in the centuriate assembly as well.[3] Elaborate, systematic, closely supervised, and rigorously open, the Roman decision-making process was the product of a timeless and uniquely Roman view of popular government.

How this complicated process, in which some voters were passed over at random, resulted in legitimate law, binding on the entire Roman population, forms our quest in this chapter. All Roman males between the ages of seventeen and sixty in possession of full citizen rights (*cives optimo iure*) were in principle able to cast votes in any of Rome's scheduled voting assemblies. Many must have done so, for convening in assemblies of various sorts and voting allowed the primary expression of citizenship. Some voting assemblies were regular occurrences throughout the year, namely, the electoral assemblies on which the selection of Rome's leadership depended. Some were irregular occurrences, like the judicial assemblies that, until the early second century, decided guilt or innocence in select criminal cases. More crucial across the centuries were the randomly scheduled lawmaking assemblies at which the Roman people publicly resolved issues that could not be resolved in the traditional manner by the Senate or officeholders serving in a wide variety of official offices. But whether summoned to elect new leaders, to adjudicate state crimes, or to accept or reject bills, all voting assemblies were for hundreds of years alike in most respects. They demanded time, energy, and a considerable amount of knowledge in order to engage in the intricate rituals and procedures required. On these occasions political leaders interacted with citizens in order to discern the sovereign will of the Roman people. Over hundreds of years, they provided an essentially unchanging structure for all public actions by the Roman people.

WHO VOTED?

When the senator and scholar M. Terentius Varro wrote his popular treatise on farming around 70, he plausibly cast the final book as a conversation among a group of senators waiting to learn the results of an assembly convened in the

Campus Martius to elect aediles. Two of the waiting senators were members of the same tribe (*tribules*) who had already cast their ballots and now waited to escort their candidate home. Another was an augur who, by his ready presence to interpret divine signs, played an essential part in the process. As the group sat in the shade of the Villa Publica and talked about plantation farming and farm management, an abiding interest of Roman senators, some of its members were called away while still other acquaintances passing by joined in the conversation. In Varro's description of senators interweaving their ordinary concerns with the business of an electoral assembly we gain a sense of the regular place of voting in the life of the city. We gain a sense also of the special atmosphere that elections generated in Rome: the excitement and anticipation, the high tension as the murmur of the crowd swelled and subsided across the city, following the announcement of results that stirred the emotions.

Over hundreds of years, voting assemblies occasioned a sense of political urgency. Varro's description of an annually occurring election for aediles provides a case in point. While the voting process unfolded, the voters were subject to the incessant exhortations of candidates for office or supporters and opponents of a proposal of law. The temporary platform occupied by the handlers of the voting urns, the custodes (and earlier by the rogatores until the lex Papiria tabellaria of 130 introduced the written ballot)—made narrower by the tribune C. Marius in 119 so that there was too little room for the custodes and thus less opportunity for them to influence individual voters—gives us some indication of the pressures on voters at the end of the second century before that typically practical Roman solution.[4] On certain occasions for some voters it doubtless took nerve and a deep commitment to participate.

On any occasion, voting presented citizens with a formidable task whose exigencies though unmentioned by Varro were certainly well known to him. Scheduled to coincide with market days, when the many market areas throughout Rome were bustling with buyers and sellers from rural areas and from beyond Italy, an assembly began at dawn with the summons to a preliminary meeting held before the voting began, heralds crying the venue from the city walls, the Capitoline hill, and the Forum. People had already begun to gather the day before, if the issues and personalities warranted. Hence the Forum or other meeting place, as well as the places of assembly (the Forum, Circus Flaminius, Campus Martius, or Capitoline hill), could be crowded with all manner of people, not all citizen voters—men, women, and children, slaves and foreigners. Hawkers and vendors of food and drink circulated among the crowds, listening to public orators, waiting to hear the outcome of the lottery, waiting to vote or to hear the outcome of the vote. In Varro's day it took hours for all the voters present to cast their ballots (especially in the lawmaking assemblies, where the tribes voted consecutively) and for the enumerators to laboriously and scrupulously count them. Or people simply waited: The crowd and the atmosphere may have been reason enough for many to be on hand. But some people might leave the area, whiling the time away in another part of the city or simply avoiding the crowds and the sun and heat, especially during July, when the electoral assemblies met. By the standards of the modern Western world, voting in Rome was remarkably tedious.

Voting also assumed familiarity with a set of singularly elaborate voting arrangements. Unlike any other Italian community, or Greek city-state for that matter, Rome over time devised not one but three primary citizen voting assemblies distinguished by their convening magistrates and constituent voting units.[5] As the plebeian tribal assembly (concilium plebis), summoned by the chief officers of the Roman plebs, tribunes, the Roman plebs voted in tribes from which patricians, who formed a relatively small group among the elite families of Rome, were in principal excluded.[6] When summoned to vote in their tribes by consuls or praetors, the chief magistrates of Rome, Romans constituted another kind of tribal assembly that presumably included all citizens; this assembly, as we saw in chapter 1, is called by modern scholars the comitia tributa. In the centuriate assembly (comitia centuriata), summoned by consuls or praetors, citizens voted in centuries, units defined by citizen property ratings. We are entitled to wonder at the level of basic knowledge required to form the right voting unit in any assembly.[7]

Similarly the Roman people knew the sometimes subtle differences in the purposes of the various assemblies. The people met as centuriate assemblies to make decisions about war and peace and to elect consuls and praetors as well as "curule" aediles (so-called to distinguish them from the plebeian aediles). A centuriate assembly was the assembly Varro had in mind. The Roman people met as tribal assemblies to make decisions about law; to elect the lesser magistrates as well as the military tribunes and, after 107, priests; and to pass judgment as a "people's court" (iudicium populi) on the guilt or innocence of individual Romans, whose crimes against the State were laid before them. When the Roman people met to make decisions about law they are conveniently called a legislative or lawmaking assembly by modern scholars. After 287, the plebeian tribal assembly became the most important lawmaking assembly in Rome, followed by the full tribal assembly. Seldom did the centuriate assembly enact law.[8] However, the declarations of war, which were usually made by the centuriate assembly, were also called leges and are included in the category "public law."[9] When the people met to elect magistrates, they are conveniently called an electoral assembly. Again, the centuriate, the tribal, and the plebeian tribal assemblies could all be electoral assemblies. In spite of the different bases of their basic voting units, tribal membership in one case and property rating in the other, common to all assemblies was the corporate body from which each was assembled: the Roman people (populus Romanus). Nonetheless, the Roman people were subject to, and had to know, infinitely changing, overlapping, and a bit confusing (to the modern mind) arrangements for the purpose of making different kinds of decisions affecting the entire community.

The complexity of the procedures associated with the actual vote, detailed at the beginning of the chapter in the imaginary assembly convened by Rullus, made even more strenuous demands on the voters. Not only did voters have to know the candidates or the details of proposed bills upon arrival in Rome, but they had to be familiar with the complicated choreography of each intended voting event. Voters had to command an extraordinary range of incredibly minute operations even beyond those concerning the nature of the particular assembly simply in order to participate in the process. In particular, the execution of the vote, involving voting bridges (*pontes*), tribal order, ballots, voting urns, and more, assumed an impressive amount of information on the part of the participants. The array of essential detail that elected officials and voters had to know and understand in order to participate was astonishing. The relatively effortless observation of all these complicated procedures throughout our period of interest suggests that they were clearly understood by all voters at a very deep level. What manner of men these voters were is a question well worth asking.

In the late first century, the Roman voting population, more precisely the corporate body known as the Roman people (populus Romanus), held a broad spectrum of status, property, and territorial groups among the citizenry that by then included most inhabitants of Italy. A voter at any of Rome's assemblies could be a poor man or rich. He could be a resident of Rome or of any one of many lesser towns and villages; or he could be a rural inhabitant of Italy. He could be Roman, Latin, Italian, or foreign in background. He could be freeborn or ex-slave, a tenant farmer or private landowner, a laborer, a merchant, or craftsman, a senator or equestrian. Whatever his legal, social, or economic position and whatever his place of residence, he was nonetheless a Roman citizen: He was male, registered in a tribe and property class, and liable to military service between the ages of seventeen and sixty. Voting in Rome was restricted to citizens, a very precisely defined group in Roman society, just as citizens were in other ancient Mediterranean societies.

Yet in striking contrast to other ancient societies, the pool of Roman voters had expanded significantly over the years in pace with the territorial expansion of the Romans in Italy and the incorporation of new citizens. Down to 91, the growth in citizen numbers was slow but steady. Then, in 90, the size of the Roman citizen population more than doubled in size, when almost all the peoples of Italy became citizens through a public law enacted by the Roman people with the result that Rome's voters, numbering 394,336 by the census of 115 and 463,000 by 86, increased to 910,000 in the census of 70.[10] Thus while the pool of voters was vast even before 90, by the standards of ancient Mediterranean communities, after 90 the size of the pool was simply phenomenal.[11] Furthermore, as the number of voters expanded, so too did the geographic area from which they were drawn. Citizens sometimes resided hundreds of kilometers from Rome. Nothing like this had been seen in the world to date.

As numerous and as scattered as Roman citizens came to be by the first century, the formal presentation, debate, and decision about the election of officials, enactment of laws, and handing down of justice took place only in Rome throughout my period of interest. On the rare occasions when assemblies met outside Rome the reaction was swift and adverse: following one such assembly the people immediately enacted that Rome was the only venue for legitimate assemblies.[12] As a corollary, a citizen cast his vote only in one of the voting venues in Rome. Voters, who were increasingly drawn to voting from all parts of the Italian peninsula, had to make their way to Rome for the duration of the voting if not the entire electoral or lawmaking process in order to vote in the annual electoral assemblies and the frequent lawmaking assemblies. In terms of the planning required to get there and the knowledge such a journey assumed, voting in Rome came to be a very demanding affair. We might well wonder how many voters made the journey.

The limitations of space in voting locations throughout Rome make the question of how many voted more pressing still. Before 200, the tribal assemblies met in the precinct of the Temple of Jupiter Best and Greatest on the Capitoline hill, an area of about fifteen hundred square meters.[13] After 200, the tribal assemblies met in the Comitium, about sixteen hundred square meters, and later in the Forum, seven iugera or approximately twenty-five hundred square meters in extent.[14] Throughout the Republic, the centuriate assembly met in the Campus Martius, outside the city's sacred boundary. Modern historians have observed that the space available in these areas could hold only limited numbers of people: the Campus Martius, the largest of the three locations for Roman voting assemblies, could accommodate anywhere from roughly forty thousand to seventy thousand people, standing room only.[15] The Forum, which was the regular meeting place for the tribal assembly after 200, was considerably smaller. It appears that Rome could hardly hold its voters if they all came at once to vote, many times a year.

From a strictly practical standpoint, the practice of voting in the assemblies must have been restricted to relatively few citizens. Considering the space limitations, 4 percent at most could have attended Rullus's imaginary assembly in 63, that is, seven years after the last census, when roughly 910,000 citizens were enumerated.[16] Considering the knowledge required to participate, how many citizens could attempt the process? Although modern scholars make much of such matters, from the Romans' perspective neither numerical representation nor knowledge appears to be an issue. The number of contributing voices mattered relatively little in the pronouncement of the Roman people's commands (iussa populi) while the most detailed knowledge of the voting process by the voters is simply assumed.[17] Given the modern tendency to diminish the mental capacity of any crowd and to equate the expression of popular sovereignty with majority rule, the curious observer wonders therefore about the Roman perceptions of political action that generated the arrangements and procedures detailed earlier and led citizens to participate in these uniquely devised, uniquely Roman assemblies.[18] Vitally important to any understanding of voting patterns in lawmaking assemblies is the paradoxical role of the Roman people in the production of law.

THE PEOPLE

The force of the arguments and the complexity and volume of detail in Cicero's first public speech as consul in January of 63, *De Lege Agraria* 2, are unexpected, if either are regarded as a measure of the voters' interest in public business or of their sophistication.[19] Historians do not often credit them with either.[20] Despite a conventional understanding of Roman citizens that minimizes the importance of issues in drawing a crowd, Cicero's *De Lege Agraria* 2 indicates otherwise. The focus of Cicero's arguments, detailed in the previous chapter, indicates a deep interest in P. Servilius Rullus's land redistribution scheme. Moreover, when Cicero concerns himself with concrete issues of drafting he must take it for granted that the Roman people can appreciate technical details and that it matters to them what exactly the law says. This was no recent development. Earlier, in the third century, when the comic poet Plautus admonished his audience to decide on the best production fairly, he phrased his request in the language of public law and delivered it in the resonant patterns familiar from a public lawmaking session where the herald intones the law to the assembled crowd.[21] Mimicking a lex de ambitu in language and rhythm, the Latin verses are remarkably close to the real thing. We find in other plays by Plautus, whose plots are mostly the reworked stories of Greek productions, other comic allusions and deliberate references to Roman public law, which could have been effective as comedy only if these resonate with an existing attitude toward and appreciation of public law on the part of the Roman people. As an index of convention and behavior, comedy is invaluable.

The ancient testimony presents us with a set of apparent contradictions about the people's role in Rome's energetic public lawmaking process—at least from a modern perspective, informed by the workings of twentieth-century CE Western democracies. As represented to us by an elite writer like Cicero, the people's role appears somewhat ambiguous. In *De Lege Agraria* 2, for instance, the sovereign will of the people was on the one hand paramount, once the voters had cast their vote and made their decision. On the other hand the people were malleable in the right hands. Cicero is evidently unconcerned about what appears to a modern historian to be the incongruity between the two views of the Roman people, whose judgment is at one and the same time confidently supreme and pliantly infirm. Cicero juxtaposes popular sovereignty and infirmity of judgment constantly, most notably in the discourse *De Legibus* (On Statutes). To be sure, *De Legibus* is a theoretical essay on laws and lawmaking, not a description of actual lawmaking in Roman political life.[22]

Nonetheless the prevailing attitude among some political leaders about the role of the people in making decisions about law was by our standards strongly elitist. The people's knowledge about public law and the lawmaking process was not regarded as "serious" knowledge, whatever depth or range it did acquire (which we cannot know). In *De Lege Agraria* 2, Cicero openly dismisses the people's capacity to understand the public law of Rome. Behind this pervasive line of argument is a rather convoluted set of assumptions. As we read Cicero's speech, we can see that he took it for granted that what the people thought Rullus's proposal was and what he knew the proposal was were two different commodities. Cicero assumes that two states of general knowledge existed in Rome about law and lawmaking, one belonging to the Roman people and the other to Cicero, a member of Rome's political elite. Whether the people shared the assumption we cannot know for sure. They probably did not.

The corollary to Cicero's assumption is of course that the people ought to rely on the knowledge of Rome's political leaders. According to Cicero the people could not participate knowledgeably or ably in making decisions about law—that is to say, they could not act in the best interests of the state—without the guidance of Roman leaders.[23] This is not Cicero's opinion alone; it pervades the writings of others in the same class. Moreover it was a view apparently shared by the masses of Roman voters as indicated by their apparent satisfaction with group voting (discussed in the next section). To all Romans, the beneficent and guiding influence of the Roman aristocracy flowed naturally down, never meeting an opposite flow. Roman political leaders occasionally even thought to regulate conventional behavior. Cicero advocated such regulation in his treatise *De Legibus*, whose readers were men of his own class.[24]

The many-layered objectives of the debate might appear to confirm this. As we saw in the previous chapter, public oratory was an exercise in persuasion. At the same time, political leaders clearly saw the debate as the primary occasion for informing Roman voters about the matters at issue. Magistrates furnished specific information about laws that was assumed or hidden in the context of a speech but was clearly derived from the text of the proposal under discussion, whether it was conveyed as a paraphrase of the law, a direct quote, or a public reading from the text itself. The method of conveying this information in meetings appeared to rely entirely on the magistrates, via their assistants as intermediaries. In such public meetings the people depended on magistrates and other members of the political elite for the information needed in the public argument about laws. Indeed, they expected their political leaders to mediate between themselves and the leader who proposed the law by providing the information required to make a decision in public lawmaking events. In effect each magistrate told the people what they needed to know, from his point of view, hoping for a response from the people, pro or con, depending on his position on the law. The scope for independent action from the people was narrow at best. No wonder their political vigor has long been disregarded.

Yet it is worth stressing that in situations that allow popular attitudes to emerge, there is a wide range of options in the way in which leaders assert their superior positions and the majority population receives them. On lawmaking occasions the people could be aggressive. The people could be forceful in the expression of their wishes, even in the face of opposing wishes on the part of that most unified body of Roman leaders, the Roman Senate. Despite the active opposition of senators and even his father, C. Flaminius as tribune in 232 won the people's approval of his land redistribution bill.[25] The events surrounding Pompey's nomination to the supreme military command against the pirates in 67 by a law proposed by the tribune Gabinius illustrate the point more forcefully.[26] The Senate disapproved of Pompey's nomination and announced their disapproval. The people, supporting Gabinius's proposed law, would not accept this and mobbed the Senate House. No formal decision from the Senate about their collective opinion was issued. But the people evidently hoped for such an opinion and that it would support the bill. At the final public meeting convened before the law was put to the vote, Gabinius coerced two tribunes into keeping quiet and afterward invited Catulus, the princeps senatus, to speak, hoping he—and, represented in him, the Senate—would be persuaded by the experience of the tribunes to give his public approval of the proposal. Throughout this incident it quite obviously did matter to the people and to Gabinius that the Senate should publicly approve the plan to give the command to Pompey. Despite their intention to go ahead with it anyway, the action by the people and Gabinius at the Senate House and at the final meeting was aimed at persuading the Senate to support the arrangements they wanted. In turn, Rome's political leaders clearly took the Roman voter very seriously, and, although the public argument and voting on laws were directed and articulated by Rome's rulers, the interest and involvement of the Roman people were critical. To the extent that voter behavior was shaped by influence and persuasion, influence and persuasion worked both ways. Magistrates influenced public opinion, but they were themselves influenced by it. The prime reason is obvious. Lawmakers needed the support of public opinion for the success of their proposals of law.

To be sure, although Roman voters determined absolutely the success or failure of bills, they had virtually nothing to do with developing them. Whether single-handedly or in collaboration with elected officials and senators, ordinary Romans never formulated or drafted bills. They never initiated law proposals, as their counterparts had done in the Ekklesia of Classical Athens. Most important, they never orated publicly about law proposals. Formally, the Roman people were merely asked to make a yes or no decision about a bill presented to them in advance by one of their elected officials and debated in their presence by other political leaders. They made no other contributions. This was understood. Rather, the production of law was firmly directed by Rome's elected officials and senators. These men initiated the process in private workrooms and on the floor of the Senate. They brought the fruits of their labors into the light of day through the sponsor who, in the presence of the Roman people, promulgated his bill by announcement, recitation, and posting. The Roman people merely stood by and listened, an audience of voters. The Romans clearly accepted the respective roles of the people and their political leaders. A passage from another play by the comic poet Plautus is instructive, in which a "hanger-on" (*parasitus*) named Saturius sets out to draft a statute. He starts to formulate his statute but finally quits his efforts, saying, in effect, "this is a job for our elected leaders."[27] Here we see reflected the real division of labor in the patterns and procedures involved in public lawmaking, understood by all Romans.

Nonetheless, the people were considerably more than passive actors in the process. Voters, like their elected officials, regularly brought a fairly sophisticated, technical level of knowledge to public lawmaking sessions. To be sure, the levels of knowledge of Roman political leaders and the Roman people, as they are exhibited on such occasions, were different: the Roman voters did not themselves need the same information, that is, the same command of detail or the same knowledge of precedent, since they did not participate in lawmaking in the same way. But such differences arise from a mutual understanding of the proper, reciprocal role of each group in the public lawmaking arena. They do not diminish the extent to which, to the Roman mind, the voters were making a choice. The people listened to one officeholder or another; different points were aired that they heard and approved or rejected. In all such occasions of give-and-take we can see the extent to which the people were actively engaged in ensuring that society work as they believed it should, in 67 no less than in 200. The Roman people's behavior on lawmaking occasions may only have been a matter of choice about which leader to heed, but it combined with a reaction to events as well as an intuitive understanding of the ordering of Roman society. Hence, the reality of voter participation was far more complicated than the elitist position would have it. We are entitled to wonder therefore why it is that the political voice of the Roman people at public lawmaking sessions was expressed in the manner in which it was.

THE GROUP VOTE

Any customary assumptions underlying community action and common patterns of association that determined the clustering of participants in lawmaking events were vastly complicated by a steady movement of citizens and foreigners in and out of the city. To an extent not yet recognized participation in assemblies was tied to this movement; predictably, therefore, Rome's voting population was a changeable and, to modern observers, an erratic body.[28] Contemporary observers, however, grasped intuitively the range of considerations behind individual decisions to participate in public lawmaking assemblies. One such observer was Cicero. In a trial speech delivered in 57 to the tribunal investigating an allegation of political violence laid against his client, Cicero claimed that the Roman people had shown so little interest in a certain bill proposed by the tribune Vatinius in 59 that some tribes could not vote until substitutes from other tribes had filled out the numbers.[29] In the same year, Cicero claimed that "all of Italy" (*tota Italia*), by which he infers the better classes from municipia in all corners of Italy, had converged on Rome to vote in their centuries on the bill proposed by the consul to recall Cicero from exile. In the vastly different levels of reported attendance at two lawmaking assemblies (one rarely used for the purpose, namely, the centuriate assembly) lies the point of departure for our exploration of Roman voting patterns: the group vote.

No Roman voted as an individual but rather as a member of a group, most salient for lawmaking purposes one of the constituent voting units of Rome's principal lawmaking assemblies, the thirty-five rural and urban tribes to which all Romans belonged.[30] When he cast his ballot in a tribal assembly, a Roman voter engaged in the process of exercising not his own views but the will of his tribe. His decision and the decisions of a majority of like-minded fellow tribesmen gave expression to the harmonious voice of the Roman tribe, determining the official vote of the tribe. "One tribe, one vote" was the rule in Rome's tribal assemblies, up to a total of thirty-five possible votes. So critical was the tribe as an intact unity that the number of voters present to vote in any tribe was immaterial, so long as they had a basic number to make a tribal presence viable. (We have no idea what this number was although the Romans clearly did, witness Cicero's disparagement of the assembly convened by Vatinius.)[31] No matter how many or how few members of any tribe voted, the tribe still carried a vote that weighed equally with the votes of other tribes.

Correspondingly, a majority of tribes, not men, made decisions in Rome's lawmaking assemblies. A bare majority of the assembled tribes—eighteen out of thirty-five—was deemed sufficient to express the will of the whole Roman people.[32] The conviction is far removed from the premises of representative politics in Western democracies. Its vigor throughout the Republic, however, is demonstrated in the unwavering assent by Romans of all periods to the lex Hortensia, a decision by the Roman people in 287 to make laws approved in the plebeian tribal assembly binding on the whole community. To the extent that the vote of each tribe (and each man's vote within the tribe) carried the same weight, the tribal assemblies were structurally egalitarian, unlike the century-based centuriate assembly, and offered the only formal setting where the popular voice could be heard. Nonetheless it was a group voice.

The notion of a group consensus is a distinguishing feature of Roman civic culture, visible first and foremost in the voting units to which all Romans belonged. The notion extends far beyond such formal units, however. To a degree unparalleled in modern Western societies, the Romans in Cicero's day formed various clusters beneath the umbrella of the Roman state. Groups of men sharing the same status or cult, ethnic origins, or occupation were basic units of informal allegiance and loyalty in the Roman world, from the priestly colleges of elite Romans (*sodalitates*) to the clusters of dangling members of society, forming the networks in an adoptive society that we call associations and the Romans called *collegia*.[33] Among such groups the Roman tribe was preeminent. Other groupings in Roman society were less precisely defined in any corporate sense: ethnic or regional groups and groups based on personal ties or common objectives. All clusters, formal and informal, exhibit specific interests and aspirations. They share common loyalties. They form the locus of discussion and decision. Above all they are held together, top to bottom and side to side, by bonds shaped by mutual respect, deference, and obligation among all members. Intrinsic to all Roman groups were the time-honored attachments that made the group voice viable.

These attachments lodged their deepest and most tenacious roots in the Roman tribes, each of which accommodated the full spectrum of Roman status and property classes. Within the tribe, ordinary Romans and high status Romans lived side by side. Within the tribe were acknowledged tribal leaders, reputable men of respectable or high status, whose recommendations and opinions other tribesmen for the most part respected. Such men were elected annually to be the tribe's foremost officials, *curatores tribuum*, five in each tribe.[34] Described by Mommsen as middlemen between the people and the elected officers of the state, the curatores tribuum were undoubtedly brokers among groups within the tribe as well.[35] Tribal leaders knew their fellow tribesmen, their circumstances, and their needs. They regularly distributed cash, grain, and oil to their fellow tribesmen, gifts that had become standardized at an early date and placed under the management of the *divisores* who were responsible for their distribution. As in the larger society, so in the tribe mutual ties of deference and obligation linked ordinary tribesmen and tribal leaders. Ordinary tribesmen heeded the recommendations and opinions of acknowledged tribal leaders; it was characteristic of Rome's close-knit and hierarchic sociopolitical order that ordinary Romans should defer to men of rank, reputation, and proven merit.[36] If not a formal covenant, it was by and large a customary one and was continually reinforced at the tribal level, as we shall see in chapter 5.

Lending a certain tension to tribal attachments in first-century Rome was the sheer number of groups. Cutting across the immediate relationships among Roman tribesmen for instance were others, derived from the membership of tribesmen in other clusters. Some clusters were incorporated within, some intersected with, and some were altogether outside the tribe. The voting centuries, incorporated within the tribes, provide a significant case in point, as we shall see in chapter 5. City associations (collegia and *vici*) in Rome and in other towns in Italy also held Roman tribesmen. In Cicero's day, as a result of the grant of citizenship to all Italians in 90, tribesmen held a range of regional and ethnic identities. In short, within their tribes Romans were arranged in varied and overlapping groupings along a descending spiral of rank and wealth.

When a Roman stood alone before his tribe's supervisor at the voting bridges, or perhaps especially then, he was first and foremost a tribesman. The tribal loyalty is assumed by the custom of formally naming a man to vote first in a tribe selected by lot as the principium, or "first tribe." In this context belong those shadowy individuals in Rome's political history—Q. Fabius Q.f., A. Gabinius Capito, and Sex . . . L.f. Virro, of unknown nomen—who at one time or another were chosen "first voter" in the tribe selected by lot to vote first in a lawmaking assembly.[37] Fabius, Gabinius, and Virro, among a scant handful of reported first voters, owe their slender renown to the chance survival of the formal headings attached to laws enacted by the assemblies in question.[38] Here, in terse language, stands the record of each man's achievements: he "cast the first vote of endorsement for his tribe" (*pro tribu . . . primus scivit*), which was the first tribe to vote (*principium fuit*).[39] The remaining members of this very small group, Cn. Plancius and C. Fidulius, are hardly less shadowy than their epigraphic comrades even though they emerge from somewhat detailed narrative reports about lawmaking assemblies in 59 and 58.[40] Yet over our period of interest, thousands of Romans formally cast the first ballot in as many tribal assemblies, and the names of hundreds of first voters, engraved on bronze tablets in letters often many times larger than the text of the law itself, greeted the eyes of passersby in the central public areas of Rome.[41] The identities and functions of these men may be hidden from view, but we are clearly dealing with a practice of fundamental significance. Viewed as harbingers of the tribe's collective vote, the ballots cast by first voters were in principle decisive.[42] For the unspoken acceptance by voters of the lead taken by men of wealth and standing in part determined how the tribe voted.

But needs and interest also played a part and were clearly instrumental in determining which voters from any tribe might converge to form a particular assembly. By way of illustration, consider the audience facing Cicero in 63 as he delivered his oration *De Lege Agraria* 2. Cicero refers to his listeners directly throughout his public speeches. He addresses them regularly as Quirites and populus Romanus; three times he describes them as the plebs Romana (2.5.12, 2.25.66) or the plebs urbana (2.26.70). These terms are relatively unrevealing, encompassing as they do an undifferentiated group of Roman citizens, in the first instance, and in the second, the city dwellers of Rome, equally undifferentiated. Who were the individuals behind these terms in the crowd that faced Cicero? Precisely we may never know, especially in view of the substantial increase in voter numbers following the enrollment of new citizens finally, only seven years before, in 70. But some significant amplification is possible, along lines suggested by the fundamental issues that Cicero presented to his listeners in January of 63 and the expectations on which they rested.

Specifically Cicero's speech points emphatically to groups with a keen interest in the allocation of Roman resources. The events of 63, when debt was widespread and land and resources were very big issues, allow a more precise description. Explaining why the city population of Rome supported Catiline's plans for a coup in that year, Sallust, a historian writing thirty years after the event, began with a commonplace. In times of riot and civil disturbance, he wrote, the plebs live without worry, because poverty is easily maintained.[43] The remark exposes the improvident disregard of a bogus leader for the desperation of individuals who have nothing left to lose. What follows in Sallust's monograph on the Catilinarian conspiracy is more explicit: Catiline found support in the city among men who were conspicuous for shamelessness and impudence, men who had squandered their patrimony, men whose dark crimes led them to seek anonymity in Rome, reckless souls and criminals.[44] The moral high tone of an elite Roman in describing his social inferiors is commonplace in Roman narratives. Here, Sallust appears to resort deliberately to the cliché in order to reinforce the seriousness of Catiline's threat to men of Sallust's class, an impression confirmed several sections along when he notes, contradicting himself, the enthusiastic response that the plebs made to the arrest of several leaders of the conspiracy in Rome. The senator Sallust tended to see the city population as a lowly and undifferentiated group.

Obviously it was not. Sallust himself identified specific reasons for the support that members of the urban plebs gave Catiline, and from these we get a strong sense of the different aspirations of some of the men in Rome that year. There were new citizens who came from communities where access to land was access to life: for these men, remembering how Sulla's soldiers had profited from their commander's victory in Italy in 82, military service was the road to landholdings. There were young men who according to Sallust preferred to live on the public grain dole and the handouts of patrons in Rome than farm in rural Italy. Finally, there were men who had lost their property and status in 82 and the sons of such men.[45] What they all have in common is membership in rural tribes and a fundamental desire for restitution and subsistence. To all these men Catiline offered hope. It was noteworthy to Sallust that at the battle near Pistoria, Catiline's final stand with his ragtag army in January of 62, not a single soldier ran. In its aspirations the crowd listening to Cicero in 63 was quite like the men Sallust listed among the urban supporters of Catiline later in the same year. A few desperate men, in particular the men proscribed or dispossessed by Sulla or their sons and some of the old Italian allies, formed the core of disaffection on which Catiline rested the success of his coup. For a larger group of rural tribesmen in the same year the driving interest was simply access to land resources.

Clearly, interest in a particular issue determined group attendance and participation in both the lawmaking meeting and assembly. The varied descriptions of voters and others present at meetings, most often accompanying ancient reports of land redistribution or similarly charged issues brought to the people for their decision, indicate that participants were generally specific to the issue. The voters who approved the lex Sempronia in 133, for instance, were predominantly rural tribesmen interested in land redistribution. And, since the disposition of ager publicus was a burning concern to landholders without the franchise, too, the crowds present also included Italians who could not vote.[46] Again, in 103, the voters who accepted the colonization bill of L. Appuleius Saturninus included discharged soldiers, who had served with C. Marius in North Africa and southern France. Given the enormous diversity within the population of Roman Italy, which embraced a wide range of statuses and holdings, from citizen to noncitizen, elite to nonelite members, and rich to poor, different people found different points of entry into the lawmaking process (as we might expect) and had different motivations for participating. But always they were present as fragments of various groups.

In turn, each individual voting assembly presented a uniquely complicated and immediate set of issues for the participants. When meetings were held and assemblies convened, always for specific purposes, voters interested in specific issues attended these specific meetings and assemblies. As our sources confirm, different crowds or groups of varying size regularly turned out for these occasions: An ever changing population of participants rallied for the public debate representing different groups who responded, in different numbers, to the vastly different issues that were presented to the people. Romans voted, in other words, when it was in the interest of their group—or more precisely the group to which they owed the greatest allegiance at the time—to vote. Not surprisingly, the Roman voting population was as fluid and changeable as the groups that constituted it and the issues with which they wrestled.

The political leaders of Rome fully recognized the importance of groups in Roman voting. No political leader spoke as an individual in the Senate House or in the Forum. He like all Romans belonged in a group. A leader gathered in his person as in his comportment and actions the collective expectations of a throng of dependents, friends, relatives, and supporters who encircled him at various distances of intimacy, need, and support. Although such a man held or had held high office when orating to the people in particular, the ties linking him to individuals in the audience were highly personal, usually antedating office, and derived from a range of associations including inherited links to a region or community, the experience of military command in combat, and service in legal matters. In every public arena, every action carried out by a Roman leader was the distillation of the desires and hopes of various clusters of people whose expectations were articulated by the leader. This was his essential function in all areas of life, religious, economic, political, and military. Roman leaders' own political futures depended on the demonstration of ability and success that only popular support could affirm, encourage, and promote.

Indeed, leaders were absolutely dependent for their positions in society on their varying abilities to articulate the will of the people. To the extent that they could do this, leaders garnered the support of different groups among the Roman population.[47] Reporting the land redistribution scheme of Ti. Gracchus in 133, the biographer Plutarch notes that Ti. Gracchus drafted his land measure in 133 partly in response to the express desire of poor Romans and Italians to possess land.[48] The numbers of rural inhabitants of Italy who traveled to Rome confirmed Gracchus's success in correctly discerning the will of the people. The success of the lawmaking efforts of M. Licinius Crassus and Cn. Pompeius Magnus in 70, C. Cornelius and A. Gabinius in 67, and C. Julius Caesar and P. Vatinius in 59 is tied not only to the presence of recently discharged soldiers in Rome and the attachments between the law sponsors and those same veterans, formed in the camp and on campaign, but more so to the sponsors' ability to articulate a set of critical needs that appealed to the broadest number of groups.[49] There were legitimate needs, legitimate complaints and solutions, and officeholders who represented them. For every public law proposal, for every approved or rejected bill, there were voters whose support or opposition depended on the highly complicated relationships linking the various groups to which they belonged, the lawmaker, and the issues.

A Roman voter therefore held various identifications within a complex mesh of status, economic, occupational, and family clusters, expressed in a certain degree of patterned behavior. Romans, in particular political leaders, developed a sense of the predictability of a Roman voter's behavior as a result of membership in these groups. From the lawmaker's perspective, most critical among all groups were the tribes whose responsibility it was to determine the fate of his bill. Within his own tribe the lawmaker was (ideally) recognized, esteemed, and persuasive. His tribesmen as well as the diverse crowd behind him expected him to field their interests.[50] As senator or elected officeholder he also had formal attachments to Romans in every tribe. Thus, all the tribes occupied his political attention. Mediating between the lawmaker and the thirty-four other tribes were his political associates, senators, and elected leaders. When Plutarch records that Lucullus was voted a triumph in 66 only because "the most important and most powerful citizens mingled with tribes and persuaded the people to let him triumph," undoubtedly each man headed for his own tribe.[51] His rank and authority carried a special weight for his own tribesmen. Similarly, when a law sponsor named a first voter in a tribe selected by lot, he chose a man of repute who not only backed his law but appealed to a sizable number of voters within that tribe. In every tribe were found reputable men closely associated with one political leader and at odds with another.

Given the complexity of the Roman sense of identity and the controversial nature of most of the issues introduced at public lawmaking sessions, it is obvious that the behavior of voters expressed through their tribal or other leaders was never entirely predictable. The extent to which law sponsors labored to make a case for their bills confirms this. Nor did every first voter, who presumably always voted in support of a bill, invariably rally his fellow tribe members behind him. The reasons for this are obscure, for we are never appraised of the intricate connections binding the Romans present at any assembly that derived from their membership in various clusters, including the tribe. But our Roman at the voting bridge was undoubtedly juggling other loyalties as he cast his vote. Individual attachments to or within various groups were mutable, especially in the first century.[52] Clearly, the shifting arrangement and membership of sundry groups making up society were critical in determining not only who voted in public lawmaking assemblies but how they voted.

Hence leaders might try to form a predictable crowd of voters, from their perspective, for any given assembly. Illustrations of the care taken by both law sponsors and others to ensure the attendance or nonattendance of specific people and groups are numerous. Voters were sometimes brought great distances to Rome, or assemblies were convened when certain groups were already present in Rome—discharged soldiers above all.[53] The presence in Rome in 133 of a resolute crowd of Romans and Italians played a crucial role in determining Ti. Gracchus's course of action in the face of opposition to his proposal from other magistrates and senators. In 122, when C. Gracchus proposed a statute giving Roman citizenship to Latins and Italian allies, the Senate decreed that only those with the right to vote should stay in the city or closer to the city than forty stades while the proposal was being discussed and voted.[54] Even the presence of nonvoters in large numbers was viewed with suspicion. What Roman leaders could be sure of at all times, though, was a varied crowd of voters ready to hand. The practice of selling grain at a fixed, low price in Rome for Roman citizens introduced by C. Gracchus and modified by various officeholders over the next one hundred years confirms the Roman leadership's recognition of the constant flow of citizens into and out of Rome.[55] By the Gracchan period, elected officeholders and the Roman Senate itself recognized the political implications of the large numbers of temporary and permanent migrants to the city of Rome.

Although our sources report the existence of specific groups, rarely do they report numbers in attendance at assemblies or the proportional size of a particular group relative to another that was present. Only when consensus was overwhelming do we get some indication of crowds so large they overburdened the city's temporary housing. Why? Clearly numbers were of limited importance, for the passage of law was determined not by numbers but by a customary and divine process in which elite members of society succeeded or failed in discerning the sense of the voters present on a specific issue. This was achieved when each tribe weighed in with its own sense of what should be done, presaged usually by the vote cast initially by a first voter, a reputable man selected by the sponsor, of a first tribe selected by lot. The practice takes for granted that all tribesmen present for the vote will fall in line behind their social betters to make the right decision whether in electoral or lawmaking assemblies. A majority of tribes expressing themselves did not mean that a decision was reached by a majority per se—especially when some tribes held more members than others—but that a majority of tribes reflected the accepted Roman view of what should be. Evidently, Romans had an intuitive sense of the representative size of a sufficient group.

Numbers alone, to reiterate the point, were unimportant. Rome was no democracy, except perhaps in a Roman sense: a voting event was one in which the gods, the Roman people, and their leaders came together to discern the sense of the Roman people on a particular issue that drew a particular crowd interested in that issue.[56] No wonder the Romans regarded leges saturae, bills addressing disconnected issues, as antithetical to the process of discerning the people's will. No matter how many voters cast their ballots, all understood that the final decision represented the sovereign will of the entire Roman people.[57]

BALANCE AND CEREMONY

All assemblies in Rome were convened and directed according to set procedures scrupulously executed. Consider this set of instructions from an old handbook on consular procedure, preserved by Varro, informing consuls on the proper way of convening the centuriate assembly.

> He who is about to summon the citizen-army shall say to his assistant, "Gaius Calpurnius, call all the citizens hither to me with an . . . 'invitation.'" The assistant speaks thus: "All citizens, come ye hither to the judges, to an invitation meeting." "Gaius Calpurnius," says the consul,

> "call all the citizens hither to me, to a gathering." The assistant speaks thus: "All citizens, come hither to the judges, to a gathering." Then the consul makes declaration to the army: "I order you to go by the proper way to the centuriate assembly."
>
> (*Ling*. 6.86–88; Loeb trans.)

Vividly detailed in these descriptions are the scrupulosity and precision characteristic of Roman public life in all areas. Whether in the enactment of ritual or the conduct of assemblies, the Romans adhered to prescribed patterns of performance and speech.

Today, the patterns of Rome's lawmaking process seem peculiarly cumbersome. Promulgation (*promulgatio*), a formal declaration of intent, required the formal display of a proposal or "query" (*rogatio*), publicly and in writing; the formal recital of the proposal by a herald; and the declaration of the date of the voting assembly. These ceremonial events initiated and concluded the public stages of the production of law.[58] Over the next three Roman weeks (*trinundinum*) or more the display stood in the Forum, and at each of the three required meetings, held on market days (nundinae), the bill was recited.[59] On the day of the assembly, the law sponsor—the one who "asks the question" (*rogator*)—called the people to a meeting at which the proposal was debated and posed the question to the people: "Do you desire and order it to be?" (*velitis iubeatisne*). The bill was read, as we saw earlier, for the last time. If no magistrate vetoed the bill, and if no senator or magistrate announced a religious flaw in the proceedings to prevent the bill, the sponsor called his assistant to dissolve the meeting and reconvene the people in their voting units, using the formulaic language placed in the mouth of P. Servilius Rullus in our opening paragraph: "The law has been read." So Cicero concluded his hopeful set of regulations for a rejuvenated Rome, bringing an end to the imaginary recital.[60]

In such time-ordained patterns, which governed lawmaking assemblies as well as all other assemblies in the late Republic, the legitimacy of actions taken by the Roman people was firmly grounded. Only a law properly displayed and recited before the vote was a valid law. Only an assembly properly convened and conducted in accordance with customary procedure was a "legitimate" assembly.[61] Only public law generated in such an assembly was legitimate.[62] Confirmation of legitimacy is conveyed in the testimonial to the lawful conditions of its passage introducing every statute generated in an assembly of the Roman people: "Titus Quinctius Crispinus, consul, duly asked the people if they wanted this law and the people duly accepted it."[63] The Roman understanding of the Latin *iure*, meaning "lawfully" and rendered in English as "duly," is clear. The assembly was rightfully convened and conducted, in accordance with procedures established by custom and reiterated by enactment; the lawmaker rightfully presented his proposal, again in accordance with accepted procedures established by custom and enactment; and the people rightfully responded.

Closer examination of the constitution of lawmaking rightfully performed suggests that iure entails, to an as yet hidden degree, the affirmation of a long-standing arrangement between Rome and her gods that was carefully managed. Many of the complex procedures found in public lawmaking directly involved the gods in decisions taken by the Roman people. Even the lottery, as Lily Ross Taylor notes, placed the selection of the first tribe or first century to vote in the hands of the gods, although the precise relationship between the lot and Roman religion is uncertain.[64] More familiar are the requirements to meet in an inaugurated spot (where a line of communication with the gods existed), to take the auspices, and to watch for bad omens. The centuriate and full tribal assemblies met in consecrated areas, where it was permissible and possible for the convening consul or praetor to take the auspices prior to convening the assembly. Plebeian tribal assemblies did not do so, necessarily, because tribunes did not have the capacity to take the auspices. Nonetheless, the plebeian tribal assembly did sometimes meet in the precinct of the Capitoline temple, and tribunes did consult the augurs. Such procedures were essential no matter the purpose for which the assembly had been convened in order to, common wisdom held, ensure that the proceedings had Jupiter's protection.[65]

Whether divine sanction suffices as a comprehensive explanation for all such practices and procedures is unresolved.[66] On a pragmatic or functional level, it is clear that divination in all its forms (taking the auspices or *extispicium*) allowed the Romans to decipher the silence of the gods on particular matters of importance. Prayers, vows, and sacrifice, equally important ritualized actions, allowed the Romans to regulate their divine alliance. If the signs were foreboding or if the actions were incorrectly performed or flawed—for instance, if the priest stumbled when repeating the words of the prayer recited to him by his attendant or if a noise interrupted the prayer—the repetition of the performance was essential. A blunder in the performance of ritual action or conduct could be quite minor by modern standards—as for instance when a flamen's ritual cap (*apex*) fell off and the Romans found it necessary to divest the priest of his sacred position.[67] Likewise, the augur's reading of the signs was absolutely necessary: if the augur pronounced "another day" (*alio die*) the scheduled assembly was postponed. The college of augurs as a result came to hold the authority to declare enactments illegitimate if in their view statutes had not been properly enacted with respect to the gods. The relationship between men and the gods tolerated no uncertainty.

Similar concerns appear to surround some of the ceremonial, that is nonreligious, procedures of assemblies.[68] In the late Republic, no assemblies were held before a lengthy and formal airing of bills, candidates, or legal causes. The law proposal had to be publicly displayed. It had to be read. The veto, which took the form of physical intervention by a tribune at a particular moment (when the herald began proclaiming the text of a proposed law), had to terminate the course of the law. Except for the tribune's veto, these procedures did not necessarily involve the gods, but they are similarly ritualized acts and, given contemporary reactions, much of the same effect was felt if they were obstructed.[69] Whether occurring in lawmaking, electoral, or juridical arenas, any mistakes, oversights, or obstructions to these procedural requirements vitiated the performance in much the same way it did in the case of religious ritual. Precision of performance and speech rendered any event and its outcome, whether the issue was law or leadership, legitimate. This fact made the procedural requirements of all such occasions, especially lawmaking occasions, as we shall see in chapter 9, highly susceptible to disruption.

But if the various religious and ceremonial procedural requirements of assemblies to some extent reflected a need for control and predictability in the sphere of divine and human interaction, to a greater extent they secured, over more than four hundred years, the foundations of Rome's uniquely representative political character. Think for a moment about the functions of the lottery that determined the voting order of tribes.[70] Inasmuch as Rome's thirty-five tribes held fixed positions on a censorial roll, the selection of a tribe to vote first in a tribal assembly decided the order in which all the remaining tribes would vote.[71] That the medium of selection was an arbitrary lottery meant that no one knew in advance which tribe would vote first or the order of voting thereafter. Every tribe had an equal chance to be the first tribe, as determined by the gods, specifically Jupiter, not by men.[72] Random selection in effect provided the basis for open and fair decisions of the Roman people, reached by vote, in which every voting unit had an equally random and divinely sanctioned chance to participate. Given the principle of group voting, the Roman lottery bears little comparison with the deliberately democratic use of sortition in fifth-century Athens. Only the Roman lottery, however, operating in an increasingly large-scale society, was instrumental in conserving an effective popular government, which diffused effective power among all thirty-five tribes. When properly handled, the gods ensured the success of the Roman people, but men always had to work at making success possible. Given its overtly conservative nature, the system proved extraordinarily flexible over time.

To an even greater extent, therefore, such procedures assisted in creating, recreating, and somehow fixing the order of Roman society along the lines of a perceived ideal. When properly performed they channeled the political energies of ever expanding numbers of Roman citizens into long-standing tribal and other structures. They buttress the Roman certitude that the production of law or the election of leaders was not possible without the participation and common sanction of the Roman people expressing themselves as members of their voting unit. Hence, the formal emphasis on publication and information in the lawmaking process in particular was profound.[73] Not only were all public stages of the lawmaking process directed to the Roman people, but great care was taken to guarantee public access to the lawmaking process, through the meticulous communication of the full text of proposed laws to them, by posting written notices in the Forum and publicly reading laws before the voting assemblies were convened. For a statute was legitimate only when it was enacted with full publicity in the procedurally prescribed manner: proposals were publicly posted and read for a period of three Roman weeks, and arguments for and against laws were aired in public meetings. Once enacted, laws were engraved on bronze tablets under a formal heading that declared the public conditions in which the people had endorsed them, and the tablets were displayed in Rome's central areas.[74] In brief, the legitimacy of statutes, as of all actions taken by the Roman people and their elected officials, derived from the divinely sanctioned, unencumbered expression of the sovereign will of the Roman people. All the world understood the key role of the Roman people in public lawmaking events.

CONCLUSION

Cicero's blistering attack against M. Antonius in 44, circulated in the orations titled *Philippics*, returns time and again to the illegitimacy of the decisions Antonius forced on the Roman people as sanctioned law following the assassination of Julius Caesar. Laws were presented to voting assemblies even when thunder resounded all around; laws were voted by assemblies from which the people had been excluded; laws were even engraved before they had been publicized for the requisite twenty-seven or more days (trinundinum). In Cicero's resolute list of improprieties, the fundamental requirements of legitimate law are crystal clear: the bill, correctly promulgated in Rome for the period of time fixed by law; the gods, present and suitably disposed to the proceedings; and above all the people, convened as an assembly in the proper setting in Rome and summoned to cast their ballots openly and unhindered.

As a central process in facilitating the functioning of Roman society, public lawmaking assemblies reflected many of the most fundamental features of Roman life over a very long time. In the first century no less than the fourth, the officeholders who proposed the law and guided the discussion were the same group of leaders who managed the society, whose prestige at the session reflected their prestige in society. The necessity for divine approval on the times for their performance, the forms of the rituals, and many of the formal acts that took place during each stage reflected the importance of religion, constant across our period. The elaborate debates and the complicated voting procedures required to discern "the will of the people" reflected the authority and importance of Roman citizens. Voting itself was clearly the product of a society that placed a great deal of importance on group membership and customary procedures. To engage in the elaborate rituals and procedures involved in the entire public lawmaking process, participants, be they leaders or members of the majority population, had to possess time, energy, and an intuitive knowledge of rites, rules, principles, and traditions. Whether religious or practical in motivation, strict formalities and conventions shaped every step leading to the production of law. Always in lawmaking assemblies, a delicate balancing act was staged by the leaders of Rome, who tried to measure the desires of the Roman people and balance them off with the religious dimensions of all human activity and in turn deal with real problems. The flexibility in the system was provided by the shared religious life of the Roman people and their leaders and the common recognition of what the gods required. The striking recognition and general observation of these features, constant across our entire period of study, underscore the extent to which the lawmaking process reflected the values and assumptions of the society at large. We might wonder how this continued to be possible as the scale of Roman society increased.

Around 130 in Rome, on the occasion of a much-heckled public speech about land reform, Scipio Aemilianus reportedly rebuked a crowd of haranguers with the charge that they were only the "step-children" of Italy. His insult is commonly understood by modern scholars to mean that Scipio's audience that day was perceptibly foreign in its composition: its members, drawn from the urban population, were neither Italian, Roman, nor Latin. Instead, Rome had by then become a city populated mostly by ex-slaves drawn from the conquered lands of the eastern Mediterranean—complete outsiders to the traditional Roman system. While this is inherently unlikely, certainly a man did not have to be Roman to be a Roman citizen. By 130, Latins, Italians, and even foreigners had been randomly entering the citizen population for over two hundred years. Within fifty years, all Italy with its diverse and distinguishable groups would be Roman. But to a leader like Scipio the "Roman-ness" of these new citizens was suspect. Confronted by such hints of transformation in the groups constituting the Roman population when penetrated by outsiders, we are entitled to wonder how public processes such as lawmaking, which certainly demanded intuitive understanding of the various stages from all participants, continued to unfold purposefully and effectively.

Given the expanding size of the Roman citizen population, especially in the first century, the increased resort to public lawmaking assemblies in Rome during the same period is remarkable. The detailed and time-consuming public law proposal, the complexity of the generally understood procedures at all stages, the implicit acknowledgment of divine oversight, and the respect for social standing all underscore the immensity of the Roman achievement in absorbing so many conquered peoples into such a system. One of the best indicators of the high level of absorption achieved is the degree to which outsiders participated in and recognized the proceedings at public lawmaking assemblies. This was not an amalgamation that had taken place overnight. In part 2 we turn to lawmaking during the growth of Rome to explore the avenues that led to the wide-scale acceptance of Rome's public lawmaking process.

Notes

1. The best description of the arrangements in voting assemblies is provided by L. R. Taylor, *Roman voting assemblies from the Hannibalic war to the dictatorship of Caesar* (Ann Arbor, MI, 1966), 35–84, esp. 70–78, on tribal lawmaking assemblies. See also Staveley 1972, 143–76; and G. W. Botsford, *The Roman assemblies* (New York, 1909).

2. *Custodes:* Mommsen, *R.St.* 3.406.

3. It was far more cumbersome in Rullus's day than it had been before the introduction of the written ballot in137. Until that innovation, voters had formed in lines and each voter walked in turn from the head of his line to the pontes, where the responsible tribal leaders, the rogatores, simply asked how he voted and recorded the response.

4. Cic., *Leg.* 3.38. This is believed by some to be a lex tabellaria, or ballot law: A. Lintott "Political history, 146–95 BC," *CAH* 9, 2d ed. (Cambridge, New York, New Rochelle, Melbourne, and Sydney, 1994), 86; cf A. Lintott, "Electoral bribery in the Roman republic," *JRS* 80 (1990): 7. See Taylor 1966, 39–46, for the probable arrangements.

5. I omit here a fourth assembly, the curiate assembly, whose functions and membership were restricted.

6. Taylor 1966, 61–62 with n. 7.

7. Time was a critical factor, according to modern historians, in the more frequent recourse to the tribal assemblies for elections, where the units cast their votes simultaneously. It took far less time to tally and announce thirty-five tribal votes than 193 centuriate votes. The voting process in the centuriate assembly was eventually speeded up by the construction of the "sorting pens" known as the Saepta Iulia in the Campus Martius, completed early in the reign of Augustus in 26. L. Richardson, Jr., A

new topographical dictionary of ancient Rome (Baltimore and London, 1992), 340–41. The voting process in electoral assemblies has been reconstructed in Taylor 1966, 47–58.

8. See chapter 1.

9. Declarations of war voted by the people: J. Rich, *Declaring war in the Roman republic in the period of transmarine expansion* (Brussels, 1976), 13–17. Rich identifies eight soundly attested "war votes" between 264 and 44.

10. See chapter 7, n. 1.

11. It was initially an increase in principle only, because at least two decades passed before all of the new citizens were registered, the essential prerequisite to full use of the citizen's franchise and without which the decision to grant citizenship had little meaning. Chapter 8 addresses various efforts to restrict the voting rights of new citizens.

12. Livy 7.16.8.

13. Area Capitolinus: S. Platner and T. Ashby, *A topographical dictionary of ancient Rome* (Oxford, 1929), 48.

14. Comitium: F. Coarelli, *Il foro romano: Periodo arcaico* (Rome, 1983), 148. Forum: Varro, *Rust.* 1.2.9: . . . *primus populum ad leges accipiendas in septem iugera forensia e comitio eduxit*; cf. Cic., *Amic.* 25, 96.

15. R. MacMullen, "How many Romans voted," *Ath.* 53 (1980): 454–57; Taylor 1966, 52–54.

16. But, as has been pointed out, the voting units voted consecutively, not simultaneously, in legislative assemblies; hence the voters need not all be present in the voting enclosure at the same time: Taylor 1966, 128–30 n. 26, summarizing conclusions reached by P. Fraccaro, "La procedura del vota nei comizi tributi romani," in *Opuscula* 2 (Pavia, 1957), 235–54, original edition, *Atti della R. Accademia delle Scienze di Torino* 49 (1913–14): 600–622; cf. A. Yakobsen, *Elections and Electioneering in Rome* (Stuttgart, 1999), 49 n. 78.

17. Numbers: Cicero's claims on various occasions that, for instance, the votes of tota Italia made his return possible or some laws were approved although the requisite minimum of voters were not present to fill the tribes (discussed later), make the point negatively.

18. Because proportionally few Romans could have voted at every assembly, modern scholars long supposed that popular participation in Roman government was severely limited and relatively unimportant: see, for example, M. I. Finley, *Politics in the ancient world* (Cambridge, 1983), 84–92. The recognition that the people did have a significant voice has gained ground over the last twenty years: Williamson 1984, 1990; see also note 56, this chapter.

19. An earlier version of this section was first published as part of Williamson 1990.

20. See in particular the presumptions in Syme 1939 and Taylor 1949.

21. The admonishment comes in the introduction to a popular play, *Amphitro* 64–74, esp. "sive qui ambissent palmam histrionibus / seu quoiquam artifici (seu per scriptas litteras / seu qui ipse ambisset seu per internuntium), / sive adeo aediles perfidiose quoi duint, / sirempse legem iussit esse Iuppiter, / quasi magistratum sibi alterive ambiverit." The alliteration of the underlined words and the term *sirempse* are reminiscent of legal Latin. See M. McDonnell, "Legal language in Plautus," *AJP* 107 (1986): 564–76.

22. On this treatise see most recently Lintott 1999, 225–32.

23. Cic., *Leg.* 3.4.11 and 3.19.43.

24. At the other extreme, C. Gracchus proposed a measure in 122 to replace the current hierarchic voting order of the centuries in the centuriate assembly with a system of randomly calling centuries from all the classes to vote. Again, the measure was never made law. Sall., [*Ad. Caes.sen.*] 2.8.1; Mommsen, *R.St.* 3.294.

25. Sources in *MRR* 1.225.

26. Sources in *MRR* 2.144–45.

27. *Persa* 68 ff.

28. The interpretation of Roman voters presented here, namely, the voting population conformed to the structures of life and movement in Italy generally, rests on my arguments in chapter 6 about the city of Rome. It is more commonly believed that the largest group of steady voters were the small shopkeepers (*tabernarii*) and craftsmen (*opifices*) in the vicinity of the Forum and former slaves resident in Rome—the "plebs contionalis," as defined by Meier, which is very evident in the ancient accounts of political life and voting in Late Republican Rome. Otherwise only wealthy Romans who had the time and interest regularly came to Rome to vote from outside the city. As Taylor put it: "The largest number available at all the comitia were from the men always on hand in the four urban tribes, which included the lower population of the city and all the freedmen." Taylor 1966, 54. Plebs contionalis: C. Meier, *Res publica amissa: Eine studie zu Verfassung und Geschichte der späten römischen Republik*, 2d ed. (Wiesbaden, 1980), 114–16; Vanderbroek 1987, 86–93; Pina Polo 1996, 130–32. Most recently Millar has attempted to refine the identities of these Roman voters with reference to locales and "zones" in and around the city: Millar 1998, 13–48, esp. 28–30.

29. Lawmaking of Vatinius: chapter 9.

30. Group vote: Staveley 1972, 133–42. I return to the mesh of tribe and century in chapter 5.

31. Otherwise Cicero's charge that so few tribesmen attended an assembly voters had to be drafted into some tribes wouldn't make sense (whether he was exaggerating or not).

32. Or the majority of any group in any assembly, whether defined by tribes or centuries (the differences between the egalitarian tribal and hierarchic centuriate assemblies notwithstanding).

33. *Sodales:* J. North, s.v. "*sodales*," in *OCD*3, 1420, and briefly Lintott 1990, 9. Professional associations in Rome: see chapter 6.

34. Mommsen, *R.St.* 3.190–92; cf. Taylor 1960, 15, 16, 74. See chapter 5.

35. Mommsen, *Die römischen tribus in administrativer Beziehung* (Altona, 1844), 23.

36. Similar links enmeshed tribesmen in each of the four urban tribes, whose leadership and membership are far more discernible to modern historians than those of the rural tribes, especially in the Late Republic. See further on the urban tribes and their leadership in chapters 6 and 7.

37. First voters: Staveley 1972 164–69; C. Nicolet, *Le métier de citoyen dans la Rome républicaine* (Paris, 1976), 383–85; J.-C. Dumont et al., *Insula sacra: La loi Gabinia-Calpurnia de Délos (58 av. J.-C.)* (Rome, 1980), 53–56; J. Linderski and A. Kaminska-Linderski, "A. Gabinius A.f. Capito and the first voter in the legislative comitia tributa," *ZPE* 12 (1973): 247–52.

38. The lex Agraria of 111, the lex Gabinia Calpurnia de Delos of 58, and the lex Quinctia de aquaeductibus of 9, respectively. Discussion of these and other testimonia are provided by Dumont et al. 1980, 53–56.

39. Formula: Dumont et al. 1980, 53–54.

40. Plancius: Cic., *Planc.* 35; Staveley 1972, 165 with n. 320. Fidulius: Cic., *Dom.* 79–80; Stavely 1972, 166 with n. 322. See also Dumont et al. 1980, 54–55.

41. Bronze tablets engraved with law: C. Williamson, "Monuments of bronze: Roman legal documents on bronze tablets," *CA* 6 (1987): 160–83; and C. Williamson, "The display of law and archival practice in Rome," in *Acta colloquii epigraphici latini*, ed. Heikki Solin, Olli Salomies, and Uta-Maria Liertz (Helsinki, 1995), 239–51.

42. Staveley 1972, 168. First voters also served as guarantors of the assembly results: Nicolet 1976a, 383; Dumont et al. 1980, 53; Williamson 1995, 239–51.

43. Sallust, *Cat.* 37.3.

44. Sallust, *Cat.* 37.4–5.

45. Sallust, *Cat.* 37. 6–9.

46. See chapter 1, note 11.

47. See Pina Polo 1996, 140–50, and Yakobsen 1999, 65–111, for different assessments of a clearly very complex relationship.

48. Plutarch, *Ti. Gracch.* 8.7.

49. Soldiers as voters: Gruen 1974, 377–78.

50. The idea that elected officials sponsored laws, paid citizens to vote, or rearranged tribal membership in order to win clients misses the complexity of the relationship between Roman leaders and the majority population: Taylor 1960, 133–38, esp. 137 (Ap. Claudius Caecus). Cf. Eckstein 1987, 10–11 (C. Flaminius).

51. Plutarch, *Luc.* 37.1–2.

52. See chapter 7.

53. Voters from rural Italy: Taylor 1960, 47–68, 79–131; cf. Nicolet 1976a, 391–401; cf. Millar 1998, 29 (voters from Gallia Cisalpina).

54. Appian, *B.C.* 1.23.

55. See chapter 6.

56. The term "democracy," as understood by ancient Greeks or twentieth-century historians, inadequately describes the Roman political experience. Nonetheless, as the only term available, it has provided a starting point for numerous efforts in the past twenty years to examine anew the political character of Rome from a Roman perspective and in particular to assess the "democratic" element of the Roman government structure. See in particular F. G. B. Millar, "The political character of the Roman republic," *JRS* 74 (1984): 1–19; F. G. B. Millar, "Politics, persuasion and the people before the social war," *JRS* 76 (1986): 1–11; F. G. B. Millar, "Popular politics at Rome in the late republic," in *Leaders and masses in the Roman world*, ed. I. Malkin and Z. W. Rubinsohn (Leiden, New York, and Köln, 1995), 91–113; Millar 1998; A. Lintott, "Democracy in the late republic," *ZRG* 117 (1987): 34–52; and J. North, "Democratic politics in republican Rome," *Past and Present* 126 (1990): 3–21; cf. Williamson 1984. Discussion of the debate is provided in M. Jehne, ed., *Demokratie in Rom? Die Rolle des Volkes in der Politik der römischen Republik* (Stuttgart, 1995).

57. The idea that whoever was present to vote represented the entire citizen population has been adopted somewhat hesitantly by Millar 1998, 196; cf. 45, 48.

58. From Cicero's description in *Leg. Agr.* 2.5.13 ("*legem contionemque expectabam: lex initio nulla proponitur, contionem in pridie Idus advocari jubet*") and 2.5.13 ("*Aliquando tandem me designato lex in publicum proponitur*") it appears that the posting was expected

to coincide with a meeting because the significance of his remarks is that it did not. On the introduction of the written display see chapter 7.

59. Publication on market days (nundinae): Macrobius 1.16.34. The stipulated elements of oral publication are a public meeting (contio) and repetition on three occasions (*in trinum nundinum*), i.e., in three public meetings. However, we only ever hear about the performance that concluded the public meeting before the voting assembly. Length of trinundinum: A. Lintott, "Trinundinum," *CQ* 59 (1965): 281–85; cf. Lintott 1999, 44 with n. 20; Mommsen, *R.St.* 3.375–76; A. K. Michels, *The calendar of the Roman republic* (Princeton, 1967), 191 ff. (restating Mommsen's view that it was a set interval of time, incorporating a fixed number of days).

60. Cic., *Leg.* 3.11.

61. Assemblies were called by proper magistrates only on appropriate days, designated dies comitiales, and held only during the hours of daylight. On the calendar of days see Michels 1967. On all matters related to procedure in voting assemblies, the best guide in English is Taylor 1966; cf. Staveley 1972 and Botsford 1909.

62. Hence Cicero complained in 44 that the laws Antony enacted that year were not legitimate: see comments at the end of this chapter.

63. *RS* 2 No. 63, ll. 1–4: *T. Quinctius Crispinus consul populum iure rogavit populusque iure scivit.*

64. Taylor 1966, 73.

65. Taylor 1966, 7.

66. Purposes of divination: J. North, "Diviners and divination at Rome," in *Pagan priests: Religion and power in the ancient world*, ed. M. Beard and J. North (Ithaca, NY, 1990), 51–71, esp. 60–65.

67. Livy, *Epit.* 54.

68. The distinction between ceremony and religious ritual was often blurred in Rome: D. J. Gargola, *Lands, laws, and gods: Magistrates and ceremony in the regulation of public lands in republican Rome* (Chapel Hill and London, 1995), 5–6.

69. The stylistic features of statutes also reflect the concern for recognizing and maintaining a preexistent world. The characteristically precise language and phrasing of enactments is a byproduct of the concern for precision. From a modern perspective the language and phrasing are very legalistic and remarkably modern. But the motive force behind the Roman style of lawmaking was uniquely Roman: Williamson 1984, 102–23.

70. Sortition in tribal assemblies: Taylor 1966, 70–74. In Rome generally: Staveley 1972, 230–32. See also G. Forni, "Considerazioni sui comizi romani," *Rendiconti di Istituto Lombardo, Accad. di scienze e lettere* 106 (1972): 543–66.

71. Order of tribes: Taylor 1960, 69–78.

72. Not only was Jupiter the presiding divinity at assemblies, but the augurs played a role in the sortition process: Taylor 1966, 73.

73. Williamson 1984, 12–80, 196–226; Williamson 1990, 266–76, esp. 268 and 272; cf. Millar 1998, 45, 115.

74. Williamson 1987, 160–183, and 1995, 239–51.

PART TWO

THE EXPANSION OF ROME

CHAPTER FOUR

The Conquest of Italy

OUR FINDINGS IN PART I raise a number of questions central to any examination of the importance of lawmaking assemblies in Roman history. How do we explain the persistence of such events over the most unsettled centuries of growth in Roman history? What role did public lawmaking assemblies play in making this expansion possible? How did ever increasing numbers of new members throughout the expanding Roman state come to share the deep understanding of Roman social order, civic structures, and political culture required to engage in lawmaking assemblies? Any comprehensive effort to identify the considerations that underlay this achievement must await the completion of a detailed history of the entire Roman experience from the widest possible range of scholarly perspectives. Nevertheless a start must be made.

In this chapter I explore the extent to which the absorption of Italian peoples was to a large degree the result of Roman settlers doing things in the usual way in a physical environment that had over time produced a level of common behavior among all inhabitants of Italy. The Roman perception of the degree to which outsiders shared these values played an important role in decisions to draw some peoples, perhaps most, into an ever expanding political unit and to annihilate others. Of the utmost importance in the absorption of outsiders, also, was the Roman genius for adapting customary ways to the exigencies of expansion and growth, which permeated down through society at all levels: it was a rare issue, as we shall see, that Romans could not resolve without resort to customary Roman ways. And one of the most obvious examples of the Roman potential for adjusting to the most complicated demands of absorbing outsiders can be seen in their eventual resort to public lawmaking assemblies to develop and legitimize a solution to an otherwise intractable problem. In their resort to such an all-encompassing and complicated public airing and resolution of otherwise intractable issues the Romans differed significantly from other Mediterranean peoples or indeed probably peoples anywhere in the world at the time. To understand an accomplishment of this magnitude we must go back to the beginnings of Roman settlement and expansion.

ENVIRONMENT AND MOBILITY

Over three centuries before the Italian War, on the eve of the Roman expansion in the fourth century, Italy was to all appearances an impressively diverse place.[1] In the north, in the area later called Cisalpine Gaul, Gauls made up most of the population, relative newcomers to Italy since 500, when tribal groups of Celts crossed the Alps to settle in the Alpine foothills and the lowlands of the Po River basin (MAP *1*).[2] In the north also were the Veneti, at the head of the Po River, and Ligurians, along the narrow Tyrrhenian coast and inland in the valleys and mountains of the northwestern Apennine range below the Po River basin. These represented the most southerly tier of Ligurians, who inhabited an area of Europe stretching from Italy to the Pyrenees, and were divided in Italy among two chief tribal groups speaking a common, non-Italic language.[3] Peninsular Italy south of the Po River basin, including the lowlands along the Tyrrhenian and Adriatic coasts and the central and south-central Apennine region, held the four largest language groups on the peninsula. Etruscans occupied the region called Etruria, lying along the central Tyrrhenian coast and inland. Adjacent were Umbrian speakers, centered primarily on the region called Umbria (Umbri) but also farther south in the Apennines bordering Etruria and Latium (Sabini, Hernici, Volsci, Aequi) and in the central Apennines (Marsi). Latins occupied southern Etruria and Latium, spreading also into the foothills of the central Apennines. The Romans in their city on the Tiber River were a smaller group within the larger body of Latins. The culturally and linguistically diverse Oscan-speaking peoples of central and southern Italy lived in the mountain valleys, plateaus, and mountainous ridges of the Apennines (Marrucini, Vestini, Paeligni, Frentani, Pentrian Samnites); to the north in a part of the region called Picenum (Picentes, Praetutti); in the plain of Campania (Aurunci, Sidicini, Samnites); and across the wooded plains

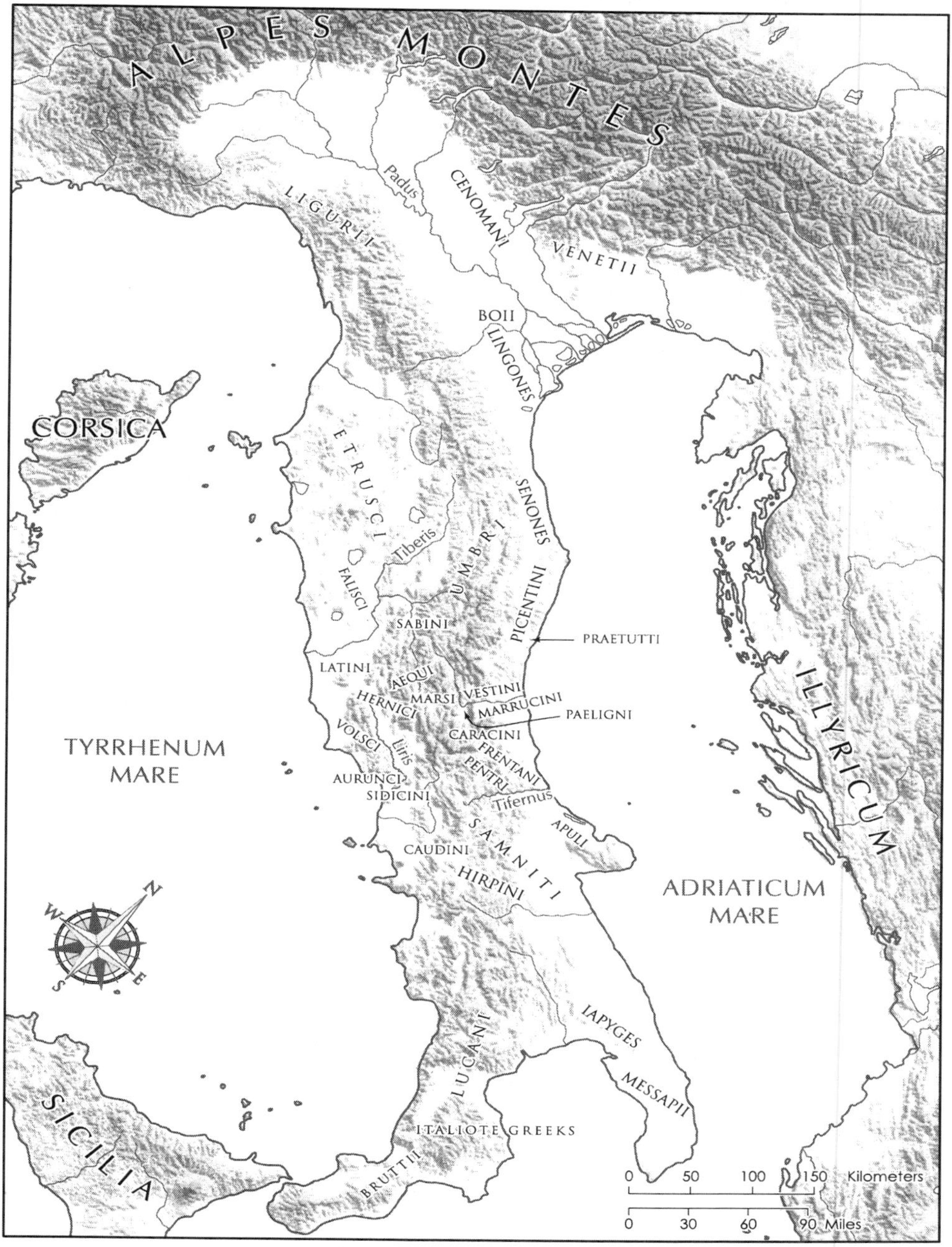

Map 1. Italy's Peoples, ca. 400

and mountains of the south (Samnites, Lucani, Bruttii).[4] Along the southern coast were Italiote Greeks, whose ancestors had come as colonists in previous centuries and who lived among Oscan-speaking Italians and other peoples. The latter included the Iapyges and Messapians of southeastern Italy (in Apulia and Calabria), whose linguistic and cultural affinities lay outside Italy, in the Balkans. Nonetheless, by 91 the great majority of Italians had been absorbed into the Roman system to the point where they were prepared to die in war to claim full inclusion in the Roman state.

The development of the shared universe of common beliefs that underlay the emergence of a pan-Italian Roman state can be traced to the impact of the physical environment on organized human communities, from the first recorded settlements throughout Italy, as geography forced a common response to their surroundings by the different groups of settlers. The main features of this environment consisted of the Apennine mountain range with its high plateaus, river valleys, and ridges covering much of the peninsula south of the Po River and the lowlands along either coast.[5] No more than narrow ribbons along some stretches, these lowlands also included four major plains: the Po River valley in the northeast, lying between the Alps and the Apennines and following the course of the river to the Adriatic Sea; the plain of Latium along the central Tyrrhenian coast; the plain of Campania, farther south along the same coast; and the plains of Apulia and Calabria along the Adriatic Sea in southeastern Italy. The Apennines rimmed by coastal lowlands, sometimes widening into plains that with river valleys penetrated the foothills and high ridges of the mountains, were a dominating presence for the inhabitants of Italy. Above all, the Apennines and the lowlands, neither sufficient in themselves to allow for maximum effective exploitation of the land, as we shall see, created a reciprocal relationship between the permanent inhabitants of mountain and plain that had a profound impact on the development of communities and states.[6]

Notwithstanding sharp regional variations in cultural, political, and economic structures, once population levels required the maximum exploitation of land resources—at different times in different places—the diverse Italian peoples came to share a common adjustment to their geographical placement. Climatic and geographic conditions throughout Italy encouraged the movement of herds, or transhumance, the seasonal migration of animals from one set of pasture lands to another. Lowlands, limited to narrow coastal strips including the three main plains and river valleys in mountainous areas, were too dry in the summer to provide adequate fodder; sheep in particular were susceptible to the arid conditions of summer in the lowlands. Conversely, highlands were snow covered in winter. Consequently it was impossible to sustain herds in permanent pastures in a mountain or lowland location, especially if animals were herded in any number. Producing fodder even for a few plow animals put an almost impossible strain on lowland farmers in the first century.[7] Transhumance therefore was both critical and widespread, from the very beginnings of animal rearing during the Neolithic. Throughout Italy goats, sheep, or cattle were herded between summer pastures in the Alpine foothills or the Apennines from late spring to early autumn and winter pastures in the lowland river valleys and coastal areas, from autumn to spring.[8] This age-old migration of Italians had created patterns of subsistence farming and herding, characterized by the seasonal movement of animals, long before the fourth century, after the apparently haphazard advent of agriculture that occurred initially in the fourth millennium in the lowlands east of the Apennines and next in the lowlands on the west coast.[9] These patterns intensified when population levels increased in the seventh and sixth centuries, a phenomenon linked to agricultural and other changes introduced by Greek settlers.[10]

Accordingly, on the eve of Roman expansion, transhumance had become a way of life to one degree or another for most Italian peoples, whether lowland or plain dwellers, such as most Etruscans, Latins, Campanians or Apulians, or mountain dwellers, such as Ligurians and Gauls in the north and the Oscan-speaking peoples of central and south Italy. But the level of engagement in seasonal migrations with herds varied somewhat from one Italian group to another. The peoples whose permanent settlements were in the mountain and lowland areas of central and southern Italy—the Paeligni, Marsi, Marrucini, and Vestini (collectively called the Abruzzi peoples after the modern name for the region) and the Samnites, Sidicini, and Lucanians—were especially dependent on transhumance for survival. Limited amounts of arable land in their regions of the Apennines, confined to narrow strips of arable land along the edges of valleys between the heavy soils of the valley bottoms, too heavy to plow, and the scant dirt of mountain ridges, made the Apennine peoples dependent on the lowlands both for winter pasture and for arable land. Far more secure than these mountain dwellers were the permanent inhabitants of arable plains along the coast, the site of the winter pastures. Nonetheless, transhumance was as much a part of life to the urbanizing populations of the plains, including the plain of Latium, as it was to the Apennine tribesmen.[11] In all these regions herding continued and with it the need for moving herds between seasonal pastures. The early importance of transhumance endured, unobstructed albeit transformed, as we shall see, by the extension of Roman dominion across Italy.[12] The ubiquitous shrines to Hercules, patron of herders, found along the cattle trails of Italy, are also found in the city of Rome.[13] As late as 1961–62, the archeologist R. Ross Holloway reports sighting "the huts of shepherds from the mountains of the Abruzzi, who were wintering with their flocks in the Roman Campagna," alongside the airport of Guidona east of Rome.[14]

Thus, the distinctive regions and peoples of Italy were drawn by geography into a common world requiring the reciprocal seasonal movement of flocks of sheep, goats, or cattle. From the Alpine foothills in north Italy, Celtic herders moved cattle, sheep, and goats between winter pastures in the Po River valley lowland and summer pastures in the foothills of the Alps or higher still. On the south side of the Po River, their herds traveled between winter pastures in the valley and summer pastures in the Apennines. The Ligurians moved herds between summer pastures in the mountains, where their permanent settlements were located, and winter pastures in the lowland coastal areas and river valleys.[15] The movement of herds in central and southern Italy was similarly pervasive and widespread, covering the entire region with a network of trails, some of them in continual use from the late Neolithic to the mid-twentieth century CE.[16] Herds were moved short distances at times, especially in the Alpine foothills and in the Apennines, where herds were often moved from river valley bottoms to pastures higher up. The rapid movements of Hannibal's army from the Po River valley to Apulia, via southern Etruria, Umbria, Picenum, and the central Adriatic coast, in 218, along with the high visibility of cattle among his portable booty, attest to the ubiquitous presence of livestock trails along his route.[17] It was still possible to traverse all central and southern Italy on livestock trails in the first century, when transhumance continued to be widespread.[18] When Varro relates a story in his handbook on farming, written around 37, about the fidelity and perseverance of sheep dogs and involving a flock of sheep newly purchased in lower Umbria whose owner had it moved to Metapontum, many rough kilometers away in Bruttium, he incidentally records the existence of trails in his day that made such long-distance movement possible. Two centuries before, the distances covered were often equally impressive.[19]

Not surprisingly, transhumance required interaction and cooperation between the various Italian peoples along the routes. Over centuries, the interdependence and interaction of lowland and mountainous areas were firmly established. The common practice of transhumant herding within and between the discrete regions of Italy saw the emergence of similar agricultural and social systems involving the primarily farming populations and the seasonally transhumant herders with permanent settlements in the highlands.[20] Interaction between the more settled farmers—the first to adapt the more sophisticated agricultural techniques and newer crops brought by outsiders—and the transhumant herders occurred on a great many levels: the daily exchange of agricultural or animal products and the exchange of information and ideas. Trade followed the same routes. Later, the introduction of mixed crop cultivation did not substantially diminish or alter seasonal movement of herds: Herding continued and with it transhumance. The importance of pasture land to the settled populations of the plain of Latium is evident in a range of details: the Roman tradition of Rome's foundation by Romulus, who assembled a population from Latin shepherds; the shrines or temples to Hercules in Rome; the continued existence of livestock trails, noted later in the chapter; and the wars fought between Romans and Samnites, two Italian groups experiencing particularly rapid population growth, for control of arable and pasture lands between 350 and 260.[21] Over the same period, as communities expanded, the reciprocal interdependence between lowland and mountain dweller became more established and traditional patterns of migration intensified. Long before the Romans expanded across Italy a complicated network of trails and roads facilitated the movement of peoples and the interaction between them to a degree that astonishes the modern observer.

URBAN AND TRIBAL ITALY

(See MAP 2 for towns and sites referenced in this section.) On the eve of Roman expansion, Italy remained a diverse place whose peoples differed with respect to tribal or urban base, oligarchic or monarchic leadership, and subsistence agriculture or market economy.[22] Especially sharp differences in social, political, and economic organization distinguished the urban Etruscans, Latins, and Campanians in particular from the tribal Italians dwelling in the central and southern Apennines, as well as the Ligurians and the migratory Celts. As we shall see, the Romans made a profound impact on and a very selective adjustment to the patterns of life found among both tribal and urban peoples. While archaeologists and historians still have a long way to go in fully uncovering the complexity of these patterns, a review of findings to date is essential to understanding the social and political organization of conquered lands and the reasons for the Romans' success in absorbing them.[23] I begin in this section by sketching in broad outline the basic urban and tribal patterns found in Italy before moving to examine patterns of Roman conquest. Of particular interest is the ongoing adaptation to urban culture by one or another Italian tribal group, often in the process of expanding its territorial reach into the plain. Chief among these were the Hernici, Aequi, and Volsci along the edges of the plain of Latium and northern Campania; the Samnites, who had moved into Campania; and the Lucani, who dominated south Italy in the fourth century.[24]

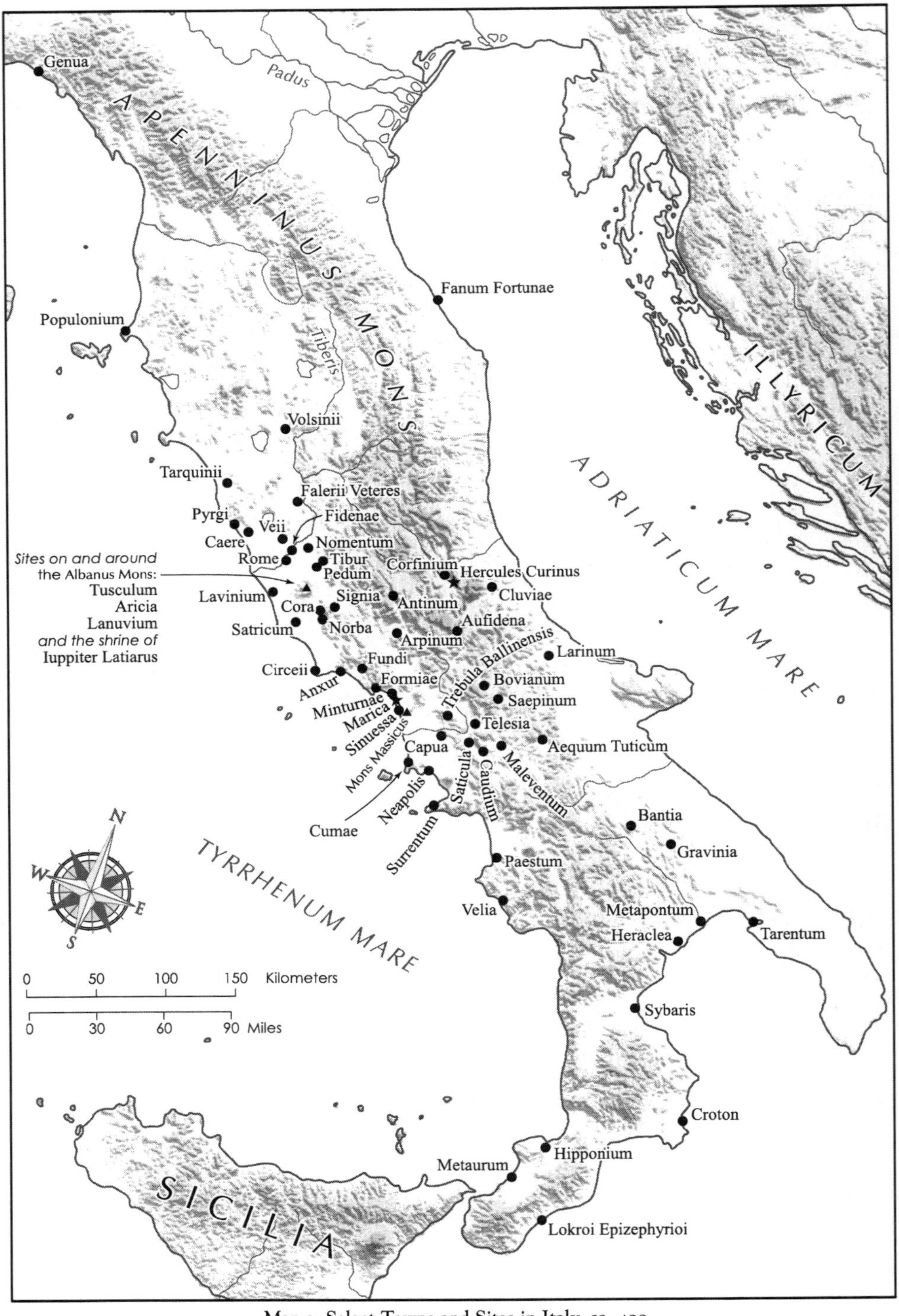

Map 2. Select Towns and Sites in Italy, ca. 400

Patterns of life for the urban peoples of Italy were set before the fourth century. Over the centuries following the beginnings of Greek migration to Italy, roughly 800, Etruscans, Latins, and Campanians adapted and developed the urban culture of the Italiote Greeks.[25] Among these coastal and lowland communities, the arrival of revolutionary ideas about markets and farming, borne by Greek traders and settlers who began to arrive in critical numbers in the eighth century, had promoted profound social and cultural changes, which were accompanied by significant agricultural changes in Italy. Mixed crop cultivation of olives, vines, and wheat was introduced, crops that, prior to the arrival of the Greeks, were seldom cultivated because of the labor investment required. The success of these crops depended on regional markets, found in towns whose proliferation in Italy was spurred by the arrival of the Greeks as well. The combination of vines, olives, and cereals grown for profit and regional markets in cities and towns came to be a dominant feature of Etruria, Latium, and Campania. Markets and mixed crop cultivation were found also in other areas with a strong Greek presence or contacts: in particular Apulia on the Adriatic. The inhabitants of these regions develop other characteristic economic, social, and political structures toward the end of the seventh century. As among the Greeks, life among the Etruscans, Latins, and Campanians centered on urban centers—often walled, beginning in the sixth century, in response to new military techniques—which controlled a surrounding hinterland. These centers provided a marketing node for the agricultural products of the immediate region, as well as for items of longer distance trade. Urban centers also formed the focus of religious and civic life, which unfolded in the public areas and sacred buildings beginning to adorn the city in the last decades of the seventh century.[26]

The impact of this transformation was evident in Rome in a pattern of urbanization perhaps spurred by the more sophisticated Etruscans.[27] The earliest attested stone walls are sometimes dated to the first half of the sixth century, the initial draining and paving of the Forum to the end of the seventh and beginning of the sixth century, and likewise the construction of the original meeting place (Comitium) and Senate House (Curia).[28] But in Rome and elsewhere, other characteristic social and political structures emerged long before.[29] The first appearance of the hierarchic family structure typical of the Roman aristocracy in later centuries—clans, or gentes, in the Roman context—is linked to wider social changes throughout Etruria and Latium in the eighth century.[30] These include the family ownership of land—that is, private ownership as distinct from tribal use of the land—encouraged by the increased agricultural productivity of the land and providing in turn an impetus to the stabilization of the community and the stratification of families in the community. Private landholding is associated with both the emergence of extended family groups as well as relations of dependency between large landholders and people restricted to marginal landholdings.[31] The system of clientage that many scholars believe characterizes Roman social relations throughout the Republic is thought to have its origins in such developments, occurring among the Latins, Etruscans, and Campanians.[32]

By the mid-fourth century, towns and cities had been established for over three centuries along the coasts of southern Italy and in the lowland areas of Italy west of the Apennines: Latium, Etruria, and Campania. In each of them the everyday lives of their inhabitants were geared to the rhythms of the urban-rural environment—the seasonal demands of farm and flock meshed with the civic and religious activities happening in the public and sacred areas of the city. In most, political life was firmly directed by elite families with the equally firm commitment by ordinary citizens. In Rome, for example, the operation of a complicated tripartite political system—assemblies of male citizens, Senate members, and elected officeholders drawn from the same pool as the senators—was fueled by sensibilities attuned to the hierarchic family structure of Rome, whose great clans possessed wealth and status and claimed high office. Although the territorial limits of each city generally determined the boundaries of attachment for the citizens, among cities whose inhabitants belonged to the same language group, such as Latin, Etruscan, or Campanian, individual horizons were broader. A recognized feature of west-central Italy was its "openness to intra- and inter-regional contacts."[33] Elite families in particular formed social and economic links with elite families in other cities. These attachments sometimes transcended cultural affinity as witnessed in the well-known marriage links between elite Romans and Campanians in the third century.[34] Interaction on this level between elite Latin and Etruscan families is attested as early as the seventh century.[35]

Similarly, while the cities of any one cultural and language group were largely independent from each other with regard to formal political linkages, they found shared venues for interaction. Common sanctuaries were a feature of life in central Italy by the sixth century. Some sanctuaries invited commercial interaction with foreign groups, including Phoenicians, Carthaginians, and Greeks.[36] Furthermore, cities often formed leagues for defensive and religious purposes. The Etruscan cities, all independent, were joined in a federation. The Latin cities formed the Latin League for several purposes, among them the celebration once a year of the Latin Jupiter (Jupiter Latiaris), chief god of the Latin people, at a common sanctuary at Albanus mons.[37] Moreover, the citizens of such cities shared mutual privileges: the right to change domicile, the right to intermarry, and the right to make contracts. In this way, as a member of the Latin League in the fourth century, Rome shared privileges with other Latin communities. In turn, the ordinary interaction among different cities included military conflict as cities sought to expand their territories and access to resources across a wider area. The Etruscans first imposed a kind of dominion on Italy to the north, west, and south of Etruria in the sixth century, extending as far south as Capua in Campania. In the fifth and fourth centuries, the Latin cities were seeking more land. In economic prosperity the cities of Italy matched and sometimes rivaled the cities of the Greek world. Among these urban centers, Rome, the largest city in Italy by the fourth century, provided the conditions and genius for a unique experiment in state formation.[38]

In sharp contrast to the urban patterns of life found among the Etruscans, Latins, and Campanians stand the transhumant patterns understood by the Apennine inhabitants of Italy, whose young men were soon to make a vital contribution to Roman military might.[39] Although a similar pattern was shared by the Celts, Ligurians, and others in the Po River valley, the following discussion focuses on the Apennine Italians, who on the one hand played a key role in the success of the Roman expansion, by providing many of its most stalwart military allies, and yet presented the most formidable challenge to the survival of the Roman state by forming the nucleus of the revolt against Rome in 91–89.[40] The very success of the Romans established the commonalities that underlay the desire of the Apennine Italians to win full Roman citizenship or to die in the attempt.

The linguistically diverse Apennine inhabitants occupied lands in central and southern Italy, in the rugged terrain of the Apennines. Commanding territories of varying extent, these peoples formed several distinct tribal groups, chief among them the Oscan-speaking Samnites (Pentri, Hirpini, Caraceni, Caudini, and Frentani) and including also the Oscan-speaking Aurunci, Marrucini, Paeligni, Vestini, Lucani, and Brutti and the Umbrian-speaking Praetutti and Marsi. Among these tribal groups, towns on the scale of towns in Latium, Etruria, or Campania were lacking, for the most part, and markets on the scale we find among plain dwellers were not viable. Instead, the Apennine peoples tended to live in small, mountain valley settlements (vici) that had grown up around shrines, water, or arable land or in scattered habitation across traditional lands (*pagi*).[41] Hill forts (*castella*) commanding mountain passes or valleys with arable and pasture lands provided centers of refuge and defense.[42] While town centers (*oppida*) emerge by the fourth century in areas where regional markets were viable or urban ideas current (for example, the Frentani town of

Larinum near the Adriatic coast), and there are signs of rural settlement around central market towns elsewhere in central Italy (for example, in the south, at Gravinia, modern Botromagno, in the territory of the Lucani), this is not universal.[43] On the west-central coast of Italy and in the coastal plains traversed by migrating herders there are few signs of urban settlement and market development before the Romans appropriated the land.[44] Instead here and elsewhere, common sanctuaries located near cattle trails, often situated along rivers, at river mouths, or at the confluence of valley trails and frequented by more than one group, served as marketing nodes prompted by increased exchange with Etruscan and Greek cities after the seventh century.[45] Such a sanctuary stands at the mouth of the Liris (modern Garigliano) River in northern Campania, sacred to the goddess Marica and used by the migrating Aurunci tribesmen, whose permanent settlements were near Roccamonfina and the Mons Massicus, during the winter pasturage.[46] Another stands at the mouth of the Savus (modern Savone) River.[47] The Paeligni situated a common sanctuary to Hercules Curinus, visited also by the Sabines who lived in the same valley, along a shared cattle trail.[48] Though the Greek influence that spurred the urban development of Etruria, Latium, and Campania is also manifest in central Italy, for instance in the cult of Hercules and the assumption of the Greek deities Castor and Pollux, the Apennine peoples on the whole lived in scattered rural settlements.[49] Engaged profitably in trade and in the exchange of ideas with neighboring groups as well as foreigners—modern archaeologists have expressed amazement over the unexpected levels of wealth found in sixth-century tombs in the Molise and Abruzzo regions, given the unimposing structures associated with settlement—they nonetheless tended to endure the sparse lives of subsistence farmers and herders.[50]

The Apennine world was created by inhabitants reacting to the demands of periodic migration of herds. Nearly all Apennine tribal groups had engaged in a transhumant pastoral existence for centuries. The limited availability of arable or year-round pasture land in the vicinity of permanent settlements brought about an accommodation with the environment that may be termed "traditional." In this traditional accommodation, the Apennine Italians drew their subsistence from a mix of herding and farming. The staple grain crops were emmer wheat, barley, and millet because of their hardiness, ease of cultivation, and varied growing seasons.[51] Arable land was held collectively and its use allotted to individual families by the larger group. Understandably, as the allotments were merely farmed not owned, the land itself was uninheritable, although the use of it might have been. Furthermore, the limited availability of land necessitated the temporary migration of some members of the community, both to pasture lands higher up in the mountains or on the coastal plains and also to arable fields at some distance from the settlement. These treks were undertaken both by animals and their herders, usually young men. Migrating from valley bottoms and lowlands to higher pastures in the Apennines, males often spent up to six months a year with their herds. Absent from families and communities, they lived temporary lives that revolved around the supervision, care, and breeding of their animals and the production of cheese or other products.[52] Where highland dwellers had to move to arable land in lowland regions in order to cultivate cereals—typically traveling long distances, spending days en route—women and children as well as men might participate in the seasonal migration. In all cases, families had adjusted to the movement of family members away from the community and especially to the absence of young men for long periods. While part of a subsistence survival strategy, this migration also helped determine the characteristic family system of the Apennine inhabitants.

Regularly, peoples engaged in transhumant herding in other places throughout the world develop a characteristic family structure that experts have labeled "independent" to distinguish it from the "extended families" characteristic of more sedentary farming populations, which also have strong notions of private ownership of land.[53] Independent families tend to be accustomed to independent action and decision within a larger group, as one might expect in a population that includes herders living temporary and solitary lives for half the year.[54] Their attachment to land was based on use rather than ownership, in contrast to the settled, farming people typically inhabiting the lowlands. When land was held collectively by the tribal group rather than privately by individual families, families were less likely to accumulate wealth in the form of land at the expense of neighbors. Consequently there were probably fewer socialized attachments to community members outside the immediate family group. There were probably fewer vertical ties of dependency and responsibility characteristic of the patron-client relationship attributed by scholars to more sedentary, urbanized Italians, notably Latins. In sum, the fundamental structures of life, that is, family, community, and the relationship to land, took different directions among transhumant Apennine tribesmen and the farming and town-dwelling Etruscans, Campanians, and Latins. The Apennine peoples of central Italy nonetheless also lived in a mesh of relationships with family members, with other families, and with the tribal group at large, enjoying a strong sense of membership in a larger group. If not always a common language, Apennine tribesmen shared with other mountain dwellers regular patterns of seasonal movement, as well as similar customs including religious worship of the gods and goddesses Feronia, Angitia, Hercules, and Mefitis, who watered herds.[55]

Clustered in their permanent settlements in the mountains, nodes of habitation or defense around water, shrines, or arable land collectively held, they also formed federations for religious and defensive purposes.[56] The modern identification of distinct groups notwithstanding, the groups themselves were probably less mindful of distinctive cultural differences.

Movement played a large part in the Apennine connectedness. Ranging over territories of varying extent and indeterminate limits, the Apennine tribesmen recognized territorial limits that were in all likelihood fluid, determined by use and movement along regular routes rather than by the fixed and marked boundaries characteristic of Roman territory.[57] (Modern studies generally assume territorial holdings with fixed boundaries.) Thus, Paeligni, Vestini, and Sabini coexisted in the upper Aternus valley. In contrast to farmers settled permanently on arable land, the Apennine peoples described earlier exhibit a fluid sense of location. Some sense of this fluidity may be gained from the territorial range of certain tribal groups, notably the Ligurians and Gauls, for whom migration was essential for survival. This impressive level of tribal mobility obscured an even more extraordinarily high level of personal and family movement. The obvious territorial range of the misfortunate "Iceman" who succumbed, probably from wounds inflicted by attackers, in the late Neolithic to reemerge from an Alpine glacier in north Italy in the 1990s is clear indication that long treks were common. There were to be sure traditional places of settlement in traditional lands. In the territorial range of each tribal group, settlements grew up for reasons of defense, as we have seen, or for control of arable land and routes of communication, or around springs, shrines, or graves. These were villages, around them regions of scattered rural settlement. But these locations were determined by a sense of family and tribal membership and continuity.

Even in the same valley different tribes might take different directions. An idea of traditional routes may be gained by examining the adaptation of alphabets. Most Apennine groups adapted either the Etruscan or the Greek alphabets to their languages, but some used the Latin alphabet.[58] The use of writing among the Marsi, for instance, was evidently tied to fourth-century Roman contact.[59] Latin letter forms were in vogue also among some of the Frentani, Samnites whose traditional lands were adjacent to the lands of the Pentrian Samnites.[60] But they moved on different routes than their Samnite kin, the Pentri, following instead the same routes as the Marrucini, the Paeligni, and the Marsi, who lived to the north and west. Indeed, the Frentani were never in the Samnite League but were perhaps members of the Sabellian League (with the Paeligni, Marsi, and Marrucini), which signed a treaty with Rome in 304.[61] Likewise the Paeligni, Marsi, Marrucini, and the Sabini, who coexisted in the upper Aternus River valley with the Paeligni, Latinized early on.[62] The Samnites of the Samnite League on the other hand moved south and west toward Apulia and Campania. They adapted the Greek, not the Etruscan, alphabet. The cultural and interest divide between two Samnite tribes, the Frentani and the Pentri, in the lower and upper Biferno (ancient Tifernus) River valley respectively confirms that each group pursued different routes in search of pasture and subsistence.

Alongside significant differences between urban and tribal Italians there are also significant commonalities. In particular, continual movement seems to have characterized the lives of the majority of Italians, whether urban or tribal, as changing patterns of resource availability led one group or another to move from place to place, some for short periods of time, others for good.[63] In his narrative of Roman expansion across Italy Livy regularly notes the sequence of possessors of various locales—for instance, the Roman colony established at Luna in 177 was located on land taken from Ligurians that had previously belonged to the Etruscans.[64] A Roman colony at Gravisca, in Etruscan territory, was on a site previously held by people of Tarquinii.[65] Already in the sixth century, as noted, the Etruscans expanded beyond their center in the Tyrrhenian plain. In the fourth century several groups, urban and tribal, were in the process of expansion with two noteworthy corollaries. Most notable of course is the Roman conquest of all Italy. But equally important is the encounter of tribal Italians with urban culture. The movement of one group over the traditional lands of another—the Samnites, above all, into Campania but also the Volsci and Aequi into Latium and northern Campania and the Lucani across south Italy (during their expansion a secondary group formed, the Bruttii)—ongoing in different regions, had dramatic consequences for ordinary life, even before the Romans entered the picture. Inevitably the composition of a local population changed with the admixture of new members. By the mid-fourth century, the Campanians, for example, were a long-time mix of Italians indigenous to the plain, emigrating Greeks, and migrating Aurunci and Samnites. Some tribal groups began to urbanize, notably the Samnites in Campania but also the Volsci in northern Campania, whose towns were taken by the Romans, the Aequi, whose towns were destroyed by the Romans, the Sabines and the Hernici.[66] But while some Samnites moved into the urban centers of Campania, becoming "hellenized" like the Etruscans and the Latins as they adapted the urban culture of the Greek, others remained in their traditional Apennine locale or in scattered rural settlements in Apulia.

In the midst of these ongoing and common social changes early in the fourth century, the Romans emerged from their corner of Latium to embark on a course of expansion across Italy. While Roman action against the Etruscan city of Veii in 396 marks a beginning of steady Roman expansion, the effort intensifies during the wars against the Samnites and Latins between 343 and 338. From then until 218, the beginning of the Second Punic War, the Romans gradually brought most of the Italian peoples under Rome's dominion, overwhelming in turn and at times with considerable effort other Latins, Etruscans, Volsci, Aequi, Sabines, and Campanians dwelling in and around the coastal plains of western Italy, as well as the Umbrians, Picentes, Ligurians, and Celts to the north and center, the Samnites and various other tribal groups living in the central Apennine region and south Italy, and the Italiote Greeks in south Italy.[67] Among the important changes brought by Roman conquerors as they expanded in Italy were alliances formed with other inhabitants of the peninsula. Between ca. 350 and 218, most of the peoples of Italy became allies of Rome at different times and under different circumstances.[68] But the relationships that were established by treaty between Rome and the Italians always placed each Italian people in a dependent position, whether they were Italian allies (*socii*) or allies of the Latin Name (*socii Latinis nominis*).[69] Defensive in aim, the alliances entailed one primary obligation: the supply of troops for service in the Roman army. While the demands and losses engendered by the Second Punic War were onerous, in particular straining the relationship between the Romans and their Italian allies, they were not so high as to prevent the Romans from consolidating their dominion in Italy in a number of ways after their victory over Hannibal in 202, including the confiscation of even more land from some of the peoples of south Italy who had assisted Hannibal. Reinforced by the common endeavor of successful conquest, the expanding Roman state on the whole flourished. The land and peoples of Italy, however, were transformed in the process.

ORGANIZING THE NEW LANDS

(See map 3 for colonies referenced in this section.) Laying claim to the productive lands of Italy, the Romans embarked at once on a systematic process of confiscation and incorporation. By 218 they had annexed territory held by near and far neighbors in an area extending south to the Silarus River at the southern edge of Campania, east across central Italy to the Adriatic Sea, and north to the Po River basin. At the end of the Second Punic War the Romans took still more land from cities in south Italy.[70] As subjected Latins, Italians, and others ceded jeopardous amounts of territory over a period of 140 years, the Romans realized a tenfold increase in their own lands.[71] In time this massive shift in vital resources would put the continuing survival of the peoples of Italy in question. For Rome, however, the immediate challenge was the effective transfer of these resources, many far from Latium.

Map 3. Roman and Latin Colonies, 338–100

From the early days of conquest the principal mechanism of transfer was the distribution of parcels on newly acquired territory to settlers.[72] Although land was sometimes distributed on an individual basis (*viritim adsignare*), land grants in colonies were more common and indeed had a long history: already in the fifth and early fourth centuries the Romans and other Latins jointly established colonies on lands in and around the plain of Latium that they reclaimed from the encroaching Aequi and Volsci.[73] Following the Latin War the Romans amplifed the practice, founding colonies initially in Latium (Antium, 338, and Tarracina, 329), which were known as citizen colonies because the settlers retained the rights and privileges of Roman citizens optimo iure. But the Romans also established so-called Latin colonies, which joined Latin and Roman settlers in new foundations on annexed land outside Latium. The earliest of these were situated in the corridor along the Liris River between Latium and Campania (Cales, 334; Fregellae, 328; Luceria, 314; Suessa, Pontia, and Saticula, 313; Interamna, 312; and Sora and Alba, 303) and in the lowland valleys of the central Apennines in territory annexed from the Aequi, north of the Fucine Lake (Alba Fucens), and from the Samnites, between Samnium and Apulia (Luceria).[74] More distant settlements accompanied third-century and early-second-century appropriations of Italian land, scattering Romans across the peninsula.

While the placement of colonies and the availability of land for distribution necessarily hinged on the chances of conquest, settlement was by no means haphazard. Through the agency of individual commanders, the Senate, or the Roman people, the state assigned land to selected citizens and Latins—usually veterans of recent campaigns. Specifically, the Senate might issue a decree on its own initiative, confirm by decree the arrangements made by a commander in the field, or instruct an officeholder to bring the matter to the people.[75] Or an officeholder might take the initiative to present a public law proposal regarding colony foundation or land settlement to the people.[76] The specific agent of a given assignment generally emerged from the circumstances of the day. Although recipients of land grants might migrate on their own initiative to individual allotments, the so-called viritane allotments, more commonly the migration of settlers to colonies, were planned and assisted by the state. Numbers involved were calculated: citizen or Roman colonies were small, including generally three hundred colonists and their families; Latin colonies, generally farther from Rome, were larger, containing anywhere from two thousand to six thousand colonists and their families.[77] Although we are not provided with similar details by our sources, the number of individual grants was no doubt similarly projected.[78] No matter how achieved, the settlement of conquered lands was a matter of societywide interest and obeyed a common community mandate.[79]

For that reason, the visual patterns of Roman land settlement across Italy are suggestive. Map 4 superimposes the areas of colonization and individual land parcels, arranged in increments by region, on a population map of pre-Roman Italy. Between the fourth and second centuries, an ever widening spiral of new foundations radiated from the city of Rome.[80] Especially thick layers of settlement occurred between 338 and 283 (thirteen Latin and six citizen colonies), mostly in west-central Italy; between 232 and 218 (the viritane settlements of 232 and two Latin colonies) in Picenum and the Po River basin; and between 199 and 180 (fourteen citizen colonies and four Latin colonies) mostly in south Italy and the Po River basin. The pattern is testimony to the growing expanse of the ager Romanus, Roman state land, as it took in adjacent lands confiscated from defeated Volsci, Aequi, Latin, Etruscan, Sabine, and Campanian communities and discontiguous parcels appropriated from defeated Italian, Greek, and Gallic peoples all across the peninsula. More important, Roman settlement wrapped irrepressibly around the detached nations of Italy like a shoot from the sturdy honeysuckle.

Newly settled ager Romanus eventually acquired a distinctive appearance. Wherever the Romans determined to establish colonies on annexed land or to grant the land to Roman citizens, Latins, or sometimes Italians on an individual basis, teams of surveyors went out to mark the land, sent from the staffs of the colony's three men for leading out the colony (*tresviri coloniae deducendae*), provided for by Senate decree, edict, or enactment, or the ten commissioners associated with viritane grants.[81] The surveyors first meticulously fitted the landscape to a grid pattern whose boundaries were visibly marked out by lanes, trenches, stone walls, and boundary markers (*termini*).[82] The grid emanated from a focal intersection of two lines, the *cardo maior* (running north-south) and the *decumanus maior* (running east-west). New towns were laid out in accordance with the grid and centered on the focal intersection. The procedure, known as centuriation, imposed squares of varying size on the land—two hundred square iugera was standard although the size varied from place to place—within which settlers received their plots, also of varying size, by lot. Centuriation developed in pace with Roman expansion across Italy.[83] The earliest examples accompany early settlements before the Latin War, but not all settlements were so treated. Centuriation was becoming systematized when seen at the Roman colony of Tarracina, established in 338 on the Tyrrhenian coast and on the ager Falernus of Campania, where the Romans also established settlements in the late fourth century. The procedure is more consistently developed in Cisalpine Gaul, settled by individual settlers and colonists in the third century, and likewise in south Italy, where ager publicus distributed under the lex Sempronia

Roman and Latin Colonies by Name and Date of Foundation

Colony	Date	Type
Antium	338	Roman
Ostia	ca. 338	Roman
Cales	334	Latin
Tarracina	329	Roman
Fregellae	328	Latin
Luceria	314	Latin
Pontia	313	Latin
Saticula	313	Latin
Suessa	313	Latin
Interamna	312	Latin
Sora	303	Latin
Alba Fucens	303	Latin
Narnia	299	Latin
Carsioli	298	Latin
Minturnae	295	Roman
Sinuessa	295	Roman
Venusia	291	Latin
Hatria	290–86	Latin
Sena Gallica	289–83	Roman
Paestum	273	Latin
Beneventum	268	Latin
Ariminium	268	Latin
Cosa	264	Latin
Castrum Novum	264	Roman
Firmum	264	Latin
Aesernia	263	Latin
Alsium	247	Roman
Pyrgi	247	Roman
Fregenae	245	Roman
Brundisium	244	Latin
Spoletium	241	Latin
Cremona	218	Latin
Placentia	218	Latin
Sipontum	194	Roman
Volturnum	194	Roman
Puteoli	194	Roman
Buxentum	194	Roman
Croton	194	Roman
Liternum	194	Roman
Salernum	194	Roman
Tempsa	194	Roman
Copia	193	Latin
Vibo	192	Latin
Bononia	189	Latin
Potentia	184	Roman
Pisaurum	184	Roman
Parma	183	Roman
Mutina	183	Roman
Saturnia	183	Roman
Aquileia	181	Latin
Graviscae	181	Roman
Luna	177	Roman
Auximum	128?	Roman
Heba	128?	Roman
Fabrateria Nova	124	Roman
Minervia	122	Roman
Neptunia	122	Roman
Dertona	ca. 109	Roman
Eporedia	100	Roman

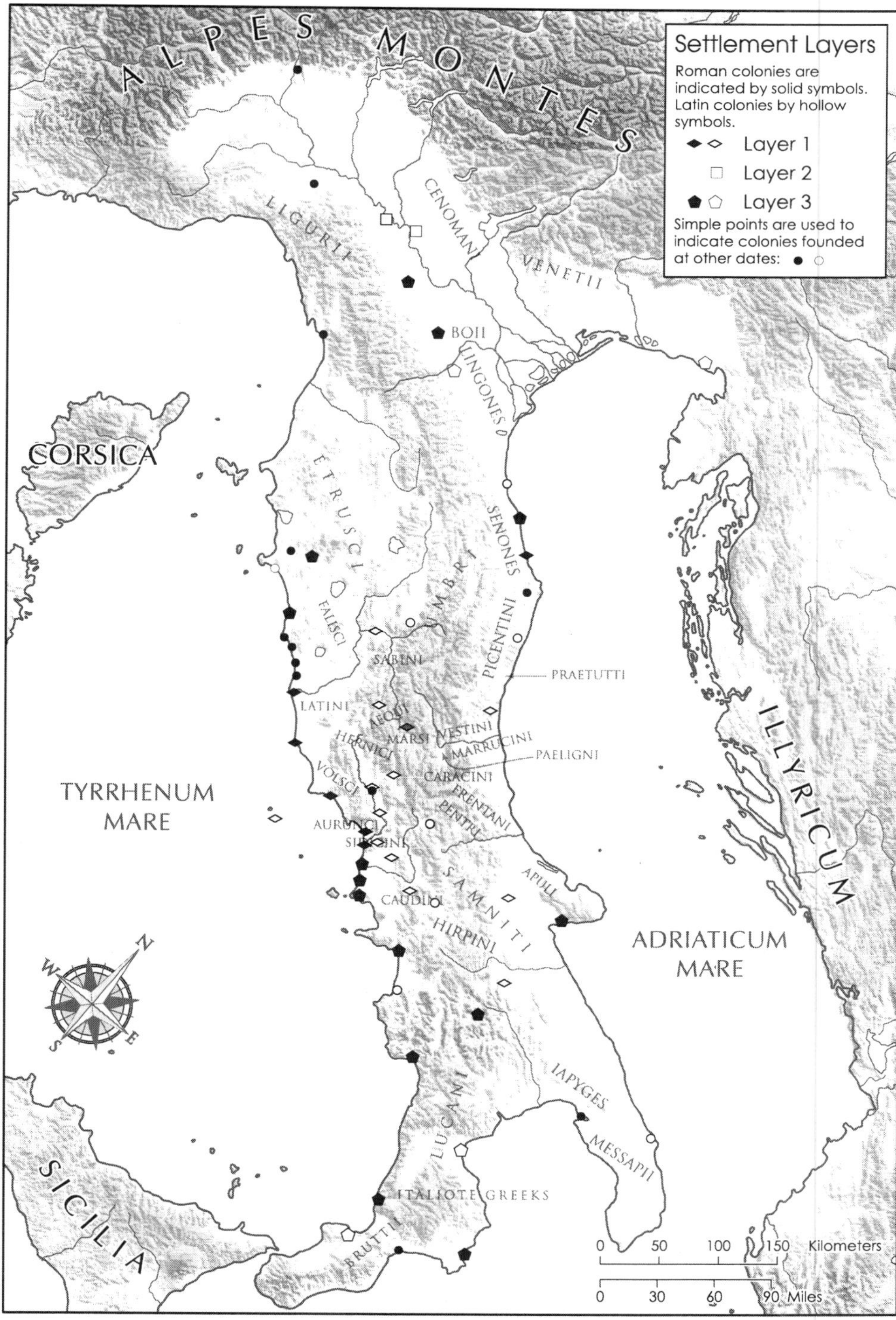

Map 4. Layers of Roman Settlement, 338–100

agraria of C. Gracchus of 123 was centuriated beforehand. Surviving boundary markers have been found at a number of locations.[84] The Romans developed not only the procedure, mastered by surveyors (*agrimensores*), but also a highly complex system of agrarian law to which it pertained.[85]

It has been suggested that the Romans used centuriation deliberately to put their mark especially on land annexed from difficult enemies.[86] From the Roman perspective, centuriation imposed the ritual divisions of the skies used by the Roman augurs to determine the gods' disposition on appropriate occasions on the ground, on ager Romanus.[87] When seen from the air, a vantage first revealed in air reconnaissance photos taken for military purposes in 1914–18 and 1939–44, the extent of centuriation in some regions of Italy—the Tavoliere in Apulia, annexed in 200 and settled thereafter, shows the centuriation most clearly—provides striking visual testimony of the Romans' imposition of order on their physical world. Centuriation also served to standardize measurement, thus facilitating and rationalizing the process of comparing output, hence the value, of different parcels of land.[88] It is relevant that the developing use and Roman production of coinage, another more obvious medium for rationalizing exchange, parallels the development of centuriation. Whatever the Roman motives prompting centuriation, a significant improvement in food output generally followed.

Much of this improvement in output was the result of improvements in drainage, which allowed the Romans to use the land more intensively than former possessors had. Drainage of flat lands along rivers and in low-lying plains, previously unproductive beyond the requirements of subsistence farming and herding, permitted the cultivation of cereals, vines, or olive trees, producing grain, wine, or olive oil for the market.[89] Excavations in northern Campania, a region whose domination the Romans contested with the Samnites in the late fourth and third centuries and one of the regions earliest settled by the Romans, reveal signs of such drainage before the land was surveyed and distributed.[90] At Gravinia in southern Italy (Apulia), Roman ditches were laid in before the land confiscated from the local population after the Second Punic War was surveyed, boundaries marked and colonies founded.[91] These state-managed drainage projects, undertaken before settlement, attest to the Romans' intention to increase their arable land resources by appropriating and settling the territories of conquered neighbors.[92]

New settlers therefore transformed patterns of land use. Above all they created a stable food supply in some areas that previously had been utilized primarily for herding and subsistence farming. Mixed crop cultivation of olives, vines, and cereals appears to have been the regular mode of farming in the areas brought under cultivation by the Romans, terrain and climate permitting, whether in the environs of Rome, in southern Etruria, Latium, the foothills of the central Apennines, or farther afield.[93] The kinds of land uses envisaged by the Romans in particular areas are indicated by the size of the allotments reported for different colonies.[94] In Roman colonies, colonists were usually allotted small plots—two, five, six, and eight iugera are reported and once ten iugera was reported to colonists at Saturnia, established in 183—while in Latin colonies the plots were generally larger. The size of allotments appears to be determined by the cultivation or pasturage potential of the land. Thus, allotments in regions suited to extensive polyculture—that is, arable lowland such as that found south of the Po River and in other river valleys (when drainage or irrigation was applied) as well as in broad coastal plains—tended to be much larger than allotments in regions in which farming was probably secondary to herding. This was the case in the citizen colonies along the coast, sometimes called "maritime colonies," whose settlers had relatively small plots but probably greater access to common pasture land (*ager compascuus*). The range of sizes demonstrates something of the complexity of any explanation for Roman expansion: at stake in varying degrees were the necessity of securing a food supply, of defense, and of encouraging members of an expanding Latin and Roman population to migrate to new homes. In brief, a variety of measures applied when the Romans allocated use of the land and determined the size of the lots. Among them was the kind of agriculture a given area could support.

Concurrently, Roman victories brought changes in the existing urban settlement of Italy. Prior to the Roman annexations of Italian land, autonomous towns and cities were for the most part restricted to the plains and coastal regions, as we have seen. After annexation, this urban pattern was extended and transformed by the foundation, sometimes deliberate and sometimes spontaneous, of new towns (oppida). New towns were often built for settlers in colonies either because the Romans destroyed any preexisting settlement or because none was there in the first place. The Romans destroyed all the settlements of the Aequi in the fourth century, but not all those of the Volsci. One, Antium, received Roman citizen colonists in 338.[95] Roman settlement in the lower Liris River valley, an important communication corridor leading out of the central Apennines, introduced urban centers for the first time.[96] Excavators at Fregellae, the Latin colony founded in 328 near the juncture of the Liris and Sacco Rivers, have found no signs of settlement in the area prior to the arrival of the Romans. Indeed, throughout this important corridor between Latium and Campania, settlement of any kind was sparse before the arrival of the Romans, who not only undertook drainage projects, as noted earlier, but established three Latin colonies along the Liris River in the late fourth century, first at Fregellae (328), then downriver at Interamna (312), and finally upriver at Sora (303).[97] Colonies were also at times imposed on existing Italian towns. The Latin colony of Luceria was established at a preexisting Samnite fortified settlement (castellum). From one oppidum, Aquileia, founded in 181 at the head of the Adriatic Gulf on the site of a briefly preexisting Gallic town (it was established in 189), comes a rare surviving frieze commemorating the foundation that depicts priests leading the oxen around the town site in order to plow the sacred perimeter (*pomerium*) encircling all Roman towns. Thus if a town was already in place, the Romans reconfigured it in Roman fashion.[98]

The foundation of such new or reconstituted towns regularly accompanied colonization. A less deliberate consequence of the extension of state land by confiscation and of granting parcels of state land to Roman citizens on an individual basis was to spur the creation of villages and towns, providing local market and community centers for far-flung Romans. Some, *conciliabula*, appeared spontaneously; others, fora, were established by magistrates along the roads linking Rome and Roman state land whose construction belongs to the same period or by conquering commanders.[99] The relationship between these towns and Rome is pursued in chapter 6.

As a result of Roman settlement, the varied landscape of Italy acquired still more variety, in the third and second centuries, in the complicated mix of large and small holdings constituting rural habitation.[100] The complexity of such patterns of settlement is very apparent in a sparsely inhabited region of Italy, the Biferno River (ancient Tifernus River) valley, running from the Adriatic coast to the eastern ridge of the central Apennines, for which we have somewhat detailed archeological evidence.[101] The surveys and surface excavations carried out in the1970s and later indicate that more intensive settlement of the lower valley began only in the second century, coinciding with Roman land confiscations in the area made after the Second Punic War. In an early publication, the excavator Graeme Barker speculated that intensive settlement thus is probably related to these confiscations.[102] Settlement by whom? Perhaps the increased density of settlement is due to an influx of settlers, Romans or others, on confiscated land. Or perhaps settlement reflects changing settlement and life patterns among the Frentani, whose traditional lands these were, as a result of agricultural changes in the area. The increasing prosperity and market importance of the nearby Frentani town of Larinum may be associated with the same phenomenon. The fact that excavators cannot always determine with absolute certainty whether (or at what point in time) increased settlement was local or Roman, based on the excavated remnants that reveal culture, is a significant measure of the degree of absorption or assimilation experienced by the

Frentani that followed Roman expansion (see chapter 5) or of the existence of a common culture.

In any event, the increased settlement is clearly owed to increased farming in a region devoted also to herding. Based on excavation data, mostly from the upper Biferno valley, home to Pentrian Samnites, which touches the edge of the Apennines, farmstead and villa sites were clustered in parts of the valley that could be easily plowed.[103] The land was used primarily for cereal and legume cultivation and stock raising. There were few vines and no olives in the upper valley because the climate was not suited.[104] In the lower valley, however, there is some suggestion of mixed crop cultivation of vines, olives, and cereals. Farm sites here were located close to fields, indicating a desire to maximize efforts by living close to arable land.[105] There is strong evidence also for transhumant herding in the Biferno valley. Seasonal campsites were situated on the valley floors, where the soil was too heavy to plow but provided good grazing. While the owners of the villa sites identified by archeologists on the edges of these areas were presumably involved in stock rearing, the seasonal camps might also have been used by long-distance herders. Trails from Apulia to the summer pastures of the Apennines cross the Biferno valley.

A similar pattern is visible in the river valleys of west-central Italy, in the region stretching from Rome to the Silarus River to the eastern rim of the Liris River valley—that is, from the northern edge of the plain of Latium to the southern edge of Campania and inland to the foothills of the Apennines—where rural habitation had increased well before the second century. This was the first area extensively colonized by Rome as well as the location of some of the earliest urban development in Italy. Here the foundation of new towns was accompanied by a denser rural population.[106] Rural habitation came to include luxurious villas, large and small farmsteads, and hovels attesting to both large- and small-scale market farming as well as subsistence agriculture.[107] Villas, few in number until the late second century, obviously represent the country dwellings of the largest landowners, wealthy men whose holdings in the first century, known primarily from narrative reports, were scattered across different regions in Italy and produced cash crops of oil, grain, or vines. As in the Biferno River valley, the identity of the occupants of smaller farmsteads and hovels, lesser landholders, whose presence is amply confirmed in excavation reports, is unknown. Whether free or slave, tenants or freeholders, certainly they were people of a demonstrably lower status and level of wealth as measured in the size of their presumed habitations.

At the center of the complex networks of settlement and land use were markets, both regional and local, which built up in layers corresponding to the phases of Roman settlement.[108] Rural settlement and agricultural change were always supported by changes in market conditions. In turn, the pockets of cultivation created by Roman expansion were intensified by the establishment of markets in the various new towns (oppida, conciliabula, fora) associated with settlement. There were many such regional markets, serving as nodes of commerce and exchange for Apennine Italians, we may imagine, in a similar fashion as the pre-Roman sanctuaries, which served as market centers for these mountain dwellers. By the first century, when permanent calendars were put up in town centers, markets were regularly held in different towns on different days in an effort to regularize economic life throughout Italy. To be sure, regional markets were already in existence in Italian towns, especially in Etruria, Campania, and south Italy, or were given a new impetus as a result of Roman expansion.[109] Yet the new towns brought a significantly Roman dimension to the relationship between markets and land use.

SOCIAL AND ECONOMIC ADJUSTMENT TO ROMAN EXPANSION

In their expansion across Italy, between the fourth and second centuries, the Romans conquered a wide variety of peoples, each with their own history and traditions. Following conquest, the conditions of Roman contact and the Roman perception of a group's history and traditions, in particular its amenity to Roman ways, determined patterns of absorption by the conquerors. In this process the Romans often displayed an uncanny talent for adopting courses of action that inevitably strengthened them and weakened neighboring peoples at a fundamental level.

Settling Romans on annexed Italian land is a case in point. The establishment of citizen colonies along the Tyrrhenian coast, in positions indicated by the Carthaginians' offensive and commercial domination of sea routes in the third century, enabled the Romans to set up a defensive net around the coasts of Italy. At the same time these defenses formed a military buffer between the Romans and other Italians, specifically the Samnites, and brought the arable land essential for the maintenance of their own food supply under Roman control. To these ends, colonies enabled the Romans to control both the necessary winter pasture areas used by migrating groups and the arable land on which the local population depended for existence. The establishment of Roman colonies in the foothills of the central Apennines and in mountain valleys surrounding Samnium achieved similar aims: by settling these areas the Romans controlled arable land and pastures essential both to their own expanding population and to the Samnites. Earlier in the fourth century, the Samnites had themselves encroached on the lowlands adjacent to their mountainous region, in Campania and in Latium, when the Romans intervened. The series of wars between the Samnites and the Romans, settled irresolutely by treaty, were wars for control of arable and pasture lands.[110] After the establishment of colonies, seasonal migration between the lowland pastures and pastures inland was no longer the same regular movement governed by tradition and convention, entailing the mutual advantage of groups occupying winter and summer pasture areas. For the lowlands were increasingly, from the late fourth century, under new management. This was the case in the coastal colonies, which more than anything ensured Roman control of the important winter pasture areas of the central Apennine peoples.[111] A corollary to the Romans strengthening their strategic position on the Italian peninsula by moving out into surrounding lands was the impact of that movement on the integrity of many allied and citizen communities.

The most extreme disruptions followed difficult wars, as the Romans destroyed towns and cities, exterminated or enslaved entire populations and confiscated their lands, or relocated the former enemies. Fairly close to Rome, some of the Aequi and Volsci were eliminated in the fourth century. By decision of the Roman people, in 319, the recently incorporated but rebellious Latin town of Satricum was punished by disenfranchisement. Several years earlier, in 323, the people had rejected a more extreme bill directed at newly Roman, rebellious Tusculum, which envisaged the extermination of the town's male population and the enslavement of its women and children.[112] Also in the fourth century, the population of Falerii Veteres, situated on a defensible plateau in southern Etruria controlling a primary route running south to north across the eastern edge of Faliscan territory, ager Faliscus, was relocated to a new site on the plain that became the town of Falerii Novi.[113] Roman settlement in the area followed, rendered more secure by the elimination of an Etruscan strong point.[114] In the third century, in 283, the Romans established Sena Gallica near the Adriatic coast at the southern edge of the Po River basin, in the territory of the Senones, a Gallic tribal group, but not before the Romans had exterminated all male Senones and sold the women and children into slavery.[115] Fifty years later, in 232, viritane allotments were made on the land of the Senones, too, by enactment of the Roman people (lex Flaminia).[116] Meanwhile, in 269 a large portion of the Picentine population, which had rebelled against the Roman annexation of lands in the area, was relocated to a stretch of the Tyrrhenian coast between Surrentum and the Silarus River, taken earlier from the Lucani. The region was called henceforth ager Picentinus.[117]

Picentine land in Picenum became public property of the Roman people. In 180, the proconsular commander in Liguria, M. Baebius Tamphilus, relocated the Apuani Ligurians to Samnium, and, in 179, the consul Q. Fulvius Flaccus relocated about forty thousand Insaures Ligurians to Roman state land in Apulia.[118] In all these areas the removals or exterminations opened the way for new settlers drawn from the Roman and Latin peoples.

While it takes little imagination to envision the impact of extermination on group cohesion and identity, considerably more is needed to envision the consequences of relocation. For all the relocated peoples of Italy, and others elsewhere similarly treated, we can imagine that forced relocation must have had a devastating effect on social organization and on individual lives and relationships, making it unlikely that they would again challenge the Romans. Determining the impact of relocation in a more detailed way is difficult. Nevertheless, the attempt must be made if we are to understand the fundamental changes that made possible the emergence of a Roman state in Italy whose inhabitants shared the most fundamental Roman beliefs. Doubtless, not only the populations directly involved were affected but also the local populations in the regions to which the Romans relocated them. As a result of Roman confiscation followed by an infusion of Roman or Latin settlers and sometimes by a local purging, the population in these regions both changed and increased, often dramatically. But what kinds of relationships were shattered for those who were forcibly moved, and what new relationships were formed?

To some degree such peoples retained a sense of group identity. While much of the town at Falerii Veteres was destroyed, the old temples and shrines continued to stand and function as the primary site of ritual for the Faliscan population, which had been relocated in Falerii Novi. As late as the first century the Faliscan population worshipped at the temples of Juno and Mercury and other shrines.[119] More significantly they maintained a sense of Faliscan identity. The relocated Picentes gave support to the Carthaginians during the war with Hannibal and were punished by the Romans. Clearly they were still functioning as, and seen by the Romans as, an identifiable, viable group. We might imagine that the relocation of forty-seven thousand Ligurians near Beneventum was absolutely disruptive of the traditional customs and networks of the Ligurians. Torn from the shrines of their gods and graves of their ancestors, they were set down in a Samnite frontier.[120] Yet it was a similar region in respect to the most important dimension of their previous lives: throughout Samnium, as Liguria, transhumance was the way of life. A sense of Ligurian identity continued into the second century CE, judging by the persistence of Ligurian names. Clearly cult, family, and custom persisted on some level, even when a population was forcibly moved.[121] Some accommodation had been found by the relocated peoples, which permitted their survival.

The nature and extent of this accommodation in the face of severe disruption are most easily seen in the case of Rome's new Italian allies from whom the Romans simply confiscated land. Forced to relinquish their most arable lands to the dominant partner in a new alliance, the Romans, entire communities were henceforth restricted to a portion of their previous holdings. At the same time, young men of the community were obliged to leave their regular routines of farming and herding for obligatory service with the Roman army, the demands of which in terms of manpower and time increased dramatically during the Second Punic War and the century that followed.[122] The adjustment resulting from these demands was nonetheless minor compared with the broadscale transformation caused by the looming presence of economic and political structures almost exclusively Roman.[123] The impact of Roman and Latin settlement on the patterns of traditional life among Apennine dwellers, transhumant herders, was especially momentous, and their experiences may be seen in many ways as typical of the Roman impact on all the peoples of Italy and of the kind of transformation forced on Rome's allies.

To an extent never seen before with the territorial expansion of any earlier group in Italy, Roman settlement widely redirected the subsistence strategies of transhumant herders by choking off the traditional agricultural and pastoral system of most central Apennine peoples. Accustomed to moving seasonally from their summer pastures in the mountains to winter pastures in the lowland and accustomed also to subsistence farming on arable lowland, the central Apennines inhabitants quickly found their traditional lowland haunts closed to them as the newcomers appropriated the best land, bringing new forms of land use and economic interaction. In the lowlands, pasture areas were not open for use in the same ways they had been before. Instead, herders were liable to pay grazing taxes for the use of ager publicus, which were collected locally—usually, we think, by Roman officials in the lowland or valley towns serving as Roman administrative centers, many of which appear to have been situated near the trails used in seasonal migration of herds—and paid into the Roman treasury.[124] Or the use of pasture lands and arable was mediated through individuals who leased their own land. Imagine the predicament of migrating herdsmen traversing the Liris River valley after 300 who encountered three Latin towns and much denser rural settlement along the way. Thus the continued practice of transhumant herding required the annual payment of a tax or the renting of pasture and farmland directly from private owners. Similarly when Apennine dwellers sought lowland arable for subsistence farming, new avenues of access had to be uncovered, compatible with Roman ownership and rents. The subsequent adjustment rippled through mountain villages and tribal communities, disrupting life on all levels, especially that of the family. And similar disruption undoubtedly occurred in Italy's cropland areas.

Inevitably, previous inhabitants were dispossessed and forced to withdraw to marginal land, less suited for farming, wherever confiscated land was surveyed by the Romans and allotted to settlers or rented to new possessors. The territorial boundaries of transhumant herders, which though fluid nonetheless had enclosed enough land resources needed to sustain the particular group through herding and subsistence farming, were now restricted. Where private property rights were already established, as in Etruria, Umbria, Apulia, and other urbanized areas, fixed territorial limits were drastically diminished. Previous inhabitants in brief had fewer land resources at their disposal. Of necessity some, the least powerful, retreated to marginal lands in marsh areas, on rocky slopes and ridges, and other inhospitable reaches.[125] While it is difficult to find the remains of such settlements throughout all of Europe—none was built for posterity—remnants of apparent hovels have been noted in Etruria, away from the Roman roads cutting through productive lands holding the large estates that produced grapes and olives.[126] Although the newcomers never seem to have deliberately imposed Roman legal standards of landholding on preexisting landholding patterns, disruption was unavoidable under the circumstances.[127] To the modern observer, the Roman impact creates a considerable dilemma that deepens over time. How in particular were the Romans able to disrupt local patterns of existence among the same groups that sent vast numbers of their young men to fight Rome's wars?

In the teeth of catastrophe, Italians developed strategies of accommodation. Mountain-dwelling herders in particular, faced with want and with restricted access to pasture lands and to tribal lands, were forced to seek out alternative means of survival. Fortuitously the arrival of the Romans created new options for livelihood as well as the necessity for seeking them out. New agricultural practices initiated by the Romans brought a stable food supply as the new Roman and Latin towns provided a focus for locals trying to confront an uncertain world. At the regional markets associated with these towns, individuals could exchange their labor for cash or produce. Some groups developed rather unpredictable occupational patterns as a result. The Marsi, Marrucini, and Paeligni living on the western slope of the Apennines, for example, volunteered to serve as oarsmen in Scipio Africanus's expedition to North Africa in 204. How had such land-locked people come by this maritime skill? Did they go from making ships' masts to working in the boats?[128] The demand for rowers in Rome's serial fleets during the First Punic War, and subsequently the possibilities of a labor market in an expanding world, offers one explanation.

But military service provided the prime alternative for survival to people loosed from the land and overwhelmed by Rome. Although our sources often record the bitter objections of local Italian leaders to the military service required by treaty, they also reveal a high level of involvement by Italian males in the Roman army. In the latter part of the third century, when the Romans faced their biggest military challenge from the Carthaginians and Hannibal during the Second Punic War, the Latin and Italian allies formed nearly two-thirds of the total Roman military force. The Abruzzi tribesmen, Samnites, Lucanians, and Apulians (Messapians), called on regularly in times of military need, formed more than half of the allied contribution.[129] The number of troops the Italians eventually supplied, between 218 and 91, the period for which the best evidence exists, was extraordinarily high and was the prime factor in Rome's successful conquest of the Mediterranean.

Why did so many go, voluntarily? It is only within the context of family disruption and survival accompanying the arrival of the Romans that the high level of involvement in military service becomes understandable. Roman military service provided young men with a means of family survival—like service as mercenary soldiers, a common alternative throughout the Mediterranean.[130] Obviously, booty, through successful campaigns, and land allotments in Italy—albeit less land than Romans and Latins received—were powerful incentives to military service in hard times. Most important, to transhumant peoples military service represented an extension of traditional patterns of male departure and return and provided, therefore, a means of survival that was less disruptive of traditional family patterns than other alternatives. Seasonal migration required younger males in Apennine and Alpine communities to stay away for up to six months each year. Over time their respective societies had adjusted to such departures. The departure of youths for increasingly longer periods when called by the Roman military levy similarly required the development of a new ploy in an age-old migratory adaptation to their world. During the second century, when the Romans conquered the eastern end of the Mediterranean, terms of military service for Romans and Italians were extended to an estimated six years on average. While onerous and at times resented, the regular military service required by treaties between their communities and Rome still represented a variation on a traditional pattern of adaptation to life by younger males and their families. Eventually the variation itself became traditional: As late as the reign of Augustus (31–CE 14), the poet Vergil saw Roman legionaries in Sicilian herders (*Georgics* 3:339, 349). In Italy and elsewhere, Roman demands for military manpower from her allies thus meshed with the regular individual and familial patterns of adaptation of a transhumant population.

The interaction underscores one of the unique aspects of the Roman experience: the deeper potential for assimilation and growth presented to a subjugated tribal group by the new Roman system. Introducing new survival options for newly conquered peoples, the Romans initiated a process of absorption that lasted in some places for centuries. Over time the Roman impact produced a significant element of new citizens loyal to Rome, the subject of chapter 5. Yet Roman success was made possible primarily because the reciprocal manner in which such imperialism was carried out allowed both the Romans and their allies to adjust to the process within a context of beliefs and patterns of behavior that both understood.

The permanent migration of a certain number of Samnites and Paeligni—four thousand families according to their leaders—to Fregellae offers an opportunity to further explore this idea. In 187, leaders of both the Paeligni, whose territory lay in the upper valley of the Aternus River and on the slopes of the Gran Sasso where they controlled the eastern end of the main pass over the central Apennines, and the Samnites, whose territories lay farther south in and around the central Apennines, reported at Rome that some of their peoples had moved to Fregellae, on a plateau over the Liris River in west-central Italy. According to ancient report, a desire to avoid the Roman draft prompted the migration.[131] Realistically, these families (whatever their actual number) had relocated in response to the fundamental changes wrought by the Roman annexation of Samnite and Paelignian lands in the fourth century and perhaps the more recent uncertainties caused by Hannibal's progress through central Italy.[132] The Samnites suffered additional losses of territory again after the Second Punic War. In the case of the Paeligni, who were customarily transhumant herders like others in the Apennines, Romans settlement had not affected their mountain lands.[133] But the Romans had settled in the lowland areas all around, in the Liris River valley and the coastal plain, thus altering the traditional relationship between highlands and lowlands.[134] These families appear to be responding to such a crisis or the later crisis of Hannibal's march in familiar ways within the context of their own traditional behavior. In the case of each group, the regular patterns of seasonal movement shared by all, as well as a common language, religious rituals, and customs, understandably prompted them to migrate to the same place. Significantly, in their migrations they followed a long-established route to an area of traditional farming and herding activity in the Liris River valley and the coastal plains to which it led, now dominated by Fregellae.[135] Faced with deprivation and want, they nonetheless adjusted in line with patterns traditional to their way of life. In Fregellae the four thousand migrating Paelignian and Samnite families presumably settled on marginal lands as tenants or sharecroppers and thus continued the subsistence farming with which they were familiar. Others went elsewhere—some Paeligni went to the sea, for instance, as oarsmen—but they are unlikely to have gone alone. Like seasonal migrants and allied soldiers, oarsmen departed and returned in groups or serially in a process of chain migration reminiscent of transhumance movement.

Rome's actions against her allies in the latter part of the Second Punic War provide memorable confirmation of the Romans' intuitive adoption of courses of action that inevitably strengthened themselves and weakened neighboring and other Italians at a fundamental level. Hannibal's thirteen-year campaign in Italy presented the most dangerous external threat the Romans had faced. At the end of the Second Punic War, the Romans confiscated ten thousand square kilometers in the south of Italy in Samnium, Apulia, and mostly from Lucanians, with whom a treaty had been made in 300. It was the single largest appropriation of land in Italy to date. While we may reasonably see these steps as intended to provide land for immediate and future needs, ancient recorders indicate more complex motives on the part of Rome. Specifically, the confiscations were part of a deliberate program to punish those allies who had assisted Hannibal or lagged in their support of Rome. We can well imagine that confiscations on such a scale were extraordinarily disruptive of everyday life in the affected areas. Subsequently, Roman settlers moved into the area: In 201, the Senate decreed that the land would be distributed to an estimated 40,000 veterans of Scipio Africanus's campaign against the Carthaginians in North Africa and, to this end, appointed a commission of ten men to survey lands in Samnium and Apulia and to assign lots on an individual basis.[136] There is no record of land assignments on this scale again until Sulla provided land for 120,000 veterans in 81.[137] In addition to this distribution, ten citizen colonies were established, some by public law, between 199 and 150, in southern Italy, mainly around the coast, significantly the largest group of foundations made in any fifty-year period before the first century.[138] The locations encourage us again to suppose that the Romans gained control of winter pastures and arable land, specifically.

The punishment of faltering allies in south Italy took other forms. In some cases, adjustments were made to the military levies arranged by treaty. In 204, the Romans imposed a larger levy (plus additional tax and stricter census requirements) on Latins who had supported Hannibal, specifically the communities of Nepet, Sutrium, Ardea, Cales, Alba, Carsioli, Sora, Suessa, Setia, Circei,

Narnia, and Interamna—most of them Latin colonies and all within one to three days' journey from Rome—and removed the Picentes, who had been forcibly relocated to south Italy a century before, from the lists altogether.[139] The consequences of either action are comparable. Taking no soldiers from communities whose young men entered military service as an alternative to seasonal migration with herds is a hardship if the pattern of seasonal migration is already disrupted; taking more soldiers from communities whose members are primarily farmers disrupts farming life. In either case the Romans seemed to fasten on a course that was most disruptive of community cohesion at a personal level, at the level of everyday life. Significantly, the courses of action they chose were reciprocal in their impact: As the targeted communities weakened, the Romans grew stronger.

Rome's disruptive program in south Italy exhibited another dimension in the urbanized area of Campania. The fate of prosperous Capua at the end of the Hannibalic War was more decisive, and more controversial, than the earlier relocation of Etruscan Falerii Veteres. Undoubtedly, a delicate combination of factors—including the city's Roman citizen status, the economic potential of the surrounding region, and Capua's perceived rivalry with Rome—prompted the Romans to convene in a lawmaking assembly during a difficult wartime year, in 210, to advise the Senate to determine the fate of this rebellious ally. Rather than relocate Capua the Romans completely dismantled its governing apparatus. No longer an effective urban center, Capua was administered by Roman prefects (*praefecti Capuam Cumas*). Its fertile and flourishing lands, the ager Campanus, capable of producing four crops a year, became the jewel among the public properties of the Roman people. The systematic Roman effort to absorb the resources of Capua, whose pattern of life was shaped by regional markets, trade, and intensive production, underscores the strength of the Roman impulse to deal with rivals in ways that strengthened the Roman state.

As earlier, disruption on such a scale necessitated accommodation by the local population. In Apulia, a large indigenous settlement at Gravinia, flourishing and newly walled in the mid-third century in anticipation of Rome or Hannibal, was replaced by a private villa after the Roman confiscations at the end of the Second Punic War. Visible here is the impact of the changed legal status of the land under Roman domination, which forced the local population to seek other homes, most of them on less desirable land—probably in nearby marshes and rocky foothills. Herding, their primary source of livelihood, continued on the same scale in the region based on faunal remains in the pre-Roman and Roman occupation levels.[140] But whether the herdsmen are the inhabitants of the pre-Roman community continuing their traditional migrations with herds or whether the herdsman are slave or hired herdsmen in the service of the large landowner who occupied the villa and fielded large herds for profit is unknown. Some combination of the two is probable, as the previous inhabitants reached an accommodation with the changed conditions of life they were forced to confront as a result of Roman action. And the confrontation endured. In 132, almost one hundred years after Rome's punitive confiscations in south Italy, the consul P. Popillius Laenas erected a commemorative marker lauding his new road between Rhegium and Capua and advertising, among other past achievements, that ager publicus by his efforts was finally taken from herders and given to farmers.[141] In 122, C. Gracchus enacted a law distributing more ager publicus in the region to farmers. While landless Romans benefited from such land distributions, transhumant herders, now in Lucania and Bruttium, were once again, or to an even greater extent than before, cut off from traditional patterns of existence.

As ever, military service was the most promising alternative for those young men for whom it was an option. Immediately after the Second Punic War the Romans conscripted large armies for campaigns in Greece and Asia. Many conscripts must have come from the Lucanian and Apulian communities of south Italy. The presence here of a large slave workforce in the second century indicates clearly that there was by now a shortage of freemen in the area because so many had turned to military service in the Roman army. In turn, the introduction of a large slave labor force throughout south Italy reveals the extent of disruption wrought by Roman penalties. Between 196 and 186, thousands of slaves were brought into Apulia and Lucania, where they worked as herders of sheep and cattle, the property perhaps of wealthy landowners, who modern scholars believe were now beginning to move vast herds in lucrative grazing ventures as many are reported to have done in the last century, or of smaller freeholders or tenants of ager publicus who we may identify with the forty thousand recipients of land grants in 201. The willingness of Romans to employ slaves is open to question: Rome's leaders were clearly wary of slaves in such numbers. Livy reports that the consul Postumius, touring south Italy in the aftermath of the crisis surrounding the Bacchanalian crisis in 186, executed seven thousand slave adherents to the cult of Bacchus. Whether or not the cult found members among the slave herders is no more demonstrable to us than it probably was to the Romans. What is certain is that the Roman Senate reacted to a perceived threat to Roman order by massacring a large body of slaves, whose foreign origins made them obvious targets. Taken together, the confiscations, the retributions, and the imposition of Roman settlements are all actions that caused considerable turmoil for the groups involved. A more effective program of destabilization in a traditional world is hard to imagine—all the more reason to wonder therefore at the degree of accommodation manifest by conquered Italians, even to the point of accepting Roman ways of conflict resolution, including, as we shall see next, public lawmaking.

EXPANSION AND PUBLIC LAW, BETWEEN THE FOURTH AND SECOND CENTURIES

Between the fourth and the second centuries, the Romans annexed lands amounting to nearly one-third of all Italy from conquered Italians, established many colonies on annexed land, distributed an incalculable amount to citizens in viritane grants, and created fourteen wholly new tribes as well as tribal extensions.[142] At the same time they embarked on the unparalleled gamble of overseas expansion, whose success depended on the fighting men of all Italy. All of this was done in the ordinary course of business as the Romans extended alliances or citizen grants to most of the peoples of Italy, without resort to any systematic agenda of expansion. Often, local initiative on the part of the Roman commander, or a decision by the Roman Senate, or consular or censorial edict appears to determine what steps were taken to smooth the progress of Roman domination.[143] But on some occasions, the massive transformations in life and society that accompanied this expansion were carried through by vote of the Roman people in lawmaking assemblies.[144]

Table 4.1 lists a number of issues that in one way or another deal with the Roman conquest, integration, or management of enemy lands and peoples. All the laws on the list are efforts to resolve some contentious matter, ranging from Roman appropriation of Italy's land resources to improper conduct by Roman officials (*res repetundae*), from alliances to war declarations, and from citizenship to disenfranchisement. First in frequency among the issues in table 4.1 is declaring war, which accounts for 16 public lawmaking sessions during the entire period although none, significantly, after 111.[145] The extension of Roman citizenship or citizen liberties to the peoples of Italy forms the next most frequent issue—to which we will turn in chapter 5—with 15 sessions, followed by the foundation of colonies (9 sessions) and land-related matters (13 sessions). The public laws relating to land resources are examined later. Smaller but significant clusters, in terms of a Roman sense of balance, are the 8 public lawmaking sessions concerned with the wrongdoing or misbehavior of Roman commanders vis-à-vis conquered peoples and the 4 sessions in which the Roman people considered the punishment of rebellious towns or cities (Tusculum, Satricum, and Capua), and of a mutinous Roman garrison (table 4.1). Given that Roman political leaders summoned the Roman people to consider at least 243 public law proposals between 350 and 100, it is noteworthy that almost one-half (109) of those proposals reported, collected in table 4.1, dealt with issues raised by the interaction between Romans and other inhabitants of Italy during the course of Roman expansion.

We can reasonably assume that these laws and proposed laws stand at the tip of a mountain of decisions by the Roman Senate, magistrates, or promagistrates with imperium, as well as Roman voting assemblies on the particular topics involved. That the number of reported declarations of war (sixteen), for example, is far less than the number of wars fought attests to the fact that at some times wars were approved through regular political and religious action.[146] Only when public support for a particular war was in some doubt did Romans seem to resort to the legitimizing action of a public lawmaking assembly. The debate and vote over war with Carthage in 264, "*la più antica lex de bello indicendo che sia esteriormente attestata, al dire del Mommsen*," recorded by Polybius, as well as the contested declaration of war against Jugurtha in 111, provide obvious cases in point.[147] It is also clear that communities or peoples were punished on more than the four occasions listed in table 4.1, often instantly. At times, uncompromising action against an enemy population seems to be a measure of the hardships encountered in military ventures: Rome typically took the most viciously punitive measures against those who stood against her. It is clear, too, that citizenship was granted on a small-scale basis on more than the eight listed occasions when public laws were proposed or enacted or that the citizen status of Latins or the extension of Roman civil liberties, provocatio, to allies was debated, as an alternative to citizenship, in venues other than the public lawmaking arena, on more than seven occasions (table 4.1).[148] And it is clear that the large-scale expulsion of allies from Rome or Roman towns was an issue dealt with in other ways than through the successful or unsuccessful intervention of lawmaking assemblies, as in 177 and 126 (table 4.1). With few exceptions, the structure of decision making in Roman society goes unrecognized by contemporary reporters, suggesting that such structures were largely taken for granted by ancient recorders.

At the same time, the kinds of issues and the circumstances of those issues indicate that public lawmaking assemblies represented a process of particular resort. Although discordance seems to have been tolerated for some time before an issue became pressing enough to invite action beyond the usual Roman structure of decision making, inevitably such occasions arose. When critical issues achieved a certain threshold of importance or pain, an enterprising officeholder might seize the initiative and propose a law to remedy the situation at a public lawmaking assembly and thus involve individuals on all levels of society in developing a resolution. The public debate about the punishment of Capua in 210 is instructive (discussed previously). The most frequently aired issues in table 4.1—taken together with the repeated and individual sessions to pass laws to send requested military assistance (to the Mamertines), to approve treaties, to confirm peace, or to ameliorate the conditions of military service—reveal the important role of public lawmaking in creating the essential social and political consensus, which made it possible for the Romans to conquer and absorb the surrounding peoples.

Corroboration is provided by a uniquely documented progression of events in Roman efforts, at the end of the second century, to deal with conflicts arising out of a 250-year Roman effort to organize lands outside of the city of Rome. In 117, a two-man Senate commission settled a land dispute in Liguria, northwest of the Po River basin. In 111, the Roman people adopted an innovative proposal regarding the disposition of Roman public property, ager publicus, in Italy, Africa, and Greece. While both events involve disputes concerning the possession and ownership of land there are major differences not only in scale and in the number of people affected by the outcome but more important in the ramifications of any decision in the future of the Roman state. Let us look first at the Roman adjudication of a local land dispute in Liguria.

Liguria was a region inhabited mostly by transhumant herders, with a long and often difficult relationship with the Romans. As we have seen, the Romans resorted on more than one occasion to the relocation of one or another Ligurian tribe (180 and 179); one Roman commander had unlawfully enslaved another group, prompting a request from the Ligurians in question that the Roman people intervene, which they did in a public law proposal establishing a commission of inquiry. In 117, the town council of Genua, a Ligurian coastal town, sent two of its leading citizens to Rome to request intervention in their dispute with the Viturii Langenses, another Ligurian tribal group, regarding the control of the land used by the Viturii Langenses and claimed by the Genuates. Similar requests were frequently entertained by the Senate and by local Roman officials both in Italy and outside in the second century.[149] The Romans were recognized far and wide as peerless experts in boundary arbitration. In this instance, two brothers, Q. and M. Minucius Rufus, were assigned by decree of the Roman Senate to render a decision.[150]

The complexity and sophistication of the brothers' subsequent decision, recorded in Latin and engraved on a bronze tablet, are as striking as their genius for adapting customary ways to the exigencies of expansion and growth. The boundaries of the land described as the private land of the Viturii Langenses were established. The boundaries of the land described as the public land of the Viturii Langenses were also established. The rent (*vectigal*) that the Viturii Langenses ought to pay the Genuates was established. Payment of the assigned portion by current possessors of the public land to the Viturii Langenses was established. Possessors of their public land were to be determined by vote of the Viturii Langenses. Possession and cultivation of the public land were limited to Genuates and Viturii Langenses. Use of common pasture land (ager compascuus) by the Viturii Langenses and four other Ligurian tribal groups was established, and decisions about the use of this land were placed in their hands. Finally, Viturii Langenses who were in chains as a result of the dispute or who had been fined were to be released and absolved.[151]

These adjustments fit a complicated, transitional world. Looking beyond the Genuates' understanding of their position in the region—which appears to be modeled on Roman practice—we see patterns of behavior and expectations that are entirely in keeping with a transhumant society. From a hilltop fortress (castellum), the Viturii Langenses farmed and herded animals. The pasture land was held in common by themselves and four other tribal groups. We may well imagine that these tribal groups and their ancestors had been engaged in farming and herding in the same region for centuries. But some of the land they occupied and used for farming and herding was claimed by the Genuates in 117.[152] The arrangements eventually reached by the two Roman arbitrators are striking in several respects. First, they maintain the autonomy of the tribal groups over decisions regarding the use of traditional lands—in particular the lands described as the public property of the Viturii Langenses, over which Genua exercised control. No outsiders may cultivate traditional lands, only Viturii Langenses and Genuates; and the decision about who may hold the public property of Genua rests not with the Genuates but with the Viturii Langenses. Similarly, decisions about the common pasture lands on the public property of Genua rests with the herders: the Viturii Langenses, Odiates, Dectunines, Cavaturines, and Mentovines. The boundaries of land described as the private land of the castellum of the Viturii Langenses and as their ager publicus show more of the transhumant dimension of the society represented in the document. The location of the castellum, not indicated in the document, is thought to be modern Langasco.[153] The private land of the castellum seems to be centered on the via Postumia, the Roman road connecting Genua on the coast with the Roman colony Dertona, established a brief three years before in the Po River valley across the Apennines. This private land also appears to be in the lowlands. The public property in contrast seems to comprise the mountainous interior.

How meaningful Roman categories and arrangements were to the Ligurians is worth considering. The notion of fixed boundaries, marked by boundary markers (termini), is out of place among a people dependent on unhampered movement in search of pastures. For such a people boundaries are necessarily more fluid and permeable when others in the region are also engaged in the same activities as they are and in search of both arable and pasture land. It is worth wondering, also, whether the land identified by the Roman adjudicators as private and qualified as land that could be sold and bequeathed was in fact the lowland area traditionally cultivated by the Viturii Langenses from their hilltop fortress, held collectively and cultivated in plots allotted to family groups by the tribal group. Are the adjudicators attempting to make sense of a Ligurian situation in Roman terms and finding that it does not quite fit? When we set aside the Roman character of the decisions themselves, the situation that gave rise to them appears to be governed by the traditional relationships and patterns of a transhumant society.

Whatever the situation, we can be sure of a tension, clearly reflected in the document, between Roman categories and agricultural change and the traditional, transhumant society on which they were superimposed. In the case of Genua, the Romans were adept at recognizing and preserving the traditional relationship between the Genuates and the Viturii Langenses and at the same time removing impediments to eventual Roman dominion, by imposing a Roman understanding of boundaries.[154] Time and again across Italy, similar tensions between the Romans and subject Italians were consistently resolved in the Roman way. But only under certain conditions did the Roman way call for the intervention of public lawmaking assemblies. These conditions are clarified by the second of our two select events in Roman efforts to deal with conflicts arising out of the long Roman venture to organize conquered lands outside of the city of Rome: the enactment of the lex Agraria of 111.

In 111, the Roman people enacted a momentous statute that transformed the legal status of the public property of the Roman people (ager publicus populi Romani). Through the confirmation of individual holdings on ager publicus, all such land became private property (ager privatus). In the fifty-eight surviving clauses of this lex Agraria, as it is known, the lawmakers drafted in minute detail the provisions governing the shift of all occupied ager publicus, privately held as of 133, from possession (*possessio*) to ownership (*dominium*), in a final effort to resolve the conflict dividing the Roman community since 133 over the legitimate possession of ager publicus. Recognized in the arrangements of the lex Agraria are the claims of a comprehensive range of inhabitants of Italy, notably Roman citizen, colonist, Italian ally, and ally of the Latin

Name. In the nearly three hundred years that had elapsed since the beginning of Roman expansion in Italy, the Roman people had mooted at least twenty-seven laws on the subject of the colonization, settlement, and distribution of land in Italy and abroad to the inhabitants of Italy, listed in table 4.2.[155] Each one, like the lex Agraria of 111, was offered at a critical moment in the Roman community. The lex Agraria is unique among other such land bills because a substantial portion—perhaps one-third of the entire law—has survived, allowing us a rare glimpse of the eventual outcome of the most consequential change introduced by the Roman conquest of Italy: the triumph of Roman notions of private land ownership over local traditions and patterns of landholding.

From the arrangements of the Sententia Minuciorum six years before it is clear that, rather than completely replacing traditional landholding patterns, the Romans usually harnessed indigenous conditions throughout the conquered lands to the Roman system. The complexity of the amalgamation is reflected in the passage in 111, after centuries of interaction and Roman dominion, of the lex Agraria to resolve complicated issues of landholding on the part not only of Romans but of conquered Italians and Latins south of the Po River. In this instance, unlike the Ligurian dispute resolved in one of the customary Roman ways, through the intercession and adjudication of a commission of senators named by the Roman Senate at the request of the parties involved, the issues required a public lawmaking assembly. From internal evidence there is no doubt that the lex Agraria was enacted in 111 or that it in general confirmed individual holdings on ager publicus by making such lands in possession, as of 133, ager privatus. Nor is there disagreement that it was the legal closing of a twenty-year controversy in Rome about the legitimate possession of ager publicus, initiated by the lex Sempronia agraria of 133 and reconsidered in a series of later proposals and enactments including the lex Sempronia agraria of 123 (table 4.2).[156] Although these earlier measures were enacted they were not easily implemented—the land commission created by the law of 133 found the task of determining legal possession of ager publicus nearly impossible, according to Appian—or in the case of the law of 123, as we shall see in a later chapter, their arrangements were abrogated or altered bit by bit by later public laws, including the lex Agraria of 111 (table 4.2). For my purposes, these certainties about the generation of the lex Agraria are sufficient because I am interested here primarily in what the law reveals about the adaptation to a changed environment by both Romans and Italians and in the role of lawmaking in achieving that adaptation. In the economic and legal relationships determining access to land resources that had emerged in Italy by the end of the second century, as documented by the lex Agraria, it appears that at some level the traditional mobility characteristic of Italian life continued alongside new patterns of Roman life, including patterns of private landownership. At the same time, the document presents a snapshot of the intervention of a public lawmaking assembly in the adjustment between the Romans and the conquered peoples of Italy.

Roman acceptance of the Italians on the one hand and Italian integration into the Roman system on the other is especially apparent in changing access to land resources. Private land ownership by Romans interrupted similar previous ownership patterns among the Etruscans, Campanians, Greeks, and others, as well as the traditional systems of communal land use in the mountain regions, whose inhabitants were transhumant herders. Italians whose territories were severely reduced by Roman appropriation were required to pay rent to use lands once their own or to confine themselves to marginal lands. At the same time, however, access to land was expanded for many Romans and Italians, in particular soldiers. Ager publicus throughout Italy, acquired by right of conquest from the Italians over the period between roughly the fourth and the second centuries, was at times distributed to soldiers on their discharge from military service. Colonists were often recently discharged soldiers. In order perhaps to guarantee the stability of these grants, not only to veterans but to other Romans without land, the recipients were prevented from disposing of the land by sale or bequest. By the second half of the second century, land in conquered regions outside Italy was similarly distributed. The lex Agraria records such distributions in Greece and North Africa. In 100, the tribune L. Appuleius Saturninus unsuccessfully presented a public law proposal to distribute similar lands in Gaul to the veterans of Marius who conquered it (table 4.2).[157]

In addition to state distributions, the unoccupied portions of ager publicus in Italy were available for use by Romans or Italians on payment of a rent to the Roman state either for pasturage on public pasture lands or for a portion of the produce of the land they farmed. The land in question in the lex Agraria, private holdings of ager publicus, was the public property of the Roman people occupied without contract. Significantly, such ager publicus, over time, had received owners and possessors drawn not only from the ranks of the Roman conquerors but from those of the conquered—Latins and Italians who at one and the same time relinquished their claims to traditional territories yet gained access to the annexed lands of other conquered Italians (and conquered peoples outside Italy eventually) through military service in the conquerors' army. When they returned to the land they entered a new Roman world of settled farming.

By 111, after more than two centuries of appropriation in Italy, after centuries of letting ager publicus to previous holders or to newcomers, and of allotting land in outright ownership to colonists, the Romans institutionalized the interruption of traditional movement by the imposition of boundaries and private landownership. Private land, defined in 117 as land that could be sold and bequeathed, suggests some combination of sedentary agriculture, extended families, and land-based wealth.[158] At the same time, the notion of traditional use continued: For instance, the drafters of the lex Agraria recognized *ager patritus*, sometimes understood to be traditional lands of the Italian peoples, and exempted it from the arrangements of the law.[159] Likewise the rural servitudes in Roman law—the rights of way across land, for humans by foot and for animals, and the right to draw water—attest to a world of commonly shared resources.[160] Present in the Twelve Tables, servitudes are also confirmed in the lex Agraria. In this period, too, the Romans were also developing personal servitudes, in particular the idea of *usufructus*, the legal notion that the profits or produce of something could be utilized by someone who did not have quiritary ownership of the resource that generated them.[161] We may see how this idea could emerge out of a landscape accustomed to yielding wood for charcoal, or lime, or some other necessity to a number of groups who ranged in common over the land. In brief, to a significant extent the common use of land persisted.

The underlying mobility of the Italian population, contingent on the geographic constraints of Italy, also continued. Transhumance involving small herds continued on the part of Italians through the third and second centuries and later still. The lex Agraria of 111 offers significant protections to herders with small herds in particular. People pasturing ten or fewer large animals, or an unknown number of small animals will not be subject to a renting tax on the state land in Italy reserved for pasturage.[162] By this time large herds managed by slaves were typical in Apulia, Calabria, Lucania, and Bruttium.[163] Nonetheless the attention to small herders is a striking recognition of the persistence of a transhumant way of life for mountain peoples.[164] Significantly, these patterns that now coexisted with state and private landownership were becoming institutionalized as well, through public laws such as the lex Agraria. The institutionalizing of such relationships had probably begun much earlier. How much earlier may be indicated by the fortuitous description of legal and economic relationships on a personal level transmitted to us by M. Porcius Cato in his handbook on estate farming, ca. 160, to which we shall return in chapter 7.

While traditional mobility continued, the Romans also introduced new wrinkles. People settling along the new Roman roads occupied their land, ager publicus, under special conditions. Called "people living alongside roads" (*viasiei* or *vicani*), they appear to be responsible for road maintenance.[165] Numbered among these individuals were perhaps Italians whose traditional routes were now covered by Roman roadway. They had entered into a new relationship to the route. Traditional movement from winter to summer pasture and the attachment to traditional routes and fields were interrupted by the private ownership of land assigned by the state not only in various regions of Italy but also abroad. Ex-soldiers were settled in the Balearic Islands off Spain, in North Africa, in Greece, and in southern France before 100. Thus, movement continued as before to the extent that soldiers moved from one region to another, but it was driven now by the contingencies of state settlement and military perquisite.

One of the single most persistent issues presented to the Roman people between the fourth and second centuries involved the disposition of land resources.[166] The lex Agraria of 111 transformed the possession of land that was public property as of 133 into private ownership. This was the culmination of social changes of monumental proportions stretching back for hundreds of years whose beginnings we considered earlier in this chapter. A noteworthy feature of the Roman solution to conflict within the community over access to land, reached in the lex Agraria of 111, is the extent to which Italians and Latins accepted the Rome-imposed conditions of relationship to land that had been taken from them. The lex Agraria provides a reminder of the level of commitment of the peoples of Italy to the state created in Italy by the Romans. However, the lex Agraria was but one of a range of proposed public laws that attempted to resolve inconsistencies with the Roman way in the conquered lands. We can hardly question that public lawmaking events, the traditional Roman mechanisms for making adjustments to the system, were crucial in resolving the social tensions surrounding Roman expansion, especially as it involved one of the most critical aspects of legitimate access to land.

CONCLUSION

As they moved beyond their boundaries, the Romans not only displayed an ability to maintain a distinct sense of themselves, but they also exercised a unique genius for bringing diverse groups of people into the Roman cultural orbit. Sometimes the Romans exterminated entire populations and confiscated their lands; sometimes a group was relocated; more often enough land was left to them to survive in their old areas or patterns of transhumance were adjusted to place conquered peoples firmly under Roman control. But in every case, the Romans displayed a remarkable talent for imposing themselves on a conquered people in such a way as to harness the indigenous productive potential and bring them firmly into the Roman structure, thus creating the basis for an expanding and prosperous society increasingly centered on the city of Rome.

That wars were fought almost continuously, increasing numbers of military raised among the conquered peoples, new peoples subjugated, frightful casualties endured, taxes collected from Roman citizens throughout Italy (up to 167), extensive trade carried on, and land divided and used productively in the Roman way, all in the presence of relatively few representatives of the Roman state and the absence of any discernible agenda of empire, suggests the emergence of a Roman culture with an extraordinary potential for adaptation in the face of change and expansion. Facilitating this adaptation was the unique geography of Italy and the resiliency of Roman culture, social structure, and ways of resolving crises, especially crises that threatened the way of life within the Roman state.

Throughout the period of Roman expansion lawmaking assemblies operated within a complicated structure of Roman crises resolution that made possible the unprecedented absorption of conquered peoples during the creation of the Roman state. When the inhabitants of Italy, Roman and non-Roman, failed to resolve a conflict on the local level arising from Roman expansion, an appeal could be made to any number of Roman elected officeholders, to agents deputized by the urban praetor (*praefecti*), or to the Roman Senate to settle the issue. As a final resort an issue could be brought by an elected official of Rome to the attention of a public lawmaking assembly. Hence, despite evidence of a Roman genius for bringing together groups of people with diverse cultures to support a single imperial state, such an amalgamation was not achieved overnight. In many cases, hundreds of years after the initial arrival of the Romans crucial questions of the interaction were still being debated—sometimes in public lawmaking sessions in Rome.

The obvious importance of a great many of the issues involved suggests that the process served as a mechanism for the resolution of conflicts that might otherwise have sundered the Roman state, particularly during its most vulnerable years. It is difficult to imagine the continued productive and unchallenged use of conquered lands without the arrangements enshrined in the lex Agraria or for that matter the very different arrangements attempted before the lex Agraria in the long series of enacted laws and public law proposals since 133 that also dealt with the controversial issue of land resources. The Romans' continual recourse to public lawmaking assemblies to consider the issue of access to land resources in Italy underscores the importance of reaching a collective decision when attempting to resolve such a critical issue. Indeed it is fair to say that without public lawmaking assemblies the Roman experience would have been much different and far more circumscribed. A great many of the issues involved in public lawmaking sessions in Rome throughout the period of Roman expansion suggest that the process served as a mechanism of last resort for many conflicts that might otherwise have seriously impeded Roman growth.

The broad acceptance of public lawmaking assemblies throughout conquered lands as a mediating authority, to the point at times where Italians agitated for the passage of laws in Rome, provides an index of the amalgamation of outsiders. Lawmaking was one aspect of a deep process of adaptation of Roman ways by conquered peoples. Crucial to understanding the development of the knowledge and assumptions necessary for the widespread acceptance of public lawmaking assemblies is flexibility of Roman citizenship.

TABLE 4.1 Laws Relating to Roman Expansion, 350–100

Declaration of war (16)	Status of landholdings (2)	The extension of the lex Fannia to all Italy
The foundation of colonies (9)	Mutiny by soldiers	Rejection of peace and surrender of commander
Grant of citizenship to outside group (8)	Renewal of treaty with Samnites	Jurisdictio of three men for granting and assigning lands
Confirmation of peace (7)	Treaty with Lucani	Use of bequest of King Attalus
Special commission of investigation (6)	Election of three men for founding a colony	The expulsion of foreigners from Rome
Distribution or assignment of land (6)	Punishment of legio Campana	The conditions of military service
Civil liberties (5)	Military aid to Mamertines	Port duties
The crime of repetundae (5)	Treaty with Hiero of Syracuse	The construction of new roads
The distribution of grain to citizens (5)	Stipend of censured equites	The vectigal imposed on state land by lex Sempronia
The citizen status of marginals (2)	Punishment of Campanian rebels by the Senate	Foreign participation in the cult of Jupiter Capitolinus
Suspension or circumvention of law (2)	Authorization to make peace with Carthage and recall army	Stopping a colony foundation
Punishment of community (2)	Authorization to negotiate a peace	Abrogation of an existing statute
Grant of citizenship to individuals (2)	Extension of Roman laws on debt to allies and Latins	The inalienability of redistributed land under lex Sempronia
Lease of ager Campanus by censors (2)	Expulsion of Latin and Italian immigrants from Rome	Land boundaries
The term of military service (2)	Appearance of M. Popillius Laenas before quaestio	

Source: See appendixes A and C.

TABLE 4.2 Laws Relating to the Appropriation, Settlement, and Distribution of Land and Resources by Year, 350–100

Year	Latin Name	Subject
296	Plebiscitum de triumviris coloniae deducendae	Election of three men for founding a colony
232	Lex Flaminia de agro Piceno et Gallico viritim dividendo	Distribution or assignment of land
210	Plebiscitum de agro romano	Lease of ager Campanus by censors
196	Lex Atinia de coloniis quinque deducendis	The foundation of colonies
(194)[a]	Lex Baebia de coloniis deducendis	The foundation of colonies
193	Lex Aelia de coloniis duabus latinis deducendis	The foundation of colonies
172	Lex Lucretia de agro Campano	Lease of ager Campanus by censors
146	Lex Livia de agris Africanis	Distribution or assignment of land
140	Rogatio Laelia agraria	Distribution or assignment of land
133	Lex Sempronia agraria	Distribution or assignment of land
133	Lex Sempronia agraria altera	Jurisdictio of three men for granting and assigning lands
133	Rogatio Sempronia de pecunia regis Attali	Use of bequest of King Attalus
123	Lex Sempronia agraria	Distribution or assignment of land
123	Lex Sempronia frumentaria	The distribution of grain to citizens
123	Lex Sempronia de coloniis Tarentum et Capuam deducendis	The foundation of colonies
122	Lex Rubria de colonia Carthaginem deducenda	The foundation of colonies
122	Rogatio Livia agraria	The vectigal imposed on state land by lex Sempronia
122	Rogatio Livia de coloniis duodecim deducendis	The foundation of colonies
122	Rogatio Livia frumentaria	The distribution of grain to citizens
121	Lex Minucia de colonia Carthaginem deducenda	Stopping a colony foundation
121	Leges Minuciae de legibus Semproniis abrogandiis	Abrogation of an existing statute
(121)	Lex agraria	The inalienability of redistributed land under lex Sempronia
119	Rogatio frumentaria	The distribution of grain to citizens
118	Lex de colonia Narbonem deducenda	The foundation of colonies
(111)	Lex Thoria agraria	Status of landholdings
111	Lex agraria	Status of landholdings
(110)	Lex Octavia frumentaria	The distribution of grain to citizens
109	Lex Mamilia de limitibus	Land boundaries
104	Rogatio Marcia agraria	Uncertain or conjectural
103	Lex Appuleia de coloniis in Africam deducendis	The foundation of colonies

(*continued*)

TABLE 4.2 *(continued)*

Year	Latin Name	Subject
100	Lex Appuleia agraria	Distribution or assignment of land
100	Lex Appuleia de coloniis in Siciliam, Achaiam, Macedoniam deducendis	The foundation of colonies
(100)	Lex Appuleia frumentaria	The distribution of grain to citizens

Source: See appendixes A and C.
[a]Dates in parentheses are approximate. See appendix C.

Notes

1. Pallottino 1994 provides an introduction to the history of pre-Roman Italy down to the fourth century. On the Italian peoples see also E. T. Salmon, "The iron age: The peoples of Italy," *CAH* 4, 2d ed. (Cambridge, 1988), 676–719; E. T. Salmon, *The making of Roman Italy* (London, 1982), 1–39; and J.-M. David, *The Roman conquest of Italy* (Cambridge, MA, 1996), 13–34. More specialized bibliography is cited in note 23, this chapter.

2. Celts in Italy: E. Campanile, ed., *I Celti d'Italia* (Pisa, 1981); C. Peyre, *La cisalpine gauloise du IIIe au Ier siècle av. J.C.* (Paris, 1979).

3. Italic and non-Italic language groups in Italy: M. Lejeune and D. Briquel, "Lingue e scritture," in *Italia, omnium terrarum parens*, 2d ed., ed. C. Ampolo et al. (Milan, 1991), 435–76. See also V. Pisani, "Le lingue preromane d'Italia. Origini e fortune," in *PCIA*, ed. A. L. Prosdocimi and A. Marinetti, 6.1.15–77; and G. Battista Pellegrini, "Toponimi ed etnici nelle lingue dell'Italia antica," in *PCIA*, ed. A. L. Prosdocimi and A. Marinetti, 6.1.80–127.

4. The foremost Oscans in the fifth and fourth centuries, the Samnites, were divided into five tribal groups: the Frentani, Pentri, Caudini, Hirpini, and Carriceni. Samnite areas: G. Tagliamonte, *I Sanniti: Caudini, Irpini, Pentri, Carricini, Frentani* (Milan, 1997), 50–116; E. T. Salmon, *Samnium and the Samnites* (Cambridge, 1967), 23–27.

5. Geography of Italy in antiquity: H. Nissen, *Italische Landeskunde*, 2 vols. (Berlin, 1883–1902). A general description of the geography of Italy in the mid-twentieth century is provided in the four large volumes on Italy prepared during World War II by the British Naval Intelligence Division as part of its *Geographical Handbook* series, in particular vol. 1, 187–405. Briefer but more accessible is D. S. Walker, *A Geography of Italy*, 2d ed. (London, 1967).

6. The classic statement on the importance of environment is F. Braudel, *The Mediterranean and the Mediterranean world in the age of Philip II*, trans. S. Reynolds (New York, Evanston, San Francisco, and London, 1972), part 1, "The role of the environment," 25–352. See also P. Holden and N. Purcell, *The corrupting sea: A study of Mediterranean history* (Oxford, 2000), a study challenging and refining Braudel's vision, which appeared after I wrote this chapter.

7. This is revealed indirectly in the importance placed by both Cato and Varro, in their handbooks on estate farming, on access to both winter and summer pasturage.

8. In general see G. Tibiletti, "Considerazione sulle popolazioni dell'Italia preromana," in *PCIA*, ed. M. Pallottino et al., 7.33–39 (Rome, 1978); J. E. Skydsgaard, "Transhumance in ancient Italy," *Analecta Romana Instituti Danici* 7 (1974): 7–36; and M. Pasquinucci, "La transumanza nell'Italia romana," in *Strutturie agrarie e allevamento transumante nell'Italia romana (III-I sec. A. C.)*, ed. E. Gabba and M. Pasquinucci (Pisa, 1979), 79–182.

9. I am summarizing archaeologist Graeme Barker, who addresses the early and continuing importance of transhumance. See in particular G. Barker, *Landscape and society: Prehistoric central Italy* (London, 1981), and G. Barker, "Stability and change," in *Roman landscapes: Archaeological survey in the Mediterranean region*, ed. G. Barker and J. A. Lloyd (London, 1991). Cf. Braudel 1972, 85–95.

10. T. W. Potter, *The changing landscape of southern Etruria* (London, 1979), 58–79 (population increase in Etruria); cf. E. Zubrow and J. Robinson, "Chance and the human population: Population growth in the Mediterranean," in *Reconstructing past population trends in Mediterranean Europe*, ed. Bintliff and Sbonias (Oxford, 1999), 133: "In this region [the Mediterranean] the transition to successful agriculture involved both a technological and a demographic revolution." For a general discussion of causality (whether an increasing population drives agricultural and/or technological innovation or vice versa) see M. Livi-Bacci, *A concise history of world population* (Cambridge, MA, and Oxford, 1992), 74–99.

11. I am not here concerned with the traditional view of early Rome as a pastoral society, disputed by some scholars: C. Ampolo, "Rome archäique: Une société pastorale?" in *Pastoral economies in classical antiquity*, ed. C. R. Whittaker, Cambridge Philological Society, Suppl. 14 (Cambridge, 1988), 120–33. The issue is the interdependence of plain and mountain. See, in the case of Latium, J. W. Bouma et al., "The economy of an early Latin settlement, Borgo Le Ferriere-Satricum, 800–200," in *Settlement and economy in Italy, 1500 to AD 1500: Papers of the fifth conference of Italian archaeology*, ed. N. Christie, Oxbow Monograph 41 (Oxford, 1995), 185–87 (landscape presupposes a strong dependence on domestic stock raising, transhumance, or both). Pasquinucci observes that transhumance must have been practiced whenever animal rearing is attested, even if the regular movement of herds between summer and winter pastures is not: Pasquinucci 1979, 146.

12. The view of transhumance commonly presented by ancient historians assumes that the coming of Rome played a key role in the disruption of short-distance transhumance and the emergence of long-distance transhumance. In particular, long-distance transhumance emerged only in the second century and was entirely dependent on (a) men who could make a large capital investment in herds; (b) large regional markets for animal products; and (c) a centralized political authority that could protect the migrating herders. Such arguments reveal a fundamental misunderstanding of transhumance as a system for coping with economic constraints on survival posed by geography and climate and fail to address the variety of ways uncovered by the regional peoples of Italy, over time, to live as effectively as possible given the environmental circumstances they confronted. See, for instance, P. Garnsey, "Mountain economies in southern Europe," in Whittaker, ed., 1988, 206: "Geographical facts do not account for long

range transhumance or even for the existence of a pastoral economy at all." Cf. P. Halstead, "Traditional and rural economy in Mediterranean Europe: Plus ça change?" *JHS* 107 (1987): 77–87. Instead such arguments view transhumance as a capital-eating venture akin to modern ranching. See in particular E. Gabba, "Sulle strutture agrarie dell'Italia romana fra III e I sec. a.C.," in Pasquinucci and Gabba, eds., 1979, 15–73, reiterated in "La pastorizia nell'età tardo-imperiale in Italia," in Whittaker, ed., 1988; cf. A. G. Toynbee, *Hannibal's legacy: The Hannibalic war's effects on Roman life* (Oxford, 1965), 2:286–95; and D. S. Spurr, *Arable cultivation in Roman Italy* (London, 1986), 125–26. The position is taken or assumed by others, e.g., C. Letta, *I Marsi e il Fucini nell'antichità* (Milan, 1972), 87–88; D. P. Kehoe, "Pastoralism and agriculture," *JRA* 3 (1990): 386–98 (rev. of Whittaker, ed., 1988); E. Dench, *From barbarians to new men* (Oxford, 1995), 116–25; and E. Curti, E. Dench, and J. Patterson, "The archaeology of central and southern Italy," *JRS* 86 (1996): 180–81.

13. Hercules in Italy: note 55, this chapter. Hercules in Rome: chapter 6.

14. R. Ross Holloway, *The archaeology of early Rome and Latium* (London and New York, 1994), 51.

15. Strabo 4.6.2; Cass. Dio 5.39. See S. Dyson, *The creation of the Roman frontier* (Princeton, 1985), 88–90.

16. Correspondence between ancient, medieval, and modern tratturi: Skydsgaard 1974, 12 with figure 1; Pasquinucci 1979, tavole 1, following 182; Barker 1981, 27 with figure 9. Transhumance in mid-twentieth century: Walker 1967, 173, 190; Skydsgaard 1974, 28 with figure 2; Barker 1981, 27–29.

17. On his route see Polyb. 3.86.8–11. Noted by R. Chevallier, *Roman roads* (Berkeley and Los Angeles, 1976), 131 n. 1, in terms of fodder and pasture. He had considerably more than two thousand head of cattle, the number expended on his stratagem: Polyb. 3.92.4. Sometimes Hannibal got lost.

18. This seems to be the prevailing view among geographers, archaeologists, and social historians despite those who argue that geography and climate are but weakly related to patterns of life, in particular transhumance (note 12, this chapter). A summary of the positions taken by scholars in different disciplines on long-range versus local transhumance is provided by M. Corbier, "La transhumance entre le Samnium et l'Apulie: Continuités entre l'époque républicaine et l'époque imperiale," in *La romanisation du Samnium aux IIe et Ier Siècles av. J.-C.* Actes du colloque organisé par le Centre Jean Bérard (Naples, 1991), 149–51.

19. For instance, pigs were herded to Rome from the Po River valley: Strabo 5.1.12; see Pasquinucci 1979, 164.

20. On these interactions see the work of Frederik Barth, in particular, "A general perspective on nomad-sedentary relations in the Middle East," and "Ethnic groups and boundaries," in F. Barth, *Process and form in social life: Selected essays of Frederik Barth* (London, Boston, and Henley, 1981), 1.187–97, 198–227.

21. Skydsgaard 1974, 26–29.

22. See note 1, this chapter.

23. As a starting point, the several volumes of *Popoli e Civiltà dell'Italia Antica* (*PCIA*) provide an essential digest of archaeological fieldwork and analysis of the various regions and peoples of pre-Roman Italy. The analyses in volume 7 are particularly valuable. Other useful collections include D. Ridgway and F. Ridgway, eds., *Italy before the Romans*

(London and New York, 1979); C. Ampolo et al., eds., *Storia della società Italiana. I.* Dalla preistoria all'espansione di Roma (Milan, 1981); Ampolo et al. 1989; *Crise et transformation des sociétés archäique de l'Italie au Ve siècle av. J.-C.* (Rome, 1990).

24. Omitted from this discussion are the *oppida* in north Italy characteristic of the Celtic world as a whole; on these proto-cities see Peyre 1979, 56 ff.

25. A selection of the growing number of studies include *Studi sulla città antica: Atti del convegno sulla città etrusca e italica preromana* (Bologna, 1970); *La formazione della città preromana in Emilio Romagna* (Bologna, 1988); M. Frederiksen, *Campania* (London, 1984), 31–33, 68–77, 85–116 (Campania); "La formazione della città in Lazio. Seminario tenuto a Roma 24–26 giugno, 1977," *Dial. di Arch* (1980): 2.1–2, and P. Attema, "Notes on the urbanization of Latium vetus," in *Urbanization in the Mediterranean in the ninth to sixth Centuries*, ed. H. Damgaard Andersen et al. (Copenhagen, 1997), 279–95 (Latium); *Studi sulla città antica: Atti del convegno sulla città etrusca e italica preromana* (Bologna, 1970), and H. Damgaard Andersen, "The archeological evidence for the origin and development of the Etruscan city in the seventh to sixth centuries," in Anderson et al., eds., 1997, 343–82 (Etruria).

26. See M. Torelli, "Archaic Rome between Latium and Etruria," *CAH* 7.2, 2d ed. (Cambridge, New York, Port Chester, Melbourne, and Sydney, 1989), 37.

27. Rome and the Etruscans: C. Smith, *Early Rome and Latium. Economy and society c. 1000–500* (Oxford, 1996), and C. Ampolo, "Rome e il Latium Vetus nel VI e nel V Sec. a.C.," *PCIA*, ed. C. Ampolo, A. Bottini, and P. G. Guzzo, 8.391–467. T. J. Cornell, *The beginnings of Rome: Italy and Rome from the Bronze Age to the Punic Wars (c. 1000–264 BC)* (London and New York, 1995), 151–72, offers a different model for the relationship between the Romans and Etruscans.

28. Urban development of Rome: Cornell 1995, 92–97. On the replacement of mound-and-ditch defense works with walls of stone block, generally in the first half of the sixth century, see Torelli 1989, 34–37; cf. Cornell 1995, 198–202.

29. For a discussion of the issues raised in the following paragraphs see Cornell 1995, 81–118, 230–31.

30. A. M. Bietti-Sestieri, "The Iron Age cemetery of Osteria dell'Osa, Rome: Evidence of social change in Lazio in the 8th c.," in *Papers in Italian Archaeology IV: The Cambridge Conference* (Oxford, 1985), ed. C. Malone and S. Stoddart, 111–44. On the clans see also Cornell 1995, 81–86; and Torelli 1989, 34–35.

31. Mommsen, *R.St.* 3.1.22–23: "Vermögensrechtlich ist das Geschlecht wahrscheinlich für das private Bodenrecht der älteste Träger gewesen." Essential reading is the classic study of the origins and consequences of private landholding from a sociological perspective by M. Weber, *Die römische Agrargeschichte* (Stuttgart, 1891; reprint Amsterdam, 1962); cf. Weber, *The agrarian sociology of ancient civilizations* (London, 1976), 260–305, esp. 265–72. A helpful survey of the various theories of Mommsen, Weber, and others is provided by O. Behrends, "Bodenheit und privates Bodeneigentum im Grenzewesen Roms," in *Die römische Feldmeßkunst. Interdisziplinäre Beiträge zu ihrer Bedeutung für die Zivilisationsgeschichte Roms*, ed. O. Behrends and L. Capogrossi Colognesi (Göttingen, 1992), 201–13. Also useful is the discussion of Weber's views on private landownership by J. R. Love, *Antiquity and capitalism: Max Weber and the sociological foundations of Roman civilization* (London and New York, 1991), 15–18.

32. Torelli 1989, 38–39. For a discussion of other modern theories about the origins of the Roman system of clientage see A. Drummond, "Early Roman clientage," in *Patronage in Ancient Society*, ed. A. Wallace-Hadrill (London, 1989), 89–115. See also Brunt 1988, 382–442, with whose arguments about the flexibility of hereditary Roman patron-client ties and the "disintegration of a putative social harmony" I am in general agreement.

33. The observation, made by archaeologist Bietti-Sestieri with reference to Iron Age society, applies equally to all periods: A. M. Bietti-Sestieri, *The Iron Age community of Osteria dell'Osa* (Cambridge, 1992), 3, and "The role of interregional contact in the development of latial society in the early Iron Age," in Christie, ed., 1995, 353–64.

34. F. Münzer, *Römische Adelsparteien und Adelsfamilien* (Stuttgart, 1920), 46–62; Scullard 1973, 10, 32.

35. See for instance C. Ampolo, "Demarato, osservazioni sulla mobilità sociale arcaica," *Dial. di Arch.* 9–10 (1976–77): 333–45.

36. A convenient discussion of these is provided in Cornell 1995, 108–12.

37. On the religious foundations of the league see B. Liou-Gille, "Naissance de la ligue latine: Mythe et culte de fondation, " *RBPhil* 74 (1996): 73–97.

38. Already ascendant in the sixth century: Cornell 1995, 198–214.

39. On Italian society see Tibiletti 1978 and M. Cristofani, "Società e istituzioni nell'Italia preromana," in *PCIA*, ed. M. Pallotino, 7.51–112. Cf. David 1996, 22–29.

40. The focus is conventional: The peoples of central and southern Italy were generally regarded in antiquity and by modern scholars as singularly "attuned" to each other; specifically they shared a certain, common cultural outlook to which the Celts, Ligurians, and other Celticized inhabitants of the Po River valley were not privy. See the comments of David 1996, 14–18.

41. *Vici* and *Pagi*: M. W. Frederiksen, "Changes in the pattern of settlement," in *Hellenismus in Mittelitalien*, ed. P. Zanker (Göttingen, 1976), 341–55 (meaning of terms); E. Gabba, Urbanizzazione e rinnovamenti urbanistici nell'Italia centro-meridionale del I sec. a.C.," in E. Gabba, *Italia Romana* (Como, 1994), 68–69. Settlement patterns: David 1994, 22; Tagliamonte 1996, 156–78 (Samnites). Cf. E. Antonacci Sanpaolo, "Landscape changes: Romanization and new settlement patterns at Tiati," in Keay and Terrenato 2001, 27, citing previous publications regarding settlement patterns at Tiati.

42. Hill forts: S. P. Oakley, *The hill forts of the Samnites*. Archaeological Monographs of the British School at Rome, 10 (London, 1995).

43. Larinum: Salmon 1982, 21. Gravinia: A. Small, ed., *Gravinia: An Iron Age and Roman republican settlement on Botromagno, Gravina di Puglia, excavations 1965–74*. Archaeological Monographs of the British School at Rome, 5 (London, 1992), 1.12. See note 23, this chapter.

44. P. Arthur, *Romans in northern Campania*. Archaeological Monographs of the British School at Rome, 1 (London, 1991), 30.

45. Sanctuaries were located along drove trails: E. Fabbricotti, "Storia di un tratturo," in Christie, ed., 1995, 197. On the functions of sanctuaries see Arthur 1991, 20, 29.

46. Excavated in the early part of this century. See P. Mingazzini, "Il santuario della dea Marica alle foci del Garigliano," *Mon. Ant.* 37 (1938); P. Talamo, "L'Area aurunca nel quadro dell'Italia centromeridionale: Testimonianze archeologiche di età

arcaica," BARS 384 (Oxford, 1987); Arthur 1991, 32–33. Three settlements: Salmon 1982, 10. These shared a common shrine perhaps to Marica: Livy 8.11.11.

47. On the similarities with other sanctuaries in south Italy and their role see G. Pugliese Carratelli, "Santuari extramurani in Magna Graecia," *PP* 17 (1962): 241–46; Arthur 1991, 46.

48. F. van Wonterghem, "Le culte d'Hercule chez les Paeligni," *Ant. Class.* 42 (1973): 36–48. On Curinus, thought to be a Sabine name, see F. van Wonterghem, "Archäologische Zeugnisse spätrepublikanischer Zeit aus dem Gebiet der Peligner," in Zanker, ed., 1976, 147, 151; A. La Regina,"Il Sannio," in Zanker, ed., 1976, 242; and J.-P. Morel, "Le sanctuaire de Vastogirardi (Molise) et les influences hellénistiques en Italie centrale," in Zanker, ed., 1976, 261 n. 18.

49. Castor and Pollux among the Marsi and Paeligni: E. Vetter, *Handbuch der Italischen Dialekte* (Heidelberg, 1953), no. 22. Hellenization: Zanker, ed., 1976 is still fundamental; see also the useful study of ancient and modern perspectives on the Apennine inhabitants by Dench 1995. A summary of more recent scholarship on the issue is provided by Curti, Dench, and Patterson 1996, 181–89.

50. D. Ridgway, rev. of *PCIA* 4 and 5 in *JRS* 71 (1981): 210: "Nor do such strays [rich artifacts found elsewhere] throw any light at all on the circumstances that permitted the individual or communal accumulation of reserves represented by the phenomenal quantities of bronze used in the manufacture of the receptacles, personal ornaments, arms and armour found in the Campovalono graves. The contrast between the fortunes of the Abruzzo and Molise region in ancient and modern times could hardly be more striking."

51. Spurr 1986, 1–22, 90–96.

52. The most useful discussion is Pasquinucci 1979, 161–69.

53. R. Middleton and M. F. Nimkoff, "Types of family and types of economy," *AJS* 66 (1960): 215–25.

54. Cf. Braudel 1972, 38–41.

55. See A. L. Prosdocimi, "La religioni degli Italici," in Ampolo et al., eds. (1991), 477–595; U. Bianchi, "Gli dei delle stirpi Italiche," *PCIA*, ed. M. Pallottino, 7:195–236. Hercules: Prosdocimi 1989, 529; A. De Niro, *Il culto d'Ercole tra I Sanniti Pentri e Frentani* (Rome, 1977).

56. Sabellian League (Paeligni, Marsi, Marrucini, Frentani): Letta 1972, 65–69. Samnite League (Pentri, Hirpini, Caudini, Carraceni): Letta 1972, 69–82 ; Salmon 1982, 14. On the designation Sabelli for Oscan-speaking peoples other than Samnites, current at the time of the Italian War, see Pallottino 1994, 154.

57. Ancient description of regions: Pliny, *N.H.* 3.12–110; cf. V. Cianfarani, "Culture arcaiche dell'Italia medio-adriatica," *PCIA*, ed. Cianfarani et al., 5.35–39.

58. On this subject see Lejeune and Briquel 1991, 468–71. Etruscan: N. Oscan, Latini, Falisci, Sabini, Umbri, Veneti, Rieti, Liguri, Piceni. Greek: Messapii, S. Osci, Siculi, Sicani, Elini. See also M. Pandolfino and A. L. Prosdocimi, *Alfabetari e insegnamento della scritture in Etruria e nell'Italia antica* (1990), and J. H. W. Penney in *CAH* 4, 2d ed. (1988), 720–38.

59. Salmon 1982, 23, 56; Cf. Crawford 1981, 158.

60. Tagliamonte 1997, 226 with references: "In area frentano si riscontra tuttavia, accanto all'impiego della scrittura epicoria, anche una precoce utilizzazione dei caratteri

dell'alfabeto coloniale latino nella notazione di testi in lingua osca" (third century, Larinum, and later, Casacalenda, Montenero di Bisaccia, Torino di Sangro).

61. Salmon 1982, 24.

62. Salmon 1982, 23, 25, 55–56. See comments of Crawford 1981, 158, with reference to the unlikely, independent adaptation of Victory and Apollo by the Marsi.

63. Pallottino 1994, 99–105. These movements are part of a "fifth century crisis" that saw the expansion and sometimes urbanizing of Apennine groups and the simultaneous, economic waning of the Etruscan and Campanian urban centers.

64. Livy 41.13.5

65. Livy 40.29.1.

66. Samnites: Frederiksen 1984, 98–100, 134–57; Lucani: A. Pontrandolfo Greco, *I Lucani: Etnografia e archeologia di una regione antica* (Milan, 1982), 127–65; *La formazione della città preromana in Emilia Romagna. Atti del convegno di studi, Convegno e Colloqui, novi serie 8, Bologna—Marzabotto 1985* (Bologna, 1988). Central Apennines: A. Campanelli, "La nascita della città in Abruzzo: Tradizioni, insediamenti e nuovi modelli (IV–I sec. A. C.), in Christie, ed., 1995, 493–98.

67. I am simplifying a very complicated process in this paragraph. K. J. Beloch, *Römische Geschichte bis zum Beginn der punischen Kriege* (Berlin, 1926), is essential. A. Afzelius, *Die römische Eroberung Italiens (340–264 v. Chr.)* (Copenhagen, 1942), 136–96, provides a detailed discussion of the course of Rome's conquest in the fourth and third centuries. See also Cornell 1995, 322–26, 345–68.

68. For the experiences of individual communities and a list of allies (excluding Latins) in 218 see K. J. Beloch, *Der italische Bund unter Roms Hegemonie* (Leipzig, 1880), 158–77.

69. On the dynamics of the relationship see especially E. Badian, *Foreign clientelae (264–70)* (Oxford, 1958), 15–32.

70. Only a part taken: Appian, *B.C.* 1.7.26; see Brunt 1971, 538. The annalists say one-third, one-half, or two-thirds. For a list of the Italians whose land was taken see Salmon 1982, 59 with n. 262.

71. Incremental growth of ager Romanus: Beloch 1926, 321, with discussion and adjustments of earlier work in Beloch 1880.

72. The mechanics of organizing the new lands are described in detail in Gargola 1995.

73. Cornell 1995, 301–4, argues that the initiative was Roman.

74. In general see E. T. Salmon, *Roman colonization under the republic* (London, 1969); Liris valley: F. Coarelli, "Fregellae e la colonizzazione latina nella valle del Liri," *Arch. Laz.* 2 (1979): 197–204.

75. The ancient evidence, in particular Livy, does not support the idea that such projects were ever exclusively managed either by the Senate or the people, notwithstanding the report of Velleius Paterculus (1.14.1) that all colony foundations prior to 133–121 were initiated by the Senate: see Gargola 1995, 53 with nn. 3 and 4. On the involvement of the Roman Senate in the fourth century see the detailed analysis of Hölkeskamp 1987, 155–56 (colony foundations) and 170–203; cf. Hölkeskamp 1993, 33.

76. Gargola 1995, 51–58 and 102–6 provides a useful summary of these laws.

77. One, the colony of Venusia in Apulia, founded in 291, included twenty thousand colonists and their families, according to Dion. Hal. 16.17.5; it is so large a group that modern scholars usually reject the figure (but see Afzelius 1942, 133).

78. On the selection and numbers of settlers and mechanisms of land distribution involved in viritane and colonial allotments see Gargola 1995, 64–70 and 107–113.

79. The penalty levied against the mutinous legion in Rhegium provides a case in point.

80. See the summary of Velleius Paterculus 1.14–15, who conflates the settlements (called *coloniae militariae*) with grants of citizenship.

81. The creation, membership, and functions of the colonial commissions, and the commissioners set in charge of viritane distribution projects enacted by law, are addressed by Gargola 1995, 58–63 and 106–7.

82. What follows is a rough summary of a much more elaborate and developing process known from the technical writings of its practitioners and from traces of ancient surveying on the landscape. The fundamental study is now B. Campbell, *The writings of the Roman land surveyors: Introduction, text, translation, and commentary* (London, 2000). A summary of how the surveyors worked is provided in Gargola 1995, 39–41.

83. On this see E. Gabba, "Per un'interpretazione storica della centuriazione romana," *Ath.* 63 (1985): 255–84, and "Storia e politica nei Gromatici," in Behrends and Capogrossi Colognesi 1992, 398–409. Modern scholarship on the developing practice of land surveying and centuriation is extensive. Useful collections of the last twenty years include *Misurare la terra: Centurazione e coloni nel mondo romano*, 4 vols. (Modena, 1983, 1984, 1985); M. Clavel-Lévêque, *Cadastres et espace rurale: Approches et réalités antiques. Table rond de Besançcon, mai 1980* (Paris, 1983); G. Chouquer and F. Favory, *Les paysages de l'antiquité. Terres et cadastres de l'occident romain (IVe s. avant J.-C./IIIe s. après J.-C.)* (Paris, 1991); and Behrends and Capogrossi Colognesi 1992. A comprehensive bibliography is included in Campbell 2000.

84. These are collected in Campbell 2000, 452–53, appendix 2, "List of Inscribed Cadastral Stones."

85. See Campbell 2000, 472–74 (appendix 5, "Types of Land"), and 475–77 (appendix 6, "Surveyors and the Law"). The legal aspects as they relate to land in private ownership are well covered in Behrends 1992, 192–284. The complicated degrees of legal ownership and possession in the later period are cogently analyzed by M. Kaser, "Typen der römischen Bodenrechte in der späteren Republik," *ZRG* 62 (1942): 68–73; "Eigentum und Besitz," *ZRG* 68 (1948): 131 ff; and F. T. Hinrichs, *Die Geschichte der gromatischen Institutionen: Untersuchungen zu Landverteilung: Landvermessung, Bodenverwaltungund Bodenrecht im römischen Reich* (Wiesbaden, 1974). See also Weber 1891.

86. N. Purcell, "The creation of provincial landscape: The Roman impact on Cisalpine Gaul," in *The early Roman empire in the west*, ed. T. Blagg and M. Millett (Oxford, 1990), 7–29, esp. 14–20.

87. W. Hübner, "Himmel und Erdvermessung" in Behrends and Capogrossi Colognesi 1992, 140–71. Cf. Gargola 1995, 42–50. For other interpretations see also J.-P. Vallat, "Ager publicus, colonie et territoire agraire en Campanie du nord à l'époque républicaine," in Clavel-Lévêque 1983b, 187–98, and M. Clavel-Lévêque, "Studio di un catasto nell'ager Falernus," in *Misurare la terra: Centurazione e coloni nel mondo romano* (1983), 1.227–30.

88. The terms of the land lease contracts in Cato, *Agr.*, which require different amounts of produce depending on the assessed output of the land, as well as the rents specified by the *Sententia Minuciorum* (discussed later in this chapter), with regard to equivalent produce, as well as the testimony of the *agrimensores*, for whom *ubertas*, productivity, is the basis of land valuation, make this clear. See further on land valuation in chapter 5.

89. Similar drainage systems are found in Latium, of uncertain date: S. Quilici-Gigli, "Sistemi di cunicoli nel territorio tra Velletri e Cisterna," *Arch. Laz.* 5 (1982): 112–23; J. W. Bouma et al. 1995, 185. As late as 160, the Romans drained the Pomptine marshes: Livy, *Epit.* 46.

90. Arthur 1991, 60.

91. Small, ed., 1992, 14.

92. Earlier drainage projects are attested southeast of the Astura River, in the Pontine region: P. Attema, *An archaeological survey in the Pontine region: A contribution to the early settlement history of south Lazio 900–100* (Groningen, 1993).

93. Spurr 1986. Some scholars hesitate to assume that the Romans introduced mixed crop cultivation in the absence of explicit archeological evidence that they did so: M.H. Crawford, et al., "Excavations at Fregellae, 1978–1984," *PBSR* 54 (1986): 40–68.

94. Alternatively, the size of the plot was determined by the Roman intention to create either agriculturally self-supporting Latin communities or citizen colonies, materially dependent on Rome: G. Tibiletti, "Ricerche di storia agraria romana," *Ath.* 28 (1950): 183–266, endorsed by E. Gabba, *CAH* 7, 2d ed. (1989), 215–16. Other common explanations of Roman motivations in distributing different sized plots are examined, with reference to C. Flaminius's land law of 232, by Feig-Vishnia 1996, 25–34.

95. Salmon 1982, 8–9, sees this as an indication of the relative urbanization of the different groups.

96. Antinum, to the north, was a Volscian settlement: Letta 1972, 27–28 with n. 16.

97. The absence of previous settlement around Fregellae is reported in M. Crawford et al., "Excavations at Fregellae, 1978–1984," *PBSR* 52 (1984), 23.

98. Gargola 1995, 71–101, provides a thorough discussion of the ways in which the Romans gave a familiar external shape and internal structure to new foundations.

99. See chapter 6.

100. On the density of Roman rural settlement see the comprehensive remarks and bibliography of G. Barker, "Landscape Archaeology in Italy—Goals for the 1990s," in Christie, ed., 1995, 1–3, and J. Lloyd, "Forms of rural settlement in the early Roman empire," in Barker and Lloyd, eds., 1991, 233–40.

101. See G. Barker, ed., *A Mediterranean valley: Landscape archaeology and annales history in the Biferno Valley* (London and New York, 1995).

102. G. Barker, J. Lloyd, and D. Webley, "A classical landscape in Molise," *PBSR* 46 (1978): 42.

103. J. A. Lloyd, "Farming the highlands: Samnium and Arcadia in the Hellenistic and early Roman empire," in Barker and Lloyd, eds., 1991, 180–93.

104. Barker, Lloyd, and Webley 1978, 44.

105. Barker, Lloyd, and Webley 1978, 45.

106. Surveys in the area are reported in E. Wightman, "The Lower Liri Valley: Problems, trends and peculiarities," in *Archaeology and Italian Society*, ed. G. Barker and R.

Hodges. British Archaeological Reports, International Series 102 (Oxford, 1981), 275–87, and Arthur 1991.

107. Lloyd, "Forms of rural settlement," in Barker and Lloyd, eds., 1991b, 233–40.

108. The short study by J. Frayn, *markets and fairs in Roman Italy* (Oxford, 1993), provides a comprehensive analysis dependent on ancient sources and modern "central place" theory. See also Spurr 1986, 143–44.

109. E. Gabba, "La colonizzazione Romana tra la guerra latina e la guerra annibalica: Aspetti militari e agrari," *Dial. di Arch.* 6 (1988): 21–28; cf. Gabba 1994b, 69–70, and *La città nell'Italia settentrionale in età romana* (Trieste and Rome, 1990).

110. Skydsgaard 1974, 7–36.

111. Reassessment of the Roman view of colonies as military garrisons: B. Isaac, *The limits of empire: The Roman army in the east* (Oxford, 1992), 311–15 (they were not garrisons).

112. These two laws, enacted by the plebeian tribal assembly, are considered apocryphal by some scholars, on the grounds that only a centuriate assembly could levy such harsh punishments (as a iudicium populi): Humbert 1998, 232; Mommsen, *R.St.* 3.351 n.2.

113. Potter 1979, 98–101.

114. Strong point: M. W. Frederiksen and J. B. Ward Perkins, "The ancient road systems of the central and northern Ager Faliscus," *PBSR* 25 (1957): 135–36. Similar destruction occurred in north Etruria in the third century: I. Attolini et al., "Political geography and productive geography between the valleys of the Albegna and the Fiora in northern Etruria," in Barker and Lloyd, eds., 1991, 144.

115. The immediate justification was the military contribution of the Senones as mercenaries to the Etruscans. In addition, the Gauls had made common cause with the Samnites against the Romans, fighting in the Apennine region of Etruria and Umbria. App., *Sam.* 6.1; *Hann.* 11; Polyb. 2.19.5–13; Livy, *Epit.* 11.

116. T. Frank, *Economic survey of ancient Rome* (Baltimore, 1933), 1.60–61.

117. Strabo 5.4.13; U. Laffi, *Asculum* (Pisa, 1985), 1.xvi—ii.

118. 180: Livy 40.36.7, 37.8–38.9; Nissen 1883–1902, 2.814 f.; 179: Livy 40.44.3 or 40.53.1–6. See A. Barzanò, "Il trasferimento dei Liguri Apuani nel Sannio del 180–179 BC," in *Coercizione e mobilità umana nel mondo antico*, ed. M. Sordi (Milan, 1995), 177–201.

119. Potter 1979, 99–100; Frederiksen and Ward-Perkins, 1957, 129–33.

120. Livy 40.38.6, 413.

121. A. Luisi, "La presenza dei 'Ligures Baebiani' nel Sannio," in Sordi, ed., 1995, 203–14.

122. The number of troops fluctuated with the number of Roman troops called up; generally the allies furnished the same number of infantry as the Romans but more cavalry. The consequences of the organization and deployment of Italians alongside the Romans will be discussed in chapter 5; suffice to say here that it furthered the absorption of a conquered people.

123. The impact of Roman settlement varied greatly from region to region and is revealed only through detailed archaeological investigation. On the range of possible outcomes, from disruption to cooperation, see J. R. Patterson, Review of *L'ipogeo dei Vimini di Canosa (Adrias II)*, by E. M. de Julius, and six other books, *JRS* 83 (1993):

189–93 (review of recent work on the archaeology of Roman Italy). More and more studies on this topic are now appearing: see the useful collection of papers in Keay and Terrenato 2001. The work of Emilio Gabba remains important: Gabba 1989, 197–243, and Gabba 1994b, a collection of articles published in the last twenty years.

124. Supervision of the pasture areas by tax farmers, who collected directly from herders, is another possibility. On the collection of grazing taxes see Corbier 1991, 152, and Pasquinucci 1979, 137–40. The state revenues derived from pasture land are the subject of C. Trapenard, *L'ager scripturarius: Contribution à l'histoire de la propriété collective* (Paris, 1908); cf. C. Nicolet, *Tributum: Recherches sur la fiscalité directe sous la république romain* (Bonn, 1976), 81.

125. The apparent population decrease in Etruria in the third century (based on survey and excavation), attributed to the Roman relocation or massacre (unreported), of the local population might also reflect the dispersal of the inhabitants to marginal lands. Relocation or massacre: Potter 1979, 100–101; cf. P. Perkins, "Reconstructing the population history of the Albegna Valley and Ager Cosanus, Tuscany," in *Geographical information systems and landscape archaeology*, ed. M. Gillings, D. Mattingley, and J. van Dalen (Oxford, 1999), 113.

126. Potter 1979, 44. The practice of field walking and field surveys has confirmed the ubiquity of rural habitation and settlement: Barker 1995, 1.

127. See for instance W. V. Harris, *Etruria and Umbria* (Oxford, 1971), 147.

128. Livy 28.45.19. See Letta 1972, 93.

129. Based on the contributions of 225, recorded by Polyb. 2.24.10–17.

130. See T. Gallant, *Risk and survival in ancient Greece* (Stanford, CA, 1991), 135–36, 137–38; Letta 1972, 1–95, on military service and emigration. Gauls from Italy as well as Campanians and Bruttians fought as mercenaries outside Italy in the third century.

131. Livy 41.8.8–9.

132. See F. Coarelli, "I Sanniti a Fregellae," in *La Romanisation du Samnium aux IIe et Ier siècles av. J.-C.* Actes du colloque organisé par le Centre Jean Bérard (Naples, 1991), 177–85 (on the episode, 179–80).

133. Only one source reports (unreliably) the annexation of Paelignian land: Cass. Dio 20.90.3. On this episode see H. Galsterer, *Herrschaft und Verwaltung im republikanischen Italien* (Munich, 1976), 160. While the report raises a number of related questions—When and under what circumstances had they gone? How often were heads counted for the purpose of compiling a list of men for the military levy?—the crucial point it makes concerns migration. On the census see Galsterer 1976, 110–17.

134. Livy 8.22.2; 23.6.

135. Coarelli 1991, 177–85, esp. 177: "La media valle del Liri costituisce, da sempre, un luogo di transito privilegiato per la transumanza proveniente dalle zone appenniniche confinanti, e in particolare dalla Marsica, attraverso l'alta valle del fiume (Val Roveto). Vie secondarie di penetrazione corrispondono ai passi in direzione di Atina e di Casinum."

136. Livy 31.4. 1–3; see Brunt 1971, 70 n. 1; 281.

137. The number of men receiving land is based on legions at full strength. Brunt 1971, 305, proposes that eighty thousand is a more "credible maximum" on the grounds that the legions would not be at full strength.

138. Three in Campania (Volturnum, Liternum, Puteoli), six in Lucania and Bruttium (Salernum, Buxentum, Tempsa, Vibo, Croton, Copia), and one in Apulia (Sipontum).

On the colonies founded in 194—Puteoli, Volturnum, Liternum (300 each), Salernum, Buxentum on land confiscated from the Campanians, Sipontum on land taken from the Arpini, Tempsa on land taken from the Bruttii, and Croton on Greek land—see Livy 34.45.1–5.

139. Latin towns: Livy 29.15.5–10.

140. Small, ed. 1992, 15–16.

141. *ILS* 23 = *ILLRP* 454. Most scholars agree that this consul built the road, although Wiseman has argued cogently that T. Annius built it, as praetor, propraetor, and consul between 131 and 128: T. P. Wiseman, "Viae Anniae," *PBSR* 32 (1964): 21–37, and "Viae Anniae Again" *PBSR* 37 (1969): 82–91.

142. See chapter 5.

143. See the useful discussion by Gargola 1995, 12–24, and note 75, this chapter.

144. I leave aside declarations of war and peace. The frequency of laws on issues of war and peace in the fourth century and their relative infrequency in later centuries does not, in my view, bear out the contention of many scholars that the Senate came into "control of the government" late in the fourth century, as a result probably of the lex Ovinia of ca. 339–332. See Cornell 1995, 370: "before the late fourth century government appears to have been conducted by the magistrates acting in concert with the popular assemblies." On the pattern of lawmaking in the fourth century see chapter 1.

145. Table 1. 3 (chapter 1) and appendix A.

146. J. Rich, *Declaring war in the Roman republic in the period of the transmarine expansion. Collection Latomus* 149 (Brussels, 1976); see also W. V. Harris, *War and imperialism in republican Rome*, 327–70 (Oxford, 1979), 166–74 (fetial law), 263 (war votes in the centuriate assembly).

147. Polyb. 1.11.3; *LPPR* 244.

148. Citizenship and citizen grants will be discussed more fully in chapter 5.

149. Foreign requests for intervention in boundary disputes came from North Africa, Greece, and Spain. Within Italy Roman expertise was tapped by peoples of Cisalpine Gaul, north of the Po River. Cases: 168: *quinqueviri finibus cognoscendis statuendisque* in a boundary dispute between the town of Pisa and the colony of Luna (Livy 45.13.10–11); 164: dispute between Sparta and Megalopolis in Greece; 153 and 151: dispute between Carthage and King Massinisa; 135: Sex. Atilius Serranus as proconsul of Gaul regulates boundaries of Vicetia and Ateste (*ILS* 5945); 141 or 116: the proconsul of Gaul, L. Caecilius Metellus (Diadematus?), regulated boundaries between Patavium and Areste (*CIL* 1^2.2.633; 634; 2501); ca. 86: *tabula Contrebiensis* from Spain. See Campbell 2000, 454–67, which collects evidence from both the Republic and Empire.

150. *CIL* 1^2.584, 5.7749; T. Mommsen, *Gesammelte Schriften* (1903), 1.383–91 (= *CIL* 1.199); Kaser 1942, 68–73.

151. See discussion of this document in the context of legal Latin by Crawford, *RS* 1.16–19.

152. An alternative explanation of the relationship between the Genuates and the other Ligurians is offered by E. Sereni, *History of the Italian agricultural landscape* (Princeton, 1997 [1962]).

153. Mommsen 1903, 390.

154. For an explanation of the relationship in legal terms see Mommsen 1903, 389.

155. The lex Flaminia, 232, public laws arranging for lease of ager Campanus in 210 and 172; a proposed land redistribution law in 140, never enacted; the lex Sempronia in 133 and a related law concerning the jurisdiction of the IIIviri; the lex Sempronia of 123; at least two laws changing certain provisions of the lex Sempronia in 122 and 121; and ten colony foundation laws, between 350 and 111.

156. See the recent discussion of the date and identity of the law in Lintott 1992, 282–86; cf. 48–49.

157. Whether or not the intention was to benefit allies by "providing for the participation of Italians on a large scale" is discussed in Brunt 1988, 131.

158. Sententia Minuciorum: Bruns[7] no. 184, ll. 5–6.

159. Lintott 1992, 231–33, commentary to lex Agraria l. 28. Crawford does not think there is "an entity known as ager patritus" and takes patritum to be a "hereditary contract": *RS* 1.166.

160. On servitudes see M. Kaser, *Das römische Privatrecht* (Munich, 1955), 370–75.

161. Current legal scholarship places the origins of usufructus in the necessity of providing for widows in a marriage without manus, after ca. 150: A. Watson, *The law of property in the later Roman republic* (Oxford, 1968), 203 (Watson stresses that the arguments for this connection are weak); J. A. C. Thomas, *Textbook of Roman law* (Amsterdam, New York, and Oxford, 1976), 202–3 with n. 70.

162. *RS* 1 No. 2, ll. 14–15 (ager compascuus) and 25–26 (ager publicus).

163. "Organized transhumance": Barker, Lloyd, and Webley 1978, 47.

164. Transhumance in lex Agraria: Pasquinucci 1979, 102–6.

165. There are problems associated with this interpretation: *RS* 1.160.

166. Chapter 1.

CHAPTER FIVE

Incorporation: Citizenship and Military Service

AMONG THE MOST implacable of the Italian allies facing Rome during the Italian War of 91–89 were the Lucani, a federation of Oscan-speaking tribal peoples inhabiting south Italy. Refusing to accept Roman citizenship or peace following the decision of the Roman people to incorporate all inhabitants of Italy into the Roman state, the Lucani like their Samnite kin instead remained in a state of war with Rome, insisting on the restitution of traditional lands. The determination of the Lucani to topple Rome rather than fully enter the Roman state is not hard to understand. During the course of the fourth century the Lucani had themselves been conquerors, dominating south Italy, overpowering Italiote Greek cities, and overrunning the region as far south as the heel of Italy. In the late third century, the Lucani eagerly aided Hannibal, although they were now allies of Rome. They suffered, as a result, the most severe of the penalties levied by Rome at the end of the Second Punic War. With the deterioration of local conditions, the number of Lucani regularly drawn into Roman military service in all probability exceeded the forty-four thousand troops, almost 10 percent of the total allied contribution, the federation had committed to Rome in a time of military crisis before 218.[1] Reluctant allies, the leaders of one town, Bantia, drew up a town charter in the Oscan language, not long before the Italian War, and had it engraved on a bronze tablet for public display to proclaim, as modern commentators speculate, the sovereignty of this particular Lucanian community in an atmosphere of intensified alienation from Rome.[2] Despite the proven disaffection of the Lucani, less than fifty years after the Italian War the geographer Strabo could still conclude his description of them with the terse observation "but now they are Romans."[3]

From the early days of Roman expansion the Romans had pursued a course of action that included the absorption of conquered peoples. In this chapter I shall pursue the avenues leading to the final stage of that absorption: incorporation in the Roman state as full members, citizens of Rome. The grant of full citizenship to all allies south of the Po River in 90 expanded and reinforced changes already effected in the Roman citizen body. Since the fourth century Romans by birth had been joined in citizenship by a trickle of outsiders—mostly Latins, who shared a common language and culture with the Romans, and other Italians. These newly created citizens entered individually or as members of incorporated communities. Some foreigners, including slaves brought unwillingly to Rome, stayed on as Roman citizens when freed. The massive changes introduced by the general grant of citizenship in 90 were brought to completion in 49 by another decision by Roman voters, approving a proposal that extended full citizenship to Italians north of the Po River, the Transpadani, who had earlier received Latin rights through a law sponsored by Cn. Pompeius Strabo in 89.[4] Now all Italy was Roman, and all Italians shared the privileges and obligations of Roman citizenship.[5]

Of major importance in making citizenship acceptable to an increasingly large element in each of the conquered Italian peoples was the requirement for Roman military service. The organization and deployment of Italians alongside the Romans were vital in furthering the absorption of a conquered group by making Roman citizenship acceptable to a great number of people. Equally important in making citizenship acceptable was the flexibility of the institution itself. Being Roman entailed both the integration of new citizens as members of a Roman tribe and property class, giving them full access to the vote and the political process, and the continual reintegration of failed citizens as effective members of the Roman state. Through such mechanisms, the Romans absorbed the new citizens into the social and political structure of Rome, to the point in particular where they embraced public lawmaking assemblies as fully as the Romans themselves.

CITIZEN GRANTS BEFORE THE ITALIAN WAR

The lex Iulia of 90, granting citizenship to allies who remained loyal, was the culmination of a development that began three centuries earlier. From 381 onward, new citizens began to enter the Roman state at a slow but steady rate, admitted by formal grants of citizenship to non-Romans either by Senate decree or by enactment of the Roman people.[6] Initially, new citizens were admitted as members of groups to whom the franchise was extended wholesale over time. The first such groups were Latins in a few nearby Latin towns to whom citizenship was granted early in the fourth century: the town of Tusculum in 381 was the first, receiving initially restricted citizenship and, in 340, full citizenship.[7] The Roman extension of citizenship to Tusculum is regarded as the "prototype" for similar grants later.[8] After Rome's victory over the Latin League in 338, the Latin towns of Lanuvium, Aricia, Nomentum, and Pedum were also given full citizenship.[9] While these communities continued to exercise local autonomy and observe traditional cults, in these sweeping grants they also became Roman, their territories added to that of Rome.[10]

A different group of newcomers in the Roman state was the new class of citizen with restricted citizenship created after the same victory in 338. At this time, the Romans maneuvered several Italian towns (beginning with Etruscan Caere) into an innovative relationship with Rome.[11] The inhabitants of these municipia, as they came to be called, became citizens in a limited sense. They were obliged to furnish troops and taxes (tributum), like other citizens. They shared, moreover, basic community privileges with the Romans: they could intermarry with Romans (*ius conubii*); make contracts and wills with Romans (*ius commercii*); and take up residence in Rome (*ius migrationis*). Most important, they shared with other Romans the fundamental civil liberty of provocatio ad populum, which protected citizens against physical abuse by elected officials.[12] But they could not vote or hold office in Rome and thus were termed "citizens without the vote" (*cives sine suffragio*).[13] Among the first such municipalities in the late fourth century were Campanian and Volscian towns; most of the Sabines were accommodated within the Roman state by this fiction in 290; so too were the Praetutti.[14] In this way, these towns received a different political and administrative cast at the hands of the Romans. In other respects, however, they continued to be what they had been before: market, ritual, and governmental centers for a wide hinterland. Further community grants of restricted citizenship were not made after roughly 275 BCE.[15]

Both community and individual grants of full citizenship, however, continued as the Romans gradually drew more of the peoples of Italy into the Roman state. Some communities previously granted restricted citizenship were fully incorporated several generations later. Some Sabini became full citizens in 268 and others by 241. In 188, the Roman people enacted a law granting full citizenship to the Volscian towns of Fundi, Formiae, and Arpinum—home later to Marius and Cicero. These towns had received restricted citizenship soon after the Latin War of 338.[16] Some men entered citizen status on an individual basis, even though their communities had not. By the end of the third century, first reported during the Second Punic War, the Senate or assembly began to grant citizenship to foreigners by way of reward for special services, usually in wartime.[17] Beginning in the late second century, Latins became citizens regularly as a result of holding office in their community.[18] At the same time citizenship was awarded to successful prosecutors in cases of res repetundae involving Roman senators and elected officials; the privilege was accompanied by registration in the tribe of the convicted man.[19] Latins and Italians were sometimes rewarded with allotments in citizen colonies, which carried with them the privilege of citizenship. A slave of a citizen who was manumitted through a certain legal form became a citizen himself.[20] Evidently almost anyone could become a Roman through any one of a number of routes.

Although the exact aims underlying such citizen grants are somewhat difficult to uncover, the Romans were clearly selective in bringing outsiders into the Roman citizen body. It is a useful reminder that citizenship grants were relatively rare before the Italian War. Indeed, as Rome expanded across Italy, most of the newly forged relationships with conquered Italians rested on the formal alliances Rome established with individual Italian towns or tribal groups. Whether the allied community was Latin or Italian, by the terms of the treaty the allies (socii) were required to contribute men to Roman military ventures. The relative sizes of the Roman and allied forces give us some idea of how many of the inhabitants of Italy were formal partners of the Romans: together the Latins and Italians came to contribute nearly one-half of the manpower required by the Roman army. Citizenship, in other words, was by no means the predominate form of attachment. The majority of the peoples of Italy, both Italian and Latin, were allies of the Romans.[21]

There must have been a developing sense of citizenship in Rome between the fourth and the first centuries. At least, accepted wisdom about essential preconditions for receiving citizenship or the aims of giving citizenship to conquered peoples appear to change at different stages in the extension of Roman citizen boundaries.[22] The situation of the settlers in Latin colonies is instructive. After the Latin War of 338, the new Latin colonies, like the original Latin colonies, became allies of the Latin Name (socii Latini nominis).[23] Like other allies these Latins owed military and financial obligations to Rome. To be sure, they also had a unique relationship to the Romans, to which we shall return shortly (in language and culture Latins and Romans were indistinguishable).[24] On occasion Roman officials made a circuit of Latin colonies as they did of Roman market towns and villages in the tribes.[25] Generally, however, Latin towns and their territory remained locally autonomous.

In spite of all this, most colonists in Latin colonies, perhaps as many as three-quarters according to Peter Brunt, were Romans who by going out to these colonies lost Roman citizenship.[26] Such a loss, viewed by modern scholars as a drop in status, was probably not an issue to the fourth- and third-century Romans who migrated some distance from Rome to settle. For at this time the privileges of citizenship tended to be tied to a community that typically occupied a fixed and defined geographic location.[27] Thus the new Latins, once Roman, lost Roman citizen rights not by way of penalizing them in relation to Romans in Rome but because at the time citizenship in any community, as demonstrated especially by voting and holding office, had meaning only within the geographic boundaries of that community. It is not surprising therefore that the Romans, in 338, had not taken the further step of detaching citizenship from location. This step was not long in coming, however: once the Romans began confiscating land several days' march from the city and turning it into Roman state land, inhabited by citizens, the link became attenuated.

The idea that citizenship might be more flexibly detached from location comes to light in two developments of the late third and early second centuries: the creation of tribal extensions after 241 on confiscated land at some distance from Rome and the establishment of 2,000–3,000-man citizen colonies beginning in 184. Citizen colonies were now as large as Latin colonies. More citizens now lived at great distances from Rome. Citizen settlers retained the prerogatives and obligations of all Roman citizens. In particular, they were obliged to perform military service, unlike settlers in the earlier 300-man citizen colonies. Perhaps to this period, when Romans also went out in numbers to Latin colonies, belongs the right acquired by Latins, when in Rome, to vote in a tribe chosen by lot on the day of the assembly. As a result they were able to exercise in Rome the prerogative of full citizens, namely, voting.[28] They could also acquire Roman citizenship by migrating to Rome permanently. The flexibility of the relationship between citizenship and location was acknowledged roughly a century later, when elite members of Latin towns gained access to full Roman citizenship through holding office in their communities. This was a development from, and replacement of, the older right to change one's town of residence and so acquire citizenship.[29] The Roman understanding of citizenship as a function of location had been irrevocably transformed.

The situation of the Latins in other respects, in particular in relation to the situation of incorporated Italians, also raises questions about the connections, in the Roman mind, between apparent cultural affinities and citizenship. When the Romans began making new citizens in the fourth century, the one group we might expect to lead the rush, the Latins, did not do so, with the exception of a few communities. This is surprising because in other respects the boundaries between the Roman and Latin communities were by this time blurring more and more, as their joint colonizing ventures might indicate.[30] Romans and Latins who migrated from Latium to settle on newly acquired Roman territory left the nodes of traditional family networks—their families, the graves of their ancestors, and their traditional shrines—to do so. But in migrating, men acquired the essential resource for survival, land. The impact of Roman and Latin settlement throughout Italy on Romans and the Latins of Latium was momentous in other respects.

The shared culture of all Latin-speaking peoples, Romans and others from the plain of Latium, scattered throughout the colonies and municipalities of Italy rested solidly on common religious practices and observance. Thus religion as much as language bound all Latins. Indeed, one of the purposes of the Latin League before its dissolution by Roman victory in 338 was the joint observance of common cult: the row of same-size altars at Lavinium, dating between the sixth and second centuries, is highly suggestive of the egalitarian nature of this cult center to which Latins came regularly from their respective communities to attend to matters of ritual, each man at his own community's altar. Rome, too, had an altar here. Latins and Romans shared a bewildering swarm of common gods and goddesses, ritual observances, and prohibitions. Among others was Jupiter, the chief god of the Romans, who was the tutelary god also of many other Latin communities. The Roman epithet "Best and Greatest" (*Optimus Maximus*) refers to the Roman Jupiter's victory over the primary Latin Jupiter, Jupiter Latiaris, when the Romans defeated the Latin League in 338. Even so, the continued importance of the Latin Festival for one thousand years—when sacrifices of milk, sheep, or cheese and figurines (*oscilla*) were made annually in April to Jupiter Latiaris—is indicative of the central position of a common Latin culture in the Roman world.

Hence Latins and Romans, previously sharing the same language and culture, were even before 338 merging into one group. Latins and Romans both shared a number of community privileges generated by their common cultural and ancestral bases—specifically the right to intermarry, to change residence, and to make contracts, all of which had their origin long before 338. For both Romans and Latins, colonization involved a gradual dissolution of social and political boundaries. At the same time, many colonists in the Latin colonies established by Rome were drawn from the Roman population, blurring the boundaries between Roman and Latin still further. "Latin" became a rather artificial group—Sherwin-White speaks of a "later Latinity" after 338.[31] Yet from the perspective of shared language and customs, they were still the same people.

Sharing culture and language with the Romans, and ancestral settlements in the plain of Latium, Latins were nonetheless formally excluded from the Roman system. The Romans did not incorporate Latin communities as a rule after the war with the Latin League in 338. With some exceptions, the Latins remained in a special relationship to Rome that fell short of civic merging: they were neither full nor restricted citizens. On the other hand they could become citizens simply by migrating to Rome; and when in Rome temporarily they could vote in the assemblies in a specially selected tribe. Similarly, in the second century, a later stage of citizenship grants, the Romans often granted full citizenship to individuals within Latin communities. Officeholding in particular, as noted, became the regular gateway to full Roman citizenship. The odd relationship between Romans and Latins requires explanation, given that other peoples whose bonds with the Romans were weaker than those of the Latins were not excluded from citizenship.

From the Roman perspective a complicated set of issues appears to be involved in bringing the Latins in through the back door. Immediately, Romans viewed Latins with suspicion because they were neighbors competing for limited resources—jealousy not infrequently emerges in the Roman tradition as a Roman motive for hostility, for instance toward Capua. The suspicion was justified in the fourth century, for the Latins did instigate war with Rome. Yet at the same time Romans and Latins formed a culturally and linguistically homogeneous group. Given their common culture the extension of citizenship should have been a small step. But the Romans did not take it until almost two hundred years had passed, in 90, when the consul L. Iulius Caesar carried a measure in a lawmaking assembly extending citizenship to all Latins. In contrast, some Etruscan, Volscian, Sabine, and Campanian communities were more smoothly admitted to Roman citizenship although they did not share comparable ties with the Romans.

The common explanation involves the sophistication of a particular incorporated community's political development in the late fourth century. At this time a few Latin towns were fully incorporated. At the same time, Volscians and Campanians, and later other Italians, were incorporated subject to restrictions as cives sine suffragio. Restricted citizenship is viewed as a necessary stage on the way to becoming full Roman citizens for peoples who did not share Roman understandings of political and social organization. Latins—some Latins—could become full citizens (*cives optimo iure*) immediately, because they shared a common culture with the Romans. But Italians could be admitted "only after a probationary period during which these peoples were brought under the influence of Romano-Latin discipline and culture."[32] Never mind that these communities had begun already to urbanize. The Romans extended restricted citizenship to town dwellers, not scattered tribal groups. Never mind also that most Latins, of both the old and new variety, were excluded. The explanation can be deepened. By excluding Latins as a group yet bringing some Latins and Italians into the Roman state in these ways, the Romans achieved complementary ends: They strengthened the Roman state by increasing the number of male citizens, and they nullified the potential as well as the actual threat posed earlier by the Latin League and later by neighboring Italians.

Other considerations were also operative. Latin colonies and towns entered into a relationship with Rome that was defined by formal alliances yet still held out the ties and promise of community membership. Latins could become Romans through migration. Similarly, by the later grants of citizenship to individual Latin political leaders, or to Italians who successfully prosecuted Roman senators under the lex Repetundarum, the Romans created a powerful group of supporters in the heart of Latin and Italian communities.[33] In this way the elite members of Latin colonies and Italian towns, and subsequently their sons and descendants, were absorbed by the Romans as citizens no matter where they lived. Maintaining residence in their hometowns these local elites were also Roman. Firmly attached to elite Roman families by shared ideas about status, privilege, and wealth, some of these families as we shall see in chapter 7 henceforth not only belonged to the Roman aristocracy but aspired to and in many instances reached the high offices and Senate of Rome. But whatever the intention, such towns, whether Latin towns or new Latin colonies, as well as incorporated Italian municipalities, became citizen towns of a particular kind. Drawn into Rome's civic orbit to varying degrees through a variety of means, these towns were self-supporting. Nonetheless their inhabitants looked to Rome, whether because of the formal military and tributary obligations or, in the case of the Latins as we have seen, because of the cultural and personal ties binding the separate communities to Rome.

The issue of citizenship, vital in Rome from the fourth century to the first century, was to all appearances a singular matter decided only by the people. At certain moments, an elected officeholder would advance a public law proposal to extend citizen privileges and rights to one or another group or individual. The recorded proposals between 350 and 91 are collected in table 5.1. Common to all these occasions is the absence of agreement on how, or whether, to admit a specific group or individual as well as the belief, surfacing at such moments, that decisions about the admission or expulsion of citizens were the prerogative of the Roman people. When Capua, a municipium since the fourth century, fell to Rome during the Second Punic War, the Romans agreed to follow the precedent set in the punishment of Satricum, another rebellious Roman town, in 319. At that time it was the Roman people, convened in a voting assembly, who decided that Satricum should be punished and voted a public law instructing the Roman Senate to determine the penalty. The same, it was agreed in 210, should be done in the case of Capua. The Senate's determination was the most rigorous penalty imaginable, short of total destruction: Capua's governing structures were dismantled and its people reduced in status.[34] Again, in 188, the tribune C. Valerius Tappo successfully defended his public law proposal to admit the restricted citizen inhabitants (cives sine suffragio) of Formiae, Fundanum, and Arpinum as full citizens (cives optimo iure) when some of his colleagues threatened to veto the proposal, on the grounds that the Senate had not given its sanction. The sponsor insisted that only the people could decide on such matters, and the bill was approved.[35] Time and again, too, major innovations in the granting of citizenship were approved by the Roman people in a public assembly. The grant of citizenship to successful Italian prosecutors of Roman senators, for instance, including the manner of tribal assignment and stipulation of rights, is part and parcel of the complicated arrangements enacted in the lex Repetundarum of 123. To be sure the Roman Senate often recommended that laws be brought to the people, and in the Late Republic Rome's military commanders sometimes pronounced grants of citizenship independently, usually to allied soldiers.[36] Nonetheless, the prime instrument in making the incorporation of new citizens possible was the lawmaking assembly.

Correspondingly, the frequent internal opposition to the incorporation of conquered peoples during the Roman drive across Italy was resolved in the public negotiation of lawmaking assemblies. In 126, the question of inclusion in the Roman state was clearly reaching troublesome proportions. In that year, the Roman people accepted the lex Iunia expelling Italians from Roman towns, a bill opposed by C. Gracchus and perhaps intended, Peter Brunt posits, to keep Italians away from an anticipated assembly to consider a proposal by the consul Flaccus to extend citizenship to the Latins.[37] In 122, the Latin colony of Fregellae revolted in response to the failure of Flaccus's proposal.[38] Yet force was not the only Roman approach to the vexing issue of citizenship in the 120s. Efforts were also made to find a solution by giving allies the Roman citizen rights of provocatio—involving protections against physical violence and coercion from officeholders and military commandeers, which had been expanded earlier in the century in lawmaking assemblies for Romans themselves—to allies (table 5.1). These efforts were unsuccessful at the time, but that the situation was contained is some measure of the acceptance by the inhabitants of Italy of the collective voice of the Roman people expressed in a public lawmaking assembly.

From the Roman side, the award of citizenship reflects a reciprocal solution to the problem of maintaining the Roman community during a period of rapid change, reached over time on a strictly ad hoc basis governed by the framework of customary behavior that the Romans understood: the benign approach to coexisting with neighbors was to make them Roman. When the Acerrani were made cives sine suffragio in 332, following the Latin War, the Roman historian Livy, a contemporary of Strabo, described the grant as "making them Roman": "*Romani facti sunt*" is in fact a contemporary expression of this process of absorption and assimilation that had fully entered the vocabulary of accommodation in the first century.[39] To be sure, attitudes to Roman citizenship on the part of the non-Roman inhabitants of Italy continually changed between the late fourth and the second centuries.[40] In the fourth century some were dissatisfied with Rome's citizen arrangements. In 306, the Hernici, offered a choice between incomplete citizen status or continued alliance with Rome, chose to remain allies. They preferred autonomy to restricted membership in the Roman state. Around the same time the Aequi went to war in order to avoid incomplete citizen status.[41]

By the second century, however, hints of such dissatisfaction fade. In 177, the Roman people enacted a bill expelling twelve thousand Latins who had moved to Rome to claim citizenship. In 125, the Latin colony of Fregellae revolted over the Roman refusal to extend citizenship and was utterly destroyed by the Romans, who dismantled even the town's temples. In 95, the consuls carried a law setting up a court to investigate the citizenship claimed by allies resident in Rome; ten thousand men and their families left the city.[42] In 91, the Italian allies went to war because they were refused membership as full citizens in the Roman state. In time, it appears that the developing process that admitted outsiders to the Roman citizen group was fortified by the recognition on the part of outsiders, in particular Latins and Italians, as well as Romans of the mutual advantages of expanding the Roman citizen population by the incorporation of new citizens.

Indeed, on the part of most Italian peoples, the commitment to the Roman way was so deeply rooted that they eagerly accepted the grant of citizenship to loyal allies in 90, in wholehearted accord with the sovereign will of the Roman people as expressed in a public lawmaking assembly.[43] But the case of the Lucani with which we began this chapter raises a question. Given the opposition of the Lucani to Rome, it is not axiomatic that the Romans should have included the Lucani, or others similarly hostile, when they offered full citizen rights to Italians in 90, nor is it axiomatic that the Lucani would ever accept the offer (they did finally accept, in 87). We are entitled to wonder how the Romans could imagine the effective incorporation of outsiders bent on the destruction of Rome and how, in turn, such people could become effective Romans. It is time now to consider some of the Roman mechanisms of integration that made possible the wide acceptance of Roman citizenship on the part of Italians over time, along with the practical acceptance of a Roman way of life and the assumptions, values, rights, and duties that came with citizenship.

ITALIAN ASSIMILATION

Composing his geography late in the first century from secondhand information, the Greek Strabo was not particularly familiar with Italy or its inhabitants. But he knew enough to recognize that the core of the Roman empire was an amalgamation of Italian peoples who were once distinct in regard to language, organization, and custom. In Strabo's day, the distinctions in the case of the Lucanians, Bruttii, and Samnites of southern Italy had deteriorated in pace with their settlements. But even fifty years before, at the time of the Italian War, we might wonder at the depth of the differences separating some Romans and Italians. Consider the town charter of Lucanian Bantia, written in Oscan and engraved on bronze, a public display of Lucanian autonomy as we noted at the beginning of this chapter. Significantly this same charter reveals the progress of change following the Roman expansion across Italy. Not only were the offices and procedures in the surviving fragments of the charter clearly modeled on the Roman charters of Latin colonies established in the region in earlier centuries, but the elite Lucanian draftsmen were by now probably equally conversant in Latin and Oscan. Alienated from Rome, these Lucani were nonetheless adapting Roman ways even before the Italian War.

The Sententia Minuciorum, the record of Roman adjudication of a local land dispute in Liguria, in 117, opens a window onto the process of Italian acculturation.[44] On the one hand the document, as we saw in the previous chapter, reflects a transitional, traditional world of herding. On the other hand it reveals an extraordinarily deep understanding of Roman ways. The Genuates, whose town was a flourishing regional market, sent legates to the Roman Senate to request intervention and adjudication in a local dispute over the use of lands around Genua. The act reveals a recognition on the part of the Genuates of the traditional Roman way of solving community problems, through the mediation of elite Romans. The Senate's selection of two of its members who were brothers, both from the same Minucius family that in an earlier generation had produced a commander who had defeated and arranged satisfactory terms for the Ligurians, reflects the Roman understanding that the personal ties of patronage governed relations between the Roman aristocracy and local elites in Italy.[45] From the language and instructions of the final adjudication in 117 it is clear that some prior merger of cultures had eased the acceptance of a Roman outlook by the local elite situated in the city of Genua.

To a large extent, however, this merger was dependent on the urban status of Genua. Genua and towns like it were hubs for change. With the Roman conquest of Italy, Italian towns and market centers became part of a constellation of communities centering on Rome. Here new relationships and patterns were formed in a changing world. In particular, the local leaders in towns became involved in the apparatus of Roman dominion—administration. Towns served as regional administrative hubs in particular for purposes of the Roman military draft. Inasmuch as the Romans required their Italian allies and allies of the Latin Name to supply troops in numbers set by the original treaty, local leaders counted heads periodically, just like the Romans did at the quinquennial census in Rome. The conscription of Italian troops began with this local registration of young men in the various towns of Italy by local leaders. Furthermore, service as *praefecti sociorum* joined these men in military service with their Roman counterparts, as we shall see later in the chapter, in a setting in which Latin was the language of command. The immediate consequence for elite members of Italian towns and tribal groups was growing familiarity with and use of the Latin language, as well as Roman commercial, legal, administrative, and military practices—that is, acculturation. Thereupon we may imagine that their participation turned to commitment as they were increasingly drawn into the Roman system. Throughout the peninsula the acculturation of Italians to Roman ways began with local leaders whose primary avenue of accommodation was town life and urban culture.

The gradual spread of the Latin language among local elites in Italy provides a measure of the stages of absorption of elite Italians into the Roman state. Before the Italian War of 91–89, Latin tended to be a second language to elite members of Italian communities, whose primary languages were Oscan, Umbrian or related dialects, and Etruscan. Latin was moreover a spoken language: these Italians ordinarily did not write in Latin. Instead they were literate in their primary language.[46] Surviving inscriptions from the sixth to the first centuries in Etruscan, Oscan, and Umbrian and related dialects attest to the widespread and increasing application of writing, introduced initially by the Greeks, to all languages.[47] While the main avenues for the dissemination of writing throughout all Italy were three in number in the sixth through fourth centuries—namely, Greek, Etruscan, and Latin—only one avenue, Latin, became so broad thereafter as to accommodate additional tasks. The Latin language, which earlier had merely provided an alphabet for rendering different dialects, by the second century was seen to be the language of power.[48] In 180, the Oscan-speaking political leaders of Cumae in the ager Campanus petitioned Rome to adopt Latin as the language of official pronouncements.[49]

But language is only one cultural indicator of absorption. Such men also shared a common culture with Romans of their class. Like their Roman counterparts, local Italian elites inhabited a world structured around a hierarchy of status and wealth. Inevitably the aristocracy of wealth embraced all men of wealth and standing in Italy, who were linked in a network of trade and large landholdings. These are the men who received citizenship first. Significantly, however, the most distinctive, common cultural attributes were Greek in origin. A veneer of Greek culture was adapted increasingly in the second century by Romans and Italians alike.[50] Most visible in the elite-sponsored town building projects—baths, temples, and basilicae—in developing urban centers across Italy in the second and first centuries, and in the Greek-based education of high-status Romans, Latins, and Italians, this Greek veneer might suggest an external stimulus for the acculturation of Roman and Italian.[51] Indeed, the process of adapting the characteristic ideas, norms, and structures of contemporary Greek culture, "Hellenization," was a shared phenomenon among all urban peoples of Italy, now as earlier. But now, the phenomenon was clearly boosted by the Roman military occupation of the eastern Mediterranean and the ramifications of that occupation (because of the influx of gold, slaves, books, etc.) in a Rome-dominated Italy. The expansion of Rome from the fourth century onward was the catalyst for Hellenization as for other processes.

Notwithstanding a common base of cultural understandings, particularly apparent in their shared religious life and their interaction in such arenas as public lawmaking, elite and nonelite members of society came to inhabit separate worlds in some respects: local leaders in a Rome-bound world of privilege and domination; the majority of the population in a much less secure world, whose traditional ties to land and community were disrupted, for whom life was generally unpredictable because of the new conditions for access to resources imposed by the Romans. We might suspect, then, that the larger society had different experiences of the assimilation process. Language again provides an index of the acceptance by nonelite Italians of superficial attributes of Roman culture. The everyday use of Latin was clearly restricted to elite members of such communities, men who presumably dealt directly with Romans. The practice of staging plays in Etruscan, Oscan, and Umbrian into the first century and beyond demonstrates the persistence of these dialects among most people in the non-Roman towns of Italy. Yet the wide acceptance of Roman ways by ordinary people by the late second century is clear.

A telling indicator of assimilation is the extent to which public law proposals addressing issues raised by Roman expansion involved conquered peoples as well as Romans, as reflected in their efforts to involve themselves in public law assemblies. Although Roman *ius civile* was by definition centered on Rome and restricted to Romans, public lawmaking sessions soon embraced Roman and non-Roman in a common effort. The importance of lawmaking assemblies as the ultimate mediating authority in Roman society was eventually recognized by the non-Roman inhabitants of Italy, as can be seen on the occasions when Italians agitated for or against the passage of laws in Rome. Presumably the initiative came from local elites, some of whom might have had Roman citizenship and thus sought to make their influence felt at Rome to the benefit of their standing at Rome and at home. In 177, the Latin communities around Rome sent envoys to the Senate to formally request that a law be passed requiring Latins who had migrated to Rome to return to their home communities. The Senate instructed the consul to propose such a bill, which the people enacted as law. In 172, Ligurians petitioned the Romans for relief from wrongful enslavement by the Roman commander M. Popillius Laenas. The tribune M. Marcius Sermo carried a bill in a lawmaking assembly instructing the Senate to establish a special court of investigation (*quaestio*) presided over by the praetor C. Licinius to adjudicate a resolution.[52] A second proposal by M. Marcius ordering M. Popillius Laenas to come before the court was never presented to the people because Popillius appeared anyway.[53] A generation later a similar court of inquiry was proposed, in 149, unsuccessfully, to look into the enslavement of some Lusitanians from Spain, presumably at the request of Lusitanians. Even outside Italy, conquered peoples had some sense of the role of Roman lawmaking assemblies—and certain familiarity with the route and circumstances, perhaps when the Senate's reaction had been negative or noncommittal—that led straight to the Roman people. An uncounted throng of supporters and opponents converged on Rome in 133 for the assembly announced by the tribune Ti. Sempronius Gracchus to consider his land proposal. They included rich men who stood to lose some of their holdings on ager publicus, long in their possession even if irregularly held; men of military age, soldiers, and ex-soldiers without land; Roman and Latin colonists and restricted citizen inhabitants of municipia; and Italians interested in the disposition of such land.[54] Similarly, in 122, in trepidation over the appeal of C. Gracchus's proposed citizenship law, the Senate decreed that Italians must stay at least forty stades away from Rome on the day of the voting assembly. We must wonder at both the size of the noncitizen crowds the Senate anticipated as well as the Senate's fears that these noncitizens could influence the outcome of a voting assembly in which they could not participate.[55] Clearly, the conquered peoples embraced also the Roman ways of resolving division in the community through public lawmaking in Rome.[56] In this context the strident Italian demands for citizenship throughout the second century, which would enable them to participate fully and equally with their Roman compatriots in such events, are more comprehensible.

Italian acculturation at lower levels of society took place along two major and inextricably intertwined avenues: economic changes resulting in the emergence of an Italy-wide economy and participation in the Roman military draft. The conquered Latins, Italians, Italiote Greeks, and others were subject to a developing range of conditions imposed by Rome usually worked out in the Roman Senate: the appropriation of a part of their territories by Rome and the formal attachment of some communities to Rome most commonly by treaties of alliance but sometimes by incorporation through the grant of citizenship.[57] In all instances military obligations as well as specified legal and economic relationships were dictated.[58] All were required to supply troops according to a *formula togatorum* worked out, it is believed, at the time of the original treaty.[59] As we have seen, Roman expansion in Italy necessitated considerable adjustment on the part of Italians in order to survive and flourish. For some Italians, military service with the conquering army of the Romans became an alternative to traditional ways of movement. At the same time, Italians exchanged their labor for the goods and produce available in Roman and Latin towns. Sometimes they migrated to towns. Such alternatives, widely accepted by conquered Italians, involved the acceptance of both superficial and deep attributes of the dominant Roman culture. Some of these we saw earlier, including the adoption of the Latin alphabet to local languages, agricultural changes, and the intensification of a market economy accompanied by monetization. The acceptance of Roman legal categories is manifest in the decision recorded in the Sententia Minuciorum.

The adaptation of the Italians to these Rome-borne changes may be seen as a measure of human determination to survive in a changing world. But what of their acceptance of the deeper attributes of Roman culture to the extent that by the end of the second century we see not only a general desire on the part of all Italians to become Roman but the acceptance of public lawmaking?

Some process was under way among nonelite members of Italy that involved the loosening and remolding of traditional ties with region, community, and leaders. This process, involving the formation of effective relationships between nonelite Italians and the Roman state, was fundamental in allowing the peoples of Italy to accept the new connections offered by Rome, including Roman ways of resolving society wide problems as well as citizenship and the arenas of civic action. The experiences of Roman military service were crucial in the formation of these relationships. Indeed, Roman military service, which for more than two hundred years joined Romans, Latins, and Italians in a common venture, was the main avenue to absorption for an important segment of the nonelite population.[60]

THE ROLE OF MILITARY SERVICE IN ITALIAN ASSIMILATION

After 218 most Roman, Latin, and Italian males participated at some point in their lives in the ongoing conquests of the Roman state. Over the period in question, when the Romans conquered the Mediterranean world, Romans, Latins, and Italians were involved in the military to a degree that astonishes the modern observer. Between 200 and 146, when the Romans were first pushing aggressively into the eastern Mediterranean, the proportion of Roman males serving in the military fluctuated with military needs and ranged from 7 percent, the usual peacetime figure, to 50 percent per year of the entire male population during times of heavy demand.[61] In times of civic crises between 100 and 44 the demands ranged as high as 60 percent. Given that the base population for these percentages is virtually the entire male Roman citizen population of all ages, a figure as high as 60 percent means that the entire male Roman working population in their prime producing years, between the ages of seventeen and forty-five, was serving in the military.

Other Italians were drawn into military service as well. The size of the military manpower pool Rome created in this way was staggering. In 225, more than one hundred years after Rome's conquest of Italy began, the Romans directed all eligible males ages seventeen to sixty to stand by for a call to arms when faced with a serious threat in north Italy from the Gauls.[62] The Greek historian Polybius reports that 273,000 Roman males were listed as eligible for military service during the ensuing crisis.[63] At the same time, eligible males in the same age range among the Latins, Rome's closest allies, numbered 111,000. The Samnites followed in Polybius's list with 103,000; then the Apulians with 75,000; the Abruzzi peoples with 45,000; the Etruscans with 72,000; the Umbrians with

29,000; and the Lucanians with 44,000.[64] Poised to conquer the Mediterranean, the Romans presented a formidable assemblage drawn from all the peoples of Italy as a result of the system of alliances instituted by the Romans and pursuant on conquest.

After 200, the Roman demands for manpower and Roman success overseas involved the male population in a cycle of military mobility in vast numbers. We have figures on the combined participation of Romans, Latins, and Italians in Roman military service. Out of an estimated 850,000 men in Italy between the ages of seventeen and forty-five on average in the first fifty years of the second century, the numbers called up each year ranged from a high of 182,000 (21 percent of total) to a low of 5,500 (2 percent of total). Rarely do we see a year where less than 10 percent of the entire male population of Italy—Romans, Latins, and Italians—is engaged in military service, for increasingly long periods of service.[65] Clearly, a significant proportion of Roman and Italian males in their prime producing years was continuously siphoned off to serve in the army.

That the military experience directly shaped the lives of these men over time is beyond doubt. The extent to which the Roman army was engaged in road and engineering works across Italy and elsewhere, building infrastructures essential for Roman expansion and prosperity, suggests the difficulty of separating military service from a wider Roman experience. This is also apparent in the more prosaic, administrative aspects of army life experienced by the fighting man. All Roman males ages seventeen to sixty were liable for military service, their names and eligibility entered on a military list based on the quinquennial enumeration of citizens. In practice only males ages seventeen to forty-five (iuniores) were called up. Older men ages forty-six to sixty (seniores) were excused from actual service, along with priests, except in times of military emergency, and at age sixty a citizen's military obligation as well as other civic obligations ceased altogether.66 But the younger men were obliged to fight in sixteen campaigns by the time of the Second Punic War, and by the end of the second century soldiers spent on average six years away from home, by modern estimates.67 The number of males involved in the military every year, especially between 218 and 44, was considerable: For over two hundred years Roman military needs drew heavily and constantly on the population of Roman males ages seventeen to forty-five. The draw on fighting men among Rome's Latin and Italian allies was likewise heavy, for these groups provided at times roughly half the troops in Rome's armies. For all males in Italy, military service was a constant fact of life.

For everyone concerned, military demands meshed so closely with community routines that some facets of military service were customarily matters of personal rather than state obligation. In Rome the stages of military preparation from conscription to muster rested to a large extent on ordinary Romans. The regular levy for the four new consular legions formed every year occurred on the Capitoline hill in Rome in March, until the second century, when January became the first month of the year. In this location Roman males eligible for military service assembled in their tribes to be selected, four at a time from each tribe, and assigned one at a time to one of the four legions by the military tribunes.[68] Outside this regular event in Rome, which required males to travel to Rome, military tribunes traveled out from Rome or back to Italy from military encampment to Roman towns and other Roman settlements in Italy to conscript more legionaries as needed, again from the eligible males.[69] Whether in Rome or in Roman territory the recruitment of the new legionaries was sealed simply by the military oath (*sacramentum*) binding them to their commanders—and underscoring the personal dimension of leadership in the military sphere from an early date. Once signed on in this fashion, the soldiers were sent away with orders to report at a specified future date to a muster point where the legion would form up for deployment in Italy or abroad. Until the second century recruits for the most part also equipped themselves initially, providing their own weapons, armor, and clothing.[70] Throughout the campaign, the legionaries paid for their own rations. Only at the end of the campaign did they receive their compensatory stipend. Thus individuals were responsible for presenting themselves for conscription and getting themselves to the legion in a state of armed readiness.

Yet eventually transcending the customary role of individual obligation was a level of state-managed organization that far exceeded levels attained in any other ancient military force.[71] This organization, resting in some of its aspects on an expanded use of writing, is visible in all facets of military activity, from conscription to deployment and supply. Conscription itself depended on a list of eligible males, noting ages and property qualifications, that was compiled every five years from an enumeration of citizens. In 225, the list held the names of 273,000 Romans, a rather large number of bodies to keep track of in a largely oral society. Moreover the numbers changed regularly as the output of citizens' land fell below or climbed above the minimum property qualifications and as new citizens entered or left the pool. Traditionally a large area was designated on the edge of the Campus Martius in the late fifth century, the Villa Publica, for the purpose both of taking the census and reviewing the citizens, as well as holding military levies. The area continued to hold these combined functions in the last century. Surrounded in due course by a colonnaded portico the Villa Publica was thus largely an open space for assembly, conscription, and enumeration, the nearby Temple of the Nymphs serving as an archives to house the growing body of records generated by the need to enumerate the male population.[72]

The Roman military generated other records. Probably before the third century, the Romans had developed a sophisticated and rigorous system of record keeping to identify the current status of their legionary manpower in the field.[73] On the level of the basic unit of organization in each legion, the century, holding one hundred men, the unit commander, a centurion, kept a daily log on each trooper. Daily the centurions noted the presence or absence as well as the conduct of individual troopers, and daily they submitted these unit logs to the military tribunes commanding the maniples, and later cohorts, into which the centuries were grouped. In turn, the ranking tribune submitted the record of soldiers present and absent for the entire legion to the commander so that from day to day he knew exactly how many soldiers were on hand.[74] Not for a thousand years did European armies begin to employ a similar level of personal accounting.

Supply, too, required a high level of administrative organization. Supply was of primary concern to commanders, whose first task at the beginning of a campaign was to contract for the grain, oil, wine, and other staples needed to maintain the legions and the allied contingents in the field. Once the legions began to fight regularly outside Italy in Europe, North Africa, and western Asia after the First Punic War, sources of supply and supply routes became rather complicated and difficult. Yet commanders continued to contract for supplies in Rome, with state or private suppliers, the latter Roman or Italian. We can see how the necessity of moving grain to a Roman army in Syria or Illyria required these private suppliers to seek markets in foreign lands, building ever expanding networks of trade that centered on Rome. Similarly, shipping the grain acquired as tribute from the grain-growing provinces of Sardinia and Sicily to such an army required a large-scale and dependable transport system. Commanders saw also to the equipment of their troops, apt to wear out or disappear in the course of any campaign. In wartime, the output of enemy arms factories could be diverted to Roman use, or allies called on to supply Roman soldiers, or the soldiers set to producing their own gear. In the first century these supplies were also produced by private contractors.[75] So important was military supply in all its aspects that the Romans developed, in ad hoc stages over time, a fairly sophisticated administrative apparatus and staff, managed by a quaestor, to carry it.[76] Of the five centuries of noncombatant specialists on the military lists, one, composed of attendants (*accensi velati*), is thought to have housed the low-level administrative personnel required by military supply.[77]

Associated with these developments is an expanded use of writing. Writing, adapted by Latin speakers over the seventh and sixth centuries to restricted uses, now made possible the collection and transport not only of vast quantities of grain but of the Roman legions themselves. As Roman conquests proceeded, careful and accurate methods of record keeping emerged, making extensive use of writing, simply to keep track of the military pool and to maintain an efficient force especially as the length of military service increased and with it the number of men fighting. The use of writing as a fundamental tool of administration first reached a significant scale in the service of Roman military manpower.[78] Writing was fundamental to Roman military organization. In turn, Roman military organization was a prime factor in the unification of Italy.

Inasmuch as the military experience of Italians resembled that of Romans, the demands of military service imposed a common administrative structure on these outside peoples. For the Latin and Italian allies, meeting the demands of Roman military service entailed an accommodation to Roman standards of organization, beginning with their conscription and deployment. Every allied community was required to contribute infantry and cavalry on request, whose numbers were fixed by the original treaty with Rome.[79] Furthermore, each community kept a list of men ages seventeen to forty-five eligible for military service, like the Roman list, and based also on enumerations of the male population.[80] Until 204, the lists were made locally in Latin and Italian communities. But after 204, the census in the twelve Latin colonies came under the jurisdiction of Roman censors, and the census of the Italian allies may have done so, too, during the course of the next century, although this is uncertain.[81] Roman organization was taking over.

The conditions of military service brought Italians in close proximity to the Roman system. The contingents of allied troops and cavalry conscripted from each community were attached to the legions as supporting units called *alae sociorum*. Initially, these allied contingents were under the general leadership of the consul commanding the Roman legion to which each was attached, but more immediately were under a joint Roman and Italian command consisting of three Italian subordinate commanders from the same community as the soldiers and three junior Roman military commanders, praefecti sociorum, who were equivalent in rank and function to the military tribunes commanding the cohorts in the legions.[82] Later, like the legions, the allied contingents were composed of cohorts, led by Italian commanders, *praefecti cohortum*.[83] The language of command was Latin; the clothing, armor, and weapons of the heavy-armed and light-armed troops were the same in the legions and the allied contingents. While the legionaries received a stipend from which they paid for rations, the allies received a monthly grain allowance of four *modii* of wheat. Training was the same. At the end of a day's march everyone constructed the typical Roman fortification, designed not only for maximum security and rapid deployment of the cohorts but for accountability: every man and every cohort were in their proper places in a Roman camp, ranged neatly in a regular hierarchy of cohorts around the commander's quarters and the camp shrine, where the standards reposed, ritual center of the encampment.[84] The rigorous discipline of Roman military life, the demanding obedience to authority represented in centurions, military tribunes, and commanders, broke down the cultural norms of non-Roman troops and fostered Roman values in their place. Fighting for Rome almost continually in the period from 264 (First Punic War) to 91 (Italian War), Italians eventually came to share much in common with their Roman comrades.

Inevitably the long involvement with the Roman army shaped the assimilation experience of many ordinary members of Italian society. As a result of campaigning with the Romans, Italian allies firmly embraced the Roman sense of organization, regularization, and order. These deep attributes of Roman culture, embodied in the Roman military, held out the promise of security in somewhat precarious lives, as did supply and labor markets in towns. Taken on by non-Romans, these attributes were reinforced by the tangible rewards of military service, land, and cash. Italians and Latins as well as Romans received allotments of land either in colonies or as individual grants. Usually they were resettled in the same units in which they had served. Regularly they received gifts of cash, donatives, from the booty acquired on successful campaigns. These donatives could be quite substantial at times, given the unsophisticated monetary economy of Roman Italy. Such an infusion of cash in the lower levels of society must have contributed greatly to social change in Italy, reinforcing the market economy set in place by Roman expansion and altering conditions of landholding and acquisition by enabling these men to purchase land.[85] Concurrently, military service opened up access to the resources of Rome for many allies and their families as they adapted to Roman ways.

More important, the land grants and colonies preserving the integrity of units that had campaigned together provide an index of the deeper social cohesion fostered at the lower levels of society among all the peoples of Italy by military service. Italians and Latins eventually merged with their Roman comrades. Especially after 200, soldiers show a remarkable unity of interest and loyalty to a Roman system in which men have access to the resources of a conquering state. After the Italian War this unity deepens, notwithstanding social and economic upheaval in Italy as well as increasing conflict within the ranks of Rome's leaders. Even during the Roman civil wars of the first century, both in the period from 87 to 80 and in the period from 50 to 44, soldiers in opposing legions show a great reluctance to fight one another. Instead at the first opportunity they combine forces. Military service had become the chief unifier of Italy by the time of the Italian War.

Such was the assimilation of allies through military service that by the second century the fighting men of Italy formed a large group among the majority population keenly disposed to full inclusion in the conquering Roman state. As a citizen of Rome a soldier was privileged. Roman soldiers received more land and more cash. Outside the military camp, citizens could avail themselves of grain at a fixed price beginning in 123; later grain was free.[86] Roman soldiers had legally defined civil liberties or, more loosely, civil rights—a phrase that conveys the meaning (though not the limited scope, by U.S. expectations) of provocatio to the Romans—and enjoyed more legal protection than Italians.[87] In particular, they were protected from physical punishment (flogging) by a lex Porcia carried in the second century. At times, some Romans sought to ameliorate conditions of military service for the Latin and Italian allies, too, in a variety of ways: by limiting terms of service and ages of conscription or by sharing Roman civil liberties with them. The public law proposals presented on the latter issue in the late second century failed. Of greater concern to the allies were the public law proposals offering citizenship itself. As soldiers fighting alongside the Romans, the allies were well aware that Roman citizenship itself opened up greater access to resources. But the primary way to express power as a citizen was voting, and to do this as well as to exercise all the prerogatives of Roman citizenship, a man had to be duly declared and registered in Rome as a member of a tribe and property class.

TRIBES AND PROPERTY CLASSES

On at least two occasions, under uncertain circumstances and through unreported mechanisms, the Romans lowered the minimum property qualifications for registration in the bottommost infantry rating, Class 5. The reductions—implied by the differences in the minimum property qualifications reported by Fabius Pictor for early Rome, by Cicero for sometime probably before 129, and by Polybius for some intervening date—are reliably linked to military manpower needs.[88] In all likelihood the admission of citizens with no infantry rating (*proletarii*) into the class of landholders (*assidui*)—the practical outcome of lowering the minimum qualification—was accomplished by the determination of a consul or proconsul to conscript men with a rating of 4,000 asses instead of 11,000 asses (or 1,100 denarii) in 214 and of some later commander sometime before 129 to conscript men with only 375 sesterces (equivalent to 1,500 uncial asses).[89] Whatever the mechanism, these reductions are testimony to a widening gap between effective and ineffective citizens in Rome. The predicament, an outgrowth of Roman expansion, would seem to bode ill for the future. Nonetheless the state flourished, its legions replenished from the ready and numerous proletarii, many of them new citizens, by the simple act of lowering the property qualifications. That the step was taken without visible recourse to a lawmaking assembly suggests it was uncontroversial. Certainly the state's defensive needs (not to mention the interests of public harmony) provide compelling reason to boost a large class of military-ready men to a viable level of citizen performance. But like the continual admission of new citizens, which often was controversial, these reductions bear witness to the bedrock of Roman success: the purposeful adjustment of the state's most important resource, the Roman people, to permit the continued growth of Rome.

Making such adjustment possible was the flexibility of two structures that form our subject in this section, the Roman tribes and property classes. Every Roman belonged to one of thirty-five voting districts, or tribes (*tribus*), and one of several status and economic brackets, or property classes (*classes*), formal and legally conceived groups of closely regulated membership. Together the tribes and the property classes, the latter variously divided for political action into 193 small units called centuries, formed the bases of civic participation in Rome. To a large degree they were overlapping bases, although the tribes, whose corporate identity and structure were critical to the effective operation of the state, formed the more important unit of Roman citizen organization.[90] The mesh of tribes and centuries in the first century was ceremoniously displayed on the occasion of the quinquennial enumeration and review of citizens. Assembled in their thirty-five tribes, systematically arranged in accordance with custom and geographic location, the Roman people stood before the censors in ranked order by property classes and centuries.[91] More important was the discreet mesh of tribes and centuries in the reformed centuriate assembly, to which we shall return shortly. Here let us begin with the tribes.

The Roman tribes, an institution believed to be unique in Italy to the Romans, were in origin territorial districts into which Roman state land owned by Roman citizens was ordered.[92] In the fifth century, the hinterland of the city of Rome, an area measuring roughly four thousand square kilometers, was divided into seventeen rural tribes, and the city itself was divided into four urban tribes.[93] Between the fourth and second centuries, however, the geographic relationship of the tribes and tribesmen to Rome changed when the state appropriated more and more Italian land and assigned it to citizens, scattering Roman-owned properties at some distance from the city. In the subsequent adjustment of the Roman tribes to fit the new lands, the Romans played around with the original tribal organization of Roman territory, creating fourteen new tribes on recently confiscated territory that abutted onto the original tribes. Four tribes were created in 387 on land taken from Veii (Livy 6.5.8). Insofar as we can determine, more were created in pairs of two in 357 (Livy 7.5.12), 332 as noted later (Livy 8.17.11), 318 (Livy 8.20.21), 299 (Livy 10.1.3), and 241, with the result that Roman tribes now extended from south of Capua and the Volturnus River to lacus Ciminius in the north and west to Reate on the via Salaria. Jumping the central Apennine ridges, another tribe was located farther west still, along the Adriatic coast. After 241 the Romans created no more new tribes on confiscated land but allocated Roman-owned land among existing tribes in what can be called "tribal extensions." This was done first in 232, in connection with the viritane allotments granted to citizens by the lex Flaminia, on territory taken from the Senones in north Italy. The mechanisms for creating the new tribes and extensions are obscure, perhaps because the necessity was recognized throughout the Roman community without question. The censors, responsible for tribal registration, are the most likely agents of the new additions.[94] In fact, Livy, commenting on the census of 332, notes that the censors at this time added two new tribes for recently conquered lands.[95]

In any event, the process of tribal expansion entailed gradual and clearly deliberate adjustments. Initially the Romans created new tribes around Rome. Then they stretched the boundaries of both old and new tribes. Finally, when the extension of tribal boundaries into adjoining areas around Rome was no longer possible, because Roman state land abutted onto the territory of a Latin town or an allied Italian people, the Romans created tribal extensions at some distance from the original tribe.[96] Such extensions were regularly adjacent to or near the territory of Latin colonies; Latin colonies, in turn, which might have walled urban centers (oppida), were often situated near new tribes in order to offer protection against hostile encroachments.[97] Through this process, territories seized from defeated Italians, on which private Roman landholdings were established, were fitted to the existing structure of Roman tribes. In the development of a new relationship between the conquered lands and Rome, the Roman flair for defining new circumstances within a framework of customary behavior shows itself again.

As the tribe in origin was a territorial district, so each citizen in principle belonged to the tribe dictated by his landholdings and thus his place of residence.[98] If he owned land in the city of Rome itself, resided permanently in the city and owned no land, or stood on the margins of Roman society, he belonged to one of the four urban tribes whose membership was for the most part restricted to urban inhabitants and select groups such as former slaves.[99] A random and unchanging selection of Romans in the various tribes by no means follows from this principle, however. From the beginning of the Republic there were great disparities among tribesmen with respect to wealth and status. In the rural tribes, filled with men who owned land in that tribe, a few tribesmen were equites while most, the men called assidui, were enrolled in Classes 1 through 5. The rural tribes also held Romans whose valuation fell below the minimum property qualifications for the infantry classes. These were proletarii, the men "below the classes" (*infra classem*).[100] The ownership of land, not the assessed value of the land, determined membership in a rural tribe.

Over time, the varying life circumstances confronted by individual Romans altered other traditional patterns of tribal membership. In the first place, tribesmen on new tribes and tribal extensions included citizens previously registered in another tribe who were now recipients of land allotments as colonists, or on a man-by-man basis (viritim). Among them also were Romans from leading clans, whose willing transfer to new tribes secured the hierarchic principle of the voting districts.[101] Significantly, the dispersal of citizens across Italy in private landholdings and the creation of additional tribes were managed in such a way as to maintain a balance in Rome's voting assemblies—including public lawmaking assemblies. More critical, a rather high level of personal mobility brought about by land settlement and military service produced a situation by the late second century where residency in a rural or urban tribe, that is, a specific geographic location, was not accompanied by membership in that tribe. For, despite individual migration, a Roman's tribe remained the same. Neither the censors nor the Roman people ever transferred citizens from one tribe to another, with the exception of settlers on new tribes, including noble Romans reassigned to new rural tribes, or former slaves. (The review of these rural immigrants' property ratings is another matter, however.) Hence, citizens in rural tribes who migrated permanently to Rome were not placed in urban tribes. Permanent city residents, such Romans nonetheless remained in their rural tribes. They were not reassigned to urban tribes.[102] Nor, after the lex Iulia of 90, were new citizens from the municipia of Italy who migrated to Rome registered in Rome's urban tribes. Their tribe was the tribe of their townsmen. Increasingly tribal affiliation was simply inherited, having little to do with place of residence or ownership. By the first century, the principle of tribe as territorial district had effectively collapsed. All the same, it would be revitalized following the Italian War, at least for a while, owing to certain developments, to which we shall return.

The changing character of the Roman tribes notwithstanding, the primary attachment of every citizen to the Roman state was his tribe. Born into the tribe of his father and registered on the tribal rolls at birth or age one year, a citizen could expect to spend his life in the tribe.[103] From the age of citizen responsibility onward, seventeen years, he performed every civic activity—from voting to military service, from the payment of a land tax (discontinued in 167) to state ritual observance—as a tribe member. His political voice found its purest expression in the group vote of Rome's tribal assemblies. His welfare rested first and foremost on the human network within the tribe, which provided housing for the immediate relationships linking family members, friends, and neighbors, people and leaders. His tribe, and the tribe of each Roman, was his principal community.

While the basis of civic participation was registration in a Roman tribe, the degree of participation was determined by economic or property rating. Information pertinent to the property classes, in the period between roughly the Second Punic War and ca. 140, when the sesterce replaced the *as* as the "normal official unit of reckoning of the Roman state," is presented in table 5.2.[104] Until the late second century, the assignment to a particular property class reflected a citizen's ability to arm himself for war, placing him in the cavalry (equites), infantry (Classes 1 through 5), or support units (infra classem), as appropriate. Every year when four new legions were formed for the two new consuls, the infantry was drawn from citizens in five numbered property ratings, called *classes* (sing. *classis*), and the cavalry and support units from two unranked ratings, shown in table 5.2, column 1. Men who served as legionaries, the heavily armed soldiers forming the main strength of Rome's army, had property qualifications that placed them in Classes 1 through 3. Men in Classes 4 and 5 were lightly armed skirmishers. Beneath these five infantry ratings was an unranked class for Romans with insufficient means to qualify for assignment in a ranked property class and thus described in Latin as citizens infra classem. The support units were drawn from this class. Ranked above the five infantry classes, in addition, stood a single rating for citizens who could (in origin) maintain a horse. Citizens in this group were cavalrymen (equites), more commonly called equestrians. Included in their number were the leading families of the state whose members supplied Rome's political leadership throughout the Republic. Testimony to the defense priorities of a small-scale community, the property classes of early Rome assumed an economically, socially, and numerically stable male population. Over time, however, the classes encompassed a population whose shifting configuration was unimagined by the originators of the Servian Reform.

In pace with the social and economic transformation attendant on Roman expansion in our period of interest, the customary census of Roman citizens envisaged by the property ratings changed. In particular, the number of Romans registered in the highest and lowest classes multiplied, as new-sprung extremes of wealth and penury appeared in Roman society. Most visibly affected was the membership of the equestrian class, the highest social and political status group, whose membership soon formed the most important pool from which new political leaders emerged.[105] There were few equites at the time of the Servian reform, early in the fourth century, when an equestrian rating determined responsibility for cavalry service. (The early Roman military organization probably needed about 1,600 equites annually.[106]) At that time, according to Roman tradition, a formal body known as the "equestrians with a public horse" (*equites equo publico*), numbering 1,800, came into existence, whose members were registered in the first eighteen centuries of the centuriate assembly and periodically reviewed by the censors as to their qualifications.[107] Under the year 225, the Greek historian Polybius records that 23,000 Romans qualified as equites, out of an able-bodied male population of 250,000. The larger-than-might-be-expected figure, nearly 10 percent of the male population, is doubtless owed to a combination of factors, including the role of money, trade, and war booty in creating an aristocracy of wealth in the Roman population over the preceding century and the enfranchisement of men from Latin and Italian towns with the same rating as their Roman counterparts.[108] Nonetheless, the Romans continued to restrict membership in the elite group of equestrians with a public horse to 1,800 or 2,400 men.[109] Perhaps the traditional ceiling reflected Roman belief over the centuries that this number represented the traditional dimensions of Rome's highest status group; or it represented an effort to control entry into that group.[110] Not surprisingly the men whose wealth qualified them for registration in the equestrian class far exceeded that restricted group. These men, technically labeled *tribuni aerarii*, also come to be called equestrians even though they were formally registered in Class 1.[111] In short, entry into the highest property class was somewhat flexible.

Correspondingly flexible was entry into and removal from Classes 1 through 5, given the changing economic prospects and resources of ordinary citizens as reflected (eventually) in the assets needed for membership in these property classes. At some point, the Romans expressed the requirements of the various classes in asses (and, after the adjustments in Rome's coinage, sesterces), as shown in table 5.2. By the time these equivalents become known to us there are huge gaps between some classes. In the late third and early second centuries, the minimum worth of an equestrian was fixed at 1,000,000 asses, ten times that of Class 1, fixed at 100,000 asses (this was later raised to 120,000).[112] At the same time Class 4 was 25,000 (or 20,000) asses, over five times higher than

Class 5, 4,000 asses. By the end of the second century, Class 5 had been lowered to 375 sesterces, six times less than Class 4. Here in microcosm is the growing disparity among members of Roman society right before Rome's greatest overseas expansion.

What the monetary rates replaced is not known, but land values certainly underpin the amounts on our table: Worth was always measured in terms of land. More precisely, the rates reflect a valuation of land based on the fertility (*ubertas*) of land in ownership, that is, the output or productivity, as attested by the landholder in his declaration (*professio*) to the censors.[113] In the same way, land rents were based on yields, not acreage.[114] Sadly, we do not know the formula Roman censors employed to assign a money equivalent to the given set of assets whose valuation constituted a citizen's census or whether the "fertility" in question was tied to the potential or the actual productivity of specified properties. The developing practice of centuriation between the fourth and second centuries, when the Romans were appropriating lands of varying agricultural qualities and uses, implies a conscious effort to systematize the business of measuring potential output. Men used to the friable soil of Latium needed a way of evaluating the wet plains of the Po River valley. Well before any such need becomes evident, however, and continuing long after, the frequency of Rome's distinctive census, to which we now turn, points to actual yields.

With puzzling regularity, Roman men traveled to Rome to declare themselves, their families, and their holdings to the censors.[115] Based on his personal declaration (professio), the censors weighed each man's current economic standing and assigned or reassigned him to the appropriate property class.[116] Such a task we may readily imagine was not performed by the censors alone, notwithstanding the report of Pliny the Elder about one Roman censor of prodigious memory who knew the name of every Roman citizen. In point of fact, the censors depended heavily on the knowledgeable assistance of that small number of Romans whose role in civic life, although virtually unreported, was of fundamental importance, namely, the 175 curatores tribuum from Rome's thirty-five tribes. Elected tribe by tribe, to the number of five in each tribe from each of Rome's five numbered classes, the curatores functioned as supervisors of their classes.[117] As each tribe was summoned for review and the tribesmen filed by the censors to make their declarations, man by man, the tribe's curatores stood by, ready to confirm a man's personal declaration or to fill in the gaps for absentees. Keeping track of local changes affecting a tribe's membership, the curatores had firsthand knowledge about the status of private property in the tribe and about the circumstances of fellow tribesmen in their classes. The curatores' function as ready sources of information on such matters accounts for the tribal unit of assessment employed at the census. In this way, the censors scrupulously reviewed a citizen population numbering, by the end of the second century, about three hundred thousand men. The chief product of this review was a listing of all citizens, citizen households, and citizen assets from which was developed a separate listing of all available fighting men (males between the ages of seventeen and sixty) and their classification. The objective was twofold: the review kept the Roman Senate and elected leaders fully and accurately informed about the number of Rome's fighting men, and it determined the voters for the 193 centuries of the centuriate assembly. Astonishingly, the lengthy process required to meet this objective was repeated every five years, down to the first century.[118]

The regular, five-year cycle of review, unusual even in antiquity, merits examination, particularly in view of the eventual size of the Roman population and the land area over which it spread.[119] Other ancient states and empires, including the Roman Empire, experienced more leisurely cycles of enumeration and assessment—fourteen years in the case of Ptolemaic Egypt—if indeed there was a regular cycle at all.[120] Since the advent of the modern census in the eighteenth century, the customary cycle is ten years in length.[121] Although the rationale for a cycle of ten years' duration is nowhere explicitly stated, before the twentieth century, it most likely reflects different social, political, and economic exigencies than Rome experienced.[122] These differences, at any rate, probably explain the ten-year cycle adopted by the drafters of the U.S. Constitution, who established a census for the purpose of determining the number of representatives elected in the individual states of the new United States.[123] The men attending the Constitutional Convention proposed cycles of five to seven, ten, fifteen, and twenty years. They settled on a ten-year cycle.[124] Facing comparable restrictions with respect to communications and transportation, the Roman state nonetheless mounted a full-scale assessment of its people every five years. What explains the significantly shorter length of the Roman cycle?

From the Romans' perspective, a five-year cycle most closely encompassed the chaotic spins and twists to which Roman citizens were subject, especially with respect to the land. Between the fourth and second centuries, Romans individually experienced rapidly changing circumstances. During this period Romans went to war in high numbers and with increasing frequency. The Roman population dispersed and increased, as new land resources became available. Migrants encountered varied climatic and soil conditions across central Italy, where by 241 Rome had created fourteen new rural tribes. Roman farms and ranches in the Velina tribe, along the mountainous eastern coast, faced different conditions than their counterparts in the Falerna enjoying the rich soil of Campania. Sweeping variations in Italy's arable land ensured that the changeable character of Roman life became highly localized, too, a trend reinforced by the creation of self-regulating tribes and tribal extensions. All the same, Romans everywhere faced the common adversities of premodern life: crops failed, animals and men died, and war intervened. Farmers in all the tribes experienced good years and bad, and the smaller the farm the slimmer the buffer between continuation and disaster. A productive farm could slide quickly into ruin, leaving its owner with insufficient assets for registration in the same class. Conversely, a land grant in a new colony could provide a man with sufficient assets for registration, perhaps for the first time, as an *assiduus*. In effect a man's census, monitored during the regular enumeration of citizens, encapsulated the circumstances of the previous five years and gave him a "place" in the military and political structure of the state for the next five years.[125]

A tenacious link between the property ratings and land yields persisted long after the monetization of the system, as the reductions described at the beginning of this section attest. The first reduction was most likely made in 214, in response to heavy losses during the Second Punic War.[126] The second may be tied to Rome's wars in the years immediately before 133, when the tribune Ti. Gracchus attempted to increase the number of citizens available for military service in the infantry (Classes 1 through 5) through the redistribution of ager publicus. As with the ratings themselves we are uncertain about the underlying circumstances. Did more men have less land and thus fell below the classes? Most modern historians take this scenario for granted. Or did an uncontrolled influx of hard cash into Italy contribute to a decrease in prices and a corresponding decrease in the valuation of the output of existing holdings, so that Romans with land found that their assets were insufficient for registration as assidui?[127] In any event, even when the Class 5 qualification was lowered to 1,500 uncial asses (375 sesterces), sometime before 129, the sum is still substantial in terms of first-century buying power, considering that a month's ration of wheat, 5 modii, cost HS 3 at first-century prices.[128]

The disparity among members of Roman society reflected in the property ratings underlies the organization of the centuriate assembly, which, unlike the tribal assemblies, reflected the economic and status divisions in Roman society. For the purpose of voting the property classes were divided into a disproportionate number of centuries, each of which carried one vote. (Table 5.2. displays the close relationship between property classes and centuries in the first century). The higher the property class, the more centuries it contained. Hence, as measured by centuries, well-to-do Romans had more voting power than Romans who were less prosperous, although, as A. Yakobsen has conclusively shown, the voting power of ordinary Romans was significant.[129] What the table does not show is the further disparity between the concentration of centuries in the highest property classes and the number of men holding those ratings. In particular Class 1, which held comparatively few citizens, nonetheless had the most centuries, 80 out of 193, and consequently the most votes. Below the men of Class 1 were the much more numerous members of Class 2, divided into only 20 centuries; above them were the equites equo publico, restricted to 1,800 to 2,400 men but divided into 18 centuries with eighteen votes. To all appearances we are dealing with an explicit formula calculated to ensure that the outcome of the voting in the centuriate assembly reflected the will of the most prosperous Romans.

The formal pivot of the union of Roman, Latin, and Italian in Roman citizenship was the tribal system. The potential of the Roman tribes in absorbing new citizens is revealed in the reform of the centuriate assembly toward the end of the third century.[130] Within a generation of the creation of the last two tribes in 241, the 170 centuries constituting Classes 1 through 5, which formed the core of the centuriate assembly, were disbanded and reconstituted in such a fashion that in each class each century held members from only one tribe and in each class each tribe supplied two centuries—one of fighting men (iuniores) and one of reserves (seniores).[131] Thus, Class 1 held 70 centuries, two from each of the thirty-five tribes, as probably did Class 2 and also Classes 3, 4, and 5. Yet, as we shall see later, centuries were conflated into voting units in such a way that the total voting capacity of the five classes remained what it had been before, namely 170 votes, despite the actual increase in the number of centuries.

Significantly omitted from this reform were the highest- and lowest-ranking members of Roman society, neither of whom served in the infantry. Above Class 1 were the equites equo publico, in eighteen centuries, whose numbers included senators until 129. Below Class 5 stood five noncombatant centuries—four of them technicians of a sort, namely, engineers (*fabri*); trumpeters (*liticines*); horn blowers (*cornicines*); and servants (*accensi velati*); and the last the Roman proletarii, so called because they could provide only children (*proles*) for the state, thought to comprise a majority of the Roman people from the second century onward. Thus, the cavalrymen and the noncombatants formed an exception to the tribal basis of the new organization of the five classes of foot soldiers in that they filled centuries indiscriminately, without regard to tribal affiliation. Notwithstanding the exception at either end of the social range, the essential difference between the old and the new centuriate assembly was provided by the cohesive force of the tribe. In the new assembly, citizens cast their votes not only as members of a property class but also as tribesmen.

The ramifications of this tribe-oriented reorganization become evident when we consider the complicated voting procedures of the centuriate assembly.[132] Voting commenced with one century of fighting men drawn by lot from Class 1, called the *centuria praerogativa;* the results of their vote were announced on completion.[133] Then followed voting by the remaining sixty-nine centuries in Class 1, perhaps successively and hierarchically—that is, the thirty-four remaining centuries of fighting men cast their votes first and after them the thirty-five centuries of reserves. Next came the twelve centuries of equestrians with a public horse, and then the noncombatant century of engineers (fabri), which might have voted with the thirty-four centuries of fighting men. When these centuries had voted, the results of the vote were announced, the herald calling on a spokesman from each century to relay how the century had voted.[134] The next centuries to vote were the six centuries, six hundred men, of equestrians with a public horse, who constituted the elite group known as "six votes" (*sex suffragia*). The results of the vote were again announced. At this point the voting procedure of the reformed assembly changed.

Beginning with the votes of the men of Class 2, the principle of "one century one vote" gave way to a different principle. Once the 70 centuries of Class 1, the 18 centuries of cavalrymen, and the single noncombatant century of engineers had voted, 89 votes had been cast out of an absolute total of 193. There remained 104 possible votes. But after the reform there were considerably more centuries still to vote. Consequently, beginning with Class 2 and extending through Class 5 as well as the four remaining noncombatant centuries—the trumpeters, the horn blowers, the servants, and Romans without a ranking (proletarii)—the centuries voted in combination. Lily Ross Taylor, building on earlier suggestions by Mommsen and drawing on the procedure detailed in the draft statute of 11 CE known as the Tabula Hebana concerning the procedure for voting honors to the dead Germanicus, has contrived this likely reconstruction: Before the men of Class 2 cast their votes, which were probably twenty in number, the names of the thirty-five tribes were drawn by lot to determine in which of ten urns members of the thirty-five centuries of fighting men would deposit their ballots and in which of ten urns members of the thirty-five centuries of reserves would deposit theirs. The voting of Classes 3 through 5, as well as that of the four noncombatant centuries (perhaps included with Class 5), were handled in the same fashion, by combining the centuries by lot.[135]

Playing throughout these complicated procedures, as an essential but unvoiced measure, were the thirty-five tribes. Each century in the five classes that voted in effect voted as the subunit of a tribe. Each tribe held ten centuries for the purposes of the centuriate assembly, tribesmen forming two sets of five centuries according to age and property class. How the centuries of a given tribe voted was a matter of immediate public knowledge. The tribe, at specific points in the proceedings, mattered: first, on the selection of the first century to cast its vote (centuria praerogativa)—made by drawing a name from the urn for the lots, which held the names of all thirty-five tribes—which voted first and whose vote was announced in advance of the other voting; and second, on the announcement of the voting results from Class 1, which also entailed identifying the tribe of each century. Presumably, identifying the tribes had a similar impact in both instances. For the announcement of voting results for each century of the first class was an announcement of how the wealthiest members of each tribe voted. Knowing the importance that Romans attached to status in the voting and any other arena, we may imagine the effect on the Romilian century of fighting men, say, of Class 2 when the Romilian century of Class 1 voted in favor of a particular slate of candidates. Of course, in the case of the centuria praerogativa, selected by lot, the effect was tempered by divine intervention; Jupiter was again instrumental when the tribes entered the procedure of the centuriate assembly for a third time.[136] The centuries of Class 2 did not vote as single units but as combinations: seventy centuries, representing the tribesmen of thirty-five tribes, cast twenty votes. The combination of centuries was achieved randomly by placing the names of the thirty-five tribes into the urn for the lot and drawing names out again, once for the centuries of fighting men and once for the reserves. In summary, the voting procedure of the centuriate assembly turned at crucial moments on the tribes. Fully mindful of the importance of the tribes, Q. Tullius Cicero advised his brother to learn the tribal locations and memberships in order to campaign effectively for high office.[137]

Behind its organizational framework of centuries and property qualifications the reformed centuriate assembly hid the fundamental unifying role of the tribe in building the assembly.[138] Arguably this was because the tribal role subsumed a panoply of assumptions shared by the Roman people that were never voiced; rather, they were taken implicitly for granted. Whatever the explanation, the fact remains that the potential cohesive force of the Roman tribes was built into the reformed centuriate assembly in the mid- to late third century.

In the reform of the centuriate assembly, the tribal potential for cohesion is critical but submerged. This cohesive force is more easily identified in the functions of the tribal assembly, where the tribes formed the actual voting units and were not submerged in the centuries. In consequence of the lex Publilia of 471, which made tribes rather than curiae responsible for the election of plebeian officials, the foremost political manifestation of tribal organization is the full tribal assembly of the Roman people (comitia tributa) and its modified version, the plebeian tribal assembly (concilium plebis).[139] The steadily increasing role of the tribal assemblies thereafter provides compelling evidence of the weight of the tribes in Roman political life. Among the business handled by the tribes, public lawmaking was of primary importance to the direction of the Roman state. Routinely as well the tribal assembly met (in July like the centuriate assembly) to elect the minor officeholders of Rome (*magistratus minores*): quaestors and military tribunes (*tribuni militum*); tribunes and plebeian aediles when the tribal assembly was constituted as the plebeian tribal assembly, presided over by tribunes and rid of patricians; at different times, *decemviri litibus iudicandis*, *quattuorviri praefecti* C.C., *tresviri capitales*, and *tresviri a.d.a.*; and in different combinations of tribes (to the number of seventeen) selected by lot, the priests (pontifices) and even the chief priest (pontifex maximus). Noteworthy about the lesser magistrates selected by the tribes is their immediate involvement in the legal, military, and administrative routines of the Roman state. These are the officials with whom most people might expect to come into contact, in the city, in colonies, or in military camp. Doubtless the election of Rome's minor officeholders was important to Romans, despite the inattention of our sources to these elections compared to the elections of praetors and consuls in the same month, because the candidates over time came more and more from municipalities. For such men, success at the polls provided an opportunity for entry into the ruling circle. Success depended, however, on their ability to tap into vital tribal networks.

The personal relationships maintained at the tribal level are borne out by the requirements of civic life. Official confirmation of status and worth, as a freeborn member of the Roman state, required a man's physical presence at the quinquennial census, when the Roman censors reviewed the citizen list and noted the property and family of each man who presented himself, with the help of the curatores tribuum (discussed previously). Every Roman was known to the officials of his tribe. In the second century, the Romans began to regularly include tribal affiliation as part of their formal self-designation. The lex Repetundarum of the Gracchan period instructed the praetor to post the names of 450 jurors, giving not only their filiation and cognomina but their tribal affiliation.[140] The practice, we know from other epigraphic material, was observed until the imperial period.[141] It is apparent that tribal affiliation came into play in the changing legal procedures of the second and first centuries, although how it did is regrettably obscure. We have the impression from a number of laws that the parties to a suit paid attention to tribal affiliation when selecting jurors from the larger panel.[142] The impression is reinforced by the special tribal elections enacted by the lex Plautia in 89 to select 15 jurors from each tribe, that is, by the tribesmen of each tribe, for the standing court instituted by the statute of Q. Varius to decide cases of treason and held again in 81 to choose the 300 equestrians for Sulla's expanded Senate and again in 70 to select the jurors of the three panels instituted by the lex Aurelia.[143] Routinely, too, the tribes selected the 105 men—3 from each tribe—who sat as the centumviral court or court of One Hundred Men (*centumviri*).[144] In matters of law, in particular of legal decisions, the Romans were clearly conscious and careful of the tribal voice and tribal loyalties. In such arrangements it is clear that the tribes had become the central locus for maintaining the social and political networks of the new Roman state by the second century.

More compelling evidence of the growing importance of the tribes in Roman political life is the greatly increased role of the tribal assemblies and the greatly diminished role of the centuriate assembly after the late third century in enacting law.[145] Even after the demise of the Republic, Roman tribes for a time retained a symbolic importance. In the late first century BCE, honors decreed to foreigners who had aided Rome in times of military need and to non-Roman veterans sometimes included citizenship and the privilege of enrollment in a tribe.[146] Long before then, the tribes had also become the chief mechanism for the absorption of new citizens.

New citizens like new lands had to be accommodated to the tribal system. As long as the numbers of new citizens were small, such accommodation was relatively direct. Newly created tribes or tribal extensions were sometimes filled with new citizens. The Quirina tribe, created in 241 on territory confiscated from the Sabini, was filled with Sabini, granted incomplete citizenship at the beginning of the third century, and now made full citizens.[147] But when the gradual accretions to the Roman citizen population became an avalanche as a result of the statutes of 90 and 89, the matter of tribal assignment was controversial because the new citizens outnumbered the old. We shall return to the controversy and its resolution in part 3. Suffice to say that arrangements for new citizens were slow in coming over the years between 86 and 49, and they came at great cost.[148] Always the Romans strove to maintain the integrity of the traditional system.

But over time the registration of new citizens in the Roman tribes entailed a massive yet assiduously practical shuffle. Lily Ross Taylor has assembled a convenient list of Italian communities, organized by Augustan region, identifying their tribes and including dates of full incorporation, when known; many are not known.[149] Towns in regions that were previously Roman territory, and thus already had a tribal affiliation, kept the same tribe. Latin colonies were enrolled in the tribes to which their leading magistrates already belonged.[150] The Italian peoples tended to be enrolled in tribes that were nearby or adjoining their lands already. Thus, the Aurunci were enrolled in the Teretina, established in 299, along the coast between the Volturnus and Liris Rivers in territory confiscated from that people.[151] Often, too, the principle was followed of putting the same peoples in the same tribes. Most of the Hernici, for instance, were enrolled in the Poblilia, established in 358 on land confiscated from the Hernici, after a few of their numbers had entered the tribe in earlier generations. By 90 the Poblilia was "already recognized as the tribe of that people."[152] Similarly the Vestini were enrolled in the Quirina; and the Paeligni and Marsi in the Sergia. The outcome was a solidly ethnic infusion in many of the individual rural tribes—usually viewed as a way of diminishing the importance of the tribe's vote.[153] In some districts the Roman tribes took on a distinctly Italian cast. As a result, the tendency for membership in a Roman tribe to provide a group identity was reinforced by the influx of new tribesmen who were in possession of a strong sense of group or ethnic identity to begin with. While the initial considerations determining the new tribal assignments and their political results vary greatly from one region of Italy to another, what is most striking is the Romans' recognition of local ties and local political culture in the registration of new citizens in Roman tribes, both before and after 90.[154]

Accordingly, several generations after the reform of the centuriate assembly the cohesive potential of the tribes manifested itself more fully. Different meanings had been attached to tribal membership in the second century. Still more changes ensued as a consequence of the grant of citizenship to Italian peoples in 90. Hereafter, the diversity in form and local function of town centers changed, as the Romans imposed a greater political uniformity on Italy. The notion of tribes as territorial districts made up of the private landholdings of citizens was transformed. Tribes became the districts of individual towns, municipia where some of the tribal functions such as census registration once carried out in Rome now occurred, certainly by the time of Caesar.[155] In accepting Roman citizenship, Italian communities also accepted Roman law and administrative organization. Local offices and tribal positions were modified to conform to a Roman system of administration. *Quattuorviri* or *duoviri* replaced *meddici*, for example, as local officials assumed the titles of Roman counterparts.[156] By the middle of the first century, Italy was becoming a region of municipalities, on the model of earlier Latin municipia and coloniae, as the complexities of fora, conciliabula, oppida, vici, and pagi were disappearing. The process called the "municipalization" of Italy had begun, by which modern historians understand the creation of a bureaucratic apparatus centered on towns that made Italy an administrative whole.[157] Scholars believe that towns replaced tribes, after 89, as the focal point for social and political relationships, especially where tribal lands were widely scattered across Italy.[158] But, whether in the accommodation of Italian towns to Roman tribes or the modification of the names of Italian administrative offices along Roman lines, manifest in these Italy-wide changes, Roman flexibility in the face of existing conditions as well as Italian adaptation to Roman ways are clearly visible. The Roman genius for using customary arrangements to deal with the challenges of geographic and demographic expansion as they arose had again produced a potentially resilient, functioning, and effective political and social system.

CONCLUSION

Beginning in the fourth century, the Romans expanded across Italy in a broad-scale effort, redirecting traditional life to function along Roman lines. The foundation of this program was constructed on individual alliances with the various Italian groups whose primary requirement was that conquered peoples furnish an assigned number of troops to serve alongside Romans in further campaigns of conquest. Equally important were the periodic grants of citizenship that Romans had for centuries extended to select communities and elite members of Italian communities together with tribal membership and registration in the highest property classes. Although less readily granted to the majority population, citizenship was nonetheless desired, and sometimes achieved, by many members of the larger Italian society, especially those who had served with the Roman army. The success of the Roman absorption of Italians is seen not only in the eventual increase in the number of citizens but in the prosperous expansion of the Roman state.[159]

The magnitude of the Roman achievement in bringing the Italian peoples together as Roman citizens was matched by the commitment of the newcomers to the Roman system and the degree to which they became fully functioning members of the Roman state. The passions and commitment of the combatants on both sides in the Italian War reveal firm agreement among the peoples of Italy about the primary importance of citizenship in opening access to the privileges of full membership in the Roman state. The bedrock on which these achievements rested was the Roman practice of allowing both new and rehabilitated citizens full access to the vote and the political process as members of a Roman tribe and property class. On receipt of citizenship outsiders formally entered the Roman state through registration in a Roman tribe and property class, achieved by making declaration of their property holdings and places of residence before the censors in Rome on the occasion of the quinquennial census. By the first century, grants of citizenship, military service, and the everyday demands of life in the Roman world had created a wide variety of structures of accommodation—economic, political, and military—between Romans and Italians on all levels.

The permeability of Roman citizenship made possible the erection of Roman structures of order in Italy. While citizenship grants were sometimes a result of action by the Roman Senate, just as adjustments in property ratings were probably achieved by a commander's fiat, at other critical moments when the decision was somewhat controversial the incorporation of outsiders was approved by vote of the people in a lawmaking assembly. The most critical moment came during the Italian War of 91–89. Called together in a voting assembly to consider a proposal of law, Romans agreed as a people to a major redirection of their goals on granting citizenship. Allies could henceforth be Roman. Thus in the process of incorporation, as on other aspects of the expansion across Italy, public lawmaking assemblies gave the Romans a forum for developing community consensus on many of the more controversial decisions. Equally important, citizens from throughout the conquered lands were provided with an institutional means to focus their political energies on Rome, thus strengthening support for Roman decisions in dealing with the conquered territories, to the point where the Italian allies were eventually prepared to die in their struggle to acquire full Roman citizenship. The organization and deployment of Italians alongside the Romans were vital in furthering the absorption of a conquered group by making Roman citizenship acceptable to a great number of people. The grant of citizenship that signaled a finish to the Italian War represented the tail end of a process of military service and selective citizenship grants that had characterized the interaction between Romans and Italians for centuries. Equally important in making citizenship acceptable was the flexibility of the institution itself, which allowed for the continual reintegration of failed citizens as effective members of the Roman state.

Overall the magnitude of the Roman achievement in bringing the Italian peoples together as Roman citizens was matched by the commitment of the newcomers to the Roman system and the degree to which they became fully functioning members of the Roman state. We can see how public lawmaking assemblies, which gave legitimacy to many of the more controversial decisions by the Romans to expand citizenship, were in turn strengthened by the expansion and reinvigoration of the citizen body. Public lawmaking assemblies gave all citizens an institutional instrument for developing communitywide consensus that was unprecedented in ancient Mediterranean societies. New citizens in particular were thus provided with an institutional means to focus their political energies on Rome. Among the more important indices of the successful absorption of Italian lands into the Roman system was the growing strength of this focus throughout Italy. By their reinterpretation of the concept of citizen, that is, divorcing it from territory, and by reordering their traditional tribal system to incorporate new citizens, the Romans imposed themselves on local networks, creating a society increasingly centered on the city of Rome. Showing their unique talent for resorting to customary procedures to control their expanding possessions, the Romans adjusted traditional institutions to create a Roman state in Italy whose focus was the city of Rome.

TABLE 5.1 Laws Relating to Citizen Status and Citizen Liberties, 350–91

Year	Latin Name	Subject
342	Lex Valeria militaris	Mutiny by soldiers
332	Lex Papiria de civitate Acerranorum	Grant of citizenship to outside group
329	Lex de civitate Privernatibus danda	Grant of citizenship to outside group
323	Rogatio Flavia de Tusculanis	Punishment of community
319	Lex Antistia de Satricanis	Punishment of community
306	Lex de civitate Anagninis danda	Grant of citizenship to outside group
300	Lex Valeria de provocatione	Civil liberties
270	Lex de praesidio rhegino	Punishment of legio Campana
215	Lex de civitate equitum Campanorum	Grant of citizenship to outside group
211	[Plebiscitum] de civitate Sosidi et Merico danda	Grant of citizenship to individuals
210	Plebiscitum de civitate Mutini danda	Grant of citizenship to individuals
210	Lex Atilia de dediticiis	Punishment of Campanian rebels by the Senate
(199)[a]	Lex Porcia de provocatione	Civil liberties
(198 or 195)	Lex Porcia de provocatione	Civil liberties
189	Lex Terentia de libertinorum liberis	The citizen status of marginals
188	Lex Valeria de civitate cum suffragio Formianis et Arpinatibus danda	Grant of citizenship to outside group
177	Lex Claudia de sociis	Expulsion of Latin and Italian immigrants from Rome
Before 177	Lex de civitate latinis danda	The citizen status of marginals
133	Rogatio Sempronia de provocatione	Citizen liberties
126	Lex Iunia de peregrinis	The expulsion of foreigners from Rome
125	Rogatio Fulvia de civitate sociis danda	Grant of citizenship to outside group

(*continued*)

TABLE 5.1 (*continued*)

Year	Latin Name	Subject
122	Rogatio Livia de provocatione latinis concedenda	Civil liberties
122	Rogatio Sempronia de civitate sociis danda	Grant of citizenship to outside group
122	Rogatio Sempronia de civitate sociis danda	Grant of citizenship to outside group
96	Lex Valeria de civitate Calliphanae Veliensi danda	Grant of citizenship to individuals
95	Lex Licinia Mucia de civibus redigundis	Expulsion of Latin and Italian immigrants from Rome
91	Rogatio Livia de civitate sociis danda	Grant of citizenship to outside group
(91)	Lex Minicia de liberis	The citizen status of marginals

Source: See appendixes A and C.
[a]Dates in parentheses are approximate. See appendix C.

TABLE 5.2. Property Ratings and Voting Units, ca. 200–140

Rating	Monetary equivalent (in asses)	Centuries (total 193)
Equestrian (cavalry)	1,000,000	18 centuries
Assidui (infantry)		
Classis I	100,000	80 centuries
Classis II	75,000	20 centuries
Classis III	50,000	20 centuries
Classis IV	25,000	20 centuries
Classis V	4,000	30 centuries
Infra classem (support)	none	5 centuries

Source: Nicolet 1966–74, vol.1, and Brunt 1988 (monetary equivalent of equestrian rating); Rathbone 1993 (monetary equivalent of classes 1 through 5); Taylor 1966 (centuries).

Notes

1. Polyb. 2.24.10–17

2. H. Galsterer, "Die lex Osca tabulae Bantina: Eine Bestandsaufnahme," Chiron 1 (1971): 191–214; RS 1 No.13. Such displays, along with the economic advances of the second century manifested in the adornment and expansion of Italian towns, have led to the presumption that Italians did not want to be included in the Roman state, e.g., Crawford 1981, 159. The recent study on the ideological underpinnings of alternative

points of view by Mouritsen 1998 covers the topic thoroughly. However, a sense of being Italian does not preclude any desire to be included in the Roman state.

3. Strabo 6.1.2–3.

4. Taylor 1960, 123–24. On the law of 49 see chapter 9.

5. The issues surrounding Roman citizenship are exceedingly complex. The indispensable guide is Sherwin-White 1973.

6. The suggested figures in Brunt 1971, 26–43, are useful as a rough guide.

7. Livy 6.25.26; Dion. Hal. 14.6.2; Festus p. 155L.

8. Salmon 1982, 46.

9. Livy 8.14.2–4.

10. For a brief summary see Salmon 1982, 47.

11. On this topic see M. Humbert, *Municipium et civitas sine suffragio: L'organisation de la conquête jusqu'à la guerre sociale* (Paris, 1978).

12. Humbert 1978, 280–81. Cf. Lintott 1999, 33–34: "Provocatio was later regarded as one of the principal rights of the individual Roman citizen, a theoretical guarantee against execution without trial and, after the lex Porcia of Cato the Censor, against flogging." Provocatio: D. Cloud, "The constitution and public criminal law," *CAH* 9, 2d ed. (Cambridge, New York, New Rochelle, Melbourne, and Sydney, 1994), 493–94; A. Lintott, "Provocatio: From the struggle of the orders to the principate," in *ANRW* 1.2.226–67.

13. Cives sine suffragio: Sherwin-White 1973, 38–58; Humbert 1978, 164–208.

14. Grant of full citizenship to the Sabines: Vell. Pat. 1.14.7; Sherwin-White 1973, 50–51.

15. Humbert 1978, 209–50.

16. Livy 8.14.10.

17. Sherwin-White 1973, 291–92.

18. Sherwin-White 1973, 111.

19. Lex Repetundarum: *RS* 1 No. 1, l. 77.

20. Sherwin-White 1973, 322–24.

21. Sherwin-White 1973, 120: the Romans attached most of the Italians to the Roman state through individual alliances, in particular the Oscan-speaking peoples, "the mainstay of their federation."

22. For these considerations see especially Sherwin-White 1973, 58–73, on the incorporation of outside communities and the consequent changes in their internal political organization and life.

23. They continued to share significant privileges with the Romans: intermarriage, making contracts and wills, and migration to Rome. These in fact are the privileges that members of municipia also shared with the Romans, clearly derived from the shared community privileges of the inhabitants of Latium, including Romans.

24. As a corollary the inhabitants of Latin towns were not registered on the Roman tribal rolls at the quinquennial census in Rome for which every citizen presented himself. Instead the Latin rolls—used for purposes of military service and taxation—were compiled by the municipal magistrates and sent to Rome.

25. Similarly, beginning in 204 the censors of the twelve Latin colonies founded around 268, who at times have been thought to hold inferior status, submitted the local censuses under their jurisdiction to the censors in Rome and apparently continued

to do so thereafter—as did other municipalities it appears. On the inferior position of the twelve colonies see Mommsen, *R.St.* 3.623 ff; Beloch 1880, 155 ff. Sherwin-White disagrees that there were any "special grades of Latinity": Sherwin-White 1973, 102–8, esp. 104. Census of other municipia: Galsterer 1976, 110–16.

26. Brunt 1971, 29.

27. Cf. Sherwin-White 1973, 292–93.

28. Livy 25.3.16 first mentions it during the Second Punic War, although Dion. Hal. considers the right to be ancient in origin (8.72.4): see Sherwin-White 1973, 35 and 112.

29. The ius migrationis or ius mutandae civitatis: Sherwin-White 1973, 111 and 112.

30. On the joint Roman-Latin colonies of the fifth and early fourth centuries see Cornell 1995, 301–4, who notes Beloch's belief that at least half of the colonists were from Rome and the remainder Latin or Hernican. Beloch 1880, 134, 152.

31. Sherwin-White 1973, 96–116.

32. Sherwin-White 1973, 61; cf 57: the Romans were unwilling in the fourth and third centuries to incorporate non-Latin people completely. Individual grants to non-Romans appear first at the end of the century as rewards to foreigners who helped the Romans in the war with Carthage.

33. Sherwin-White 1973, 292.

34. The proposed destruction of Tusculum in 323, presented unsuccessfully to the people by the tribune M. Flavius, has been interpreted by Mommsen, followed by Taylor, as an attack on the town's full citizen status granted less than a generation before when one of its member presented himself as a candidate for consul. See Taylor 1960, 302.

35. Livy 38.36.7–9. Not since 329 had full citizenship been extended to a community by public law.

36. These are collected in Badian 1958, 302–8, from the later Republic. Such grants only occur in the later period, beginning with Marius: Sherwin-White 1973, 294–95.

37. Brunt 1988, 98.

38. It was after this event, Brunt suggests, that the Romans extended to Latins the right of acquiring full citizenship through holding local office, "as a conciliatory gesture": Brunt 1988, 96.

39. Livy 8.17.12. The phrase, which applies specifically to the cives sine suffragio, appears first in the poetry of Ennius: Sherwin-White 1973, 41–42.

40. The meaning of restricted citizenship: Sherwin-White 1973, 49–50; Humbert 1978, 205–7.

41. Livy 9.45.7.

42. This created a situation, in Sherwin-White's estimation, that exacerbated the allies' demand for equality with Romans and Latins in Italy: Sherwin-White 1973, 140.

43. Allies who remained loyal and those who stopped fighting: Gabba 1994a, 123 ("it may be that the condition was met principally by the Etruscans and Umbrians").

44. On Italian acculturation generally see David 1996. David places more emphasis on the aristocracy than I do here and identifies somewhat different "mechanisms of unification." See also M.H. Crawford, "Italy and Rome from Sulla to Augustus," in *CAH* 10, 2d ed., ed. A. K. Bowman, E. Champlin, and A. Lintott (Cambridge, 1996). The important contributions of archaeology to the topic are presented in the

survey article by Curti, Dench, and Patterson 1996, 170–89. Recent studies (in English) addressing the process of acculturation in specific regions include G. Bradley, *Umbria* (Oxford, 2000), 190–245, and Keay and Terrenato 2001.

45. Badian 1958, 146–49.

46. Salmon 1982, 140–41; W. V. Harris, *Ancient Literacy* (Cambridge, MA, 1989), 177–79. On Umbria see Bradley 2000, 203–17.

47. Vetter 1953, P. Poccetti, *Nuovi documenti italici* (Pisa, 1979).

48. Language and acculturation: E. Benelli, "The Romanization of Italy through the epigraphic record," in Keay and Terrenato 2001, 7–16.

49. Although Greek, the language of the original Greek colonists who established Cumae, appears to have been regarded as the language of status, Oscan and other languages continued in common use if we go by the evidence of inscriptions. Greek: K. Lomas, "Urban elites and cultural definition," in *Urban society in Roman Italy*, ed. T. Cornell and K. Lomas (London, 1995), 110–11.

50. Zanker 1976 is fundamental. See also K. Lomas, *Rome and the western Greeks, 350–AD 200* (London and New York, 1993), 161–87; Lomas 1995; and the discussion of recent scholarship in Curti, Dench, and Patterson 1996, 180–89. Mouritsen 1998, 60–67, provides a useful overview of the topic.

51. This is assumed in many studies addressing quite different topics, for instance, E. Rawson, *Intellectual life in the late Roman republic* (Baltimore, 1985), and E. Gruen, *National Identity in Republican Rome* (Ithaca, NY, 1992).

52. Livy 42.21.4.

53. Livy 42.22.7.

54. See chapter 1, note 11, on Appian's *Italiotai*.

55. Cf. the lex Iunia of 126, which was probably intended to send Italians away from Rome before the vote on Flaccus's citizenship bill: Brunt 1988, 96.

56. Cf. the effort of Etruscans and Umbrians who came to Rome in 91 to discourage voters from accepting Drusus's land and colonization measures: Appian, *B.C.* 1.36. See Brunt 1988, 106; Harris 1971, 212 ff.

57. On these conditions see Beloch 1880, 158–77, and further the analyses by W. Dahlheim, *Struktur und Entwicklung des römischen Völkerrechts im 3. und 2. Jahrhundert v. Chr.* (Munich, 1968), and Galsterer 1976. More briefly see Salmon 1982, 39–72, which notes (p. 59) that we cannot prove how much land the Romans took. Only rarely were the conditions enacted as law in lawmaking assemblies.

58. Military obligations: Galsterer 1976, 105–10; see also V. Ilari, *Gli Italici nelle strutture militari romane* (Milan, 1974).

59. D. W. Baronowski, "The formula togatorum," *Hist.* 33 (1984): 248–52; Brunt 1971, 545–48; Beloch 1880, 202–7.

60. This idea is not new, in the Roman context or generally: Preface, note 10. The shared experiences of infantrymen in bloody battle are less important in this connection than the mechanical routines of daily life in base camps, which consumed most of their time under arms. S. A. Stouffer et al., *The American soldier: Adjustment during army life* (Princeton, NJ, 1949–1950), offers a detailed analysis of the ways in which marginal groups effectively entered American society through military service. The anthropologist L. Pospisil also makes useful observations on this point in *The anthropology of law: A comparative theory* (New York 1971).

61. The figures used in the following discussion of the proportion of Roman and Italian men in military service are based on the reported number of Roman legions under arms every year, the full-strength complement of a legion at different times, and the estimated size of the allied component of the Roman army, collected in Brunt 1971, 416–514. I discuss these figures in an article in preparation, "The Roman population, 225–31."

62. Ordinarily, males ages forty-six to sixty who in principle qualified as reserves (seniores) were exempt from military service, like priests: see discussion by Brunt 1971, 21.

63. Polyb. 2.24.10–17. The Roman figure includes Romans and Campanians, the latter partial citizens (sine suffragio).

64. Brunt 1971, 54; recorded in Polyb. 2.24.10–17.

65. Williamson, "The Roman population, 225–31," article in preparation.

66. Military emergency was defined specifically as a Gallic invasion (*tumultus gallicus*): Appian, *B.C.*, 2.150. On the end of military obligations: Polyb. 6.19.2; Livy 43.14.6.

67. Brunt 1971, 399–402.

68. We owe our information about the annual levy of troops for legions 1–4 to Polybius, who describes the event purportedly as it happened in his day. See further chapter 6.

69. E.g., Julius Caesar in Transpadane Gaul, during his campaign in Gaul, but in this case conscripts were not citizens but Latins.

70. General coverage of all aspects of equipment and supply: L. Keppie, *The making of the Roman army: From republic to empire* (London, 1984). Equipment: M. C. Bishop and J. C. N. Coulston, *Roman military equipment* (London, 1993), 183.

71. The Macedonians under Philip II and Alexander came closest: N. Hammond, *The Macedonian state* (Oxford, 1989); and D. Engels, *Alexander the Great and the logistics of the Macedonian army* (Berkeley and Los Angeles, 1979).

72. Villa Publica: L. Richardson, ed., A *new topographical dictionary of Rome* (Baltimore and London, 1992), 430–31; *Aedes Nymphae*: Richardson 1992, 269.

73. Military strength reports: A. K. Bowman and J. D. Thomas, "A military strength report from Vindolanda," *JRS* 81(1991): 62–73.

74. Appian, *B.C.* 3.43. These daily record books, directed to and collated by the military tribunes, are discussed by A. von Premerstein, s.v. "Commentarii," in *PW* 4.726. For a similar accounting of troops kept by Macedonian kings after Philip (in the Royal Journal) see Hammond 1989, 132, 190.

75. Bishop and Coulston 1993, 183.

76. J. Kromayer and G. Veith, *Heerwesen und Kriegsführung der Griechen und Römer* (Munich, 1928), 452.

77. Kromayer and Veith 1928, 268.

78. On the uses of writing see Harris 1989 and the more focused studies in J. H. Humphrey, ed., *Literacy in the Roman world* (Ann Arbor, MI, 1991).

79. There is some question whether the number was periodically revised or not.

80. Galsterer 1976, 110–17.

81. Livy 29.37.7; Beloch 1880, 311–12; Mommsen, *R.St.* 2. 351; Galsterer 1976, 110.

82. Kromayer and Veith 1928, 276. See Polyb. 6.26.5.

83. Kromayer and Veith 1928, 267.

84. The cult of the standards and shrine are attested only in the imperial period: A. von Domaszewski, "Die Religion des römischen Heeres," *Westd. Zeit.* (1895): 9ff.

85. On the role of the military in the diffusion of coins throughout Italy see Crawford 1985, 36–38; on the mechanisms of diffusion see Crawford, "Army and coinage in the late republic," *La romanisation du Samnium aux IIe et Ier siècles av. J.C.* (Naples, 1991), 135–37.

86. Sherwin-White 1973, 134–39, observes that it was these benefits, not citizenship as such, that made citizenship attractive to the allies. When the citizenship was not forthcoming, however, they went directly for their goal, equality in Italy with the Romans.

87. See note 12, this chapter.

88. See Brunt 1971, 75–77, 402–6; and E. Gabba, "The origins of the professional army at Rome: The 'proletarii' and marius' reform," in *Republican Rome: The army and the allies*, ed. E. Gabba (1976), 2–10. The most recent discussion of these reductions in terms of property values and size of landholdings is D. Rathbone, "The census qualifications of the assidui and the prima classis," in *De agricultura: In memoriam P.W. de Neeve*, ed. H. Sancisi-Weerdenburg et al. (Amsterdam, 1993), 121–52, esp. 139–46.

89. Brunt 1971, 403–5; Rathbone 1993, 125.

90. The most important studies of the Roman tribes are Mommsen, *R.St.* 3.161–98, revising his earlier *Die römischen Tribus in administrativer Beziehung* (Altona, 1844); and Taylor 1960.

91. Taylor 1960, 74–75. The necessary ritual purification of the tribes followed. Representations of the ritual acts required by the *lustrum* are collected and discussed in I. Scott Ryberg, *Rites of the state religion in Roman art* (Rome, 1955), 104–19.

92. Tribes as a unique Roman institution: C. Ampolo, "La nascita della città," in *Storia di Roma*, ed. A. Momigliano and A. Schiavone (Turin, 1988), 1.153–80.

93. Taylor 1960, 35–46, provides the best discussion.

94. Contra Taylor 1960, who argues (chap. 2) that new tribes had to be created by vote of the Roman people on the presumptive grounds that only the people could make such a societywide change. The censors' oversight over land leases and the bronze forma or survey maps (Gran. Lic. 28.36: *forma in Atrium Libertatis*) suggests the likelihood of a more extensive involvement. Gargola 1995 shows clearly the complexity of the arrangements necessary to incorporate new lands into the Roman state.

95. Livy 8.17.11–12: *Tribus propter eos additae Maecia et Scaptia; censores addiderunt Q. Publilius Philo Sp. Postumius.*

96. The decision to create no more new tribes is probably also related to the reform of the centuriate assembly: Taylor 1960, 68.

97. Taylor 1960, 47–68 (new tribes), and 79–100 (tribal extensions before the Italian War). On the proximity of Latin colonies see Taylor 1960, 49.

98. So much so that it is sometimes argued that any Latin or Italian who came to own land through purchase or inheritance in a Roman tribe also gained Roman citizenship: J.S. Richardson, "The ownership of Italian land: Tiberius Gracchus and the Italians," *JRS* 70 (1980): 1–11.

99. Urban tribes: Taylor 1960, 132–49; see further chapter 6.

100. Hence, an assiduus need not be a landowner per se but a landowner with a valuation that places him in Classes 1 through 5: A. Berger, *Encyclopedic dictionary of Roman law* (Philadelphia, 1953; reprint, 1991), 351, s.v. "Assidui."

101. Taylor explains the voluntary transfers of nobles to the new tribes as a move to "establish control of new tribes": Taylor 1960, 299.

102. Staveley 1972, 136–37; cf. Vanderbroek 1987, 70; Brunt 1988, 25–26; Millar 1998, 36; Yakobsen 1999, 147 n. 82. This is not directly attested in the sources, however.

103. Age at registration: Brunt 1971, 113–20.

104. The stages of adjustment in Rome's basic money standard is summarized in Rathbone 1993, 123.

105. Equestrian class: C. Nicolet, *L'ordre équestre à l'epoque republicaine* (Paris, 1966), vol. 1; Brunt 1988, 144–93; T. P. Wiseman, "The definition of 'eques Romanus' in the late republic and early empire," *Hist.* 19 (1970): 67–83.

106. Based on the presumed number of cavalrymen accompanying the four consular legions at this time.

107. Mommsen, *R.St.* 3.1.250–51, 272–73.

108. Polybius explicitly lumps the Campanians who were "citizens without the vote" together with the Romans.

109. Mommsen, *R.St.* 3.1.107 with n. 3, 259; Brunt 1988, 146.

110. See chapter 7.

111. *Tribuni aerarii* considered equestrians: Brunt 1988, 146 with 515–16, and 210 with n. 40. The tribuni aerarii are believed to be "old tribal officers" who collected the tributum from each tribe, before 167, and paid it to the army: Mommsen, *R.St.* 3.189–91; Taylor 1960, 8 with n. 16; cf. Nicolet 1976, 46–55.

112. ClassI qualifications: Rathbone 1993, 121–52, esp. 126–37.

113. Valuation based on fertility: Campbell 2000, 136.10; 170.4 (*pro aestimio ubertatis*); 160.33; 202.22; 202.17 (*ad modum ubertatis*). Declaration of valuation: Campbell 2000, 136.10; 170.4; 174.5. These examples are from the reigns of Augustus and Vespasian, but they are no less valid for Republican practice; cf. the following note and Tabula Heracleensis (declarations). On the property assessment determining a citizen's census see G. Pieri, *Histoire du cens jusqu'à la fin de la république Romaine* (Paris, 1968), 47–50. On land values see also P. W. de Neeve, "The price of agricultural land in Roman Italy and the problem of economic rationalism," *Opus* 4 (1988): 77–109; P. W. de Neeve, *Colonus: Private farm tenancy in Roman Italy during the republic and the early principate* (Amsterdam, 1984), 171–73.

114. Rents: Cato, *Agr.* 136; Sententia Minuciorum (Bruns[7] no. 184), ll. 25–28 (assessing payment of rent in terms of produce).

115. Brunt 1971, 40–43.

116. K. J. Beloch, *Die Bevölkerung der griechisch-römischen Welt* (Leipzig, 1886), 312–19; see discussion of P. Brunt 1971, 15–25.

117. Mommsen, *R.St.* 3.190–92; cf. Taylor 1960, 15, 16, 74. The curatores were summoned with the citizens for the census: Varro, *Ling.* 6.86.

118. Regular census cycle: Brunt 1971, 15. Census in the first century: T. P. Wiseman, "The census in the first century BC," *JRS* 59 (1969): 59–75.

119. I do not discount the role of tradition in the persistence of the five-year cycle, nor the modern observation that, in the first century, regular enumerations fell victim to the size and dispersal of the Roman population.

120. Cycles of twenty years were observed in the standard enumerations of the Ottoman Empire, with shorter periods employed in certain circumstances: M. Kiel, "The Ottoman imperial registers: Central Greece and northern Bulgaria in the 15th–19th

century: The demographic development of two areas compared," in Bintliff and Sbonias, eds., 1999, 195.

121. The first examples of the modern census "in large countries" were conducted in Spain (1787) and the United States (1790): Livi-Bacci 1992, 30. Common wisdom holds that the modern census differs from earlier enumerations because it is used for long-term planning purposes involving an entire population, whereas earlier enumerations counted only restricted groups (e.g., men of a certain age) for specific, immediate purposes (taxation, military service). Hence the Roman census, which counted primarily men for the limited purposes of military service, taxation, and political participation, is not comparable to a modern census. It is undeniable, however, that the census of the Roman Republic enabled the Romans to effectively organize their military.

122. In the twentieth century, the United Nations recommends enumerating a population every ten years to ensure that demographic data are reliable: United Nations, Statistical Office, *Principles and Recommendations for National Population Censuses*. Statistical Papers. Series M, No. 27. (New York, 1958).

123. U.S. Constitution, art. 1, sec. 2., para. 3. Census taking in the United States.

124. M. Farrand, ed., *The records of the federal convention of 1787* (rev. ed., New Haven, CT, 1966), 1.201, 205 (five to seven or ten years), 576 (fifteen years), 589–90, and 596 (ten or twenty years).

125. It is also relevant that the groundwork necessary for a Roman census was largely built into the process. Preparations for the assessment were in the hands of the tribesmen, who traveled to Rome to give the necessary information to the censors, and the tribal supervisors, who traveled to Rome to confirm and supplement the information of their fellow tribesmen. Correcting and updating the lists undoubtedly required effort and time, but this was an administrative chore performed in Rome by the censors' staffs using the records of the censorial archives. The point is that the five-year cycle envisages a relatively low level of beforehand preparation as well as a high level of volatility in the assets needed for registration in a Roman property class.

126. Brunt 1971, 66, finds confirmation for the date in the increased number of assidui assumed by the enrollment of five or six new legions or "some 27,000 soldiers." He argues that "some proletarii were now called up."

127. See the discussion of these reductions in terms of property values and size of landholdings in Rathbone 1993, 121–52, esp. 139–46.

128. K. Hopkins, *Conquerors and slaves* (Cambridge, 1978), 39 n. 52.

129. Yakobsen 1999, 48–54.

130. Dion. Hal. 4.21.3; see Taylor 1966, 87–90.

131. Taylor 1960, 67–68.

132. Taylor 1966, 85–106, is fundamental.

133. This may have been only in consular elections: Develin 1978, 377; cf. Yakobsen 1999, 52.

134. Taylor 1966, 96–97.

135. For the system of conflating centuries into voting units see the discussion of Taylor 1966, 88–90, building on Mommsen.

136. See chapter 3.

137. See comments of T. P. Wiseman, *New men in the Roman senate*, 139–AD 14 (Oxford, 1971), 130–42; and especially Taylor 1960, 297–315.

138. For a similar interpretation, although couched in terms of the debate about democratic tendencies in the Roman political structure, see A. Yakobsen, "Dionysius of Halicarnassus on a democratic change in the centuriate assembly," *Scripta Classica Israelica* 12 (1993): 139–55; and "Petitio et largitio: Popular participation in the centuriate assembly of the late republic," *JRS* (1992): 32–52.

139. See chapter 3.

140. *RS* 1 No. 1, ll. 14, 18.

141. Taylor 1960, 21–23.

142. See chapter 7.

143. Lex Plautia: Asc., *Corn.* 79 C; cf. Ps. Sall., *Cic.* 2.3.

144. Mommsen, *R.St.* 3.1.189 with n. 2 for all but lex Aurelia. Lex Aurelia: Asc. 17C; cf. Schol. Bob. 94 St. (cf. Cic., *Fam.* 8.8.5; Pliny, *N.H.* 33.31). Centumviri: Brunt 1988, 234–35.

145. Lawmaking in various assemblies: Taylor 1966, 5–6. The conclusions reached in the recent detailed examination of lawmaking in the centuriate assembly by Paananen are unconvincing: Paananen 1993, 9–73.

146. E.g., *FIRA* 1 No. 55, l. 24: honors granted to the naval captain Seleucus by Octavian; *FIRA* 1 No. 56, ll. 10–11: honors granted to veterans by Octavian. Cf. Taylor 1960, 18–22.

147. Some in 268, others by the Italian War; not all Sabines, however, were registered in the same tribes. Citizenship: Taylor 1960, 65–66.

148. The overall costs, to be considered in chapters 6 and 7, refute Taylor's supposition that the men who came to Rome to be registered had to be wealthy, mostly men of the first class; she explains in this fashion the slight increase in the census of 86 (463,000) over that of 115 (394,336): Taylor 1960, 105.

149. Taylor 1960, 159–64.

150. Taylor 1960, 101–17.

151. Location of Teretina: Taylor 1960, 57–58; enrollment of Aurunci: Taylor 1960, 157.

152. Location of Poblilia: Taylor 1960, 50–53; enrollment of Hernici: Taylor 1960, 157.

153. Tribal enrollments of allies: Taylor 1960, 111 ff. (with reference to earlier views of Beloch and Kubitschek, who see the eventual arrangements as penalizing the new citizens).

154. For a list and discussion of "ethnic considerations" in the tribal enrollments of new citizens see Taylor 1960, 67 and 157, which notes that the tribes often already existed in the region.

155. Taylor 1960, 120 n. 7.

156. Reorganization of local governments and adoption of Roman terminology: U. Laffi, "I senati locali nell'Italia repubblicana," in *Les "bourgeoisies" municipales italiennes aux II et Ier siècles av. J.-C.* (Paris and Naples, 1983), 70 ff.

157. On this complicated process see Crawford 1996.

158. Cf. Taylor 1960, 158.

159. The census enumerations of the period tell the story: from 394,336 in the census of 115 and 463,000 in 86, the Romans expanded to 910,000 in the last census of the "free Republic" in 70 BCE. See chapter 7, note 1.

CHAPTER SIX

Convergence: The City of Rome

TOWARD THE END of the civil war of the 80s, a tribune revealed the secret name of Rome. Soon thereafter the tribune died, to the satisfaction of his contemporaries, expiating his transgression with death. The episode draws attention to the importance of the many unspoken associations and attachments that Rome held for her people. This sometimes mystical respect for Rome probably explains much of the power and functioning of the Romans' most fundamental institutions, whose integrity was inextricably bound up with an intense focus on Rome. Citizens throughout Italy looked to Rome for the central events of community life. Statewide religious ritual, civic performances, and decisions affecting the entire state transpired chiefly in Rome. Among these was the passage of laws in public lawmaking assemblies. The fate of the loquacious tribune suggests that the image of Rome shared by many Romans went far beyond what can be explained by any general discussion of changing patterns of economic, ritual, social, and political life of the city. Nevertheless such a discussion does provide, in however overly simplified a manner, an appreciation of the importance of the structure and function of the city to a Roman population totaling in the millions, by 50, and the central role it played in the strength of Roman institutions. The legitimacy of all Roman institutions, particularly public lawmaking assemblies, is related to the degree to which they were embedded in the life of the city of Rome. An understanding of the manner in which Rome functioned within the Roman system and the attractions of Rome to Romans, Italians, and foreigners is essential to any effort at understanding the vital role of public lawmaking assemblies in that same system.[1]

The patterns of economic, social, and religious life in the city of Rome during the fourth century, as the Romans begin the process of expanding throughout Italy, form my starting point in this chapter. The unique conditions of Roman expansion, in place by the third century, and the developing attractions of the city of Rome produced a city population that ebbed and flowed with the movement of citizens and foreigners. At this time the city's chief attraction was its role as the hub of an imperial system of religion, administration, and justice. In the second and first centuries, the special attractions of Rome combined with the breakdown in traditional ties and access to resources to produce permanent and nonpermanent migration to Rome. The result was a city whose population was at least three times larger than the total population of the next largest city in the ancient Mediterranean basin. The role that public lawmaking played in the growth of Rome concludes my examination.

ROME, CA. 300

Boasting walls unmatched by any fortifications in Italy at the time, Rome in 300 was well on the way to becoming an urban center on a unique scale. Living and working within the walls was a large and cosmopolitan population. Romans and Latins dwelled cheek-by-jowl with slaves, drawn at this point mostly from defeated neighbors, and with indeterminate numbers of other Italians, attracted willingly to the city. The diversity of this population was increased further by the immigration of people from outside Italy. The topography of Rome's neighborhoods (vici) and archaeology confirm the extent of foreign habitation.[2] The vicus Tuscus, "Etruscan Way," a street running between the Forum and the Circus Maximus, was home to Etruscans at an early date (fifth century).[3] The presence of a shrine to Carna on the Caelian hill supports Etruscan settlement here, too.[4] Greeks may have lived on vicus Sandalarius, "Sandal Makers' Row," and Carthaginians in several locations.[5] To some extent Rome's diverse population reflects the customary movement among regions and towns in Italy, particularly that between Etruria and Latium. It is also clear, however, that the high visibility of resident foreigners, in particular Carthaginians and Greeks, reflects the city's extensive trading connections both within and outside Italy.

Indeed, Rome's primary attraction at this time was its function as the hub of a wheel of trade and movement in all directions.[6] The Tiber River and the wide plains of southern Etruria and Latium provided the chief means of access from the sea to the mountainous interior of Italy and from north to south. Although Rome was not a seaport, her location on the Tiber made her the most important trading city in Italy.[7] From an early date, Rome boasted the staging areas necessary for such a movement of goods and produce. These were the markets whose presence in Rome was so prominent. Chief among them was the cattle market (Forum Boarium), situated along the Tiber, which appears to have been the central market area for livestock, salt, and olive oil. Adjacent to the market were the salt magazines (*salinae*), serving as a storage facility for salt from the pans at the mouth of the Tiber. The city of Rome in 300 resembled a nineteenth-century U.S. frontier settlement. Like St. Louis on the Mississippi River, Rome on the Tiber was a gateway through which goods and people were funneled to an expanding interior hinterland.[8]

Many of the goods traded in Rome were manufactured there as well. Roman neighborhoods located manufacture as well as the presence of foreigners: In addition to Sandal Makers' Row there was the vicus Iugarius, where animal yokes were made, and the vicus Lorarius, whose residents produced harnesses, saddles, and whips. Some areas of the city of Rome were named according to the specific items marketed there: *inter lignarios*, *inter falcarios*, *inter vitores*, and *inter figulos* were areas within the perimeter of the city where timber (firewood?), scythes and pruning hooks, baskets, and pots were sold.[9] To produce these and other goods Rome needed specialized craftsmen, provided by slaves, whose importance as a skilled labor force was long established by 300, and by other foreigners as well, such as the stonemasons from Greek Syracuse engaged to construct Rome's defensive circuit in 378. So the city population grew, replenished by the migration of Italian and foreign craftsmen and traders; Etruscans and Sabines; as well as Greeks, Carthaginians, Phoenicians, and many others from all sections of the Mediterranean who came to Rome by choice to live and work permanently or temporarily.

Romans in turn migrated temporarily or permanently to other cities, primarily as traders. Inevitably, this complementary movement between Rome and other cities changed all of them. Most noticeably in the case of Rome, it deepened the ongoing adaptation of various Greek institutions and skills. Enmeshed long before 300 in the money economy of the Greek cities of southern Italy, the Romans began to mint coins regularly themselves not long after, around the beginning of the First Punic War in 264. Greeks from southern Italy and Sicily formed a significant presence in Rome, before 300, including not only such men as the stonemasons referred to previously, skilled workers recruited for a major building project, but high-ranking Greek priestesses, invited to Rome to tend to the cult of Ceres. Few arenas were untouched by the continuous interaction between Romans and non-Romans, as manifest in the city of Rome.

Cults provide a useful index of migration into the city. At an early date Etruscan and Sabine cults were present in Rome, as well as Greek and other foreign deities and rituals. The shrine to Carna provides a case in point. While not all these cults came with migrating Etruscans, Italians, or Greeks, even cults that were deliberately moved to Rome underscore the prevalence of migration to and from the region of origin of the particular god: the Romans appropriated gods much as they did land.[10] The gods or goddesses deliberately sought out were usually Italian or Greek. The goddess Ceres was both: already present in Rome, she was given a new temple on the Aventine hill, early in the fourth century, and "Greek rites," whose performance required the Greek priestesses already referred to.[11] But the arrival of many other foreign divinities took place in a more gradual and personal way, arriving through the spontaneous efforts of individuals rather than state initiative. So it was with Hercules, whose popular cult, linked both to Carthaginian traders and the migrating herdsmen of Italy, was important in the lives of ordinary working men. Initially managed by one of Rome's prominent families, the earliest cult of Hercules, situated at the main altar known as the *ara maxima* in the Forum Boarium (because of the close relationship between Hercules and cattle), was transferred to state control in 312.[12] The wide variety of gods, resident also in one or another area of Roman settlement in Italy and popular for one reason or another with the larger society, meant that a newcomer often found that his local gods had arrived in Rome before him. The shared panoply of gods facilitated the process of integration. Already by the fourth century, Rome was attracting and absorbing Latins, Etruscans, Sabines, and other Italians by a process of religious and cultural acculturation.[13]

Over the next century, as Rome was increasingly at war, more gods and goddesses entered for the first time or underwent modification in Rome.[14] In this period, for instance, Rome's political leaders expanded the cult of Hercules. More temples and shrines to Hercules, constructed at state expense, mushroomed in Rome in the third and early second centuries, often in or near the Forum Boarium.[15] The evidence suggests a connection between the state's intervention and Roman victories over the Samnites, for whom Hercules was a tutelary god. Other foreign gods were newly introduced, among them Greek Apollo and the Phrygian Great Mother, a phenomenon explained in part by the Romans' practice of celebrating or placating the gods of their enemies, now quite numerous.[16] In part, too, the introduction of so many foreign gods to Rome is explained by the use of ritual as a vehicle of consensus. New gods (*di novales*) and festivals to celebrate them provided a focus for people who had come to share a common identity as Romans.

Thus by the beginnings of Roman expansion in Italy, the city of Rome was the product of a long-term process of migration, economic growth, and regional expansion as a religious and market center. Rome attracted people as well as trade by virtue of its location, which made it a gateway to central Italy and a staging area for a wide range of goods and products from Italy and abroad. The result of this migration was a varied and shifting population. How large we cannot say for sure, although colonization efforts in the fifth and fourth centuries provide evidence of population pressures on local arable land. Over time, foreigners integrated with Romans and Latins in a process of adaptation and accretion, to form by the end of the fourth century a distinctly cosmopolitan Rome. The mechanisms for even greater integration and growth were in place. This organic regional growth of Rome was modified by two new and singular factors that emerged from historical developments in the third and second centuries: the demands of civic and ritual obligation and the influx of grain, riches, and other products from an expanding empire. Both factors enhanced and strengthened the development of a society centered on Rome in a manner unique in world history.

THE FURTHER DEVELOPMENT OF ROME AS CIVIC AND RITUAL HUB

In 114, Publius Elvius was returning with his family to their home in Apulia after attending the Roman Games (*ludi Romani*) in Rome. While crossing the ager Stellas near Cales, along the via Latina, his young daughter was struck by lightning, an incident so portentous that the head priest (pontifex maximus) in Rome had it entered in the priestly record of annual prodigies.[17] The circumstances may have loaded the girl's death with more meaning than the lightning itself. For the set of games from which she had just come in Rome was one of the most important religious events of the year, celebrating the chief god of the Roman people, Jupiter Best and Greatest. Every year in Rome half of the month of September was devoted to sacrifice, horse races, and athletic competitions in honor of Jupiter Best and Greatest. The festivities began on 5 September with a huge procession from the Capitoline temple, the ritual center of Rome, to the Circus Maximus, led by the consuls followed by the athletes and other competitors. Next in line were the gods resident in Rome, carried on floats, while the sacrificial animals brought up the rear of the procession. On

13 September the college of priests called *epulones*, created by law in 196, organized a grand dinner party for Jupiter and the goddesses Juno and Minerva, who shared his temple on the Capitoline hill. The ritual banquet in the temple was attended only by Roman senators and magistrates, as well as the Capitoline triad, but celebratory meals were laid out on plank tables in all the neighborhoods of Rome so everyone in the city could participate. When the games finally ended on 19 September, several days more were designated on the calendar for markets in Rome. For the duration of the games and the markets the city must have been crowded with tourists, including pious Romans like P. Elvius and his family, who made the journey of more than three hundred kilometers between Apulia, in the south of Italy, and Rome.

Once the conquest of Italy had begun an already mobile city population expanded and became still more transient. The dissemination of Roman citizens across Italy accompanied by an increase in numbers was a significant factor in this growth and movement. The state-sponsored or individual migration of Romans and Latins away from the city and its environs to fill the colonies, towns, and villages established on Roman state land was balanced by a return movement, sometimes of new colonists dissatisfied with settlement life. For these people, the focus of their world after migration continued to be Rome. Not surprisingly they maintained close ties with families in Rome: the family and state cult of the Lares presumes a concern with the graves of dead ancestors. Some even abandoned the colonies and returned permanently to Rome. In 186, one of the consuls who was in south Italy restoring order after the religious outburst among the population that the Roman Senate found so dangerous, the Bacchanalian conspiracy, discovered that Buxentum, a colony established in 194, was now deserted. Where had the settlers gone? Unless we suppose that a hostile, local population had exterminated them, and there is no record of such an event, it is reasonable to assume that they had simply gone home.[18] Such a mass departure is probably the exception. For most Romans living outside Rome the return movement was temporary, a periodic feature of life in Roman Italy.

In pace with Latin and Roman settlement in Italy the population of Rome ebbed and flowed. With the creation of new tribes and tribal extensions on conquered and newly annexed Italian land, as well as municipia of restricted citizens (cives sine suffragio) and Latin colonies, the Romans brought the diverse and scattered members of the Roman community into the civic orbit. The tribes and tribal extensions in particular were firmly attached to Rome through an extended system of roads and depots. The tribal extensions spurred the establishment of communities, providing local market and community centers for the far-flung Roman tribesmen. Some, called conciliabula, appear to spring up spontaneously, in step with Roman settlement, as communities of Roman citizens on or near newly conquered lands. Modern scholars believe they came to function as markets and regional headquarters in the tribal extensions necessitated by the territorial discontinuity now experienced by the tribes.[19] Other communities, fora, were deliberately established by magistrates along the roads linking Rome and Roman state land, whose construction belongs to the same period, or by conquering commanders.[20] Like conciliabula, fora were established for a variety of purposes related to the implications of scattering Romans far and wide across the Italian landscape. In some intangible way they may have served as way stations, physical and emotional, on the way to Rome. Among more tangible uses, the fora served as markets, like conciliabula, and as locales for the adjudication of disputes, thus providing a base of operations for legal services. Thus, both conciliabula and fora were communities that originated for the ordinary market and communal needs of the Roman inhabitants of the tribes. Significantly, Rome remained the center of all administrative and judicial activity for all inhabitants of the rural tribes. From Rome came messengers to announce assemblies, decrees, proposed and approved bills; recruiting officers; and other officials. From Rome came justice dispensed by itinerant prefects, *praefecti iure dicundo*, appointed by the urban praetor and deriving their jurisdiction from him, who visited the fora on a regular basis to hear cases. The system was used also in the administration of Roman colonies.[21] Citizens traveled to Rome for the resolution of more complex legal problems. In the operational links between the city of Rome and the scattered conciliabula and fora, the Romans adapted a traditional system of management focused on Rome to new conditions in which they found themselves stretched over a much larger area.

The Roman colonies, the conciliabula and the fora inhabited by full Roman citizens, situated on the far-flung ager Romanus, organized in thirty-one rural tribes by 241 and looking to Rome for administration, were altogether distinct and distinguishable from the municipia. These were communities of men who were citizens in all respects, save their ability to vote or hold office, or Latin colonies with territories of their own. Yet the citizen, partial citizen, and Latin tracts, forming large and small pockets in the peninsula of Italy at varying distances from Rome, shared one thing in common. They all had a fixed orientation toward Rome. Striking to the modern observer, and presumably as obvious to the Italian tribesmen, is the close association between the towns and Rome that grew up in the small pockets of Roman and Latin territory by the second century.

Most important therefore in explaining the return movement to Rome is that the obligations and activities of citizenship continued to be uncompromisingly bound to the city of Rome. Out-migrants returned regularly to Rome to perform civic and ritual responsibilities. Despite the scattering of citizens on distant Roman lands, most essential of these obligations was the annual military draft. The only citizens exempt from the draft were settlers in the small citizen colonies established before the second century. Rome was also the venue for other tribal matters. All thirty-five tribes maintained tribal headquarters and tribal burial grounds in Rome.[22] Central tribal rituals occurred only in Rome, specifically the *lustrum,* crucial to the well-being of the city. Fleeting reference is made in the ancient testimony to other tribal rituals performed annually in Rome.[23] Similarly, several times a year men, women, and children celebrated their gods with sacrifices, games, and other festivities that eventually, after the third century, could last up to fifteen days.[24] Every year in July citizens elected their chief magistrates and priests in the centuriate assembly and their lesser magistrates and priests in the tribal assemblies. Every five years, citizens from the various parts of Italy, where Rome's far-flung territory extended, made their way to Rome to present themselves before the censors in the Campus Martius and to give an accounting of their holdings and families. The city of Rome also provided the only venue in Italy for Roman public lawmaking sessions, attended by citizens who returned to Rome at random intervals to participate. Participation was not invariably restricted to citizens optimo iure: Latins, too, by the second century could vote in electoral and legislative assemblies. In summary, both the central events that constituted citizen life, such as registration on the tribal rolls, declarations of property, enrollment in a legion, voting, and festivals, and the prosaic affairs of daily life, such as the conduct of legal business, transpired in the presence of the proper officials and their assistants in their designated locations in Rome. Mobility was built into the lives of the settlers as the conditions of Roman life and citizenship spurred a continual movement back to Rome. It was impossible for any Roman to participate fully without traveling to events in Rome.

In turn, Romans were highly resourceful in meshing state ritual and civic performances with the routines of everyday life. Consider the celebration of festivals, which drew significant numbers of citizens away from their homes and farms.[25] While festivals were prominent and regular occurrences, they were only one among many such recurrent events drawing large crowds to Rome. The religious calendar of the Romans was full of festivals, cults, and other activities honoring the gods.[26] The performance of the religious obligations these activities represented was an urgent part of daily life.[27] For the security of Rome hinged on the benign demeanor of the gods toward the city, which could only be maintained by the constituent parts of festivals and other cult activities, ritual, sacrifice, and prayer. While the performance of many of these activities was located in a specifically individual or family context, or could unfold in a Roman town or colony, others were tied to the heart of the Roman community and occurred only in Rome. This was the case with the great state games, a special form of recurring festival. In 300, the Romans celebrated three sets of major games during the year: the Games of Ceres (ludi Cereales) on 19 April; the Roman or Great Games (ludi Romani or Magni) in honor of the Roman's chief god, Jupiter Best and Greatest, on 13 September; and the Plebeian Games (ludi Plebeii), also in honor of Jupiter Best and Greatest, on 14 November.[28] Over the next two centuries the number of days devoted to these games steadily expanded and other games were added, sometimes by public law.[29] By 70, the Roman Games lasted fifteen days. The Romans gradually devoted so many days to ritual activity throughout the year that their success in other arenas is a genuine credit to the Roman aptitude for manufacturing the conditions they believed necessary for the growth of Rome.

One visible measure of the importance of state festivals from an early date to the elite members of Roman society who organized and staged them is provided by the regulation of festival management.[30] An initial function of the curule aedile, for instance, a new elective office established in 367 by public law, was festival related. The curule aedileship was the single new administrative office created in Rome in the fourth century and the last new office for another one hundred years. The two curule aediles administered the markets, temples, and city streets, supplementing the two existing plebeian aediles. They also initially staged the Greek-style dramatic productions, recently introduced in the games honoring Ceres in order to mitigate the effects of the plague and other ills, which from now on were to become an essential part of the great festivals. Similarly, in 196, a public law of the tribune C. Licinius Lucullus instituted the new priesthood mentioned previously, the epulones, three men responsible for orchestrating Jupiter's annual dinner party on 14 November.[31] The concern and outlay associated with festival activities on the part of Rome's political leaders mirror their significance to all Romans.

Although we have little evidence about the individual obligations entailed on these occasions, attendance was high.[32] People flocked to Rome in large numbers and as a matter of course, several times a year, in order to attend the great state games and festivals. As is clearly revealed by the story about the misfortunes of the family of P. Elvius, citizens residing in pockets of Roman and Latin territory across Italy routinely made regular trips to Rome for festivals. Not all in attendance at festivals, however, were Roman: souvenirs of these and lesser festivals, in the form of mass-produced cups (*poculi*) inscribed with the names of new gods and goddesses, have turned up in Etruscan as well as Latin towns and as far away as Aleria on Sardinia.[33] Other motivations must have brought some of these visitors to Rome, specialized markets to name the most obvious.

From a Roman perspective, however, the regular ritual and civic performances in Rome were central acts of citizenship. Membership in the Roman community presumed common obligations to the gods of the state: All Romans shared responsibility for sustaining the goodwill of the gods of the state. Membership obliged men who owned land in Roman tribes to declare their holdings and family members at the quinquennial census and, if eligible, to appear for the regular tribal military levy in January. Membership involved participation in voting assemblies, for the primary way of expressing power as a full citizen member of the Roman state was through voting. Thus, citizens went to Rome not only for state festivals and games but for the military levy, the census, and the various voting assemblies. But for all who did come, in particular citizens, for whom such regular treks were tied up with their sense of being Roman, we must wonder how they incorporated this level of movement in their lives.

Doubtless, Romans sensed little conflict between the performance on the one hand and the time or energy investment required for the performance on the other.[34] The time spent was simply part of whatever process the Romans were engaged in, whether the census, military conscription, festivals, or the more random public lawmaking assemblies. Life unfolded at a very different pace than in the modern world. As a result it is not surprising that the establishment of Roman settlements across Italy was accompanied by the institutionalization of mobility to and from Rome. Yet the distances that Romans and others were required to travel, as well as the investment in time, spurred significant adjustments in traditional routines over time simply to ensure the continuation of those routines.[35]

For instance, the major state festivals, the regular voting assemblies, and the military levy tended to occur at relatively slow times in the Italian agricultural year, usually winter and summer. In these seasons the military levy and elections were scheduled, similarly many of the most important state festivals. It appears then that Romans had developed patterns of work on the farm and with their herds that allowed them to leave and return for citizen performances in Rome, as they did for military service. As long as the customary campaign season occupied the summer months, as was the case until the great overseas expansion of the second century, these performances were generally not impeded by military service itself. Moreover, civic and ritual performances were often combined with markets. The days on which public lawmaking assemblies or judicial assemblies were scheduled, the only randomly scheduled civic events, had to be announced over a period of three market days, three nundinae or trinundinum, roughly equivalent to twenty-seven or more days, in order to let as many know as possible. Given that such assemblies were announced by herald in the fora and conciliabula throughout the Roman territories in Italy, the requirement of a trinundinum presumes the customary movement of outlying rural inhabitants to Rome for weekly markets.[36] The assemblies themselves were then frequently convened on an appropriate market day. By the end of the Republic the three biggest sets of games, the Roman Games in September, the Plebeian Games in November, and the Games to Apollo in July, were followed by three, three, and six days of market, respectively. In the calendars these blocks of days in September, November, and July were marked "market" (*mercatus*). The July electoral assemblies were usually held during this period. Thus, while markets were regular occurrences, at eight-day intervals in Rome as elsewhere, on occasions when exceptionally large numbers of citizens were in Rome, the market days were extended and electoral assemblies were held in the same period. These combinations and piling on of events show the Romans scheduling performances in a practical way to take advantage of the greatest number of visitors to the city. By a glance at the public calendar, a Roman in Apulia would know which days were *fas* and *nefas*, *dies comitiales*, and so determine his journey. In this fashion a solid relationship emerged between commercial attractions on the one hand and ritual and civic attractions on the other. In turn these attractions inspired a massive flow of people at regular times during the year. Not surprisingly the peak month for such mobility, July, was also the renewal date for leases on city apartments. Thousands were now on the move to and from Rome.

The city's central role in managing the resources of Italy further intensified and redirected the mobile population of Italy. When, for example, Roman ager publicus was rented, leases were drawn up and renewed only in Rome by the censors. Contracts for building projects, for supplying the armies or the city (until the Second Punic War), or for collecting taxes in Italy (prior to 167) were also tied to Rome. The censors again handled these. Justice was in some respects centralized in the jurisdiction of the city praetor or peregrine praetor in Rome, notwithstanding the deputies or prefects sent to outlying communities whose jurisdiction derived from the former. Only in Rome could *iudicia legitima* be held.[37] In all other locations beyond the first milestone, verdicts in trials presided over by prefects or others were delivered within the time limits of the justice giver's office (*iudicia quae in imperio continentur*). Most consequential, the city assembled and exported thousands of troops annually, drawn from all Italy, on brutal campaigns of conquest. Another draw was added to the many attractions of Rome.

Enhancing the civic and ritual attractions that Rome held for Romans and Latins were the attractions that Rome, the imperial city, held for all the inhabitants of Italy. By the end of the third century huge external supplies of oil, grain, wax, and other supplies as well as slaves, coins, and luxury items poured into Rome. Rome was thus the focus of commerce, the premiere market especially for luxury items and slaves and a labor market involving men of all classes and economic means. The import of huge amounts of external supplies as well as the export of thousands of troops annually required an intensification of record-keeping efforts as well as the archives to keep and maintain records. The Romans began to develop the resources and apparatus needed to manage an overseas empire. The Aerarium at the Temple of Saturn, long the repository for Senate decrees and state treasures, came also to be the central archives in Rome for records relating to the financial management of the provinces, as well as other legal documents. Record keeping, in turn, called for a body of workers both to produce and manage records, at their source in the provinces, with the Roman commander; or at the ports of entry, with the quaestor supervising imports; or at the assemblies or meetings held in Rome—that is, wherever costs and expenditures were tallied or decisions were made. This body of workers was formed by the now emerging corps of clerks and copyists, men generally of lower status than the political leaders of Rome, often new citizens. The control center of the empire, Rome provided the sole arena in which most administrative matters pertaining to this management could be resolved. As a result, Italians joined the Romans and Latins who regularly made their way to the city, their customary mobility redirected as an outgrowth of Roman expansion. Already a civic and ritual hub for the thousands of Romans and Latins settled in distant regions, Rome as the center for the control and allocation of resources exerted a commensurate pull on citizen and noncitizen inhabitants of Italy alike by the third century.

Soon after the beginning of their expansion across Italy, the Romans commenced building the infrastructure necessary to support such a movement to Rome, beginning with roads. Roman roads, built by military engineers, regularized and improved travel on the already extensive network of routes across Italy.[38] Most Roman roads followed the course of existing roads or routes by which the Romans like other Italians had been for centuries firmly connected to the various regions and peoples of Italy. Existing roads leading out from Rome in the fourth century included routes to nearby Etruscan and Latin towns and longer ranging routes to the northeast and south. The sophistication and extent of the graded routes across the urbanized regions of Italy are indicated by the road systems of the Faliscan territory (ager Faliscus) in southern Etruria, connecting towns of the area and providing routes between the mountains and the lowlands.[39] Predating Roman conquest, these routes formed the basis of Roman road building after the fourth century.

Many routes also were drove trails, criss-crossing the entire peninsula of Italy.[40] The via Salaria (Salt Road), in particular, was a drove trail used continuously from the Neolithic leading from the salt marshes at the mouth of the Tiber through Rome northeast to Reate in the territory of the Sabines, Asculum in that of the Picentes, and the Adriatic coast. Thus the via Salaria connected the winter coastal pastures with the highlands and in turn served as the primary route by which salt, one of the fundamental necessities of life, reached the transhumant herders of the central Apennines.[41] We should hardly wonder that the middle portion of Italy, stretching from the Tyrrhenian to the Adriatic coast, came earliest under Roman domination. By 218, the via Cornelia (later Aurelia), once a drove trail, extended about 150 miles up the coast to Populonia. This was one of the longest roads in Italy before the Second Punic War, together with the via Appia to Brundisium (by 244) and the via Flaminia, built in 220, to Fanum Fortunae, in Roman territory on the Adriatic coast, and on to Ariminium.[42] In short, starting at Rome, the Romans gradually pulled their holdings into them by grading, extending, and paving the roads that led out from Rome.

The earliest paved roads in Italy, extending south from Rome, facilitated the movement of citizens and allies to and from Rome. The via Appia, planned in 312 on the course of an existing road to the Latin town of Norba, passed through Roman territory (Forum Appi was on the road) to the citizen colony at Terracina founded in 329, before reaching its initial destination, Capua. In 296, citizen colonies were established along the route in existing towns, which were renamed Minturnae and Sinuessa. Paving of the via Appia began in 295. The via Tiburtina, begun in 307, led through Roman and allied territory to the town of Tibur on the Anio River. The road was extended soon after across Latin and allied territory to the Paelignian town of Corfinium. All these roads, and all roads generally, were planned and constructed under the supervision of Rome's highest magistrates in their military command capacity; most road builders were consuls and proconsuls. The exceptions are roads established or improved by public law: a law of C. Sempronius Gracchus in 123 or122 ordained the construction of new roads, and a law proposal and law of the first century addressed road maintenance, the rogatio Scribonia of 50 and a lex Visellia (see table 6.1).[43] Eventually, Roman territory was linked to Rome by an ever expanding network of roads, drawn out by the establishment of colonies or assignment of individual allotments. Road builders provided stopovers (*tabellaria*) on the way for travelers.[44] The fora built along roads, serving as markets and administrative centers for Romans, also provided Roman nodes for Romans en route between larger Roman towns and Rome. Roads confirmed the orientation of the Latin and Roman pockets in Italy toward Rome.[45] In this way the regular mobility of Roman citizens, into which the people of Italy were drawn, was facilitated and reinforced by a network of roads.

Construction in the city over the second century also met the needs of a mobile people. Insofar as we can discern large-scale building projects, as well as the funds used for construction, priority was given to an infrastructure supporting the large crowds visiting Rome for both civic and ritual performances and for markets. We happen to have a detailed record of building programs in Rome between 194 and 168, reported by Livy. These were managed by the Roman censors, drawing funds from state income derived from property taxes (tributum; ceasing in 167 by enactment of the Roman people), from taxes on salt (instituted in 204 by enactment of the Roman people), on inheritance and on manumission (the latter instituted by enactment of the Roman people in 304), from taxes on provincials, from booty, and to a small extent from rents on state land. The censors elected in the first half of the second century let contracts on a variety of projects intended to expand or improve the structures of city life. Roads formed one project: In 189, the Appian Way was repaved to the third milestone, and in 174 the city streets were graded, paved, and given curbs, and all dirt roads leading into the city were for the first time graveled. Another project was the water and sewer system: In 184, the censors cleaned and paved the main holding tank as well as the sewer system, which they extended to the Aventine hill. These censors also corrected abuses by levying fines on wealthy Romans in Rome and farmers along the route of the existing aqueducts (the aqua Appia and the aqua Anio vetus, both underground until they entered the city) who were wrongly diverting public water. Again in 179, the censors undertook to expand the water system in unknown ways.

The most impressive projects undertaken by Rome's censors involved the city's market, ritual, and civic facilities. In 179, the censors M. Aemilius Lepidus and M. Fulvius Nobilior let a flurry of contracts, embracing all three areas. They constructed a wooden bridge (pons Aemilius) across the Tiber to carry traffic going west, toward Etruscan Caere. Alongside they constructed port facilities for the river traffic, which was now so heavy that the riverbanks provided insufficient space to handle the movement of goods. As aedile in 193, with his brother, Aemilius Lepidus had already built a proto-warehouse there, the Porticus Aemilia. The censors also contracted for rebuilding the old Forum

Piscarium, thought to be the fish market, an area that had burned in 210, adjoining the large market (Macellum) erected after the fire, northeast of the Forum.[46] The additions to the water system undertaken by these censors may have been related to these refurbishments in the market facilities along the Tiber. In addition, Aemilius Lepidus and Fulvius Nobilior built a basilica (Basilica Fulvia et Aemilia), *post argentarias novas*, used for court cases. The censors also concerned themselves with ritual facilities, building collapsible seats and a permanent stage at the Temple of Apollo in the Field of Mars (Campus Martius) near the Forum Boarium, where the Games of Apollo were celebrated every July. Nearby they constructed a portico so that the crowds at the festival could come in out of the sun.[47] To date these efforts were the biggest seen in Rome. Of course the censors of 179 also let contracts for similar projects in Roman colonies. Nevertheless most of their attention, and that of later censors, was focused on Rome, where they built facilities unmatched by the facilities of any other Roman town, serving crowds seen nowhere else.[48]

The army of workers and managers required for these and similar projects has gone unreported.[49] So, too, has the precise original impetus for such building. Did the censors act on their own initiative or the Roman Senate's? Were they responding to public demand? If so, the demand rarely found expression in a lawmaking assembly. Clearly we see in the furbishment and embellishment of Rome a resolute concern on the part of Roman political leaders to associate themselves, particularly their reputations, with projects that were of primary benefit to the Roman people. The development of an infrastructure to support the games became a priority of the state, in particular of Roman censors and other leaders, over the course of the third and second centuries. While self-aggrandizement clearly plays a role in such efforts, of greater consequence seems to be the desire to ameliorate city conditions for the majority population. An interdependent relationship had to exist between the elite members of Roman society and ordinary Romans to encourage such behavior.

It is useful to survey the manner in which the city's infrastructure expanded as a result of these and other building efforts. By the second century there were no fewer than four specialized market areas in Rome: the fish market (Forum Piscarium), the vegetable market (Forum Holitorum), the cattle market (Forum Boarium), and the Roman Forum, the civic center of Rome that also served as the venue for money lending and where vendors sold a wide variety of manufactured goods. Port and storage facilities supplemented the market districts. As grain and oil arriving as tax (tributum) from the provinces were becoming the staple diet of the city population and the legions, more and more storage was needed. And, in the mid-second century, more storage facilities for oil from Spain and North Africa were constructed near the Forum Boarium, supplementing those built twenty years before. The Temple of Hercules Victor ad portam Trigeminam (called also Olivarius, Hercules of the Olive Traders), constructed in the second century in the port area just beyond the Forum Boarium and the oldest surviving temple in Rome, is testimony both to the prominent place of oil among other commodities and to the importance of Hercules to traders. Elite Romans also built warehouses to store grain and oil, purchased abroad and handed out to the population at their own expense. Transportation networks were refined and refurbished. All the streets in the city were paved and the roads leading into the city paved or graveled. Bridges connected the right and left banks of the Tiber at a number of points. Several times between 184 and 125 projects were begun to improve and expand the city water supply. Markets and access routes to the city were clearly of primary concern to the sponsors of such projects. Water, too, was a fundamental priority in Rome.

Other building projects served Rome's civic and ritual events. In the first half of the second century three law courts, or basilicae, were constructed on the perimeter of Rome's market districts. Many temples were constructed between 300 and 100, vowed by commanders on the field of battle for the most part. Porticos provided shade in those regions where ritual and civic activity was most intense: near the Temple of Apollo on the Campus Martius, along the ascent to the Capitoline hill. The settings for dramatic productions as well as games and races were in place. Stages were built and collapsible wooden bleachers for theatergoers provided. A censor in 159 even contracted to build a permanent stone theater, but this was scratched by the Senate, which regarded such places as potentially destabilizing. No permanent theater was constructed in Rome until 59, built by Pompey. The Circus Maximus was transformed from a simple grassy flat to an arena equipped for chariot races or animal hunts.[50] Another circus was built, the Circus Flaminius. In the ancient Mediterranean context, Rome was not only a modern city, but by 100 the largest and most sophisticated modern city in the Mediterranean. Overall we have the impression of careful attention on the part of the rulers of Rome to the structures that supported Rome's preeminence as the trading center of Italy and the civic and ritual center of a dense and highly mobile population.

LEVELS OF MIGRATION

A high level of movement in and out of Rome was the order of the day. The Roman experience of such movement in the period of greatest territorial expansion, from the end of the Second Punic War to the conquest of Gaul, roughly

200 to 50, was unique in contrast both to Rome's own past experience and to that of other cities precisely because of the high rate of growth attested in the city population and the complexity and strength of the networks connecting it to the countryside. From an estimated two hundred thousand in 200, the city population had swollen to one million by 50, it is believed, due primarily to in-migration.[51] In this section I propose to examine the dynamics of migration throughout this period and its implications for the persistence and increasing frequency of public lawmaking. The migration of citizens, Latins, Italians, and foreigners to the city tended to be of short duration, mirroring the movement of citizens to Rome described previously. Although the number of city residents was increasing, the population of Rome remained fundamentally unstable as people migrated, often on a short-term basis, joining those who simply visited the city, and then left again. In brief, the rough modern estimate of the population in Rome in 50, approximately one million people, obscures a far more important demographic phenomenon, the movement of millions of people who came to the city and left again in the years between 200 and 50. Movement underlay the Roman system.

While the personal motivations spurring such movement are irretrievable, we do know that migration in ancient Italy, like migration generally, followed established patterns and involved selected groups. Some of these select groups of migrants to Rome and the circumstances of their migration between 200 and 50 are distinguishable. Foreign slaves form one such group, specifically skilled slaves whose provenance, between 200 and 146, was mostly the Greek East and whose import from abroad may be viewed under the rubric of in-migration although their entry into Rome was forced. Working as craftsmen, teachers, performers, and other professionals before they were freed, these individuals apparently stayed in Rome to continue working as before. Since a manumission tax of 5 percent that was instituted by public law as early as 304, before the great influx of slaves, and payable by the slave, turned manumission into a lucrative prospect for the state and slaveholders, such slaves must have been quite often freed. A public law of this kind, setting up the conditions for the continued prosperity of Rome, again demonstrates the Roman talent for taking optimum advantage of a new situation. In this case, the slaves contributed skills the Romans wanted. Yet the numbers of skilled slaves and hence ex-slaves in Rome itself were doubtless few in relation to the total urban population.[52] Indeed, the impassioned opposition by many Romans to the registration of ex-slaves in rural tribes suggests that many had property outside the city or that they were registered in their previous owner's tribe. Another group was formed of foreign traders and craftsmen, artists, and teachers who followed the influx of wealth into Rome especially in the first half of the second century. Periodically they come to our attention in the occasional decrees of the Roman Senate expelling them from Rome, in times of dearth. Although an obvious focus for the Roman Senate, their numbers, like the numbers of slaves, were insignificant in proportion to the whole. Instead it is the peoples of Italy, Roman and non-Roman, who furnished migrants in numbers large enough to sustain the expansion of the population of Rome.

Unfortunately our sources provide few details that explain which Italians and Romans migrated to Rome and the circumstances surrounding their decisions. Why and how had they come? How long did they stay or intend to stay? How did they survive in the city? It seems reasonable to suppose that many migrants to the city were attracted by economic incentives. Their movement thus reflected the ebb and flow of the economic expansion of Rome: they were part of that growth and at the same time contributed to further growth. But regardless of motivation, Rome like all cities doubtless attracted many who stayed a short period, particularly in view of the cyclical patterns of life throughout the year in Rome. Personal motivations for migration were bound to be complex. What all migrants have in common is that they generally belong to self-selecting groups and represent a Roman version of chain migration. Such a chain undoubtedly led many more than the twelve thousand Latins, for instance, expelled from Rome in189 to the city over the following generations. The twelve thousand were the fortunate few who were able to survive in the city. Millions more came and went, a lost horde of migrants.[53]

Among the rural migrants to Rome, three sometimes overlapping groups tend to emerge more than any others from the shadows: (1) military veterans, both soldiers who were recently demobilized and others; (2) Italians and Latin allies, before the Italian War; and (3) men who were dispossessed of their land, in particular sons and families of the more than four thousand men who were proscribed by Sulla in 81. Soldiers form a special group among migrants to Rome because of both the composition of the Roman army and the accustomed recompense for military service. Before the Italian War the core soldiers of Rome, infantrymen, were both Roman and allies; afterward, at least by 70, all were Roman. Thus as a group soldiers were more diverse in respect to citizen status or ethnic identification than other self-selecting immigrant groups. Furthermore, their migration to Rome was often directly tied to the conditions and rewards of their military service, transformed by successful Roman expansion. Soldiers might for instance march to Rome at the end of a campaign, still under arms, to participate in the triumph of their commander, camping outside the sacred perimeter in the Campus Martius until they entered the city in triumphal procession. Unless a triumph was decreed by the Senate or voted by the people, it appears that soldiers generally returned home at the end of a campaign, in the period before the mid-second century, taking with them their formal share of the booty determined by the generosity of the commander and anything else carried away from successful conquest. The question of course is, Where was home? Before 167, when the tributum required of citizens was canceled, Roman soldiers also received their *stipendium* at the end of a campaign from tribal officials, who hand-delivered pay to the soldier's front door, to the man directly or to his survivors if he had been unlucky. As the Romans expanded across Italy between the fourth and the second centuries, Roman soldiers were frequently settled in their service units in colonies throughout Italy, most commonly by Senate decree, sometimes by public law. We have the impression that most of these were from Rome and the surrounding region in Latium. The experience of Italian soldiers was roughly similar except that their share of the booty was less, and they received no stipendium from Rome. The Roman state supported allies in the field with monthly allotments of food but no more. The rest came from the allied communities themselves.

Specific notice of the presence of soldiers or ex-soldiers in the vicinity of Rome in any numbers, that is, soldiers who saw military service in the same campaign serving under the same commander, occurs from 133 onward and is generally tied to public lawmaking assemblies or civil war conditions. By this time the average length of service is believed to be six years and military campaigns were usually outside Italy. On returning from such campaigns, did soldiers decamp as soon as they arrived in Italy and return to their homes? Did they march directly to Rome in anticipation of recompense, which more and more meant land and money allotments? Clear only is that more soldiers were in Rome during the first century—usually in relation to specific campaigns—than at any time before. The passage of certain kinds of public laws is a direct outcome of that circumstance.

Some particulars surrounding the migration of Italians and Romans who had been dispossessed of their landholdings surface in 63, in connection with the plan engineered by L. Sergius Catilina (Catiline). Catiline's supporters among the city population of Rome included men for whom farming had become impossible for any number of reasons.[54] Perhaps they had no land and were moreover without any other local alternative; they may have been veterans young or old who were unable to make it on the allotments assigned them at the end of their military service. Many Sullan veterans in Etruria were indebted in 63, for a variety of reasons, including the poor quality of the land assigned to them. They were also men who had been dispossessed twenty years before by Sulla. Migration was an alternative pursued by people who had suffered economic ruin, sometimes accompanied by disfranchisement. In this case citizens were the victims of Sulla's proscriptions, who numbered, according to Appian, forty senators and sixteen hundred equestrians.[55] Valerius Maximus gives a total figure of forty-seven hundred men proscribed by Sulla, probably including men below equestrian rank who were nonetheless wealthy men.[56] Thus many in Class 1 suffered losses. Undoubtedly they went to Rome with wives, children, and other family members. These individuals with their collective misfortune are readily identifiable in the ancient sources. Arguably, the disasters they experienced represent the singular disasters of others that go unreported. But they were probably not marginal people in the Roman system. Indeed they were citizens and at one time, if no longer, assidui.

It is clear that, for most rural immigrants in the second and first centuries, the city of Rome presented a special set of attractions whose pull, over time, grew more intense in pace with successful Roman military expansion in the Mediterranean region. One such deepening attraction in the second and first centuries was the growing labor market in Rome. As the censors and others contracted for more and more extensive building projects, the need for construction workers in Rome skyrocketed. As the market, warehouse, and port facilities expanded so too did the need for porters, stevedores, and a more specialized work force. Workers were hired and paid in cash, with which they purchased essential supplies. Rome offered the largest and most stable labor market in Italy. A more immediate attraction was the availability of food supplies. Before the late third century, the size of the city population was directly related to the ability of Rome's hinterland to feed it. But once the Romans had established external markets for the city food supply the relationship of dependency with the farms of Latium and all Italy was broken. Rome in the second and first centuries was Italy's super-warehouse, filled to overflowing with the produce of Spain, Sardinia, Sicily, and North Africa, as well as Italy itself.

To all the peoples of Italy, Roman and non-Roman, the existence of one city where food was always available must have been a tremendous reassurance and a powerful attraction. Certainly the people of Italy saw Rome as an accessible food supply point, especially after 123, when C. Gracchus carried the first bill establishing a fixed, low grain price for all citizens. Over the next one hundred years the state-funded store of inexpensive and eventually free grain for citizens was modified time and again and was even briefly terminated by Sulla. But the understanding that Rome was a dependable source of food continued. Witness, for instance, the response of local towns when Julius Caesar crossed into Italy with his legions in 50, precipitating civil war. From across Italy townspeople fled to Rome, where they felt they could be more certain of food.[57]

After 200, Rome provided the most reliable food market in Italy as well as the steadiest and largest labor market. All the markets of Rome exerted an inestimable pull on the people of Italy.

Moreover, access to the labor markets and dependable food supplies in Rome was certain. Rome was easily reached by land across an extensive network of the best-graded and best-paved roads in the Western world. For all inhabitants of Italy, Rome was readily accessible through a sophisticated road system promoting transport to and from the city. When rivers were undependable for travel and transport, these roads provided the ready means of traveling to Italy's warehouse and of transporting grain away from the city.[58] This complex and mutually reinforcing network of roads and rivers centered on Rome was unique: nothing like it existed anywhere else in the Mediterranean basin. Indeed, the need for a work force, the quantities of grain and olive oil regularly imported into Rome, and the advanced road system leading into the city from all parts of Italy were unparalleled in the ancient Mediterranean region.[59]

Equally unparalleled over time was the special attraction of public lawmaking, one of many vital events occurring only in Rome, the civic and ritual hub of the Roman state in Italy. As we have seen, inhabitants across Italy converged on Rome for various reasons and varying lengths of stay with the result that many citizens were regularly on hand to vote, whether temporary migrants or permanent city residents. Voting in lawmaking assemblies came to exert a unique pull on citizen and noncitizen alike as rural conditions in Italy deteriorated for small landholders over the second century. After the Italian War of 91–89 and the Sullan restoration of 82–80, when many immigrants had experienced adversity in civil war, participation in public lawmaking sessions held a powerful attraction for citizens with particular needs or grievances as long as there were elected officials to address them. Many immigrants to Rome came in hopes of getting land, which they might reasonably expect to be allocated by decision of the Roman people, that is, by their own decision, as Roman tribesmen and voters. Thus former soldiers and rural tribesmen attended the public lawmaking assembly convened by Ti. Gracchus in 133 to enact the bill redistributing ager publicus in Italy, roused perhaps by the sponsor's concern for the dwindling numbers of rural citizens eligible for infantry service. The soldiers of Marius who fought the Gauls attended the assemblies convened by L. Appuleius Saturninus in 103 and 100, occasions marked by considerable violence—testimony to the division in the Roman community about the grants. In 81, Sulla settled as many as 120,000 veterans in about twenty colonies in central and southern Italy.[60] At other times soldiers might be discharged abroad and rewarded with land abroad, by decree of the Senate or commander's fiat. Thus some of Pompey's troops received land grants in Asia in the late 60s. But others had to wait until Julius Caesar as consul successfully enacted a land distribution scheme in Italy that included them. Among their number were family men, given priority by Caesar in 59, who proposed to allot land to citizens with at least three children.[61] Land typically was allotted on the basis of need as well as status and service. In this case, men with children—an individual's primary contribution to the Roman state's chief asset, namely, its population—were taken care of first. Always, public lawmaking sessions were scheduled only in Rome to address vexed issues of communitywide interest, sometimes involving the disposition of resources and affecting all the inhabitants of Italy.

Accordingly, in the second and first centuries, an important reason why dispossessed or landless citizens migrated to Rome rather than to one of an estimated four hundred other towns of Italy was precisely in order to participate in assemblies. People went to Rome to vote or simply to be present on lawmaking occasions because it meant so much within the framework of the Roman system. This was one of the primary ways of sharing in the benefits of empire. In fact, of all public law issues between 133 and 44, almost 20 percent involved resources.[62] The expectation that wrongs may be righted, that rewards may be had, that shares in the profits of empire may be available in Rome seems to have been strongly held by the majority population of Italy.

The expectation, moreover, was shared by political leaders, whose successful leadership rested on their ability to effectively recognize and facilitate the needs and wishes of the people expressed in Rome. Consider public laws addressing city food supplies, specifically the many grain laws. From the third century onward, Romans with political aspirations encouraged votes through gifts of oil, grain, and cash handouts to tribesmen. The election of P. Cornelius Scipio Africanus and his brother as aediles in 213 was secured by the gift of Spanish oil sent by their father from Spain and distributed to the population. Warehouses were built by elite Romans to store grain or oil imported at private expense for distribution.[63] Every tribe had its officials for handing out perquisites, underscoring the political potential of distributions, which were customary at the tribal level. Selling such essential supplies to citizens at a stably low price, or giving it to citizens free of charge, diminished the utility of distributions of food. Thus C. Gracchus's public law fixing a low price for grain removed that particular avenue of political advantage for ambitious, competitive Romans. In turn Gracchus reaped credit as lawmaker for the same benefaction his bill denied individual patrons.[64] Indirectly, the law introduced predictability and stability in the city food supply at a time when a new level of migration brought an untold number of citizens and outsiders to Rome. That the statute subsidized the cost of grain up to a stated amount for citizens reflects a common Roman perspective on the importance of being Roman. But from the codification, so to speak, of an existing situation, doubtless the bill subsequently encouraged even more movement to Rome, where grain once only predictable was now also predictably cheap. It is not coincidental that Gracchus purportedly carried another bill to improve the road system in Italy.

For outsiders, particularly Latins and Italians, citizenship itself presented a strong pull to Rome. By the second century, Italians were migrating at times some distance across Italy in order to claim or confirm their citizen status, legitimately or fraudulently, in order to exercise the prerogatives of Roman citizenship. Many Italians became permanent residents of Rome, and many tried (and clearly succeeded) in registering on the citizen lists in Rome. Since registration on the tribal rolls required a man to make a declaration to the censor in Rome, in a face-to face encounter that involved tribal leaders, reputable men who would vouch for his identity, these Italians passed muster: someone accepted them as citizens. Given that confirmation of an individual's status and identity for the purposes of registration depended on the personal affirmation of a man of repute, probably a tribal official, we are entitled to wonder about the complicity of Roman tribal leaders in the questionable registration of outsiders.[65] Even more extraordinary is the inherent permeability of the Roman tribes and property classes. Roman citizenship was inextricably tied to the city. Latins could claim full Roman citizenship by registering in a Roman tribe that initially required residency in Rome.[66] Only in Rome could men register themselves and their families at the quinquennial census. Even after citizenship was gradually detached from Rome the relationship between Rome and Roman citizenship continued. Rome's Italian allies formed another large group of migrants to the city, drawn by the possibility of entering the conquering state via the quinquennial census. The expulsion of thousands of irregular citizens over the period confirms the value of Roman citizenship to all members of Italian communities—and the expectation of survival in the city if not the possibility of registration.

Underlying the attractions of Roman citizenship to the Italians who migrated to the city was access to resources and participation in assemblies that made decisions about the allocation of resources on a hierarchical scale: citizens and Latins received more land and more booty than Italian allies, in particular. Registration in a Roman tribe was the gateway to participation in the privileges of Roman citizenship. After 167, when the riches of the Macedonian kings flooded Rome, the tribes no longer collected tributum for the state treasury. The removal of this civic burden was seen as a privilege shared by all tribe members. Empire paid off on a directly personal level but always through the mediation of citizenship and tribal registration.

Such a constellation of attractions intensified as rural conditions in Italy steadily deteriorated from the second half of the second century onward. Sallust's description of Catiline's supporters among the urban population in 63 provides a case in point. Now, when food sources for many rural inhabitants were increasingly undependable in the face of tenuous landholdings and growing indebtedness, migration is thought to have become a more common solution in the effort to ensure survival. But migration in the first century was an option not for people at the very lowest levels of society but rather for those whose lives were redirected as a result of military service or shattered by disaster. It is reasonable to suppose, as ancient authors have indeed implied, that the simultaneously increasing frequency of lawmaking activity after 133, increasing level of rural migration, and new concern for fixed, low grain prices for citizens in Rome were no coincidence.

THE INTEGRATION OF NEWCOMERS: SOCIAL NETWORKS, TRIBES, AND VICI

In response to a formal request in 177 from the councils of several Latin towns, the consul Claudius Pulcher promulgated a bill requiring all Latins and allies as of the census of 189 who had migrated to Rome to return to their home communities. The Roman people duly accepted the proposal as law, and the consul, in implementation, gave one of the praetors the task of investigating Latins and allies who failed to comply.[67] While this is the only known occasion when the Roman people enacted a law at the request of outsiders, in this case Latins, to return immigrants to their hometowns, it is not the first or only time that the Romans expelled immigrants from Rome. In 187, the Senate set up a commission of inquiry that expelled twelve thousand Latin and Italian allies.[68] In 95, the consuls carried a bill establishing a procedure for challenging the citizenship claimed by allies; ten thousand allies resident in the city were expelled.[69] A similar measure in 65 sent allied Transpadani home.[70] In a society lacking modern means of verifying personal identification, the detection of so many Latins and Italians through the investigations of courts of inquiry is unexpected. The modern historian wonders at the low level of internal order in a city population as large and diverse as Rome's and still more at the Roman achievement in maintaining that order when so many people were moving in and out of the city. Central to any explanation are the structures of accommodation to city life encountered by migrants to Rome.

Of the millions who migrated annually to the city, how many stayed to join the ranks of permanent city residents? The most cursory inquiry into the exigencies of life in Rome that had developed by the last two centuries of the Republic shows the extent of the challenge facing newcomers. At this time the city held a permanent population of men, women, and children numbering in the tens of thousands and including Romans, Italians, and foreigners, citizens and allies, the freeborn, freed slaves, and slaves, rich and poor. For all of them the essential medium of daily life was cash, and to all appearances most of them had a marketable skill or calling that enabled them to exchange goods or services for cash. With cash, city dwellers bought grain and other comestibles; with cash, they paid millers to grind their grain and bakers to bake their bread and other food; with cash, they paid their entry fee at the baths, bought sacrificial victims and dedicatory offerings, and paid the itinerant teachers of grammar and arithmetic who taught their children. In short, cash enabled city dwellers to procure all the necessities and advantages of life in an urban setting. Above all, city residents paid rents, the most burdensome requirement of city life as attested by the struggle over rents during the civil war years from 49 to 46.[71] Under the circumstances, some lived better than others in the city of Rome. Newcomers especially must have found the immediate prospects for survival daunting.

Crucial, therefore, to understanding the adaptation of a highly mobile population to the order of city life is the potential for survival in Rome that developed over the centuries. Undoubtedly migrants found opportunities to work for wages on arrival in Rome, even those migrants whose metiers extended no further than farming, herding, or soldiering and who are presumed to form the majority of immigrants in the late second and first centuries. In a city undergoing so much expansion and importing such a quantity of goods by sea, river, and land, workers were needed to haul, lift, and carry as we have seen. There was a need as well for laborers to undertake the projects of building and repair in the city that fell within the purview of elected officeholders as well as private initiative. With only his labor to sell, however, and no guarantees of regular work, the unskilled migrant's prospects of survival by exchanging labor for cash were most likely temporary. Far more important was his ability to enter a social network in Rome, which cushioned the shock of entry, opened ready access to the means of support, and facilitated the process of acclimatization.

The numerous inhabitants of Rome found themselves inextricably bound to each other in complicated layers of networks that, insofar as they are manifested in the city, derived from a variety of fundamental relationships and social ties prevalent in the larger society. City residents with a common origin, or from the same region, town, or village within Italy or outside, or in the same occupation, shared ties of family, regional, cultural, or occupational loyalties that formed the basis of reciprocal support systems located first and foremost in the neighborhoods (vici) of Rome. Some of the earliest neighborhoods were the vicus Tuscus, vicus Argentarius, and vicus Sandalarius, the names, as we saw earlier, testimony to the tendency for the constituent members of the city population to cluster in self-selecting groups by origin or occupation. During the imperial period, boatmen, fishermen, divers, dock workers, and Jews lived in tenements built below the Janiculan hill, along the other side of the Tiber River bank, marginal groups by reason of low-status occupation or foreign origins.[72] If not precisely these, then other clusters probably lived here as early as the settlement of the left bank in the third century, group following group in the regular pattern of serial migration.

While the clustering by ethnicity or occupation might have provided the original logic behind Rome's earliest neighborhoods, in later centuries they accommodated a more diverse population. By the late Republic, city neighborhoods hosted a mix of professions and occupations as well as culture and status groups. A shoemaker, an ironworker, a seller of wool, and a herald, all freeborn Romans or Italians, are attested among the occupants of the long and bustling Subura in the first century.[73] Julius Caesar lived in modest quarters here, too, until he was elected pontifex maximus in 63, some measure of the neighborhood's attractiveness to an up-and-coming political leader.[74] Despite significant neighborhood clustering on the basis of origin, occupation, or status, all inhabitants of the city of Rome experienced a great deal of contact and interaction with each other in all periods. But despite their growing internal diversity, the various neighborhoods continued to provide varied harbors for newcomers with common ties to earlier arrivals. We may well imagine that select groups among Rome's countless immigrants in every period were drawn to particular vici where they found relatives or members of their native regions or home communities and, increasingly in the late second and first centuries, even Roman rural tribes.

If in general then the migrants who stayed in Rome were those who succeeded in broaching the human network necessary for survival, that network for citizens in particular centered on the tribes. Membership in one of Rome's thirty-one rural and four urban tribes entailed a range of vertical and horizontal ties with fellow tribesmen of differing statuses, maintained through the corporate organization and various functions of the tribe, the most important occurring in Rome. Predicated originally on residency in a rural or urban tribe, that is, a specific geographic location, tribal networks had become far more pervasive by the first century. A man's tribe was the tribe of his father, even if his property lay in a different tribe. In particular, immigrant rural tribesmen had transported the networks of rural tribes to Rome itself. Very little is known about the circumstances of Romans from rural tribes in Rome or their links with fellow tribesmen in the city, but their presence in Rome for particular events and occasions is known. For most, migration was probably temporary. That at least some rural tribesmen of all stations and means resided in Rome, however, is certain. Roman aristocrats provide the best known case in point. The group of city residents who served as Clodius's cadres in the late 60s and early 50s included two new citizens, one Samnite and another Marsi, who belonged presumably to rural tribes.

The strength of tribal networks in Rome itself is suggested by the practice of *ambitus*, electoral bribery whose political efficacy, in the final analysis, was an outgrowth of both the need for cash and the limited amounts of cash during the last two centuries. Not only were the divisores of each tribe and the clearinghouses for the monies of the various candidates, established before each election at the home of various middlemen (sequestres) between candidates and divisores, concentrated in Rome, but more significantly the distributions themselves occurred only there. When money in hand was an essential condition of life in Rome, what better boon for down-and-out Romans from rural tribes? Overall, it is easy to picture a newcomer to the city, aggrieved but Roman, making his first stop on arrival a neighborhood where he knew fellow tribesmen (tribules) lived, from whom he might expect immediate relief and assistance. Arguably Caesar, a member of the rural Fufia tribe, lived in the Subura precisely because this district housed a clustering of fellow tribesmen who had migrated to Rome. Embracing rich men and poor, the powerful and the powerless, the tribes in all periods provided a support system for citizens in Rome, whether temporary migrants or city residents.

At the same time, newly arrived migrants found it expedient to reinforce or recast their prior, traditional relationships of family and community in comprehensible ways. New networks took shape not only in the neighborhoods but also in the associations called collegia, whose members generally shared a common calling or trade and included citizens as well as slaves and former slaves.[75] Such associations are characteristic of a mobile population whose members have migrated away from a home community to relocate elsewhere.[76] Associations emerge from the interdependency of interest, resources, and needs characterizing a particular group, whether the group members are joined by common origins in a village; common profession, craft, or skill; or common aim such as burial. In Rome most collegia overlap with the city neighborhood insofar as their membership conforms to the majority population of a given neighborhood, defined by occupation. The collegia both replace and supplement the more familiar groupings and built-in social networks of home, especially for foreigners, former slaves, and Italian allies but also for poorer citizens. Notwithstanding their prior ties, these newcomers from other parts of Italy as well as abroad were quickly integrated into the social fabric of Rome through these associations. The striking incidence of associations in Roman social and political life attests to the role of such networks in absorbing and sustaining migrants to the city.

These networks supplemented, and to some extent transcended, the traditional Roman hierarchic relations of dependency, the patron-client nexus, associated with the elite members of Roman society. How much more the associations were out of the control of the Roman leadership than the traditional social networks is indicated in the Senate decree of 64 dissolving them and in the lex Clodia of 58 restoring them. By the first century, the Roman Senate viewed the membership of the collegia as dangerously independent.[77] Even outside the patron-client nexus, elite Romans believed that they and the majority population should exist in a symbiotic relationship. Later still, under the emperors, all collegia were required to have an elite Roman as patronus, a reliable way of attaching them firmly to the traditional Roman hierarchy.

High levels of migration notwithstanding, the city population found a basic structure of order in the vici of Rome. Habitation in Rome was confined primarily to the hills and the edges of the market areas, where people lived in tenements on streets that, from one intersection to another, formed neighborhoods. From the earliest days, these neighborhoods formed discrete organizational units in the expanding city whose cohesion was ensured by the shared interests or common background of the inhabitants. What we must suppose is a core group of residents in each neighborhood whose own coherence, especially if they were foreigners, was not inimical to the Romans' need for order and control in the city. Residents of each neighborhood elected one of their number to perform local administrative and ritual functions as headman (*vicomagister*).[78] Each neighborhood maintained a shrine at the intersection to the Lares Compitales, whose regular worship was managed by the headman. In matters regarding the order and stability of the city, the headman of each vicus mediated affairs between his neighborhood and the elected city officials responsible for the five regions (*regiones*) into which the city of Rome was divided, especially the marketplaces in those regions, namely the four aediles and the five-man commission called the "five men for this and that side of the Tiber" (*quinqueviri cis uls Tiberim*). Hence the headman appears to be the next lower level of management. Below him were the inhabitants of his vicus on whose behalf the headman performed the divine and secular obligations of the collective. With their corporate structures, headmen, and voting members, these neighborhood associations were fundamental units of daily life in Rome.

The neighborhoods also played an important role in the unfolding religious life of the city, providing in particular the venue for many of the activities and rituals of the state cult as well as the neighborhood shrines. In 46, Julius Caesar provided dinner for the city residents as part of the festival celebrating his triumph, for which he set out twenty-two thousand dinner couches, each holding several reclining diners, in the neighborhoods of Rome. He also staged plays in the various neighborhoods in the Latin language as well as other Italian languages and Greek. Most local rituals and celebrations were more regular, including the daily worship of the Lares Compitales and the all-important Compitalia celebrated in January. The persistence of such ancient rituals as well as the general level of participation in the complex religious life of Rome in the first century confirm the successful integration of newcomers of different backgrounds at the level of the Roman neighborhoods. All residents were drawn into citywide, and indeed Roman territorywide, patterns of ritual observance at the neighborhood shrines as well as at the myriad cult centers sprinkled thickly throughout the city.

In the common experience of city life, in the necessity of forging connections with other city residents, and in the relationships and structures of neighborhood, cult, association, and, in particular, tribe, lie the bases for the remarkable order in the city of Rome. But how it was regulated and by whom is a subject of some discussion among modern historians.[79] For instance, how was it possible for courts of inquiry in 177 and 95 to determine who should be expelled as an illegal resident? The neighborhood officials (vicomagistri) spring to mind as repositories of information about neighborhood residents. Above the neighborhood level, all city residents were managed on a similarly personal level by various strata of elected and appointed officials, drawn from the elite members of society. It is apparent that issues of law and order were generally maintained in the city initially through family (or patronage) networks and next at a fairly local level by officeholders whose primary purview was the markets.[80] But their management was relatively loose, until the elite members of Rome detected a threat to the system.

PUBLIC LAW AND THE PROSPERITY OF ROME

Vitally important in creating the conditions that the Romans believed had made their city grow and prosper was the public lawmaking process. Table 6.1 lists the issues brought to public law assemblies that smoothed the progress of urban achievement. The listing reflects the haphazard pattern of development of Rome: Romans had no urban plan or agenda for expanding the city. But many of these laws clearly removed impediments to Rome's continued central position in an expanding empire. It is easiest to detect the impact and scope of public laws in the arena of actions seemingly inspired by an economic motive. To be sure, all of these actions had rather more complex motivations.

Overall, we need not impose a modern conception of an economy on the Romans to recognize that they viewed their city and the conquered lands as a common region where considerably more than the simple exchange of goods took place. The range of issues with economic implications passed at lawmaking assemblies and applicable to the entire Roman state is listed in table 6.1. Although the issues vary in their motivation and their direct applicability to market concerns, the listing suggests a desire to establish standards and to bring a certain amount of predictability to areas where there was little agreement or where confusion would impede the operation of a market common to Rome and the conquered lands. Through the passage of public laws in Rome, which affected life throughout Italy, currency was adjusted and the value of coins was fixed, debts were regulated, rules were established for specified leases, port duties were controlled, and new roads were constructed, as noted in table 6.1. Among such laws, one-time issues emerge from time to time that are to all appearances politically or personally motivated, even though they impinge on the commercial life of Rome—for example, the attempt in 168 to annul all state leases and contracts entered into by the current censors. A significant block of laws in table 6.1, involving the city's food supply, appears only from 123 onward. More significant, however, is the consistency of issues in table 6.1 over time.

One such regular concern throughout the roughly two-hundred-year period between the First Punic War, when the Romans began to mint coins on a regular basis, and the end of the Republic was state control of Rome's money supply, as reflected in laws altering the basic money standard (four), limiting individual outlay on luxury goods and activities as well as gifts (fourteen), or placing restrictions on gambling (three). Equally constant were efforts to accommodate the negative and widespread effects of owing money, seen in laws on debt (eleven) and suretyship (six). Public lawmaking assemblies also addressed specific issues of private law that appear fundamental to the regularization of relationships involving the transfer and ownership of property across Italy. At least twenty-seven in number, these include suretyships, the creation of actions at law (*legis actiones*) for specific circumstances involving the recovery of money or property, fraud perpetrated against minors, the appointment of guardians, the ownership of stolen property, the wrongful ownership of a citizen or citizen's slave, the capacity of women to inherit property, and other matters involving inheritance. Fundamental in recognizing the vastly more complicated world of grievance and restitution, and the need for more streamlined procedures, was the public law carried sometime between 149 and 125 that established the formulary procedure.[81]

While the Romans paid careful attention to the scheduling of events throughout the year, to permit the uninterrupted flow of economic life and legal business, they did not often do so in lawmaking assemblies. In 287, a lex Hortensia allowed the conduct of legal business, including lawmaking assemblies, on market days.[82] Perhaps in 191, a lawmaking assembly assigned to a knowledgeable senator the occasional task of bringing the calendar, which periodically fell behind, in line with the solar year. In 98, the consuls carried a public law requiring that public law sponsors observe the trinundinum in scheduling their voting assemblies. For the first time, in 58, the tribune P. Clodius Pulcher enacted that public lawmaking assemblies could be scheduled on any *dies fasti*, thus increasing the number of days during a year when such events were permissible. While the political aspects of most of these laws are better known, each has implications as well for a smoothly running economic life, given the relationship between markets and days when legal business or assemblies were viable. Rather than any attempt to intentionally further an agenda of economic growth, however, these efforts were inspired by the same motives as Roman actions in other arenas of life. The Romans were seeking to recreate throughout all of their possessions the conditions that they believed allowed the growth of their city.

So also with the remarkably high number of public laws concerned with the officeholders, on whose judgments or functions the regularization of economic life often depended, listed in table 6.2. The number and kinds of offices, as well as the responsibilities of the officeholders, came under frequent revision due to the increasing pressures on office resulting from greater numbers of elite Romans.[83] But need, obviously, played a role as well. Such was the size and increasing complexity of the city population of Rome beginning in the fourth century that an impressive expansion in the number of new offices and officials took place in the third and second centuries. More lesser officeholders, magistratus minores, were created or modified in the collective that modern scholars call the Vigintisexvirate, originally the Vigintivirate.[84] The first new magistracies since the office of curule aedile in 367 appeared between 272 and 218, when the Romans established four lesser offices both to carry the increasing administrative burden of the higher offices—those of praetor, aediles, and censors—and to perform once random tasks on a perennial basis. One office, the "three men for casting and striking bronze, silver, and gold" (*tresviri monetales*), reveals the Romans at last minting coins on a regular rather than ad hoc basis for daily rather than exceptional needs.[85] Others were the "three men for night-time crime" (*tresviri nocturni*, later *capitales*), selected by the praetor, and "five men for this and that side of the Tiber" (quinqueviri cis uls Tiberim). The new offices of the third century reflect predictable areas of concern to a flourishing trade center with a burgeoning population.

A more powerful and prestigious office created in this period confirms that this burgeoning city population included a significantly foreign element. The office of the "praetor for resolving disputes between Romans and foreigners" (*praetor inter peregrinos* or peregrine praetor) was established, perhaps by enactment of the Roman people, around 242 to handle legal cases involving foreigners in Rome.[86] The office attests both to an increase in litigation in Rome, especially involving property, with the result that the existing praetor (from now on called the city praetor) was overworked, as well as to an increasing number of foreigners in Rome, temporarily or permanently, who had the right of making contracts with Romans. Such foreigners included Latins and Italian allies, first and foremost, and also any other people with whom the Romans had trading agreements at this time, such as Greeks, Carthaginians, and others. Like the five men (quinqueviri) concerned with order in the market places, the peregrine praetor is testimony to a commercial pull in the movement of noncitizens to Rome.

Attesting to the growing complexity of Roman society and an increased need for administration as well as adjudication in pace with Roman expansion, existing offices were also expanded or modified over the next two centuries. The tribune Papirius, sometime between 241 and 123 (Festus p. 347), carried a bill enacting that the people elect the tresviri capitales in a tribal assembly convened by the peregrine (?) praetor and that the tresviri capitales, in addition to their regular duties, be responsible for collecting the money fines exacted in the *legis actio sacramento* process (table 6.2). The perceived need for low-level administrators with a wider range of responsibilities doubtless arises from contemporary recognition of a more complex, rapidly expanding city population. In this period and later the number of praetors was gradually increased.[87] Two more praetorships were added after 227, and two more again after 197, to command armies and administer Roman justice in the growing expanse of Roman overseas territories. These praetors, like the urban and peregrine praetors who were the chief legal officers in the Roman state, had both power of command (imperium) and investigative authority (*jurisdictio*) by grant of the Roman people. In 81, a further two praetors were created, to make a total of eight praetors, six of whom headed up the newly developing criminal courts (table 6.2). Likewise the number of quaestors, the first rung in the *cursus honorum* and from 81 the office of entry into the Roman Senate, expanded from two to six in 267 to even more thereafter in order to manage abundant state resources in Italy and the provinces. In 81, a lex Cornelia created twenty quaestors (table 6.2). Public law proposals addressed other administrative offices or commissions. The ad hoc nature of many of these is apparent, particularly the creation of one-time extraordinary boards during the Second Punic War (table 6.2). Some positions were inevitably political, notably the creation of an extraordinary command against the pirates in 67, whose powers and scope were modeled on the command the Senate established for M. Antonius in 102. Another ad hoc office was the official designated by public law to oversee the grain supply in 57 (table 6.2).[88] Nonetheless, such positions at all times filled a genuine need.

So too did the special commissions of inquiry. When matters arose that were not accommodated automatically within the existing system of justice, a more frequent occurrence after the Second Punic War, the Romans instituted commissions of investigation. Sometimes these commissions were set up by Senate decree, in response to outside request or inside concern, appointing consuls, praetors, or senators without office to head up the inquiry. Sometimes, too, the commissions were instituted by public law, as listed in table 6.2. Special commissions of investigation form one of the single most commonly recurring public law issue between 338 and 44. Products of the inherent flexibility in the Roman system, these commissions were a key mechanism allowing the Romans to modulate the unanticipated grievances and conflicts accompanying Roman expansion.

Over time, other arbiters and courts became part of the regular administrative and legal apparatus of the Roman state. These, too, were subject to creation, regulation, or attempted regulation by public lawmaking assemblies, listed in table 6.2. The quattuorviri praefecti Capuam Cumas, who administered justice in the ten districts of Campania, were created by the Senate following a public law in 210 instructing that body to impose penalties on Capua. From 124, the tribal assembly elected these administrators; before that the praetor selected them.[89] More enduring than the special commissions of inquiry were the permanent courts (*quaestiones*) (addressed more fully in chapter 7), also products of Rome's lawmaking process, beginning with the lex Calpurnia de repetundis of 149. The court established by the lex Calpurnia was followed by courts concerned with treason (*maiestas*), in 103 and 90, and thereafter by a range of others. All were initially created and subsequently revised and revised again in regard to their scope, procedure, and jury composition by decision of the Roman people. These courts to a large extent replaced the special commissions as well as the selective use of popular assemblies as "popular courts" (iudicia publica) in adjudicating state crimes involving elite Romans.[90] Like the commissions of inquiry, the courts provide further demonstration of the resiliency of the process of public law in responding to continually new situations.

Strikingly absent from our listings in tables 6.1 and 6.2, given the obvious concern for the regularization of economic life, is evidence of any overt agenda of city management as found in municipal laws of the Late Republic, exemplified in the Tabula Heracleensis. The city's water supply provides a case in point. Given the size and pattern of growth of Rome, water understandably was a major concern. Indeed the lex Quinctia de aquaeductibus of 9 established a massive fine on purloiners of public water. Yet this public law from the reign of Augustus is the only law regulating the water supply known today in any detail. While there may have been others—a lex Sulpicia of unknown date is identified as such a law (*RS* 2 No. 42)—it appears more likely that, just as aqueduct maintenance and water use were left entirely to the oversight of the aediles and censors, such rules as developed were issued entirely by order of these magistrates or Senate decree.[91] Some lawmakers attempted to regularize areas of everyday life, for instance, the sponsor of the lex Silia, a third-century measure establishing the aediles' oversight over weights and measures, and the tribune Scribonius in 50, whose proposals also addressed the oversight over weights and measures and roads. For the most part, however, a somewhat personal management was the order of the day, until some crisis or other prompted action. The regulation of religious life by public laws presents such a situation. Many gods and their cults arrived somewhat spontaneously in Rome. Only when ritual observance was elevated to the level of state cult, as it was in the institution of regular state festivals in the third century on set days of the year, or when it became necessary to regulate the management of ritual by political leaders and the necessary adjustments could not be made by a consensus among the leadership, was recourse had to public lawmaking sessions. Laws addressing, among other related matters, the number and qualifications of augurs and priests, the creation of the epulones, a board of three priests responsible for Jupiter's dinner party at the Roman games, the selection of Vestals, and the co-optation or election of priests are collected in table 6.2.

In the circumstances, surprisingly few rules generated by elected officeholders, the Senate, or people regulated the internal order of the city. Public lawmaking assemblies in particular played a very small role in shaping various facets of city life, and then only when city disorder disturbed the order of the entire Roman state. The Bacchanalian conspiracy provides a case in point. To a remarkable degree Rome was unmanaged, the city's many and varied inhabitants coming to share a common base of customary relationships and customary ways of interaction. Overall, the continuing basis for the formal regulation of order in Rome as much as order itself was provided fundamentally by a strong sense of the underlying relationships among different groups of people. Belonging to family and kin groups, patronage networks, neighborhoods, tribes, associations, and other groups, the people of Rome were firmly attached from top to bottom. The strength of the bonds uniting Romans of all levels made possible the fairly loose control of public order by elite Romans. While the increase in the number of low-level administrators over time is hardly surprising given the increasing scale and complexity of Roman society, it is noteworthy that the formal apparatus of justice thereby created always relied heavily on the individual judgment of elected officials and their deputies. Accordingly, the regulation of order at the lower levels was not often directly facilitated by public law. Only when issues of justice directly affected elite Romans, or disrupted or threatened to disrupt statewide community order, that is, when the potential disruption transcended the city of Rome itself, were issues involving public order taken to public lawmaking assemblies.

CONCLUSION

The city of Rome as it appeared by the end of the Republic, the product of a process of population movement, adjustment, and settlement stretching back hundreds of years, served as the focal point in Italy for activities encompassing the most important spheres of Roman community life: economic, political, and religious. Rome was the imperial center of empire, the focus of the administration of colonies and of provinces. Rome was the ritual center of the wide-flung Roman population, staging the chief festivals and celebrations required by Roman religious life and building temples to house a growing pantheon of gods. Rome was likewise the civic center of empire, the sole venue for voting, for citizen registration, and for the performance in brief of the central obligations and activities of citizenship. Public lawmaking belonged among the most important of the attractions Rome presented to citizens. Expansion resulted in a city of phenomenal size and kaleidoscopic movement while Romans struggled to manage in a traditional Roman way. Nevertheless, the infrastructure and mechanisms allowing massive overseas expansion were in place.

The importance of the regular civic and ritual performances in Rome, central to life in the Roman community, was intensified by the role of Rome in managing the resources of Italy. Specialized regional markets attracted buyers and sellers from throughout Italy. By the second century huge external supplies of grain, slaves, coins, and luxury items poured into Rome. In turn the city assembled and exported thousands of troops, drawn from all Italy, on brutal campaigns of conquest. In these movements, we catch a glimpse of the fundamental motive force behind the Romans' expansion of empire: the striking mobility of all kinds among people on all levels and the degree to which customary networks expanded to accommodate this mobility and growth and helped create a city remarkable in the ancient Mediterranean by virtue both of its size and the role it played in a vast hinterland peopled by citizens and others sharing an increasingly common outlook.

The rapid movement of individuals in and out of the city of Rome provides an index of the extent to which the Romans succeeded in redirecting traditional patterns of life throughout Italy to center on Rome in a manner unprecedented in the ancient world. The more we examine the details of this movement, the more we confront this question: How did the city of Rome not only stay together but also grow so impressively over the period? Within the city of Rome diverse groups lived in a loose relationship to central authority—Rome's political leaders. As the city expanded and the population grew more diverse, the chief elected officeholders and the Senate relied on small-scale structures to help maintain order. Romans lived in proximity to others like themselves, sharing customary relationships and customary ways of interacting with others. Like their rural countrymen, permanent urban residents were joined to the system by their rights and duties as citizens and by their membership in a tribe. City residents were joined also to one another by a series of reciprocal ongoing contacts involving the search for food, land, jobs, and survival. The Roman way of life was a group experience.

Surprisingly few formal regulations of any kind were necessary in such a system, and surprisingly few were decreed by the Senate (*senatus consulta*) or dictated by elected officials (*edicta*). Even fewer public laws were presented in lawmaking assemblies to address issues of order in the city. In general, individual or family wrongs were dealt with through family, kin, or patronage networks. The behavior of both rural and urban populations was controlled by somewhat autonomous local authorities, who in turn were responsible to a diffuse layer of elite Romans serving in various public offices. When this diverse resilient system proved incapable of dealing with a larger challenge, enterprising political leaders often proposed a public law to restore the balance. Similarly, officeholders paid attention to ensuring, often through public law, a balanced mesh of the many ritual, market, and civic events essential to the functioning of the city.

Thus, public law played an infrequent but crucial role in maintaining the vitality of the structures underlying Rome's preeminence as the trading center of Italy and the civic and ritual center of a dense and highly mobile population. Attendance at voting assemblies in Rome reflected the rapid movement characterizing the Roman world. Recourse was had to lawmaking assemblies primarily when issues affected Rome as center of Roman state and empire. Then, public law served to develop and maintain a collective voice on the fundamental institutions that allowed the city to prosper, specifically the festivals, assemblies, courts, and markets. While day-to-day workings of city life were managed by low-level and high-level officials, public laws regulated the details of life that transcended the city itself, especially in regard to state cult, grain distribution, offices, and courts and crimes involving elite Romans. The viability of this Roman system rested on deeply held assumptions that permeated all levels of society at lawmaking assemblies. All Romans understood the necessity for resolving potentially disruptive issues in lawmaking assemblies, which represented in microcosm the balance of forces in the city of Rome. Within Rome and throughout the Roman state, public lawmaking assemblies were deeply embedded in a system of economic, ritual, social, and political institutions centered on Rome. The smooth and effective functioning of public lawmaking assemblies reflected the legitimacy of those institutions. When Rome's institutions began to buckle under the impact of the great influx of new citizens into the Roman state after the end of the Italian War, the result was obvious in the disruptions at public lawmaking assemblies. In part 3 of this study on the decline of the Roman Republic we shall explore further the extent to which the public lawmaking process both reflected the balance of forces in Rome and helped maintain that balance.

TABLE 6.1 Laws Advancing the Prosperity of Rome by Topic, 350–44

The distribution of grain to citizens (9)
Settlement or remission of debts (6)
Regulation of suretyship (5)
Modification or extension of legis actiones (4)
Creation of extraordinary commission (3)
Permissible gambling (3)
Cost of food at dinner parties (3)
Food and guests at dinner parties (3)
Remission of rents in Rome (2)
Port duties (2)
Assignment of oversight over grain supply (2)
Oversight over weights and measures (2)
Dissolution of debt bondage
Legal business on market days
Damage to property
The election and responsibilities of IIIviri capitales
Expensive clothing
Carrying weight of boats owned by senators
The value of bronze coinage
Women's clothing and jewelry, horse-drawn carriages
Gift giving by clients on the Saturnalia
Gifts from defendants in law cases, value of gifts
The size of legacies
Abrogation of the lex Oppia
Extension of Roman laws on debt to allies and Latins
Money lending
Assignment of responsibility for intercalation
Assignment of guardians by urban praetor and tribunes
The number of guests at dinner parties
The capacity of women to inherit
The annulment of state leases and contracts made by censors
The return of a widow's dowry
The ownership of stolen property
Fraud perpetrated against minors
The formulary procedure
The extension of the lex Fannia to all Italy
Lease of state contracts in Asia by censors
The construction of new roads
Victory on a coinage issue
Remedy of manus iniectio against creditors
Wrongful ownership of a citizen or his slave
Abrogation of the lex Licinia
The addition of bronze to silver coinage
The introduction of the semiuncial as (coin)
Interest payments on the principal of debts
A ceiling on senators' debts
Limitations on suretyship
Confirmation of heirs
The crime of falsa
The crime of peculatus
Responsibility for letting state contracts
Debt and land distribution
Comitial days and their interruption
Personal expenditures by senators
Cost of travel equipment
Supervision of roads
Acquisition of servitudes through usucapio
List of eligible grain recipients
Extending the pomerium of the city

Source: See appendixes A and C.

TABLE 6.2 **Regular Offices, Extraordinary Boards, and Special Commissions of Inquiry, ca. 350–44**

331	Lex de quaestione extraordinaria instituenda	Special commission of investigation
311	Lex Decia de duumviris navalibus	Creation of two-man board for outfitting and repairing fleet
300	Lex Ogulnia de auguribus et pontificibus	Number and qualifications of augurs and priests
287–218	Lex Silia	Oversight of weights and measures by aediles
267	Lex de quaestoribus octo creandis	Expanding the number of quaestors
Before 241	Lex Plaetoria	Jurisdictio of urban praetor
241–123	Lex Papiria	Election/responsibilities of IIIviri capitales
216	Lex Minucia de triumviris mensariis	Creation of extraordinary commission
215	Lex Sempronia de duoviris aedi dedicandae	Creation of extraordinary commission
215	Plebiscitum ut servi publice emerentur	Creation of extraordinary commission
212	Plebiscitum de quinqueviris et triumviris	Creation of extraordinary commission
Early 2d c.	Lex Plaetoria	Creation of extraordinary commission
196	Lex Licinia de IIIviris epulonibus creandis	Creation of a three-man priesthood
187	Lex Petillia de pecunia regis Antiochi	Special commission of investigation
181	Lex Baebia de praetoribus	Number of praetors elected in alternate years
179	[Plebiscitum] de latrocinio duorum equitum	Special commission of investigation
172	Lex Marcia de Liguribus	Special commission of investigation
(154)[a]	Lex Caecilia	Special commission of investigation
149	Rogatio Scribonia de Lusitanis	Special commission of investigation
145	Rogatio Licinia de sacerdotiis	The election of priests
141	Lex Mucia de L. Hostilio Tubulo	Special commission of investigation
123	Lex Sempronia de P. Popillio Laenate	Special commission of investigation
113	Lex Peducaea de incestu virginum Vestalium	Special commission of investigation
109	Lex Mamilia de coniuratione Iugurthina	Special commission of investigation
104	Lex Domitia de sacerdotiis	The election of priests
103	Lex Norbana de auri tolosani quaestione	Special commission of investigation
103	Lex Appuleia de quaestione extraordinaria instituenda	Special commission of investigation
81	Lex Cornelia de sacerdotiis	Number of priests and restoration of co-optation
81	Lex Cornelia de praetoribus octo creandis	Expanding the number of praetors
81	Lex Cornelia de XX quaestoribus	Expanding the number of quaestors
70	Lex de legatis decem mittendis	Creation of extraordinary commission

(*continued*)

TABLE 6.2. *(continued)*

67	Lex Gabinia de bello piratico	Creation of command against pirates
(65)	Lex Papia de vestalium lectione	The selection of Vestals
63	Lex Atia de sacerdotiis	The election of priests
62	Rogatio Iulia de cura Capitolii restituendi	Reassignment of oversight over temple reconstruction
61	Lex Pupia Valeria de incestu Clodii	Special commission of investigation
61	Lex Fufia de religione	Special commission of investigation
61	Rogatio de repetundis	Special commission of investigation
59	Lex Vatinia de Vettii iudicio	Special commission of investigation
57	Rogatio Messia de cura annonae Cn. Pompeio mandanda	Assignment of oversight over grain supply
57	Lex Cornelia Caecilia de cura annonae Cn. Pompeio mandanda	Assignment of oversight over grain supply
56	Rogatio Porcia de quaestione extraordinaria instituenda	Special commission of investigation
54	Rogatio de tacito iudicio	Special commission of investigation
50	Rogatio Scribonia alimentaria	Assignment of oversight over weights and measures
50	Rogatio Scribonia viaria	Supervision of roads
(46)	Lex Iulia de sacerdotiis	Eligibility for selection to priesthood

Source: See appendixes A and C.
[a]Dates in parentheses are approximate. See appendix C.

Notes

1. I am not concerned in this chapter with any particular model of an ancient city. However, theoretical supports for the many-layered view of Rome presented here may be found in two insightful studies, D. Engels, *Roman Corinth: An alternative model for the classical city* (Chicago and London, 1990); and N. Morley, *Metropolis and Hinterland: The City of Rome and the Italian Economy, 200 BC-AD 200* (Cambridge, 1996).

2. On vici see further in this chapter.

3. So the Romans believed. A modern explanation of the derivation of the name attributes it to the fact that the vicus Tuscus was a main road to Etruria, beyond the Tiber: Richardson 1992, 429. However, an ancient statue of the Etruscan god Vortumnus here reinforces the idea of an Etruscan neighborhood: Varro, *Ling.* 5.46; Cic., *Verr.* 2.1.154; Propertius, 4.2.1–10. Location of statue: M. C. J. Putnam, "Vortumnus," *AJA* 71 (1967): 177–79.

4. An inscription ca. 300 provides the names of an apparently Etruscan couple living on the vicus Longus: *CIL* 6.100023.

5. Greeks: (inscriptional evidence from the reign of Augustus) *CIL* 6. 761 = *ILS* 3308; Carthaginians in Rome: R. E. A Palmer, *Rome and Carthage at peace*. Vol. 113 of Historia Einzelschriften (Wiesbaden, 1997).

6. On the geographic importance of the site see Walker 1958, 21.

7. In the late third and second centuries, Puteoli in Campania on the Bay of Naples (modern Pozzuoli) becomes the major port serving Rome: Frederiksen 1984, 46. No adequate port facilities existed at Ostia until the reign of Claudius: see R. Meiggs, *Roman Ostia*, 2d ed. (Oxford, 1973), 54–57.

8. A comparison made also by Holloway 1994, 165.

9. *Inter lignarios:* Livy 35.41.10; *inter falcarios:* Cic., *Cat.* 1.8; *Sull.* 52; *inter vitores:* *CIL* 14.4535.3; and *inter figulos:* Varro. *Ling.* 5.154.

10. Appropriating gods: R. E. A. Palmer, *Roman religion and Roman empire: Five essays* (Philadelphia, 1974), 3–56; M. Beard, J. North, and S. Price, *Religions of Rome* (Cambridge, 1998), 1.73–87.

11. Beard, North, and Price 1998, 1.70.

12. Livy 9.29.9–11.

13. The openness of Rome to new cults: North 1976; Beard, North, and Price 1998, 1:63, 75.

14. Beard, North, and Price 1998, 1.79–87.

15. Hercules: R. E. A. Palmer, "Cults of Hercules, Apollo Caelispex and Fortuna in and around the Roman cattle market," *JRA* 3 (1990): 234–44, esp. 236–40; F. Coarelli, *Il foro boario dalle origine alla fine della repubblica* (Rome, 1988), 75.

16. See further in this chapter.

17. Julius Obsequens 37.

18. Such was also the case with Placentia, established in 218 and refilled in 190: Livy 37.46.9–47.2.

19. Taylor 1960, 49, and Sherwin-White 1973, 74–75, both following Beloch 1880, 103–4.

20. Fora: R. Laurence, *The roads of Roman Italy: Mobility and cultural change* (London and New York, 1999), 29–38; E. Ruoff-Vanäänän, *Studies on the Italian fora* (Wiesbaden, 1978). The best discussion on conciliabula and fora remains Beloch 1880, 102–16. See also Gargola 1995, 109–11.

21. Sherwin-White 1973, 52–53; Humbert 1978, 382–90.

22. Taylor 1960, 69. Burial grounds for the Pollia tribe were uncovered along the via Salaria: Taylor 1960, 14–15.

23. Argei: Taylor 1960, 75.

24. Festivals: W. Ward Fowler, *The Roman festivals* (London, 1899); Scullard, 1981.

25. General discussion of the place of these festivals in city life: Beard, North, and Price 1998, 1.40–41; J. E. Stambaugh, *The ancient Roman city* (Baltimore, 1988), 221–33.

26. Calendar: Michels 1967. Calendar of festivals: Scullard 1981.

27. Performance: Beard, North, and Price 1998, 1.42–54.

28. ludi Romani and Plebeii: Beard, North, and Price 1998, 1.40–41, 66–67.

29. In the third century, the Games of Apollo (ludi Apollinares) were instituted. First staged in 212 on the occasion of a plague, during the Second Punic War, these games were made annual in 208 by a public law brought by the praetor P. Licinius Varus (Livy 27.23.7). By 190, the games lasted four days, from 13 to 16 July, and by the 40s they extended over eight days. In the second century, two more sets of games were instituted on an annual basis: the Megalesia, in honor of the Great Mother (Magna Mater),

from 4 to 10 April, became annual in 194; and the Games of Flora (ludi Florales), from 28 April to 3 May, became annual in 173.

30. Beard, North, and Price 1998, 1.101.

31. *Epulum Iovis:* Warde Fowler 1899, 216–34; Scullard 1981, 186–87.

32. Individuals and festivals: Beard, North, and Price 1998, 1.48–51.

33. The cups include elephant cups as well as cups with a cupid, inscribed with the names of Laverna, Vesta, Fortuna, Ceres, Juno, Minerva, Vulcan, Saturn, Aesculapius, Concordia, Salus, Bellona, and Venus. They have been found (many in graves) in Clusium, Vulci, Tarquinii, Capena, Lanuvium, Aleria, Teanum, and Carsioli.

34. Notwithstanding the tendency of modern scholars to doubt the regular movement of citizens (except wealthy ones) to Rome. On this basis Brunt raises objections to the feasibility of filling the legions in Rome: Brunt 1971, 625–35. Rawson effectively counters this position: E. Rawson, "The literary sources for the pre-Marian army," *PBSR* 39 (1971): 37–39.

35. Time and distance: Laurence 1999, 78–94.

36. Macr., *Sat.* 1.16.34.

37. The term appears first in the leges Iuliae iudiciariae: Gaius 4.104, 107; Kaser 1955, 1.545; Thomas 1976, 92–93.

38. Road building: Laurence 1999, 11–26; T. P. Wiseman, "Roman republican roadbuilding," *PBSR* 38 (1970): 122–52.

39. Potter 1979, 79–87; Frederikson and Ward-Perkins 1957, 67–198.

40. The via Cornelia, later named Aurelia, was most likely in origin a drove trail along the coast: Potter 1979, 80. J. André, "Les noms latins du chemin et de la rue," *REL* 28 (1950): 105–8 (*calles*).

41. Via Salaria: Chevallier 1976, 66–67, 131, 134. The salt trade along this route was controlled by Rome from early in the fourth century, who took it over from the Latin town of Fidenae, near Rome, located on the route.

42. Chevallier 1976, 30.

43. Road building of C. Gracchus: Laurence 1999, 49–51.

44. *CIL* 1^2.638.

45. Cf. Laurence 1999, 27–38; Purcell 1990, 12–14. General discussion of roads: Chevallier 1976, 132–37. Roads were built for strategic reasons, in pace with military conquests; they came in the "wake of conquest and subsequent political unification and economic development."

46. This was constructed with funds derived from penalties exacted from two equites who defrauded the state in the exercise of wartime contracts. The ancient sources are collected in Richardson 1992, 169, s.v. Forum Piscarium.

47. On these projects see Livy 40.51.

48. Discussion of the current state of knowledge about urban growth of Rome: J. R. Patterson, "The city of Rome: From republic to empire," *JRS* 82 (1992): 186–215.

49. Labor force: P. Brunt, "Free labour and public works at Rome," *JRS* 70 (1980): 81–100.

50. *Lexicon Topographicum Urbis Romae* (Rome, 1993), vol. 1, s.v. "Circus Maximus."

51. It is based on the city's water supply, its land area, and in particular a handful of references to the number of permanent city residents receiving free grain. For discussion of these issues see Morley 1996, 33–39.

52. Although many scholars have assumed the opposite: see, for instance, Brunt 1971, 69, 386.

53. The most systematic work on the "effectiveness" of migration—the ratio of those who stayed in a city to those who moved there for a short time—to urban areas in preindustrial society seems to have been done in the United States and shows that only about one in fifteen migrants to a city stayed permanently: Stephan Thernstrom, *The Other Bostonians* (Cambridge, MA, 1973).

54. Sall., *Cat.* 37.8–9. See chapter 3.

55. Appian, *B.C.* 1.95 with commentary in Gabba 1958. See Brunt 1971, 301–2.

56. Val. Max. 9.2.1, with Brunt 1971, 302.

57. Cass. Dio 40.59–66. Regrettably, the refugees from civil war were wrong. Food supplies to the city were severely cut between 50 and 46 with the result that not only the newcomers but the permanent city residents melted away. When Caesar held a census of the city population in 46, taken neighborhood by neighborhood, 150,000 men were counted, down from 320,000 in 50. In the absence of a steady food supply, the population had dropped from roughly one million to half a million, in four years, based on the enumeration of citizens eligible for the grain handout: Livy, *Epit.* 115; Suet., *Iul.* 41.3; Plut., *Caes.* 55.3; Cass. Dio 43.21.4, 25.2; Appian, *B.C.* 2.14.102. How many died and how many left cannot be determined.

58. Rivers undependable for transporting goods and produce: Walker 1967, 14.

59. The relationship was established by Mommsen, *R.St.* 2.2.1029–33.

60. Brunt 1971, 305–9; the figure is Brunt's estimate. Half the colonies can be named although the locations of only four are certain, Arretium, Faesulae, Pompeii, and Praeneste. The colonies were established on state land and in towns on the losing side, whose cultivated lands were appropriated, divided, and assigned to the victors: Appian, *B.C.* 1.96, 100.

61. The ancient sources are collected in *MRR* 2.188.

62. See tables 1.9 and 1.10 in chapter 1.

63. G. Rickman, *Roman granaries and store-buildings* (Cambridge, 1971).

64. When Sulla in 81 annulled the previous grain law he opened the field up again.

65. The complex human as well as political dimensions emerge in a few well-known episodes: Marius and Mamertine cohorts; the work of the censors of 97. On these see E. Badian, "Caepio and Norbanus," in Badian 1964a, 34–70 (= Badian 1964b), esp. 47–49.

66. While this appears to have been recognized practice after the Second Punic War, by the time of the Italian War the privilege is no longer commonly claimed: Sherwin-White 1973, 110–11.

67. Livy 41.9.9–12. The praetor was L. Mummius, who had been assigned the province of Sardinia.

68. Livy 39.3.4–6.

69. Figure from Diod. Sic. 37.13, who reports that Poppaedius Silo marched on Rome with ten thousand allies who had left, fearing the outcome of a judicial inquiry. Cic., *Corn.* fr. 10 and Asc., 67–68C; Cic., *De Or.* 2.257; *Sest.* 30; *Balb.* 48 and 54; *Off.* 3.47; *Brut.* 63; Sall., *Hist.* 1.20M; Schol. Bob. 129 Stangl. On the episode see Badian 1964, 48 with nn. 130 and 131, and 49, and Brunt 1988, 99–101.

70. The lex Papia: Cic., *Leg. Agr.* 1.13; *Arch.* 10; *Balb.* 52; *Att.* 4.18.4; *Off.* 3.47; Cass. Dio 37.9.5; Schol. Bob. 175 Stangl; Val. Max. 3.4.5.

71. See chapter 9.

72. R. Lanciani, *The ruins and excavations of ancient Rome* (Boston and London, 1967 [1897]), 544.

73. Lanciani 1897, 389. *CIL* 6.1953 (1956), 9284, 9399, 9491, 9526. All appear to be Roman or Italian.

74. Suet., *Iul.* 46.

75. See J.-M Flambard, "Collegia compitalicia: Phénomène associatif, cadres territoriaux et cadres civiques dans le monde romain à l'époque républicaine," *Ktema* 6 (1981): 144–66; and Vanderbroeck 1987, 52–66. More generally see S. G. Wilson, "Voluntary associations: An Overview," in *Voluntary associations in the Greco-Roman World*, ed. J. S. Kloppenburg and S. G. Wilson (London and New York, 1996), 1–15. The classic study of the types, organization, and membership of the various collegia, though outdated with respect to twentieth-century anthropological and sociological literature on their significance as a measure of individual mobility, is J.-P. Waltzing, *Étude historique sur les corporations professionnelles chez les Romains* (Paris, 1895–1900, reprint 1970), 4 vols.

76. In Italy, they are found in all towns of any size, symptomatic of the high level of mobility throughout Roman Italy. On the phenomenon, characteristic also of the towns and cities of ancient China, see L. A. Fallers, ed., *Immigrants and associations* (The Hague and Paris, 1967).

77. See chapter 9.

78. The organization described here was revived by Augustus. Its operation earlier is not directly attested but is probable, given, for example, the customary organizational role of vicomagistri in the Compitalia: Cic., *Pis*. 8.23; Livy 34.7.2.

79. W. Nippel, *Public order in ancient Rome* (Cambridge, 1995).

80. Nippel 1995, 4–46.

81. Formulary procedure: A. Watson, "Development of the praetor's edict," *JRS* 60 (1970): 105–19.

82. Macrob., *Sat.* 1.16.30.

83. Chapter 7.

84. Minor magistrates: Lintott 1999, 137–44.

85. Crawford thinks the censors minted coins before this, but the length of tenure and five-year gap between censorships made it impossible to anticipate needs. Consequently, the coinage minted (generally outside Rome) prior to the creation of the tresviri monetales was used only outside Rome, to pay for the fleet: Crawford 1985, 25–27.

86. This is conventional. Brennan 2000, 85–89, offers a different hypothesis (a second praetorship needed for the province of Sicily).

87. Brennan 2000.

88. On the extraordinary boards during the Second Punic War see chapter 1, and on Pompey's command against the pirates see chapter 9.

89. M. Kaser, *Das römische Zivilprozessrecht* (Munich, 1966), 127. Whether their jurisdictio was restricted is unknown, as is the date of their disappearance after the Italian War.

90. See P. Birks, "New light on the Roman legal system: The appointment of judges," *Cambridge Law Journal* 47.1 (1988): 36–60.

91. The former were thus leges datae: *RS* 2.43.

PART THREE

THE DECLINE OF THE REPUBLIC

CHAPTER SEVEN

A Roman Balance

A SELECTION OF EXTANT enumerations of Roman males carried out by the Roman censors highlights the principal outcome of incorporating new citizens into the Roman state during the third through first centuries. In 204, 214,000 men were counted; in 154, 324,000 men; and in 115, 394,336 men. The number then increased to 910,000 in the enumeration of 70, following the grant of citizenship to all Italians twenty years before, and almost astronomically to 4,063,000 in the enumeration of 28.[1] Although it is only with the census enumerations of the late first century that we see a significant citizen population increase unmistakably owed to in-migration, it is possible to view incorporation at all times as part of a Roman strategy to maintain the male population, which was prone to high levels of mortality in war. The results clearly are that the Roman male population was on the whole steady and even experienced a slight increase over time until the dramatic increases following the grant of citizenship to all Latins and Italians in 90.[2] No wonder the Romans were able to send thousands of men to war, year in and year out, for nearly two hundred years.

The degree to which the Romans were able to maintain a functioning, expanding society, during the fourth through first centuries, through the incorporation of new members was unrivaled in world history. Equally striking was the degree to which the harmony and growth of the Roman state rested on deeply held assumptions shared by political leaders and people, chief among them the viability of the public lawmaking process as a flexible instrument for resolving social and political problems. Yet the stability that the Romans brought to their society in this fashion came at a cost to the small-scale world of Rome. Concurrent with the growing numbers of members in the highest and lowest classes, the original military basis of the classes slipped away, with consequences especially for Rome's leadership. While the highest offices of consul and praetor were the traditional preserve of Romans belonging to a handful of noble clans, numerous lesser offices and positions, routine but essential, were held by members of Rome's equestrian class. Primarily the economic managers of empire, equestrians also became officeholders and administrators. Most served as military tribunes and junior elected officeholders, as well as (after 149) jurors for the permanent courts. Some attained higher office as aediles and quaestors. A few came even to occupy the praetorship and consulate as new men (novi homines), that is, men whose immediate antecedents had not attained the office of praetor or consul. The presence in society of more men with political qualifications and aspirations was ominous. The tensions introduced in Roman society by its growing and increasingly diverse citizen population, particularly as regards traditional relationships linking Rome's political leaders and the Roman people, proved almost insurmountable in the long run. In part 3 we explore the changes in Roman society that required new efforts to sustain the Roman understandings that gave public law its force and the role of public lawmaking in those efforts. Underlying our quest is the question that forms the subject of the present chapter: How did the Romans, numbering in the hundreds of thousands and experiencing a slow but steady inflow of members drawn from other communities in Italy, work to maintain the integrity of the Roman system? Our starting point and primary focus is the Roman leadership, whose members were drawn ever more frequently from families and communities outside Rome and whose experiences and circumstances were as a result considerably altered.

AN EXPANDING LEADERSHIP

The requirements of a larger and more complex Roman state placed heavy demands on the political families of Rome. Imperial expansion, as we saw in the previous chapter, was accompanied throughout the period by an increase both in the number of offices in Rome and in temporarily appointed or elected commissions. More men were required in the ranks of Rome's elected or appointed officials, especially at the junior levels, in all areas of government. At the same time as the number of administrative positions was growing, senatorial and equestrian families were experiencing heavy losses in Rome's continuous wars. During the early years of the Second Punic War in particular, after Hannibal's entry into Italy, senators and their sons made up a high number of casualties in battle: At the Battle of Cannae alone, in 216, more than eighty senators died, including one of the consuls, and twenty-nine military tribunes.[3] Throughout the third and second centuries, mortality rates among such men (and Roman men of all classes) were high. The inevitable result was that sons of established equestrian or senatorial (particularly noble) political families were in short supply and their long-term availability for administrative positions uncertain.[4]

This combination of circumstances ensured that the narrowly restricted political hierarchy of early-fourth-century Rome, resting on wealth, status, and exclusion, was gradually loosened. From here on out, Rome's governing classes were roughly equivalent to all families possessing the property rating of equestrians. Some men belonged to the elite equites equo publico; many more were wealthy tribuni aerarii, registered in Class 1.[5] From the late third century, the chances of equestrians with no previous personal or indeed family experience entering leadership positions grew, sometimes rapidly. The Roman disaster at Cannae provides a case in point: Although we have no explicit testimony, the numbers lost from the Roman Senate were undoubtedly made up, and the source turned to at this time, as later, was the small group of equites equo publico. Moreover, an increasing number of these equestrians, and hence political leaders, were newer citizens from Latin colonies and Italian municipalites. For the equestrian class itself, as we have seen, was expanding. War not only depleted the ranks of a traditional leadership, it intensified the rate of entry of new citizens into the leadership pool. At no time were the boundaries of Rome's elite circle impermeable, but the casualties suffered among their number at the end of the third century meant that greater numbers of new members entered than at any time before. For the local elites throughout Italy, an equestrian property rating determined access to the pool from which political leaders emerged.

Not only was the membership of this pool expanded by more and more men drawn from all communities of Italy with a Roman equestrian property rating, but new members willingly entered the competitive race for political office in Rome—an indicator of the degree of assimilation achieved. New clans emerged in Roman political life, drawn from the newer Romans of the near and far municipalities, to supply candidates for elected office and thus membership in the Roman Senate.[6] After the Second Punic War, as after earlier wars, new families appear on the political scene.[7] The pattern clearly follows the widening spiral of Roman citizenship grants: the first clans to penetrate Roman political elite ranks came from nearby Latin towns, some granted citizenship early in the fourth century.[8] The elite families of Tusculum, for instance, the first Latin town to receive Roman citizenship in 381, had penetrated the rulers' innermost circle, the small group of nobiles, in Rome by 198, the year M. Porcius Cato attained the office of praetor. Others had reached lower office before then. In the case of Cato as well as others, it is apparent that such a rise was by no means rapid considering how long the local elites had been Roman citizens.[9] In fact, throughout the period, the nobiles of Rome presented an impenetrable facade to political newcomers. The entrée of these political newcomers into the society of Rome, and in some instances into the ranks of the higher leadership itself, for the most elevated among them, the new men, was gained before the Italian War mostly through the patronage of the leading clans in Rome. But although relatively few newcomers were willingly tolerated at any one moment, their access to the ranks of the political leadership was inevitable.

In fact, the voters of Rome ensured their eventual entry, despite the reluctance of the Roman nobility to allow political newcomers into its own ranks before the Punic Wars. The Roman people were far more ecumenical toward political newcomers than were the nobility. Regardless of a tendency toward privileging members of the entrenched clans at the polls, because of tribal loyalties and the local relationships between these clans and the communities where their lands were situated, voters looked also to competence, ability, and merit in the men they chose as leaders. Since these qualifications were demonstrated in a man's performance during military service and officeholding, the junior legal and administrative offices as well as the junior military rank of military tribune were crucial stages in a man's career. In all the junior offices, held by new men and sons of nobles, a man formed a reputation through performance and public oratory, which he later expanded in the public arena in Rome.[10] Within a noble clan, accordingly, there were winners and losers in the eyes of the voters. With the wider field of players introduced by the expanding numbers of equestrians and simultaneously an expanded and dispersed majority population, both winners and losers in the old noble clans—and also, it should be stressed, in the new families—faced considerable challenges.[11]

Neither existing nor new political families among the Roman leadership faced these challenges lying down, however. Indeed the changes in the equestrian pool and thus in Rome's potential leadership, already long under way in the first half of the third century and intensified by the habitual competitiveness of elite Romans for authority and wealth, certainly motivated the enduring frictions that typify the Roman leadership. Friction between patrician and plebeian, noble and new families, goes back to the beginnings of the

Republic in the Roman annalistic tradition about the "struggle of the orders." It is likewise evident already in the fourth century, in the form of political animosities between the informal groupings called factions by modern historians. Doubtless, the growing number of newly incorporated men and families whose wealth and status made them potential rivals of Roman families of longer standing had crept into Roman awareness long before the Second Punic War. The stability of the Republic was eventually undermined by almost insurmountable friction at this level. But the sources of such friction are most plain in efforts beginning in the fourth century and picking up steam in the third and later centuries to regulate access, frequently through recourse to public lawmaking assemblies, to positions of leadership.

These efforts begin with the leadership pool itself, where we see an effort to strike a balance between the growing number of men with an equestrian property rating and the elite character of the equestrian class. Membership in the equestrians with the public horse never exceeded (by much) the traditional figure of eighteen hundred, even when the numbers of wealthy men had grown into the thousands, and probably in the late third century the property qualification of an equestrian was set at the astronomical sum of one million asses.[12] Evidently some Romans hoped to restrict entry into the group, which regularly contributed junior officials and new senators, in light of the growing number of men whose resources qualified them for registration. Senate purges reveal similar tensions within the Senate, where the striking of senators from the list reflects both the animosities generated by the different origins of new senators and an awareness that some senators fell short of the mark. Reported revisions of the Senate list between 200 and 91 usually note the expulsion of nine or, more commonly, fewer senators.[13] In 115, the censors removed thirty-two senators from the list, a full 15 percent of the Senate membership.[14] To all appearances, a continuous effort was under way almost from the beginnings of Roman expansion in Italy to regulate qualifications for admission to the group that furnished the future political, religious, and military leadership of the community.

While the Senate or officeholders, in particular the Roman censor, probably generated many of these reforms, the most assiduous engine of reform was the public lawmaking assembly. Table 7.1 collects all public laws creating new offices, expanding the number of officeholders, modifying the conditions of selection or qualification, and addressing Senate or equestrian class membership throughout the period. The seventeen public law proposals involving Rome's leadership between 218 and 201 are best understood in the context of the exigencies of wartime pressure. But the necessity of casting the net widely for the best possible military and political leaders is in some measure also a reflection of the growth in number of men eligible for leadership positions. Other items in our listing in table 7.1 suggest similar forces at work, in particular laws proposed or enacted making adjustments in the regular selection of commanders in times of war. Still more items—laws assigning new responsibilities and creating more offices—reflect the practical need for more administrators.

Other items indicate a growing pressure on offices and honors—and a resolution of the problem to the advantage of newer equestrian families in the broader-based leadership pool. Notably, the admission of plebeians to the offices of consul and censor was accomplished in the late fourth century through lawmaking assemblies. Other items include laws regulating the ages for holding office, laws admitting equestrians into the Senate or jury panels, laws regulating equestrian honors, and laws regulating the conditions for holding triumphs: All provide confirmation of the competitive drive for office and position from a larger group of competitors (table 7.1). The bill of 129 removing the public horse from senators, in particular, reveals the pressures from an expanded equestrian class on positions of honor as well as the tensions created by senatorial appropriation of those honors. Henceforth, the small group of equites equo publico would draw its membership only from men of equestrian rating outside the Senate. In turn a number of laws curtailing the authority of the censors to remove men from the Senate confirms the depth of the concern among senators to police themselves. Efforts are also made through public lawmaking assemblies to control officeholders and other elite Romans, for instance, by prohibiting public law sponsors or their family members from holding positions created by a law they sponsored or by making senators on state business liable for prosecution in Rome (table 7.1).

The developing position of military tribune, which was both nonelective and elective and counted among the lesser offices of Rome, magistratus minores, is especially indicative of such pressures.[15] This position was often though not always held before the quaestorship, the first rung in the cursus honorum and the office that after 81 provided entry into the Senate.[16] Junior officers in the Roman army, the military tribunes' functions were exercised in a strictly military arena. The office was also a vital step in a man's political career because of the opportunities it offered him to reinforce the public support already demonstrated through his success at the polls in the first place by forging critical relationships with Rome's fighting men. A significant index of the importance with which the positions were viewed is the attention paid in lawmaking assemblies to the manner of selection and qualifications of military tribunes. Initially selected by the consuls, eventually all of the tribunes came to be elected in the tribal assembly—a law in 362 enacted that the people would elect six initially; another law in 311 enacted that the people would elect sixteen; and finally, in 207, all twenty-four (of whom fourteen must be equestrians, testimony to the clout of equestrians). Between these dates other laws modified the selection (or election) process, usually in times of critical need.[17] No fewer than six recorded statutes between the fourth and second centuries addressed the elective position of military tribune, a critically important office for ascendant Romans with political ambitions, including new citizens. Indeed, the military tribunate was instrumental in the elevation of municipal leaders to the rank of Roman equestrian, before and after the Italian War.[18] Other elective positions were also the subject of lawmaking assemblies. The number of statutes listed in table 7.1 regulating the manner in which men were chosen to fill the lesser offices attests to the importance with which these offices, like the military tribunate, were viewed by elite Romans and the Roman people. The bigger issue was the growing number of Romans competing for office. Significantly, the outcome of these laws was to broaden the avenue of access to elected office, enabling more equestrians from different backgrounds to enter the political leadership.

IMPLICATIONS FOR THE PRODUCTION OF LAW

Considering the customary manner of formulating and drafting law before it entered into public view, it is worth asking how members of Rome's political leadership continued to become privy to public lawmaking conventions when officeholders were drawn from distant communities. Traditionally, imparting the arts of government to young aristocrats entailed an apprenticeship in which the youth followed an elder relative or family friend in order to observe and to learn. Senators' sons attended sessions of the Senate. Legal experts who sat at home or strolled through the Forum and delivered advice to Romans who sought advice were attended by aristocratic youths. Early military service for young aristocrats, which began at roughly age sixteen and was expected to last ten years, was a period of training on the same principle: in the field, adolescent boys served on the commander's staff, sharing a tent with an older man. Thus, after a process of learning by observation and participation, young aristocrats were familiar with the kinds and arenas of interaction expected of them when the time came to present themselves as candidates or nominees for the military tribunate and the junior offices in Rome.

For all types of training except military the venue was Rome. In Rome were to be found the best teachers of rhetoric, the art of public speaking, included among the essential equipment of aristocrats. Consequently, municipal aristocrats who entertained political aspirations for their sons sent them to Rome for the same kind of apprenticeship enjoyed by aristocratic Roman youths. Such was Cicero's experience, recorded by Cornelius Nepos in his biography of Atticus. Moreover, in Rome, and only in Rome, was found the primary gateway to political leadership: the electoral voting assemblies. The offices in the cursus honorum and the tribunate were the most elevated in a competitive political career whose peak was the consulate. But other elective offices, offices through which aspiring leaders advanced before they reached the topmost rungs of leadership, were sought and held by many men of equestrian rank. These include the military tribunes of the first four legions and, beginning in the late third and early second centuries, many of the positions in the Vigintisexvirate. The men who succeeded at the polls might not necessarily advance further in a significant political career, or they might advance only as far as the quaestorship, tribunate, or aedileship and no further, but they were nonetheless playing essential roles in the administration of Roman society. At the same time they were enhancing the present status and future potential of their families. Thus, elected office in Rome presupposed long-term exposure to a process of learning and selection that began at an early age. Moreover, an increasing number of individuals had to be exposed to this process for, in spite of our patchy impressions of Rome's administrative apparatus, we are clearly dealing with a structure that made extensive demands on the uppermost strata of Roman society from the third century onward.

Undoubtedly the entry of more and more new aristocrats into the system between the fourth and the second centuries brought some changes to a customary training process if not to the conventions of leadership themselves. But this is not yet in evidence in the second century, when leaders prepared for rule in a customary but evolving process involving a number of legal and administrative positions that underwent significant changes over time. Where public law is concerned, law sponsors over time came from more varied backgrounds, confirmation of the widening access for political newcomers to the traditional training grounds of the Roman lawmaker: political office and judicial responsibilities. Interestingly there are no obvious signs of any significant breakdown in the conventions of rule during the second century, no complaints that these newer political leaders, some from newly incorporated communities, utterly lack the understandings and tools to be leaders of Rome.[19] So successful had been the assimilation of new citizens at elite levels during the period down to roughly the mid-second century.

Perhaps we should not expect any breakdown at such a stage of Roman development, for the momentous repercussions of Mediterranean conquest are still a generation away. The extraordinary display of wealth and training in Greek rhetoric, which set the political and social leadership of Rome apart from the rest, came to be common only during the second century. Until then, there was greater homogeneity among the senators, equites equo publico, and other men with an equestrian rating with respect to mode of life and outlook, as well as intellectual training and skills. More important, the scale and demands of rule were not yet as complex as they later became. In 218, Roman administration extended only as far as the Po River in Italy and the islands Sicily, Sardinia, and Corsica. While the Romans made adjustments to their ruling apparatus in order to accommodate this expansion, the modification required was small compared to that required after 146. Of greater consequence, however, to the customary grasp of Roman ways was the devastation of senatorial families in the first century, to which we shall return in chapter 8. Suffice to say here that at that time the commitment to Roman ways appears to have changed. Nonetheless the entry of more and more new elite families into the system between the fourth and the second centuries undoubtedly had significant consequences for the group's hold on the conventions of leadership. That such a development would also have repercussions in the workings of a traditional Roman system goes without saying. Of fundamental concern was an awareness that holding the loyalties of the majority population required new efforts. Let us turn then to the critical relationship between leaders and the Roman people.

ATTENUATING ATTACHMENTS

In a two-year period, between 123 and 121, C. Sempronius Gracchus and five other Roman tribunes presented at least twenty-seven public law proposals to the Roman people, over half of them successfully, in rapid-fire succession.[20] Not since the Second Punic War, and even then never on this scale, had Roman voters considered so many public law proposals in such a brief span of time. Gracchus himself presented an unrivaled sixteen proposals in 123 and 122, carrying all but four. No one lawmaker would again field so many public laws until L. Cornelius Sulla in the 80s. Another pioneering feature of this surge of lawmaking is the replication of issues addressed by different lawmakers. The tribunes M. Livius Drusus in 122 and M. Minucius Rufus in 121 in particular aired similar concerns as C. Sempronius Gracchus, between them presenting bills on rents, on the possession or redistribution of public property of the Roman people (ager publicus), on colony foundations, on subsidized grain distributions, and on citizen rights that reversed or nullified—in one case unsuccessfully, in the other not—laws carried by Gracchus. Given that lawmakers sought to develop public law proposals that would appeal to all thirty-five tribes, we must wonder at the expectations of Rome's leaders in regard to the Roman voters: How is it that M. Livius Drusus in 122 could think that the voters would endorse his proposals so soon after they had wholeheartedly embraced those of C. Sempronius Gracchus? How then could M. Minucius Rufus in late 122 or early 121 successfully carry measures similar in aim to M. Livius Drusus? The volatile record of the lawmaking over 123 to 121 highlights the changes in progress that forever changed the mechanisms of reciprocity between the growing number of groups potentially in attendance at lawmaking assemblies in Rome, to whom such a wide variety of public concerns appealed, and the growing number of officeholders who sought to garner their support.

Our point of departure in examining these changes is M. Porcius Cato's depiction of rural Italy in a handbook on estate farming, *De Agricultura,* the best available literary evidence for such an inquiry, written about 160.[21] Twice consul, censor in 184, and wealthy landowner, Cato had official and personal familiarity with the socioeconomic interactions attendant on estate management, particularly in the area of west-central Italy, where he situates his guidelines. Accordingly, the population and practices that Cato takes for granted tell us much about the world Rome had created here by 160, almost two centuries after Roman settlement.

De Agricultura is populated by estate owners, slaves, lesser landholders, and free laborers. Since slave labor was the preferred work force in most circumstances on large, capital-generating estates in his day, Cato is concerned primarily with slaves and slave overseers. Nonetheless he touches on a wide range of landholdings and relationships among free individuals, which makes it very clear that cash crops and slaves existed in a much more complicated rural context. He takes for granted for instance the existence of some kind of local market, which involved exchange between the estate and its neighbors. Most likely these neighbors were villagers or poorer farmers on marginal lands rather than other wealthy landowners because Cato assumes that they will buy firewood and lime, two essentials for everyday existence during most of the year.

Hence, *De Agricultura* offers a contemporary perspective on everyday dealings between ordinary rural inhabitants and their social betters in Roman Italy. Of particular interest is Cato's coverage of the suggested labor agreements into which his estate owner might enter, characterized by a precision of language and phrasing that is probably owed to Cato's tenure as censor.[22] (The Roman censors customarily handled state contracts.) In *De Agricultura,* Cato identifies a variety of situations arising in the course of ordinary estate management that called for formal arrangements. If the construction of farm buildings necessitated the hire of a builder, the estate owner and builder should agree bilaterally to terms that Cato conveniently provides, which spell out in precise, legalistic language the respective promises of the estate owner and the builder. The production of lime also involved an agreement, again articulated by Cato: The estate owner is responsible for the materials, the burner is responsible for the kiln, and each takes a share of the lime for his efforts. The estate owner's share, as noted, sufficed for his own uses and for sale to neighbors in the region. Labor contracts for picking olives involved several parties, specifically the estate owner; a labor contractor, that is, an individual or group who acts as some kind of middleman by assembling workers; and the olive pickers. The responsibilities of both middleman and workers are precisely detailed, up to and including a stipulation that the workers must swear not to steal the produce. Contracts for pressing olives are similar. Earning capital from the land itself involved the estate owner in other contracts, which Cato also provides. One stipulates the lease of land for winter pastures. To whom, we wonder? To smaller farmers, doubtless, and perhaps even to Apennine herdsmen. As described in chapter 4, a reciprocal relationship had emerged, in centuries past, between peoples dwelling in the summer and winter pasture areas. It is reasonable to speculate that such leases in *De Agricultura* indicate the continuation of these traditional transhumance patterns, by way of contractual agreement. We have seen already how the institutionalization of traditional transhumance networks appears to be reflected in the arrangements of the lex Agraria and the Sententia Minuciorum.

The labor contracts preserved in *De Agricultura* suggest a much deeper transformation in society. Such formal arrangements move us far away from imagining a world in which wealthy, powerful estate owners are supported by a net of dependents who owe them certain work obligations. Conspicuously absent from Cato's depiction of the prosaic business of estate management, which at times depended on specialists or seasonal labor, is a sense that his estate owner could find building experts or extra hands among a ready group of his client-tenants. Indeed, labor contracts seem to rule out the operation of any such patron-client ties of dependency in a rural setting.[23] The high incidence of legally defined relationships in *De Agricultura* indicates that relations between big landowners and ordinary men in the mid-second century were not merely socially defined. Instead the laborers sought by estate owners for particular jobs appear to be unattached men. The absence of social attachments between the work force and the landowner explains why they are required to swear an oath that they will not steal the harvest. Oaths presuppose a certain level of autonomy and mutual independence. Oaths establish a relationship if not between equals at least between men who recognize the independent worth of each other's station and actions. They establish a relationship outside that determined by ties of family or village. Thus soldiers swear oaths of loyalty to their commander and Rome. Returning to the more prosaic situation of the olive pickers, surely we might imagine that an oath promising not to steal would be extraneous if the workers were clients in a traditional work relationship with the middleman or the estate owner. In short, the requisite bilateral agreements and oaths, the defining features of legal relationships, suggest a society some of whose members for whatever reason tended to be rather loosely linked.

Why this was so in a society commonly termed "traditional" calls for some elaboration. In fact, Cato reveals a world in which the traditional ties characteristic of preexpansion Rome have to some extent come undone for ordinary people, creating a more fluid situation open to the formation of different bonds among men.[24] Increasing density of settlement in the region due to in-migration provides one explanation. In particular, Oscan-speaking migrants from the Apennines who had a tradition of independent family structure did not quickly develop the reciprocal, vertical relationships believed characteristic of Roman and other sedentary farming and urban populations. More important is the high level of mobility and disruption accompanying Roman expansion over two centuries and the absence of young males in military service, returning to land grants in unfamiliar regions.

Roman military service tended to break down old loyalties and foster new ones in their stead. The process was far more dynamic after the Second Punic War, when Roman overseas expansion drew more men into long periods of service away from Italy. Over time military obligations imposed on Latins and Italians transformed the foundations of traditional order and community loyalties in Latin and Italian communities. As soldiers fought longer and longer campaigns, usually outside Italy, the Roman army became the focus for the formation of alternative social networks among men, as a result of both the duration and intensity of the attachments to comrades-in-arm forged in military service. The continuous and long wars of the first century in Italy and outside intensified the tendency; even more so the long-time practice of settling discharged soldiers from the same unit together in a single colony or region. Commonly veterans from the same units were settled together in Roman and Latin colonies. The earliest large-scale grants occurred at the end of the Second Punic War, when forty thousand veterans of the campaign against Hannibal were given confiscated land in south Italy.[25] Most land distributions were smaller. In 123, three thousand troops who had served in Spain were settled in a Roman colony on the Balearic Island of Spain.[26] In 100, the discharged soldiers of Marius's campaigns against Jugurtha, and against the Cimbri and Teutoni, were settled together in North Africa. While the largest such settlements, in which soldiers of the same unit passed from camp to colony, were features of the first century, the point remains: for a long time the soldiers of Rome had formed self-identified groups with collective interests. For veterans, immediate loyalties were no longer determined by region, town of origin, or ancestral ties of dependency, but by military units, ever subject to loss and replenishment, and commanders, whose duration in command might be fleeting. That these more fluid loyalties prevailed after soldiers crossed the perimeters of military camps and entered the civic arena is clear—and explains why Caesar, in 47, scattered the land allotments given to soldiers from a mutinous legion.[27] In a world of changing relationships, Roman military service had assumed great importance.

Moreover, an institutionalized reciprocity generally prevailed over any customary regional or family links between ordinary men and their social betters. The civil rights and privileges of ordinary Roman citizens—in particular provocatio, but also the range of legal protections and opportunities of redress outlined in the Twelve Tables, enshrined in the praetor's annual edict and in countless public laws—transcended any reliance on the deference owed to Roman senator or elected official, for his own sake. This is not to say that Rome was becoming a society of individuals with an unmediated attachment to the state, as in modern Western democracies. Rather, the mesh of traditional relationships enwrapped a more fluid population, made up of more numerous and ramified groups. Not only reciprocity but merit and continuous realignment featured in the relationships that leaders forged with ordinary men.[28]

These features explain the unsettled character of Roman patronage, whose conspicuous failings in late Republican Rome led Brunt to doubt that the institution held any real significance in political life.[29] In the quintessential patron-client union (as projected in modern studies), the patron in Rome and elsewhere was protector, benefactor, and master of his client, who in turn owed him the respect and bidding of a son to his father. The client also performed certain services, which from a modern perspective appear intangible at times. Clients of an aspiring or ascendant political leader, for example, would present themselves at his home in the morning and accompany him in a great throng on his daily rounds about the city of Rome, thus serving to publicize his status and importance. Clients of lesser patrons in lesser towns performed similar services. In return the patrons handed out daily allowances, new clothes, and other necessities of life. Hierarchically ranged, patrons and clients alike straddled the gamut of Roman status groups. All Roman senators, officeholders, and equestrians (equites equo publico and men assessed with an equestrian rating) functioned in varying degrees as patrons to clients who were lower-ranking senators or equestrians, ordinary freeborn citizens, or ex-slaves. These reciprocal obligations and relations were in a manner of speaking fixed.

At the same time, however, the population involved in such relations was one whose members, under pressure of historical circumstances, began to enter and exit formal status positions in a highly volatile pattern. Nevertheless, the necessity of delineating relationships in a population comprising newer citizens, varied cultures and languages, as well as citizens in changed circumstances was met by drawing on prior, customary relations. Elite Romans took clients and patrons for granted; yet all Romans were not clients (or patrons). Town dwellers and former slaves were most often in the fides of a patron.[30] Or the relationship was rather fluid: veteran soldiers and their commanders come to mind. In brief, vertical ties in the Roman population were somewhat broken by the advent of a larger, more diverse population and a larger leadership.

Roman leaders were aware that long-established relationships were slipping. For in all periods we hear murmurs about the vital importance of maintaining a proper balance in the community through understood habits of interaction between the leadership and the people. Before the Italian War this balance was firmly held by men from politically known clans, nobiles, who carefully controlled the admission of political newcomers or new men (novi homines). Such a balance we might imagine was believed by some elite Roman to be threatened by the incorporation of outsiders, as they regarded Latins and especially allies, who were not privy to the understandings of Romans or whose loyalties were divided between Rome and their own local leaders. A passing comment of Cicero, in a speech delivered in 56, offers a glimpse of a firm Roman attitude to men of uncertain attachment. Commending himself as consul in 63 for upholding the statute of Sulla that barred the sons of proscribed Romans from standing for office, Cicero justifies his actions, which had been unpopular with ordinary Romans but popular with the Roman Senate, on the grounds that those sons, "though brave and patriotic, had passed through experiences which would probably have led them to shatter the constitution, had they obtained office" (*Pis.* 4; Loeb trans.). These are men who had in a sense been tossed out of the system: What of men who had only recently entered? The capacity of established political leaders, in particular men belonging to the noble clans, to lead was doubtless diminished by the expansion of the Roman citizen population to include men of uncertain attachments at all levels. For the traditional dimension of leadership, as understood by the leaders, which depended on the personal dependency of individual families or defined groups—Roman or Latin colonies, municipia, or tribes—to a specific clan over time, was diluted when an expanded citizen population made such attachments harder to maintain. Now there were more potential leaders, each with a changeable crowd of friends, associates, and dependents.

One index of the uncertainties confronting the political leadership is the appearance and increasingly widespread prevalence of campaign bribes, ambitus.[31] The common practice of giving gifts to tribal members had already become institutionalized in the creation of tribal officers called divisores, who were responsible for sharing out benefactions.[32] But by the Middle Republic the practice came to be redirected to facilitate the election of men to high office who could not count on the strength of the votes of their fellow tribesmen. Such bribes confirm some kind of breakdown in the loyalties mediated by tribal leaders and expressed by ordinary Romans for a customary leadership drawn from established and acceptable clans.[33] Gone, modern historians postulate, were the firm ties of clientage among tribal members that linked ordinary Romans with their high-status tribules and ensured the political elevation of men from select clans with the support of their fellow tribesmen. In their place now appears the lure of cash, reducing the rank order of tribal loyalties to a monetary transaction between voters and ambitious candidates. Such a scenario, however, tends to miss the complexities and conservatism of Roman social change.

For although hierarchy remains a constant feature of Roman social organization throughout our period of interest, the vertical ties of hierarchy were considerably ramified as a result of the incorporation of new citizens and in particular the admission of new members into Rome's leadership pool. At the same time, if the increase in numbers of would-be leaders diminished or dispersed the strength of vertical ties, it had no observable effect on horizontal ties. Indeed, such ties were enhanced over the course of the Republic by the superimposed networks of the legions and colonies on the Roman tribes, characterized by reciprocal horizontal and vertical ties involving not only citizens but, before the Italian War, Italian and Latin allies. Arguably, it was the endurance of horizontal ties among tribesmen that encouraged Rome's political leaders to disburse more and more cash to voters before elections. They recognized the endurance of bonds among ordinary citizens as well as a growing divide between themselves and such citizens, even in their own tribes.

To restore a balance to the system, the Romans adjusted their most fundamental institutions. We saw earlier (chapter 5) how the Romans lowered the property qualifications for Class 5, reabsorbing poorer Romans as effective citizens. Among similar reforms, now directed at the leadership, most important was the manipulation of voting units in the centuriate assembly, which reflected the property classes. This assembly, whose voters elected Rome's highest leaders and whose decisions therefore were of crucial importance to would-be consuls, praetors, and curule aediles, first felt the impact of the newly incorporated citizens. The reform of the centuriate assembly, sometime in the mid-third century, through which the centuries were brought into closer alignment with the Roman tribes, was undoubtedly an effort to maintain the integrity of the system by restoring a customary Roman balance to the voting potential of the various centuries of each class.[34] Concurrently, Romans in Class 1 were given the privilege of voting first, before the equites equo publico. This was not a democratic reform, as some scholars believe, but a realistic acknowledgment of the growing numbers of men with an equestrian property rating, many of them new citizens, in Class 1. As a result of the reform, new citizens who were generally registered in all the tribes were caught in the existing net of tribal loyalties that enmeshed tribesmen of different status groups.

Even before the reform of the centuriate assembly, and continuing long after, the tribal assignments of new citizens were also subject to adjustment.[35] For some citizens were deemed unassimilable by some Romans except perhaps as dedicated clients of powerful Roman leaders.[36] Witness the rigorous opposition of a group of noble senators in 312 to the decision of the censor, Ap. Claudius Caecus, to enroll former slaves and city of Rome shopkeepers throughout all the tribes.[37] Although the censors of 304 again restricted these citizens to the four city tribes, the assignment of freedmen continued to be an issue until the end of the Republic.[38] The incident reveals a divided mind about new citizens among Rome's leaders late in the fourth century, some of whom were determined to control the voting power of these men through the regulation of tribal assignments. The basis for their hostility to these particular Romans bears thought.[39] After all, in 312, former slaves were likely to be victims of war in Italy—Etruscan, Latin, Samnite, or other Italian; Greek or possibly Gaul; perhaps even Romans who had the misfortune to fall into binding debt—hence, people who for the most part (except Gauls) in other circumstances might be perfectly acceptable citizens or allies. Assets were not an issue, since freed slaves were likely to be men of property, nor indeed were origins: the Roman people deemed sons of freedmen eligible for citizenship optimo iure, enacting a law to that effect in 189 and registering these new citizens throughout all the tribes.[40]

The slave condition, however, was in itself suspect: like proscribed men in the first century, former slaves at all times were men of uncertain attachment. And their misfortunes were sometimes compounded by foreign origins. Could they be privy to the understandings that knit Roman society together at the top and elevated the best men to office, especially high office? Evidently not, for Livy credits them with the election of the clerk Cn. Flavius, son of a former slave, as aedile in 304—an outcome greeted with unambiguous animosity on the part of Roman nobles. By their opposition to enrolling former slaves throughout all the tribes, such leaders clearly sought to narrow the avenue to political participation by people whose ability to make the right decision as determined by the better classes of Roman society was in a sense unknown. In the long run, however, the real danger to the Roman system came not from ordinary people but from men of highest status.[41]

SETTING LIMITS ON THE LEADERS

In 149, the tribune Calpurnius successfully proposed the first of Rome's celebrated public laws addressing the crime of res repetundae, the unlawful seizure of property belonging to provincials by a Roman governor. For the first time the lex Calpurnia defined as criminal the habitual, somewhat rapacious behavior of Roman leaders abroad and established a procedure to investigate charges of such behavior brought by aggrieved provincials before the praetor peregrinus in Rome. Over the next one hundred years, the Romans further developed the definitions of the crime, the range of individuals (initially Roman officeholders or senators and their sons, but expanding by the end of the Republic to include members of a governor's staff) liable to prosecution, the trial procedures, and most notably the Roman citizens who were to have the right of trial, judgment, and assessment of damages. At least sixty-four high-ranking Romans were brought to trial before the end of the Republic.[42] Masters of the world, the Romans astutely recognized the need to temper force with justice and provided a remedy for official abuse in the leges repetundarum.

Although Roman officeholders had always been liable for specific acts of misconduct or failure, no single category of official behavior was consistently defined as a crime against the state, with the exception of the long-standing capital offense of perduellio, adjudicated by the Roman people. Complaints about the behavior of individual officeholders or senators were spontaneous, and the Senate or people might create special commissions of investigation to adjudicate them on an ad hoc basis. Or an aedile or quaestor would convene the people as a judicial assembly to adjudicate complaints, again on an ad hoc basis. By the second century, however, the expanding number of potential Roman leaders and the increasing competition among such men invited efforts to control present and former officeholders through the identification of sustainable crimes against the state. These efforts always involved lawmaking assemblies. Ambitus, campaign bribery, was the earliest such crime, addressed in a series of laws beginning perhaps in the fourth century and certainly on record in the early second century (see table 7.2).[43] The only known feature of the first secure lex de ambitu, the lex Baebia of 181, is the penalty attached to the crime, disqualification from office for ten years.[44] The next sustainable crime, res repetundae, was defined by the lex Calpurnia, as seen previously. For the first time a permanent court of investigation, quaestio, was established, specific to the crime. Thereafter, the identification of other state crimes would be accompanied by the establishment of a unique, permanent court of investigation, staffed by jurors (iudices) drawn from an evolving list of eligible Romans: maiestas (103), falsa (81), sicarii and venefici (81), iniuria (81), peculatus (81), vis (70), sodalicia (55), and parricidium (ca. 50).[45] Over time, the Romans modified the definitions of some of these crimes, as they did the *crimen repetundarum*, the range of individuals liable to prosecution, the trial procedures, and the Roman citizens who were to have the right of trial, judgment, and assessment of damages. These adjustments, engineered in lawmaking assemblies, confirm a societywide concern to set limits on an irrepressible aristocracy. At the same time, the series of laws initiated by the lex Calpurnia reveals an even more delicate balancing act within the ranks of Rome's leaders and would-be leaders, senators, and equestrians.

Fortunately, we have a clear view of these tensions in the fine detail of the so-called lex Repetundarum of the Gracchan period, 133–121, which modified the procedure and jurors of the permanent court established by the lex Calpurnia in 149.[46] Best known of the extortion laws by virtue of its lacunose survival (it was engraved on the front of the tablet that also preserves the lex Agraria), the lex Repetundarum precisely renders an array of persons, relations, and conditions that come under the law. The sheer number of these, a striking feature of the law, attests a finely honed awareness of qualities that set Romans apart. Accused men belong to a group that exhibits overlapping characteristics. First and foremost they are elected officeholders (except quaestors), elected military tribunes, or elected or appointed commissioners with juridical powers; that is, dictator, consul, praetor, master of the horse, censor, aedile, tribune, one of the three men for night-time crime (tresvir capitalis), one of the three men for the granting and assigning of lands (tresvir agris dandis adsignatis), or military tribune of legions 1–4. Second they are senators, by family association if not in fact, for the son of any of the identified officers is liable under the law only as long as the father is a senator. Office then is critical.

Turning to the selection of jurors, patrons, and witnesses, office again is a primary criterion, though not the only one. The 450 men placed by the praetor on the annual list of jurors (*album iudicum*) may not be or have been any of the named officers liable under the law or a quaestor (in other words, officers not automatically identifiable as senators). Other conditions must also be met. Jurors may not be or have been in the Senate; they may not have received a payment or been condemned in a quaestio and iudicium publicum so that they cannot be enrolled in the Senate; they may not be under thirty or over sixty; they must legally reside in Rome or within one mile; they may not be or have been father, brother, or son to any of the previously mentioned magistrates or of a man in the Senate or overseas. The jurors must be published in a list, with each juror identified by name, father's name, and tribe. The lex Repetundarum instructed the praetor to group them by tribe, tributim, as well: "He shall have all these names written on a white-washed board in black ink, including their father, tribe and cognomen, and organized by tribe."[47]

Even more restrictions hedge the business of selecting jurors for an individual trial. The jurors selected from this list may not be related to the accused as son-in-law, father-in-law, stepfather, stepson, cousin, or closer blood relation or be a sodalis to him or be in the same collegium.[48] Nor may they be related to the prosecutor, or he to them, as father-in-law, son-in-law, stepfather, stepson, cousin, or closer blood relation or be a sodalis to him; nor may jurors be or have been tribune, quaestor, tresvir capitalis, tresvir agris dandis adsignatis, or military tribune; nor be or have been in the Senate; nor have been elected tresviri for founding a colony under the lex Rubria; nor be absent on public business or be overseas; nor be more than one from a family; nor be a man condemned under the lex Calpurnia or lex Iunia, earlier extortion laws, or because he has been prosecuted under this statute.

Likewise, the patronus, or representative assigned to a prosecutor, and the witnesses for the prosecutor are tightly defined. A patronus must be a freeborn Roman citizen. He cannot be related to the accused as son-in-law, father-in-law, stepfather, stepson, cousin, or closer blood relation; or be a sodalis to him or be in the same collegium; or be in his fides or have ancestors who were in his ancestors' fides; or have been condemned in a quaestio and iudicium publicum so that he cannot be enrolled in the Senate; or be a juror under this law or have been appointed patron already under this law. While there is only one patron, there may be up to forty-eight witnesses. The conditions a witness should meet are equally lengthy (although there is a lacuna in the text of the law here): A witness who gives evidence may not be someone in whose fides the accused is, nor can the accused's ancestors have been in the fides of the witness's ancestors; he may not be someone in the fides of the accused or someone whose ancestors were in the fides of ancestors of the accused or someone who pleads his case, up to one, or someone who is the freedman or woman of him or his parent.

The entire display of particulars in the lex Repetundarum calls attention to the brittleness of Rome's governing classes or, more precisely, of the ties linking members and groups within those classes. The strongest ties are the immediately personal ones: ties of association, ties of clientage, and above all ties of family prevail. So important is the last of these that the panel of jurors may contain only one man from a given family. In defining degrees of permitted and forbidden relationships so closely, the draftsman must intuitively know, and the law sponsor and the Roman people know, that such bonds determine the strongest attachments of Roman equestrians. The loyalties of senators also are determined by family and patronage, as well as by membership in the Senate and priestly college. Equestrians or senators in any of these relationships to the prosecutor or accused cannot be expected to judge impartially, to advise impartially, or to give testimony impartially, nor can Romans who are not in the prime of life or who have suffered infamia (with the result that they were removed from the Senate), that is, men of uncertain attachment. Like Cicero's sons of proscribed Romans, high-status Romans who had suffered infamia were unpredictable, their ability to make the right decision suspect. Such men are excluded as jurors in the lex Repetundarum. Tribe is also important. With a glance at the album, prosecutors and accused senators alike can know the tribe of each juror. Presumably this knowledge helped the accused man choose the jurors for his trial. These ties, however, are evidently not as fundamental as the prescribed degrees of relationship: never bound by the obligations of pietas or fides, tribesmen were somewhat loosely connected.

Conversely, an oath is required of every participant at practically every stage of the proceedings. The praetor peregrinus must swear openly that he has chosen the 450 jurors as the statute requires. The prosecutor, a non-Roman, must swear he is not making a false accusation. The accused, a senator or son of a senator, must swear in the presence of the prosecutor that he has identified among the jurors everyone related to him in the ways proscribed by the statute. The prosecutor must swear before the praetor in the presence of the people that the 100 jurors he has selected are not related to him in the ways described or are not the individuals listed. The jurors must swear before the proceedings begin that they will behave, listen to the witnesses, and make a judgment. The jurors must swear again before the deliberations begin. At every stage an oath: What of trust among men of repute? It would seem that the scale and diversity of Roman society at all levels made trust a tenuous commodity in the late second century. We are left with the strong sense that among themselves Roman aristocrats were rather loosely attached.

Ironically, the tensions within a like-minded leadership, reflected in the lex Repetundarum, belie a practical reality that some Romans recognized. The long and relatively well-documented struggle over jury composition on Rome's permanent courts provides illustration. Often the struggle was played out in public lawmaking assemblies, as shown in table 7.2. On the establishment of the first permanent court in 149 (table 7.2), the Romans published a list of jurors (album iudicum) that for the next twenty-five years effectively replicated the current list of senators. The position of iudex was restricted to senators until the Gracchan period, when jurors were drawn, with some exclusions, from the equestrian class. The furor in ancient Rome from this time onward over the men who should be included on the album iudicum calls attention to the inescapable realities fueling the expansion of the Roman leadership.[49]

Setting aside the emotional and political arguments that centered around the control of the political leadership by the Roman Senate, the matter of jury composition addressed in the bills in table 7.2 came down very practically to numbers. In order to staff the thirty- to seventy-five-man juries of the permanent courts in process of formation after 149, the Romans had to move beyond the boundaries of the Roman Senate in its present configuration of three hundred men. Given that senators already served as individual judges and jurors, recuperatores, members of the centumviral court, members of extraordinary commissions and special commissions of investigation, minor and major magistrates, priests, augurs, and military leaders, they were doubtless hard-pressed to take on additional legal tasks. One resolution to the problem, perhaps introduced in an uncertain public law proposal by C. Sempronius Gracchus, involved augmenting the number of senators by adding new members from the equestrian class. The men selected were presumably equestrians with a public horse, from whose numbers senators had been excluded by a law of 129. Whether this was achieved by the lex Sempronia iudiciaria of 122 is doubted by scholars.[50] Sulla, however, enlarged the Senate to six hundred members in 81 by adlecting equestrians (lex Cornelia iudiciaria; see table 8.2 in chapter 8) and instituted jury panels of senators exclusively. Another resolution was simply to include equestrians directly on the slate of jurors. This was done by the lex Repetundarum, undone by other laws, then done and undone again. In 70, the lex Aurelia projected a list of jurors comprising men from three groups: Roman senators, equestrians with a public horse, and tribuni aerarii, who were considered equestrians although they were formally registered in Class 1 (table 7.2).[51] The lex Iulia in 46 again restricted jurors to senators and equestrians, the latter now including both equites equo publico and tribuni aerarii. Throughout this decades-long struggle the need for more administrators was obvious. The crux for elite Romans, however, was who among their numbers could judge the highest ranking among them, the Roman senators. The permanent courts, as well as the selection or election process of decemviri and centumviri, and the composition of jury courts, all instituted by public law, are another feature of the efforts by Roman leaders to manage the extensive changes in Rome's highest property class and political leadership.

RESTORING THE CONDITIONS FOR A COMMUNITY CONSENSUS

The perceived gravity of the problems confronting Rome's leadership is highlighted by the introduction of the written ballot. Between 139 and 130, three tribunes presented bills to the people introducing written ballots in electoral assemblies (139), then in most assemblies convened as popular law courts (137), and finally in lawmaking assemblies (130) (table 7.3).[52] All three were enacted by Roman voters. As a result of these laws, voters cast their votes by dropping a ballot marked, in the case of lawmaking assemblies, antiquo ("no") or uti rogas ("yes"), or simply "A" or "U," in an urn watched by selected reputable men from each tribe, the custodes. Issued two ballots apiece when his voting unit was called forward, each voter returned his ballot of choice as he filed by the urn. No longer were votes given orally to the tribal or other official "asker of the question" (rogator) and recorded before the tally. Now the ballots were simply collected and counted by other reputable men, the counters (diribitores). In this way writing made its appearance in another sphere of Roman civic life.[53] What purposes were served by written ballots?

Our main ancient informant, Cicero, suggests that all three ballot laws were the work of demagogues currying political favor with voters at lower levels. Written ballots made the vote secret, thus guaranteeing the independence of the voters.[54] Pursuant on Cicero's account, modern scholars (with some exceptions) generally conclude that the ballot laws were the work of "democratic-minded" lawmakers and belong to "il movimento democratico" in Rome.[55] The fact that all three bills are reported to have wide support among voters seems to support the idea. Moreover, in the second century the Romans were emphatically proclaiming the importance of being Roman in terms of political power as exercised in the voting assemblies. The catchphrase "iussa populi," popular sovereignty, derives from these years.[56]

What is known about the circumstances of the three ballot laws, however—which is very little, except for the names of the sponsors—does not fully corroborate the mid-first-century interpretation. The sponsor of the first statute in 139 was the tribune A. Gabinius, a political newcomer, the first Gabinius known to hold any office in Rome. The family, which appears to have low-status origins in Cales (slave or ex-slave potters named Gabinii are attested here in the third century, and the tribune was reputed to be the grandson of an estate-born slave woman), owed its entry into the governing classes to the tribune's father, a successful officer named prefect of the Roman army at Scorda by the propraetor L. Anicius Gallus in 167.[57] The tribune also had a successful military career; he was one of a group of officers serving under Q. Caecilius Metellus Macedonicus in Macedonia in 146 sent by the proconsul to talk the Achaean League out of war. Gabinius probably held no other offices after his tribunate, although his descendants advanced to the praetorship in the second century and the consulate in the first. The sponsor of the second ballot law in 137, L. Cassius Longinus Ravilla, belonged to a plebeian clan ennobled in the previous generation.[58] Consul in 127 and censor in 125, he was a man of commanding reputation in the community. Although a fellow tribune and one of the consuls, Lepidus, opposed Cassius's proposal, it had the support of Scipio Aemilianus.[59] The sponsor of the third ballot law in 130, the tribune Cn. Papirius Carbo, called a "rabble-rouser" by Cicero, demonstrated (as consul in 120) his commitment to the best men by successfully defending L. Opimius (cos. 121) against a charge of unlawfully executing Romans.[60] These then are the sponsors of Rome's first ballot laws. The lineup hardly suggests any uniformity of intent.

The absence of any common thread linking the sponsors—other than new citizens, in the case of Gabinius and Cassius—suggests that closer scrutiny is in order.[61] As a practical measure the written ballot in electoral, judicial, and legislative assemblies achieved one clear end: it removed the rogator from the job of asking for and transcribing votes. In the competitive atmosphere of second-century Rome, when men with political aspirations would set themselves at an advantage in any way possible in those venues where citizens made critical decisions, namely, voting assemblies, when there was, as Astin writes, a "growing sense that those in the assemblies could be won over and that social pressures could be outweighed by personal appeal and emotive incitement," the written ballot thus diminished the power of tribal leaders, who had previously recorded the oral votes of the voters.[62] More precisely, in light of the circumstances created by Rome's expanding leadership, the written ballot removed the tribal leader from determining the vote or impeding the vote.[63] How could the people express their will effectively when unknown or possibly corrupt tribal leaders pressured new and old tribal members? How could the Roman people express their will effectively when the influx of newcomers to a tribe could so vastly expand the power of tribal leaders that they had the capability of skewing any such expression? Like the laws on campaign bribery (ambitus), the ballot laws addressed Roman concerns, particularly concerns of elite Romans, on this score by ensuring that the process of voting unfolded properly to allow the voters to give unencumbered expression to the will of the Roman people. In effect the written ballot effectively restored the circumstances in which the voting could proceed as it should.

Like many similar adjustments the ballot laws restored a balance to the political arena. At stake were the collective interests of Roman leaders, who now comprised a larger and more fluid group. From the perspective of politically ambitious men, a written ballot leveled the playing field for all contenders, whether from leading clans or newer families, in small town municipalities no less than Rome. The written ballot was premised on the assumption that by accurately recording the votes of the Roman people, through a secret ballot previously defined by elite Romans, they would make the system work as it should, from the viewpoint of elite Romans. Hence the sponsors of ballot laws should be viewed as furthering the self-interest of their own group within the governing classes, not as "demagogues" currying political favor from the Roman people. The first such law was sponsored by a political newcomer. The second was sponsored and supported by nobiles with known attachments to the Italian allies. Rather than reflecting a newly emerging popular dimension to Roman political life, the introduction of writing shows the conservative assumptions by which society (to the Roman mind) operated.

Contrariwise, Cicero at the end of the 50s saw the written ballot as a dangerous step that eroded the authority of elite members of Roman society. Secret ballots encouraged the Roman people to make decisions independently from their rightful leaders. They restricted the traditional relationship between leader and ordinary citizen in the voting arena. In *De Legibus*, Cicero condemns such restrictions, disparaging the ballot laws and their sponsors and lauding his own grandfather for opposing the efforts by Marius Gratidianus to introduce the written ballot in Arpinum. But it is doubtful whether Cicero's perspective was precisely that of elite Romans living two generations earlier.[64] In all periods Roman political leaders belonged to a privileged group in a society all of whose members recognized the hierarchy of status and prestige. Still, much had changed for the Roman elite between the 130s and the last decade of Cicero's political life. For instance, their own membership in Cicero's day was even larger and more fluid, the citizen population was three times larger, and Rome's leaders were more obviously out of control. Cicero's censure of the ballot laws in *De Legibus* reflects his sense of a changed political reality. It is a measure of his disappointment in the turn of events.[65] At some level the customary symbiotic passage of knowledge and information between leaders and people was not operating in the 40s, at least not in the way Cicero thought it should. Accordingly he included it as a provision in the ideal law presented in *De Legibus*: "presiding officers . . . shall instruct the people in regard to the matter in hand, and allow them to be instructed by other magistrates and private citizens" (*qui agent . . . rem populum docento, doceri a magistratibus privatisque patiunto*).[66] For Cicero, the dependency of the Roman people on its proper magistrates for information and understanding of laws appeared to be slipping away. He did not consider that it might instead be the final failing on the part of the leadership.

The ballot laws of the 130s, however, were passed by a generation trying to restore their own notion of control to the realm of voting, now complicated by the emergence of leaders from newer families and voters from newly admitted communities. Under pressure, elite Romans utilized the tool of writing as a response to the need to accommodate a wider membership in the circle of elite Romans and the resulting changes in traditional relationships between leaders and the Roman people. Related adjustments made through lawmaking assemblies to balance competing leaders and groups, listed in table 7.3, focused on other aspects of voting. Although the laws, which span almost 250 years, address apparently different issues ranging from the conduct of assemblies to participation by voters, most of those issues reveal a common concern with ensuring that the lawmaking process work the way it was supposed to, that is, in conformity with Roman understandings of the vital interaction between political leaders, tribal leaders, and the Roman people. Hence in the fourth century the Roman dictator Publilius Philo carried a bill prescribing the announcement of the Senate's opinion or sanction (*auctoritas patrum*), which probably amounted to confirmation that the proposed law had no religious flaws, before a lawmaking assembly (table 7.3). Some fifty years later, the prescription was carried over to electoral assemblies. These measures were doubtless attempts to allow the unfettered expression of senatorial opinion to guide the decisions of the Roman voters.[67] The announcement of the collective opinion of the Senate prior to electing officials or enacting law was understood to have a tremendous influence on the outcome of the vote, because of the respect for the authority of the Senate. Similarly, the so-called leges Aelia et Fufia of ca. 153 (table 7.3) prescribed the appropriate response to the announcement of adverse omens (obnuntiatio), namely, an immediate end to the proceedings, and the appropriate days for assemblies. Directed primarily at the proper conduct of assemblies, the laws also suggest a perceived need to regularize business, ritual, and market days.[68] As table 7.3 indicates, the frequency of such measures increases noticeably around the mid-second century. Additionally, the issues that they now address provide a far more significant indicator of changes in Roman society.

From now on, all measures governing the production of law are aimed at seeming deviations from custom introduced by the elite managers and participants of the events. We have discussed already the significance of campaign bribery, ambitus, involving tribal leaders in the disbursement of cash handouts from individual candidates to tribal members in order to win the vote, as a reflection of a kind of breakdown in (or rearrangement of) traditional ties. In the case of bribery laws and ballot laws, as previously noted, the concern with a network of traditional relations among tribesmen and between citizens of different classes and status groups, that is, the personal dimension of the lawmaking process, is also clear. Similar public laws address the voter's ability to cast his vote without hindrance—for example, Marius's public law, the lex Maria, narrowing the width of the voting bridge (pontes), whose aim we have discussed, as well as the divine and legitimating conditions of lawmaking. In every case public laws relating to voting assemblies attempt to restore a situation so as to maintain an understood balance between the various elements involved in the process. Significantly, most of the laws in table 7.3 attempt to regulate elite behavior. But as with the auctoritas patrum and the written ballot, the focus of concern in correcting such deviations is the Roman voter—just as the voter is the focus of the Roman leader's concern in his efforts to adjust to the changing scale of Roman society.

These laws, as well as the opposition to them, attest to the importance both the Romans and their eagerly created compatriots, the Latins, Italians, and ex-slaves, attached to voting, especially at public lawmaking assemblies, over two and a half centuries.[69] Furthermore, the accepted importance of public lawmaking as a mechanism for making societywide adjustment explains the necessity of imposing such rules to ensure that the event flowed as Romans believed it should. In the face of changes in the Roman leadership such a flow was increasingly difficult at the level of personal interaction between political or tribal leaders and the Roman people.

The same conservative impulses prompting the Romans to regulate voting procedures underlie concerns to preserve the open conditions deemed essential for the production of legitimate law. Voting occurred only in Rome because the uncoerced expression of community consensus was possible only in Rome. Outside Rome, citizens under arms and convened by a commander with imperium, the only conditions under which an assembly had ever been convened outside Rome, in 357, were hardly in a position to voice the sovereign will of the Roman people.[70] Moreover, voting assemblies were perforce held in the full light of day, following prior announcement over a period of three Roman weeks, because the expression of a valid community consensus required open meetings, advertised in advance. Assemblies convened without the requisite advertising period were un-Roman, although some political leaders at the end of the second century ignored this. As a result the lex Caecilia Didia of 98 (table 7.3) regulated the customary observance of the three-market-day advertising period.[71] Clandestine meetings and meetings held in the dark of night were viewed by the Romans as totally contrary to the spirit of community consensus. Cicero roundly condemned the tribunes of 63 because, he claimed, they met in the dark of night to draft the rogatio Servilia agraria. In this context, Caesar's edict as consul in 59 to publish the proceedings of the Roman Senate provides an interesting contemporary perspective on the Roman Senate as a collective that no longer heeded, no longer in fact articulated, the sovereign will of the Roman people.[72] Without disclosure of the transactions and debates of these closed meetings, the desires of the Roman people would be distorted.

The Romans had clearly become aware some generations earlier that a traditional openness, no doubt related to the smaller dimensions of an earlier Rome, was vanishing. This is hardly surprising given the size and dispersal of the citizen population, which made it difficult for the Romans to conduct community business in the presence of all citizens. Moreover, political leaders were not above manipulating the system. But there was clearly a concern on the part of some Romans to restore the open conditions believed essential to the expression of community consensus on some matters. Often they resorted to public law. In the lex Repetundarum, for instance, open conditions in the matter of trials for res repetundae were closely regulated by the law. Where jury selection is concerned, the law instructs the praetor, in the current year and every year, to have names of jurors he has selected written on white-washed boards (*alba*). Likewise, the praetor must have the names announced in a meeting, and he must swear that the men he has chosen are suitable and chosen according to the statute. Then, the prosecutor must swear before the praetor in the presence of the people that the one hundred jurors he has selected are not related to him in any of the proscribed ways. The law further instructs the praetor to openly serve notice of trial to the person who has been accused, telling him what day it will be. Next, before the trial begins the jurors must swear before the praetor in the Forum in front of the rostra. The praetor must then have the names of the jurors who have sworn announced in a meeting, and he shall have them displayed openly in the Forum. The praetor must also declare his opinion regarding a juror whose selection has been questioned in a public meeting in the presence of the jurors. The voting procedures instituted by the law also reveal a deep concern with openness. An urn is placed on the platform. The praetor gives a ballot openly to each juror. The juror marks his ballot and with a bare arm places it openly (with the letter covered) in the urn. The juror selected to count the votes takes each ballot out, shows it to the people so that they can see all of it, and declares the vote. He then hands the ballot to the nearest juror, who hands it to the praetor. If we needed reinforcement of our earlier impression that the Roman aristocracy appears to bear close watching, the lex Repetundarum provides it. More interesting, however, is the function of writing in determining open conditions.

While the utility of writing as a tool is obvious, its adaptability to the Roman sense of procedure is less so. Over the fourth and third centuries, the political leaders of Rome (and their assistants) had gradually introduced writing into the administration of Roman affairs in order to manage the rapidly expanding resources at their disposal and to control the rapidly changing circumstances accompanying the influx of new members into Roman society. By the second century, writing was used extensively in the management of the Romans' growing world, and they continued to adapt its uses further, most noticeably in the political arena. Already we have seen that the written ballot, introduced in 139, allowed the uncoerced expression of community consensus. In effect, writing offered a means to keep traditional Roman public processes operating in the customary way that Romans felt they should. Part and parcel of a larger turn toward the use of writing as well was the publication of public law proposals on white-washed boards (alba), used for all forms of written public announcement in Rome.

In routine use from the second century onward, the written display of proposed laws probably belongs to the same period as written ballots and was most likely motivated by similar concerns.[73] Like the written ballot, too, written displays of law have been viewed as a democratic feature of Roman lawmaking, because they made the law accessible to anyone.[74] Certainly these notice boards were intended to be read, for routine publicizing instructions include the formulaic admonition to place the boards "where they could be read from ground level" (*unde de plano recte legi possit*). Whether they were, in fact, read by your average Roman is of little consequence. From a Roman perspective, the requisite recital of the law draft was more critical in achieving the practical goal of publicizing information about law. Despite the pervasiveness of writing, Rome remained a predominately oral culture whose primary agents of publication were heralds and whose primary means of publicizing information were proclamation and debate. In 103, the tribune C. Servilius Glaucia advised the people to listen for certain key phrases in a proposed law as the herald read it in order to determine whether the proposal affected them or not.[75] Such advice belongs to a world long accustomed to processing information received by proclamation and word of mouth. Nonetheless the formal requirements of lawmaking, instituted by the Roman leadership, demanded the written display of law proposals. What is to wonder at is not the curious combination of notice boards and recitals but the formal persistence of recitals. Even after the introduction of writing in the lawmaking arena, public readings of the law continued as a requirement of promulgation. In the lawmaking arena, as in all others, the Romans appear reluctant to discard customary practice after the introduction of new practices.

The contemporary importance of the posted texts lies rather in their meaning to the elite members of Roman society. Whether read or not, the vital presence of posted texts of proposed law demonstrates the importance to the rulers of Rome of making information available to the Roman people in an open way. Information, as transmitted by rightful leaders, was essential for the uncoerced expression of community consensus. The public display of written law drafts limited the opportunities for political leaders to manipulate the people's vote by skewing the information because it ensured that the law presented to the assembly was the same law recited at the first lawmaking meeting. The public display of written information, like the written ballot, leveled the playing field for all contenders by allowing the process to unfold as it should.

Concurrently, the rulers of Rome appear to be making information available to the Roman people in a way that determined who those people ought to be. Complicated Latin law drafts required sophisticated Latin readers. Even hearing the draft recited would be useless without a spoken command of the language. Similarly, the written ballot discouraged non-Latin readers from voting. Its creators did not contemplate voters who did not speak Latin. Thus, in the 130s, written ballots were also an effort to determine who voted: men who were conversant with the language of power, Latin. As late as 92, when the censors issued an edict banning instruction of rhetoric in the Latin language these considerations held force.[76] Although most local aristocracies spoke Latin by 90, they still wrote their mother languages. Only at the end of the century were local languages, whether written or spoken, for the most part completely replaced. But in the 90s, some Romans viewed Latin rhetorical training, which was taking place in the roving schools set up in the Forum and other public places, as a deviation from the standards and areas of instruction established by tradition. Like the institution of the written ballot, such a prohibition made access to the techniques of public speaking, that is, to the tools of the right kind of oratory, harder to come by for all but the elite members of Roman and Italian society, for whom Greek education was common. In both cases, we are witnessing an intense effort on the part of Rome's political leaders to restrict access to a basic tool of leadership at a time when membership in their own ranks was expanding. Competition among elite Romans accompanied the expansion of the Roman state almost from the beginning.

CONCLUSION

As an expanding leadership confronted new conditions of rule, in particular a momentous increase in the number of ordinary Romans, the problems in Roman society mounted. Often fundamental corrections to the Roman system were introduced directly by an elected officeholder. A significant example is the lowering of minimum property qualifications for membership in Class 5, implemented twice by decision of an unknown commander seeking recruits for infantry service, and the reform of the centuriate assembly, accomplished by the censors. The issues in these instances were doubtless uncontroversial. But controversial issues could be brought to the attention of a public lawmaking assembly by an elected official of Rome. Many such issues involved the leaders themselves. A sense of the privileges of status pervaded Roman society and is especially visible in the Roman drive to limit political participation by new Romans at the level of the ruling elite, struggling to control the influx of new members.

The extent to which the Romans perceived a general need to set firm limits for an irrepressible aristocracy is obvious in the wide range of laws addressing the Roman leadership. An increasingly more rigorous definition of certain kinds of behavior as criminal, usually on the part of Romans of high status, was accompanied by the institution of courts staffed by high-status Romans to judge that behavior. Matters that had been responsive to one-time special commissions of investigation or judicial assemblies were now so pervasive as to justify permanent courts and juries. Increasing numbers of elite Romans became involved in dispensing justice in matters involving elite Romans through service on jury panels. The use of popular assemblies as courts of justice in those same matters gradually disappeared, signaling an intensified effort on the part of elite Romans to maintain the traditional relationship between themselves and the wider population, which had become weakened by the growth in citizen numbers. Limits were set on the opportunities for manipulating the system to personal, political advantage of oneself and one's group. Public laws introduced a number of reforms into the voting arena in particular, though other arenas were not neglected. The grain distribution laws, initiated in 122 by C. Gracchus, clearly belong in the constellation of laws that attempted to regulate the manipulation of a traditional system by an increasing number of ambitious Romans whose relationship to the majority population, itself increasing in size, had become attenuated. It is no surprise that the preponderance of public laws address issues relating to political leaders and other elite Romans.

Concurrently the tensions surrounding Rome's expanding leadership helped ensure that public lawmaking came into its own as a mechanism of adjustment. A growing number of political leaders accompanied by the attenuation of traditional relationships in Italian communities gave new importance to the resiliency of Roman public lawmaking. Lawmaking provided an arena where needs were met and concerns aired. A fluid political leadership was in place, comprising more men outside the shadow of Rome' great families, men with a foot in the military camps, of proven competence and merit, able to sway a crowd with words. There were more potential leaders, each with a crowd of friends, associates, and dependents. Voting decisions now depended on an even more complicated set of expectations, understandings, alignments, and other considerations on the part of the Roman people as well as their elected leaders. By the second half of the second century, the ramifications of these developments in the lawmaking arena were considerable.

Clearly the process itself was changing, as the lawmaking activity over the years of C. Gracchus's tribunate makes clear. From this time onward, the Roman people met ever more frequently to make decisions about more and more issues. Other wrinkles in the traditional lawmaking process were to follow. In 100, the tribune L. Appuleius Saturninus carried a bill to distribute lands in Transalpine Gaul annexed by C. Marius from the conquered Cimbri to the discharged soldiers of Marius who had fought them. Among the provisions of the measure was one requiring all senators and elected officials to swear publicly within five days to uphold the law. Ten years later an epitaph of C. Livius Drusus, the murdered tribune of 91, states that he was a member of a ten-man land commission in accordance with his own law and a member of a five-man land commission the same year in accordance with a lex Saufeia: *Xvir a.d.a. lege sua et eodem anno Vvir a.d.a. lege Saufe[i]a.*[77] That very year, the Roman Senate annulled all public laws carried by Drusus on the grounds that they were illegal.

Unmistakable in this varied set of efforts to undo enacted public law at the end of the second century are signs of shifts in the acceptance of public law, especially by elite Romans, which appear to reflect broad social change in Roman society. Equally apparent is the universal recognition that the end products of Roman lawmaking assemblies were the public expressions of common agreement about issues of concern to the Roman people. On the occasions singled out in the previous paragraph, such expressions could be nullified in a variety of ways: through the voters' acceptance of a contrary public law, through nonobservance by senators, and through annulment on procedural grounds. The lawmaking of 123–121 signals the onset of changes in public lawmaking, which became more and more frequent in the first century. Yet no matter what stratagems were employed, including the nullification of law, they all rest on the assumption that a statute was legitimate only when it was enacted with full publicity in the procedurally prescribed manner. And behind all the efforts to restore a balance to the system was the belief that if allowed to vote in an unencumbered way Roman citizens of all kinds would make the proper decisions. Only under these conditions did the resounding response of "uti rogas" by the assembled voters give unobstructed voice to the sovereign will of the Roman people. The persistence of this belief even while Roman society was undergoing its most rapid change is visible in the lawmaking activity of the period from 91 to 44, the subject of chapters 8 and 9.

TABLE 7.1 Laws Adjusting Office and Position by Year and Subject, 350–92

342	Interval between consecutive offices, plebeian consuls
339	Opening censorship to plebs
327	Prorogation of imperium
313	Censors' authority to review Senate membership
311	Election of the military tribunes of legions 1–4
295	Prorogation of imperium
(287–218)[a]	Oversight of weights and measures by aediles
267	Expanding the number of quaestors
266	The surrender of a commander
265	Iteration of the censorship
252	Stipend of censured equites
Before 241	Jurisdictio of urban praetor
241–123	The election and responsibilities of IIIviri capitales
223	A triumph for a commander
217	Suspension or circumvention of law
217	Election of a dictator
217	Abrogation of a dictator's imperium
217	Equalizing the imperium of the dictator and magister equitum
215	Proconsular imperium for a praetor
211	The selection of a commander
211	Extension of proconsul's imperium until his ovatio
210	Election of a dictator
209	Abrogation of a commander's imperium
208	Prorogation of imperium
205	The assignment of a province
204	The selection of two commanders
203	Exculpating C. Servilius from knowingly breaking the law
202	The selection of a commander

(*continued*)

TABLE 7.1 (*continued*)

201	The selection of a commander
200	The selection of two commanders
200	Suspension or circumvention of law
192	The reassignment of provinces
By 181	The ages for holding office
181	Number of praetors elected in alternate years
180	The ages for holding office
Ca. 179	The necessary conditions for a triumph
177	Abrogation of a commander's imperium
171	Suspension or circumvention of law
168	Annulment of leases/contracts made by censors
167	Extension of commander's imperium until triumph
167	Privileges for individuals
Ca. 151	Reelection to the office of consul
(149)	Membership of tribunes in the Senate
147	Suspension or circumvention of law
147	The assignment of a province
134	Suspension or circumvention of law
133	Removal of tribune(s) from office
131	The selection of a commander
131–123	Reelection of the previous year's tribunes
(130)	Iteration of office by tribunes
(129)	The public horse of senators
123	Addition of equestrians to Senate
123	Magistrates deposed by the people
123	Allotment of consular provinces by the Senate
(122)	The ages for election as military tribune
Before 113	Liability for trial of individuals away on state business
107	The selection of a commander
105	Abrogation of a commander's imperium
105	Selection of military tribunes by consul
104	Expulsion of senators losing imperium
(100)	A sponsor's election to the extraordinary office he created
(100)	A sponsor's election to the extraordinary office he created
100	The exile of individual(s)
100	The assignment of a province
91	Addition of equestrians to Senate and jury composition

Source: See appendixes A and C.

[a]Dates in parentheses are approximate. See appendix C.

TABLE 7.2 **Crimes, Courts, and Juries by Year and Subject, 200–44**

181	The crime of ambitus
159	The crime of ambitus
149	The crime of repetundae
ca. 149–123	The crime of repetundae
133	Jury composition
123	Addition of equestrians to Senate
122	The crime of repetundae
122	Jury composition
ca. 133–91	Jury matters
ca. 133–91	The crime of repetundae
106	Jury composition
103	The crime of maiestas
103	Special commission of investigation
(101)[a]	The crime of repetundae
91	Addition of equestrians to Senate, jury composition
90	Special commission of investigation
89	The election of jurors by the tribes
88	Addition of equestrians to Senate
81	Establishment of standing courts and/or jury composition
81	The crime of falsa
81	The crime of sicarii and venefici
81	The crime of iniuria
81	The crime of maiestas
81	The crime of repetundae
81	The crime of peculatus
74	Abrogation of an existing statute
70	Jury composition
(70)	The crime of vis
67	The crime of ambitus
67	The crime of ambitus
(65)	The crime of ambitus
63	The crime of ambitus
61	The crime of ambitus
61	Special commission of investigation
61	Special commission of investigation
61	Special commission of investigation
59	The crime of repetundae
59	Jury selection
59	Special commission of investigation
59	The voting order of jurors
56	Special commission of investigation
55	Jury composition
55	The crime of repetundae
55	The crime of sodalicia
54	Special commission of investigation
52	The crime of vis
52	The crime of ambitus

(*continued*)

TABLE 7.2 (*continued*)

(50)	The crime of parricide
Mid-1st century	The crime of repetundae
46	Jury composition
46	The crime of maiestas
46	The crime of vis
Perhaps 46	The crime of repetundae
44	Jury composition
Unknown	The crime of repetundae

Source: See appendixes A and C.
[a]Dates in parentheses are approximate. See appendix C.

TABLE 7.3 Laws Relating to Voting Assemblies by Year, Latin Name, and Subject, 350–92

Year	Latin Name	Subject
339	Lex Publilia Philone de plebiscitis	The general validity of plebiscites
339	Lex Publilia Philone de patrum auctoritate	Announcement of auctoritas patrum in legislative assemblies
(287)[a]	Lex Maenia de patrum auctoritate	Announcement of auctoritas patrum in electoral assemblies
287	Lex Hortensia de plebiscitis	The general validity of plebiscites
287	Lex Hortensia de nundinis	Legal business on market days
181	Lex Cornelia Baebia de ambitu	The crime of ambitus
159	Lex Cornelia Fulvia de ambitu	The crime of ambitus
(153)	Lex Aelia de modo legum ferendarum	Obnuntiatio in law making assemblies
(153)	Lex Fufia de modo legum ferendarum	Obnuntiatio in law making assemblies
139	Lex Gabinia tabellaria	Voting by written ballot
137	Lex Cassia tabellaria	Voting by written ballot
130	Lex Papiria tabellaria	Voting by written ballot
122	Rogatio Sempronia de suffragiorum confusione	The order of voting in the centuriate assembly
119	Lex Maria de suffragiis ferendis	The pontes used by voters
107	Lex Caelia tabellaria	Voting by written ballot
98	Lex Caecilia Didia de modo legum promulgandarum	The trinundinum and unrelated measures in one proposal

Source: See appendixes A and C.
[a]Dates in parentheses are approximate. See appendix C.

Notes

1. Census figures: Brunt 1971, 13–14. Historians have contested the meaning of the figure of roughly four million returned in 28 BCE. I agree with E. Lo Cascio (following Mommsen) that it represents men only: Lo Cascio 1994 and 1999, 161–164. Brunt (following Beloch) argues that the figure includes women and children as well as

men: Brunt 1971, 113–20. The two positions are summarized in W. Scheidel, *Measuring sex, age, and death in the Roman empire: Explorations in ancient demography*. *JRA* Supp. 21 (Ann Arbor, MI, 1996), 167–68.

2. Population trends: Lo Cascio 1999, 166–71. Let me emphasize that it is almost impossible to distinguish the relative contributions of in-migration, in the shape of enfranchisement, and natural increase to the growth of the Roman citizen population until the first century BCE. For a very complicated and ultimately unsatisfactory effort to do so, with reference to previous efforts, see Brunt 1971, 61–99. Similarly the effects of mortality and out-migration, in the shape of resettlement in Latin colonies, are difficult to weigh. All these factors play a role in the pattern of growth revealed in Roman census enumerations.

3. Livy 22.49.15–17.

4. G. Burton and K. Hopkins, "Political succession in the late republic (249–50 B.C.)," in *Death and renewal*, ed. K. Hopkins (Cambridge, 1983), 31–119.

5. Tribuni aerarii considered equestrians: Brunt 1988, 146, 515–16 (endnote 1), and 210 with n. 40.

6. The progress and changing fortunes of these relative newcomers between the fourth and mid-second centuries have been traced in the important studies of Roman prosopography by Münzer, Scullard, and Badian. See also Hölkeskamp 1987 and David 1996, esp. 99–136.

7. Scullard 1973, 11.

8. Münzer 1920, 46–78.

9. Münzer 1920, 47: Marius was the first consul from Arpinum; the first Paelignian entered the Roman Senate in the reign of Augustus.

10. David 1992.

11. References in chapter 1, note 57. See also T. P. Wiseman, "Domi nobiles and the Roman cultural elite," in *Les "bourgeoisies" municipales Italiennes* (Paris and Naples, 1983), 299–308.

12. Equites equo publico and equestrian class: chapter 5. Equestrian property qualification: Nicolet 1966, 46–68; Brunt 1971, 700, and 1988, 146; Crawford 1974, 623; Wiseman 1971, 66. Nicolet points to the rough equivalence between HS 400,000, known from the lex Roscia of 69, and the 1,000,000 asses of Livy 24.11.7, possession of which obliged a Roman to contribute the upkeep of seven ships' crews for a year in 214. Following Nicolet, Brunt agrees the rating might already have been the equivalent of HS 400,000 at the time of the Second Punic War: Brunt 1988, 146; cf. Wiseman 1971, 66. Or the rating was increased in the second century, when the property qualification of Class 5 was lowered: Brunt 1971, 700. Crawford insists that the equestrian rating of HS 400,000, expressed only in sesterces, was set after the Romans retariffed their coinage around 141.

13. *Lectiones senatus:* Willems 1885, 1.381–95.

14. Revision of 115: Liv., *Epit.* 62; see Wiseman 1971, 5–6. Willems 1885, 1.231, attributes the high number to the presence in the Senate of tribunes, admitted by the lex Atinia, of unknown date but approved, Willems argues, before 115. Since they were not adlected by censors, the censors of this year threw them out.

15. Minor magistrates: Lintott 1999, 137–44.

16. Mommsen, *R.St.* 1.545.

17. A law of 172 restored the right of selection temporarily to the consuls. A lex Rutilia of uncertain date made similar arrangements.

18. S. Demougin, "Notables municipaux et ordre équestre," in *Les "bourgeoisies" municipales italiennes* (Paris and Naples, 1983), 279–307.

19. The animosity to Cn. Flavius, elected aedile in 304, is a notable exception. But his status was at issue, never his competence or knowledge of routine administrative matters.

20. See appendix A.

21. Cato's handbook: E. Rawson, *Intellectual life in the late Roman republic* (Baltimore, 1985), 134–37; K. D. White, "Roman agricultural writers," *ANRW* (1973): 1.4.439–97.

22. Cato's contracts: U. von Lübtow, "Catos leges venditiones et locationi dictae," *Eos* 48.3 (1957): 227–441.

23. The distinctions between tenants and clients holding or using land at the discretion of their patronus are addressed in de Neeve 1984, 13–15, 187–92, and in the recent commentary on de Neeve's work by P. Rosafio, "The emergence of tenancy and the Precarium," in *De agricultura: In memoriam P.W. de Neeve*, ed. H. Sancisi-Weerdenburg et al. (Amsterdam, 1993), 164–76.

24. The "relaxation of ties" in the Middle Republic: Brunt 1988, 414–24.

25. By law and Senate decree: Livy 31.4.1–3, 31.49.5.

26. Strabo 3.5.1; Pliny, *N.H.* 3.77.

27. Plut. *Caes.* 51; Suet., *Iul.* 35.

28. Yakobsen 1999, 78–84.

29. Brunt 1988, 441–42; cf. Yakobsen 1999, 66–71, 78–84.

30. Peasants as clients: P. Garnsey and G. Woolf, "Patronage of the rural poor in the Roman world, " in Wallace-Hadrill, ed., 1989, 153–70.

31. Ambitus generally: L. Fascione, *Crimen e quaestio ambitus nell'età repubblicana* (Milan, 1984); E. Bauerle, "Procuring an election: Ambitus in the Roman republic, 432–49 BC" (Ph.D. diss., University of Michigan, 1990).

32. See briefly Taylor 1960, 15; and A. Lintott, "Electoral bribery in the Roman republic," *JRS* 80 (1990): 7–8. Divisores: Mommsen, *R.St.* 3.196.

33. The problem intensified in the first century when the divisores took money from candidates from other tribes. The best-known illustration derives from Cicero (*Verr.* 1. 23), who accused Verres of summoning the divisores of all the tribes to his house to enlist them to the cause of his candidacy. Most refused. See Taylor 1960, 122, 264.

34. Reform: A. Yakobsen, "Dionysius of Halicarnassus on a democratic change in the centuriate assembly," *Scripta Classica Israelica* 12 (1993): 139–55; L. J. Grieve, "The reform of the comitia centuriata," *Hist.* 34 (1985): 278–309; F. G. B. Millar, "The Constitution of the Roman republic," *JRS* 74 (1984): 1–19; cf. Feig-Vishnia 1996, 159, on the tribal reform of 179 reported in Livy 40.51.9.

35. See chapter 8.

36. So Taylor on law removing citizenship from Tusculani: Taylor 1960, 302.

37. Livy 9.46. On the composition of the groups benefitting from his action (*forensis factio, humiles urbani, turba forensis*) identified in the context of the election of Cn. Flavius as aedile in 304, see Taylor 1960, 134–37.

38. Livy 9.46.

39. Taylor argues that Ap. Claudius was creating political support for himself, and this is what his fellow senators objected to: "A blatant attempt to obtain control of the entire tribal vote was made by the . . . censor . . . when he registered in all the rural tribes lowly men, and particularly freedmen." Taylor 1960, 299.

40. Plut., *Flam.* 18.1.

41. J.-M. David, *La république romaine de la deuxième guerre punique à la bataille d'Actium* (Paris, 2000).

42. Alexander 1998 s.v. Index of Procedures.

43. Livy 7.25.12–13 reports a lex Poetelia de ambitu in the fourth century, which some believe is genuine or at least not unlikely: Hölkeskamp 1987, 28 with n. 133, accepted by Cornell 1995, 469 n. 33.

44. Livy 40.19.11. Penalty: Schol. Bob. 2.78 Stangl.

45. Most recently on the topic see A. Riggsby, *Crime and community in Ciceronian Rome* (Austin, TX, 1999).

46. Lex Repetundarum = *RS* 1 No. 1.

47. "Ea nomina omnia in tabula, in albo atramento script<o>s, patrem tribum cognomenque tributimque d<i>scriptos hab[eto" *RS* 1 No. 1, l. 14.

48. On collegium as priestly college in this context see *RS* 1.98.

49. See Brunt 1988, 194–239.

50. The rogatio Sempronia iudiciaria: Plutarch, *C. Gracch.* 5.2–3; Livy, *Epit.* 60. The law is uncertain (*RS* 1.98).

51. Other arrangements had been made by earlier laws, e.g., the lex Acilia and the lex Servilia Glaucia, but this was the first time the tribuni aerarii were included. See Brunt 1988, 210–11.

52. The voters accepted a fourth public law in 107, presented by the tribune C. Coelius Caldus, extending the written ballot to judicial assemblies deciding cases of perduellio or treason (table 7.3).

53. See chapter 5 on writing and military organization. On the significance of the written ballot in the context of Roman literacy see Harris 1989, 167–70.

54. Cic., *Leg.* 3.15–16, 34–35, is strongly negative; cf. *Leg.* 2.4; *Sest.* 103; and *Planc.* 16, which draw a connection between written ballots and libertas. Libertas in the political arena: C. Wirzubski, *Libertas as a political idea at Rome* (Cambridge, 1950).

55. J. A. O. Larsen, quoted by Taylor 1966, 35: the laws "represent a more general popular movement." Serrao groups the laws with others indicative of "il movimento democratico." F. Serrao, *Classi partiti e legge nella repubblica romana* (Pisa, 1974), 181–93, esp. 184. Harris credits a "democratic-minded legislator" with ensuring that the ballots required only a single letter, "V" or "A," "A" or "C": Harris 1998, 168.

56. J. Hellegouarc'h, *Le vocabulaire latin des relations et des partis politiques sous le république* (Paris, 1963), 313–20.

57. Cic., *Leg.* 3.35; *Lael.* 41; Livy, *Epit.* 54. See E. Badian, "The early career of A. Gabinius (cos. 58)," *Philol.* 103 (1959): 87.

58. Münzer 1920, 219.

59. Cic., *Brut.* 97, 106; *Leg.* 3.35–37; *Sest.* 103; Asc. 216 Stangl.

60. Sources in *MRR* 1.523.

61. Cf. M. Jehne, "Geheime Abstimmung und Bindungswesen in der römischen Republik," *HZ* 257 (1993): 593–613; Yakobsen 1999, 126–33.

62. A. E. Astin, "Roman government and politics, 200–134 BC," *CAH* 8, 2d ed., ed. A. E. Astin (Cambridge, 1989), 193.

63. This is usually understood in terms of the control elite Romans exercised over their clients or other Romans in the voting arena: After the introduction of the written ballot, the citizen could vote as he liked, and his patron knew nothing about it. Taylor 1966, 35. Cf. Bleicken 1975, 278 ff: The ballot laws broke the link between social dependence and electoral behavior.

64. Cf. Yakobsen 1999, 127–29.

65. His criticism conflicts with his neutral assessment of the ballot laws in the speeches. See Millar 1998, 26–27.

66. *Leg*. 3.4.11; cf. 3.17.38–39 on the dangers of the written (and thus secret) ballot.

67. Cornell 1995, 341 (cf. 249) sees the effect of the law as curtailing the power of the patres but maintaining elite control of the process.

68. *MRR* 1.452–53 s.v. Tribunes.

69. Cf. Millar 1998, 204: "the thesis which is put forward in this study is precisely that the most important type of collective decision in Rome was not electoral, but the voting of leges."

70. Livy 7.16.8.

71. Cic., *Dom*. 41; *Sest*. 135 with Schol. Bob. 140 Stangl; *Phil*. 5.3. The same or a second bill also prohibited the passage of laws addressing unrelated issues in the same assembly (per saturam): Cic., *Dom*. 53. The impetus for the bill was most immediately offered by the actions of the tribune Saturninus in presenting one (unadvertised) proposal to a voting assembly on the heels of another. As Taylor notes, nobiles were liable to do the same thing: Taylor 1949, 207 n. 61.

72. Suetonius, *Iul*. 20.1.

73. The bare fact that these boards were put up, whether to advertise laws or anything else, is regularly and frequently attested in the phrase *tabulam proponere*. For discussion see W. Riepl, *Das Nachrichtenwesen des Altertums, mit besonderem Rucksicht auf die Römer* (Leipzig and Berlin, 1913), 336 ff.

74. See chapter 3, note 73.

75. Cicero, *Rab. Post*. 6.14.

76. Edict of 92: Aul. Gell. 15.11.2 (from Suet., *Rhet*. 1.1); Cic., *De Or*. 3.93–95. In 166, the Senate decreed to expel all teachers of rhetoric and philosophy from the city. Greek learning was at that time a dubious commodity, despite the intensity with which Roman senators engaged in its study and, more significantly, its pursuit in the assemblies and law courts of Rome.

77. *ILS* 49.

CHAPTER EIGHT

Crisis and Restoration, 91–70

ROME HAD FACED a grave crisis in Italy during the Second Punic War, but the Italian War fought between 91 and 89 was far more calamitous. In the only war of record the Romans faced a genuine manpower shortage; two consuls in consecutive years were killed in battle; and for the duration senators in Rome laid aside their togas to wear military dress instead. Roman and Italian armies collided in battle after battle, devastating the settled landscape of central and southern Italy as hundreds of thousands died. Writing one hundred years later, the historian Velleius Paterculus reported that three hundred thousand soldiers were lost on both sides; no one has counted the civilian dead.[1] Velleius's contemporary, the geographer Strabo, described ghost towns and villages in Etruria, Campania, and Samnium that were once flourishing market centers and communities.

Inspired by the resolute demands of Rome's Italian allies for full membership in the Roman state, the Italian War was unprecedented, forcing peoples who shared essentially the same cultural expectations and outlook to confront one another with violence. Long association with Rome had shaped Italian cultural expectations and outlook. Together over the centuries Italians and Romans had reached an accommodation to the social and economic changes introduced in Italy by Roman expansion. Together they had conquered the Mediterranean, sharing the experience of Roman military discipline and organization. In the months leading up to the outbreak of hostilities, Romans and Italians had served harmoniously as comrades-in-arms in seven full-strength legions, perhaps as many as forty-two thousand Romans and eighty-four thousand allies, on Roman military fronts around the Mediterranean engaged in the joint venture of world conquest. Elite members of Italian communities and their Roman counterparts enjoyed a common base of wealth, status, and education. Although periodic grants of citizenship had for some time been made to limited numbers of Italian allies, as we have seen earlier, Romans were adamant in their opposition to granting citizenship to all Italians. The Italian War broke out because the fervid pursuit of full Roman citizenship on the part of Rome's allies in Italy met an equally strong opposition on the part of the great majority of Romans. How could the predicament be resolved?

This chapter and the next explore the interaction between public lawmaking and events over a period whose limits are set by significant historical events: the Italian War beginning in 91 and the assassination of Julius Caesar in 44. Conspicuous among the problems of this turbulent period are the widespread frictions accompanying the expanding Roman population. Conspicuous among the attempted solutions are the numerous public law proposals addressing a wide range of issues, the great majority dealing with the restoration of the Roman way as interpreted by different groups of elite Romans. The entry of new citizens into the pool from which political leaders emerged, intensified by the convulsive toll of war and civil war on the political leadership over the decade from 91 to 80, brought about a radical transformation in the numbers and composition of the oligarchy. The struggle to absorb unprecedented numbers of new citizens at all levels had profound consequences for customary ways. This transformation underlay changes in the public lawmaking arena, involving the politically obscure origins of many officeholders who proposed laws, the issues they presented to lawmaking assemblies, and the conduct of the assemblies. Thus a prime factor in these changes was the expansion of the Roman community accompanied by the attenuation of the traditional balance among the various tribes, classes, and status groups.

This transition eventually led to the emergence of a new office, the "dictator for writing the laws and restoring the Roman state," whose holders, first Sulla and next Caesar, for the first time appropriated the process by which the Roman people had acted in unison with duly elected officials to enact legitimate law. The typically infrequent use of the public lawmaking process for resolving otherwise intractable issues and crises was transformed as lawmaking became more frequent and highly politicized. For ambitious leaders, both those new men from less elevated background and men like Sulla, Pompey, and Caesar with a heightened sense of the linkages among different Roman groups, public lawmaking provided an avenue to popular support and political advancement. Concurrently it became increasingly difficult to develop a community consensus on critical issues. Yet the deeply shared Roman faith in public lawmaking remained as Romans struggled initially through the appointment of dictators and later through the acceptance of an emperor to recreate the process as an expression of the collective will of the Roman people.

THE LAWMAKING OF 91–89

As the war progressed it appeared that the allies would destroy Rome. In June of 90, P. Rutilius Lupus, the consul commanding Roman operations along the northern Adriatic coast, died in battle. In the same year, Rome lost the support of her allies, the Etruscans and Umbrians, to the north, as well as some of her allies to the south, who threatened to join in the war on the side of Rome's adversaries, the hostile Apennine tribal groups led by the Samnites and the Marsi. Rome would be surrounded by enemies except for her Latin allies, who shared far deeper ties of culture, language, and kinship with the Romans than any other group in Italy. An indication of Roman fears for the survival of Rome at this time is the highly irregular conscription of several thousand former slaves to garrison towns and cities on the Tyrrhenian coast of Italy, from Cumae to Rome.

At the bleakest moments of this crisis, when the Roman state appeared to be on the brink of destruction, the Romans found deliverance in a law proposed and passed in a public lawmaking assembly. Following the latest disasters in 90, the consul L. Iulius Caesar, commanding Roman operations against the Samnites in southern Italy, returned quickly to Rome, where he held a hurried meeting with the Senate and drafted and promulgated a public law proposal granting citizenship to the Latin allies and to all Italian allies who to date remained loyal.[2] Posted in the Forum and intoned by a herald during the required period of three weeks, the bill was doubtless the object of intense scrutiny and debate by senators and elected officials in the presence of the Roman people in public meetings convened for the purpose. A more effective way to strengthen the loyalties of Rome's wavering allies and appease those Italians who had already committed to revolt was unthinkable.[3] Despite the unusual circumstances and the likely interruption in the regular flow of Roman civic events caused by war throughout Italy, voters assembled in the usual ritualized manner in Rome to make their decision. With so many men under arms the voters on this occasion were fewer in number. Those present nonetheless gave clear voice to the collective will of the Roman people as articulated in the consul's proposal and legitimated through the complicated traditional procedures of the lawmaking process. With no recorded opposition the measure was accepted as law. The dam had burst.[4]

That the most severe crisis to date in Roman history, the Italian War, was resolved by a grant of citizenship proposed and approved at a lawmaking assembly underscores the deep faith shared by all Romans in this key process for establishing consensus in the resolution of an otherwise intractable crisis and underscores the use of such gatherings as instruments of last resort.[5] By 90, both the necessity for opening wide the gates of full citizenship and the magnitude and the complexity of the Roman problems with their Italian allies came into clearer view. Although the Romans were now slowly winning the struggle the costs were extraordinarily high. The death of the consul L. Porcius Cato early in 89 in an unsuccessful engagement against the Marsi was an unexpected blow, but a number of other tensions had been gathering for some time.

Of the sixteen critical issues raised at public lawmaking sessions over the years 91 to 89, as noted in table 8.1, one-quarter (four) were designed to deal with economic issues, two were concerned with matters relating to Roman tribes, and one each covered the assignment of members to the Senate and to jury duty, the foundation of colonies, and the appointment of a special commission of investigation. The repercussions of war with the allies were felt in all areas of life. The cash needs of the Roman state in wartime had resulted in a serious problem of deflation and indebtedness among a population making sacrifices to meet them. After the failure of an earlier law, passed in 91, to manipulate the money supply by adding bronze to silver coins, a public law measure of 89 established a smaller denomination coin, the semiuncial as. That two different tribunes, M. Livius Drusus and C. Papirius Carbo, as noted in table 8.1, took it upon themselves to address the issue in public lawmaking assemblies within two years of each other underscores the pervasiveness of the issue. In an effort to neutralize the adverse effects of the convictions by the standing court created the previous year by the lex Varia de maiestate, designed to root out men of high status complicit in "inciting" the Italians to revolt, M. Plautius Silvanus also carried a measure instituting the selection of fifteen men from each tribe for jury duty in the court. In the future the court's decisions were made by elite Romans drawn from all the tribes. The newly constituted body as a result convicted Q. Varius Hybrida himself, the sponsor of the lex Varia, of diminishing the grandeur (maiestas) of Rome.

But the big issue at public lawmaking assemblies between 91 and 89, as we might imagine, and one covering almost half of all proposed public laws, concerned citizenship grants and the tribal assignments of new citizens. As hoped, the lex Iulia of 90 defused (in the short term) the immediate cause of the Italian War, a demand for parity between the Romans and their Latin and Italian allies or the destruction of Rome. Only the Samnites, Sabellians of Nola in Campania, and Lucanians refused to agree to terms unless the Romans agreed to the return of lands appropriated in the past. In 89, the year after enacting the lex Iulia, the Roman people were asked to extend citizenship to still more inhabitants of Italy, when the tribunes C. Papirius Carbo and M. Plautius Silvanus promulgated a measure granting citizenship to all foreigners resident in Italian towns (*adscripti*) who made declaration before a praetor within sixty days.[6] That same year, in a rare display of common resolve with the tribunes, the surviving consul, Cn. Pompeius Strabo, proposed a bill confirming the citizenship of Gallic towns in Cisalpine Gaul south of the Po River and the Latin status of Gallic towns north of the Po River (table 8.1). The tribune L. Calpurnius Piso carried a bill confirming individual grants of citizenship made in the field by Roman commanders to reward soldiers for bravery.[7] All these measures were enacted as law. Another bill created two new tribes for the new citizens. The lex Iulia of 90 had reportedly created ten new tribes for new citizens while the lex Plautia Papiria of 89 reportedly placed new citizens in eight old tribes.[8] But none of these tribal arrangements was ever implemented, and without membership in a tribe citizenship was of limited value.[9] Unmistakably, although the lex Iulia brought an eventual end to the Italian War, there were deeper divisions in society that continued after the war. In particular the problems accompanying the incorporation of new citizens into tribes and classes were never resolved before the end of the Republic and were the single biggest factor in the continuing civil dissension in the Roman state. Every major struggle or crisis of the period, as we shall see in the following sections, was related in some way to the challenge of absorption.

THE RESTORATIONS OF SULLA, 88 AND 81

The Italian War was the beginning of a long period of civil dissension in Italy. The Italy-wide struggle over citizenship was soon followed by a second episode of civil conflict and war, between 88 and 82, initiated now by the political leaders of Rome. The immediate cause of this second phase of conflict was competition between Rome's two most celebrated military commanders, C. Marius and L. Cornelius Sulla, over the command of a military expedition voted against King Mithridates of Pontus. Eventually, all Italy became involved, a strong indication that the crux of the struggle rested on much deeper and more widespread concerns, as we shall see it did. The second phase of conflict was manifested in several eruptions over related issues, beginning with Sulla's hostile march on Rome in 88 to forcefully invalidate the recent enactment by the tribune P. Sulpicius to replace him in the command against Mithridates with Marius. The next eruption came in 87 with the siege of Rome by the authoritative Marius, five times consul, now nearly seventy years old, supported by the consul L. Cornelius Cinna and the proconsular commander Cn. Pompeius Strabo; the siege was accompanied by the murders of a number of senators. There followed a year of civil war, once Sulla returned from Asia in 83, in which Roman legion battled Roman legion across Italy. Civil war was conducted in a faraway arena as well, the province of Spain, where the Roman commander Q. Sertorius continued the fight until his assassination in 72. Within Italy, Sulla was eventually victorious in 82, whereupon he turned to the task of the restoration of the Roman state. While the civil war of 83–82 is an index of the social and economic upheavals all across Italy in the recent Italian War, to an even greater extent, the entire episode opens an important window onto the predicament of the Roman leadership, nearly two hundred years after the beginning of Roman expansion in Italy, in its efforts to lead a larger and more diversely populated state.

The war against Mithridates brings the predicament of the Roman leadership, now heading a greatly expanded citizen population, into focus. War in Asia was eagerly sought in 88, because of the heavy cost of the Italian War to both Romans and Italians. Throughout the 90s, Mithridates had acted to reassert a local dominion over western Asia, which had been under Roman dominance for nearly one hundred years. While his single most hostile action of record, the murder on the same day by prior arrangement of all Italians in Asia, numbering many thousands, is believed by modern historians to be an apocryphal story, it illustrates the Roman determination to find just causes for war with Mithridates. Given the devastation that the Italian War brought to the monetary economy of Italy, a military campaign, in a region as rich in wealth as western Asia, offered the most promising avenue to restoration that the Romans understood.

Military campaigns often played a significant role in maintaining social order and cohesion in Roman society. Since the First Punic War, military campaigns in sequence offered Romans a quick and direct way of exporting potentially disruptive, armed, and trained fighting men who otherwise might threaten public security. In addition to the obvious incentive of employing the huge numbers of men who had been under arms in the Italian War, a successful military campaign would improve the economic situation by bringing in booty from prosperous cities and regions. The success of the maneuver is reflected in the striking fact that the Romans were far less likely to use public lawmaking assemblies to establish consensus when they were successfully, that is, profitably, fighting abroad.[10] Military success therefore provided a powerful instrument for bringing about stability in Rome. Under the circumstances, the command against Mithridates in 88 held tremendous potential for the man chosen to hold it, if he was successful. Such a man held the key to the restoration of Rome. Such a man was the ideal Roman leader.

The consuls elected for 88 were Q. Pompeius Rufus and the most successful Roman commander of the Italian War, the patrician Sulla. On his election to the consulate Sulla had been assigned the province of Asia with the command against Mithridates, King of Pontus, and was waiting for his army to assemble at Nola when a tribune, the noble P. Sulpicius, presented four controversial bills.[11] Clearly aiming at reconciliation and the restoration of some balance in the expanded Roman community after a trying war, Sulpicius proposed one measure recalling the men exiled following investigation by the court established by enactment in 90 to assign blame in inciting the allies to revolt, another registering new citizens and former slaves throughout all the tribes, and a third setting a lid of two thousand denarii on the amount of money senators could owe. The people's ultimate acceptance of such bills reflected a communitywide desire to integrate some new members in controlled ways, to reconcile old, and to conserve the Senate membership at a time when indebtedness threatened to force the expulsion of some senators. In particular P. Sulpicius, an acutely observant risk taker, had accurately discerned the wishes of Roman equestrians, whose personal attachments and business interests tied them most closely to their counterparts in Latin and Italian towns. But there was unmistakable dissent within the community as well, centering on the registration of new citizens in all the tribes. Violent disagreements marked the public lawmaking sessions at which magistrates and senators publicly aired the arguments about these three proposals of the tribune Sulpicius. The consuls were especially outspoken in their opposition to Sulpicius's measures.

Even more dissension surrounded Sulpicius's fourth and last public law proposal, which transferred the command against Mithridates to the elderly Marius, as another tribune had done twenty years earlier in 107, when the Roman people replaced the proconsular commander and noble Q. Caecilius Metellus Numidicus with the consul and new man Marius in the command against Jugurtha. Notwithstanding his age Marius offered the kind of leadership many Romans, in particular equestrians, thought imperative in the coming war with Mithridates. Ancient and modern commentators on the events of 88 believe that Sulpicius promulgated this particular measure to consolidate equestrian support for the other three. But before any of these measures came before a voting assembly the consuls as per their right declared the suspension of all public business (*iustitium*), thereby neutralizing the tribune's proposed measures by preventing him from formally presenting them to the Roman people. A riot ensued, encouraged by Sulpicius and Marius, in which Romans died and the consuls feared for their lives. The consul Sulla at length canceled the iustitium, Sulpicius convened the voting assemblies, and the measures passed, notwithstanding the displeasure of the consuls.[12]

The reaction to the approval of these measures was unprecedented in Rome. The consul Sulla, holder of Rome's highest elected office, quickly went to Nola and roused the troops, most of them probably Sulla's own veterans from the Italian War, to march against his political enemies in Rome. These citizens under arms had not been on hand in Rome to vote. The troops unanimously resolved to follow Sulla and capped their steadfast loyalty to their commander by murdering the legate, M. Gratidius, who was sent to take command of the army for C. Marius.[13] But most of Sulla's officers withdrew, refusing to serve on a mission of dubious legitimacy despite the authority of the consul's office. The Senate in Rome was likewise horrified and ordered two praetors to Nola to forbid the advance. Abused by the soldiers the praetors were forced to return.[14] At Rome Sulla's army encountered opposition from city inhabitants, who stoned the troops from rooftops, and from men quickly armed and led by Marius against Sulla's legions, to no avail.[15] For the first time a commander entered Rome at the head of his legions without formal dispensation from the Senate or Roman people to do so. Never before had duly enacted laws elicited such a patently lawless response from one of Rome's highest elected officials. A grimmer setback to the legitimate expression by the Roman people of their sovereign wishes was unimaginable.[16]

More was to come as Sulla set out on his own program of restoration. Joining with his colleague Q. Pompeius Rufus, Sulla had the tribune P. Sulpicius killed. The enactments carried by P. Sulpicius were annulled on the grounds that they had been carried during niustitium. Other enemies in the Senate to the number of twelve were killed or exiled, including C. Marius, who fled to Africa.[17] With much of the elite opposition out of the way, Sulla resorted to an immediate use of public lawmaking assemblies. The exile of Marius and others was presented to the Roman people by the consuls and enacted as law. Far more significant were the measures, which offered quite a different version of reconciliation and restoration than the earlier measures of P. Sulpicius.

In particular, in a series of three public law proposals the consuls dramatically changed the entire process of public lawmaking assemblies, which was so critical in establishing consensus. In future all bills presented to the people were to be approved by the Senate. The centuriate assembly, in which citizens assembled in centuries and voted according to wealth, rather than the plebeian tribal assembly was to enact law. The tribunes' authority was to be restricted. Roman voters enacted all three bills as law. Other bills added three hundred new members drawn from the equestrian class to the Senate; founded colonies for veterans; and established that interest payments on debts were to apply to the principal.[18] At this time, if not several years later, Sulla may also have proposed a bill on suretyship (*sponsio*), which appears to address the same issue as P. Sulpicius's measure on senators' debts.[19]

We might wonder at the about-face the approval of these measures presumes on the part of the voting population now in Rome. Were the same voters present? Ancient recorders report that citizens already in Rome when Sulla marched on the city were hostile to Sulla's proposals and that these same citizens later rejected candidates he endorsed at the electoral assemblies.[20] But there was now another group of voters on hand for the lawmaking assemblies, namely, Sulla's soldiers, who formed a significantly large group. Accordingly, at the voting assemblies convened to vote on the consuls' measures, the sovereign will of the Roman people was again duly expressed. Once before, between 123 and 122, had Romans engaged in the kind of "competitive" lawmaking so unmistakable in 88. In one respect, however, the lawmaking of 88 was as unprecedented as Sulla's march on Rome. Never before had Roman consuls turned to public lawmaking on such a scale, under such circumstances, as a deliberate corrective to a prior public and legitimate expression of communitywide wishes. Nor had Roman consuls ever before challenged so many aspects of the public lawmaking process.

Although momentous in their implications for the future, the changes instituted by the consuls were tolerated only briefly in the short term. The presence of so many men under arms especially in the vicinity of Rome had played a crucial role in Sulla's successful effort to restore order to Roman society and to transform the public lawmaking process. Consequently, with Sulla's legions gone, and the legions of Cinna, Marius, and Strabo on hand holding a large number of new citizens, Sulla's laws were annulled in 87 and Sulpicius's laws reenacted. But these changes were also relatively short-lived. Four years later Sulla came back to Italy, and the order first suggested in 88 eventually prevailed in the most lavish outpouring of public laws in Roman history to date.

Bringing the campaign in Asia against King Mithridates to a temporary conclusion, Sulla returned to Italy in 83 at the head of six Roman legions.[21] All Italy mobilized for war. The consuls L. Cornelius Scipio Asiaticus and C. Norbanus and the praetor Q. Sertorius hastily marched their legions south to engage Sulla. Cn. Papirius Carbo was proconsular commander in northern Italy and Cisalpine Gaul, heading an army from what was left of the corps of nearly twenty legions holding by modern count one hundred thousand men, mobilized in 85 and 84 from the new citizen communities of Italy to defend against Sulla.[22] Sulla was joined by elite Romans who had retired to rural estates or fled Italy during his absence: Cn. Pompeius, son of Cn. Pompeius Strabo, and Q. Caecilius Metellus Pius. He also recruited more troops from among new citizens—before returning Sulla had assured the former allies that he would uphold the registration of new citizens begun in the census of 86.[23] From the beginning the war went badly for the consuls and other commanders facing Sulla. Scipio's army deserted him at Teanum and joined Sulla's troops. Norbanus was defeated near Mt. Tifata and withdrew to Capua, where he withstood a siege for a time. Cn. Papirius Carbo was forced back to Rome by Pompey, who had conscripted troops from among his father's veterans in Picenum, where his family's estates were located. Other elite Romans joined Sulla. Sensing disaster, Sertorius, a new man from Sabine Nursia, left Italy with his legions to take up his assigned command in Spain.[24] Civil war continued throughout the remainder of this year and the next as Sulla fought his way north, meeting stout resistance only from former Italian allies, especially Samnites, the core of resistance to Rome during the recent Italian War. Never having formally agreed to terms with the Romans, the Samnites in that earlier war had fought Sulla in many difficult battles. The Roman commanders opposing Sulla found their legions gradually whittled away as troops deserted in numbers to join Sulla. Even so, new consuls were elected in 82 to continue the fight—C. Marius, now twenty-six years old, the son of C. Marius; and Cn. Papirius Carbo, consul for the third time. After a series of reverses Carbo fled alone to the Roman settlements in Africa established almost twenty years before for veterans of his colleague's father. Marius was killed in the siege of Praeneste. With the opposition leadership neutralized, routed, or killed, Sulla was victorious.

To the Romans under arms, Sulla had proven himself to be the right leader. The primary issues of the civil war ensuing from the competition between Marius and Sulla for military command—the rightful leadership of Rome and the restoration of social order—had also reflected powerful divisions on all levels and between groups throughout Italy. Under these circumstances, the extent to which all society, new citizens and old, at some level pulled together to fight the external war is remarkable: all were deeply committed to the war against Mithridates. It is not surprising therefore that ordinary Romans and Italians, who had difficulties in remaining loyal to Cinna and the other rulers in

Rome between 86 and 83, showed no hesitation in joining Sulla before and after he returned from Asia. The pattern of mutiny and desertion that begins with the murder of L. Valerius Flaccus, the "legitimate" commander of the province of Asia by his legate Fimbria, whose troops then deserted to Sulla, and continues with the murder of Cinna by soldiers in 84 comes to typify the last years of the civil war, as legion after legion of fighting men chose to serve with Sulla rather than the commanders who levied them. No other leader, after the death of Marius, had the right stuff in the view of so many.

In Rome, the interrex L. Valerius Flaccus convened the people in the centuriate assembly to enact a public law creating a new position for Sulla and legitimizing his actions to date. By the end of 82, the Roman conqueror of Italy, who had previously been declared an outlaw and seen his consular laws of 88 annulled, entered Rome to assume the unprecedented office of "dictator for writing the laws and restoring the Roman state."[25] Over the next year, Sulla took direct action on a number of fronts. The Samnite troops who had surrendered to him were called to assemble in the place of military levies in Rome, the Villa Publica. Believing that they were to be conscripted for military service about ten thousand Samnites responded. Instead they were massacred, a familiar Roman action regularly taken against her most intractable enemies. In the present case, extermination provided, in the Roman context, a sensible solution to pressing claims for parity within the Roman community by groups the Romans thought they could not absorb. Sulla dealt quickly with Roman adversaries as well. Sulla published a list of names of men who could be killed with impunity, entitling their killers to a reward. At least forty senators, sixteen hundred Roman equestrians, and a total of forty-seven hundred men from these and the next highest property ratings were proscribed, their properties confiscated and sold.[26] Henceforth proscriptions, like foreign wars, served to infuse the treasury with needed capital and provide capital and land for veteran troops.

In addition, Sulla laid penalties on whole communities, fining or retracting citizenship from some towns in Italy that had opposed him; dismantling the walls of others; and confiscating lands and buildings in still others. Some of these measures were presented by the dictator to the people, who enacted them as law.[27] Other steps were actions taken by Sulla as proconsular commander, legitimized by the lex Valeria; still others appear to rest on the annulled laws of 88, which the lex Valeria reinstated. About twenty colonies were established in such towns, and the confiscated lands and buildings, as well as still available public property of the Roman people (ager publicus), allotted to around 120,000 soldiers discharged from Sulla's legions at the end of the fighting and settled in their military units.[28] One ancient recorder, Appian, identifies the primary motivation behind these settlements as Sulla's desire to control Italy with veteran soldiers loyal to him. We discussed similar Roman actions in chapter 4 during the first phase of Roman expansion across Italy, as well as at the end of the Second Punic War. At the same time these settlements provided a rather large number of able men, potentially drifting and dangerous members of an agrarian society, with their primary access to resources—land. Most of these and earlier arrangements in Asia were ratified by the lex Valeria, which made Sulla dictator.

But Sulla's enduring restoration of the core of the Roman community was made through the public lawmaking process, using the centuriate and tribal assemblies.[29] Sulla sponsored at least eighteen laws in 81, shown in table 8.2, the largest number ever promulgated by a single individual to date. Some were revivals of laws he had carried as consul in 88, which had been annulled. All suggest a new use of public lawmaking assemblies in ways that might not have been tolerated by the people at less disrupted times. One of Sulla's laws corrected losses in the Senate by creating new senators from the equestrian class. Such an infusion may have been proposed first by C. Gracchus in 123 for the purpose of indirectly including equestrians on the panel of jurors for the standing court.[30] Gracchus's public law proposal failed in that year, but he carried a similar bill in 122 that added equites equo publico directly to the list of jurors. Another public law known as the lex Cornelia de XX quaestoribus increased the number of quaestors to twenty and made the office of quaestor the office of entry into the Senate. A portion of this enactment is extant on one surviving bronze tablet from the set of tablets on which the law was engraved. Sulla carried other bills relating to offices and officeholding: the ages for holding the quaestorship, praetorship, and consulship were regulated, as were the order in which the offices were held, the interval between the offices, and repetition of the consulship; the tribunes' right of veto was restricted, their right to sponsor law was removed, and their ability to hold further office was removed. Still other laws passed over 81 increased the number of augurs and priests (pontifices) and restored the selection of new members by the college rather than election by the people; and regulated expenditures on luxury items. A public law abolishing the distribution of state-supplied grain restored to tribal leaders, senators, and elected officials an important avenue for enhancing the political support of the majority population.

Among the most consequential of Sulla's "new laws" (leges novae) as Appian describes them, an expression whose meaning we will consider later, were the series of enactments further defining capital crimes previously handled by the urban praetor or tresviri capitales (depending on the status of the miscreant) or the permanent courts de repetundiis and de maiestate and establishing or modifying the courts in which such crimes were investigated. The identification and articulation of crimes against the state had been an emerging concern of the Roman leadership since the mid-second century. Among the listing in table 8.2 were enactments that formed or reformed permanent courts (quaestiones) to consider accusations of extortion (de repetundis) against elected officials and senators; of murder (de sicariis et veneficis); of forgery (de falsis); and of embezzlement (de peculatu).[31] Sulla also carried several laws on maiestas, conventionally translated as treason, and the quaestio de maiestate. In these laws of the "dictator for writing laws and restoring the state," scholars have seen what appears to be, for the first time in Roman history, a systematically thought-out program rather than the customary reactions to immediate situations.[32] It is more likely that the laws were designed to allow Sulla and the Senate to control undesirable members of the Roman elite by accusing them of crimes that could be sustained.

While the aims of this program are complex, let us focus on what it achieved in regard to the most pressing problem of the day for Roman senators, namely, the Roman leadership. The scale of the administrative challenges facing senators and the highest levels of society generally was growing ever larger. At the same time the admission of new citizens into the highest property classes had intensified the native competitiveness of the governing classes. Now elite Romans were forced to face these issues in a distressingly direct way in consequence of the exceptionally high mortality rate among senators and men of equestrian rating during both the Italian War and the civil conflict of the 80s. Casualties during the Italian War included an unreported, though probably high, number of senators and equestrians. The number multiplied in 88 when Sulla marched on Rome, murdered some men, including P. Sulpicius, and exiled others, including Marius. The next year, Marius and Cinna marched on Rome and proceeded to murder senators and equestrians who had opposed them. While the reports of the massacres are probably exaggerated by their source (ultimately Sulla's memoirs), we nonetheless know the names of about ten senators who died. Thereafter new senators were probably added by the censors elected in 86, L. Marcius Philippus and M. Perperna; but Sulla certainly had many of these senators killed in 82 when he again entered Rome.[33] Unlike Marius and Cinna, Sulla devised a legal sanction for his vengeance, the proscription list. As a result of the accumulation of combat casualties and murders throughout the decade between 91 and 81, both the three-hundred-man Senate and the class of equites equo publico were depleted and undermanned.[34]

New members had to be found. We have seen Sulla's solution in regard to the Senate, a public law as consul in 88 adding three hundred equites to the Senate. While this law was almost immediately annulled, Sulla then revived it as dictator and it was enacted in 81, in the lex Cornelia iudiciaria. To be sure, the Senate held fewer than three hundred senators by this time, thanks to Sulla's proscriptions, so that when Sulla expanded the Senate membership by adlecting three hundred equites equo publico, he presumably also adlected an indeterminate number of equites to bring the Senate up to its new full complement of six hundred.[35] As for the class of equites equo publico, enough men of equestrian rating were available to keep the numbers up: The proscriptions enriched some men at the expense of others. Sulla's grant of citizenship optimo iure to ten thousand freed slaves of the proscribed and his land grants to the veterans of twenty-three legions are but two of the best-known instances of the redistribution of resources. New equites equo publico and thus potentially the replacements for the senators were mostly equestrians of obscure background and municipal origin; some were new citizens.[36]

This second, successful attempt by Sulla to bring three hundred equestrians into the Senate addressed directly and indirectly two immediate concerns: the depleted ranks of the Roman Senate as a result of war and the controlled entry of new citizens in the highest classes. Since each man selected was approved by the vote of the Roman tribes, Sulla created a new aristocracy, drawn from the equestrian class and validated man by man by the Roman tribes.[37] Other bills relating to offices and officeholding exhibit similar concerns. The lex Cornelia de XX quaestoribus, noted previously, made this office the regular entry into the Senate and increased the number of annually elected quaestors to twenty. On this basis it has been estimated that twenty vacancies occurred yearly in the six-hundred-member Senate and that Sulla's reform of the quaestorship was intended to maintain the Senate at strength.[38] Such a law removed the need for the customary revision of the Senate list (*lectio senatus*), a review of the senators' qualifications and character conducted by the Roman censors every five years before the interruptions of the previous decade.

Although the fighting men of Italy made an unequivocal commitment to Sulla, the dilemma of leadership continued, for Sulla himself and all Roman leaders. Efforts to resolve the dilemma took many forms, some more deadly than others. One solution, as we have seen, was extermination. The murder of thousands of Roman senators and equestrians by Sulla in 82, as well as many more thousand Samnites, and Sulla's extensive reprisals against Etrurian and other towns reflect a general determination to rid Roman society of difficult elements at all levels. In a more benign fashion, the determination to prevent the increase in citizen numbers from upsetting the traditional relationship between groups is reflected in the efforts to keep new citizens from voting by preventing their registration in property classes and controlling the tribal vote. Sulla's attempts to deal directly with these issues exacerbated the difficulties in maintaining the Roman way, at a time when the death of many Romans in war necessitated the creation of a renewed Roman political aristocracy and the solution to the Italian War had in fact brought about an impressive expansion on all levels of society.

The repercussions of Sulla's program continued to pound at the highest levels of society over the next thirty years. Immediate crises involved the social integrity of the leadership. In 77, the proconsular commander of Transalpine Gaul, M. Aemilius Lepidus, after failing as consul in 78 to undo the changes instituted by the laws of Sulla through his own proposals of law to restore the powers of the office of tribune and compensate men whose lands had been confiscated by the measures of Sulla and to restore the grain dole, attempted to do so by force of arms. Marching on Rome with his legions in 77 he was defeated by Q. Lutatius Catulus. Lepidus escaped to Sardinia, accompanied by many of his soldiers, but died there. The soldiers then followed his legate M. Perperna Vento to Spain, where they joined Q. Sertorius. Between 77 and 72, the civil war concluded in Italy by 81 continued in Spain, as Sertorius battled ably against the successive Roman commanders sent from Italy, Q. Caecilius Metellus Pius and Cn. Pompeius Magnus. War ended only when Sertorius was murdered by one of his officers in 72. Before his death, thousands of Roman troops were called to fight under the commanders sent from Rome.[39] In these actions and in the loyalties of the ordinary Roman soldiers who participated in them, it is obvious that legitimate leadership continued to be a critical issue. Leadership would continue to be the prime divisive issue in the Roman state down to the creation of the position of emperor by the adopted son of Julius Caesar, C. Julius Caesar Octavianus, after his victory over M. Antonius at Actium in 31.

More significantly for the future of the Roman public lawmaking process, Sulla's use of the lawmaking capacity of the Roman people signifies an awareness on the part of Sulla of the political potential of public lawmaking assemblies. Sulla clearly equated his public law proposals and his own political advancement with the advancement of the Roman system. This was something probably all political leaders had always done; the performance of the "popular" tribunes C. Flaminius in 232, Ti. Gracchus in 133, even more his brother C. Gracchus in 123–122, and L. Appuleius Saturninus in 103 and 100 are cases in point. But earlier, elected officials were kept in line by the overwhelming power of the collective body of Roman senators. Now with Sulla, the attenuation of the traditional system made a more directly political use of public lawmaking possible. At the same time, the dramatically increasing frequency of public lawmaking assemblies—eighteen in 81 alone—involving Roman participation for most of the year politicized the process to an extent never before possible. Like their leaders, Romans increasingly came to see public lawmaking assemblies as a public instrument of value in the day-to-day struggles within Rome.

NEW CITIZENS, 91–70

Over most of their history, some Romans were hostile to newly made citizens, fighting to exclude or at least contain such men even when the community as a group was deliberately bringing them in. The restricted tribal assignments were directed not only against ex-slaves but also against Latins, who voted in a single tribe chosen by lot, and particularly against the thousands of Latins and Italians made citizen in 90 and 89. The fierce opposition displayed toward the tribal enrollment of new citizens provides a measure of the threat to the Roman system induced by the challenge of new members at all levels. Without an understanding of the attachments linking ordinary people and Roman leaders, how could new citizens participate? Hence at all times the most apparent, because the most articulate, locus for hostility to newcomers was the Roman leadership. In the second century, leaders at times articulated their fears in public oratory, stridently opposing any influx of newcomers into the Roman citizen body on grounds that old citizens would find their perquisites diminished and their customary arenas overrun. Arguing against a bill proposed by C. Gracchus in 122 to extend Roman citizenship to allies, the consul C. Fannius warned that city residents would be crowded out of their meetings, games, and festivals if the law was approved.[40] They had to guard their votes against the Latins and Italians, who would outnumber them if granted the citizenship. A similar sentiment surfaces two generations later, in the consul Cicero's speech *De Lege Agraria* 2, delivered in 63. Cicero advised city dwellers that it was not in their interests to forsake the perquisites of city life for a plot of land. Whether these expressions accurately reflect the fears of ordinary Romans we are not likely to know for sure. That they were aired at such events suggests that they were somewhat popular on lower levels. Certainly, they reveal a rather consistent position on the part of Roman leaders over a long period.

Actual resistance to new citizens took different forms and attained different levels of hostility depending on the particular group. Its primary expression was the legal restriction of the new citizen's participation in community life. Continuous efforts were made to contain new citizens, who were variously Latins, ex-slaves, or Italians, through restrictions on tribal assignments. The question of inclusion, and who to include, went back and forth over a long period. By the late second century, the threatened impact of massive numbers of new citizens—almost triple the number of old Romans, roughly one million voting men—rippled through Roman society on all levels, creating a considerable dilemma for Romans. On the highest levels of society, the issue of absorption entailed more precisely the rightful leadership of Rome, brought increasingly into question as a result of the continuous admission of Latins and Italians into Roman citizenship and the highest property classes. But on lower levels, the issue entailed the customary relationship between the leaders and the led, a far more troublesome matter to political leaders.

In turns some Romans worked to ensure control of society by the right sort of men, the *boni* and *optimates* in Rome's political vocabulary, and to rid the community of undesirable members, while other Romans worked to reestablish community cohesion through the recall of exiles, the accommodation of new citizens, and the purification of the ranks of the leadership. Some Romans were fiercely resistant to the idea of incorporating Latins and allies, while others were fiercely determined to incorporate them. Before the Italian War, a tribune, Minicius, probably in 91, carried a bill assigning the children of marriages between a Roman and someone from a group without the "right of legal marriage" (ius conubii) to the status of the non-Roman.[41] There must have been a sufficient number of such individuals to make their citizen status a matter of concern. The efforts, in 91, of the tribune M. Livius Drusus to incorporate the Latins and allies through a promised bill, which was never promulgated, exemplifies both the general efforts of Roman leaders of the latter group over the previous generation or two as well as their acceptance of the realities of the Roman state in Italy.[42] Drusus's murder in 91, by an unknown assailant, followed by the Roman Senate's immediate annulment of his successful enactments—a sequence of events that sparked the Italian War—underscore the passions of the group of Romans opposed to incorporation. The anticipated bill and eventual murder of M. Livius Drusus in 91; the commission of investigation established by the enactment of Q. Varius Hibrida in 90 to set up a special commission of investigation to prosecute senators and equestrians who encouraged allies to revolt; and the enactment of P. Sulpicius to recall men who had been exiled by the commission are all episodes in the struggle between proponents of community purification and community cohesion.[43] The issue surfaces most overtly, of course, in 91 with the Italian demand, backed by arms, for incorporation.

Although the crisis over inclusion in the Roman state as we have seen was resolved through the lex Iulia of 90, the dilemma involving the Roman leadership was far from over for Romans. Throughout the decade from 91 to 81, a time of almost continuous civil conflict and dissension, beginning with the Italian War and ending with the civil war fought between L. Cornelius Sulla and his Roman opponents, the fundamental point at issue was the absorption of new citizens into the Roman state. Absorption continued to occupy Romans not only across the decade to 81 but down to the end of the Republic, posing a considerable dilemma for elite Romans, to which we shall return. Suffice to say here that the Romans resolved it only at the expense of the Roman Republic.

Here let us focus on the recourse to lawmaking assemblies to facilitate the absorption of new citizens into the Roman state between 91 and 70. Table 8.3 collects the public law proposals concerning new citizens over the period. In the period of the Italian War, the primary battleground for the tensions surrounding the absorption of new citizens was the public lawmaking assembly, convened repeatedly over a five-year period to address the registration of new citizens in tribes and property classes. In the past, tribal assignment was determined by statute only when the assignment of marginal members of the Roman community was at issue, ex-slaves in particular. But after 90, when as a result of the lex Iulia the new citizens would outnumber the old by about two to one, the question of tribal assignments for new citizens was sufficiently explosive to require the intervention of public lawmaking assemblies.[44] While sheer numbers, in and of themselves, were relatively unimportant in determining the tribal vote, as we have seen, they were critical to the customary relationship between tribal leaders and tribesmen and in particular to the ability of tribal leaders to focus the loyalties of tribesmen on the right decision to be made in electoral or lawmaking assemblies. If all tribes were flooded with large numbers of new citizens the traditional balances essential for the effective working of the assemblies could be lost.

Accordingly, the Romans initially envisioned restrictive tribal assignments. The lex Iulia of 90 probably registered new citizens—Latins and allies who had remained loyal to Rome—in ten new tribes (table 8.3).[45] The lex Plautia Papiria of 89, which extended citizenship to adscripti, does not appear to have addressed tribal assignments. But another tribune, L. Calpurnius Piso, may have proposed the creation of two new tribes, presumably to hold new citizens (table 8.3).[46] Over the next three years there followed a public debate that nearly destroyed the Roman state. The restrictive new tribes (because they would have voted after the thirty-five existing tribes) were eliminated in 88 by the tribune P. Sulpicius, who enacted a bill permitting all new citizens and ex-slaves to register in all the tribes (table 8.3).[47] Within a short time the consuls of 88, L. Cornelius Sulla and Q. Pompeius Rufus, rescinded this and other statutes brought by P. Sulpicius. They carried further measures, as we shall see, that controlled the admission of new citizens in another way. The consul Cinna in 87 presented the matter again (table 8.3), unsuccessfully; his proposal was vetoed. When he pushed ahead with the voting assembly, his colleagues for the first time in Roman history, sent armed men into the Forum to scatter the voters.[48] The episode precipitated the civil war of 87–86. But when Cinna and Marius returned to Rome the public laws of Sulla and Pompeius were in their turn rescinded and the measures of Sulpicius reinstated. Thereafter the question of tribal assignment was resolved not by lawmaking assemblies but by the censors, the Roman Senate, and the key figure in the decline of the Republic, L. Cornelius Sulla, consul in 88 and dictator in 82–81.

During Sulla's absence from Italy, the question of the incorporation of new citizens at the lower levels had continued to dominate the concerns of the rulers of Rome. Indeed, although the immediate causes of the civil conflict between 88 and 82, stemming from competition between two Roman leaders over a military command, appear on the surface to be unrelated to the Italian War, the fundamental point at issue had been the incorporation of new citizens in the Roman state. Censors were elected in 86, the first in twenty-nine years (since 115), who appear to have registered new citizens throughout all the tribes. And reportedly by Senate decree in 87 the new citizens were permitted to vote.[49] That all it took to implement the intention of the lex Julia was a decree of the Roman Senate, not another public law seems surprising. After all, the lex Iulia redirecting Roman goals on granting citizenship had been made, and the flurry of public law proposals concerning tribal enrollments were advanced and decided in an atmosphere of civil war between 90 and 86. Even so it is a good indicator of unanimity among the current crop of senators about allowing new citizens to exercise their power as voters.

However, Sulla clearly considered this solution to the question of incorporation untenable. Notwithstanding his earlier assurances to the former allies that he would accept the registrations of 86—which conveyed an implicit recognition of all the rights and privileges of full citizenship, in particular voting—he effectively nullified them through a set of revolutionary changes involving Rome's electoral and legislative assemblies. Specifically he blocked the traditional avenues to effective citizen participation as voters in the centuriate assembly and in the plebeian tribal assembly, the chief lawmaking assembly, through restrictions on the censorship and the tribunate. Without recourse to a lawmaking assembly, the office of censor was simply set aside: no censors were elected in 81, the next regular census, nor were any censors elected again until 70. In this way Sulla thwarted any further registration of new citizens in Rome's property classes and perhaps also in the tribes at the regular time of the quinquennial census. It was a deliberate move, scholars believe, calculated to slow the entry of qualified Italians into the equestrian class and Class 1 (since only the censors in Rome could assign new citizens to a class) and thence into the corresponding voting centuries of the centuriate assembly.[50] Registration in a property class was a prerequisite for voting in Rome's centuriate assembly. It was likely also to hinder the enrollment of new citizens in the tribes and consequently their ability to vote in tribal assemblies.[51] Although it is sometimes believed that tribal assignments were made locally, that is, automatically, it is hard to see how new Romans could vote unless new tribal leaders were in place in the tribal government to confirm them as tribe members in Rome. No doubt the local supervision of the tribes was in disarray.[52] In any case, even if new citizens were able to vote in the full tribal assembly and so enact law or elect low-ranking officials under the leadership of consuls or praetors, they were excluded from voting in the centuriate assembly.

Equally damaging to the ability of former allies to fully exercise the rights and privileges of citizenship were Sulla's innovations in regard to the tribunate. As we have seen in 88, Sulla carried bills placing stringent restrictions on the office of tribune and on the functions of the plebeian tribal assembly. Specifically, the lawmaking capacity of the officers of the plebeian assembly, the tribunes, was eliminated and the primary organ for enacting public law, the plebeian tribal assembly, was replaced by the full tribal and centuriate assemblies (table 8.2).[53] Annulled in 88, the laws were restored in 81 (table 8.2). All lawmaking business was henceforth conducted in the centuriate assembly or the tribal assembly convened by consuls or praetors.[54] Concurrently, Sulla's restrictions on the tribunate, in particular the removal of the tribunes' authority to bring bills to the people, neutralized the communitywide feature of public lawmaking by tribunes as well. Indeed, only 14 public law proposals, or 6 percent of the total number (230) across the period 91–44, were presented to the people in the years 79–70 (table 8.4), in assemblies convened by praetors or consuls. Thus the effective incorporation of new citizens at all levels, to the point where they could exercise their power as voters in lawmaking assemblies, was slow in coming. While new citizens were promised registration in all the thirty-five tribes in 86, the whole process of formal incorporation through tribes and property classes was put on hold until 70.

The reluctance to grant citizenship to the allies until there appeared to be no other solution and the reluctance to allow former allies to fully participate in voting assemblies after 90 reflected deep-seated and widespread fear as to the impact of the absorption of such vast numbers of new citizens on the society. There was a reality here. With the inclusion of 740,000 Italian and Latin allies, the Roman male citizen population of roughly 394,000 would jump in principle to 1,134,000, some of whom sought access to elite levels, and now included dozens of diverse groups.[55] In fact, when the censors of 70 held an enumeration at last of citizens, old and new, 910,000 were registered, up from the 463,000 Romans who had presented themselves before the censors in the previous census of 86, attesting to the widespread interest on the part of new citizens to present themselves before the censors in Rome.[56] The fundamental problem in bringing masses of new citizens into Roman society, some of whom qualified for higher status, was how to do it while maintaining the traditional Roman way, especially the balance between elements that allowed the development of a community consensus best seen in times of crisis in the public lawmaking process. Bringing new citizens, especially in such large numbers, into the various tribes threatened the status of the elites within their primary political base of power, the tribes. Expanding the various hierarchies of elites further shook the nexus between political leaders, tribal leaders, and tribesmen. The various crises that unfolded over the years from 91 to 44—the crisis of military leadership of 87, the civil war of 83–81, the attempted coup of M. Aemilius Lepidus in 78, the slave rebellion led by Spartacus between 73 and 71, and the Catilinarian conspiracy of 63—were all in one way or another an outcome of the failure to accord full citizenship to qualified newcomers and to effectively manage their absorption into Roman society.

Over these same years, as shown in table 8.4, public lawmaking events reached the unprecedented average of almost five laws per year as Roman lawmakers sought to restore the rapidly disappearing political balance. For hundreds of years such assemblies had been used successfully to develop a community consensus on controversial issues. This time, however, the outcome would be different: the more legislation was passed the more complicated and intractable became the problem. The problems accompanying the incorporation of new citizens after the Italian War were never resolved before the end of the Republic and were the single biggest factor in the continuing civil dissension in the Roman state.

CONSEQUENCES OF THE SULLAN RESTORATION

Sulla's program of "restoration" had produced tensions at all levels of society, centering on access to resources in Italy. The heavy reparations levied on some communities by Sulla, including the confiscation of private and municipal property, mostly in central and south Italy, and the settlement of thousands of soldiers in colonies imposed on penalized towns in the same areas, as well as the proscriptions of individual Romans and Italians, intensified the disruption of the war itself, extending its impact across two generations. Some already wealthy, elite members of Roman society profited from confiscations in the short term. Even nonelite members of society might profit, like Chrysogenus, the ex-slave of Sulla who made millions by buying up confiscated estates at a fraction of their value and reselling them at full value. The approximately 120,000 veterans who received land allotments appear to have benefited in the short term. Some doubtless even thrived. Yet chronic indebtedness among the rural population of Italy, which becomes increasingly evident after 81, combined with settlement on marginal lands made success an elusive outcome for veterans. In the long run these men faced the same challenges as other small landholders. We may imagine that survival was difficult for anyone put down in a new environment where the land was mediocre, even if it was possible to create familiar networks of cooperation—a likely possibility since veterans were settled in their military units. The contemporary historian Sallust's contention that Sulla's veterans, settled on lands in Picenum, Etruria, and Apulia, were impoverished by 63 seems plausible.

Debt in fact appears to have been a constant companion to many Romans, especially rural inhabitants, in large part because of the restricted cash flow in a limited monetary economy. When available stocks of bronze, silver, and gold were used up, especially in payment of desperate military endeavors, difficult times followed for all. Major wars whose successful conduct or conclusion failed to bring gold and silver into the Roman treasury were followed by widespread indebtedness among rich and poor, urban and rural dweller alike. This was true not only of the civil wars of 91–89 and 87–81 but of most wars fought between the 130s and the 60s. There was little loot except for what infantrymen could carry off themselves from pillaged villagers and townsmen. The public outrage at the disappearance of the gold from Tolosa, in Gaul, in 104 while en route to Rome, reportedly into the pockets of the commander Q. Servilius Caepio, provides an insight into the public interest in loot.[57] The cost of continuous war, accompanied by fewer war profits, introduced a new level of indebtedness into Italy. Rural inhabitants of Italy, old and new citizens alike, experienced debt and debt bondage. In turn, while rural land tenure continued to be insecure anyway after the lex Agraria of 111, which had primarily confirmed the status quo of 123, the reparations Sulla demanded from Italian communities especially in Etruria, Picenum, and Apulia had again raised the question of access to ager publicus. The accumulation of wealth in the hands of senators and a growing number of men with the equestrian rating further intensified tensions within the uppermost stratum of Roman society. Concurrently, since the civil wars of 91–81, new citizens had been frustrated in the full realization of Roman citizenship by barriers preventing their registration in property ratings and tribes. Thus, both new and old citizens numbered among the rural inhabitants of Italy had been increasingly distanced from the rewards of Roman empire.

As before, but to an even greater extent, military service continued to be the chief route to survival for all affected inhabitants of Italy threatened by debt or subsistence crises. In 86, Cinna conscripted one hundred thousand Italians. Cn. Pompeius Magnus raised three legions in 83 from the rural inhabitants of Picenum, clustered on the marginal lands of his family's vast estates. Throughout the period between 80 and 50, the Romans, now including Italians, were deeply committed to external wars, from Spain to Asia—paradoxically, in view of both ongoing internal crisis as well as the particularly heavy losses in manpower during the Italian War. Before 58, the largest commitment of troops was found in the eastern Mediterranean, primarily fighting Mithridates, King of Pontus, with whom war had resumed in 74. In 67, Rome also mounted a major campaign against the pirates based in Cilicia, placing Cn. Pompeius Magnus in command. The following year they rolled this campaign into an all-out Roman bid to annex the eastern Mediterranean with its untold wealth. In 58, Rome mounted a similar assault on Gaul, under the leadership of C. Julius Caesar, while M. Licinius Crassus in 54 led an attack on Parthia. On average, one hundred thousand Romans marched to war every year between 80 and 50.[58] More legions were conscripted between 79 and 65 than at any other time in the history of the Roman Republic.

Now, however, military service did little to alleviate the situation. The social churning resulting from many departures from Roman society, an estimated 272,000 men from 83 to 81 alone, as well as the constant drain across the period, was intensified by combat casualties. Several years witnessed heavy losses in battle. In 74, M. Cotta was defeated by Mithridates at Chalcedon by land and by sea, with reported losses of 5,300 (Memnon) and 4,000 (Plutarch) men. In 73 and 72, the slaves in Italy vanquished six Roman armies, including those of the two consuls of 72 and a proconsul. The number of casualties is unreported, but successive defeats at the hands of slaves undoubtedly brought considerable shame to Rome. In 67, Mithridates destroyed a Roman army in Pontus, killing 7,000 Romans, including 150 centurions and 24 tribunes. In 53, Gauls ambushed a Roman army, killing the two commanders. Also in 53, in the biggest single Roman defeat of the era, Crassus lost 30,000 men—20,000 killed and 10,000 taken prisoner—by the Parthians at Carrhae. Many more thousands died in the civil wars between 50 and 46.[59] While individuals might indeed benefit from war, Roman society as a whole did not.

What routes to survival other than military service attracted impoverished Romans? We might expect a surge of migration to market towns or to Rome. But migration always appears selective of those a notch or two from the very bottom of society. As noted in chapter 4, during the initial phase of Roman expansion many displaced Italians seem to have stayed in their regions of origin: when the best arable land was taken by the more powerful, the powerless moved to marginal lands. So, too, in later centuries. In 81, when similar disruptions occurred in Etruria, the original Etruscan inhabitants of the Apennine town of Faesulae, who were dispossessed of their land and citizenship by Sulla in favor of his veterans, remained in the area. They then rose against the new inhabitants in 78.[60] How and where they had survived in the meantime is a matter for speculation: probably on the marginal mountain highlands or in swamps and marshes, as had been the case in other parts of Europe. But clearly, they had stayed put in the region. The impoverished citizens of Etruria and Picenum, whose numbers were large enough in 63 to provide Catiline with a base of support, also stayed on the land. The praetor Q. Caecilius Metellus Celer conscripted troops from the ager Picenus and ager Gallicus in 63.[61] Among them were Sullan veterans who though deeply indebted were nonetheless still in possession of their lands. The continued existence of small landholdings in Italy, which point to the continued presence of independent or tenant farmers, has been amply confirmed by archeological excavation. The conclusion that long-distance migration in this period was an option for specific individuals with particular experiences, and was not the rule for all Italians, is unavoidable.[62]

The divisions within the Roman leadership presented another alternative for hard-pressed Romans in the years between 80 and 50, namely, rebellion. While military service had become a major unifier of Italy by the time of the Italian War, service had also intensified the gap between elite and nonelite members of the wider society. Again during the Roman civil wars, both in the period from 87 to 80 and in the period from 50 to 44, soldiers in opposing legions exhibit confusion about "legitimate" causes and leaders, largely because their own interests converge but jointly diverge from the elite-centered interests of many of their leaders from the Roman aristocracy. The political competitiveness in particular of elite Romans appears to be a concern unique to that group. To be sure, the loyalty of a legion to its commander was often unshakable. But such steadfastness depended absolutely on the commander.

Notwithstanding the divergent interests of the leaders and the led, both loyalty and leadership in Roman society had a strong personal dimension.

Some leaders accordingly inspired strong support. In 78, L. Aemilius Lepidus capitalized on the legacy of disruption and debt in his efforts to bring a new leadership to the helm in Rome, first through his public law proposals and, when they failed, through war. The crisis of continuing dissension in Italy was compounded between 73 and 71 when a slave revolt led by the Thracian Spartacus broke out in Italy. Italy again had a grave need for troops. In 73, the armies formed by Spartacus around a core of slave gladiators and prisoners from Capua defeated three hastily conscripted Roman armies. In 72, the slaves again defeated the armies of the two consuls as well as two legions in Cisalpine Gaul commanded by C. Cassius Longinus, consul in 73. The success of these slave armies, composed mostly of Gauls and Germans, in maintaining themselves in the regions of Italy through which they passed as well as in attracting ever more fighters attests to the number of desperate Romans in the rural areas willing to join Spartacus. Something had to be done. A large army was formed. M. Licinius Crassus Dives, who had been praetor probably in 73, was placed in command as proconsul. When two legions of this army, commanded by Mummius, were again routed by slaves Crassus was provoked to order the decimation of a cohort of the survivors, an extreme punishment last used in the third century. Under Crassus's leadership, the Romans concluded the war against Spartacus in six months, in late 72 and early 71. At the end the Senate instructed Cn. Pompeius Magnus, holding a proconsular command in Spain, to return to Italy to join his army to Crassus's.[63] Although Spartacus was killed, and a grim public display was made of some of the slave survivors, the rural poverty that aided Spartacus's revolt in Italy persisted.

In 63, L. Sergius Catilina drew on the same group of impoverished men again, specifically "allies," according to Dio, that is, new citizens, and "disaffected Romans." When forced to leave Rome he headed for Faesulae in Etruria, where he took over the legion already raised by an ex-centurion. Official fears of the potential danger from armed slaves were again roused: Capua was garrisoned to protect the gladiator schools lest Catiline's supporters were to free the slaves there.[64] The praetors M. Bibulus and Q. Tullius Cicero were sent to the central Apennines and southern Italy respectively to discourage the Paeligni and Bruttii from similar actions.[65] The depth of commitment on the part of the men who joined Catiline is clearly revealed when Sallust, the historian of the uprising, marveled that not a man ran from the battlefield at the final encounter.

The failure of these uprisings is a measure of the Romans' success even now at reaching generally acceptable solutions to societywide crises in public lawmaking assemblies. As we shall see in the next chapter, dedicated and ambitious Roman leaders initiated significant lawmaking efforts in order to ameliorate conditions and promote the advancement of the Roman system. Thus lawmaking itself, requiring at least temporary migration to Rome to attend public lawmaking sessions, presented yet another, countervailing alternative for hard-pressed Romans.[66] The convergence on Rome of voters who accepted the increasing politicization of the process coincided with the politicization by Roman leaders of associations (collegia) and "clubs" (sodalitates), structures that had emerged long before in Roman society in response to the social needs of an expanding, mobile population.

Some impoverished Italians and Romans turned to outlawry to survive. Banditry as an alternative means of survival was evidently characteristic of Etruria, the region that had suffered the harshest punitive measures imposed by Sulla in 81 and had led the response to Aemilius Lepidus's call to arms in 78 and Catiline in 63. So common was banditry in the central region of Italy, home to the estates of wealthy men, that M. Terentius Varro took it for granted as an ordinary hazard of plantation farming in his handbook on farming, intended as a guide perhaps for his wife, Fundania. Banditry became more common throughout the Italian countryside in the latter part of the last century, providing a refuge and a means of survival for debtors or men from communities whose territory had been appropriated alike. After the failure of Spartacus's rebellion and Catiline's revolt, remnants of those armies still roamed less populated regions of Italy. In 60, the proconsul C. Octavius, on his way to his province in Macedonia, "mopped up" some of these outlaws in Apulia. In 59, the Senate initially allotted as provinces to the consuls Caesar and Bibulus (very much against their liking) the "woods and trails" (*silvae callesque*) of Italy, suggesting that there was a need for policing outlaws in remote regions. But before now, the growing scale of piracy throughout the eastern Mediterranean in the 80s and 70s attests to an even more widespread dislocation of peoples as well as another alternative for desperate men. The pirates of Cilicia welcomed the displaced men of Italy as eagerly as men from other regions around the Mediterranean. Pompey's resettlement of vanquished pirates in 67 as well as the increasing organization and discipline of pirate raiders suggest that they included a high number of Romans and Italians.[67]

In short, the economic crises and civil dissension in Italy arising from the incorporation of new citizens, the impact of the large-scale involvement in the military, the poor return in the form of booty for investments in military campaigns, and the impressive loss of life in war permeated to all levels of society through Italy. But to our wonder, the evidence clearly shows that masses of voters still displayed the same respect as ever for the process of public lawmaking when it came to correcting some of these societywide ills. The potential of public law to redistribute resources was especially important. Public laws established the largest land grants to soldiers, for instance, in which soldiers of the same unit passed from camp to colony or individual allotment: those of Sulla in 81 and Julius Caesar between 47 and 44. Sulla gave allotments in twenty-three colonies to approximately 120,000 soldiers; Caesar gave land grants to approximately 50,000.[68] In 44, the soldiers to whom land had been given were quartered in temples in Rome, waiting to go. In preparation they had sold their possessions and had chosen group leaders from their number to lead each group to the colonies. Sadly, when Caesar was assassinated in March their consternation was great lest his successors would annul the grant—so accustomed had Romans become to the evanescence of public law.[69]

As we shall see next, the customary avenue for resolving the inevitable tensions, public lawmaking assemblies, for the first time were undergoing a related transformation at the hands of a new aristocracy. Although the impetus for the new, more immediate use of the process seems to have come from the top, all Romans eventually shared in the new perception of the immediate political uses of public lawmaking.

THE NEW LEADERSHIP AND THE LAWMAKING OF 70

When Pompey first entered the Senate on becoming consul in 70 at the age of thirty-six, he petitioned his friend, the scholarly senator of praetorian rank M. Terentius Varro, to prepare a handbook of senatorial responsibilities so that he would know what senators did and how they did it.[70] The explanation for this surprising unfamiliarity with a Roman senator's scope of duties and their execution, on the part of a man from a consular family, was his unanticipated, utter avoidance of the traditional training grounds for the Roman Senate: the junior legal commissions and elective offices. Pompey's early career was exclusively military; and even in this regard his career path was exceptional, for after his initial customary military service on his father's staff during the Italian War, circumstances not only prevented him from presenting his candidacy for one of the twenty-four elective military tribunates but made his appointment to any of the other military tribunates politically risky. In fact, Pompey gained entry into Roman political life through his highly irregular tenure as commander pro praetore between 83 (when he was twenty-three) and 79 and as commander pro consule between 77 and 71.[71] When elected consul, Pompey had held no previous elected office. The pattern was unusual, but it draws attention to persistent irregularities in the preparation for rule of an entire generation. The reasons are not hard to find.

The Italian War and the civil conflict of the 80s produced high casualties among senators and equestrians. Combat and proscription left at least one hundred senators dead by 82, one-third of the entire Senate body. New members were found among the equites equo publico. When Sulla increased the total membership of the Senate to six hundred in 82, he did so by adlecting equites.[72] But the equites equo publico had also suffered high attrition between 91 and 82, as had the equestrian class generally: forty-seven hundred lost in the proscriptions, probably far more in the fighting. Nonetheless, the administrative demand for equestrians continued. Before Caesar's even bigger revision of the Senate in 46, normal attrition and special circumstances necessitated further additions to the Senate. It has been estimated on the basis of the lex Cornelia de quaestoribus that twenty vacancies occurred yearly in the six-hundred-member Senate and that Sulla's reform in the quaestorship was intended to maintain the Senate at strength.[73] In 70, sixty-four senators were removed by the censors.[74] Hence the avenue of entry into the Roman leadership, widened by war, remained wide open.

The men who entered were mostly equestrians of obscure background and municipal origin. Some may have been new citizens.[75] Throughout Italy the number of such men had been increasing. The north Italian town of Patavium claimed five hundred men of equestrian rank during the reign of Augustus, an exceptionally high figure thought to demonstrate local wealth: At this time the circumstances and fortunes of these individuals were greatly aggravated by civil war.[76] Not every town boasted so many rich men. Nonetheless, Brunt conjectures that men with a property rating of at least HS 100,000 in the more than three hundred towns in Italy in the first century, who comprised a class of town councilors, numbered fifty thousand.[77] We have already seen that these men were critical additions to Rome's leadership between the fourth and second centuries. They were more critical at the conclusion of the decade-long struggles in Italy between 91 and 82. At all times, and especially in wartime, when mortality rates were high, men of equestrian rank drawn from all communities of Italy provided an expanded pool in the Late Republic from which officials, officers, and administrators were drawn. The changing composition of the Roman Senate in the first century reflected this expanded pool.[78]

So too did the growing number of new men in office. In particular, many junior officeholders throughout the first century were men without any political antecedents, whose fathers or grandfathers had not held high office. The most reliable listing of known new men and men of municipal origin (some new citizens) who entered the Senate between 139 BCE and 14 CE numbers 563.[79] These men were also elected to office, rarely high office but the lower offices. A useful set of figures drawn up by Vanderbroek, based on this listing, shows that a group of eighty-seven tribunes holding office between 78 and 49, whose antecedents and careers are known, included thirty-five, or 40 percent, from obscure backgrounds, that is, men from families that had not produced a high elected official.[80] Presumably, many more such men were found among the military tribunes and Vigintisexvirate.[81] And not only were a fairly large proportion of the junior officeholders political newcomers, but an increasing number of low-ranking senators were recruited from men of equestrian rating who had not held office. It is reasonable to expect that these changes were accompanied by a transformation in the conventions of leadership followed by elite Romans.

As big as the demand for administrators had been in the second century, it was far bigger in the first century, commensurate with the number of offices to be filled. In every year after 70, eighty-four junior offices had to be filled by election: ten tribunes, twenty quaestors, four aediles, twenty-four military tribunes, and twenty-six members of the Vigintisexvirate. Every year, three hundred equestrians were put on a list of jurors by the praetor and were required to be in Rome in order to be available if called to serve on a jury. Because the offices were held for only one year, and the album iudicum was drawn up anew every year, we can imagine that the apparatus over time involved a great many equestrians, drawing deeply on the resources of the equestrian class. If only the equites equo publico, roughly 1,800 men, and some of the larger group of men with an equestrian rating, the tribuni aerarii from Class 1, were drawn in by the demanding range of legal, administrative, and political posts required to regulate and manage the Roman state, then over time we should expect a great many members of this restricted group to become acquainted with some of the materials and procedures of rule. Given that 840 men were needed for the eighty-four elected offices that had to be filled annually between 70 and 60, and that at a minimum 3,000 men (drawn from senators, equestrians, and tribuni aerarii) were on the album iudicium over the period—not to mention the men serving on special commissions as legates or envoys or as members of a recuperatorial panel, *recuperatores* (senators, scholars think)—then about 4,000 men in all would be involved over the period. Assuming a stable group and an annual turnover in positions, then every senator and every equites equo publico would be actively involved every year in the business of justice and leadership and roughly 2,000 more elite Romans outside the Senate and outside the ranks of the equites equo publico would at one time or another be privy to the conventions of rule across this ten-year period. Adding in the necessary and numerous young assistants, the number grows. Clearly a large percentage of Rome's elite members—indeed all of Rome's senators and equites equo publico, as well as many of her equestrians—were engaged year-round in the process of administration and adjudication. No wonder so many elected officeholders with the authority to convene the people could be expected to have at least rudimentary acquaintance with Rome's public law in the first century.

As the number of offices expanded throughout the period of the Republic and the requirements of Rome's system of justice at all levels, so too did the size of the pool from which such administrators came. Between the fourth and second centuries, more and more aristocrats came from the municipalities of Italy. After the Italian War of 91–89, still larger numbers of Italian aristocrats entered the pool. Accordingly, across the period from the fourth to the first centuries, the steady demand for administrators was matched by the steadily increasing number of potential administrators. By the first century, both demand and numbers were commensurately large, with significant implications for the preparation of Rome's equestrians for leadership, in particular for participation in the public lawmaking process.

The waning of the Roman Senate's paramount role in lawmaking provides an indication of the direction of change. The Senate, traditionally the repository of auctoritas, was traditionally also the main source of advice and affirmation tapped by sponsors of public law. The opinion of the Senate about public law mattered a great deal to the people throughout our period of interest. For in a hierarchic society such as Rome, the sanction or censure of this exalted body ideally articulated in advance the collective will of the people. Though the Senate continued to rank as a chief source of authority in Rome down to the end of the Republic, whose affirmation of and recommendations about public law and proposals of law mattered, other sources appeared in consequence of Rome's expanding leadership. The authority and influence of individual officeholders, and increasingly senators without office, sometimes carried far more weight than that of the Senate. The ability of individual leaders to win support over the collective wishes of the Senate emerges in the record first with C. Flaminius in 232 and characterizes the lawmaking process from the tribunate of Ti. Gracchus in 133 down to 44. While these developments are generally viewed as a fundamental change in the lawmaking process, involving both the arenas and the sources of authority, their underlying causes indicate broader changes. In particular the growing divisions within the Senate membership by the end of the second century, as individual senators began to operate to an extent on their own, signal the opportunities opened by the emergence of more groups in Roman society. Now, individual Roman leaders could turn to singular advantage the unspoken relationship between Senate and people.

In many respects, however, little appears to have changed. Where public law is concerned, when tribunes or consuls did not take their proposed laws directly to the Senate, they turned instead to the other obvious sources of expertise that they used publicly in meetings of the Roman people. These were individual elected officeholders and senators without office, men who did not always align themselves with the Senate as a collective body. From the perspective of the voters, they were nonetheless authoritative: The assumption that Roman senators collectively or individually knew the Roman mind was deeply held. Moreover, there was little difference in what they might say. The same matters were aired in the Senate and in public meetings in regard to proposed laws. Similarly, in both the Senate and in public meetings, the debate sought to develop a version of law that would appeal to the widest number of Romans. The significant difference was that Senate meetings were closed to the Roman people, a matter of growing concern to Romans by the mid-first century because it involved the conditions believed essential for the unhindered expression of community consensus.[82]

Returning to Pompey in 70, we might wonder about the nature and extent of the deficiencies in Pompey's training that he so clearly wanted to remedy. More important, why would a Roman of Pompey's position seek to remedy these deficiencies? Thirty years after Pompey's petition to Varro, Cicero argued strongly in his theoretical treatise on the laws of Rome that senators should observe three rules: they should attend sessions of the Senate, speak in turn and briefly, and have a grasp of the affairs of the Roman people.[83] By implication senators in Cicero's day were not always knowledgeable about the scope of senatorial responsibilities. Nor indeed were magistrates, for Cicero complained as well that the elected officeholders of Rome did not know the responsibilities of their office, relying on what their assistants told them.[84]

Witnessed in Pompey's request to Varro is on the one hand an acknowledgment of reality and on the other, a sense on the part of some Romans, that Rome's leadership has somehow deviated from an ideal state. Magistrates entered annually revolving offices and could not hold the same office again until ten years had passed. Low-ranking senators entered the Senate after holding the tribunate or quaestorship and never progressed beyond these offices or at most the office of aedile. These men were noticeably (to articulate contemporaries) less well equipped to carry out their responsibilities in the Late Republic than in previous generations. To be sure, the specialized knowledge demanded by other Roman institutions formed the subject of scholarly and practical treatises even before the first century. The handbook Varro produced for Pompey was not the only one of its kind, nor indeed the first.[85] Varro drew heavily in his own writings on similar didactic manuals that described in great detail the procedures consuls must observe when convening assemblies, for instance. Knowing how to perform the responsibilities of office was important. But understanding the limits of action was even more critical. In the competitive atmosphere of Rome in the Middle and Late Republic, it is easy to imagine that instruction books helped officeholders understand what they should not do as much as what they should know.

The curious investigator wonders what thoughts ran through the minds of most new senators, entering junior offices and the Senate at an especially rapid rate in the first century, as they confronted their change in fortune and even more the senatorial responsibilities accompanying the change. How many had been groomed for such responsibilities in an adolescence and young manhood shaped by the traditional apprenticeship in the arts of government as well as war and senatorial aspirations? Very few, judging by ancient report of their origins and qualifications. Nor had all of the newcomers adlected to the Senate held any office. We have to conclude that the Senate, infused with new blood in 81, emerged reconstituted as a body fully half of whose membership was not necessarily privy to the conventions of rule shared by an earlier elite group. How senators executed their responsibilities, insofar as we can see, was profoundly affected by the changes in personnel. More critical were the changes in the preparations for rule and consequently the understandings of the new leaders. Different conventions were bound to emerge at the same time that events occurring in public arenas, prominent among them public lawmaking, became even more important in the competition for office and leadership.

Indeed, to a greater and greater extent in Pompey's own lifetime the knowledge of Roman ways included public lawmaking. More Roman leaders holding the offices of consul, praetor, tribune, and, in the case of Sulla, dictator would present more public laws to Roman voters between 91 and 50 than in any earlier period of comparable length. Even before 91, the ability to accurately discern the will of the Roman people had become the cachet of a dedicated Roman leader. Such a leader was Tiberius Gracchus, murdered at the end of 133 by his fellow senators, and Gaius Gracchus, forced to commit suicide in 121. Following the Italian War, as his lawmaking program in 81 plainly shows, Sulla was another genuine leader who survived the feat. Whatever he learned from Varro in 70, Pompey's achievements as consul in that year and again in 55 and 52 place him, too, firmly in the slim ranks of Rome's most discerning lawmakers. More than most ambitious Romans, Pompey appears to have been acutely aware of the importance of lawmaking in cementing the relationship between a Roman leader and the Roman people.

The two men elected consul for 70, Pompey and Crassus, were leaders of recognized ability, tested most recently against the desperate army of Spartacus.[86] Together Pompey and Crassus delivered the Roman state from great peril. Together they stood for and won the consulate. In terms of political experience, they were an odd couple. Never had Pompey performed any of the junior juridical or administrative tasks forming the essential background to high office. Never had he presented himself as a candidate for any office. Indeed, his candidacy for the consulship was illegal under the circumstances, leading some scholars to suspect he had been granted a dispensation from the law.[87] Conversely, the noble Crassus had ascended the cursus, office by office, and was properly acquainted with the conventions of rule.[88] It was Pompey nonetheless who demonstrated the greater ability to lead in a traditional Roman way by articulating the desires and concerns of the Roman people. Orating to the people in 71, his first speech as consul-elect, Pompey declared the return of traditional government.[89] No longer would the people's tribunes endure the loss of powers stripped by Sulla. No longer would Roman administrators despoil the provinces. No longer would the courts pervert justice. The people, Cicero reports, roared their endorsement of Pompey's objectives.

These objectives were quickly implemented by the lawmakers of 70, the two consuls and the praetor L. Aurelius Cotta. In association with Crassus, Pompey enacted a measure to revive the tribunate. The severe restrictions that the lex Cornelia de tribunicia poteste of 81 had placed on the office of tribune had troubled many Romans. Although a number of attempts had been ventured to reverse the measure, none succeeded in fully restoring the intended functions to the office.[90] Most important, the tribunes still lacked the legislative and jurisdictional powers that enabled them to balance the unilateral authority of the Roman Senate. The lex Pompeia Licinia de tribunicia potestate restored the vigor of the tribunate. Henceforth, down to the end of the Republic, the office provided a busy platform for political newcomers and nobiles alike with visions of personal advance as leaders who could discern the will of the Roman people. Not only the tribunate but the courts were addressed by lawmakers in 70. Reversing another of Sulla's controversial reforms, the praetor L. Aurelius Cotta carried the lex Aurelia iudiciaria, which instituted three panels of jurors for Rome's standing courts, one each for senators, equites equo publico, and tribuni aerarii.[91] Thus was broken the Senate's exclusive hold on the right to adjudicate capital crimes alleged against its own members, instituted by the lex Cornelia iudiciaria of 81. Instead, the lex Aurelia enlarged the pool of high-status Romans capable of passing judgment on the behavior of (mostly) senators and coincidentally admitted men from a wider range of backgrounds. Some jurors might even be men whose citizenship derived from the lex Iulia of 90.

While these measures were instrumental in loosening the grip of a relatively small number of Roman nobiles on the direction of the Roman state, of far greater consequence was the consuls' undertaking to directly address the intent, at long last, of the lex Iulia of 90 by facilitating the registration of new citizens, traditionally the task of the censors, in tribes and property classes. The office of censor, however, in abeyance for nearly twenty years, had been rendered unnecessary by Sulla's legislation as part of his effort as we have seen to adjust to the expansion of the citizen population.[92] Once again, censors were elected to conduct the census, the first since 86, in which 963,000 Romans were enumerated. The figure, three times greater than the results of the last census, reflects the vast crowd of new citizens denied full membership in the Roman state until now.[93] The censors also revised the Senate list, expelling sixty-four senators. The review of the equites equo publico followed, in which an unknown but undoubtedly significant number of equestrians were cast out or enrolled. In any event, the reinvigoration of the tribunate combined with the election of censors was a powerful step toward restoring community cohesion along traditional lines.[94] It took, however, a leader of some ability and strongly in touch with the Roman people to see the utility of such restorative steps in keeping with customary Roman ways.

CONCLUSION

Together the citizenship grants of 90 and 89, advanced and endorsed by the Senate, the highest of elected officials, the Roman consul, as well as the tribunes and the Roman people, in response to the crisis of the Italian War, produced the most significant and the most wrenching change of scale ever achieved in the Roman civic body. Although the granting of citizenship through the incorporation of outside communities or their leaders had become routine since 338, as we saw in chapter 5, the practice had so far occurred on a relatively small scale. In consequence of the lex Iulia granting citizenship to loyal Latins and Italians, strengthened by later laws facilitating the further grant of citizenship to adscripti in Italian towns and Latins and allies in Cisalpine Gaul, the earlier trickle of new citizens threatened to become a raging torrent. The adjustment of Roman tribes to new citizens proved one of the most intractable problems ever taken to lawmaking assemblies. The difficulty of implementing those arrangements in the laws of 90 and 89 that appear to have addressed tribal registration provides clear demonstration that the outcome of a public lawmaking assembly was valid only when everyone believed in the solution.

Behind the facade of public agreement that accompanied the passage of public laws granting Roman citizenship to Latins and Italians in the first century, a great deal of potential conflict lay hidden. The solution to the Italian War, the public law granting citizenship to all Italians in 90, signaled an end and a beginning: the end of a traditional and relatively slowly changing Rome that could develop agreement on the resolution of apparently intractable problems through the use of public laws and the beginning of an unprecedented shift in the social and political foundations of the Roman Republic, which continued to run its course until the demise of the Republic in 44. The resolution of the Italian War by public law was very much in line with the traditional uses of public law for hundreds of years. Unfortunately, the influx of new citizens that descended on Rome as a result of the new laws, including a significant element of eligible men clamoring for inclusion in Rome's elite classes, created a situation that could not be resolved through public lawmaking.

Fearful casualties among the older Roman noble clans coincided with the appearance from municipalities throughout Italy of an impressive wave of wealthy men who met the criteria for inclusion on the highest level of Roman society to create a volatile situation among elite Romans. As they had done in similar difficult situations in the past, elite Romans turned to the public lawmaking process to resolve the challenges of the new situation in the traditional Roman way. This time, however, the size and the scale of the threat were of such a magnitude as to attenuate the linkages between the various groups that underlay the function of public lawmaking assemblies as a legitimate instrument for developing a community consensus. To the fundamental problem of assigning masses of new citizens to tribes and property classes, thus allowing full access to the benefits of Roman citizenship, was added the challenge of absorbing masses of wealthy newcomers into the various elite levels. Initially undeterred, enterprising Roman officeholders seized the opportunity to propose bills to absorb Italians as citizens on all levels. In quick succession laws were approved allowing newcomers access to traditional Roman structures of power: masses of newcomers were assigned to tribes, while many of the wealthy among them joined the Senate. Alas, as the magnitude of the absorption became apparent the journey of the new citizens to the voting arena was impeded by limited implementation of the new laws on tribal membership, while wealthy newcomers found it difficult to enter the ranks of elite Romans. Quickly it became apparent that the absorption of new Italian citizens was going to be one of the most difficult issues ever confronted by Romans.

The eventual transformation of Roman society as a result of the dissemination of Roman citizenship to Italians went far deeper than the Romans themselves perhaps expected, although it is clear they expected trouble. The inevitable increase in numbers was staggering in itself. The scale of the resulting citizen population, the largest ever seen in the ancient Mediterranean, was extraordinary. As many Romans had feared, the blanket grant of citizenship to all Italians initiated a great sorting out in the society that did not run its course until the demise of the Republic.

The ultimate failure to absorb new citizens on all levels, despite an increasingly intense use of the public lawmaking process to resolve the crisis, underlay every major social upheaval of the period 91–44 and eventually led to the transformation of lawmaking assemblies themselves. The difficult job of assigning this vast body of new citizens to tribe and property classes, which entailed opening access to the Roman leadership for wealthy outsiders—a troublesome process since the beginning of citizen grants in the fourth century—proved far more difficult after the Italian War. Customarily the Roman censors fit new citizens into existing tribes or created new tribes as the Romans expanded across Italy; infrequently assignments were achieved through public law. But after 91, when the issue became dangerously divisive, political leaders convened lawmaking assemblies to decide the question of new tribes and tribal membership. Their failure to resolve these issues presaged the eventual and fatal transformation of the lawmaking process. In years to come, the Romans found themselves attempting to resolve apparently intractable problems that required society-wide consensus through the use of an instrument that itself had become grievously flawed by its inability to deal with the massive influx of newcomers caused by the grant of citizenship to all Italians in 89. Reflecting the inability to absorb Italians, public lawmaking assemblies were now less representative of the citizen body than ever. As we shall see in the final chapter, the problems introduced in Roman society by its vastly increased scale proved almost insurmountable in the long run, despite continuing efforts to restore the integrity of the traditional Roman system.

TABLE 8.1 Public Law Sponsors and Proposals, 91–89

Year	Sponsor	Subject
91	M. Livius Drusus, tribune	Foundation of colonies
91	M. Livius Drusus, tribune	Grant of citizenship to outside group
91	M. Livius Drusus, tribune	Addition of bronze to silver coinage
91	M. Livius Drusus, tribune	Distribution of grain to citizens
91	M. Livius Drusus, tribune	Addition of equestrians to Senate and jury composition
91	M. Livius Drusus, tribune	Redistribution of ager publicus
91	Saufeius, tribune	Uncertain or conjectural
(91)[a]	Minicius, tribune	Citizen status of marginals
90	L. Iulius Caesar, consul	Grant of citizenship to outside group
90	Q. Varius Hibrida, tribune	Special commission of investigation
89	L. Calpurnius Piso, tribune	Creation of new tribes
89	L. Calpurnius Piso, tribune	Grant of citizenship to outside group
(89)	C. Papirius Carbo, tribune	Introduction of semiuncial as (coins)
89	C. Papirius Carbo and M. Plautius Silvanus, tribunes	Grant of citizenship to outside group
89	M. Plautius Silvanus, tribune	Election of jurors by the tribes
89	Cn. Pompeius Strabo, consul	Grant of citizenship to outside group

Source: See appendixes A and C.

[a]Dates in parentheses are approximate. See appendix C.

TABLE 8.2 Sulla's Laws, 88–80

88	Lex Cornelia Pompeia de comitiis centuriatis	Enactment of law in the comitia centuriata
88	Lex Cornelia Pompeia de tribunicia potestate	Restrictions on tribunes
88	Lex Cornelia Pompeia coloniaria	The foundation of colonies
88	Lex Cornelia Pompeia de senatu	Addition of members to Senate from equestrian class
88	Lex Cornelia Pompeia unciaria	Interest payments on the principal of debts
88	Lex Cornelia de exilio Marianorum	The exile of individual(s)
88	Lex Cornelia de sponsu	Limitations on suretyship
82	Lex Cornelia de proscriptione	The proscription of citizens
81	Lex Cornelia de tribunicia potestate	Restrictions on tribunes
81	Lex Cornelia de magistratibus	The order, interval, and age limits for holding office
81	Lex Cornelia iudiciaria	Establishment of standing courts and jury composition
81	Lex Cornelia de sacerdotiis	The number of priests and restoration of co-optation
81	Lex Cornelia de civitate Volaterranis adimenda	The removal of citizenship from towns
81	Lex Cornelia de provinciis ordinandis	Restrictions on provincial governors

(*continued*)

TABLE 8.2 (*continued*)

81	Lex Cornelia de praetoribus octo creandis	Expanding the number of praetors
81	Lex Cornelia de XX quaestoribus	Expanding the number of quaestors
81	Lex Cornelia frumentaria	Distribution of grain to citizens
81	Lex Cornelia sumptuaria	Cost of food at dinner parties
(81)[a]	Lex Cornelia de confirmandis testamentis eorum qui in hostium potestate decessissent	Confirmation of heirs
81	Lex Cornelia de falsis	The crime of falsa
81	Lex Cornelia de sicariis et veneficis	The crime of sicarii and venefici
81	Lex Cornelia de iniuriis	The crime of iniuria
81	Lex Cornelia de maiestate	The crime of maiestas
81	Lex Cornelia de repetundis	The crime of repetundae
81	Lex Cornelia de peculatu	The crime of peculatus
(81)	Lex Cornelia de aleatoribus	Permissible gambling
80	Lex Cornelia de reditu Cn. Pompei	A triumph for a commander

Source: See appendixes A and C.

[a]Dates in parentheses are approximate. See appendix C.

TABLE 8.3 Laws Concerning New Citizens, 91–44

91	Proposed grant of citizenship to allies
91	Grant of citizenship to outside group
(91)[a]	Citizen status of children of marriages between Roman and ally
90	Grant of citizenship to Latins and loyal allies
89	Creation of new tribes for new citizens
89	Grant of citizenship to adscripti resident in Italy
89	Confirmation of citizenship of Cispadane Gauls, Latin rights of Transpadane Gauls (*Transpadani*)
89	Permission to grant citizenship to soldiers for bravery
88	Enrollment of new citizens in all the tribes
87	Proposed enrollment of new citizens in all the tribes
81	Removal of citizenship from towns
72	Grants of citizenship by commander
65	Expulsion of Transpadani from Rome
53	Proposed grant of full citizenship/ registration in rural tribes to certain freed slaves
49	Ratification of Caesar's grant of citizenship to Gades
49	Grant of citizenship to Transpadani
44	Grant of citizenship to Sicilians

Source: See appendixes A and C.

[a]Dates in parentheses are approximate. See appendix C.

TABLE 8.4 **Number of Laws by Year and Decade, 91–44**[a]

Year	Decade	Number of Laws
	91–80	
91		8
90		2
89		6
88		12
87		4
86		1
84		1
83		1
82		2
81		18
80		1
		56 (25%)
	79–70	
78		1
75		3
74		1
73		1
72		2
70		6
		14 (6%)
	69–60	
69		1
68		2
67		14
66		3
65		4
64		1
63		7
62		5
61		5
60		3
		45 (20%)
	59–50	
59		14
58		16
57		6
56		3
55		6
54		2
53		2
52		8
50		7
		64 (28%)
	49–44	
49		5
48		7
47		2
46		9
45		4
44		19
		46 (20%)

Total laws: 225 (99%)
Total years: 47
Average laws per year: 4.8

Source: See appendixes A and C.
[a]Unknown: 9 laws.

Notes

1. Vell. Pat. 2.15.2: cf. Brunt 1971, 439.

2. Cic., *Balb.* 21; Gell. 4.4.3; Cic., *Fam.* 13.30; cf. Vell. Pat. 2.16.4.

3. So Appian, *B.C.* 1.49, commenting on the conscription of former slaves and a Senate decree promising citizenship to allies who remained loyal that preceded the lex Iulia.

4. Scholars believe that the law applied to Italians who had remained "individually loyal" to Rome. As a result of the laws most Italians stopped fighting. Those who surrendered and agreed to recognize Roman law were given citizenship by Senate decree

in 87 (Gran. Lic. p. 21 Flemisch; Livy, *Epit.* 80), except the Samnites and some Lucanians, who wanted restitution of property as well. Taylor 1960, 102 n. 4, avers that the decree would have to be followed by a law.

5. Contra Brunt, following Badian, who believes the lex Plulia came too late to make a difference and the end of the war came because of "hard fighting" by Romans, which reduced Italians to "unconditional surrender": Brunt 1988, 107–8 with n. 37.

6. Sherwin-White 1973, 151–53; Badian 1964, 75–76.

7. Cornelius Sisenna, fr. 120 Peter. See Taylor 1960, 102 n. 3, and *MRR* 2.33–34. These were grants as rewards for bravery. The earlier lex Iulia had reportedly given commanders the right to grant citizenship with the concurrence of their consilium. One possible recipient of such a grant was the great-grandfather of Velleius Paterculus, Minatius Magius of Aeculanum, who raised a legion from among the Hirpini to fight with the Romans: Vell. Pat. 2.16.2.

8. Taylor 1960, 102 with n. 6.

9. Censors were elected in 89 to register new citizens in new tribes but failed to complete the census: Cic., *Arch.* 11. The public law proposal of P. Sulpicius registering new citizens in the old tribes intervened. See Taylor 1960, 103, and Mommsen, *R.St.* 2.342 n. 3.

10. Chapter 1.

11. Sources in *MRR* 2.41–42, s.v. Tribunes.

12. The relationship among the bills and the timing of the assemblies are unknown. See Badian 1964, 34–70.

13. Val. Max. 9.7 ext. 1; Oros. 5.19.4; cf. Plut., *Mar.* 35.4, *Sull.* 8.4.

14. Plut., *Sull.* 9.2.

15. Appian, *B.C.* 1. 55–63; Plut., *Sulla* 7.1–10.2.

16. An alternate interpretation, from a strictly political perspective, is Badian's assessment of Sulla in terms of who supported him after 88, the "Sullani" (see especially his remarks on Sulla's relationship to the troops): Badian 1964, 219–21.

17. Vell. Pat. 2.19.

18. Vell. Pat. 2.19.1; Flor. 2.9.6–8 (exile); Appian, *B.C.*1.59; Livy, *Epit.* 77 (administrative measures); Festus 516L (debt).

19. Gaius 3.124, 125; see Kaser 1955, 1.555 with n. 30; and Thomas 1976, 337.

20. Hostility of city inhabitants: Plut., *Sulla* 10.

21. Brunt 1971, 441.

22. Probably more if we assume that they were at full strength. In 84 some of these were sent on campaign against Illyrians in the Balkans across the Adriatic Sea: *MRR* 2.58. This was done "to prepare them to fight Sulla": Brunt 1971, 441; Badian 1964, 227–28.

23. Plut., *Crass.* 6.2–3.

24. Sertorius: Wiseman 1971, no. 394.

25. Seager provides a useful assessment of the constitutionality of Sulla's career from this point onward: Seager 1994, 199–206.

26. Senators and equestrians: Appian, *B.C.* 1.95.442, with commentary of Gabba 1958. The total comes from Velleius Paterculus 9.2.1; on these figures see Brunt 1971, 301–2. Proscriptions: F. Hinard, *Les proscriptions de la Rome républicaine* (Rome and Paris, 1985), 17–144. Hinard has argued persuasively that the lex Cornelia de proscriptione (now *RS* 2 No. 49) was enacted in an assembly: Hinard 1985, 67–74.

27. This is discussed later in this chapter.

28. In the belief that the legions were never full, particularly when "hastily raised" during civil war, and that casualties had been high, Brunt argues that the number of troops receiving land was less, probably around 80,000. Brunt considers the figure of 120,000 provided by Appian "a paper figure for the complement of the 23 legions to whom lands were apportioned": Brunt 1971, 305.

29. The evidence is presented by Hantos 1988, 69 with nn. 2 and 3. Hantos notes that although Sulla did not have to use the assemblies for his lawmaking, he did. The lex Cornelia de civitate Volaterranis adimendis (Cicero, *Dom.* 79) addressing the citizenship of Volaterra and Arretium was certainly presented to the centuriate assembly. The lex Cornelia de XX quaestoribus was certainly enacted by the tribal assembly: see the remarks accompanying *RS* 2. No.14 (lex Cornelia de XX quaestoribus). We do not know which assembly enacted other laws.

30. The rogatio Sempronia iudiciaria: Plutarch, *C. Gracch.* 5.2–3; Livy, *Epit.* 60. The law is uncertain (*RS* 1. 98).

31. Lex Cornelia de sicariis et veneficis = *RS* 2 No. 50; see Ferrary, "Lex Cornelia de sicariis et veneficis," *Ath.* n.s. 79 (1991): 417–34. The lex de falsis is omitted from Sulla's legislation by J. Crook, "Lex Cornelia 'de falsis,'" *Ath.* n.s. 75 (1987): 163–71.

32. For a conventional approach to Sulla's legislation as dictator see Hantos 1988, 69–161.

33. Revision of Senate list: Cic., *Dom.* 84; Livy, *Epit.* 83, 89; and Cass. Dio 41.14.5. Sulla and new citizens: Wiseman 1971, 26, 140.

34. Probably at least one hundred senators died, one-third of the entire body: Hinard 1985, 116–19, 264–69.

35. Sall., *Cat.* 37.6; Cass. Dion., *Hal.* 5.77.4; Appian, *B.C.* 1.100; Livy, *Epit.* 89. See Wiseman 1971, 7.

36. Wiseman 1971, 6.

37. Appian, *B.C.* 1.100.

38. Cf. Wiseman 1971, 96, n. 3.

39. Brunt 1971, 470–72.

40. Malcovati 1967, 32 frag. 3.

41. *MRR* 2.22, s.v. Tribunes.

42. *MRR* 2.21–22, s.v. Tribunes.

43. Varius: *MRR* 2.26–27, s.v. Tribunes.

44. On the importance of the vote and tribal assignments see Brunt 1988, 125–27.

45. Appian, *B.C.* 1.49 with commentary of Gabba 1958; Vell. Pat. 2.20.3. See Taylor 1960, 102–3 based on Appian, *B.C.* 1.49.

46. L. Cornelius Sisenna, frag. 17 and 120 Peter. See Sherwin-White 1973, 153.

47. Asc. 64C, Appian, *B.C.* 1.55–56; *MRR* 2.41.

48. Appian, *B.C.* 1.64.

49. Census in first century: Wiseman 1969a. Senate decree: Liv. *Epit.* 80.

50. Taylor 1960, 119, citing earlier scholarship.

51. Taylor 1960, 105–6 and 120. Taylor suggests, however, that registration in local municipalities was sufficient to vote in the tribal assembly.

52. Mommsen believed that the census was taken locally after the Italian War (*R.St.* 2.368 ff.), a position held also by C. Nicolet, "Economy and society, 133–43 BC," *CAH*

9, 2d ed., ed. A. Lintott, J. A. Crook, and E. Rawson (Cambridge, New York, New Rochelle, Melbourne, and Sydney, 1994), 602, based on evidence in the tabula Heracleensis (dated, in Nicolet's belief, between 75 and 45). Taylor, followed by Lo Cascio, thought this was not done until Caesar: Taylor 1960, 120 n. 7; Lo Cascio 1999, 164 (summarizing arguments in a forthcoming book).

53. Cic., *Leg.* 3.22; *Verr.* 2.1.155; *Cluent.* 110; Caes., *B.C.* 1.5, 7.3; Sall., *Hist.* 3.48.8 and 12M; Dion. Hal. 5.77.4; Vell. Pat. 2.30.4; Asc. 67, 78, 81C; Plut., *Caes.* 4.2; Suet., *Iul.* 5; Appian, *B.C.* 1.100, 2.29; Livy, *Epit.* 89.

54. The first lex Cornelia Pompeia of 88, which was now reintroduced, according to some, restored the Servian basis of the centuriate assembly: Appian, *B.C.* 1.59; Livy, *Epit.* 77; cf. Cic., *Leg.* 3.9.22. *MRR* 2.40 takes Appian as meaning that the centuriate assembly rather than the tribal assembly was made responsible for voting statutes.

55. Roman census figures from 115, the last reported census before the Italian War: 394,336 Romans. Brunt estimates Italian allies at roughly 740,000 before the Italian War: Brunt 1971, 97, 90.

56. Failure of the censors of 86 to register new citizens: Badian 1964, 223. Return of 70/69: Lo Cascio 1999, 162–64 (difference between return of 70/69 and 28 is explained by new efficiency of registration).

57. A commission of investigation was set up; Cic., *Nat.Deor.* 3.74; Oros. 5.15.25.

58. Based on legions under arms throughout the period: see chapter 5, note 61.

59. Brunt 1971, 690–93.

60. Sall., *Hist.* 1.54–73M.

61. Cicero, *Cat.* 2.5–6, 26; *Fam.* 5.2.1; Sall., *Cat.* 30.5; 42.3; 57.2; Plut., *Cic.* 16.1.

62. As has been amply demonstrated for modern Italy: cf. W. A. Douglas, *Emigration in a south Italian town: An anthropological history* (New Brunswick, NJ, 1984).

63. Sources: *MRR* 2.124.

64. Sall., *Cat.* 30.5.

65. Cass. Dio 37.41.1; Oros. 6.6.7.

66. See chapter 6.

67. Little detailed work has been done on the phenomenon from this perspective. See M. Clavel-Lévêque, "Brigandage et piraterie: Représentations idéologiques et pratiques impérialistes au dernier siècle de la république," *DHA* 4 (1978): 17–32.

68. Keppie 1983, 50: ten legions, under strength, at most twenty thousand men.

69. Appian, *B.C.* 2.120.

70. Varro's praetorship: *MRR* 2.466 (probably before 76).

71. Pompey's career: *MRR* 2.603 "Index of Careers"; and *MRR* 2.64, 77, 81, 84, 90 (*pro praetore* against Lepidus, *pro consule* against Sertorius), 94, 99, 104, 112, 118, 124.

72. Sall., *Cat.* 37.6; Dion. Hal. 5.77.4; Appian, *B.C.* 1.100; Livy, *Epit.* 89. See Wiseman 1971, 7.

73. Wiseman 1971, 96 n. 3; Hopkins 1983, 47.

74. This is discussed later in this section.

75. Wiseman 1971, 6.

76. Strabo 5.1.7; see Brunt 1971, 200.

77. Brunt 1988, 245.

78. The classic presentation of the topic is Syme 1949. On new men from the late second century onward, Wiseman 1971 is essential.

79. Wiseman 1971.

80. Vanderbroek 1987, 38.

81. Military tribunes: Suolahti 1952; Démougin 1983, 279–98.

82. No decision could be made if outsiders were present in the Senate House: Cass. Dio 39.28.3.

83. Cic., *Leg.* 3.4.11.

84. Cic., *Leg.* 3.20.48.

85. Von Premerstein, *PW* 4.726 s.v. Commentarii; Rawson 1984, 233–49.

86. This is discussed earlier in this chapter.

87. That is, the leges annales. Mommsen speculated that he was given such a dispensation by the Roman Senate, not the people: Mommsen, *R.St.* 3.1232–33.

88. We do not firmly know the stages of his political career before his praetorship, which is probably dated 73. He may have been aedile in 76: *MRR* 3.120 s.v. M. Licinius P.f. M. n. Crassus. He was a legate of Sulla in 83 and probably again in 82: *MRR* 2.65 and 71. He profited greatly from Sulla's proscriptions: Plut., *Crass.* 2.3–6.

89. Cic., *Verr.* 1.43.

90. Attempts include the failed proposals of the consul of 78 and the lex Aurelia de tribunicia potestate of 75.

91. On the identification of equites and tribuni aerarii on this album see Brunt 1988, 210.

92. Mommsen, *R.St.* 2.336. Significantly, neutralizing and revitalizing the censorship had not required a public law decision as the office of tribune had: we might assume there was less dissent.

93. Lo Cascio 1999, 162.

94. Pompey and Crassus would be consuls together again in 55, when they would again enact significantly restorative consular laws.

CHAPTER NINE

The Demise of Public Law, 69–44

BEFORE THE START of an ill-fated assembly in 47, during the turbulent civil war years at the end of the Roman Republic, the "master of the horse" (magister equitum), M. Antonius, ordered his soldiers into the Forum to tear down the notice boards advertising a proposal to remit all debts and rents promulgated three weeks earlier by the tribune P. Cornelius Dolabella.[1] The removal of the boards precipitated a bloody confrontation between the soldiers and the Roman voters in support of Dolabella's measure, who had barricaded themselves in the Forum overnight to await the scheduled voting assembly. The determined fury displayed by these voters in 47 is a barometer of the extent to which the Roman people now accepted more immediate political uses of public lawmaking assemblies. But the implications for Roman public lawmaking activity of the Senate-sanctioned violence are far more significant.

Three years earlier, in 50, the Roman world had erupted in the final civil war that would eventually usher in a new Roman order under the rule of emperors. Crossing into Italy at the head of a Roman army in 50 Julius Caesar carried to its penultimate stage the final solution to uncontrolled competition among the leadership, challenging the cohesion of Roman society by attempting to set himself up as the single, all-powerful leader in Rome within the parameters of traditional Roman offices. Some measure of the initial acquiescence in his role by other Romans came on the heels of M. Antonius's slaughter of Roman citizens in the Roman Forum in 47: the Senate decreed no new laws in Rome until the return of Julius Caesar. Public lawmaking as the uncoerced expression of the people's will was for all practical purposes over.

In this chapter we continue to explore some of the developments leading to this point. Roman leaders worked hard to ensure the continued functioning of the traditional public lawmaking system. These efforts, however, were futile in face of an explosion in the citizen population, the vast changes in the pool that had traditionally provided leadership, and the growing politicization of lawmaking that culminated in the portentous lawmaking activity of the civil war years, 49 to 44. After 44, this most remarkable burst of lawmaking activity in Roman history is followed by dramatic changes in the format and focus of lawmaking assemblies. The failure of public lawmaking assemblies to reduce the level of disruption was followed by the emergence, with the ascendancy of Octavian in 31, of the first Roman emperor. Lawmaking assemblies, although not yet moribund, never again assumed the form, frequency, or function that they had held for over half a millennium.

PUBLIC LAWMAKING, 69–50

The consequences of the revisions consummated in 70 were far-reaching. As measured by the density of public laws and proposals down to 50, it is clear that Romans in the more numerous groups now constituting the Roman voting population still viewed the lawmaking process as a regular means of establishing consensus in a diverse society. Unfortunately, the emphasis of the ancient narratives on the political alliances and personal ambitions of a small number of Romans—senators, nobiles, and political newcomers competing for office—as laid bare in the lawmaking arena, masks the degree to which public lawmaking activity as well as the concerns of law sponsors reflect a communitywide interest in changing or restoring the Roman state through the traditional avenue, public law. But it was this communitywide engagement (and only this) that made possible the emergence of a new political dimension in public lawmaking activity. In particular, a more varied and irregular leadership, brought about by the diverse society Rome had become, began to use the process to advance special interests—or interests undoubtedly appearing special to other Romans for the reason that the ruptures among groups were becoming irreparable. Although the details of the politicization of public lawmaking are visible in many of the events of the next twenty years, in the following analysis I propose to focus on events in 67, 59, and 58 that prompted unusually high levels of lawmaking activity. The various issues addressed by law sponsors in the ten or more public law proposals mooted in each of these years confirm that 70 was the climacteric of Roman public law. Henceforth, the uses of lawmaking were changed forever.

THE LAWMAKING OF 67

In 68, the proconsul in Bithynia, Pontus, and Cilicia, L. Licinius Lucullus, ordered out the Roman legion XX stationed in Pontus. The soldiers mutinied because, according to report, they had already served long enough. Without them Lucullus marched into Armenia, where he won a battle and withdrew to Nisibis for the winter. There his troops were roused to air their resentment for Lucullus by one of his staff, the young P. Clodius Pulcher, now aged twenty-four, later tribune in 58.[2] Back in Rome the praetor L. Quinctius orated on the necessity of replacing Lucullus in the command against Mithridates. In these rancorous episodes, the growing dissatisfaction of Romans on all levels of society with the way Lucullus was conducting the long campaign against Mithridates is unmistakable. As a Roman leader under scrutiny Lucullus was by no means alone: since 70, the leadership of Rome had been coming under particularly close inspection and revision from many quarters. However, the situation in the east was particularly dangerous because of Lucullus's failure not only to vanquish Mithridates—indeed, the king's vitality was growing—but to control the menace of piracy in the regions assigned to his command. The organization and capability of the pirates based in Crete and Cilicia had deepened. Pirates intercepted grain ships traveling to Rome from Sardinia, Sicily, and North Africa. Among city dwellers, the fear of famine was high. Going ashore in Italy itself, pirates plundered villas and snatched wealthy Romans for ransom. In 68, pirates even captured two Roman praetors complete with insignia of office and attendants.[3] In past years the Roman commanders sent to Crete and Cilicia had failed to stop them; now Lucullus was failing too. Catastrophe was in the air. Then, in 67, Mithridates destroyed the Roman army in Pontus, commanded by a legate during the commander's absence in Armenia. Among the great many casualties were 7,000 Roman dead, including 150 centurions and 24 military tribunes. No single battle since the Second Punic War had touched so many senatorial and equestrian families in Rome and in the municipalities of Italy with the death of fathers, sons, or brothers. Mithridates, with his son-in-law Tigranes, proceeded to regain Pontus and Armenia while the Romans remained stunned, their commander,

Lucullus, paralyzed by the disintegrating morale of his troops and the defeat of his legate, C. Valerius Triarius.

In the same year, a consul and three tribunes presented at least thirteen laws to the people for their approval, listed with their sponsors in table 9.1. Despite the different issues addressed by these proposals, their primary thrust was leadership: military command in the eastern wars and more broadly the overall responsibility and privilege of Rome's leaders. The most critical measures of the year, carried by the tribune A. Gabinius, a longtime associate of Pompey and recent entrant to office, involved military commands.[4] Gabinius first sponsored a bill that gave to the consul M'. Acilius Glabrio the province of Bithynia and Pontus and some of the legions currently commanded by Lucullus. Thus the proconsul, who had gone out to Asia after his consulship in 74, came to share the command against Mithridates. Gabinius next presented a highly controversial bill creating an extraordinary command for Pompey against the pirates, similar to one held between 102 and 100 by the proconsul M. Antonius.[5] This law designated a special province, the entire Mediterranean sea and its shores, extending fifty miles inland, for a period of three years. The bill also gave Pompey the authority to draw directly on state funds and a fleet of two hundred ships, full authority to conscript rowers and soldiers, and the authority to choose fifteen legates from the Senate. Never had one man held as much power as Pompey would under the terms of the rogatio Gabinia.

The public lawmaking sessions convened to debate the tribune's bill were agitated. Reportedly the people who attended the preliminary meeting at which the Gabinius promulgated his measure were wildly enthusiastic when the terms of the law were read aloud[6]—all but the senators, who, with the exception of Caesar, were solidly opposed to the measure because of the authority it vested in one man. When the consul M'. Acilius Glabrio advised Pompey in a public oration not to accept the command he was nearly lynched. When the "first man" in the Senate (princeps senatus), Q. Lutatius Catulus, consul in 78, argued in a public oration about the danger of giving one man so much power—what if something should happen to him?—his listeners respectfully roared that they would replace Pompey with Catulus himself. When the tribune L. Roscius Otho tried to orate about the wisdom of selecting at least two commanders for this special province the people refused to let him be heard. At this critical moment when pirates blocked vital food supplies, only one strong leader, so far as the Roman people were concerned, Pompey, could restore Rome.

Thanks to the Senate, the people's sovereign will was expressed on this occasion with difficulty. Despite communitywide support for the proposal, outside a cluster of leading senators, when Gabinius convened the voting assembly one of his colleagues, L. Trebellius, vetoed the measure. In turn, Gabinius proposed a measure on the spot to remove Trebellius from office, as Ti. Gracchus had done in 133 in the course of a lawmaking session involving another popular bill. When it looked like the voters would unanimously approve the measure to depose him, Trebellius withdrew his veto. The voters at length cast their votes to accept the measure as law. Even then, the Senate obstructed the implementation of the bill. When the consul C. Calpurnius Piso discharged sailors conscripted by Pompey and impeded the equipment of his ships, the tribune Gabinius drafted another measure to depose the consul from office.[7] Tensions between Pompey and the Senate are apparent.

A leadership in conflict within itself and with the people emerges in other bills of 67 shown in table 9.1, in particular those of the tribune C. Cornelius. Like Gabinius, he had recently been in the military consilium of Pompey.[8] Like Gabinius, too, Cornelius was an active law sponsor, promulgating at least five proposals.[9] Among his initial proposals was a bill prohibiting loans by senators to foreign states, believed to be aimed at reducing the scope for corruption that such loans encouraged.[10] The bill failed when the Senate objected that the terms of the bill were already covered in a Senate decree of 94. In retaliation, according to Asconius, Cornelius proposed his next measure, which addressed the Senate's authority to give exemptions from the law—probably the law regulating the order in which offices in the cursus were held.[11] Only the people, his bill confirmed, had the power to grant such exemptions.[12] Whatever its immediate motivation, the proposal was stoutly opposed by senators.

In the public lawmaking session at which Cornelius presented this bill another tribune interposed his veto. The herald, on the point of reciting the law to the voters, stopped at once, but Cornelius took up the codex and recited the law himself. Outraged, the consul Piso and other senators objected forcefully to this breach in customary procedure. Defiant, the Romans in attendance threatened to lynch the consul. Recognizing a dangerous situation, Cornelius dismissed the assembly without calling for a vote. He subsequently presented a revised proposal, which enacted that any exemptions from the law determined by a quorum of two hundred senators must be presented to the people for their approval.[13] When presented to the voters this measure was accepted as law. The tribune's effort at conciliation without conceding the sovereign authority of the Roman people is evident. Another bill enacted that the praetor urbanus must make judgments in accordance with his edict, announced at the beginning of his year of office.[14] According to Dio, the bill aimed to prevent bribery by defendants in law cases before the praetor. This measure, too, was accepted as law.

After these bills, Cornelius presented a law on the crime of ambitus, imposing heavy fines on candidates for office convicted of bribery and also for the first time on the tribal officials, divisores, convicted of distributing bribes to tribal members.[15] The proposal evidently was inspired by a surge in the number of candidates and in electoral bribery as men who had been removed from the Senate lists in 70 tried to regain entry through election to high office.[16] Notwithstanding support for the measure outside the Senate—indeed there was a communitywide concern to correct the spreading incidence of bribery at the highest levels—it does not appear to have been enacted as law.[17] But soon after, at the time of the elections, Rome was shaken by several public episodes of bribery and violence as candidates competed for votes. Although public business was customarily prohibited during the election period, the Senate decreed that an exemption should be given to the consul Piso (who was himself reputedly elected with the assistance of lavish bribes) from the custom, so that he could present another bribery law to the people with somewhat lighter penalties attached and leaving divisores out of the terms of the law.[18] Like Cornelius's lex de legibus solvendo earlier in the year, Piso devised an accommodating bill, agreeable to voters who might have accepted Cornelius's rogatio de ambitu as well as voters who were against it. This measure was accepted.

All other measures presented to the people by the magistrates of 67 and listed in table 9.1 also involved Roman leadership.[19] Gabinius, probably as tribune in this year, carried a measure instituting the month of February as the period during which the Senate would hear foreign embassies. By reducing the length of time foreign emissaries stayed in Rome, the potential for senatorial corruption would also diminish.[20] On the same line and following the failure of Cornelius's proposal regarding loans by senators, Gabinius probably carried a similar measure prohibiting loans to foreign emissaries in Rome.[21] The tribune L. Roscius Otho addressed leadership on a different level in a successful bill to reserve seats in the theater for men of equestrian rank. The public honor of a reserved front-row bank of seats in the theater, previously held only by senators and priests, was now again extended to the wealthiest businessmen and state contractors who funneled the resources of empire back to Italy. For these men, Roscius, himself a political newcomer, reestablished the honor of reserve seats in the next fourteen rows, removed by Sulla in 81.[22] While such honors are part of the trend toward the inflation of privilege that characterizes the last years of the Republic, they are also indicative of the increasing self-importance of this identifiable sector of the community, namely, men of equestrian rank constituting the highest property class, who since 70 derived not only from Rome and those Italian and Latin communities receiving citizenship before the Italian War but the municipalities of Italy. Cicero later claimed that Roscius was responding to communitywide demand in promulgating this bill, although the demonstrated hostility of ordinary Romans to Roscius in 63 with regard to this very privilege suggests otherwise.[23] More likely the tribune's motives were to attach the men of this class more closely to the Senate. Lone among the tribunician bills of 67, the lex Roscia sought to restore the vigor of the Senate, diminished since 70.

As a group the laws of 67 reveal continued, troubling divisions among the men who constituted Rome's leadership, within and without the Senate, played out in Rome's public lawmaking arena. On one side in 67 was the consular renovator, Pompey. On the other side was the Senate, or rather a small group of high-ranking senators, principes civitates, who opposed both the resurrection of a vital tribunate and Pompey.[24] The political nature of the lawmaking activity in 67 is indisputable. Two lawmakers this year, Cornelius and Gabinius, strengthened the tribunate and Pompey. And two lawmakers were committed to an ascendant Senate, Piso, solidly hostile to Pompey, and Roscius Otho.[25] The experience of Cornelius best reveals the enduring hostilities between divided camps. Despite the success of the revised version of his lex de legibus solvendo, the tribune nonetheless faced a novel charge brought the following year by two equestrians that his actions at the earlier assembly had diminished the maiestas of the colleague who vetoed his proposal.[26] Defended by the senator Cicero, Cornelius denied that he had ignored the veto.[27] The case was dropped when the praetor failed to appear and the audience lay into the two prosecutors. Whatever the legal issues of the case, contemporaries and modern historians alike have viewed the entire episode as a political maneuver to get even with the leaders who overturned Sulla's central reform.[28]

At the same time the merits of most if not all of the measures clearly transcend politics—or more properly the clash of individual political ambitions. Cornelius and Gabinius in particular, sharing Pompey's ability to discern the will of the people, sponsored bills that were at times momentous and always attentive to the responsibilities of the leadership of Rome. Cornelius went after the Roman Senate, specifically the power of the Senate decree to remove actions (and the men who carried them out) that had societywide impact from the purview of the Roman people, to wit financial transactions that impoverished the provinces, entries for election to high office from men who had not followed the regular cursus, bribery at elections. To what extent Cornelius's individual vision or experience is reflected in his lawmaking activity we cannot gauge since we know so little about him. Gabinius, however, is more comprehensible. Surely only a man like Gabinius, who had spent nearly twenty years in the field before holding political office and was later regarded as one of Rome's vires militares, could successfully propose two unusual measures transforming the command structure ordained by the Roman Senate.[29]

In accepting the leges Gabiniae, the people's judgment (and Gabinius's) proved accurate. Pompey in particular was rapidly successful in unraveling the networks of pirate organization and clearing the seas of outlaw marauders, resettling them in underpopulated regions.[30] By the end of the year, the Roman people viewed Pompey as the leader to reinvigorate Roman expansion in the east as well, stalled under the purview of Lucullus and Glabrio. Undoubtedly the defeat of Triarius reinforced their judgment. Early in 66, the tribune C. Manilius carried a measure giving Pompey the provinces and troops of Cilicia, Bithynia, and Pontus, previously commanded by Lucullus and Glabrio, and the command against Mithridates. At the same time Pompey kept the special province created the previous year by Gabinius.[31] The overwhelming public support for the measure is unmistakable in the single public oration surviving in full, delivered by the praetor, Cicero. Although the Senate as a collective opposed the bill, only the princeps senatus, Catulus, spoke against the measure, and at the assembly the tribes unanimously accepted Manilius's proposal as law.[32] Pompey's rapid success against Mithridates, resulting in a magnificent flow of riches into the Roman treasury and firm control of the east, again confirmed the people's judgment. The leges Gabiniae initiating this string of events might be termed political in their motivations, from a modern perspective, because they served to enhance Pompey's reputation, but they also served the immediate needs and interests of the Roman state.

THE LAWMAKING OF 59

In 63, on the motion of the consul Cicero, the Roman Senate voted to execute two of its own members without trial following their arrest for inciting the Allobroges of Transalpine Gaul to rebellion. Notwithstanding the efforts of Caesar, now praetor, to mitigate the penalty, Cicero's recommendation that the senators be summarily killed as criminals caught in the act, emotionally endorsed by M. Porcius Cato, carried the day. So died the patrician P. Cornelius Lentulus Sura, quaestor in 81, praetor of the extortion court in 74, and consul in 71. Expelled from the Senate in 70 he reentered as a result of his election to the office of praetor in 63, for the second time. The senator C. Cethegus died also, reportedly a low-ranking senator of no known reputation or attainments. The equites M. Caeparius of Terracina, L. Statilius, and P. Gabinius were also executed.[33] Warrants were sworn for the arrest of several other men of all ranks who escaped capture, fleeing Rome to join the irregular army of Catiline in Etruria.[34]

In these executions urged by the Roman consul and decreed by the Roman Senate, the most radical act of the incident known as the Catilinarian conspiracy, the attenuation of the traditional linkages between members of the Roman state at all levels is clearly revealed. The precise nature of the crisis of 63 is perplexingly elusive, in spite of the voluble narrations of Cicero, himself one of the chief participants, as well as of C. Sallustius Crispus (Sallust), a younger contemporary who was tribune a decade later in 52 and praetor in 46. The issues as presented by Cicero and Sallust were moral: Catiline and his co-conspirators represented a degenerate leadership drawing on the support of base men who had squandered their resources and desperate men with nothing to lose. Given the scope of the crisis, ranging from open rebellion in Transalpine Gaul to the whispered menace of spontaneous insurrection across Roman Italy and Latin Cisalpine Gaul, the issues were undoubtedly far deeper.[35] In particular, growing disparities in the access that Romans of different status groups had to essential land resources and to the rewards of empire had intensified division over the incorporation of new members and the leadership of the Roman state. No fewer than thirty full-strength legions were under arms in 63.[36] At the beginning of his year of office, the tribune P. Servilius Rullus had proposed the most practical measure to date addressing the land problems facing Romans. Despite the conspicuous need for a measure of such unprecedented scope and notwithstanding support from ordinary Romans, Rullus withdrew his proposal rather than face a likely veto. As we saw in chapter 2, the persuasive opposition of the consul Cicero—who at one and the same time embodied the political aspirations of new citizens and championed the political conservatism of the Senate, whose most prominent members were as adverse to the idea of vesting extraordinary powers in a ten-man commission as they were in one man—was overwhelming. What crises were building? How could they be resolved? The Catilinarian conspiracy serves to direct the focus on the Roman leadership and in particular on the failings of that most important collective, the Roman Senate, in the efforts, almost unceasing from now on, to mend a society whose political foundations are trembling.

These failings come again into view in 60, when the Senate resolutely turned down requests from Caesar and Pompey in regard to matters that came within the Senate's traditional purview. Waiting outside Rome with his army, prior to entering the city in triumph, as per his right, Caesar requested an exemption from the rule that candidates for office had to present their candidacy in person (or that he be allowed to enter the city to stand for consul, then return to his army without setting down his imperium). Similar exemptions had often been made before, sometimes by public law, as for instance during the Second Punic War, and at other times by Senate decree, but on this occasion the Senate refused, forcing Caesar to forego his deserved triumph in order to announce his candidacy. Pompey for his part had requested the Senate to ratify his arrangements in the east, made on his own initiative in the absence of counsel from the usual senatorial commission. Again the Senate refused, acceding to the persuasive arguments of Pompey's rivals in military glory, Crassus and Lucullus. In the same year the Senate had supported the consul Metellus Celer's obstruction of the tribune Flavius's public law proposal to grant land to Pompey's veterans, agents of the most profitable Roman military victories since the mid-second century. In frustration Pompey promised "under oath" to support Caesar in his bid for consulship; Caesar mediated friendly relations between Pompey and the celebrated, rivalrous Crassus, and the extra-legal "three-man commission" known as the First Triumvirate was formed to promote the ambition and vision of Caesar, Pompey, and Crassus through public lawmaking assemblies.[37] Without such a coalition the Senate wielded enough authority to prevent the passage of any public law proposal deemed to undermine its collective interest. The experiences of the tribunes Rullus in 63 and Flavius in 60 provide cases in point.

While the most conspicuous measure of the Senate's failure to provide collective leadership in 60 for an increasingly complex society is the informal political coalition formed by Pompey, Caesar, and Crassus at the end of the year, the public law proposals of 59 and 58, listed with their sponsors in table 9.2, disclose the extent of the problem in a much more precise way.[38] Elected consul in 60 for 59, Caesar launched his year of office in January with an edict ordaining regular publication of Senate deliberations as well as contiones. Closed meetings and secrecy did not serve the people's interests.[39] He then laid out an array of public law proposals addressing pressing social and economic issues that the Roman Senate had set aside or obstructed in the previous years. Among the first public law proposals was a measure assigning land to Pompey's veterans, accepted as law by the tribal assembly, as were all subsequent proposals.[40] Given the consul's ability to discern the will of the people, the opposition of the Senate to Caesar's lawmaking program throughout the year, no less than their opposition to Caesar and Pompey in 60, is indicative of the level of friction now characterizing the topmost levels of Roman society that inhibited the Senate from attending to pressing social needs. When Caesar introduced a second public law proposal in the Senate in April, dealing with land distribution, he met with stony silence as the senators refused to discuss the draft.

Like the public law proposal of the tribune Rullus in 63, Caesar's proposal was an effort of scale to resolve one of the most urgent social problems of the day, access to land resources. A commission of twenty rather than ten men was instituted to divide up public property in the ager Stellas and Campanus, the last ager publicus in Italy, and to purchase land from willing sellers with money funneled into the state treasury from the booty Pompey brought to Rome from his successful campaigns. Men with three or more children were given priority in Caesar's bill; twenty thousand men at once lined up. To ensure implementation the proposal called for senators to swear an oath to uphold the law. Among the senators only Cato addressed Caesar's proposal, urging the Senate not to endorse a "new law."[41] Pointedly foregoing the Senate's formal approval, Caesar promulgated the proposal and convened meetings for the purpose of public debate. Pointedly he invited the consul M. Bibulus, elected as Caesar's colleague to "hold him in check," to endorse the measure and met with the anticipated refusal.[42] Caesar then invited his two influential associates, Pompey and Crassus, to lead off the discussion even though neither currently held an elected office. Custom required that law sponsors solicit contributions to the public argument from senators according to a rank order that placed officeholders before private citizens.[43] Three tribunes promised to veto the bill, and Bibulus pronounced a cessation from public business for the remainder of the year. Caesar disregarded both, calling the assembly as announced.

On the day of the voting assembly Bibulus, attended by his lictors, mounted the podium of the Temple of Castor and Pollux, where Caesar was orating to the crowd, in order to denounce the proposal. Bibulus was unceremoniously pushed to the bottom of the flight of stairs, his shattered fasces tumbling after. The three opposing tribunes were pummeled. The senator Cato tried in vain to orate to the crowd, who not only refused to hear him but threw him bodily out of the Forum. He lacked the presence and skill to address the crowd, according to Dio.[44] The voters, called to assemble in their voting units, enthusiastically approved Caesar's proposal. So resounding was the voters' affirmation of the lex Iulia agraria that on the day following, when Bibulus urged the Senate to annul the law, the senators would not consider the recommendation. For the remainder of his term Bibulus withdrew from his public duties, emerging only periodically from his house to resolutely announce he was watching the skies for omens, a prognostication that customarily called a halt to any legitimate assembly.

Even so Caesar promulgated and carried other laws, many of which addressed issues deliberated at one time or another in recent years by the Senate. One public law remitted one-third of their contracts to tax farmers in Asia, who had been requesting such a reduction from the Senate since the bids of 65 or 61.[45] The Senate had turned them down. Another was a measure ratifying the arrangements Pompey had made in the east on the successful conclusion of his three-month campaign against the pirates and his four-year campaign against King Mithridates, between 67 and 62. Another law confirmed Ptolemy Auletes as King of Egypt and "friend and ally of Rome."[46] In all cases Caesar carried public laws that reversed earlier Senate decisions or took action on matters the Senate had obstructed. The Senate itself was the focus of another public law, the lex Iulia de repetundis, which applied primarily to senators and imposed more stringent penalties on their proven misbehavior. Outlasting any immediate circumstances, the scope and arrangements of this law were of lasting importance.[47]

Similarly contentious matters, with respect to an entrenched Senate membership, were aired by the two other officials presenting public law proposals in 59. While the consul Caesar was an unusually active lawmaker, so was the tribune P. Vatinius, with at least six public law proposals and probably more, as we see in table 9.2. A new man, Vatinius appears to have been a second-generation Roman citizen from the Marsi inhabiting the central Apennines, one of the tribal groups forming the core of resistance to Rome during the Italian War.[48] His wife was the granddaughter of L. Iulius Caesar, consul in 90 who opened the floodgates of citizen incorporation with his public law of that year granting citizenship to Latins and faithful allies. Thus through this marriage Vatinius had some connection to Caesar, a clansman of the consul of 90. Likewise he was associated with Caesar throughout his political career. After his tribunate, Vatinius served as legate of Caesar in Gaul from 58 to 56.[49] Standing for the office of aedile in 57, Vatinius failed, prompting Cicero's cutting intimation that a man who could not carry his own tribe at the voting assembly was suspect.[50] Even so he was elected praetor in 55 and consul in 47.

In 59 we see Vatinius as a man with strong links to new citizens and to Romans advocating the incorporation of new citizens, links he shared with the consul, Caesar. As tribune he presented, in the early months of 59, a proposal concerning jury panels in criminal cases that allowed rejection of alternate jurymen.[51] The bill appears to stem from the efforts of the Senate in 61 to control the selection of jurors for the court instituted to try P. Clodius Pulcher for sacrilege.[52] Accepted by the voters, the lex Vatinia introduced a lasting reform in jury selection procedures. Another concerned the staff of provincial governors. Vatinius carried other bills establishing treaties with states, kings, and tetrarchs undoubtedly in implementation of some of Pompey's arrangements in the east.[53] When the Senate assigned unprofitable provinces to the consuls, Vatinius carried a measure giving Caesar Cisalpine Gaul and Illyricum, with three legions, for five years.[54] Although Cicero angrily denounced the lex Vatinia de provincia Caesaris as an infringement on the prerogative of the Senate to direct policy, he overstated the case: the people had made similar adjustments in the past, most recently in 67 and 66.[55] The Senate later added Transalpine Gaul and an additional legion.[56] Vatinius also carried a measure giving Caesar the authority to establish a citizen colony, Novum Comum, at Celtic Comum at the foot of the Alps in Cisalpine Gaul, which had earlier received Latin rights under a measure carried by the consul, Cn. Pompeius Strabo, extending Latin rights to the Transpadane inhabitants of Italy in 89.[57] The effort to extend citizenship and tribal membership to the region, initiated by Caesar in 68 following his return from Further Spain, where he had served as quaestor under the propraetor Antistius Vetus, and advanced by Vatinius was only completed in 49.[58]

Like Vatinius, the third recorded lawmaker of 59 listed in table 9.2, the praetor Q. Fufius Calenus, was also a new man. But the family of Fufius Calenus, from Cales, a Latin colony that received citizenship in 90, had acquired citizen rights long before by virtue of holding local office.[59] Fufius Calenus was later consul in 47, sharing that office with Vatinius. Like Vatinius, the group interests fielded by Fufius Calenus meshed with those of Caesar in 59. As tribune in 61, Fufius Calenus had carried a measure replacing the consul's controversial public law proposal regarding the constitution of the court to try P. Clodius Pulcher for sacrilege.[60] As praetor in 59, Fufius Calenus proposed a bill requiring the three classes that made up jury panels—senators, equestrians, and tribuni aerarii—to report their votes separately.[61] Like Caesar's edict requiring the publication of Senate minutes, this bill opened up to public scrutiny the decisions made by each panel. Doubtless Fufius had in mind the narrow margin of Clodius's acquittal in 61. The bill failed.

To sum up, throughout 59 we see laws carried by a consul, praetor, and tribune on matters taken originally to the Senate for decision but refused at that level; on matters involving the economic and political interests of men with an equestrian rating; and on matters involving new citizens. Equally visible is the degree to which individual lawmakers, in advancing their political ambitions, also advanced the interests of their own families, their own groups, and Roman society, as well as the interests of two widely recognized leaders, Caesar and Pompey.

As was customary, an entirely different college of tribunes and different consuls held office the following year, 58. Similarly a different range of immediate, divisive issues was aired in public law proposals (table 9.2). As in previous years, however, these issues were rooted in abiding, societywide concerns, in particular the accommodation of new citizens, the access to resources, and the rightful leadership of Rome, whose explosive potential was most recently seen in the unsuccessful Catilinarian conspiracy of 63. Nonetheless, the subtle shifts in the uses of lawmaking that lay beneath the activity of 67 and 59 were about to break the surface.

THE LAWMAKING OF 58

By the time the patrician P. Clodius Pulcher made his first bid for political office, the Senate had come to view him with growing alarm.[62] Son of Ap. Claudius Pulcher, consul in 79, and member of the urban Palatina tribe, Clodius belonged to a highly visible branch of the patrician Claudii, fortunate in its accomplishments and connections.[63] The family had an extensive hereditary clientage in the east, which Clodius, like his eldest brother, consul in 54, would later use to underwrite his political advancement.[64] Besides the advantages falling to the third son in such a family, Clodius possessed the useful ability to identify and rally the discontented, a talent he displayed for the first time while serving on the staff of his brother-in-law Lucullus in the east, in 68, when he backed the troops protesting against the length of their service.[65] Within a few years, Clodius had brought this ability to bear in Rome, whose crowded neighborhoods accommodated the bitterness and distress lingering after the defeat of Catiline in 63.[66] By the time Clodius canvassed successfully for quaestor, in July of 62, he had an organized following of militant citizens.[67] Hence, when the quaestor-elect was discovered in early December in the house of Pompeia, Julius Caesar's wife, during the state rites for the Bona Dea, and when Caesar declined to prosecute Clodius for adultery, and when the college of pontiffs decided that Clodius's presence in the house on that occasion constituted sacrilege, which carried no legal penalty, the Senate took action.

Early in 61 the consuls were instructed to propose a law (for all purposes drafted by the Senate) setting up a special court and allowing the prosecution of Clodius for incestus before this court.[68] Although the Senate had to contrive somewhat the facts of the case to fit the definition of the crime—incest in the modern sense or sexual relations with a vestal (as well as any hint of chastity compromised)—incestus had the advantage of carrying a penalty of death or exile. The Senate's resourceful invention of a sustainable crime is a reliable indicator of its determination to rid Rome of this dangerous young man. While some senators objected to the idea of any criminal prosecution at all, the rogatio Pupia Valeria contained one particularly controversial arrangement: the urban praetor would select the preliminary panel of jurors.[69] A hostile court was guaranteed. When an unwilling Pupius presented the proposal to the voters, Clodius's followers occupied the voting bridges and removed the ballots marked "uti rogas." Piso cancelled the assembly, leaving the proposal unvoted. It was soon replaced by a compromise measure (essentially the same bill except that the regular procedure for selecting iudices, established by the lex Aurelia of 70, was followed), enacted by a tribune allied to Clodius, Fufius Calenus. In accordance with the lex Fufia de incestu the court was set up; Clodius was prosecuted; and by a narrow majority of four votes he was acquitted, notwithstanding the damaging testimony of a number of prominent witnesses, among them Cicero. In May of 61, the quaestor left for his province, Sicily.

Thus P. Clodius Pulcher launched his controversial and unconventional political career. When he returned to Rome in 60, the apprehensions of the Roman Senate proved well founded. Especially sinister was Clodius's continuing recruitment and organization of citizens in Rome who were loosely attached to the larger society—primarily poor citizens and former slaves—through the neighborhood and professional associations (vici and collegia) to which city dwellers belonged.[70] Within their often overlapping vici and collegia, the men recruited by Clodius formed companies, like soldiers, and armed themselves for some events from a cache of weapons established at the tribunal Aurelia. The companies were led by a cadre of mostly low-status citizens described as "duces." Some were former slaves from abroad, some were Italian (Marsi and Samnites are identified), and some were Roman. Only one equestrian is reported among their number. According to ancient report, Clodius appealed mostly to shopkeepers, former slaves, and young aristocrats; doubtless many former soldiers were included among them, albeit little noticed by our sources.[71] Little noticed as well is the extent to which the membership of these companies penetrated all the tribes. For the associations on which they were based also absorbed the low-status or impoverished rural tribesmen living now in Rome, although registered still in rural tribes. Of course Clodius had hereditary and personal contacts of all stations among his fellow tribesmen in the urban Palatina tribe. But he also had contacts deep within every Roman tribe, through his services in 63 as middleman (sequester) between certain candidates for office and the divisores of all thirty-five tribes.[72] These shadowy, low-level officials had long-established techniques of distribution among tribesmen of all (but especially low) stations, which Clodius presumably utilized. Like Catiline in 63, Clodius galvanized the silent, marginal members of the larger society. More important, he molded them into a group with a voice, and arms, within the tribes.[73]

His ambitions appear far different from Catiline's, however: Clodius would work within the system. In 60, one of the tribunes promulgated a one-of a-kind bill to transfer Clodius to the plebs. It was vetoed. But the following year, Clodius transferred to a plebeian clan (the adoptive parent was the plebeian senator M. Fonteius) through the fiction of adoption (*adrogatio*), a transaction executed by the curiate assembly convened by the pontifex maximus; in 59, this was the consul Iulius Caesar. Contrary to custom Clodius kept his birth clan name; he also remained in his tribe. He stood for his next office and was elected tribune for 58. As tribune Clodius sponsored at least twelve public law proposals on his own, which in turn generated all other recorded tribunician proposals (at least two). If we knew nothing at all about Clodius, the number of laws alone suggests an ambitious tribune who was very aware of the potential uses of Rome's lawmaking assemblies and used them like few political leaders to date. Indeed, his activity rightly places Clodius in the small cluster of unusually prolific Roman public lawmakers, second only to the dictators Sulla and Caesar.[74]

On 10 December 59, soon after entering office, Clodius promulgated a cluster of four proposals that had been drafted beforehand. They were carefully considered. A rogatio de iure et tempore legum rogandarum established that assemblies could be convened on all appropriate days (dies fasti) and rigidly controlled some of the fundamental procedures associated with assemblies. Specifically, the bill placed constraints on using the veto at a lawmaking assembly, it prohibited obnuntiatio on the day of a legislative assembly, and it further prohibited any announcement of intent by the proper magistrate to watch the heavens for signs (which made the day unfit for a legal assembly).[75] Since the leges Aelia et Fufia (ca. 153) had first regulated these practices in order to maintain customary procedure, their uses had become politicized. The consul Bibulus had most recently demonstrated their obstructionist possibilities. Caesar, however, sustained by the prestige of Crassus and Pompey and the backing of the Roman people (among them were his own veterans from Spain), could ignore his colleague's pronouncements. In 67, the tribune Gabinius had also ignored the similar pronouncements shouted over the heads of the assembled voters by Cato from a lofty perch (he had been barred from the assembly area). Clodius's proposal addressed the abuse of traditional mechanisms for political purposes by prohibiting the use of religious injunctions and also the veto on assembly days. If watching the sky or the report of bad omens impeded the legitimate expression of the people's will, the pronouncement was illegitimate. In this way, it is generally believed, Clodius shielded his own assemblies from obstruction.

Clearly the bill would advantage other lawmakers as well, and this was also true of the rogatio de censoria notione. This bill prohibited the censors from removing anyone from the order in which he was registered without prior trial and conviction. The review of the orders was a traditional responsibility of the censors; it had, on the reinstatement of the office in 70, assumed a distinct political dimension. Undoubtedly Clodius's bill had wide appeal among the senators who had cause to worry about the possibility of expulsion. Clodius, of course, was one of these: although he had been acquitted in 61, a future censor might yet remove him from the Senate on the grounds established by the college of pontiffs in 62, sacrilege. Among Rome's lesser senators, security of position was advantageous.

On a different track from these proposals, which pertained directly only to Rome's leadership, were two measures relating to the plebs. A rogatio de collegiis restituendis novisque instituendis restored the professional and neighborhood associations, which had been prohibited by Senate decree in 64.[76] Throughout most of Rome's history, these corporations had been for the most part informally attached to the state: individuals within them might be clients of high-ranking patrons; their magistri managed certain festivals at this level of society and presumably maintained order at the neighborhood level, but the corporations themselves were fully self-governing and self-contained. In the partisan politics of the Late Republic these groups were becoming dangerously independent in their political loyalties, at least from the Senate's perspective. It was for this reason that the Senate in 64 abolished them (and later, each had to have a patron). The rogatio de collegiis restored the corporations (on which Clodius's companies were based), defined them as legitimate, and for the first time regulated the formation of new ones through a public law. Finally, a rogatio annonaria revived the notion of state-subsidized grain, which had been conceived by Gaius Gracchus and discontinued by Sulla, and established for the first time the distribution of state-purchased grain free of cost to citizens in Rome.[77] Romans would now share freely in what must have been for some the foremost privilege of empire, sustenance. Given the conditions for survival in Rome, it is hardly surprising that this particular bill was greeted with both enthusiastic general support and considerable trepidation on the part of some senators, all too aware of the scarcity of ready cash in the state treasury. On 3 January 58, the Roman people enacted all four as law in a single lawmaking assembly. Given that these measures dealt with matters salient to a diverse set of groups, the tribune's confidence in the voters presumably rested on the influencing presence of his men at the assembly. It is the case that no one offered any obstruction, although reportedly a veto was a possibility.[78]

In late February, Clodius again promulgated two proposals at the same time, both addressing the leadership of Rome. Again the voters accepted them as law. The lex Clodia de provinciis consularibus changed the provinces and commands of the consuls of 58, assigning Cilicia to Gabinius and Macedonia to Calpurnius Piso and granting each man extraordinary authority to wage war, select legates, handle funds, and adjudicate in matters involving *pecunia credita*.[79] The obvious precedent for these adjustments was the reassignment of part of Lucullus's province to Glabrio and Pompey's special command against the pirates, created by two public laws that Gabinius himself carried in 67. With respect to official practice, the law (like its precedents) was inconsistent with the arrangements in both the lex Sempronia de provinciis consularibus of 123–122, which ordained that the Senate should assign the provinces before the consular elections, and the lex Iulia de repetundis of 59, which imposed restrictions on the authority and purview of provincial commanders.[80] No one doubts that Clodius's *privilegium*, as some called it, served to dampen any consular opposition to the second of the proposals promulgated at this time.[81]

This bill, the rogatio Clodia de capite civis Romani, the most notorious of Clodius's laws, sent into exile any elected official who put Roman citizens to death without trial. While the proposal was framed broadly to include the whole Senate, all Rome understood that the measure was aimed at Cicero in particular for the death sentence passed in 63 on Cornelius Lentulus Sura and other Romans associated with Catiline. Revenge inspired the rogatio Clodia, according to ancient report: in this fashion a vengeful Clodius retaliated against Cicero for his testimony before the *quaestio extraordinaria de incestu* in 61. There were bigger issues, however, in particular the destitution and desperation of some Romans, revealed in 63. Once before the Roman people had considered such a bill, in 123, when C. Gracchus enacted the lex Sempronia de capite civis calling for the prosecution of senators responsible for the death of Ti. Gracchus in 133, under somewhat similar circumstances. In 58, Romans undoubtedly understood the implicit comparison between the two measures and the two lawmakers, separate in time. Clodius was to Catiline what Gaius had been to his brother.

Over the weeks leading up to the voting assembly, public reaction to the question of Cicero's guilt over the legal murders in 63 was extreme and divided. The consuls Gabinius and Piso, as well as Pompey, on whose public support Cicero counted, were unexpectedly reticent. Caesar condemned the executions in 63 of senators and equestrians without trial, however, condoning Clodius's proposed punishment, exile (*aqua et igni interdictio*). Crassus openly supported Clodius's proposed public law. The equestrian order sent representatives to the Senate to speak in Cicero's defense. The consul Gabinius, however, would not let them in the Senate House and admonished two senators, Hortensius and Curio, for joining the effort. Clodius likewise reprimanded the two senators in a public meeting and obstructed the tribune Ninnius's efforts to defend Cicero. Ninnius exhorted the people to put on military dress to face the armed threat of Clodius's bands. Many senators did then change into military dress—until the consuls issued an edict ordering them to put their togas back on. Cicero at length left Rome in voluntary exile, and around 20 March the voters approved Clodius's measure.[82] Within days Clodius promulgated a second proposal, the rogatio Clodia de exilio Ciceronis, calling for the exile of Cicero by name, the confiscation of his property, and the demolition of his house in Rome.[83] Furthermore, it required Cicero to approach no closer to Rome than five hundred Roman miles. Cicero, who had gone initially to Sicily, was compelled to find a more distant perch ultimately in far-off Thrace. Securing his banishment, the voters enacted the bill in April.

Within two months, on 1 June, the Senate approved one of many drafts of several public law proposals to recall Cicero. In such an atmosphere of competitive lawmaking, now a common phenomenon, the divisions within the political leadership are obvious. Whether or not Ninnius ever in fact promulgated this first proposal, a colleague promised to veto the measure and nothing came of it. In July the praetor L. Domitius Ahenobarbus announced he would propose a bill to recall Cicero, but he never did. Finally, in October, eight tribunes collectively promulgated another proposal for Cicero's recall; this was never taken to a voting assembly.[84] Clodius's response to such efforts was to post at the entrance of the Curia a copy of his law, which stipulated that any effort to contravene its provisions were illegal. All in all, Cicero's exile appears to be the most controversial lawmaking issue ever mooted in Rome.

Throughout the remainder of the year, Clodius kept up a steady pace of law production. The various enactments of record include a series of measures concerned with the east. A lex de provincia consulare assigned Syria instead of Cilicia to the consul Gabinius. Cilicia was no longer the critical assignment it had been earlier in the year because the newly annexed Cyprus had not been attached to it after all, as was evidently the original plan. Two measures were concerned with foreign kings. One bill confirmed the Senate's recognition of Deiotarus as king. As tetrarch in Galatia and ally of Rome in the wars against Mithridates, Deiotarus received the expanded Galatia as a result of Pompey's arrangements in Asia with the stipulation that his son-in-law, Brogitarus, should receive a small kingdom centered on the city of Pessinus, seat of the cult of Magna Mater. It was said that Brogitarus paid Clodius for his kingdom. Another bill ordered the confiscation of Ptolemey's royal properties on the island of Cyprus and the restoration of the Byzantine exiles and appointed M. Porcius Cato, apparently with the rank of quaestor pro praetore, to accomplish these matters.[85] There were also measures addressing matters in Rome and Italy, namely, a bill exempting a municeps, one Menula of Anagnia, from the regulations of the lex Cornelia de iniuriis of 81 and one restricting the business activities of quaestorian scribae.

In all these matters Clodius reveals himself as an astute, ambitious leader, exercising his extensive political assets in the interests of his political advancement. Like all Roman nobiles, Clodius backed his political career with other people's money. For him, the east held potent and wealthy foreign clientes. As their patron, Clodius affirmed and advanced their local dominance in a Roman world. Never mind that he interfered directly with Pompey's arrangements in the east, enacted the previous year; he needed cash. Notwithstanding, Clodius also had the people's interests at heart. Thus the scrupulously honest Cato managed Cyprus and shipped the resulting funds intact to Rome, where they were applied to the purchase of grain for distribution in accordance with the lex annonaria carried at the beginning of the year. And in Syria, Gabinius fought an important campaign against the Jews over the next two years, confirming that military exigencies were carefully considered in the reassignment.

The underlying issues of Clodius's lawmaking activity are far more momentous than the desire for vengeance often cited. They embrace not only family and tribe but the societywide schism between those Romans in favor of Italy-wide incorporation, with all its implications, and those Romans adamantly opposed. To be sure, personal motivations play a role.[86] However, they do not explain his vision, which saw a deliberate, controlled, group participation by marginal citizens in the traditional political process.[87] These were the same new citizens, former slaves, disenfranchised and impoverished Romans, and even slaves who had followed Catiline. But unlike Catiline, Clodius in effect brought Rome's dispossessed into the Roman system and, more important, devised the means of bringing these Romans into the system. Building on the fundamental units of daily life in Rome, the neighborhood and professional associations with their corporate structures, magistrates, and voting members, Clodius contrived a similar one, on a military plan. It was in fact an urban army whose internal organization and leadership mirrored the social and military networks of the larger society and whose membership intersected with the membership in the thirty-five tribes by virtue of the large numbers of dispossessed tribesmen resident in Rome. Militantly then, Clodius used lawmaking assemblies to push forward social and political changes more extreme than the insurgent Catiline's, in particular the incorporation of low-status groups within the citizen population.[88] Had Clodius lived to become praetor his intended first bill would have granted citizenship, the vote, and registration in the rural tribes to a select group of former slaves, thus expanding his organization to include all the tribes.[89]

THE POLITICIZATION OF PUBLIC LAWMAKING

Customary Roman public law sessions, convened to determine the sovereign will of the people, were wrapped in elaborate rituals of accommodation whose performance was vital to the legitimization of the end products of those sessions. Notwithstanding the clear importance of the proper observance of ritual procedure to the creation of legitimate law, and notwithstanding the untroubled observance of prescribed procedures and formalities in most public arenas, in the Late Republican lawmaking arena, political leaders had come to deviate from those procedures, repeatedly and flagrantly. At meetings and assemblies, leaders subverted conventions, ignored the auspices and omens, and inspired violence directed against magistrates. Among the better-known examples are the unprecedented efforts of Cornelius in 67 and Q. Caecilius Metellus Nepos in 62 to press ahead with the lawmaking process by intoning the bill themselves after the herald was silenced by veto and the efforts of Bibulus in 59 to terminate the lawmaking sessions of Julius Caesar by the repeated announcement that he was watching the skies. On few other occasions involving ritual procedure were disruptions so common. Significantly, electoral assemblies were the exception, where these disruptions, however, took the form of bribery, coercing the voters through violence, or stuffing the ballot box rather than interfering with procedure. Seldom in any arena other than public lawmaking was there a similar, sustained concern to regularize customary formal procedures through public law enactments.

The statutes governing the production of law and other public business in voting assemblies over the years 91–44 map the changes in the conduct and outcome of lawmaking sessions. A listing of all such statutes generated between 350 and 44, collected in table 9.3, allows us to put the specific laws of the period 91–44 in context. Typically, all the enactments appear to be responses to particular situations. Yet, every public law proposal was intended to maintain the conditions under which the lawmaking process should traditionally reflect the collective will of the Roman people. Such was also the case in the earlier period between 350 and 92 with earlier public laws and proposals relating to voting assemblies.[90] While the frequency of such measures quite obviously increases earlier, around the mid-second century, the issues that they address throughout the first century provide far more significant indicators of change. From now on all measures governing the production of law are aimed at recognizable deviations from custom introduced by the elite managers and participants of the events. A much stronger concern with electoral bribery is evident in the period, reinforced by a new concern for recently emerging political clubs whose operation, like ambitus, is defined as a crime (table 9.3).[91] The crime of violence, vis, makes its appearance. An effort to systematize the archiving of laws is under way (table 9.3). We have previously discussed the tribune Clodius's concern with the interruption of comitial days by the announcement of bad omens. The importance of public lawmaking explains the necessity of imposing such rules to ensure that the occasion played out as it should.

In the years between 69 and 44 Roman society had reached such a scale and included so many diverse groups as to render a traditional balance much more difficult to obtain. When the size of the Roman population threw the system out of kilter, because so many groups embodied the sovereign will of the Roman people, the Romans continued to make regulations, as prior generations had, geared in intention to guaranteeing that the system work the way it should. The unintended outcome was to curtail if not totally subdue the potential for group expression. Instead of keeping the system in balance the activities of individual leaders "politicized" lawmaking. In turn, the most effective control of the lawmaking arena was imposed by political leaders, not on that arena directly but on other political leaders. The native competition of elite Romans had traditionally encouraged a remarkable degree of self-policing. But conditions were different over the first century,

Bringing the changes in the period 91–44 into focus is the occurrence of irregularities or obstructions, including vetoes, in the public lawmaking process between 350 and 44. The frequent incidences of violence accompanying the passage of laws are best known because reports of such violence become pervasive in our narrative sources. The violence accompanying the proposals of the tribune Metellus Nepos in 62 was viewed by the Senate with such alarm that they passed the "final decree" (*senatus consultum ultimum*) enabling the consul to use force to bring the city to order.[92] Such episodes are relatively infrequent. More important than frequency is the fact that routine violence is a tendency found only in the later Republic.[93] And in this period, several laws dealing with violence in the conduct of public business were enacted: a lex Plautia de vi dated uncertainly to the tribunate of Plautius in 70, a lex Pompeia de vi in 52, and a lex Iulia de vi in 46 (table 9.3). Significantly the violence at issue in these laws was some other Roman's violence. Sulla, for instance, to whom is sometimes attributed the earliest such public law, was the first Roman to use force against Rome itself when he ordered his troops to take the city after the passage of P. Sulpicius's enactments in 88. In any event, through such laws many elite Romans, and some men of lesser status, were prosecuted for their role in fomenting violence at lawmaking or electoral sessions.[94] The annulment of laws is again infrequent but occurs with greater frequency in the later period too. Indeed, the outright annulment of law was unreported before 100.[95] Customarily, laws were enacted to suspend or circumvent existing laws in specific circumstances without undoing the earlier public law. During the second century, however, laws were "undone" or abrogated by the passage of another law that revised the arrangements of the law in question or returned matters to the status quo ante.[96] The legislation of C. Gracchus provides a case in point.[97] While such processes of revision continue in the period between 91 and 44, they are now accompanied, for the first time on any scale, by efforts to simply cancel outright the laws of a given lawmaker. The earliest laws to be annulled in this fashion were those of the tribune of 103 and 100, Saturninus, whose laws were annulled by the Senate after his death by stoning in 100.[98] The laws of the tribune Sex. Titius in 99 followed.[99] In 91, the Roman Senate annulled by decree the laws of Livius Drusus, after his assassination, as passed "against the auspices and existing laws."[100] The laws of P. Sulpicius, in 88, were annulled, followed by the laws of the consuls themselves in 88, Sulla and Pompeius Rufus. One of Sulla's first acts as dictator in 82 was the restoration of his laws as consul in 88. A bill carried by C. Manilius early in his year of office, 66, was annulled because he failed to observe the trinundinum.[101] Bibulus tried but failed to have the laws of Julius Caesar annulled in 59. From the perspective of the new man Cicero, such laws—he talks specifically of the leges Appuleia, Titia, and Livia—were illegal because the lawmakers were incapable of distinguishing between good and evil; they were not leaders of the "right sort."[102] From the perspective of the historian, a great deal more was obviously at stake. Lawmaking activity throughout the period, in particular in highest frequency years, comes to exhibit forms of behavior that, though not new to the Roman experience, have now reached a critical level and indicate a dramatic acceleration in the immediate, political uses of lawmaking assemblies. The "competitive" lawmaking of C. Gracchus, M. Livius Drusus, and M. Minucius Rufus in 123–121 hinted at changes to come in the lawmaking arena. The lawmaking of 88 confirms that changes had arrived.

Signs of a shift in the acceptance of public laws, particularly on the part of political leaders, become apparent with such instances of "competitive" lawmaking, that is, leaders using the lawmaking process to nullify earlier laws on a far more frequent basis than ever before or seeking annulment of public law because of procedural errors. These changes began to accelerate with the potentially dramatic increase in the numbers of newcomers into the ranks of Roman citizens after the Italian War. Hostility and resistance to newcomers accompanied incorporation at all times but especially after 90. Resistance to newcomers took several forms, but particularly obvious were the efforts to manage the voting power of the newcomers by limiting their access to tribes and property classes without which they could not vote. At issue was the difficulty of maintaining the nexus of relationships centered on the tribes.

The advent of statutes guaranteed by oaths may be seen as a Roman way of dealing with competitive lawmaking and other innovations. While the leges sacratae of the fifth century and later were a traditional form of public law, the laws of Saturninus and Caesar, which included a mandatory oath, were a new phenomenon. Like the oaths sworn by jurors and other parties involved in the business of the permanent courts, oaths attached to laws attest a certain weakening of conventions. Mandatory oaths prevented another sponsor from proposing another bill for the purpose of undoing the oath-bound law. Why was this necessary? In view of the commonly accepted mechanism of enforcing laws, the fact of the people's vote, the emergence of mandatory oaths seems to indicate a problem with enforcement or a refusal to recognize that a particular crowd present for a particular assembly voices the will of the Roman people. Oaths are both a reminder of the strength of the lawmaking process, and a way of offsetting the weakening commitment of Roman political leaders to the process.

Such convoluted expressions of the ordinary lawmaking process underscore the importance of public lawmaking to the majority population. Only senators were required to swear to the law of Saturninus in 103 and Caesar in 59. Even as the social order of the Late Republic was unraveling, the Roman people were committed to the idea that the approved means of resolving societywide problems involved the development of group consensus in lawmaking assemblies. Accordingly efforts by individual leaders to manipulate the outcome of the process—whether by ignoring procedure or adhering too rigidly to procedure—often precipitated a violent reaction from the assembled voters. The public recitation of his own law proposal by Cornelius in 67 and the removal of tablets advertising a proposed law by the magister equitum M. Antonius in 47 provide cases in point. Such was the voters' determination to ensure that the Roman people be allowed to express their sovereign will in an uncoerced fashion. Violence itself, then, as well as other forms of illegal behavior became at times the operative means to the desired end, namely, the resolution of conflict among the various groups constituting Roman society. Undoubtedly the beliefs that made this possible are the same beliefs that established lawmaking as the primary vehicle for bringing about agreement among groups of Romans. Yet our understanding of the underlying causes of such behavior on the part of Rome's leaders needs to be deepened. Why did Roman leaders take the particular intractable actions they are credited with? Why, despite the regular efforts to interfere with public lawmaking sessions, did the Roman faith in the process endure?

When the praetor M. Marius Gratidianus issued an edict in 85 establishing a method to test and remove debased coinage from circulation, the neighborhood associations in Rome offered sacrifices on his behalf at the local shrines.[103] For the first time, a living man attained cult status in Rome. In uttering this edict, however, Marius Gratidianus had preempted for purposes of self-aggrandizement a joint edict agreed to by both praetors, with the support of the tribunes. Marius Gratidianus's efforts were rewarded by his peers with resentment, obstruction over his candidacy for the office of consul, and eventually murder during the proscriptions instituted by Sulla. In 82, Catiline reportedly carried the ex-praetor's severed head through the streets of Rome to the Senate House. But in 85, the people of Rome rewarded him immediately with the honors owed to the gods, an occurrence that Gratidianus, whose ambition was presumably nothing more than the Roman consulate, probably neither expected nor sought: honoring men as gods was untypical practice in Rome at this time, although not in the Greek East, where Roman commanders had become the objects of cult by local inhabitants long before now, as the Roman troops under their command were well aware. This spontaneous reaction by the commercial sector of the city population to an elected official reveals both the mutual ties and potential misunderstandings that existed between the nonelite majority of Romans and their leaders. Clearly Gratidianus acted from a perception both of public need and personal ambition. Honored by the city population for the one, he was eventually murdered by his peers for the other.

The interaction between Roman leaders and the Roman majority in the law-making arena was just as complicated by the tensions of public need and personal ambition. The mutual dependence of magistrates and people was a pervasive and constant feature of the Roman system; they existed in a symbiotic relationship, whether engaged in public lawmaking or any other public event. In law-making that relationship was crucial to the expression of valid law. But the relationship could be dangerous for the individual who exceeded some unstated limit imposed by the larger group. When it happened that the people turned to a leader who was not an elite member of society, which occurred only once, in 44, when a man appeared identifying himself as the grandson of C. Marius and surrounded by a crowd of supporters led an emotional assault against the assassins of his presumptive cousin, Caesar, M. Antonius did not tolerate it.[104] Supported by the Senate he lynched the supposed impostor in a display of group solidarity. Even when the man was a member of the elite classes, like Marius Gratidianus in 85 (or Ti. Gracchus in 133, C. Gracchus in 121, Saturninus in 100, or Livius Drusus in 91), independence was not tolerated, if seen as potentially threatening to the larger group.

The episode of Marius Gratidianus, suggesting the extent to which the traditional understandings about social hierarchy of the Roman people were key to maintaining public order in Rome, draws our attention to one of the more striking features of Roman society. The Roman people and their rulers, two groups widely separated by the gulf of wealth and status differences, inhabited the same cultural world, and to a remarkable degree they shared the same assumptions about the workings of their common world. Often, despite the best efforts of the leadership, ordinary members of society were able to compel recognition of their problems. But in matters of public order and the public good the goals of political leaders and the majority population often clashed in a surprising way. The circumstances of the fate of the reputed grandson of C. Marius in 44 make one thing clear: When order broke down in Roman society, generally the leaders initiated it, not the Roman people.

In this context, the violence that often accompanied the Romans' pursuit of legitimacy in law and government, during the last century of the Roman Republic, is striking. At meetings and assemblies rocks were thrown, heads broken, and magistrates and senators abused and occasionally murdered, most frequently by other senators. Sometimes, senators devised methods to control each other and other political leaders in scheduled assemblies, which appear to be at variance with the legitimizing procedures through which the events of the assembly should unfold. The actions of Cornelius Scipio Nasica, chief priest (pontifex maximus), leading up to the assassination of Ti. Gracchus come to mind. After a hurried meeting of the Senate, Scipio led a band of senators to the place of assembly armed with clubs, himself in the lead with his toga pulled over his head as though he were performing a sacrifice. At the assembly they clubbed Gracchus and hundreds of his supporters to death. Following such examples, other Romans initiated similar actions: Livius Drusus had the violent support of Latins in seeking approval for his proposals in 92; P. Sulpicius coordinated the coercive activities of equestrians in 89; many other instances mark the final years of the Roman Republic. What gives meaning to such episodes is the validating, normative function of procedure. For the violence is usually associated with direct efforts to disrupt procedures, such as stopping the recitation or tearing down the posted tablets. Violence further recognizes the fundamental principal of Roman civic life—that the ultimate legitimization for any event was the will of the Roman people. To some extent violence represents the expression of that will even when the ordinary potential in normal lawmaking activity for building consensus was missing.

Another feature of such violence is its "self-help" nature, as we understand the term in early Roman law. Families, specifically the pater familias, advised by a council of elder family members, decide the crime and pass judgment on family members. At moments of deep class crisis, some leaders pass quick judgment upon their peers or inferiors and exact punishment—usually death by violence. The violent deaths of the tribunes Ti. Gracchus in 133, C. Gracchus in 121, and Saturninus in 100, together with many others who supported the same causes, at the hands of fellow senators are examples of such "self-help" action. It is symptomatic of an aristocracy whose members see themselves as the upholders of the proper social order and the ultimate arbiters of right and wrong. Among the Roman leadership, the principle flows through the legal system, initially in its lower rungs and throughout the second century in the gradual development of definitions of capital crimes and courts to investigate them. The tresviri capitales, for instance, during the third century, constituted a panel of summary judges who passed sentence on petty thieves haled before them during the night hours. Of far greater import was the institutionalizing of such action in the Senate decree, known as the final decree (senatus consultum ultimum), passed by the Senate first in 123 and only seven times thereafter at moments of extreme danger to the security of the senatorial order as interpreted by different groups of senators.[105] By the terms of the final decree, the consul was empowered to kill citizens with impunity. The death of C. Gracchus was sanctioned by this decree, as was the execution of several senators and equestrians by the consul Cicero in 63, conspirators with Catiline in the attempted coup of that year. Significantly, no Roman appears to have been fully at ease with the final decree.

Arguably at the core of this unease, and equally at the core of the inability of elite Romans to sustain the customary operation of the system, is the massive transformation in membership suffered in the first century. War and civil war had taken a convulsive toll on the political leadership of Rome. While the addition of new members to the Roman political aristocracy at the end of the civil war in 82 was necessary, it also created unanticipated strains. In particular, the addition of new members to the Senate by Sulla created divisions within the Senate itself. In 70 the censors, elected for the first time since 86, purged the Senate of sixty-four members. Over the intervening period between 81 and 70 tensions between senators and men with the equestrian rating had escalated; in 70 the praetor L. Aurelius Cotta carried a measure reconstituting the standing court juries as three panels drawn from the senators, the equestrian order, and tribuni aerarii. The moral grounds cited for the removal of some senators in 70—including Q. Curius, quaestor 71; C. Antonius, later consul in 63; Cornelius Lentulus Sura, consul in 71; and several senators associated with the trial of the equestrian Statius Albius Oppianicus in 74—probably mask the efforts of some senators to cling to an order in which lineage determined political success to a far greater degree than was now possible. The customary relationship between the Roman leadership and the people in arenas of customary interaction was changing, rendering the connections between the leaders and the led more tenuous. And to a far greater degree than ever before the new leaders display a different commitment to the proper procedures in various arenas of public life, most noticeably in public lawmaking. The commitment to customary Roman ways on the part of Rome's political leadership had become noticeably diluted.

Among the statutory rules that Cicero envisioned for a rejuvenated Rome in his treatise *De Legibus* was one giving the censor charge of the authorized version of public law statutes (*fidem legum*).[106] For, Cicero lamented, there was no such version in the records, with the result that statutes were what the clerical staff made them:

> legum custodiam nullam habemus; itaque eae leges sunt, quas apparitores nostri volunt; a librariis petimus, publicis litteris consignatam memoriam publicam nullam habemus.
>
> *[We have no guardianship of statutes, and therefore they are whatever our clerks want them to be; we get them from the copyists, but have no public memory, entered in the public records.]*
>
> (*Leg.* 3.20.46)

He went on to praise the Athenian nomophylakes, who guarded both records of statutes and observance of the law, as the Roman pontifices had done at the dawn of the Republic. This passage urging the restoration of an aristocratic watch over laws and behavior, drawn from Cicero's justification for the rules he proposed, conveys succinctly his forlorn hope to revive a tradition of oligarchy long since passed away.

Captured in Cicero's complaint is a glimpse of the concern newly emerging in the first century over the legitimacy of the statutes recorded in the state archives and engraved on bronze tablets for ceremonial display. Given the complexity of Roman society we can well imagine the scope of the problem. Statutes generated in assemblies of the Roman people addressed a wide variety of pressing issues, of concern to a varying range of groups among the aristocracy and ordinary citizens. The simple logistics alone of the storage and retrieval of a body of enactments distilling, year by year, the necessary rules and adjustments that enabled so diverse a population to maintain its cohesion, when the widely varied interests of so many were at stake, must have been phenomenal. In turn, the opportunities for manipulating the record on the part of aristocrats were numerous, primarily because an engraved or archived law was taken to be what its physical embodiment on bronze tablets or its presence in the archives declared it to be, a decision of the people, a Senate decree, or some other expression of law. The legitimacy of engraved or archived law was assumed, because it derived ultimately from the circumstances and conditions of passage.

The flutter of concern in the late 60s and 50s to safeguard filing procedures suggests that some changes were afoot. At this time, senators and clerks alike could be casual in their duties, neglecting witnesses and entering faked decrees. The registration procedure was subject to abuse. As long as witnesses could be suborned the record could be manipulated. To correct such abuses, M. Porcius Cato as quaestor in 64 insisted on proper witnessing procedures, by men of repute. He personally supervised the entry of documents in the record, paying particular attention to the witnessing of Senate decrees.[107] For it was senators who were submitting fabricated decrees, witnessed by other senators. Not until the consuls had sworn that it was a decree of the Senate did Cato allow it to be entered as such.[108] Cato was a one-man army on this campaign, and the enemies were his colleagues both in office and in the Senate.

Two years later as tribune, Cato followed the same lines he had set for himself in the office of quaestor.[109] He was the watchdog of lawful procedure in assembly business and so prosecuted the consul-elect Licinius Murena for bribery at his consular election.[110] Plutarch records also that Cato took his duties as senator seriously. On days when the Senate met he was the first to arrive and the last to leave; he never left Rome when the Senate was in session. He paid such scrupulous attention to matters that were discussed that unfair measures could not be got past him. In other years Pompey used to devise schemes to keep Cato away from meetings at which he wanted a free hand (Plut. *Cat. Min.* 19.1). Particulars of this kind abound in the tradition about Cato's exceptional conscientiousness and fairness.[111]

A Roman concern for assurances about the validity of archival records of law also surfaces in a statute brought by the consuls of 62, Iunius Silanus and L. Licinius Murena, that appears to regulate filing procedures for statutes and specifically the proper witnessing of statutes as they were entered into the public records.[112] Since Licinius Murena consulted Cato on the most important matters as consul we might assume his law draft was shaped by Cato's efforts.[113]

Unfortunately the content and intent of the lex Licinia Iunia are known only from a handful of nonspecific references; invariably the statute is coupled with the lex Caecilia Didia of 98, which enacted that the three-Roman-week advertising period should be observed in the production of statutes.[114] The lex Licinia Iunia appears to have regulated the entry of statutes in the public record by instituting some manner of supervision that guaranteed that the statute entered in the record was the same statute approved at the assembly. In other words, the lex Licinia Iunia required witnesses for the first time, in order to guarantee statutes. The absence of a requirement for witnesses would account for Cicero's lament that no "public memory" of statutes was entered and verified (*consignatam*) in the records. Verifying the text of a statute was unnecessary during the wholly public stages of lawmaking but became necessary when the statute was in transit, so to speak, from that public arena to the Aerarium. Thus, the change instituted by the lex Licinia Iunia probably had to do with the mechanism for entering statutes in the record at the Aerarium. Elsewhere in *De Legibus*, composed in the late 50s and 40s, Cicero aired his concern with filing procedure. On lawmaking occasions, Cicero thought it was desirable to bring the Aerarium into the picture at an early stage. In his ideal law he made it the responsibility of the magistrate to inform the Aerarium about a proposal of law: *in aerario cognita* (*Leg*. 3.4.11).[115]

Given the opportunities for manipulating the public record evidenced in the 60s, it is not surprising that correctives were sought. By the 40s, the registration of decrees was a solemn occasion. The Jewish historian Josephus reports that Caesar and King Herod of Judaea, who had been present in the Senate on one occasion, went together to the Capitoline hill to deposit a decree in the records and then to sacrifice. The manner of deposition was regulated, as we have seen: how successfully is unknown. Certainly the number of recorded witnesses more than doubled, some measure of the Roman determination to disseminate trust among as large a group as possible. Perhaps the sheer bulk of the material at issue overwhelmed the effort. But also the practice of engraving statutes on bronze appears, in the 40s, to have became more regular. In a chance remark, Cicero wondered how Antony could privilege the dead Caesar's notebooks over the live Caesar's decisions (*acta*), "that he had engraved on bronze, on which he desired that the commands of the Roman people and perpetual statues [should be engraved]."[116] The phrase clearly refers to the intention on the part of Caesar to make engraving a routine procedure for decisions by the Roman people. The practice was common enough already, because Cicero also charged some years earlier that Clodius had engraved statutes at home before they had been promulgated, discussed, and approved by the Roman people; before, in fact, Clodius had even been elected praetor.[117] In Caesar's concern to regularize the practice we probably see the deliberate efforts of Romans to create a bond between archival and monumental record. Bronze endowed the law with a kind of sanctity that makes sense in an atmosphere of uncertainty about what was legitimate and what was not. In view of the concern emerging in the middle of the first century to establish the legitimacy of statutes, the Romans had recourse increasingly to the legitimizing and eternalizing effects of engraving a legal document on bronze. Caesar, who also undertook to sort through and codify the laws of Rome, apparently desired that all commands of the people (iussa populi) be engraved on bronze—undoubtedly to bring them forcefully and physically into the public arena and into the view of the Roman people. Engraving statutes on bronze became one of the primary means of ensuring their legitimization.[118]

Accordingly, one solution to the social disruption inherent in the lawmaking system built on the two common ways of handling statutes once the voting assemblies had approved them: archiving them and engraving them on bronze. This produced respectively "archival records," that is, legal documents entered into the "public record" in the state archives, and "monumental records" or legal documents engraved on bronze tablets and displayed primarily on the Capitoline hill.[119] In their use of bronze tablets and in their archival reforms, the Romans attempted a kind of restorative management of law. It was manifested in the public arena by strengthening the means of disseminating the commands of the people in a permanent form, that is, by the display of law on bronze and by systematizing and strengthening aristocratic control over legal information. In their adaptation of engraving and archiving, the Romans again confirmed their genius for finding new options in customary ways of controlling their world.

PUBLIC LAWMAKING DURING THE CIVIL WAR YEARS, 49–44

In 49, when the young tribune Metellus cited the law to refuse Julius Caesar admittance to the reserve treasury in the Aerarium, Caesar retorted that there was a time for law and a time for arms.[120] Threatened with his life, Metellus judiciously retreated, and Caesar relieved the state of hard cash to supply his army. Over the next few years, arms prevailed as Caesar waged bloody battles against his enemies in the Senate. But even in war, the Romans were mindful of the law. During the turbulent years between 49 and 44 at least forty-eight law proposals were presented to the Roman people, as shown in table 9.4. Although considerably more lawmaking occasions fall in the three years following Julius Caesar's return to Rome in 46, the record shows about fourteen laws between 49 and 47.[121] In view of the turmoil of these years, we are entitled to marvel at the zeal of thousands of Romans converging on Rome's voting locales. More important, however, is the meaning of these events in their day. To appreciate this, let me begin with an overview of public laws and their context during the civil war years from 49 to March of 44, the month of Caesar's assassination.

In 49, en route to Rome following his successful campaign in Spain, where he won over the legions of Pompey, Caesar became dictator through a law proposed by the praetor M. Aemilius Lepidus.[122] Arrived in Rome, Caesar administered routine matters of government requiring an elected official's direction: he presided over the Latin festival, held the elections, allotted provinces, and selected new priests to fill vacancies in the colleges.[123] Caesar's most consequential act involved debt. He instructed the praetors with regard to suits involving the collection of debts to institute a "new mechanism . . . of appointed assessors and valuations at pre-war prices," which regulated the assessment of property and the repayment of debts and forbade anyone from possessing more than HS 60,000 worth of gold or silver.[124] Two additional mandates evidently followed in late 48.[125] In this way Caesar addressed the dangerous money crisis faced by Romans of all stations but especially aristocrats, produced by the staggering costs of war, the high level of borrowing, the determination of creditors to call in their loans, and the inability of indebted Romans to make good because of the shortage of ready cash. As we shall see, Caesar's mandate did not resolve the matter of debt.[126] Stepping down after eleven days, Caesar left in pursuit of Pompey, apparently leaving to others in Rome the business of regulating affairs through lawmaking assemblies.

Most of the laws of record in 49 were probably proposed by tribunes and praetors. As tribune, M. Antonius presented a bill that allowed the sons of men proscribed by Sulla to resume the prerogatives of their previous status, specifically to run for elected office, an issue that had been addressed in a number of earlier proposals, and another measure that restored the men condemned under the lex Pompeia de vi of 52.[127] A law was presented to the people to confirm Caesar's grant of citizenship to the Gaditani.[128] A grant of citizenship was finally made to the Transpadani, another issue that had been contested over past years. Caesar had a long involvement with the Transpadani and the question of citizenship; he was not the law sponsor, however. Ultimately the sponsor is unknown, although modern scholars often identify him as the praetor L. Roscius.[129] While our sources indicate that more laws were probably enacted in 49—for example, the lex de Gallia Cisalpina (*RS* 1 No. 28), which addressed the judicial organization of Cisalpine Gaul, might have been enacted in 49 and in any event no later than 42—these are the most visible in the record and the most certainly dated to 49.

The lawmaking activity of 48 and 47 fell during the long months of Caesar's absence, until September of 47. After the Battle of Pharsalus, probably in October of 48, Caesar was again made dictator rei gerundae causa through a public law, now for one year.[130] Caesar also was granted a triumph by a public law, in the period following Pharsalus, and he was given the powers of a tribune by another law. Another law granting privileges is dated no earlier than 48 and before 44. Scholars assign a tribunate to A. Hirtius in 48 and credit him with the lex Hirtia de Pompeianis, of uncertain content except that it concerned treatment of Pompey's supporters.[131] No further laws are recorded until late 48 and 47, when first the praetor M. Caelius Rufus, followed by the tribune P. Cornelius Dolabella, unsuccessfully promulgated a set of laws on debts and rents. This effort, culminating in the episode with which I began this chapter, requires some elaboration.

Caesar's equitable adjustments in 49 and 48, combined with the shortage of hard cash, made the repayment of debt a matter of desperate concern still to many Romans. Hence in 48, the praetor peregrinus M. Caelius Rufus announced that he would not adjudicate suits regarding the collection of debts and rents according to Caesar's instructions to the praetors in 49 but would apply his own remedies to advantage out-of-pocket debtors.[132] To that end he promulgated a bill and in so doing flouted Caesar.[133] That Caelius Rufus aimed in this way to build support for his own political advance is confirmed not only by the violence of his conflict with the urban praetor, Trebonius over the matter but by his decision to promulgate two more bills granting the full suspension of payment of debts and rents.[134] While the consul and Senate took firm action against Caelius, forcing him out of Rome, they did so without the full support of the Roman people or the tribunes.[135] In the following year, the tribune P. Cornelius Dolabella resurrected the substance of Caelius's bills in two proposals of similar intent, provoking the attack on the Forum by the master of the horse M. Antonius and the Senate's decree that there would be no laws until Caesar's return.[136] Caesar did return to Rome in September of 47, and although he made many decisions, none appears to be public law. His stay in Rome was brief, as he soon departed for Africa.

In April of 46, following his victories in Africa, Julius Caesar became dictator legibus scribendis et rei publicae constituendae, the position devised more than thirty years earlier by Sulla.[137] Unlike Sulla, Caesar was to hold the position for ten years.[138] In this capacity Caesar now turned to the public lawmaking process.[139] Already a lawmaker of distinction, with seven laws sponsored as consul in 59, Caesar is credited with at least eleven more between 46 and his death in 44, 32 percent of the recorded laws (thirty-four) for the entire period down to Caesar's death, as shown in table 9.4. The laws address a range of issues, all pertaining to the order and administration of the Roman state and including the length of tenure of provincial governors, the selection of priests, limits on luxury spending, travel abroad by senators, the crimes of vis and maiestas, jury membership, the status of herdsmen, and the imposition of port duties. Following the efforts of M. Caelius Rufus and Dolabella, Caesar at last presented his own law on debt, the lex Iulia de bonis cedendis.[140]

Between 46 and March of 44, comparatively fewer laws were presented to public lawmaking assemblies by other elected officials. One Caecilius, a tribune of 45, sponsored bills concerning Caesar's urban development plans.[141] In 44, another tribune, L. Cassius Longinus, sponsored a bill to make new patrician families. The tribune C. Helvius Cinna sponsored a bill removing two of his colleagues from office, following an incident where they removed a crown placed on the head of a statue of Caesar. Cinna also had a bill in the works at the time of Caesar's assassination that would allow Caesar to marry as many women as he wanted. Another tribune, L. Antonius, presented a law that gave Caesar the privilege of selecting half the magistrates each year.[142] Caesar's colleague in the consulship, M. Antonius, sponsored a similar bill renaming the month of Quintilis after Caesar. Of course, elected officials continued to enact laws throughout the remainder of 44, after Caesar's assassination in March. But even in death, Caesar's lawmaking activity—at least four posthumous bills appeared in his name—outstripped that of any other magistrate, except M. Antonius (table 9.4).

Notwithstanding considerable confusion about the laws and lawmakers of these years, there is a pattern. To begin, Julius Caesar's lawmaking activity between 49 and 47 is highly uncertain. Most if not all of the laws of this period are attributable to other magistrates, some known and some unknown.[143] When in Rome, however, Caesar often initiated laws sponsored by other magistrates. He also began the conflicted process of regulating the most pressing issue of the day, debt, through other magistrates, specifically the praetors. Looking at the issues addressed by the laws of other magistrates between 49 and 47—namely, the restoration of civil rights (bis: leges Antoniae, 49), the grant of citizenship to the Transpadani (49), the grant of tribunician power to Caesar (48), Caesar's triumph (48), the capacity of Pompey's supporters to stand for office (lex Hirtia, 48), the remission of rents and settlement of debts (rogationes Caeliae and Corneliae, 48 and 47), and perhaps the judicial organization of Gaul (lex de Gallia Cisalpina, between 49 and 42)—we have the impression that before the firm defeat of his enemies Caesar was careful to distance himself from the business of articulating the will of a divided Roman people on controversial matters. To be sure, Caesar was absent from Rome for most of the period between 49 and 46, except for eleven days in 49 and another brief stay in 47. Even so, the matters presented to the people by other magistrates after 47—the consul Antonius and three tribunes in 44, before Caesar's death—namely, controversial privileges for the strongest man in Rome, reinforce the impression. More important, the vigor of the Senate's reaction to the efforts of Caelius (in 48) and especially Dolabella (in 47) to resolve the enormous problem of debt through lawmaking assemblies, signals finally an irrevocable consenus at the highest levels to silence the voice of the Roman people. No new laws until the return of Caesar, decreed the Senate in 47. Significantly, it appears to be now, for the first time, that Caesar was named dictator legibus scribendis et rei publicae constituendae. The timing is hardly coincidental.

His own lawmaking efforts after 47 suggest that Caesar knew well the importance of, and had visions of monopolizing, the right of articulating the people's will on uncontested matters. When the civil war had ended in 46, Caesar began the reconstruction of the Roman state, often through lawmaking assemblies. Although it is impossible to determine in every case whether Caesar took an issue to a lawmaking assembly or dealt with it by mandate, certainly some of the most critical matters percolated through the assemblies.[144] Limits were set and opportunities created for Rome's highest classes; at the same time the damage done to their membership and privileges, diluted by the entry of lower-status Romans during the civil wars, was repaired. Predictability returned. More important, Caesar tried to restore the conditions that the Romans believed allowed the growth and prosperity of Rome. Among other laws of the period belong the lex Iulia de sacerdotiis, the lex Iulia de provinciis, and the lex Iulia iudiciaria.[145] In the course of regulating troublesome areas of Roman life and law, Caesar again enacted a law of lasting import for the Roman legal system, as he did in 59 with the lex Iulia de pecuniis repetundis, namely, the lex Iulia de bonis cedendis, which "created the rights of a debtor on which all our modern bankruptcy regulations are based."[146] Like Sulla before him, Caesar recognized the utility of public law in restoring the Roman state.

CONCLUSION

With the civil wars of 49–44 we reach a defining moment in public lawmaking in the Roman Republic. No longer was the expression of the Roman people's will in lawmaking assemblies universally and unequivocally accepted as the final authority in solving community crisis. No longer did the decisions of assembled voters have binding force on the whole community. Since the tribunate of C. Gracchus in 123, competitive lawmaking, outright annulments of law, and the infringement or disregard of procedure had gradually become common. Since 91 these convolutions of customary lawmaking practice had come more and more to typify the process. While such convolutions confirm the continued societywide acceptance of the fundamental premise of public lawmaking sessions, at the same time they indicate a dramatic shift in the uses of such sessions. In the episode of 47, when the Senate collectively opposed Dolabella's public law proposals, the ascendant Roman leadership gave firm notice that it would tolerate only the right sort of lawmaker and the right sort of law. Coming at the tail end of a generation grown accustomed to frequent public law proposals by a wider range of officeholders and individuals, it is an understandable response from leaders all too aware of the political applications of public lawmaking. Although the final disappearance of public lawmaking came only after nearly one hundred years of Roman emperors, by the time we reach the dictatorships of Julius Caesar, lawmaking is quite a different animal even than it had been throughout the preceding fifty years.

Changes in the traditional checks and balances between the various elements at lawmaking assemblies, a development best seen in the increased efforts by the leadership to use the lawmaking process in a new and more self-interested way than ever before, reflect the attenuation of social networks. This effort in turn was exacerbated by a growing level of deviation from traditional procedures in proposing laws, increasing violence at public lawmaking sessions largely inspired by political leaders themselves, a developing lack of concern with religious rituals at lawmaking sessions, and a host of laws against certain kinds of behavior, often presented as "crimes," designed to control increasing turmoil among elite Romans desperately trying to maintain their political standing where it fundamentally mattered, in the tribe, or trying to build position and reputation among the fighting men of Italy. Increasingly deviations from customary lawmaking practices became the order of the day, and lawmaking began to assume the dimensions of an everyday political tool to be used by elected officials and senators in the rough and tumble of Roman politics. Concurrently the integrity of the one institution whose strength reflected the strength of the basic connections in Roman society, the public lawmaking process, became an issue. Throughout the half-century preceding the demise of the Republic, Romans spent much if not most of their year involved in one way or another with the public lawmaking process—eloquent confirmation that the system and the process were awry.

In the specific lawmaking activity described previously we saw the chief factor contributing to the politicization of lawmaking, namely, the functions of lawmaking as a mechanism for achieving group consensus in times of crisis. The very frequency of public law sessions throughout the years between 70 and 44, in the historical circumstances of those years, just as obviously suggests a fundamental change in the role of public lawmaking, making it more a part of the ordinary political life of Rome. In turn the role of the people in determining the direction of the community was gradually lost as a few, remarkably successful individual leaders took on the role of lawmaker. The first step in the process was the singular dictator legibus scribendis et republicae constituendae, an office created by Sulla in 81 and revived briefly by Caesar in 46, which had an especially significant lawmaking capacity. Sulla was the first leader to recognize the uses of public law in enhancing his own position. The increasing lawmaking activity by both tribunes, after the office was restored in 70, and consuls demonstrates that the lesson was not lost on his contemporaries. Eventually, in the case of Pompey, as of Sulla before him and Caesar after, to name the most powerful Romans, the distinguishing edge he had over most other lawmakers was the strong support of loyal soldiers in the vicinity.

Even in civil war, all Romans understood the common avenues of establishing consensus about divisive issues and the mechanisms for modulating social changes of some magnitude. The proposal by the tribune Dolabella in 47 addressed the question of debt afresh, in a competitive effort to supplant Caesar's remedies, undertaken by the praetors regarding the repayment of debts. Arguably, Dolabella was the last Roman law sponsor to independently articulate the will of the Roman people. In 46, Caesar embarked on an intensive program of public laws matching that of Sulla in 81. His assassination in March of 44 by senators was no setback to this lawmaking activity. On the authority of Caesar's notebooks, M. Antonius had public law proposals carried as leges Iuliae. Thus although unsuccessful in the short term Caesar's solution to civil war anticipates the end of public lawmaking assemblies.

Paradoxically the final demise of the traditional lawmaking process and the changes that led up to it were brought about by the passage of laws purportedly found in the assassinated Caesar's notebooks. The compelling authority of a dead man to legitimize law sets the stage for the final adjustment leading to the end of public lawmaking assemblies, the institution of a Roman emperor. No longer would the Roman leadership unequivocally accept the decision of the Roman people assembled in a lawmaking assembly as the Roman people's will. From here on out the Roman leadership would tolerate only the right sort of lawmaker, the emperor or his delegate, who by virtue of his authority would propose the right sort of law. Public lawmaking continues during the reign of Augustus, first emperor of the Roman people and the Roman Empire, but from now until its complete disappearance public lawmaking represents not the collective voice of the Roman people but the will of the Roman emperor.

TABLE 9.1 Public Law Sponsors and Proposals, 67

Sponsor	Proposal
A. Gabinius, tribune	The assignment of a province
A. Gabinius, tribune	The creation of a command against pirates
A. Gabinius, tribune	Removal of a tribune from office
A. Gabinius, tribune	The removal of a consul from office
C. Cornelius, tribune	Loans to foreign states
C. Cornelius, tribune	The power to give exemptions from the law
C. Cornelius, tribune	The power to give exemptions from the law
C. Cornelius, tribune	The praetor's observance of his edict
C. Cornelius, tribune	The crime of ambitus
C. Calpurnius Piso, consul	The crime of ambitus
A. Gabinius, tribune	Senate audiences with foreign embassies
A. Gabinius, tribune	Loans to foreign envoys
L. Roscius Otho, tribune	Theater seats for equites
Unknown tribune	Privileges for individuals

Source: See appendixes A and C.

TABLE 9.2 Public Law Sponsors and Proposals, 59–58

Date	Sponsor	Proposal
59	C. Iulius Caesar, consul	Distribution or assignment of land
59	C. Iulius Caesar, consul	Distribution or assignment of land
59	C. Iulius Caesar, consul	Distribution or assignment of land
59	C. Iulius Caesar, consul	The crime of repetundae
59	C. Iulius Caesar, consul	Ratification of a commander's acts
59	C. Iulius Caesar, consul	Contracts of the publicani of Asia
59	C. Iulius Caesar, consul	The ruler of Egypt
59	P. Vatinus, tribune	Jury selection
59	P. Vatinus, tribune	The staff of a provincial governor
59	P. Vatinus, tribune	The assignment of a province
59	P. Vatinus, tribune	The foundation of colonies
59	P. Vatinus, tribune	Relations/foreign cities/states
59	P. Vatinus, tribune	Special commission of investigation
59	Q. Fufius Calenus, praetor	The voting order of jurors
58	A. Gabinius and L. Calpurnius Piso, consuls	Immunity for Delos
58	Unknown tribune	Dedicate a statue on Capitolium
58	P. Clodius Pulcher, tribune	The restoration of collegia
58	P. Clodius Pulcher, tribune	The assignment of consular provinces
58	P. Clodius Pulcher, tribune	The reassignment of provinces
58	P. Clodius Pulcher, tribune	Magistrates and death without trial
58	P. Clodius Pulcher, tribune	The exile of individual(s)
58	P. Clodius Pulcher, tribune	Suspension or circumvention of law
58	P. Clodius Pulcher, tribune	Comitial days and their interruption
58	P. Clodius Pulcher, tribune	Galatian king/Magna Mater, Pessinus

(*continued*)

TABLE 9.2 *(continued)*

Date	Sponsor	Proposal
58	P. Clodius Pulcher, tribune	Annexation of Cyprus as a province
58	P. Clodius Pulcher, tribune	Censors' review of Senate membership
58	P. Clodius Pulcher, tribune	Quaestorian scribae in trade
58	P. Clodius Pulcher, tribune	Distribution of grain to citizens
58	L. Ninnnius Quadratus, tribune	Recall of exile(s)
58	Unknown tribune	Recall of exile(s)

Source: See appendixes A and C.

TABLE 9.3 Laws Relating to the Conduct of Assemblies by Year, Latin Name, and Subject, 350–44

Year	Latin Name	Subject
339	Lex Publilia Philone de plebiscitis	The general validity of plebiscites
339	Lex Publilia Philone de patrum auctoritate	Announcement of patrum auctoritas in legislative assemblies
(287)[a]	Lex Maenia de patrum auctoritate	Announcement of patrum auctoritas in electoral assemblies
287	Lex Hortensia de plebiscitis	The general validity of plebiscites
287	Lex Hortensia de nundinis	Legal business on market days
181	Lex Cornelia Baebia de ambitu	The crime of ambitus
159	Lex Cornelia Fulvia de ambitu	The crime of ambitus
(153)	Lex Aelia de modo legum ferendarum	Obnuntiatio in lawmaking assemblies
(153)	Lex Fufia de modo legum ferendarum	Obnuntiatio in lawmaking assemblies
139	Lex Gabinia tabellaria	Voting by written ballot
137	Lex Cassia tabellaria	Voting by written ballot
130	Lex Papiria tabellaria	Voting by written ballot
122	Rogatio Sempronia de suffragiorum confusione	The order of voting in the centuriate assembly
119	Lex Maria de suffragiis ferendis	The pontes used by voters
107	Lex Caelia tabellaria	Voting by written ballot
98	Lex Caecilia Didia de modo legum promulgandarum	The trinundinum and unrelated measures in one proposal
88	Lex Cornelia Pompeia de comitiis centuriatis	Enactment of law in the comitia centuriata
(70)	Lex Plautia de vi	The crime of vis
62	Lex Iunia Licinia de legum latione	Archiving the law
(61)	Lex Pupia de senatu diebus comitialibus non habendo	Senate and comitial meeting days
58	Lex Clodia de iure et tempore legum rogandarum	Comitial days and their interruption
52	Lex Pompeia de vi	The crime of vis
46	Lex Iulia de vi	The crime of vis

Source: See appendixes A and C.

[a]Dates in parentheses are approximate. See appendix C.

TABLE 9.4 Law Topics and Law Sponsors, 49–44

49	M. Aemilius Lepidus, praetor	Selection of dictator
49	Unknown	Confirmation of citizenship grant to Gades
49	M. Antonius, tribune	Restoration of civil rights to individual(s)
(49)[a]	Unknown	Grant of citizenship to outside group
49	M. Antonius, tribune	Restoration of civil rights to individual(s)
48	Unknown tribune	Grant of tribunician powers to Caesar
48	Unknown	Selection of dictator
48	Unknown	A triumph for a commander
48	M. Caelius Rufus, praetor	Remission of rents in Rome
48	M. Caelius Rufus, praetor	Settlement of debts
48	M. Caelius Rufus, praetor	Settlement of debts
ca. 48–44	Unknown	Privileges for individual(s)
48	A. Hirtius, tribune	Capacity of Pompey's men to stand for office
47	P. Cornelius Dolabella, tribune	Remission of rents in Rome
47	P. Cornelius Dolabella, tribune	Settlement of debts
(46)	C. Iulius Caesar, dictator	Eligibility for selection to priesthood
(46)	C. Iulius Caesar, dictator	Length of provincial governorships
46	C. Iulius Caesar, dictator	Food and guests at dinner parties
46	C. Iulius Caesar, dictator	List of eligible grain recipients
46	C. Iulius Caesar, dictator	Jury composition
46	C. Iulius Caesar, dictator	The crime of maiestas
46	C. Iulius Caesar, dictator	The crime of vis
46	C. Iulius Caesar, dictator	The hire of shepherds of free status
ca. 46	Unknown	The crime of repetundae
46 or 45	C. Iulius Caesar, dictator	Settlement of debts
45	C. Iulius Caesar, dictator	Port duties
45	C. Iulius Caesar, dictator	Restrictions on travel outside Italy
45	Caecilius, tribune	Extending the pomerium
44	L. Cassius Longinus, tribune	Creation of new patrician families
44	M. Antonius, consul	Naming month after Caesar
44	L. Antonius, tribune	Privilege of naming candidates to Caesar
44	C. Helvius Cinna, tribune	Caesar's wives
44	M. Antonius, consul	Privileges for Caesar
44	C. Helvius Cinna, tribune	Removal of tribunes from office
44 post Ides	P. Cornelius Dolabella, consul	The assignment of a province
44 post Ides	M. Antonius, consul	The foundation of colonies
44 post Ides	M. Antonius, consul	Commission to examine Caesar's acta
44 post Ides	M. Antonius, consul	Ratification of Caesar's acta
44 post Ides	C. Iulius Caesar, deceased	Tax burden and provincial status of Crete
44 post Ides	C. Iulius Caesar, deceased	Recall of exile(s)
44 post Ides	C. Iulius Caesar, deceased	Grant of citizenship to Sicilians
44 post Ides	C. Iulius Caesar, deceased	Restoration of power to King Deiotarus
44 post Ides	M. Antonius, consul	Jury composition
44 post Ides	M. Antonius, consul	Abolition of the office of dictator
44 post Ides	M. Antonius, consul	The reassignment of provinces

(*continued*)

TABLE 9.4 (*continued*)

44 post Ides	Unknown tribune	The assignment of consular provinces
44 post Ides	M. Antonius, consul	Appeals to the people
44 post Ides	M. Antonius and P. Cornelius Dolabella, consuls	Distribution or assignment of land

Source: See appendixes A and C.
[a]Dates in parentheses are approximate. See appendix C.

Notes

1. Cass. Dio 42.32.2; Livy, *Epit.* 113; Plut., *Ant.* 9.1; Cic., *Att.* 11.23.3; *Phil.* 6.4.11.

2. *MRR* 2.139–40, s.v. Index of Careers. Clodius: see under heading "The Lawmaking of 58."

3. Effects of civil wars in Italy and Mithridates in encouraging the boldness and organization of the pirates: Plutarch, *Pomp.* 24. Capture of praetors: *Pomp.* 24.6.

4. Badian's arguments that Gabinius's association with Pompey commenced when they were both fighting for Sulla in the 80s, that he was a legate of Pompey in Spain until 71, and that he began his political career only on his return to Rome are persuasive: Badian 1959, 87–99. Cf. *MRR* 3.97, which notes the unresolved date of his quaestorship. On the late date of Gabinius's tribunate see also Wiseman 1971, 166 n. 3 with references. Gabinius, one of Rome's foremost military men, gained a consulship in 58.

5. *MRR* 1.568. He received the command as praetor and continued as proconsul.

6. Plut., *Pomp.* 25; Cass. Dio 36.

7. Plut., *Pomp.* 27.1–2.

8. Cornelius, a little-known member of a many-branched clan, was Pompey's quaestor in Spain: Asc. 57 C. On the date of his quaestorship—no later than 71 (Pompey's return)—see *MRR* 2.122. Cornelius apparently rose no further in the cursus.

9. Asc. 59.11–12 (Clark) suggests that there may have been more proposals than the four he reports. These would include the lex de ambitu, which Asconius does not report directly; we know of it in some detail from Cass. Dio. My discussion of Cornelius's lawmaking activity and its context follows M. Griffin, "The tribunate of C. Cornelius," *JRS* 63 (1973): 196–213, and Wiseman 1994, 329–38. B. Marshall, *A historical commentary on Asconius* (Columbia, MO, 1985), 215–17, provides a summary of the arguments advanced by Griffin 1973 about the order of Cornelius's measures, based on preferring Asconius's account over Cassius Dio's.

10. Asc. 57–58 C with discussion of Marshall 1985, 215–19.

11. Asc. 57–58 C.

12. Cass. Dio 36.39; Cic., *Corn.* 1, fr. 5, 27, 30–32; *Vat.* 5; Asc. 58–59, 71–72 C. Apparently the dispensations in question were granted by the Senate to advantage candidates—among them Pompey (who did not have an ordinary career pattern) and others, including most recently former senators removed from the list in 70 who were trying to

regain their rank through office—for the praetorship or consulship by permitting them to skip the preceding office: Griffin 1973, 200 with n. 32 citing previous bibliography.

13. Until the time of Augustus, there was no fixed and necessary number of senators whose presence constituted a quorum; the number varied depending on the matters at hand: Willems 1885, 2.165–66.

14. Cass. Dio 36.40.2–3. For discussion see A. A. Schiller, *Roman law: The mechanisms of its development* (New York, The Hague, Paris, 1978), 412–13.

15. Asc., *Corn.* 66.

16. Cass. Dio 36.38.2.

17. Cass. Dio 36.38.4.

18. Calpurnius was acquitted of the charge. See Alexander 1990, no. 190. On the lawmaking of 67 see especially Wiseman 1994, 331–38.

19. Cass. Dio notes, and Rotondi accepts, also a plebiscite that granted the tribune C. Papirius Carbo the privilege of wearing the insignia of a consul for successfully prosecuting M. Aurelius Cotta, consul in 74, for stealing booty when commander in Bithynia and Pontus between 73 and 70 (Cass. Dio 36. 40.3). This was more likely a privilege given to successful prosecutors under the current law. On the case see Alexander 1990, no. 192. The charge was peculatus or repetundae.

20. Willems 1885, 2.157 n. 1, dates the law to his praetorship in 61.

21. Cic., *Att.* 5.21.12; 1.1.5, and 2.7. Griffin 1973, 209, argues that this bill succeeded in doing what Cornelius earlier had failed to do with a similar measure. Whether Gabinius proposed this and the preceding measure as tribune or consul is ultimately unknowable, although most think as tribune: cf. Doumont et al. 1980, 48, n. 7.

22. See note 25, this chapter.

23. Cic., *Corn*, fr. 53P; Plut., *Cic.* 13.

24. The description and position of these few, but powerful, senators are relayed by Asc. (Clark) 60.19–21, 78.18–22, 79.18–19, and 79. 20–23.

25. The family background of the consul is obscure. He had been praetor in 71 (or 72); he was later proconsul in Cisalpine and Transalpine Gaul, following which Julius Caesar prosecuted him de repetundis: *MRR* 3.46. On his opposition to Pompey see E. Gruen, "Pompey and the Pisones," *Calif. Stud. Class. Ant.* 1 (1968): 156–59; and L. Hayne, "The politics of M'. Glabrio," *CP* 69 (1974): 280. Roscius was a new man, perhaps a member of a Latin family that had recently become wealthy through the management of mines in Spain: *ILLRP* 1262. He was later praetor in 63 (the date is uncertain), when he was revealed to be unpopular with the people (they jeered him at a theatrical performance), because of his sponsorship of the lex Roscia de theatris: for references see Wiseman 1971, 256 (no. 359) and *MRR* 2.167.

26. For details of the case see Alexander 1990, no. 203, p. 202; Asc., *Corn.* 58 and 61, Clark; Cic., *Vat.* 2, 5.

27. Cornelius claimed he was not "reading the law," *legem recitare*, but was looking it over, *legem recognoscere* (Cic., *Vat.* 2, 5). The action was the same in either case, but the intention was quite different. The phrase *legem recitare* describes the formal recital. The purpose of "looking over" the law is not clear.

28. Cornelius reportedly drafted a proposal for the tribune Manilius, elected in 67 for 66.

29. Unusual but not unprecedented: cf. commands during the Second Punic War, against Mithridates in 88, and so forth.

30. Plut., *Pomp.* 28.

31. Plut., *Pomp.* 30.

32. Cass. Dio 36.42–44.

33. On the connection between this Gabinius and the family of A. Gabinius, tribune in 67, consul in 58, see Badian 1959.

34. P. Autronius Paetus was quaestor in 75, legate in 73–72, praetor by 68, and had been candidate for consul in 65 until his candidacy was annulled by a conviction on bribery charges, together with his fellow candidate P. Cornelius Sulla. L. Vargunteius was tried and convicted for bribery in 66 though defended by Hortensius. On these see Cic., *Sull.* 6; cf. Sall., *Cat.* 28.1.

35. See chapter 8; cf. Wiseman 1994, 346–58; and R. Stewart, "Catiline and the crisis of 63–60 BC: The Italian perspective," *Lat.* 54 (1995): 62–78.

36. Brunt 1971, 449 (table XIV).

37. For grounds and timing (after the elections: Suetonius) see W. Drumann and P. Groebe, *Geschichte Roms in seinem Übergange von der republikanischen zur monarchischen Verfassung* (Berlin, 1899–1929), 3.177–78.

38. The classic discussion is Taylor 1949, esp. 132–39.

39. See chapter 7.

40. On the lex Iulia agraria of 59 (= *RS* 2 No. 54) see M. H. Crawford, "The lex Iulia agraria," *Ath.* 77 (1989): 179–90: the so-called lex Mamilia Roscia Peducaea Alliena Fabia is in fact the lex Iulia Agraria. On the chronology see L. R. Taylor, "On the chronology of Caesar's first consulship," *AJP* 62 (1951): 254–68.

41. Cass. Dio 38.2.1–3.3.

42. Appian, *B.C.* 2.9. Bibulus had been elected with the help of funds from other senators, including Cato, for the purpose of bribing voters in order to offset the effort of Caesar to finance the campaign of the man he wanted as co-consul.

43. See chapter 2.

44. Cass. Dio 38.3.1.

45. Appian, *B.C.* 2.13. Probably 61. Censors had been elected who revised the list of senators but stepped down before administering census: Cass. Dio 37.46.4. They reportedly leased contracts for tax collection in Asia, which the contractors tried to revise later: Cic., *Att.* 1.17.9.

46. Reportedly for a sum of money, HS 6,000.

47. *RS* 2 No. 55. On this and other laws see A. Lintott, "The *leges de repetundis* and associate measures under the republic," *ZRG* 98 (1981): 162–212.

48. Wiseman 1971, no. 467; Taylor 1960, 263: his background is based on his tribe, the Sergia, and the fact that his grandfather was not a citizen (not included on the fasti).

49. Earlier he had been legate of C. Cosconius in Spain in 62, and he was quaestor in 63.

50. Cic., *Vat.* 36.

51. On the scope of the law see A. H. J. Greenidge, *The legal procedure of Cicero's time* (Oxford, 1901), 451–52.

52. Cic., *Att.* 1.14.2–5. Clodius is discussed later in the chapter.

53. Cic., *Vat.* 29.

54. Suet., *Iul.* 19: silvae callesque (the "woods and trails"). See Willems 1888, 2.576 n. 5.

55. Cic., *Vat.* 36.

56. Suet., *Iul.* 22.

57. Appian, *B.C.* 2.26. The rights were contested: Taylor 1960, 125–26.

58. Suet., *Iul.* 8.A law of 65 expelling foreigners from Rome who were illegally gaining citizenship was directed at Transpadani.

59. His tribe was the Poblilia: Taylor 1960, 215.

60. See under the heading "The Lawmaking of 58."

61. Cass. Dio 38. 8.1; Greenidge 1901, 450.

62. P. Clodius Pulcher: W. J. Tatum, *The Patrician Tribune: Publius Clodius Pulcher* (Chapel Hill and London, 1999).

63. Membership in Palatina: Taylor 1960, 205.

64. On this clientage see E. Rawson, *Roman culture and society: Collected papers* (Oxford, 1991), 102–24.

65. Cic., *Har. Resp.* 42; Plut., *Luc.* 34.1–2; Cass. Dio 36.14.3–4, 17.2. Plutarch explains that Claudius did this because his invidious arrogance led him to believe Lucullus was not showing him enough honor. The troops in question had served initially under Fimbria sixteen years before.

66. In 63 Clodius was sequester for candidates seeking office, which put him into direct contact with the divisores of the tribes. He used his house as a headquarters. Cicero later suggested that Clodius was an associate of Catiline because Clodius, prosecuting Catiline in 65 on a charge of extortion, had helped select a jury favorably disposed to the defendant. Catiline was acquitted by a majority, composed of the equites and tribuni aerarii (the senators voted to convict). On the trial see Alexander 1990, no. 212.

67. They included young nobles, low-status Romans, new citizens, former slaves and some slaves. See further in the chapter.

68. I follow here the analysis of P. Moreau, *Clodiana religio: Un procès politique en 61 av. J.-C.* (Paris, 1982).

69. On the complicated sequence of events surrounding the Senate's efforts to have the people carry a measure to arrange a special court and procedure for Clodius's trial see Millar 1998, 118–19.

70. On the nature of the group so organized see H. Benner, *Die Politik des P. Clodius Pulcher: Untersuchungen zur Denatierung des Clientelwesens in den ausgehenden römischen Republik* (Stuttgart, 1987).

71. This is likely given both the military organization and Clodius's own military experience. In 67 Clodius left his brother-in-law's staff and joined Q. Marcius Rex in Cilicia, where he was captured by pirates. Clodius next served as military tribune on the staff of L. Licinius Murena in Cisalpine and Transalpine Gaul.

72. Cic., *Har.Resp.* 20. 42. On this see Moreau 1982.

73. Moreau identifies the military and civic experiences that provided Clodius's models for "une organisation inspirée de celle de la légion, de celles des collèges et de celles des divisores, et des groupes de combat": Moreau 1982, 50. In view of their organization, these were not clientes in any traditional Roman sense: Benner 1987.

74. On the goals of Clodius's lawmaking activity see Wiseman 1994, 377–81.

75. Sources: *MRR* 2.196, s.v. Tribunes.

76. Title: S. Accame, "La legislazione romana intorno ai collegi nel I° secolo a.C.," *BullMusImp* 13 (1942): 15–29.

77. The title is given by Asconius; other sources call it frumentaria. See J.-M. Flambard, "Clodius, les collèges, la plèbe et les ésclaves," *MEFRA* 89.1 (1977): 145.

78. Cicero would have induced the tribune L. Ninnius Quadratus to veto the earlier measures but did not, because Clodius convinced him that he had no intention of presenting any bill against Cicero: Cass. Dio 38.14–17. Reportedly these four measures served to consolidate Clodius's position before the bill to send Cicero into exile, by attracting support from the Senate, equestrians, and people. Cass. Dio 38.13.1 f; Plut., *Cic.* 30; Drumann-Groebe 1899, 2.203.

79. See note 85, this chapter.

80. See later discussion on Caesar.

81. Badian, "M. Porcius Cato and the Annexation and Early Administration of Cyprus," *JRS* 55 (1965): 115.

82. Cic., *Fam.* 12.25.1; Cass. Dio 45.17.3. First he dedicated a statue to Minerva Custos in the Capitoline temple. According to *LPPR* 393, his right to do so was granted in a plebiscitum de dedicatione simulacri Minervae carried by another tribune in 58. None of the sources reports such a plebiscite. He said himself that he left Rome rather than risk provoking civil war.

83. *RS* 2 No. 56; P. Moreau, "La lex Clodia sur le bannissement de Cicéron," *Ath.* n.s. 75 (1987): 465–92.

84. *RS* 2 No. 57; Moreau 1989, 151–78.

85. Badian 1965, 110–21. Badian argues on constitutional grounds (anything else would violate the lex Caecilia-Didia) that there were three bills involved, one taking Cyprus from Ptolemy, one restoring the Byzantine exiles, and one putting Cato in charge. The sources are vague: Cic., *Dom.* 20–21, 52–53, and 65; *Sest.* 56, 57, 59–61; *Har. Resp.* 59; Livy, *Epit.* 104.

86. Tatum 1999.

87. As indeed had Cornelius, some say.

88. This section draws on Flambard 1977, 115–56; and A. Lintott, *Violence in republican Rome* (Oxford, 1968).

89. Cic., *Mil.* 12.33; 32.87; Asc. 52 C; Schol. Bob. p. 346 Or.

90. See discussion accompanying table 7.3 in chapter 7.

91. Political clubs: Taylor 1949, 50–75; and Taylor 1960, 122. Effects of an expanded citizen population on campaign bribery and new political uses of collegia and sodalicia: Wiseman 1971, 130–42.

92. Cass. Dio 37.42–44.

93. L. R. Taylor, "Forerunners of the Gracchi," *JRS* 52 (1962): 19–27, emphasizes the point.

94. These trials are collected in Alexander 1990.

95. Lintott 1999.

96. On the various ways of undoing public laws see *RS* 1.12–13. On abrogation see A. Biscardi, "Aperçu historique du problème de l'abrogatio legis," *RIDA* 3e série 18 (1971): 449–70; J. Linderski, "The augural law," *ANRW* 2.16.3 (1986): 2146–312.

97. A number of laws were presented to the people between 121 and 120 to abrogate select provisions in the statutes carried by C. Sempronius Gracchus. See chapter 7.

98. Cic., *Balb*. 48, *Leg*. 2.14. Annulment of laws by the Senate: K. Heikkilä, "Lex non iure rogata: Senate and the Annulment of Laws in the Late Republic," in Vaahtera 1993, 117–42.

99. Cic., *Leg*. 2.14.

100. Cic., *Dom*. 41; *Leg*. 2.14 and 31; Diod. 37.10.3; Val Max. 3.1.2; Vell. Pat. 2.13.2; Asc. 69 C.

101. Cass. Dio 36.42.1–3.

102. Cic., *Leg*. 2.14. He compares the laws of Appuleius, Titius, and Drusus to the rules that robbers would make or the poisons administered as beneficial drugs by unskilled medical practitioners.

103. Cic., *Off*. 3. 80–81; Plin., *N.H*. 33.132, 34.27.

104. Although modern scholars commonly hold this man to have been an impostor, the possibility should not be ruled out that he was indeed the son of C. Marius (consul in 82) and the granddaughter of L. Crassus, who would have inevitably lost everything in Sulla's proscriptions. Cicero's references to this Marius, in letters written in May of 45 (*Att*. 12.49.2) and April of 44 (*Att*. 14. 8.1), do not indicate he was not who he said he was despite assertions elsewhere that he was a freedman or runaway slave (Cic., *Phil*. 1.2.5; Livy, *Epit*. 116; Val. Max. 9.15.1). His execution by Antonius suggests that Antonius believed he had reason to fear him (Appian, *B.C*. 3. 3). See S. Weinstock, *Divus Iulius* (Oxford, 1971), 364 ff.

105. Senatus consultum ultimum: Lintott 1999.

106. *Censoris fidem legum custodiunto:* Cic., *Leg*. 3.4.11. Cicero commenced writing *De Legibus* after *De Re Publica* and before his tenure as governor in Cilicia in 51 and, it is believed, never published the treatise: E. Rawson, "The interpretation of Cicero's *de legibus*," in Rawson 1991, 125–29.

107. See the discussion of this episode by M. Bonnefond-Coury, *Le sénat de la république romaine* (Rome, 1989), 571–73.

108. Plut., *Cat. Min*. 17.3.

109. Cato's career at this stage: *MRR* 2.163, 174.

110. Plut., *Cat. Min*. 21.2–5.

111. F. Miltner, "Porcius," no. 16, *PW* 22.1, 205 ff.

112. Schol. Bob. p. 140 Stangl, commenting on Cic., *pro Sestio* 133.

113. Plutarch, *Cat. Min*., 21.6.

114. Cic., *Vat*. 14.33; *Phil*. 5.3.8; *Sest*. 64.135; *Att*. 2.9.1; 4.16.5; *Leg*. 3.4.11; cf. 20.46; Schol. Bob. p. 140 Stangl.

115. Williamson 1984, 211–24. Posting bills at the Aerarium: E. Badian, "An unrecognized date in Cicero's text?" in *Mnemai: Classical studies in memory of Karl K. Hulley*, ed. H. D. Evjen (Chico, CA, 1984), 101.

116. *Phil*. 1.7.16: "quae ille in aes incidit, in quo populi iussa perpetuasque leges esse voluit." See Williamson 1987, 173 with n. 51.

117. *Mil*. 32. 87.

118. Williamson 1987.

119. Williamson 1995.

120. Plut., *Caes*. 35.6–11.

121. A useful compilation and discussion of Caesar's laws and mandates in this period are found in Z. Yavetz, *Julius Caesar and His Public Image* (Ithaca, NY, 1983), 58–160.

122. Probably rei gerendae causa: *MRR* 2.256–57. The complicated constitutional arrangements of the years 49–44 are presented in M. Gelzer, *Caesar: Politician and Statesman*, 6th ed. (Cambridge, MA, 1968), 195–333. See further note 137, this chapter.

123. Cass. Dio 41.36.2–3. Dio does not distinguish between laws enacted in assemblies and mandates of the dictator. The selection of priests to fill vacancies is not related to the lex Iulia de sacerdotiis cited by Cicero in a letter to Brutus in 43: see note 145, this chapter.

124. Sources: *MRR* 2.256–57. Debt: Cass. Dio 41.37.1–3. Gelzer identifies this as a lex data, based on the language in Caesar, *B.C.*, 3.1.2; 20.1 and 2: Gelzer 1968, 221.

125. Cass. Dio 42.51.1–2. Frederiksen places them in late 48, before the proposals of Caelius Rufus: M. W. Frederiksen, "Caesar, Cicero, and the problem of debt," *JRS* 56 (1966): 133–34. These are included in *LPPR* and Yavetz 1983 as laws, the lex Iulia de mercedibus habitationum annuis and lex Iulia de modo credendi possidendique intra Italiam.

126. On Caesar's efforts to resolve the problem of debt, introduced here and continued subsequently, I follow Frederiksen 1966, 134–41.

127. Children of proscribed Romans: Caesar, *B.C.* 3.1.3–5; Cass. Dio 41.18.2; 44.47.4; Suet., *Iul.* 41; Plut., *Caes.* 37; Zonar 10.8. Exiles: Cic., *Phil.* 2.55–56 and 98; *Att.* 10.4.8; Caes., *B.C.* 3.1.4; Suet., *Iul.* 41; Plut., *Caes.* 37; Appian, *B.C.* 2.48; Cass. Dio 41.36.2; 42.24.2.

128. Cass. Dio 41.24.1–2. See note 143, this chapter.

129. Cass. Dio 41.36.3. The attribution of the law to the praetor of 49, L. Roscius Fabatus (*MRR* 2.258), is based on the text of the Este fragment, once believed to be the law mentioned by Dio, which refers to a law brought by a magistrate named L. Roscius on 11 March (*RS* 1 No. 16. l. 13). Crawford argues convincingly that the text on the Este fragment "did not form part of a statute on Gallia Cisalpina, . . . but was originally of wholly general import." *RS* 1.317–18. Crawford also distinguishes between the lex Roscia named in the Este fragment and the lex de Transpadanis.

130. Cass. Dio 42.20.3. Again Dio does not distinguish between honors decreed by the Senate or voted by the people.

131. Cic., *Phil.* 13.32; cf. Cass. Dio 42.20.1, which places such an enactment in 48, after the Battle of Pharsalus. Various interpretations of the law: Yavetz 1983, 75–76. Tribunate of Hirtius: *MRR* 2.285 n. 3.

132. Cass. Dio 42.22. 1.

133. His recalcitrance, according to Dio, was inspired by his belief that Caesar had been vanquished by Pompey (Cass. Dio 42.22.1).

134. Caesar, *B.C.* 3.20–21; Cass. Dio 42.22.4.

135. Surrounding the Curia with soldiers, the consul P. Servilius Isauricus convened the Senate in order to pass a senatus consultum ultimum. The tribunes vetoed the proposals whereupon the consul ordered the removal of the tablets on which they were written, precipitating a fracas involving himself and the praetor Caelius. At length the consul, authorized by the Senate, removed Caelius from office. Caelius left Rome to join Milo, who was organizing an army against Caesar in Campania.

136. Cass. Dio 42.32.2. See note 1, this chapter.

137. Based on epigraphic evidence as well as the evidence of his lawmaking activity and contemporary report he was certainly dictator legibus scribendis et rei publicae constituendae in his third and fourth dictatorships: *MRR* 3.107–8. In the absence of explicit testimony and because he held the office so briefly in 49 (eleven days), most scholars believe he was dictator rei gerundae causae at other times: *MRR* 2.285 n. 1; and W. Kunkel, *Staatsordnung und Staatspraxis der römischen Republik* (Munich, 1995), 712–15. See also Hurlet 1993, 173 with nn. 9 and 10. A. Degrassi, *Inscriptores Italiae*, vol. 13, *Fasti et Elogia*, Fasc. 1, *Fasti Consulares et Triumphales* (Rome, 1947), 133, followed by Broughton, *MRR* 2.295, posits that he was dictator rei gerendae causa, not rei publicae causa, in 46.

138. Cass. Dio 43.14.3. This was extended to life in 44 (sources in *MRR* 2.317–18).

139. Sources: *MRR* 2.286.

140. Frederiksen argues persuasively that the Lex Iulia de bonis cedendis was enacted in 46 or 45: Frederiksen 1966, 135–41.

141. Cic., *Att.* 13.20.1, records that laws had been promulgated de urbe augenda; cf. 33a. 4; 35.1; cf. Cass. Dio 43.49 and Suet., *Iul.* 44. See *MRR* 2.307, corrected by *MRR* 3.35 s.v. Caecilius (or Pomponius).

142. *MRR* 2.23–24; cf. Yavetz 1983, 126–29.

143. The only law attributed by modern scholars to Caesar's own sponsorship in 49 is the lex de civitate Gaditanorum. None of the ancient sources says that he sponsored this law, however: Cass. Dio 41.24.1; Livy, *Epit.* 110; Caesar, *B.C.* 2.20–21.

144. The imprecision of the sources is reflected in *MRR* 2.293–94 and 305–6.

145. De sacerdotiis: P. Moreau, "Lex Iulia de sacerdotiis," *Ath.* n.s. 66 (1988): 365–69; *RS* 2 No. 58; de provinciis: Yavetz 1983, 108–9; de iudiciaria: Yavetz 1983, 116.

146. Mommsen, *History of Rome*, trans. of 4th German ed., 4 vols. (New York), 401, as quoted by Frederiksen 1966, 140–41.

Epilogue

FROM 350 TO 44, hundreds of public lawmaking assemblies—whether dealing with issues urgently important or to modern observers seemingly unimportant, communitywide in scope or narrowly focused on an individual or group—were held in Rome on an apparently infrequent and irregular basis. Culminating a process that was at all times cumbersome and time-consuming, from our twentieth-century perspective, that invariably demanded from its participants knowledge of the most intricate details of Roman procedures and customs, and that regularly involved participants from members of the citizenry on all levels, public lawmaking assemblies endured throughout the rapidly changing circumstances of the Roman Republic. Only the Romans fully understood the circumstances that called for a political leader to convene the people in a public lawmaking assembly. That each generation had a different sense of the appropriate circumstances attests to the resiliency and depth of the process in Roman society. The range of individuals with the authority to call public lawmaking assemblies, the range of groups involved in determining the outcome, and the number of occasions during the public lawmaking process in Rome on which participants had an opportunity to influence the outcome underscore the importance of lawmaking in Roman society for hundreds of years.

Common to the resolution of the most crucial issues that developed out of the stresses and strains of Roman expansion was the promulgation of public law. When hard-pressed during the Second Punic War of 218 to 201, the first serious threat to Roman survival in Italy, the Romans convened public lawmaking assemblies to decide critical issues in the development of agreement on the direction of Rome's campaign and thus to focus a united effort against Hannibal. Again, when the survival of the Roman state seemed in doubt between 91 and 81, the Romans promulgated a flurry of laws to resolve the differences that had brought an unprecedented level of war to the Italian peninsula. The final year of the "free" Republic, 44, one of the most politically disruptive years in Roman history, saw more reported lawmaking activity than any earlier single year. In every turn to lawmaking, whether on the scale of these years or not, the pressures and problems unique to a particular crisis were resolved. Public lawmaking was never the first response to dealing with a crisis; rather it was closer to a last resort. Indeed, the particular occasions on which resort was had to it, and the range of topics of proposals of law, suggest that the Romans used the public lawmaking process as a means for developing community consensus to resolve potentially disruptive issues that could not be bindingly resolved by the Roman Senate or by elite officeholders serving in a wide variety of official positions.

An understanding of the factors associated with the resort to public lawmaking assemblies involves an explanation of the most deep-seated elements of Roman culture and as such will probably always be "intrinsically incomplete."[1] Yet plainly crucial to any understanding of public lawmaking is the recognition that the Roman community was never a seamless whole but a fine mesh of sundry groups experiencing, especially in the period of our study, rapid changes in membership and relationship to the larger community. While the Roman tribe and property class embraced all Romans in a fundamental community organization, these basic groupings incorporated citizens in ever changing numbers and description and were themselves intersected by smaller groupings. The great clans of Roman society set the horizons of a privileged few who formed the pinnacle of the descending hierarchy of patrons and clients that penetrated the society. In towns and cities across Italy the various associations called collegia provided smaller-scale shelter and a focus of identity for the landless laborers and artisans who swelled the tribes of Rome. In towns and cities the systematic links to community life were found at the neighborhood level, where neighborhood officials (vicomagistri) managed affairs of local order and performance such as the neighborhood cult or enumerations of city residents. Men with military experience found fellowship and support in military units that had seen long service together and were settled as units on land grants at the conclusion of service. In brief, each Roman experienced his world as a member of a group or even several overlapping groups. Each Roman intuitively accepted a position within his group along a hierarchical spectrum determined by community standing, that is, by property and status. Each Roman intuitively lived according to the remembered conventions of his group with respect to the proper comportment and behavior to the gods, to other men, to other groups, and to Rome at large. The continuance of Roman society depended on the capacity of groups to connect, combine, and speak as one in all arenas. Some men served as group leaders. Foremost among the key men in various groups were Roman political leaders, the senators and elected officeholders. Numbered among the key men were also men of local wealth and standing who held an equestrian rating and included both equites equo publico and the wealthiest men of Class 1, tribuni aerarii. At lower levels of society, key men surfaced among the general population: these became the officials of collegia, chosen by the membership, and likewise neighborhood bosses, and they might be freeborn citizens or ex-slaves. These group leaders, forming at the highest levels an elite grouping of their own, forged links among separate groups.

When an issue emerged whose solution required a statewide consensus, particularly when the well-being of the Roman state was threatened, any one of a number of leaders occupying the elected offices that permitted them to convene the people, chiefly tribunes or consuls, could propose a legal remedy to be adjudicated by groups representing the entire society in a public lawmaking assembly. Such men, however, had to be able to formulate a proposal of merit not only to their own group but to leaders and members of other groups. Each political leader gave voice to the views of a core group of individuals of different statuses related to him in a variety of ways, as fellow tribesmen, clansmen, clients, tenants, friends, or political or business associates. To be sure, all decisions made by political leaders, whether individually or collectively, were in a manner of speaking fundamentally the decisions of a group. Thus the senators M. and Q. Minucius Rufus indirectly expressed the expectations of the Roman people when adjudicating a Ligurian boundary dispute in 117.

Public lawmaking, however, offered an arena for the various constituent members of core clusters to play a role in adjudicating the various options in the most important societywide decision-making process in Rome. In public lawmaking assemblies Rome's political leaders legitimized the people's will directly in a process that required the people's presence and participation. In public lawmaking assemblies Roman citizens voted as members of various groups led by men who occupied key positions within their group. In public lawmaking assemblies political leaders validated their position within the society at the same time as they validated the values and beliefs underlying the Roman system, at the same time as they sought to resolve troublesome issues. The process of public lawmaking therefore was as important as the substance of the proposal of law. Significantly, even when the number of citizens and groups in Roman society vastly expanded, we can still see the imprint of the public lawmaking process. The structure and operation of public lawmaking assemblies reflect the structure and operation of the larger Roman society.

During the last years of the Republic, the proceedings in public lawmaking sessions reveal the degree to which all inhabitants of Italy, now Romans, shared not only this common orientation to Rome but a complex set of interests and assumptions about how Roman society ought to be ordered. Cicero's public orations *De Lege Agraria*, delivered in 63, the longest and most complete set of speeches addressing the merits of a complicated public law proposal in existence, provide the template that guided Roman legal draftsmen of the day. The speeches tell us how laws should be processed: they should not be privately developed, and they should be explained by the proper people, that is, the elite, in an understandable way. The speeches also show us how a magistrate interacted with the people about a proposed law during the public stages in the production of law, unfolding in public meetings. The challenge for the leaders was to garner support by reflecting most accurately the desires of the Roman people in their institutions and confirming shared attitudes on the uses of power in their society. The strength of this reciprocal bond can be seen in Cicero's complicated oratorical display of the assumptions and emotions shared by the consul and his audience. Yet the extent to which these same Romans depended on Cicero and other aristocrats to convey the precise details of the law to them suggests a wide gap in levels of knowledge between citizens on different levels of the social structure. This reliance by the Roman people on aristocrats to publicly convey proposed laws to them gave an edge to those with effective speaking skills. Thus, as an arena in which they tested their leadership to the fullest through orating, public lawmaking sessions were critically important for aristocrats.

Roman respect for legal conventions was also on full display on these occasions as debaters paid careful attention to the substance and presentation of a public law draft. Political leaders who proposed law acquired the prerequisite knowledge of Rome's laws and essential drafting skills in a customary but evolving process involving service in a number of legal and administrative positions that underwent significant changes over time. Between the third and the first centuries the number of these low-ranking political offices dramatically increased. In this period also the apparatus of justice underwent significant revision and expansion, culminating in the establishment of permanent courts, quaestiones, to try individual, newly defined state crimes. Paradoxically after 100 changes in the membership of the Roman aristocracy meant that fewer junior magistrates, in particular tribunes, were privy to the customary training in legal matters. It is in this same period that we see the emergence of new ways of managing the technical requirements of producing law. The proposers of public law began to depend to a far greater extent than earlier on the skills and knowledge of others in the execution of their responsibilities. Roman aristocrats now worked with clerical assistants to produce the texts of proposed laws presented to the people. A specialized, professional corps of clerks emerged to assist magistrates, mirroring a general trend in law in which men of equestrian rank replaced senators as Rome's juristic experts.

Public lawmaking assemblies reflected many of the most fundamental features of Roman life. The necessity for divine approval on the times for their performance, the forms of the rituals, and many of the formal acts that took place during each stage mirrored the intensity of Rome's religious spirit. The elected officeholders who proposed the law and guided the discussion were the same group of aristocrats who managed the society. The elaborate debates and the complicated voting procedures required to discern "the will of the people" rested on the authority and importance of the majority Roman citizen population. To engage in the elaborate rituals and procedures involved in the public lawmaking process, all the participants had to possess time, energy, and an intuitive knowledge of rites, rules, principles, and traditions. The observation of these features is constant across the period. In 81, 63, and 46, no less than in 218, Romans of all stations clearly insisted upon the import of proper procedures on public lawmaking occasions. The striking recognition and general observation of the complicated choreography required at public lawmaking assemblies, the widescale involvement of all elements of the population, the public display, and the religious observances, constant across our entire period of study, underscore the extent to which public lawmaking succeeded in reflecting the values and assumptions of Roman society at large.

The knowledge and assumptions displayed by a rapidly changing Roman citizenry on lawmaking occasions, some of whose members settled away from Rome and others who were newly added from conquered Italian peoples, emerged out of the long-term process of interaction between Romans and other residents of the Italian peninsula that began in the days of earliest settlement. Long before the Romans moved beyond the boundaries of their city to conquer their neighbors the unique geography of Italy had created a reciprocal relationship between mountain and plain dweller that facilitated the emergence of somewhat common patterns of interaction between peoples. Part of the common pattern of life in Italy was that continual give-and-take enjoined by the perennial movement of people and herds across a shared environment, reflected in a complicated and extensive network of trails and roads. From an early date the Romans, like other peoples of Italy, experienced a high level of personal mobility because of the exigencies of geography and environment throughout the peninsula. Family members who made the seasonal trek away from their permanent settlements were constantly required to negotiate the terms of passage, pasturage, cultivation, and access to basic resources with others who occupied the regions they traversed or who like them were traveling in search of pasture or arable land. Sustaining this mobility was a high degree of give-and-take in the interactions among distinct groups that permitted all, on the level of everyday life, to resolve potentially disruptive encounters with other inhabitants. These patterns of interaction persisted despite the emergence and expansion of intensive polyculture and urban market centers in Italy. This process produced a veneer of common understandings among the diverse peoples of the Italian peninsula that provided the cornerstone on which the Romans built their remarkable imperial state during the initial and most critical course of their expansion. Common understandings proved vital during the Roman expansion across Italy in the absence of the resources to conquer surrounding peoples solely through force. The success of the Roman expansion across Italy rested on far more than military might or unique political institutions.

Augmenting the common understandings at each step of the advance across Italy was a unique Roman genius for redirecting indigenous ways to their own advantage. Most obvious is the ability to forestall tensions arising over land resources by providing recognizable alternatives to dispossessed Italians. Equally important was the decisive implementation of Roman ways of conflict resolution, ranging from the decisions of on-the-spot Roman commanders and prefects to the decisions of senatorial commissions, instituted by the Senate or assemblies in Rome, and finally the societywide directives of public lawmaking assemblies. At each stage further advance was possible only with support from newly conquered lands and the use of troops from previously conquered allied Italians who fought alongside the Romans. By 91, when the Italian War began, Italians made up half the troops in the Roman army and conquered peoples had been absorbed to the point where they shared the Roman recognition of the central importance of public lawmaking assemblies. In the Roman public lawmaking process, different groups came together to negotiate issues of concern whose resolution, expressed through the vote of the assembled tribes, represented a consensus that was understood to be the formal expression of the will of the Roman people. The core assumptions that allowed the Romans, unlike other ancient peoples, to expand territorially, absorb newcomers, and still retain the stability of the smaller, face-to-face community provide the basis for public lawmaking assemblies.

But if the logic of public lawmaking grew out of a common Italian experience of mobility and accommodation, we must ask how it was that the Romans succeeded in elevating their singularly Roman public lawmaking process to an Italy-wide instrument of negotiation? Arguably the uniquely Roman contribution to the process of expansion and accommodation that disseminated Roman decision-making ways throughout Italy was the permeability and resiliency of Roman institutions, in particular the Roman tribes and property classes. As they expanded across Italy the Romans gradually adjusted to a changing population by continually situating individuals, through registration in tribes and property classes at the quinquennial census, in appropriate positions in the existing Roman status structure. Between the fourth and the second centuries the Romans awarded citizenship to selected Italians and Latins in a changing pattern corresponding to the intuitive feel the Romans developed for peoples most likely to become good Romans. By divorcing citizenship from location in a manner unlike any other Mediterranean people, the Romans gave new citizens full access to voting privileges as members of the Roman tribes and property classes. In this way the Romans provided the institutional means to focus and channel the political energy of newcomers so that they strengthened rather than weakened the Roman system. Similarly as more and more Roman citizens faced changed circumstances through economic adversity and were removed from the military lists, the Romans modified effective citizen property qualifications in order to readmit such individuals at a level that permitted them to fight in the infantry. For Italians, service in the Roman army promoted assimilation to Roman ways as Roman discipline helped break down indigenous norms of behavior and custom. The benefits of service emphasized the importance of Roman citizenship for the single most significant group in Italy, men of fighting age. Over hundreds of years, the more enterprising Italians—men who rose to the rank of centurion or even military tribune and retired from military service to enter local positions of office and honor, which by the second century carried the potential for Roman citizenship and registration in the highest Roman property classes—expanded the number of citizens throughout the conquered territories. Thus the Roman genius in bringing selected newcomers into the system was matched by the loyalty of the newcomers to the Roman state as they moved into key positions within their group.

The Roman resiliency in dealing with the results of expansion across Italy and the absorption of newcomers into their system is obvious also in the means devised for the recovery of their own citizens, who experienced significant disruption in their lives. Over the years between 264 and 91, as the Romans expanded across Italy and the Mediterranean basin, frequent wars drawing steadily on Roman men as well as other inhabitants of Italy resulted in disrupted family lives and community ties as men died or remained under arms away from Italy on longer and longer campaigns. Through economic adversity, some fell out of the Roman system: Men whose property lost value, the basis for registration in the infantry classes, Classes 1 through 5, were registered at the next census "below the classes" (infra classem), as proletarii. In the second century, when overseas conquests were most extensive and most successful it became obvious even to Roman aristocrats that the military manpower pool of Italy was depleted because the men of Italy could not sustain their customary positions in the economic life of Italy as small property owners capable of arming themselves for war.

What is striking in the circumstances is the avenue to recovery chosen by the Romans: the reform of the main supports of citizen involvement, tribes and property classes, and even of Roman citizenship itself. Clearly under way were efforts to place everyone into a configuration understandable to Romans. The reduction of property qualifications for registration in Classes 1 through 5 increased the numbers available for service as infantrymen. Romans in changed circumstances as a result reentered the Roman state not at a reduced level, as proletarii, but at a functioning level, as members of one of the lower infantry classes, Classes 3 through 5. But even Romans who had fallen out of the property-holding classes altogether were presented with an avenue to recovery by the latter part of the second century, when proletarii were more and more regularly conscripted. The return on military service during successful campaigns included cash or land, perquisites that vaulted soldiers again into the propertied classes. Thus military service provided entry to higher citizen status groups as determined by the property ratings, permitting (even if it did not guarantee) civic participation by Romans who had fallen out of the system through adverse circumstances. For such individuals reentry, not permanent exclusion, was an assumed condition of being Roman. Reinforcing the implicit permeability of such restorative options for Romans themselves was the expansion of the Roman citizen population through the entry of new citizens who fortified Rome by helping maintain her manpower at a steady level. The slow but regular admission of outsiders into the Roman state and the readmission of citizens down on their luck, in such a way as to strengthen the system, explain the remarkable cohesion throughout the period of expansion and growth.

The Roman tribe provided the key corporate base for the Roman system. The tribes, providing the civic identity of Roman citizens, embraced or were themselves embraced by many overlapping group identifications—the Roman plebs and patricians; property classes; the great clans or gentes; patrons and clients; on other levels colonists or municipales; soldiers; and membership in the social and professional sodalitates, ordines, decuria, and collegia—that

Romans claimed. In the tribes, as in all Roman corporate institutions, the relationships of individual members to others were predetermined. Although individual members changed, the niches they occupied remained. The groups into and out of which individuals moved were stable in regard to the persistence of status levels within them and the prescribed relationships between different status levels. Thus, as we might expect, the membership of groups in Roman society was in constant flux, given the high level of geographic and social mobility and the high rate of absorption of newcomers.

As the symbolic cornerstone of the awesome power of the Roman people, the city of Rome became the focal point in Italy for activities encompassing the most important spheres of community life: economic, political, and religious. Here the collective voice of the Roman people resounded in the decisions of public lawmaking assemblies. As the Romans expanded across Italy between the fourth and the second centuries, the duties and rights of citizenship were permanently centered on Rome, the focus of privileges and resources. To fully engage in the rituals and events that accompanied citizenship Romans had to be on hand in the city of Rome periodically throughout the year. The voting assemblies, held only in Rome, in which citizens played a part in developing a Roman consensus on decisions involving their ways of life numbered among the most meaningful of these events. Citizens from distant Roman lands converged on Rome throughout the year for various reasons and for varying lengths of stay. This movement was intensified by an expanding influx of potentially permanent newcomers, among them former military men discharged in Rome, ex-slaves, and members of the growing surplus of citizens from the expanding population. By 50, Rome had emerged as a city of phenomenal size and remarkable stability, holding as many as one million inhabitants, whose rapid movement in and out of the city provides an index of the extent to which the Romans had succeeded in using their customary ways to redirect traditional patterns of life throughout Italy to center on Rome.

Even throughout the first century, when public lawmaking was under assault from a number of directions, all Romans shared the view that public laws were legitimate when the assembled voters gave their approval to the will of the Roman people in the procedurally prescribed manner. When Sulla, named dictator by a public law, Julius Caesar, named dictator by another public law, and Octavian, Antony, and Lepidus, named triumviri by yet another, changed (however temporarily) the governmental structure of Roman society, they did it through the agency of the public lawmaking assembly. Despite the failure at times of some of the resolutions agreed upon in public lawmaking assemblies, it is impossible to imagine Roman society without the process.

But in the strengths of this traditional process of public lawmaking lay the weakness, as colliding interests at the level of the Roman leadership made it increasingly difficult to uphold the decisions of public lawmaking assemblies. On occasion the resolution of a problem through public lawmaking created a larger problem, for example, the solution to the Italian War, namely, the series of public laws granting citizenship to all Italians passed between 91 and 89. The resolution of war by public law was very much in line with the traditional uses of public law for hundreds of years. But the failure of the Romans to agree on the implementation of these laws until 70 intensified the tendency for different groups to use the public lawmaking process to further competing interests. The influx of new aristocrats clamoring for inclusion in Rome's aristocracy joined by the influx of new citizens who descended on Rome as a result of the new laws created a situation that could not be resolved through public lawmaking—despite Sulla's turn to new remedies, again through the medium of lawmaking assemblies. Indeed the failure of the Romans to abide by the decisions of Roman assemblies in 90 and 89 in regard to absorbing the influx of new citizens signaled the beginning of an unprecedented shift in the social and political foundations of the Roman Republic, which continued to run its course until the demise of the Republic and the public lawmaking process as we knew it in 44.

Throughout most of Roman history to date the fundamental unity of the uppermost levels of Roman and Italian society had been critical to the cohesion of the state. Tying the system together was an enduring hierarchy of status led in descending order by Roman senators, equites equo publico, that is, the 1,800–2,400 members of the first eighteen centuries of the centuriate assembly, and other men of equestrian rating formally registered in Class 1, the tribuni aerarii. The relative ease with which members entered and left the uppermost Roman ranks—dependent on property qualifications and censorial review in the case of equestrians and equites equo publico and upon review and/or office in the case of senators—is notable. Local decurions from the towns of Italy and their sons, whose property holdings made them members of the Roman equestrian class, stood in line for registration in the equites equo publico, for selection or election to the posts of military tribune, and for election to the junior offices of Rome. As the first of their people to become Roman citizens, their tribal registration determined the registration of the entire community when the citizenship grants of 90 and 89 were eventually implemented in 70. This placed them in positions of considerable importance as they became the key links between Roman political leaders and the voting population. At elections and in legislative assemblies, these men commanded a new body of loyalties among the voting population.

Yet the resolution of the Italian War through the extension of Roman citizenship created problems at all levels. At the highest levels elected officeholders from old Roman families were being joined by new men of very recent citizen status, often less well versed in Roman ways because they came from towns remote from Rome and had not had the customary training requiring residence from boyhood in Rome. On the lower levels, periodic efforts to absorb even limited numbers of newcomers involved placing these individuals into the previous Roman configuration without disrupting existing networks. When the number of new citizens to be absorbed more than doubled the size of the existing citizen population, the dimensions of the problem swelled commensurably. In either case both the leaders and the led reacted adversely to the threat that the changes presented to the traditional leaders of the tribes and their constituent groups. The expansion of the Roman leadership in particular weakened the traditional attachments between local political leaders and the majority population. Ultimately traditional local attachments between the leaders and the led—at the outset sundered by defeat in war, change in citizen status, or economic disaster—were eventually replaced by the more fluid attachments between unit and legion commander and soldiers fostered by long military service, more fluid because the selection process of the groups involved transcended regional and local considerations. While the commanders of all stations were the same men who occupied positions of local leadership in Rome and in the local communities of Italy, the military environment provided a more focused, stable arena for creating long-term attachments of considerable political significance for both commanders and men. Here as in all other Roman arenas relationships were reciprocal and transmissible only under certain conditions. The attachment of Caesar's veterans to Caesar, and after his death to his chosen heir, Octavian, provides a well-known example. In 44, the soldiers to whom land had been given were quartered in temples in Rome, waiting to depart for their allotments. In preparation they had sold their possessions and had chosen group leaders from their number to lead each group to the colonies. When Caesar was assassinated in March their consternation was great lest the Senate would annul the grant.[2] At the end of the Republic it is significant that only among Rome's military forces did smaller units of men, numbered among them key men of recognized merit, still operate in the traditional Roman way. The overall result was visible at public lawmaking assemblies even before the Italian War. Not only were proper procedures flaunted or ignored, but violence disrupted the proceedings, duly enacted laws were annulled, and lawmaking reflected the dissonant commands of a fragmenting society. For hundreds of years various elected officeholders presented public laws in ultimately failed attempts to develop a community consensus for limited efforts to restore the old cohesion; these efforts intensified in the last decades of the Republic. Ultimately the attenuation of the effective links among various Roman groups weakened the essential modulating functions of assemblies.

The emergence of an emperor represented not an abandonment of Roman values and assumptions but a redirection calculated to restore a rapidly developing cohesion and thus to ensure the survival of the system. And it did. After the Battle of Actium in 31, the Romans embarked on what appears to the modern eye as a new course of political organization under their first emperor, Augustus. To the Romans, however, it represented another interpretation of the Roman way: they often resolved issues local and otherwise after a certain amount of trial and error involving previous solutions. The triumviri rei publicae constituendae Octavian, Antony, and Lepidus appear to have drawn on Sulla's and Caesar's office of dictator as a model in the lawmaking capacity they enjoyed. Finally, the first emperor of Rome, Augustus, sponsored laws at times as a tribune, on the basis of his tribunician powers, and at times as a consul, on the basis of his consular powers. With the emergence of these offices, modern scholars believe, the public lawmaking capacity of the Roman people was drastically reduced, if not destroyed. Yet these extraordinary offices reveal the significance that Roman leaders attached to the lawmaking potential of certain offices—the office of tribune in particular. In turn they reveal the importance attached to public lawmaking as a way of legitimizing political position, decision making, and social change.

L. Cornelius Sulla, C. Julius Caesar, and Augustus, first emperor of Rome, intuitively understood the legitimizing functions of the Roman public lawmaking assembly. In 81, Sulla as dictator carried a series of public laws intended to return the Roman aristocracy and the Roman state to a heading dictated by a traditional understanding of order and authority. That his laws did so primarily by regulating the behavior of Roman aristocrats, in particular restricting the lawmaking capacity of tribunes, the chief officers of the Roman people, is a measure of the troubling changes in Roman society that inspired the civil wars of the period. Julius Caesar carried many more bills between 49 and 44, some like Sulla's intended to redirect an unrestrained aristocracy and others to ameliorate long-term economic ills. Differing from both Sulla and Caesar, Augustus used public lawmaking assemblies to regulate for the first time in Roman history basic social relations and social institutions at the level of the Roman senatorial and equestrian aristocracy—a sure sign that they were seen to be threatened.

Significantly, the overall move from public lawmaking assemblies of the old kind to the new system took several generations, and it is doubtful if those passing the laws, especially in early times, realized what the outcome would be. It is unlikely that C. Gracchus and his fellow tribunes in 123 and 122 understood the ramifications of their "competitive" lawmaking efforts. Public lawmaking had continued during the civil war years of 43 to 31, and it continued also under Augustus and his immediate successors, though on an ever diminishing scale. During Augustus's reign at least twenty-four bills were presented to the Roman people for their decision. Between Augustus's death in CE 14 and the short reign of the emperor Nerva, from CE 96 to 98, a mere twenty bills are reported. After that we hear nothing more about public law enacted by the Roman people. While the end point of the Roman public lawmaking process under the emperors is indeterminate, the emergence of an emperor had clear implications for the meaning of public lawmaking. Most important, the Roman emperor spoke for the Roman people as the primary agent in maintaining the remarkable social cohesion of Roman society. The Roman emperor, the key man in all Roman groups, now embodied the sovereign power of Roman citizens, and through him, the chief lawmaker of Rome, was channeled the "will of the Roman people."

Even under the emperors, public lawmaking remained in a uniquely Roman sense what it had traditionally been, a channel for societywide agreement. The Romans understood the instrumental role of tradition in Roman history, one of the strongest bases of their persistence:

> The Romans as a people were possessed by an especial veneration for authority, precedent and tradition, by a rooted distaste of change unless change could be shown to be in harmony with ancestral custom, "mos maiorum"—which in practice meant the sentiments of the oldest living senators. Lacking any perception of the dogma of progress—for it had not yet been invented—the Romans regarded novelty with distrust and aversion. The word "novus" had an evil ring. Yet the memory of the past reminded the Romans that change had come, though slow and combated.[3]

So writes Sir Ronald Syme, identifying the Roman viewpoint reflected in the efforts of Augustus to construct a legitimate base for his position as emperor. In the present study we have explored the importance of tradition to the structures and performances of public lawmaking assemblies in all periods, including the most recent. Still, to view Roman development as "continuous and harmonious," as Augustus maintained, belies the extraordinary complexity of the changes underlying the Roman experience over time. Roman history to date had been a halting and haphazard development as the Romans encountered each situation afresh with no program to guide them except the fluid, collective memories of the deeds of their forebears held by sundry Roman groups. As Syme goes on to say, paraphrasing Cicero: "Rome's peculiar greatness was due not to one man's genius or to one age, but to many men and the long process of time."[4]

To what extent was Rome's greatness in fact peculiar? Within the ancient Mediterranean region no other peoples expanded so rapidly across so vast an area or created a cohesive society on a comparable scale embracing so many diverse groups. Nor did any other society boast an urban center of a similar size and diversity as Rome—a magnet for a highly mobile population. Nor again did any other Mediterranean society undergo such massive social changes with so little disruption to the overall cohesion of Roman society. Rome had no revolutions. And physical remains of the Roman achievement have endured: Not until the nineteenth century were Roman highways replaced in many parts of Europe. Less well known is the apparent persistence into nineteenth-century Europe of political patterns reminiscent of Rome. Comparison between Rome and nineteenth-century England seems particularly apt with respect to the common size and diversity of Rome and London, the mobility of the rural and urban population, and the degree of social and economic change in progress, generated by similar forces of expansion and social change.[5] The efforts of the Romans and the English to deal with change in similar circumstances are also eerily similar. Significantly, in England as in Rome, a similar resort was made to customary ways to restore order to a rapidly expanding society by reordering local boundaries to reflect a rapidly disappearing sense of local order.

In *The Politics of Deference* (1976), one of the few historical studies to join actions to assumptions on the level of the fundamental groups of voters in the society, as well as in several earlier articles, the historian D. C. Moore describes a situation in nineteenth-century England in which Parliament instituted wide-reaching political changes through the Reform Acts of the 1830s in an effort to maintain the traditional influence of "legitimate leaders" in determining the voting pattern of the community whose loyalties they commanded. The logic of the reforms in England, according to Moore, flowed from an involved set of assumptions. English voters behaved primarily as members of "face-to-face communit[ies] . . . composed of those men who lived in close contact with one another, who had the same occupations or were joined by the same 'interest,' and—most important of all—who recognized the same individual as their social, economic and ideological leader."[6] Moore describes these communities as "deference communities." In turn, the ideal voter was the "man who recognized himself as a member of a community and whose behavior might thus be affected by the legitimate influences of the established leaders of the community," who might be local landowners or industrialists.[7] By the First Reform Act of 1832 parliamentary seats were redistributed, the boundaries of constituencies were redrawn, and the vote was extended to more (but not all) city dwellers. In this way the ministers in England tried to "prevent those factors which they could not control"—namely, the effects on society of "accelerating industrialization, accelerating population movement, and growing intellectual ferment"—from "destroying the existing balance of power and the traditional forms of social power."[8] They sought to reestablish the "cohesion of social groups" by reconstituting voting units to "provide each member of Parliament with the constituents necessary to legitimize his behavior."[9]

That is, they did so by reorganizing existing borough boundaries and voting potential to conform to an idea of social communities whose members' behavior at the polls was conditioned by the assumption that the expressed interests of key members were also their interests. The underlying assumptions giving rise to the English Reform Act of 1832 furnish the key for understanding the purposes of the county poll books, on whose evidence Moore's arguments rest, in which for each election the ballots cast by individual voters were recorded, until the institution of the secret ballot in 1872. Poll books were "muster lists of electoral platoons, companies and battalions. They were mirrors of influence in a highly stratified society."[10] Moore's interpretation of political reform in nineteenth-century England provides an illuminating comparative case for understanding the efforts made in Republican Rome to preserve the bases of social and political order during the period of great changes accompanying Roman expansion across Italy.

Even more, the restorative effects of the First Reform Act, in which upper-class political leaders tried to restore the traditional balance of their society through "legal tools" that could be manipulated through parliamentary decision making, have very much in common with the action of leading Romans in public lawmaking assemblies. More modern, that is, twentieth-century, expectations about law and politics do little to explain the functions of Roman public lawmaking assemblies. In Republican Rome we are clearly in a different world with no comprehensive policies for dealing with any area of life: no systematic agenda of expansion, no systematic agenda for the regularization of social or political order, no systematic agenda of law enforcement. Rome had not made the imaginative leap to a society where a body of rules, legal and bureaucratic, played a pivotal role in regulation. The vast majority of decisions made in Republican Rome were made in the local arena by principal family members and community leaders, as well as by men of local standing (who might include Roman senators) acting in a private capacity as patrons or landlords.

Enforcement of law and order was primarily a local responsibility borne by the community, whose members recognized wrongful behavior and knew the proper agency, at the appropriate level, to amend it.[11] On higher levels, decisions were made by Roman senators as members of the Romans' highest collective body, the Senate, or as elected officeholders, commanders, or specially selected investigators. Roman officeholders and commanders had wide latitude to make immediate decisions in response to local conditions, even to the point of initiating war.[12] Within this diffused structure of order, public lawmaking assemblies alone served as a mechanism of regulation on a Roman statewide basis with the potential for involving the widest variety of individuals and number of groups in Roman society in community decisions.

Like the English Parliament in the early nineteenth century, public lawmaking assemblies provided an institutional way for the Romans to engage in restorative events on a continuing basis. While the public lawmaking process was significantly much more focused on immediate disruptive events, a similarly involved set of Roman assumptions operated. Roman voters behaved primarily as members of small, overlapping social communities sharing common loyalties and interests. Primary among these was the tribe, holding members sometimes from the same locale in Italy, sometimes from two or more widely separated regions. After 70, when all Italians were finally registered as citizens, the towns of Italy, each with a tribal assignment, became the local centers of tribal administration. The property classes constituted an overlapping group dependent on common status and interests, as determined by wealth. But here too the tribes provided the framework inasmuch as the membership of the property classes after the mid-third century was organized by tribe. Of increasing importance in the later Republic were the secondary groups defined by occupation and interest, especially the collegia, whose members often shared a common occupation, and the sodalitates, political clubs for aristocrats sharing the same tribal affiliations. As in nineteenth-century England, the behavior of voters, members of these overlapping Roman groups, followed the lead set by key men in the group. Unlike English voters, whose ballots were recorded in poll books, Roman voters were individually hidden. Only the name (but not the ballot) was recorded, whether of the first voter of the first tribe to vote in tribal assemblies or the first century to vote in centuriate assemblies, the centuria praerogativa. But these men were key members of their groups, in particular the tribe. To the Roman mind it was unnecessary to keep track of more intricate groupings. Clearly the Roman impulse to harmonize with a legitimate leader was taken for granted. Not all men were legitimate leaders, however, as M. Tullius Cicero's arguments in

De Lege Agraria about the shortcomings of P. Servilius Rullus reveal. A legitimate leader in 63 was identifiable by his firm loyalty to the collective authority of the Senate as well as his ability to put into words and action the desires of propertied Romans, key men in their social communities. Roman voters, as Cicero knew, intuitively recognized their true leaders. Equally, the voters and Cicero recognized that the tribes were the fundamental social communities with which political action must mesh. Accordingly, both the adjustment of property ratings, to reincorporate citizens as viable members of the Roman community, and the absorption of new citizens hinged on maintaining the social cohesion of tribes. The extent to which the Romans believed they were successful after 70 is revealed in the electioneering handbook believed written by Quintus Tullius Cicero for his brother Marcus when campaigning for office of consul in 65–64: learn the locations of the tribes as well as the identities and interests of their key members, the tribal leaders, he advised him. Traditionally the tribes were the focus of social cohesion in Roman society. And throughout the social and political changes of the Republican period, restoring the social and political balances of the tribes appeared crucial in maintaining the cohesion of society. At times by Senate decree or magistrate's edict, at moments of statewide crisis, restoration was achieved in lawmaking assemblies.

While the Romans consistently sought to restore the operations of their society in customary ways between 350 and 44, the expanding number of groups and leaders in the changing citizen body in fact made this extremely difficult. Like D. C. Moore's Englishmen, Romans assumed that individuals put in the proper environment, through placement in their proper place in the social structure, would do the right thing. But as time passed, and particularly in pressured times, the customary relationships between tribal leaders and tribal members took second place to the relationships between military leaders and troops. Eventually the scale of Roman society, with the largest citizen population ever seen in the ancient Mediterranean but more important with a vastly expanding leadership marked by competing interests, began to overwhelm the public lawmaking process and the political system as a whole. It is significant, however, that symptoms of the "decline" of the Republic, such as public laws on bribery or extortion intended to regulate aristocrats, make their appearance long before the "century of revolution," throughout which the institutions and constitution of Republican Rome are believed to be coming apart. For their appearance much earlier helps make the point that the Roman state was in a constant state of flux. Potentially disruptive events were the order of the day at all stages. We are not witnessing a progression from an ideal state in the Middle Republic to a state of anarchy in the Late Republic (except perhaps in the minds of the Romans). The Romans consistently worked at resolving tensions in understood ways, under constantly expanding conditions. What is to be wondered at is the Romans' success in keeping the system effective for so long. I have argued in this book that public laws and the process of public lawmaking played a key role in that achievement.

Notwithstanding increasing discord after 89, public lawmaking proved a remarkably resilient mechanism for reaching decisions about the direction of the Roman state throughout the period from 350 to 44. Lawmaking diffused power throughout the society by providing a process for mobilizing societywide support for the resolution of controversial and potentially disruptive issues. As a mechanism for legitimizing the assembled authority of the Roman people, the process itself was as momentous as the substance of the public law that succeeded or failed to pass muster. Indeed, the process was often more meaningful than its end products. Like other forms of Roman decision making, public law addressed immediate situations in a direct and immediate way. There was no conscious planning to produce a coherent body of public law over time in predetermined areas of Roman community life. Instead the Romans managed by accretion and adjustment: as the Roman community expanded the Romans provided necessary leadership, for instance, by expanding the number of existing offices or creating extraordinary commissions. If existing law interfered with a desired and immediate aim, the Romans often enacted more laws to suspend or circumvent existing law in order to accommodate the unique circumstances. In turn, Roman statutes do not fall into easily defined categories. There may have been many measures addressing a single subject—about elected officials, about commanders, about land, and so on—but each one addressed a singular set of circumstances in a singular way. Covering a wide range of issues and topics, these decisions share one overarching feature: a remarkable conviction in the legitimacy of group decision in maintaining the essential balance of the larger community.

From the very earliest days the Romans had begun generating a sophisticated body of decisions in public lawmaking assemblies, shaping and adjusting the bases of their social and political order. Always lawmaking started from the generally shared understanding by Romans about the members of Roman society and their relationships and activities that that order traditionally served. In a world whose order was continually shifting as the relationships within and among different groups in Italy were altered, the public laws enacted by the Roman people came to be one of the chief means of creating, recreating, and somehow fixing order along the lines of a perceived ideal and unchanging order mirrored in the

Roman reverence for the "customs of their ancestors" (mos maiorum). The Roman impulse to maintain their changing social environment in some changeless form is evident in the technique the Romans devised to accommodate awkwardly fitting situations within the fixed boundaries of custom. In 212 for instance it was necessary to conscript boys under the age of seventeen, contrary to custom. To palliate the necessity, caused by heavy losses in the war with Hannibal, the Romans enacted that boys under seventeen who swore the military oath should serve "as though they were seventeen or older." The fiction is typically Roman.[13] In effect such fictions preserve customary rules. At the same time the fictions permit the Romans to respond to new circumstances without deviating from custom. In turn, the Romans are somewhat skeptical of "new law" (lex nova). What the Romans called "new law" was an enactment without precedent, without some grounding in a previous enactment or response to some legal situation. "New law" to the mind of an aristocrat like Cicero was highly questionable unless properly handled and presented by the right aristocrats. On becoming Emperor in 31 Augustus prided himself in presenting "new laws" to the Roman people, which revived and institutionalized ancient customs.[14] Reflected here is a desire for maintaining a customary, predictable world and a sense that the public lawmaking arena was the right one for the task. Within the public lawmaking arena are exhibited the essential sources of cohesion in Roman society. Convened in lawmaking assemblies, Romans approved laws that resolved conflicts dissipating the energies that made possible the growth and prosperity of Rome. For hundreds of years, public lawmaking was paramount among the instruments allowing the Romans to move far beyond the limits of other imperial Mediterranean powers. Through the inclusion of citizens on all levels, public lawmaking assemblies were a unique and enduring Roman mechanism for the resolution of issues on a societywide basis and as such provided the pivotal event in allowing the cohesion essential to the expansion and endurance of the Roman world.

Notes

1. C. Geertz, "Thick description: Toward an interpretive theory of culture," in *The interpretation of cultures* (New York, 1973), 29.

2. Appian, *B.C.* 2.120.

3. Syme1939, 315–16.

4. Cic., *Re Pub.* 2.2

5. See the classic studies of A. Redford, *Labour migration in England, 1800–1850* (Manchester, 1964 [1926]); P. Laslett, *The world we have lost* (London, 1965); and D. V.

Glass and D. E. C. Eversley, eds., *Population in history: Essays in historical demography* (London, 1965).

6. D. C. Moore, "Concession or cure: The sociological premises of the first reform act," *Historical Journal* 9 (1966): 56.

7. Moore 1966, 56.

8. Moore 1966, 43.

9. Moore 1966, 44.

10. Moore 1966, 55.

11. Nippel 1995, 113.

12. This was also true under the emperors: Isaac 1992, 379.

13. The classic expression of legal fictions in the ancient legal context is by H. Maine, *Ancient law: Its connection with the early history of society and its relation to modern ideas* (Gloucester, MA, 1970 [1861]), 20–41.

14. *Res Gestae* 8.5

APPENDIXES

APPENDIX A

Assembling and Processing Evidence

INTRODUCTION

THIS STUDY BEGAN as a rather conventional exploration of the generation and archiving of public laws presented at Roman lawmaking assemblies. Over time the process of organizing and arranging the often scattered information on public laws turned into a monumental project far exceeding the capabilities of the usual stack of three-by-five-inch cards used by historians. Some more effective technique for handling data was called for. A few weeks spent exploring the capabilities of Macintosh HyperCard suggested the possibilities of using my Macintosh Quadra to assist in the project.[1] Fortunately not long after that most critical juncture of my research I became aware of the existence of the Statistical Package for the Social Sciences (SPSS), in my view the most comprehensive and flexible data management system available for historical research.[2] SPSS allows the historian to use information, both numerical and alphabetical, from almost any type of file to generate reports, charts, tables, and trends and gives him or her the means to rapidly edit, select, and reselect such information, thus allowing an almost unlimited exploration of possibilities for a phenomenon under examination.

The overall database generated for the project included more than ten thousand items of information gleaned from all of the available proposals and end products of Rome's public lawmaking assemblies, the roughly 780 proposals or enacted laws to which reference has survived over the entire period of public lawmaking activity from 509 BCE to 98–96 CE (details on the coding of information are discussed later). The items ranged from the reported details of individual proposals and enacted laws—including dates, subjects, offices and names of public law sponsors, names of laws, and occurrence of vetoes or other obstructions—to the ancient authors or other sources of information reporting the details and the reliability of their reportage. We owe this record to an array of contemporary and derivative sources preserving unevenly the details of laws or lawmaking occasions by a variety of different individuals: historians, epitomators, antiquarians, speechwriters, biographers, jurists, and others. Sometimes the speeches for and against proposals of law have survived to document the occasion, usually in snatches of words and phrases.[3] A small number of the laws enacted are known by their very words (*ipsissima verba*), which were engraved on bronze tablets or stone stelae or preserved in a literary or juristic text—again usually in a fragmentary state.

The process of compiling the particulars of public law proposals and enacted laws, which provided the core of my database, began with the record of attested laws and proposals assembled by G. Rotondi in *Leges Publicae Populi Romani* (1912; reprint, 1966), supplemented and corrected by a number of other standard reference tools for Roman political history and Roman law.[4] When necessary I also checked ancient sources of information, in particular to assemble information on the circumstances specific to each proposal or law. The resulting compilation of information about public law and lawmaking meetings and assemblies was processed with the help of SPSS to produce a variety of tables used throughout the text as appropriate to provide the basic framework for my discussion.

Notwithstanding my deployment of SPSS this is by no means a technical study in the sense that I used statistical techniques to give new meaning to the Roman experience. Rather I used the SPSS principally as an organizational tool to assemble the evidence for my study, to explore the resulting compilation—my "database"—and to develop straightforward measures of the frequency and content of public lawmaking activity, as well as the patterns of involvement of political leaders in public lawmaking sessions and the extent to which these patterns reflected changes in historical circumstances over time in the Roman world. My study accordingly deals with the timing and context within which manifest events involved the Roman people, as opposed to more technical quantitative studies, which often use incomplete samples to uncover patterns of life, birth rates, or life expectancy, for example, findings whose recognition by the participants themselves remains to be demonstrated. Rather than statistically accurate samples, therefore, my findings depend more on historical "snapshots," given color and depth by concrete events derived from the more conventional body of narrative, epigraphic, and legal literature available to Roman historians in conjunction with the findings of archaeological studies of Rome and Italy. Thus I seek to systematically bridge the gap between the impossible task of finding and analyzing every public proposal of law and the insights gleaned from detailed case studies of issues, participants, and procedures at single events selected from different time periods.

CODING TECHNIQUES

Information on proposals of Roman law was translated into computer-readable form through the use of a codebook—essentially a set of rules outlining how observations on particular laws will be interpreted and recorded. There are three ways to code data: (1) empirically, that is, in its original form; for example, a year or a date or other numerical measure might be coded exactly as on the original; (2) analytically, by evaluating the original information and placing it into a predetermined category; for example, a year might be coded as within a particular decade or century; and (3) free coding, that is, by assigning a unique designator, or "tag," to a particularly unique fragment of evidence; for example, in the case of Roman statutes the particularly unique and often complicated sources of information on the statute might be assigned a unique coding designator. Each form of coding displays unique advantages and disadvantages. The great advantage of coding empirically is that it allows almost unlimited flexibility in the later processing of information—"raw" items of information can be arranged and rearranged in various categories. If you begin by coding information analytically, that is, in predetermined categories, you are clearly restricting your options in terms of later rearrangement of the data. The third option, free coding, allows you to record particularly unique information on a statute with a view to possibly joining initially seemingly random fragments of information to others at a later stage or quickly accessing unusual information while the data are being processed. Finally, the SPSS program allowed recording on the database in both numeric and alphabetic form, making it possible for me to move backward and forward between both forms and thus greatly enhancing the potential for organizing information.

CODING STANDARD VARIABLES FOR EACH PROPOSAL OF LAW OR ENACTED LAW

Actual input of the information to the computer is quite similar to filling out a blank spreadsheet. Each row on the spreadsheet represents a single proposal of law with unlimited bits of information translated into "variables" by the rules set out in the codebook and recorded one to a cell in the appropriate row.

For each proposal or enacted law in my study as many as possible of the following variables as available were coded:

A. *Unique Number*

I assigned a number, or numbers, to each entry in Rotondi corresponding to each public law proposal or enacted law noted in that entry. Sometimes more than one number accompanies the entry because the consensus of scholarly opinion identifies additional proposals or laws either not included or not so distinguished by Rotondi. Following Rotondi, I include any projected bills that never reached the stage of formal promulgation; that is, they were suggested or planned but never got beyond that point. The planned laws of P. Clodius Pulcher, had he lived to be elected praetor, provide a case in point. In general on this point I was guided by the year-by-year summaries in T. R. S. Broughton, *Magistrates of the Roman Republic* (*MRR*), accompanying a magistrate's year of office. At times I turned to the more detailed entries in other reference books (Pauly-Wissowa and Drumann-Groebe) or more recent studies of specific laws, events, or lawmakers. In column L I note the pertinent modern discussions.

B. *Date*

The dates are as found in Rotondi or as corrected, generally in *MRR* or in some cases M. H. Crawford, ed., *Roman Statutes*. When the consensus of scholarly opinion holds that a proposal or law is "probably" to be dated to a particular year I have assigned it a certain date in that year (see next variable). Such dates are enclosed in parentheses in the master list.

C. *Uncertain Dates: Free Code Sheet C*

The precise dates of many laws are uncertain or unknown although there is in many cases general agreement as to their period or historical circumstances. In this column the numbers code the approximate or probable date or the range of years within which scholars usually place such laws. Probable dates, as noted previously, indicated by "perhaps" or "probably" in the codebook (and set in parentheses in my listing of laws) have also been included in the "Date" since scholarly consensus accepts such a date as very likely. Inasmuch as the lawmaking frequencies pertain to fairly broad periods in Roman history this column helps ensure that all laws are included in the appropriate period notwithstanding the difficulty of pinpointing the exact year of generation.

D. Assembly: Free Code Sheet D

In column D I code the assembly in which a law was produced. The purpose of this column is to show the incidence of legislative activity in the three assemblies in Rome in which public law was enacted, in the case of leges, the tribal assembly (comitia tributa), or the centuriate assembly (comitia centuriata); and in the case of plebiscita, the plebeian tribal assembly (concilium plebis). There are many well-attested laws whose assembly is not reported. In many instances scholars identify such laws as "probably" a plebiscitum or "probably" a lex on the basis of the measure's content and the understanding of Roman patterns of lawmaking. In my coding of the laws in this column I have tried to avoid following these accepted assignments. Instead, I have coded "assembly unknown" or "not plebeian" if there is sufficient information to determine the distinction. The number 9 is reserved for laws whose assembly is not known at all or not the object of well-founded scholarly surmise. A very few fifth-century BCE laws enacted in the comitia curiata are coded lex curiata.

E. Office of Law Sponsor: Free Code Sheet E

In column E I code the public law sponsor's office. The purpose of this column is to help determine with as much precision as possible the lawmaking activity of the offices whose holders convened legislative assemblies in Rome. These officeholders are most routinely tribunes, consuls, or praetors. When scholars are undecided about whether a lawmaker was consul or praetor but are certain he was one or the other I have coded the possibility separately as "not a tribune." When scholars surmise that a lawmaker was a tribune, a consul, or a praetor, despite the absence of sufficient information to determine his office, I have coded the individual as "office unknown."

Other extraordinary offices were involved to differing degrees in the sponsorship of law in Rome. On several recorded occasions, at different times, dictators, *triumviri reipublicae constituendae*, *xviri legibus scribendis*, and *tribuni militum consulare potestate* sponsor law. On one recorded occasion the official called the interrex, summoned in the absence of the consuls to select a dictator, makes law. Rotondi includes as law in his listing of public laws a popular decision managed by a priest (a *Xvir sacrorum*). Although scholars agree the event was not a legislative occasion, I have nonetheless coded this priesthood. Finally, the first emperor of Rome, Augustus, sponsored laws at times as a tribune, on the basis of his tribunician powers, and at times as a consul, on the basis of his consular powers. I have coded him separately.

The information to some extent reduplicates that given in column D. That is, when we know the sponsor's office we often know whether the law was a lex or a plebiscitum because certain magistrates convened certain assemblies.

F. Roman Title (Lex + Law Sponsor's Nomen): Free Code Sheet F

Column F codes the gentilicial or clan name (nomen) of the public law sponsor that gave the enacted law its title, for example, the lex Cornelia or lex Fabia. Some laws take the names of two or more sponsors, especially consular laws, less often tribunician laws. The title appears to have been used in the archiving of law. The purpose of this column is to help assemble the clans whose members over time were involved in the production of public law in Rome. It is not possible, however, to distinguish among the various, sometimes multiple branches of any one clan on the basis of title. Nor is it possible to identify the law sponsor on the basis of the law title: considerably fewer individual sponsors are reported than titles (see next variable). I do not distinguish between lex or rogatio in this column.

G and H. Name of Sponsor: Free Code Sheets G and H

In these two columns I code the name of the public law sponsor when known. Individual sponsors are coded in G. If more than one man sponsored a proposal column H codes the additional sponsor or sponsors. These columns help identify more precisely who among Rome's political leaders was involved in presenting public law proposals to the Roman people.

I. Subject: Free Code Sheet I

Column I codes the issues addressed by the laws generated in Rome's assemblies. Here I indicate the subject of a measure based on the information available about the content of a particular law or proposal. While Rotondi's summaries of the content of a measure are generally sufficient for the purpose, I have also checked ancient sources of information and consulted modern studies on points of interpretation or legal issues. Since the available information, whose sources are collected by Rotondi under each entry, rarely conveys the full scope of a measure, I have tried to stay as close as possible to simple questions in assigning subjects to each measure—what general area does the law address?—in order to come up with an overarching description of subject matter that embraces the entire content and avoids attributing motivation or aim. Obviously the effort works best when we are relatively well informed about the scope of a measure. When we are less well informed one suspects that even the baldest description of content misses the point and assigns the particular measure to an artificial analytical category rather than describes its subject matter. For instance, although many laws deal with "land distribution" their subject matters individually differ significantly: the lex Flaminia of 232 BCE addresses the distribution of recently conquered and annexed land in north Italy to poor citizens in viritane assignments; the rogatio Servilia of 63 BCE addresses the purchase of privately owned land in Italy or in the provinces and its distribution, along with the small bits of remaining ager publicus in Italy and ager publicus in the provinces, to veterans and poor citizens who are to be led out in colonies, the arrangements to be made by a specially elected commission of ten men with imperium. Notwithstanding such differences, the subject matter of some laws, like land distribution laws, appears to allow cautious conflation. I have described the subject matter of laws that establish colonies as "the foundation of colonies," notwithstanding differences as to the number of colonies, their status (Latin or Roman), their membership (poor citizens, or citizens and Latins, or veterans), and their location (Italy or abroad). Similarly I have used "the crime of repetundae," "the crime of ambitus," and so on to describe the subject matter of laws addressing these crimes, notwithstanding differences as to focus: many of such laws, when the details are known, address particular aspects of jury selection, court procedure, penalties, or individuals liable to prosecution for the crime. Similarly I have used "special commission of investigation" to describe the subject of a number of laws that set up special courts of inquiry, or quaestiones, to investigate specific misdeeds ranging from the wrongful enslavement of Ligurians and the misbehavior of the Vestals in the second century BCE to the murder of Clodius by Milo in the first century BCE. I have used "suspends or contravenes existing law" for a variety of measures setting aside existing law to accommodate a given set of circumstances. Given the differences among all the laws the result in general has been a list of frequently unique subjects.

J. Namelaw: Free Code Sheet J

In column J I code the Latin name by which the law is conventionally known, as used in Rotondi or Crawford.

K. Reliability: Free Code Sheet K

In this column I code the reliability of the recorded information with respect to the acceptance of modern scholars that a proposal or law is in fact that. The reliability of some laws noted by Rotondi is low either because the law is thought more likely to be a Senate decree or the law is hypothetical—that is, scholars have assumed that a law should have been presented to the people in certain circumstances although there is no direct or indirect evidence that such was the case—or the law is generally refuted by scholars for other reasons. Hence I have not included the tabula Heracleensis, a bronze tablet engraved with a set of municipal regulations from Heraclea in southern Italy (*RS* 1 No. 24). While part of the text on this tablet may derive from a lex Iulia of 45, the text overall is an assemblage of administrative enactments (*RS* 1:358–59). The reliability of other laws is high; that is, they are accepted without question by scholars as laws or proposals. These may be well documented or less well documented with respect to law sponsor, date, and content. Still other laws and proposals are merely probable; that is, they are generally accepted by scholars although they are poorly documented. For the purposes of measuring frequencies and ascertaining patterns for my study I have included only the items whose reliability is high or probable, including projected bills that were never promulgated.

L. *Additional Unique Aspects: Free Code Sheet L*

In this column I note the modern discussions or reference works I have consulted in checking Rotondi's entries and compiling my database.

M. *Date-Quarter*

In this column I assign the laws to a twenty-five-year block of time (based on columns B and C). If a law cannot be so assigned, I code the law as "date-quarter unknown."

N_1 *through* N_{82}. *Ancient Authors and Sources*

I have coded ancient sources of information individually. These columns include all ancient authors from all periods who record information pertaining to a public law proposal or enacted law. Included also are all epigraphic and juristic sources on laws. The sources are assembled by Rotondi at the end of each entry and, in the case of surviving laws, Crawford.

Notes

1. Apple Computer, Inc., *HyperCard: Reference Manual* (Cupertino, CA, 1993).
2. SPSS Inc., *SPSS 6.1: Base System User's Guide*, Part 1 and Part 2, Macintosh Version (Chicago, 1994).
3. These are collected in Malcovati 1967.
4. See appendix B for a discussion of sources.

APPENDIX B

Representativeness of Compilation

MY COMPILATION OF LAWS is not all-inclusive in that it does not represent the entire body of public law proposals ever considered in ancient Rome. Rather, it consists of the body of proposals of law and enacted laws available at the time of my research. How many laws were lost over the years or went unrecorded is unknown; clearly some did, as the isolation of epigraphically attested laws reveals. Those laws that we have a record of, thanks in large measure to the narrations of ancient authors, are the surviving laws from a larger body of public laws, recorded because of a conscious process of selection based on criteria that have long been forgotten.

There are basically two kinds of errors that can creep into studies based on a number of items drawn from what is obviously a larger body of the particular items: sampling errors, or errors caused by some biased method of collecting the test items; and non–sampling errors, which in the case of my study would mean errors of reportage. In regard to sampling errors, my compilation is not strictly speaking based on a sample in any modern statistical sense. Furthermore, the findings of my study depend not on statistical tests that assume a random sample but on patterns that can be drawn from the accumulation of all extant public laws at particular times and on historical "snapshots" of the lawmaking process at crucial times.

More challenging to the integrity of my compilation is the second kind of possible error, namely, non–sampling error, especially in regard to potential bias in the recording of the reported public law proposals and enacted laws. It is clear that the present availability of recorded proposals of law and enacted laws was determined to a significant degree by reportage, specifically by the interests of selected prominent Roman authors. Arguably, therefore, the patterns discernible in lawmaking activity reflect changes in the volume of existing information about different periods of Roman history. There is especially more information about lawmaking activity over the years from 80 to 43, when the most prolific of ancient authors, Cicero (106–43), was an active participant in events and a commentator on the political life of Rome. Consequently, it might be said that the trends exhibited by our recorded laws and proposals for these years do not accurately represent public lawmaking activity in Rome over the period but the biases of Cicero. In particular it may be objected that the weight of the testimony produced by Cicero, one among many ancient recorders of law, has probably skewed the picture of lawmaking activity we have by exaggerating the amount of such activity between 80 and 43. To what extent can we measure the impact of reportage on our compilation? To what extent do the frequency and subject matter of public lawmaking assemblies in different periods of Roman history reflect the degree to which ancient authors chose to emphasize a particular law or type of law in describing a particular period?

To test the impact of ancient reportage I examined my overall compilation in light of the contribution of ancient authors. The numbers of laws reported by six of the most important, including the four most prolific, ancient recorders of lawmaking activity—Cicero, Livy, Cassius Dio, Appian, Plutarch, and Polybius, in order of volume of reportage—organized by quarter century divisions, are shown in table B.1. Overall these six authors account for 359 of all recorded laws between 300 and 25, more than three out of four laws from our compilation for the period (columns 7 and 8, table B.1). As to individual patterns, Cicero alone is responsible for recording 210, nearly 45 percent of all laws for the period of which we are aware. Despite considerable gaps in the more than 100 books in which he wrote his history of Rome, *ab urbe condita*, Livy is second at 139, or almost 30 percent, of all recorded laws. Next in order of volume come Cassius Dio with 104 (22 percent), followed by Appian at 80 (17 percent), Plutarch at 79 (almost 17 percent), and Polybius at a distance with a mere 10, or 2 percent of all recorded laws (table B.1).

That there should be significant overlap between these authors is understandable: with the exception of Cicero all of them are derivative sources (and Cicero, too, is derivative when he informs us about long-ago laws). We are relatively certain about the sources of information available to these authors when their knowledge of the laws and proposals they report is not firsthand. Polybius (ca. 200–118), the earliest of our authors and a Greek, drew on some non-Roman sources but also on a number of Roman annalists, including Fabius Maximus Pictor, and the traditions recounted by Romans of his acquaintance, including a leading Roman antiquarian of the day, L. Furius Philus. When referring to public laws of earlier generations of Romans, Cicero (106–43) drew on the annalists and Roman traditions. Livy (59–CE 17 or 64–CE 12) drew on the annalists and Polybius as well as on Roman traditions; Appian (late first–early second century CE) on an unknown annalist, Polybius, Posidonius, Sallust, Asinius Pollio, and to a lesser extent Livy; Plutarch (ca. CE 50–120) on a wide variety of autobiographies and published orations as well as earlier historians depending on whose biography he was writing; and Cassius Dio (late second–early third century CE) on the annalists and Livy.

Tables B.2 and B.3 present the numbers of laws selected by Cicero and Livy, respectively, and compare them to the selections made by the other four authors for selected periods. Significantly, as we see in table B.2, Cicero and Livy, as Romans living in the period of the late Republic and the reign of Augustus, respectively, and privy to the traditions, conventions, and assumptions of their times, overlap in 49 cases, that is, 24 percent of Livy's laws are recorded by Cicero (column 2, table B.2), while Livy repeats 49, or 36 percent, of Cicero's laws (column 2, table B.3). Of the 104 (22 percent) of all recorded laws given to us by Cassius Dio, a Roman senator from Bithynia and thus a member of the Roman ruling class, 28 are also listed by Livy (column 3, table B.3), while 58 are listed by Cicero (column 3, table B.2). Of the 80 laws, that is, 17 percent of all known laws between 300 and 25, recorded by Appian—a Greek from Alexandria in Egypt, a member of the ruling elite who received Roman citizenship after holding office in Alexandria and who subsequently moved to Rome, where he became an advocate and a procurator Augusti–39 have been recorded by Livy (column 4, table B.3), and 43 are repeated from Cicero's list (column 4, table B.2). Of Plutarch's 79 laws, almost all (76) are cross-listed by Cicero (column 5, table B.2), while 37 are cross-listed by Livy (column 5, table B.3). Finally, almost two-thirds (6) of Polybius's 10 laws are also listed by Livy; 2 are listed by Cicero (column 6 of tables B.3 and B.2, respectively).

As a Greek at a considerably greater remove from Roman traditions than the later Greeks under the empire—Appian, Plutarch, and Cassius Dio—Polybius provides an instructive contrast to all other authors in our select list. One of a thousand leading Greeks taken hostage in 167 and deported to Rome, Polybius lived for the rest of his long life in Rome, as protégé of P. Cornelius Scipio

Aemilianus, where he wrote an account of Rome's rise to world power. Notwithstanding his reliance on Roman sources of information, the finished product as we have it, in fragmentary state, exhibits considerably less interest in the activities of Rome's lawmaking assemblies than in Roman authors. This can only be a reflection of the interests of his anticipated Greek audience. Compare Polybius and Livy, both of whose histories are extant for much of the period from 224 to 175—Polybius passim and Livy in books 21–45. Both authors focus on the wars in the Greek East throughout the period. While Livy mentions 56 laws in his coverage of those years, Polybius records only a handful (5). Roman public lawmaking activity was understandably of greater importance to a Roman of any period than to a Greek from outside the Roman state. Overall the reliance by ancient authors on common derivative sources did not of itself predetermine the selection of similar laws for inclusion in their writings.

Either through the accident of survival or deliberation, the listing of laws we have for each of our ancient authors is selective. As we might expect given the extensive preservation of his various writings Cicero leads the group as the most prolific: others were scarcely less comprehensive in their listings but for the accident of survival. If we had all of Livy's voluminous history of Rome, for example, it is not hard to imagine that he would have been the most diligent of recorders, exceeding even the voluble Cicero. As it is, Livy's reportage of laws in the earlier periods surpasses that of Cicero. Outsiders like Polybius had distinct habits of reportage. Nevertheless, the fact that more than half of all laws in our study were recorded by only one ancient author suggests a noteworthy level of independence in making decisions as to what laws from a particular period to include in their works.

TABLE B.1 Number of Laws Reported by Selected Ancient Authors for Selected Periods, 300–25, by Number and Percentage

Period	(1) Cicero	(2) Livy	(3) Cassius Dio	(4) Appian	(5) Plutarch	(6) Polybius	(7) Total Laws from Ancient Authors[a]	(8) Total All Laws for Period
300–275	1						1	10
274–250		1					1	9
249–225	1	1				3	3	4
224–200	4	37	2	1	3	2	39	43
199–175	5	19		3	2	3	21	30
174–150	4	10	1			1	11	19
149–125	17	14	3	9	9		27	33
124–100	33	8	2	13	18	1	42	68
99–75	33	18	6	21	10		47	67
74–50	81	20	52	17	28		102	118
49–25	31	11	38	16	9		65	67
Total	210	139	104	80	79	10	359	468
Total for each column as percentage of all laws	44.8	29.7	22.2	17.1	16.9	2.1	76.7	100

Source: See appendix A.

[a]Totals in column 7 do not equal the sum of columns 1 to 6 because of overlap between authors.

TABLE B.2 Number of Laws Reported by Cicero and Selected Ancient Authors for Selected Periods, 300–25, with Overall Total and Percentage

Period	(1) Cicero	(2) Cicero and Livy	(3) Cicero and Cassius Dio	(4) Cicero and Appian	(5) Cicero and Plutarch	(6) Cicero and Polybius
300–275	1					
274–250						
249–225	1					1
224–200	4	2	1	1		1
199–175	5	4		3	2	
174–150	3	2	1			
149–125	15	8	1	4	9	
124–100	28	5	2	6	18	
99–75	32	8	4	11	9	
74–50	81	15	34	13	28	
49–25	32	5	15	5	10	
Total	202	49	58	43	76	2
Total as percentage of Cicero	100	24	29	21	38	<1

Source: See appendix A.

TABLE B.3. Number of Laws Reported by Livy and Selected Ancient Authors for Selected Periods, 300–25, with Overall Total and Percentage

Period	(1) Livy	(2) Livy and Cicero	(3) Livy and Cassius Dio	(4) Livy and Appian	(5) Cicero and Plutarch	(6) Livy and Polybius
300–275						
274–250	1					
249–225	1					1
224–200	37	2	2	1	3	2
199–175	19	4		3	1	2
174–150	10	2	1			1
149–125	14	8	1	7	5	
124–100	8	5		4	6	
99–75	18	8	3	11	3	
74–50	20	15	13	7	15	
49–25	11	5	8	6	4	
Total	139	49	28	39	37	6
Total as percentage of Livy	100	36	20	28	27	<1

Source: See appendix A.

APPENDIX C

List of Reliable Laws and Proposals by Year, Latin Name, and Subject, 350–25 BCE

THE RELIABLY REPORTED laws and proposals in the following tabular list number 559. The year (certain or approximate) follows. Some approximate years are clear from the language. Other approximate years that are generally conceded by a majority of ancient historians are enclosed in parentheses. My primary guides in making this determination were T. R. S. Broughton, *Magistrates of the Roman Republic*, 3 vols., and in the case of epigraphically attested laws M. H. Crawford, ed., *Roman Statutes*, 2 vols. (see appendix A). Inevitably, historians will disagree about an approximate year, but in terms of the blocks of time used in organizing the information in tabular form a few years in either direction makes no difference. Laws that are excluded from tables using twenty-five-year blocks might be included in tables using conventional historical periods. The general pattern is the same. After the year I give the conventional name of the law, in Latin, again following Rotondi and Crawford. Finally, the listing identifies the subject of each law or proposal (see appendix A).

RELIABLE LAWS AND PROPOSALS BY YEAR, LATIN NAME, AND SUBJECT, 349–25 BCE

Year	*Latin Name*	*Subject*
343	Lex de bello Samnitibus indicendo	Declaration of war
342	Plebiscitum de consulibus et magistratibus	Interval between consecutive offices, plebeian consuls
342	Lex Valeria militaris	Mutiny by soldiers
339	Lex Publilia Philone de plebiscitis	The general validity of plebiscites
339	Lex Publilia Philone de patrum auctoritate	Announcement of patrum auctoritas in legislative assemblies
339	Lex Publilia Philone de censore plebeio creando	Opening censorship to plebs
332	Lex Papiria de civitate Acerranorum	Grant of citizenship to outside group
331	Lex de quaestione extraordinaria instituenda	Special commission of investigation
329	Lex de civitate Privernatibus danda	Grant of citizenship to outside group
327	Plebiscitum de imperio Publilio Philoni prorogando	Prorogation of imperium
327	Lex de bello Palaepolitanis indicendo	Declaration of war
Perhaps 327	Lex Publilia de sponsu	Regulation of suretyship
326	Lex Poetelia Papiria de nexis	Dissolution of debt bondage
326	Lex de bello Samnitibus indicendo	Declaration of war
325	Lex de bello Vestinis indicendo	Declaration of war
323	Rogatio Flavia de Tusculanis	Punishment of community
319	Lex Antistia de Satricanis	Punishment of community
318	Rogatio de foedere cum Samnitibus faciendo	Renewal of treaty with Samnites
313	Lex Ovinia de senatus lectione	Censors' authority to review Senate membership
311	Lex Atilia Marcia de tribunis militum senis denis a populo creandis	Election of the military tribunes of legions 1–4
311	Lex Decia de duumviris navalibus	Creation of two-man board for outfitting and repairing fleet
306	Lex de bello Hernicis indicendo	Declaration of war
306	Lex de civitate Anagninis danda	Grant of citizenship to outside group
304	Lex de dedicatione templi araeve	Consecration of buildings, areas, and altars

300	Lex de bello Aequis indicendo	Declaration of war
300	Lex Valeria de provocatione	Citizen liberties
300	Lex Ogulnia de auguribus et pontificibus	Number and qualifications of augurs and priests
300	Lex de foedere cum Lucanis	Treaty with Lucani
Period of legis actiones	Lex Hostilia de actione furti	Modification or extension of legis actiones
298	Plebiscitum de lege solvendo Q. Fabio Rulliano	Suspension or circumvention of law
298	Lex de bello Samnitibus indicendo	Declaration of war
296	Plebiscitum de triumviris coloniae deducendae	Election of IIIviri coloniae deducendae
295	Plebiscitum de imperio L. Volumnio prorogando	Prorogation of imperium
293	Lex de bello Faliscis indicendo	Declaration of war
(287)	Lex Maenia de patrum auctoritate	Announcement of auctoritas patrum in electoral assemblies
287	Rogatio de aere alieno minuendo	Settlement or remission of debts
287	Lex Hortensia de plebiscitis	The general validity of plebiscites
287	Lex Hortensia de nundinis	Legal business on market days
Between 287 and 223–218	Lex Silia	Oversight of weights and measures by aediles
Between 287 and Gracchi	Lex Aquilia	Damage to property
(279)	Lex Maenia de die instauraticio	Repetition of ludi romani
273	Lex de donis regis Ptolemaei	The gifts of Ptolemy to ambassadors
270	Lex de praesidio rhegino	Punishment of legio campana
267	Lex de quaestoribus octo creandis	Expanding the number of quaestors
266	Lex de deditione Q. Fabii Apolloniatibus	The surrender of a commander
265	Lex de censura non iteranda	Iteration of the censorship
264	Lex de bello Carthaginiensibus indicendo	Declaration of war
264	Lex de auxilio Mamertinis praebendo	Military aid to Mamertines
263	Lex de foedere cum Hierone faciendo	Treaty with Hiero of Syracuse
252	Plebiscitum de stipendio equitum	Stipend of censured equites
Before 241	Lex Plaetoria	Jurisdictio of urban praetor
241	Lex de lege solvendo L. Caecilio Metello	Suspension or circumvention of law

241	Lex de pace cum Carthaginiensibus facienda	Confirmation of peace
After 241	Lex Appuleia de sponsu	Regulation of suretyship
Between 241 and 123	Lex Papiria	The election and responsibilities of IIIviri capitales
Between 241 and late second century/ early first century	Lex Furia de sponsu	Regulation of suretyship
232	Lex Flaminia de agro piceno et gallico viritim dividendo	Distribution or assignment of land
228	Lex de bello Illyricis indicendo	Declaration of war
223	Plebiscitum de triumpho C. Flaminii	A triumph for a commander
(220)	Lex Metilia de fullonibus	Expensive clothing
218	Lex de bello Carthaginiensibus indicendo	Declaration of war
218	Lex Claudia de senatoribus	Carrying weight of boats owned by senators
217	Plebiscitum de lege solvendis consularibus	Suspension or circumvention of law
217	Lex Flaminia minus solvendi	The value of bronze coinage
217	Rogatio de vere sacro vovendo	Public vow of a "sacred spring"
217	Lex de prodictatore creando	Election of a dictator
217	Rogatio de imperio Q. Fabio Maximo dictatori abrogando	Abrogation of a dictator's imperium
217	Lex Metilia de aequando magistri equitum et dictatoris iure	Equalizing the imperium of the dictator and magister equitum
216	Lex Minucia de triumviris mensariis	Creation of extraordinary commission
215	Lex de imperio proconsulari M. Marcelli	Proconsular imperium for a praetor
215	Lex Sempronia de duoviris aedi dedicandae	Creation of extraordinary commission
215	Lex de civitate equitum Campanorum	Grant of citizenship to outside group
215	Plebiscitum ut servi publice emerentur	Creation of extraordinary commission
215	Lex Oppia sumptuaria	Women's clothing and jewelry, horse-drawn carriages

212	Lex Carvilia de exilio M. Postumii Pyrgensis	The exile of individual(s)
212	Plebiscitum de dilectu militum	Suspension or circumvention of law
212	Plebiscitum de quinqueviris et triumviris	Creation of extraordinary commission
211	Plebiscitum de imperio in Hispania	The selection of a commander
211	Plebiscitum de exilio Cn. Fulvii Flacci	The exile of individual(s)
211	[Plebiscitum] de civitate Sosidi et Merico danda	Grant of citizenship to individuals
211	Plebiscitum de ovatione M. Claudii Marcelli	Extension of proconsul's imperium until his ovatio
210	Plebiscitum de civitate Mutini danda	Grant of citizenship to individuals
210	Lex Atilia de dediticiis	Punishment of Campanian rebels by the Senate
210	Plebiscitum de dictatore creando	Election of a dictator
210	Plebiscitum de agro romano	Lease of ager Campanus by censors
209	Rogatio Publicia de imperio M. Claudio Marcello abrogando	Abrogation of a commander's imperium
(209)	Lex Publicia de cereis	Gift giving by clients on the Saturnalia
208	Lex de imperio C. Aurunculeio prorogando	Prorogation of imperium
208	Lex Licinia de ludis Apollinaribus	Celebration of the ludi Apollinares
205	Rogatio de provincia Africa	The assignment of a province
204	Lex Cincia	Gifts from defendants in law cases, value of gifts
204	Lex de pace cum Philippo facienda	Confirmation of peace
204	Lex de imperio in Hispania	The selection of two commanders
Before 204	Lex Silia de legis actione	Modification or extension of legis actiones
After 204	Lex Calpurnia de legis actione	Modification or extension of legis actiones
Between 204 and 169	Lex Furia testamentaria	The size of legacies
203	Plebiscitum ne C. Servilio fraudi esset quod contra legem fecisset	Exculpating C. Servilius from knowingly breaking the law
202	Plebiscitum de imperio in Africa	The selection of a commander
201	Plebiscitum de imperio in Hispania	The selection of a commander
201	Lex Acilia Minucia	Authorization to make peace with Carthage and recall army

201	Lex de pace cum Vermina facienda	Confirmation of peace
201	Plebiscitum de imperio in Hispania	The selection of a commander
200	Lex de bello Philippo Macedonum regi indicendo	Declaration of war
200	Plebiscitum de iureiurando C. Valerii Flacci	Suspension or circumvention of law
Early second century	Lex Plaetoria	Creation of extraordinary commission
(199)	Lex Porcia de provocatione	Civil liberties
(198 or 195)	Lex Porcia de provocatione	Civil liberties
198	Lex de foedere cum Achaeis faciendo	Confirmation of peace
196	Lex Atinia de coloniis quinque deducendis	The foundation of colonies
196	Lex Licinia de IIIviris epulonibus creandis	Creation of a three-man priesthood
195	Lex Marcia Atinia de pace cum Philippo facienda	Authorization to negotiate a peace
195	Lex Valeria Fundania de lege Oppia sumptuaria abroganda	Abrogation of an existing statute
(194)	Lex Baebia de coloniis deducendis	The foundation of colonies
193	Lex Aelia de coloniis duabus latinis deducendis	The foundation of colonies
193	Lex Sempronia de pecunia credita	Extension of Roman laws on debt to allies and Latins
192	Plebiscitum de permutatione provinciarum	The reassignment of provinces
(191)	Lex Iunia de feneratione	Money lending
(191)	Lex Acilia de intercalatione	Assignment of responsibility for intercalation
191	Lex de bello Antiocho indicendo	Declaration of war
Before 191	Lex Plaetoria de circumscriptione adolescentium	Fraud perpetrated against minors
189	Lex de pace cum Antiocho	Confirmation of peace
189	Lex Terentia de libertinorum liberis	The citizen status of marginals
189	Lex de pace cum Aetolis facienda	Confirmation of peace
188	Lex Valeria de civitate cum suffragio Formianis et Arpinatibus danda	Grant of citizenship to outside group
187	Lex Petillia de pecunia regis Antiochi	Special commission of investigation
186	Plebiscitum de P. Aebutio et de Fecennia Hispala	Privileges for individuals

Before 186	Lex Atilia de tutore dando	Assignment of tutors by urban praetor and tribunes
182	Lex Orchia de coenis	The number of guests at dinner parties
181 or earlier	Rogatio Pinaria annalis	The ages for holding office
181	Lex Cornelia Baebia de ambitu	The crime of ambitus
181	Lex Baebia de praetoribus	The number of praetors elected in alternate years
180	Lex Villia annalis	The ages for holding office
179	[Plebiscitum] de latrocinio duorum equitum	Special commission of investigation
(179)	Lex de abroganda lege Baebia	Abrogation of an existing statute
Around 179	Lex de triumpho	The necessary conditions for a triumph
177	Rogatio Licinia Papiria de A. Manlio imperio abrogando	Abrogation of a commander's imperium
177	Lex Claudia de sociis	Expulsion of Latin and Italian immigrants from Rome
Before 177	Lex de civitate latinis danda	The citizen status of marginals
Before 175	Lex Maevia	Uncertain or conjectural
Between 174 and 154	Lex Papiria	Consecration of buildings, areas, and altars
172	Lex Marcia de Liguribus	Special commission of investigation
172	Rogatio Marcia de M. Popillio Laenate	Appearance of M. Popillius Laenas before quaestio
172	Lex Lucretia de agro campano	Lease of ager Campanus by censors
Between 172 and 149	Rogatio de rege Attalo et de vectigalibus Asiae	Uncertain or conjectural
171	Lex Licinia Cassia de tribunis militum	Suspension or circumvention of law
171	Lex de bello Perseo indicendo	Declaration of war
(170)	Lex Aufidia de feris Africae	The importation of wild animals from Africa
169	Lex Voconia de mulierum hereditatibus	The capacity of women to inherit
169	Rogatio Rutilia de locatione censoria	The annulment of state leases and contracts made by censors
167	Lex Sempronia de triumpho L. Aemilii Paulli, Cn. Octavii, L. Anicii Galli	Extension of commander's imperium until triumph

167	Lex de ornamentis triumphalibus L. Aemilii Paulli	Privileges for individuals
167	Rogatio Iuventia de bello Rhodiis indicendo	Declaration of war
Before 162	Lex Maenia	The return of a widow's dowry
161	Lex Fannia cibaria	Food and guests at dinner parties
159	Lex Cornelia Fulvia de ambitu	The crime of ambitus
(154)	Lex Caecilia	Special commission of investigation
(153)	Lex Aelia de modo legum ferendarum	Obnuntiatio in lawmaking assemblies
(153)	Lex Fufia de modo legum ferendarum	Obnuntiatio in lawmaking assemblies
Around 151	Lex de consulatu non iterando	Reelection to the office of consul
Mid-second century	Lex Atinia	The ownership of stolen property
Mid-second century	Lex Scantinia	Sexual offenses against freeborn people
149	Rogatio Scribonia de Lusitanis	Special commission of investigation
149	Lex Calpurnia de repetundis	The crime of repetundae
(149)	Lex Atinia de tribunis plebis in senatum legendis	Membership of tribunes in the Senate
Between 149 and 125	Lex Aebutia de formulis	The formulary procedure
Between 149 and 123	Lex Iunia de repetundis	The crime of repetundae
147	Plebiscitum de lege solvendo P. Cornelio Scipione	Suspension or circumvention of law
147	Lex de provincia P. Cornelio Scipioni extra sortem danda	The assignment of a province
146	Lex Livia de agris africanis	Distribution or assignment of land
145	Rogatio Licinia de sacerdotiis	The election of priests
143	Lex Didia sumptuaria	The extension of the lex Fannia to all Italy
141	Lex de foedere cum Numantinis confirmando	Confirmation of peace
141	Lex Mucia de L. Hostilia Tubulo	Special commission of investigation
140	Rogatio Laelia agraria	Distribution or assignment of land
139	Lex Gabinia tabellaria	Voting by written ballot

137	Lex Cassia tabellaria	Voting by written ballot
136	Lex Furia Atilia de C. Hostilio Mancino Numantinis dedendo	Rejection of peace and surrender of commander
134	Plebiscitum de lege solvendo P. Cornelio Scipione	Suspension or circumvention of law
133	Lex Sempronia agraria	Distribution or assignment of land
133	Lex Sempronia agraria altera iudicandis	Jurisdictio of three-man land commission
133	Rogatio Sempronia de pecunia regis Attali	Use of bequest of King Attalus
133	Rogatio Sempronia de provocatione	Citizen liberties
133	Rogatio Sempronia militaris	The term of military service
133	Rogatio Sempronia iudiciaria	Jury composition
133	Lex Sempronia de magistratu M. Octavio abrogando	Removal of tribune(s) from office
131	Lex de bello cum Aristonico gerendo	The selection of a commander
Between 131 and 123	Plebiscitum de tribunis plebis reficiendis	Reelection of the previous year's tribunes
130	Lex Papiria tabellaria	Voting by written ballot
(130)	Rogatio Papiria de tribunis plebis reficiendis	Iteration of office by tribunes
130	Lex de regno Aegypti	The ruler of Egypt
(129)	Plebiscitum reddendorum equorum	The public horse of senators
126	Lex Iunia de peregrinis	The expulsion of foreigners from Rome
125	Rogatio Fulvia de civitate sociis danda	Grant of citizenship to outside group
123	Lex Sempronia agraria	Distribution or assignment of land
123	Lex Sempronia frumentaria	The distribution of grain to citizens
123	Rogatio Sempronia iudiciaria	Addition of members to Senate from equestrian class
123	Lex Sempronia militaris	The conditions of military service
123	Lex Sempronia de abactis	Magistrates who have been deposed by the people
123	Lex Sempronia de provincia Asia	Lease of state contracts in Asia by censors
(123)	Rogatio Aufeia [de provincia Asia]	Uncertain or conjectural
123	Lex Sempronia de P. Popillio Laenate	Special commission of investigation
123	Lex Sempronia de capite civis romani	Citizen liberties
123	Lex Sempronia de coloniis Tarentum et Capuam deducendis	The foundation of colonies
123	Lex Sempronia de novis portoriis	Port duties

123	Lex Sempronia de provinciis consularibus	Allotment of consular provinces by the Senate
123	Lex Sempronia viaria	The construction of new roads
122	Lex Rubria de colonia Carthaginem deducenda	The foundation of colonies
(122)	Rogatio Marcia de tribunis militum	The ages for election as military tribune
122	Lex Repetundarum	The crime of repetundae
122	Lex Sempronia iudiciaria	Jury composition
122	Rogatio Sempronia de suffragiorum confusione	The order of voting in the centuriate assembly
122	Rogatio Livia agraria	Vectigal imposed on state land by lex Sempronia
122	Rogatio Livia de coloniis duodecim deducendis	The foundation of colonies
122	Rogatio Livia frumentaria	The distribution of grain to citizens
122	Rogatio Livia de provocatione latinis concedenda	Citizen liberties
(122)	Lex Acilia Rubria de cultu Iovis Capitolini	Foreign participation in cult of Jupiter Capitolinus
122	Rogatio Sempronia de civitate sociis danda	Grant of citizenship to outside group
122	Rogatio Sempronia de civitate sociis danda	Grant of citizenship to outside group
121	Lex Minucia de colonia Carthaginem deducenda	Stopping a colony foundation
121	Leges Minuciae de legibus Semproniis abrogandis	Abrogation of an existing statute
(121)	Lex agraria	Inalienability of redistributed land under lex Sempronia
(120)	Lex Calpurnia de P. Popillio Laenate revocando	Recall of exile(s)
Between Gracchi and 91–89	Florence Fragment A	Uncertain or conjectural
Between Gracchi and 91–89	Florence Fragment B	Uncertain or conjectural
Between Gracchi and 91–89	Clusium Fragments	Uncertain or conjectural
Between Gracchi and 91–89	Nicotera Fragment A	Jury matters

Between Gracchi and 91–89	Nicotera Fragment B	Uncertain or conjectural
Between Gracchi and 91–89	Tarentum Fragment	The crime of repetundae
Between Gracchi and 91–89	Falerio Fragment I A	Uncertain or conjectural
Between Gracchi and 91–89	Bauer Fragment A	Uncertain or conjectural
119	Rogatio frumentaria	The distribution of grain to citizens
119	Lex Maria de suffragiis ferendis	The pontes used by voters
118	Lex de colonia Narbonem deducenda	The foundation of colonies
(118)	Lex Porcia	Uncertain or conjectural
115	Lex Aemilia sumptuaria	The cost of food at dinner parties
115	Lex Aemilia [de libertinorum suffragiis]	Uncertain or conjectural
Before 113	Lex Memmia de absentibus	Liability for trial of individuals away on state business
113	Lex Peducaea de incestu virginum Vestalium	Special commission of investigation
(111)	Lex Thoria Agraria	Status of landholdings
111	Lex Agraria	Status of landholdings
111	Lex Memmia de Iugurtha Romam ducendo	Authorization for praetor to escort Jugurtha to Rome
111	Lex de bello Iugurthae indicendo	Declaration of war
(110)	Lex Octavia frumentaria	The distribution of grain to citizens
109	Lex Iunia militaris	The term of military service
109	Lex Mamilia de coniuratione Iugurthina	Special commission of investigation
109	Lex Mamilia de limitibus	Land boundaries
107	Lex Manlia de bello Iugurthino	The selection of a commander
107	Lex Caelia tabellaria	Voting by written ballot
106	Lex Servilia iudiciaria	Jury composition
105	Plebiscitum de imperio Q. Servilio Caepioni abrogando	Abrogation of a commander's imperium
105	Lex Rutilia de tribunis militum	Selection of military tribunes by consul
(104)	Lex Clodia de victoriato	Victory on a coinage issue
(104)	Lex Marcia de fenore	Remedy of manus iniectio against creditors

104	Rogatio Marcia agraria	Uncertain or conjectural
104	Lex Cassia de senatu	Expulsion of senators losing imperium
104	Lex Domitia de sacerdotiis	The election of priests
Before 103	Lex Licinia sumptuaria	The cost of food at dinner parties
103	Lex Norbana de auri tolosani quaestione	Special commission of investigation
103	Lex Appuleia de maiestate minuta	The crime of maiestas
103	Lex Appuleia de quaestione extraordinaria instituenda	Special commission of investigation
103	Lex Appuleia de coloniis in Africam deducendis	The foundation of colonies
(101)	Lex Servilia repetundarum	The crime of repetundae
(100)	Lex Fabia de plagiariis	Wrongful possession of a citizen or citizen's slave
(100)	Lex Licinia de magistratibus extraordinariis	A sponsor's election to the extraordinary office he created
(100)	Lex Aebutia de magistratibus extraordinariis	A sponsor's election to the extraordinary office he created
(100)	Lex Latina Tabulae Bantinae	Uncertain or conjectural
100	Lex Appuleia agraria	Distribution or assignment of land
100	Lex Appuleia de coloniis in Siciliam, Achaiam, Macedoniam deduducendis	The foundation of colonies
(100)	Lex Appuleia frumentaria	The distribution of grain to citizens
100	Lex Appuleia de exilio Q. Caecilii Metelli	The exile of individual(s)
100	Lex de provinciis praetoriis	The assignment of a province
Probably late second/ early first century	Lex Cicereia de sponsu	Regulation of suretyship
99	Rogatio Porcia Pompeia de Q. Caecilio Metello revocando	Recall of exile(s)
99	Lex Titia de agris dividundis	Distribution or assignment of land
99	Lex Titia de provinciis quaestoriis	Uncertain or conjectural
98	Lex Calidia de Q. Caecilio Metello revocando	Recall of exile(s)
98	Lex Caecilia Didia de modo legum promulgandarum	The trinundinum and unrelated measures in one proposal
(97)	Lex Duronia de lege Licinia sumptuaria abroganda	Abrogation of an existing statute

96	Lex Valeria de civitate Calliphanae Veliensi danda	Grant of citizenship to individuals
95	Lex Licinia Mucia de civibus redigundis	Expulsion of Latin and Italian immigrants from Rome
91	Lex Livia de coloniis deducendis	The foundation of colonies
91	Rogatio Livia de civitate sociis danda	Grant of citizenship to outside group
91	Lex Livia nummaria	The addition of bronze to silver coinage
91	Lex Livia frumentaria	The distribution of grain to citizens
91	Lex Livia iudiciaria	Addition of equestrians to Senate and jury composition
91	Lex Livia agraria	Distribution or assignment of land
91	Lex Saufeia agraria	Uncertain or conjectural
(91)	Lex Minicia de liberis	The citizen status of marginals
90	Lex Iulia de civitate latinis et sociis danda	Grant of citizenship to outside group
90	Lex Varia de maiestate	Special commission of investigation
89	Lex Calpurnia de civitate sociorum	The creation of new tribes
89	Lex de civitate Tudertibus danda	Grant of citizenship to outside group
89	Lex Plautia Papiria de civitate sociis danda	Grant of citizenship to outside group
(89)	Lex Papiria semunciaria	The introduction of the semiuncial as
89	Lex Pompeia de transpadanis	Grant of citizenship to outside group
89	Lex Plautia iudiciaria	The election of jurors by the tribes
After 91–89	Este Fragment	Local jurisdiction in Italy
After 91–89	Falerio Fragment I B	Local jurisdiction in Italy
After 91–89	Faleria Fragment II	Uncertain or conjectural
88	Rogatio ut exules quibus causam dicere non licuisset revocarentur	Recall of exile(s)
88	Lex Cornelia Pompeia de comitiis centuriatis	Enactment of law in the comitia centuriata
88	Lex Cornelia Pompeia de tribunicia potestate	Restrictions on tribunes
88	Lex Cornelia Pompeia coloniaria	The foundation of colonies
88	Lex Cornelia Pompeia de senatu	Addition of members to Senate from equestrian class

88	Lex Cornelia Pompeia unciaria	Interest payments on the principal of debts
88	Lex Cornelia de exilio Marianorum	The exile of individual(s)
88	Lex Sulpicia de bello mithridatico C. Mario decernendo	The replacement of a commander
88	Lex Sulpicia de revocandis vi eiectis	Recall of exile(s)
88	Lex Sulpicia de aere alieno senatorum	A ceiling on senators' debts
88	Lex Sulpicia de novorum civium libertinorumque suffragiis	The enrollment of new citizens in all the tribes
88	Lex Cornelia de sponsu	Limitations on suretyship
(87)	Lex Cornelia [de IIIIviris Petelinis]	Administrative organization of municipia
87	Lex Cornelia de exulibus revocandis	Recall of exile(s)
87	Rogatio Cornelia de novis civibus	The enrollment of new citizens in all the tribes
(87)	Plebiscitum de imperio A. Claudio abrogando	Abrogation of a commander's imperium
86	Lex Valeria de aere alieno	Settlement of debts
84	Rogatio de imperio Cn. Papirio Carboni abrogando	The removal of a consul from office
83	Lex Iunia de colonia Capuam deducenda	The foundation of colonies
82	Lex Valeria de Sulla dictatore	Selection of dictator legibus scribendis et reipublicae constituendae
82	Lex Cornelia de proscriptione	The proscription of citizens
Probably before 81	Lex Titia de aleatoribus	Permissible gambling
Probably before 81	Lex Publicia de aleatoribus	Permissible gambling
81	Lex Cornelia de tribunicia potestate	Restrictions on tribunes
81	Lex Cornelia de magistratibus	The order, interval, and age limits for holding office
81	Lex Cornelia iudiciaria	Establishment of standing courts and/or jury composition
81	Lex Cornelia de sacerdotiis	The number of priests and restoration of co-optation
81	Lex Cornelia de civitate Volaterranis adimenda	The removal of citizenship from towns
81	Lex Cornelia de provinciis ordinandis	Restrictions on provincial governors

81	Lex Cornelia de praetoribus octo creandis	Expanding the number of praetors
81	Lex Cornelia de XX quaestoribus	Expanding the number of quaestors
81	Lex Cornelia frumentaria	Distribution of grain to citizens
81	Lex Cornelia sumptuaria	Cost of food at dinner parties
(81)	Lex Cornelia de confirmandis testamentis eorum qui in hostium potestate decessissent	Confirmation of heirs
81	Lex Cornelia de falsis	The crime of falsa
81	Lex Cornelia de sicariis et veneficis	The crime of sicarii and venefici (murderers and poisoners)
81	Lex Cornelia de iniuriis	The crime of iniuria
81	Lex Cornelia de maiestate	The crime of maiestas
81	Lex Cornelia de repetundis	The crime of repetundae
81	Lex Cornelia de peculatu	The crime of peculatus
(81)	Lex Cornelia de aleatoribus	Permissible gambling
Before 80	Lex Remmia de calumniatoribus	Uncertain or conjectural
80	Lex Cornelia de reditu Cn. Pompei	A triumph for a commander
78	Lex Aemilia frumentaria	Distribution of grain to citizens
75	Lex Aurelia de tribunicia potestate	Right of tribunes to seek other office
75	Lex Aurelia de iudiciis privatis	Uncertain or conjectural
75	Lex de locatione censoria	Responsibility for letting state contracts
74	Lex Aurelia de lege Aurelia de iudiciis privates abroganda	Abrogation of an existing statute
73	Lex Terentia Cassia frumentaria	Distribution of grain to citizens
72	Lex Cornelia de pecunia quam Sulla bonorum emptoribus remiserat exigenda	Remittance of purchase price for property of proscribed
72	Lex Gellia Cornelia de civitate	Confirmation of grants of citizenship by commander
(70)	Lex Plautia agraria	Uncertain or conjectural
70	Lex Plautia de redito Lepidanorum	Recall of exile(s)
70	Lex Pompeia Licinia de tribunicia potestate	Restoration of the office of tribune
70	Lex Aurelia iudiciaria	Jury composition
70	Lex de legatis decem mittendis	Creation of extraordinary commission
(70)	Lex Plautia de vi	The crime of vis
(69)	Lex Visellia de cura viarum	Uncertain or conjectural
(68)	Lex Antia sumptuaria	Food and guests at dinner parties
(68)	Lex Antonia de Termessibus	Autonomy for a foreign city
67	Plebiscitum de ornamentis consularibus Papirii Carbonis et M. Aureli Cottae	Privileges for individuals

67	Rogatio Cornelia de ambitu	The crime of ambitus
67	Rogatio Cornelia de legibus solvendo	The power to give exemptions from the law
67	Lex Cornelia de legibus solvendo	The power to give exemptions from the law
67	Lex Cornelia de iurisdictione	The praetor's observance of his edict
67	Rogatio Cornelia ne quis legatis exterarum nationum pecuniam expensam ferret	Loans to foreign states
67	Lex Gabinia de bello piratico	The creation of a command against pirates
67	Rogatio Gabinia de magistratu L. Trebellio abrogando	Removal of tribune(s) from office
67	Rogatio Gabinia de consulatu C. Calpurnio Pisoni abrogando	The removal of a consul from office
67	Lex Gabinia [de provinciis consularibus]	The assignment of a province
(67)	Lex Gabinia de senatu legatis dando	Senate audiences with foreign embassies
67	Lex Gabinia de versura Romae provincialibus non facienda	Loans to foreign envoys
67	Lex Calpurnia de ambitu	The crime of ambitus
67	Lex Roscia theatralis	Theater seats for equites
66	Lex Manilia de libertinorum suffragiis	The voting rights of freedmen
66	Lex Manilia de imperio Cn. Pompei	The assignment of a province
66	Lex Manilia de suffragiorum confusione	Uncertain or conjectural
(65)	Lex Aurelia de ambitu	The crime of ambitus
65	Lex Papia de peregrinis	The expulsion of foreigners from Rome
(65)	Lex Papia de vestalium lectione	The selection of Vestals
65	Rogatio de Aegypto	The assignment of Egypt as a province
(64)	Lex Fabia de numero sectatorum	A candidate's entourage
63	Rogatio Caecilia de poena ambitus P. Sullae et P. Autronio Paeto remittenda	The restoration of citizen rights to individual(s)
63	Lex Tullia de ambitu	The crime of ambitus
63	Lex Ampia Atia de triumphalibus ornamentis Cn.Pompei	Privileges for individuals
63	Lex Atia de sacerdotiis	The election of priests
63	Rogatio de aere alieno et agraria	Debt and land distribution

63	Rogatio de restituendis proscriptorum liberis	The restoration of citizen rights to individual(s)
63	Rogatio Servilia agraria	Distribution or assignment of land
62	Lex Maria Porcia de triumphis	The necessary conditions for a triumph
62	Rogatio Caecilia ut absens Pompeius consul fieret	Suspension or circumvention of law
62	Rogatio Caecilia de Cn. Pompeio ex Asia revocando	The recall of a commander from his province
62	Lex Iunia Licinia de legum latione	Depositing law in the archives
62	Rogatio Iulia de cura Capitolii restituendi	Reassignment of oversight over temple reconstruction
61	Rogatio Aufidia de ambitu	The crime of ambitus
61	Lex Pupia Valeria de incestu Clodii	Special commission of investigation
61	Lex Fufia de religione	Special commission of investigation
61	Rogatio de repetundis	Special commission of investigation
(61)	Lex Pupia de senatu diebus comitialibus non habendo	Senate and comitial meeting days
60	Rogatio Flavia agraria	Distribution or assignment of land
60	Lex Caecilia de vectigalibus	Port duties
60	Rogatio Herennia de P. Clodio ad plebem traducendo	Transfer of individual to a plebeian gens
59	Lex Iulia agraria	Distribution or assignment of land
59	Lex Iulia agraria campana	Distribution or assignment of land
59	Lex Iulia agraria	Distribution or assignment of land
59	Lex Iulia de pecuniis repetundis	The crime of repetundae
59	Lex Iulia de actis Cn. Pompei confirmandis	Ratification of a commander's acts
59	Lex Iulia de publicanis	Contracts of the publicani of Asia
59	Lex Iulia de rege Alexandrino	The ruler of Egypt
59	Lex Vatinia de reiectione iudicum	Jury selection
59	Lex Vatinia	The staff of a provincial governor
59	Lex Vatinia de provincia Caesaris	The assignment of a province
59	Lex Vatinia de colonia Comum deducenda	The foundation of colonies
59	Leges Vatiniae de foederibus	Roman relations with foreign cities and states
59	Lex Vatinia de Vettii iudicio	Special commission of investigation
59	Lex Fufia iudiciaria	The voting order of jurors
58	Plebiscitum de dedicatione simulacri Minervae	Authorization to dedicate a statue on Capitolium
58	Lex Clodia de collegia	The restoration of collegia

58	Lex Clodia de provinciis consularibus	The assignment of consular provinces
58	Lex Clodia de permutatione provinciarum	The reassignment of provinces
58	Lex Clodia de capite civis romani	Magistrates who put citizens to death without trial
58	Lex Clodia de exilio Ciceronis	The exile of individual(s)
58	Lex Clodia de iniuriis publicis	Suspension or circumvention of law
58	Lex Clodia de iure et tempore legum rogandarum	Comitial days and their interruption
58	Lex Clodia de rege Deiotaro et Brogitaro	Galatian king and precinct of Magna Mater at Pessinus
58	Lex Clodia de rege Ptolemaeo et de insula Cypro publicando	The annexation of Cyprus as a province, confiscation of King Ptolemy's assets
58	Lex Clodia de censoria notione	Censors' authority to review Senate membership
58	Lex Clodia de scribis quaestoribus	The involvement of quaestorian scribae in trade
58	Lex Clodia frumentaria	The distribution of grain to citizens
58	Rogatio de revocando Cicerone	Recall of exile(s)
58	Rogatio VIII tribunorum	Recall of exile(s)
58	Lex Gabinia Calpurnia de insula Delo	Immunity for Delos
57	Rogatio de revocando Cicerone	Recall of exile(s)
57	Rogatio de revocando Cicerone	Recall of exile(s)
57	Rogatio de revocando Cicerone	Recall of exile(s)
57	Rogatio Messia de cura annonae Cn. Pompeio mandanda	Assignment of oversight over grain supply
57	Lex Cornelia Caecilia de cura annonae Cn. Pompeio mandanda	Assignment of oversight over grain supply
57	Lex Cornelia Caecilia de revocando Cicerone	Recall of exile(s)
56	Rogatio Caninia de rege Alexandrino	Assignment of responsibility for restoring King Ptolemy
56	Rogatio Porcia de imperio L. Cornelio Lentulo abrogando	Abrogation of a commander's imperium
56	Rogatio Porcia de quaestione extraordinaria instituenda	Special commission of investigation
55	Lex Pompeia Licinia de provincia C. Iulii Caesaris	Prorogation of imperium
55	Lex Pompeia iudiciaria	Jury composition
55	Rogatio Pompeia sumptuaria	Personal expenditures by senators

55	Rogatio Pompeia de repetundis	The crime of repetundae
55	Lex Licinia de sodaliciis	The crime of sodalicia
55	Lex Trebonia de provinciis consularibus	The assignment of consular provinces
54	Lex Sulpicia de triumpho C. Pomptini	A triumph for a commander
54	Rogatio de tacito iudicio	Special commission of investigation
53	Rogatio Lucilia Caelia de Cn. Pompei dictatura	Election of a dictator
53	Rogatio Clodia de libertinis	The citizen status of marginals
52	Plebiscitum de imperio Cn. Pompeio et M. Crasso prorogando	Prorogation of imperium
52	Lex de imperio proconsulari M. Tullii Ciceronis	Proconsular imperium and assignment of province
52	Lex Pompeia de vi	The crime of vis
52	Lex Pompeia de ambitu	The crime of ambitus
52	Lex Pompeia de iure magistratum	Standing for office when absent from Rome
52	Lex Pompeia de provinciis	Interval between office and promagistracy
52	Lex Caecilia de censura	Censors' authority to review Senate membership
52	Plebiscitum de petitione Caesaris	Suspension or circumvention of law
(50)	Lex Pompeia de parricidio	The crime of parricide
50	Rogatio Scribonia alimentaria	Assignment of oversight over weights and measures
50	Rogatio Scribonia de itineribus	Cost of travel equipment
50	Rogatio Scribonia viaria	Supervision of roads
50	Lex Scribonia de regno Iubae publicando	Annexation of Numidia as province
50	Rogatio Scribonia de agro Campano	Distribution or assignment of land
(50)	Lex Scribonia de usucapione servitutum	Acquisition of servitudes through usucapio
Mid-first century	Lex Fonteia (Cos Fragments)	Uncertain or conjectural
Mid-first century	Guardia Vomana Fragment	The crime of repetundae
49	Lex Aemilia de dictatore creando	Selection of dictator
49	Lex [Iulia] de civitate gaditanorum	Confirmation of grants of citizenship by commander
49	Lex Antonia de proscriptorum liberis	The restoration of civil rights to individual(s)

(49)	Lex Roscia	Grant of citizenship to outside group
49	Lex Antonia	The restoration of civil rights to individual(s)
48	Plebiscitum de tribunicia potestate Caesaris	Grant of tribunician powers to Caesar
Between 49 and 42	Lex de Gallia Cisalpina	The judicial organization of Cisalpine Gaul
48	Lex de dictatore creando	Selection of dictator
48	Lex de triumpho C. Iulii Caesaris	A triumph for a commander
48	Rogatio Caelia de mercedibus habitationum annuis	Remission of rents in Rome
48	Rogatio Caelia de pecuniis creditis	Settlement of debts
48	Rogatio Caelia de novis tabulis	Settlement of debts
Between 48 and 44	Leges de honoribus Caesaris	Privileges for individual(s)
48	Lex Hirtia de Pompeianis	Capacity of Pompey's men to stand for office
47	Rogatio Cornelia de mercedibus habitationum annuis	Remission of rents in Rome
47	Rogatio Cornelia de novis tabulis	Settlement of debts
(46)	Lex Iulia de sacerdotiis	Eligibility for selection to priesthood when away from Rome
(46)	Lex Iulia de provinciis	Length of provincial governorships
46	Lex Iulia sumptuaria	Food and guests at dinner parties
46	Lex Iulia frumentaria	List of eligible grain recipients
46	Lex Iulia iudiciaria	Jury composition
46	Lex Iulia de maiestate	The crime of maiestas
46	Lex Iulia de vi	The crime of vis
46	Lex Iulia de re pecuaria	The hire of shepherds of free status
46 or 45	Lex Iulia de bonis cedendis	Settlement of debts
Perhaps 46 or soon after	Rome Fragment B	Administrative organization of the municipia
Perhaps 46 or soon after	Rome Fragment A	The crime of repetundae
45	Lex Iulia de portoriis mercium peregrinarum	Port duties
45	Lex Iulia de absentibus	Travel outside Italy by citizens ages 20–40
45	Lex Caecilia de urbe augenda	Extending the pomerium of the city

45	Lex Cassia de plebeis in patricios adlegendis	Creation of new patrician families
44	Lex Antonia de mense quintili	Privileges for individuals
44	Lex Antonia de candidatis	Privileges for individuals
44	Lex Antonio de quinto ludorum romanorum Caesari tribuendo	Privileges for individuals
44	Lex Helvia de magistratu C. Epidio Marullo et L. Caesitio Flavo abrogando	Removal of tribune(s) from office
44	Rogatio Helvia de uxoribus a C. Caesaris ducendis	Privileges for individuals
44	Lex Cornelia de provincia Syria	The assignment of a province
44	Lex Antonia de coloniis deducendis	The foundation of colonies
44	Lex Antonia de actis Caesaris confirmandis	Ratification of Caesar's acta
44	Lex Iulia de insula Creta	The tax burden and provincial status of Crete
44	Lex Iulia de exulibus revocandis	Recall of exile(s)
44	Lex Iulia de civitate Siculis danda	Grant of citizenship to outside group
44	Lex Iulia de rege Deiotaro	Restoration of power to King Deiotarus
44	Lex Antonia iudiciaria	Jury composition
44	Lex Antonia de dictatura in perpetuum tollenda	Abolition of the office of dictator
44	Lex Antonia de permutatione provinciarum	The reassignment of provinces
44	Lex de provinciis consularibus	The assignment of consular provinces
44	Plebiscitum de Caesaris actis cognoscendis cum consilio	A commission to examine Caesar's acta
44	Lex Antonia de provocatione	Appeals to the people
44	Lex Antonia agraria	Distribution or assignment of land
Perhaps end of Republic	Lex Roscia	Administrative organization of municipia
Perhaps end of Republic	Venafro Fragment	Uncertain or conjectural
Perhaps end of Republic	Lex Rubria	The judicial organization of Cisalpine Gaul
Perhaps end of Republic	Veleia Fragment III	Uncertain or conjectural

Perhaps end of Republic	Veleia Fragment II	Local jurisdiction in Italy
43	Lex Vibia de actis Caesaris confirmandis	Ratification of Caesar's acta
43	Lex Vibia de coloniis deducendis	The foundation of colonies
43	Lex Vibia de dictatura tollenda	Abolition of the office of dictator
43	Lex Titia de IIIviris rei publicae constituendae	Creation of extraordinary commission
43	Lex Titia de magistratu P. Servilio Cascae abrogando	Removal of tribune(s) from office
43	Lex Paedia de interfectoribus Caesaris	Special commission of investigation
43	Lex Paedia	Repeal of decrees of Antony and Lepidus
Perhaps 43, after 46	Lex Titia de tutela	Assignment of tutors by provincial governors
42	Lex de lictoribus virginum vestalium	Lictors for the Vestal Virgins
42	Lex Rufrena	The placement of statues of divus Iulius
42	Lex Munatia de proscriptis restituendis	The reprieve of two proscribed individuals
42	Lex Munatia	Grant of citizenship to individuals
41	Lex de bello contra Octavianum a L. Antonio gerendo	The selection of a commander
41	Lex Iulia de mercedibus habitationum annuis	Remission of rents in Rome and Italy
41	Ephesus Fragment	Privileges for individuals
40	Lex Falcidia	Minimum portion allowable to heir under a will
36	Plebiscitum de tribunicia potestate Octaviani	Grant of tribunician powers to Caesar
35	Plebiscitum de honoribus Octaviae et Liviae	Privileges for individuals
Before 32	Lex Petronia de praefectis municipiorum	The appointment of municipal prefects
30	Lex Saenia de plebeis in patricios adlegendis	Creation of new patrician families
Between 30 and 14	Lex Iulia de agris adsignandis et coloniis deducendis	The foundation of colonies
27	Lex Pacuvia de mense Sextilii	Privileges for individuals
Unknown	Lex alearia	Games of chance
Unknown	Lex Porcia de provocatione	Citizen liberties

Unknown	Lex Porcia de sumptu provinciali	The provincial governor's powers of requisition
Unknown	Lex Pesolania	Damage done by a dog
Unknown	Lex Pinaria de legis actione	Assignment of a judex after 30 days
Unknown	Lex de sepulcro C. Publicii Bibuli	Privileges for individuals
Unknown	Lex Vallia de manus iniectione	Modification or extension of legis actiones
Unknown	Lex de civitate Cn. Publicii Menandri	Confirmation of citizenship
Unknown	Lex Crepereia de summa sponsionis	Amount of sponsio before centumviral court
Unknown	Plebiscitum de repetundis	The crime of repetundae
Unknown	Lex Sulpicia	The water supply of Rome
Unknown	Lex Licinia de actione communi dividundo	Action among co-owners for division of common property
Unknown	Lex Papiria de viatoribus aediliciis	Attendants for plebeian aedile
Unknown	Lex Glitia	Children in wills
Unknown	Lex Ollinia	Uncertain or conjectural

Cited Works and Select Bibliography

Accame, S. 1942. La legislazione romana intorno ai collegi nel I° secolo a.C. *BullMusImp*. 13:13–48.

Afzelius, A. 1942. *Die römische Eroberung Italiens, 340–264 v. Chr.* Copenhagen.

Alexander, M. C. 1990. *Trials in the late republic*. Toronto, Buffalo, and London.

Ampolo, C. 1976–77. Demarato, osservazioni sulla mobilità sociale arcaica. *Dial. di Arch.* 9–10:333–45.

———. 1986. Roma e il latium vetus nel VI e nel V sec. a.C. In *PCIA*, edited by C. Ampolo, A. Bottini, and P. G. Guzzo, 8:391–467. Rome.

———. 1988a. La nascita della città. In *Storia di Roma: Roma in Italia*, edited by A. Momigliano and A. Schiavone, 1:153–180. Turin.

———. 1988b. Rome archäique: Une société pastorale? In *Pastoral economies in classical antiquity*, edited by C. R. Whittaker, 120–33. Cambridge.

Ampolo, C., et al., eds. 1981. *Storia della societa italiana*. Dalla preistoria all'espansione di Roma. Vol. 1. Milan.

Ampolo, C., et al., eds. 1989. *Crise et transformation des sociétés archäique de l'Italie au Ve siècle av. J.-C.* Rome.

Ampolo, C., et al., eds. 1991. *Italia, omnium terrarum parens: La civiltà degli Enotri, Choni, Ausoni, Sanniti, Lucani, Bruttii, Sicani, Siculi, Elimi*. 2d ed., Antica Madre, 12. Milan.

Anderson, H. Damgaard. 1997. The archaeological evidence for the origin and development of the Etruscan city in the seventh to sixth centuries. In *Urbanization in the Mediterranean in the 9th to 6th Centuries*, edited by H. Damgaard Anderson et al., 343–82. Copenhagen.

Anderson, H. Damgaard, H. W. Hornaes, S. Houby-Nelson, and A. Rathje, eds. 1997. *Urbanization in the Mediterranean in the 9th to 6th centuries*. Copenhagen.

André, J. 1950. Les noms latins du chemin et de la rue. *REL* 28:104–34.

Arthur, P. 1991. *Romans in northern Campania*. Archaeological Monographs of the British School at Rome 1. London.

Ashby, T. 1935. *The aqueducts of ancient Rome*. Oxford.

Astin, A. E. 1989. Roman government and politics, 200–134 BC. In *CAH*. Vol. 8, *Rome and the Mediterranean to 133 BC*, edited by A. E. Astin, F. W. Walbank, M. W. Frederiksen, and R. M. Ogilvie, 163–96. 2d ed. Cambridge.

Attema, P. 1993. *An archaeological survey in the Pontine region: A contribution to the early settlement history of south Lazio 900–100*. Groningen.

———. 1997. Notes on the urbanization of Latium vetus. In *Urbanization in the Mediterranean in the Ninth to Sixth Centuries*, edited by H. Damgaard Anderson et al., 279–95. Copenhagen.

Attolini, I., F. Cambi, M. Costagna, M. Celuzza, E. Fentress, P. Perkins, and E. Regoli. 1991. Political geography and productive geography between the valleys of the Albegna and the Fiora in northern Etruria. In *Roman landscapes: Archaeological survey in the Mediterranean region*, edited by G. Barker and J. A. Lloyd 142–52. London.

Badian, E. 1958. *Foreign clientelae (264–70 BC)*. Oxford.

———. 1959. The early career of A. Gabinius (cos. 58 BC). *Philol.* 103:87–99.

———. 1964a. *Studies in Greek and Roman history*. Oxford.

———. 1964b. Caepio and Norbanus. In *Studies in Greek and Roman history*, edited by E. Badian, 34–70. Oxford. First published in *Hist.* 6 (1957): 318–46.

———. 1964c. Notes on provincial governors from the social war down to Sulla's victory. In *Studies in Greek and Roman history*, edited by E. Badian, 71–104. Oxford. First published in *PACA* 1 (1958): 1–18.

———. 1964d. Waiting for Sulla. In *Studies in Greek and Roman history*, edited by E. Badian, 206–34. Oxford. First published in *JRS* 52 (1962): 47–61.

———. 1965. M. Porcius Cato and the annexation and early administration of Cyprus. *JRS* 55:110–21.

———. 1970–71. Roman politics and the Italians (133–92 BC). *Dial. di Arch.* 4–5:373–409.

———. 1972a. Tiberius Gracchus and the beginning of the Roman revolution. In *ANRW*, edited by H. Temporini, I 1:668–731. Berlin.

———. 1972b. *Publicans and sinners*. Oxford.

———. 1984. An unrecognised date in Cicero's text? In *Mnemai: Classical studies in memory of Karl K. Hulley*, edited by H. D. Evjen. Chico, CA.

———. 1989. The scribae of the Roman republic. *Klio* 71:582–603.

Balsdon, J. P. V. D. 1938. The history of the extortion court at Rome, 123–70 BC. *PBSR* 38:98–114.

Barker, G. 1981. *Landscape and society: Prehistoric central Italy*. London.

———. 1989. The archaeology of the Italian peasant. *PCPS* 35:1–19.

———. 1991. Stability and change. In *Roman landscapes: Archaeological survey in the Mediterranean region*, edited by G. Barker and J. A. Lloyd. London.

———. 1995. Landscape archaeology in Italy: Goals for the 1990s. In *Settlement and economy in Italy, 1500 to AD 1500: Papers of the fifth conference of Italian archaeology*, edited by N. Christie, 1–11. Oxford.

———, ed. 1995. *A Mediterranean valley: Landscape archaeology and annales history in the Biferno Valley*. London and New York.

Barker, G., and J. A. Lloyd, eds. 1991. *Roman landscapes: Archaeological survey in the Mediterranean region*. Archeological Monographs of the British School at Rome 2. London.

Barker, G., J. Lloyd, and D. Webley. 1978. A classical landscape in Molise. *PBSR* 46:35–51.

Baronowski, D. W. 1984.The formula togatorum. *Hist.* 33:248–52.

———. 1993. Roman military forces in 225 BC (Polybius 2.23.24). *Hist.* 42:181–202.

Barth, F. 1978. *Scale and organization*. Oslo, Bergen, and Tromsø.

———. 1981a. *Collected essays on Pathans. Selected essays of Frederik Barth*. Vol. 1, *Process and form in social life*, edited by A. Kuper. International Library of Anthropology. London, Boston, and Henley.

———. 1981b. *Collected essays on Pathans. Selected essays of Frederik Barth*. Vol. 2, *Features of person and society in Swat*, edited by A. Kuper. International Library of Anthropology. London, Boston, and Henley.

Barzanò, A. 1995. Il trasferimento dei Liguri Apuani nel Sannio del 180–179. In *Coercizione e mobilità umana nel mondo antico*, edited by M. Sordi, 177–201. Milan.

Bauerle, E. 1990. Procuring an election: Ambitus in the Roman republic, 432–49 BC. Ph.D. diss., University of Michigan.

Bauman, R. 1983. *Lawyers in Roman republican politics*. Munich.

Beard, M., J. North, and S. Price. 1998. *Religions of Rome*. 2 vols. Cambridge.

Behrends, O. 1992. Bodenheit und privates Bodeneigentum im Grenzwesen Roms. In *Die Römische Feldmeßkunst*, edited by O. Behrends and L. Capogrosso, 192–284. Göttingen.

Behrends, O., and L. Capogrosso, eds. 1992. *Die römische Feldmeßkunst: Interdisziplinäre Beiträge zu ihrer Bedeutung für die Zivilisationsgeschichte Roms*. Göttingen.

Bell, A. J. E. 1997. Cicero and the spectacle of power. *JRS* 87:1–22.

Beloch, K. J. 1880. *Der italische Bund unter Roms Hegemonie*. Rome.

———. 1886. *Die Bevölkerung der griechisch-römischen Welt*. Leipzig.

———. 1926. *Römische Geschichte bis zum Beginn der punischen Kriege*. Berlin and Leipzig.

Benedittis, G. De. 1977. *Bovianum ed il suo territorio*. Rome.

Benner, H. 1987. *Die Politik des P. Clodius Pulcher: Untersuchungen zur Denatierung des Clientelwesens in den ausgehenden römischen Republik*. Vol. 50. Historia Einzelschriften. Stuttgart.

Berger, A. 1953. *Encyclopedic dictionary of Roman law*. Philadelphia.

Bianchi, U. 1978. Gli dei delle stirpi Italiche. In *PCIA*, edited by M. Pallotino, 7:195–236. Rome.

Bietti-Sestieri, A. M. 1985. The Iron Age cemetery of Osteria dell'Osa, Rome: Evidence of social change in Lazio in the 8th c. In *Papers in British archaeology IV: The Cambridge conference*, edited by C. Malone and S. Stoddart, 117–44. Oxford.

———. 1992. *The Iron Age community of Osteria dell'Osa*. Cambridge.

———. 1995. The role of interregional contact in the development of Latial society in the early Iron Age. In *Settlement and economy in Italy, 1500 to AD 1500*, edited by N. Christie, 353–64. Oxford.

Bintliff, J., and K. Sbonias, eds. 1999. *Reconstructing past population trends in Mediterranean Europe*. Vol. 1, *The archaeology of Mediterranean landscapes*, edited by G. Barker and D. Mattingley. Oxford.

Birks, P. 1988. New light on the Roman legal system: The appointment of judges. *Cambridge Law Journal* 47 (1): 36–60.

Biscardi, A. 1971. Aperçu historique du problème de l'abrogatio legis. *RIDA* 18:449–70.
Bishop, M. C., and J. C. N Coulston. 1993. *Roman military equipment*. London.
Bitto, I. 1968. Tribus e propagatio civitatis nei secoli IV e III a.C. *Epigraphica* 30:20–58.
Blagg, T., and M. Millett, eds. 1990. *The early Roman empire in the west*. Oxford.
Bleicken, J. 1955. *Das Volkstribunat der klassischen Republik: Studien zu seiner Entwicklung zwischen 287 und 133 v. Chr.* Munich.
———. 1975. *Lex Publica: Gesetz und Recht in der römischen Republik*. Berlin and New York.
———. 1981. Das Römische Volkstribunat: Versuch einer Analyse seiner politischen Funktion in republikanischer Zeit. *Chiron* 11:87–108.
Blois, L. de. 1987. *The Roman army and politics in the first century before Christ*. Amsterdam.
Bonnefond-Coury, M. 1989. *Le sénat de la république romaine*. Rome.
Botsford, G. W. 1909. *The Roman assemblies*. New York.
Bouma, J. W., P. A. J. Attema, A. J. Beijer, A. J. Nijboer, and R. A. Olde Dubbelink. 1995. The economy of an early Latin settlement, Borgo Le Ferriere-Satricum, 800–200. In *Settlement and economy in Italy, 1500 to AD 1500*, edited by N. Christie, 183–95. Oxford.
Les "bourgeoisies" municipales italiennes aux IIe et Ier siècles av. J.C.: Centre Jean Bérard, Institut Français de Naples, 7–10 décembre 1981. 1983. Paris and Naples.
Bowman, A. K., and J. D. Thomas. 1991. A military strength report from Vindolanda. *JRS* 81:62–73.
Bradley, G. 2000. *Umbria*. Oxford.
Braudel, F. 1972. *The Mediterranean and the Mediterranean world in the age of Philip*. Translated by S. Reynolds. 2 vols. New York, Evanston, San Francisco, and London.
Brennan, T. C. 2000. *The praetorship in the Roman republic*. 2 vols. Oxford.
Broughton, T. R. S. 1984–86. *The magistrates of the Roman republic*. 3 vols. Chico, CA, and Atlanta, GA. Vols. 1 and 2 first published in 1951.
Brunt, P. A. 1971. *Italian manpower, 225 BC–AD 14*. Oxford.
———. 1980. Free labour and public works at Rome. *JRS* 70:81–100.
———. 1982. Nobilitas and novitas. *JRS* 72:1–17.
———. 1988. *The fall of the Roman republic and related essays*. Oxford.
Burton, G., and K. Hopkins. 1983. Political succession in the late republic (249–50 BC). In *Death and renewal*, edited by K. Hopkins. Cambridge.
Caldwell, J. C. 1969. *African rural-urban migration: The movement to Ghana's towns*. New York.
Cambi, F. 1999. Demography and romanization in central Italy. In *Reconstructing past population trends in Mediterranean Europe*, edited by J. Bintliff and K. Sbonias, 115–27. Oxford.
Campanelli, A. 1995. La nascita della città in Abruzzo: Tradizioni, insediamenti e nuovi modelli (IV—I sec. A. C.). In *Settlement and economy in Italy, 1500 to AD 1500*, edited by N. Christie, 493–98. Oxford.
Campanile, E., ed. 1981. *I Celti d'Italia*. Pisa.
Campbell, B. 2000. *The writings of the Roman land surveyors: Introduction, text, translation, and commentary*. JRS Monograph No. 9. London.
Cassola, F. 1962. *I gruppi politici romani nel III secolo a. C.* Trieste.
Chevallier, R. 1976. *Roman roads*. Berkeley and Los Angeles.

Chouquer, G., and F. Favory, ed. 1991. *Les paysages de l'antiquité. Terres et cadastres de l'occident romain (IVe s. av. J.-C./IIIe s. après J.-C.)*. Paris.

Christie, N., ed. 1995. *Settlement and economy in Italy, 1500 to AD 1500: Papers of the fifth conference of Italian archaeology*. Oxford.

Cianfarani, V. 1976. Culture arcaiche dell'Italia medio-adriatica. In *PCIA*, edited by V. Cianfarani, G. Mansuelli, D. G. Lollini, and M. Zuffa, 5:35–39. Rome.

La città nell'Italia settentrionale in età romana. 1990. Rome and Trieste.

Clavel-Lévêque, M. 1978. Brigandage et piraterie: Représentations idéologiques et pratiques impérialistes au dernier siècle de la république. *DHA* 4:17–32.

———. 1983a. Studio di un catasto nell'ager Falernus. In *Misurare la terra: Centurazione e coloni nel mondo romano*, 1:227–30. Modena.

———, ed. 1983b. *Cadastres et espace rurale. Approches et réalités antiques. Table rond de Besançon, mai 1980*. Paris.

Clemente, G. 1983. Il plebiscito Claudio e le classi dirigenti romane nell'età dell'imperialismo. *Ktema* 8:253–59.

Cloud, D. 1994. The constitution and public criminal law. In *CAH*. Vol. 9, *The last age of the Roman republic, 146–43 BC*, edited by J. A. Crook, A. Lintott, and E. Rawson, 493–94. 2d ed. Cambridge, New York, New Rochelle, Melbourne, and Sydney.

Coarelli, F. 1979. Fregellae e la colonizzazione latina nella valle del Liri. *Arch. Laz*. 2.

———. 1983. *Il foro romano: periodo arcaico*. Rome.

———. 1987. *I santuari del Lazio in età repubblicana*. Rome.

———. 1988. *Il foro boario dalle origine alla fine della repubblica*. Rome.

———. 1991. I Sanniti a Fregellae. In *La romanisation du Samnium aux IIe et Ier siècle av. J.C.: Notes du colloque organisée par le Centre Jean Bérard*, 177–85. Naples.

Conte Haller, G. 1978. Ricerche su alcuni centri fortificati in opere poligonale nell' area campana-sannita. *Accademia di Archeologia. Lettere e Belle Arti di Napoli. Monumenti* 3. Naples.

Corbier, M. 1987. L'écriture dans l'espace public romain. In *L'urbs: espace urbain et histoire: Ier siècle av. J.C.-IIIe siècle ap. J.C.* Rome.

———. 1991. La transhumance entre le Samnium et l'Apulie: Continuités entre l'époque republicaine et l'époque imperiale. In *La romanisation du Samnium aux IIe et Ier siècles av. J.-C.* Naples.

Cornell, T. J. 1995. *The beginnings of Rome: Italy and Rome from the Bronze Age to the Punic Wars (c.1000–264 BC)*. London and New York.

Cornell, T. J., and K. Lomas, eds. 1995. *Urban society in Roman Italy*. London.

Crawford, M. H. 1974. *Roman republican coinage*. 2 vols. Cambridge.

———. 1981. Italy and Rome. *JRS* 71:153–60.

———. 1983. Le monete romane nelle regioni d'Italia. In *Les "bourgeoisies" municipales italiennes aux IIe et Ier siècles av. J.C.*, 47–50. Paris and Naples.

———. 1985. *Coinage and money under the Roman republic*. London.

———. 1989. The lex Iulia agraria. *Ath*. n.s. 67:179–90.

———. 1991. Army and coinage in the late republic. In *La romanisation du Samnium aux IIe et Ier siècles av. J.C.*, 135–37. Naples.

———. 1996. Italy and Rome from Sulla to Augustus. In *CAH*. Vol. 10, *The Augustan empire, 44 BC–69 AD*, edited by E. Champlain, A. K. Bowman, and A. Lintott. 2d ed. Cambridge.

Crawford, M. H., ed. 1996. *Roman statutes*. 2 vols. Bulletin of the Institute of Classical Studies. Supplement 64. London.

Crawford, M. H., L. Keppie, J. Patterson, and M. Vercenocke. 1984. Excavations at Fregellae, 1978–1984. *PBSR* 52:40–68.

———. 1986. Excavations at Fregellae, 1978–1984. Part III. *PBSR* 54:40–68.

Crise et transformation des sociétés archäique de l'Italie au Ve siècle av. J.C.: Actes de la table ronde organisée par l'École Française de Rome et l'Unité de Recherches Étrusco-Italiques associée au CNRS, Rome, 19–21 Novembre 1987. 1990. Rome.

Cristofani, M. 1978. Società e istituzioni nell'Italia preromana. In *PCIA*, edited by M. Pallotino, 7:51–112. Rome.

Crook, J. 1987. Lex Cornelia de falsis. *Ath*. n.s. 65:163–171.

Curti, E., E. Dench, and J. Patterson. 1996. The archaeology of central and southern Italy: Recent trends and approaches. *JRS* 86:170–89.

Dahlheim, W. 1968. *Struktur und Entwicklung des römischen Völkerrechts im 3. und 2. Jahrhundert v. Chr*. Munich.

———. 1993. Das Staatsreich des Konsuls Sulla und die römische Italienspolitik der achtziger Jahre. In *Colloquium aus anlass des 80. Geburtstages von Alfred Heuss*, edited by J. Bleicken, 97–115. Kallmünz.

D'Armes, J. H. 1981. *Commerce and social standing in ancient Rome*. Cambridge, MA.

David, J.-M. 1983. Les orateurs des municipes à Rome: Intégration, réticences et snobismes. In *Les "bourgeoisies" municipales italiennes aux IIe et Ier siècles av. J.C.*, 309–23. Paris and Naples.

———. 1992. *Le patronat judiciaire au dernier siècle de la république romaine*. Rome.

———. 1996. *The Roman conquest of Italy*. Cambridge, MA.

———. 2000. *La république romaine de la deuxième guerre punique à la bataille d'Actium, 218–31. Crise d'une aristocratie*. Paris.

Degrassi, A. 1947. *Inscriptiones Italiae*. Vol. 13, *Fasti et Elogia*. Fasc. 1, *Fasti Consulares et Triumphales*. Rome.

Demougin, S. 1983. Notables municipaux et ordre équestre à l'époque des dernières guerres civiles. In *Les "bourgeoisies" municipales italiennes aux IIe et Ier siècles av. J.C.*, 279–98. Paris and Naples.

Dench, E. 1995. *From barbarians to new men*. Oxford.

Deniaux, E. 1983. Le passage des citoyennetés locales à la citoyenneté romaine et la constitution des clientèles. In *Les "bourgeoisies" municipales italiennes aux IIe et Ier siècles av. J.C.*, 267–77. Paris and Naples.

Develin, R. 1975. Comitia tributa plebis. *Ath*. n.s. 53:302–37.

———. 1977. Comitia tributa again. *Ath*. n.s. 55:423–25.

———. 1978. The lex agraria of 111 BC and procedure in legislative assemblies. *Antichthon* 12:45–50.

Douglas, W. A. 1984. *Emigration in a south Italian town: An anthropological history*. New Brunswick, NJ.

Drumann, W., and P. Groebe. 1899–1929. *Geschichte Roms in seinem Übergange von der republikanischen zur monarchischen Verfassung; oder, Pompeius, Caesar, Cicero und ihre Zeitgenossen nach Geschlechtern und mit genealogischen Tabellen*. 6 vols. 2d ed. Berlin.

Drummond, A. 1989. Early Roman clientage. In *Patronage in ancient society*, edited by A. Wallace-Hadrill, 89–115. London and New York.

Ducos, M. 1984. *Les romains et la loi: Recherches sur les rapports de la philosophie grecque et de la tradition romaine à la fin de la république*. Paris.

Dumont, J.-C., J.-L. Ferrary, P. Moreau, and C. Nicolet. 1980. *Insula sacra: La loi Gabinia-Calpurnia de Délos (58 av. J.-C.)*. Rome.

Dyson, S. 1985. *The creation of the Roman frontier*. Princeton.

Eckstein, A. 1987. *Senate and general: Individual decision making and Roman foreign relations, 264–194 BC*. Berkeley, Los Angeles, and London.

Eder, W. 1969. *Das vorsullanische Repetundenverfahren*. Munich.

Engels, D. 1979. *Alexander the Great and the logistics of the Macedonian army*. Berkeley and Los Angeles.

———. 1990. *Roman Corinth: An alternative model for the classical city*. Chicago and London.

Ewins, U. 1952. The early colonization of Cisalpine Gaul. *PBSR* 20:54–71.

Fabbricotti, E. 1995. Storia di un tratturo. In *Settlement and economy in Italy, 1500 to AD 1500*, edited by N. Christie, 197–200. Oxford.

Fallers, L. A., ed. 1967. *Immigrants and associations*. The Hague and Paris.

Farrand, M., ed. 1966. *The records of the federal convention of 1787*. Rev. ed. New Haven, CT.

Farrell, J. 1986. The distinction between comitia and concilium. *Ath*. 74 (n.s. 64): 407–38.

Fascione, L. 1981. Alle origini della legislazione de ambitu. In *Legge e società nella repubblica romana*, edited by F. Serrao. Naples.

———. 1984. *Crimen e quaestio ambitus nell'età repubblicana*. Milan.

Feig-Vishnia, R. 1996. *State, society, and popular leaders in mid-republican Rome, 241–167 BC*. London and New York.

Ferrary, J.-L. 1988. Rogatio Servilia agraria. *Ath*. 66:141–64.

———. 1991. Lex Cornelia de sicariis et veneficis. *Ath*. n.s. 79:417–34.

———. 1998. Chapitres tralaticiens et référence à des lois antérieures dans les lois romaines. In *Mélanges de droit romain et d'histoire ancienne. Hommage à la mémoire de André Magdelain*, edited by M. Humbert and Y. Thomas, 151–67. [Paris.]

Finley, M. I. 1983. *Politics in the ancient world*. Cambridge.

Flambard, J.-M. 1977. Clodius, les collèges, la plèbe et les ésclaves. *MEFRA* 89:115–53.

———. 1982. Collegia compitalicia: Phénomène associatif, cadres territoriaux et cadres civiques dans le monde romain à l'époque républicaine. *Ktema* 6:144–66.

———. 1983. Les collèges et les élites locales à l'époque républicaine d'après l'exemple de Capoue. In *Les "bourgeoisies" municipales italiennes aux IIe et Ier siècles av. J.C.*, 75–89. Paris and Naples.

La formazione della città in Lazio. Seminario tenuto a Roma 24–26 giugno 1977. 1980. *Dial. di Arch*. 2:1–2.

La formazione della città preromana in Emilia Romagna: Atti del convegno di studi, convegno e colloqui, novi serie 8, Bologna-Marzabotto 1985. 1988. Bologna.

Forni, G. 1972. Considerazioni sui comizi romani. *Rendiconti di Istituto Lombardo. Accad. di scienze e lettere* 106:543–66.

Fowler, W. Warde. 1899. *The Roman festivals*. London.

Fraccaro, P. 1957. La procedura del vota nei comizi tributi romani. In *Opuscula* 2. Pavia. Original edition, *Atti della Romana Accademia delle Scienze di Torino* 49 (1913–14): 600–622.

Frank, T. 1933. *Economic survey of ancient Rome*. Vol. 1, *Rome and Italy of the republic*. Baltimore.

Frayn, J. 1984. *Sheep-rearing and the wool trade in Italy during the Roman period*. Liverpool.

———. 1993. *Markets and fairs in Roman Italy*. Oxford.

Frederiksen, M. W. 1966. Caesar, Cicero, and the problem of debt. *JRS* 56:128–41.

———. 1976. Changes in the pattern of settlement. In *Hellenismus in Mittelitalien*, edited by P. Zanker, 341–55. Göttingen.

———. 1984. *Campania*. Edited by N. Purcell. London.

Frederiksen, M. W., and J. B. Ward-Perkins. 1957. The ancient road systems of the central and northern Ager Faliscus. *PBSR* 25:67–198.

Gabba, E. 1958. *Appiani bellorum civilium liber primus: Introduzione, testo critico e commento*. Florence.

———. 1976. *Republican Rome: The army and the allies*. Translated by P. J. Cuff. Oxford.

———. 1979. Sulle strutture agrarie dell'Italia romana fra III e I sec. a.C. In *Strutture agrarie e allevamento transumante nell'Italia romana (III-I Sec. A.C.)*, edited by M. Pasquinucci and E. Gabba, 15–73. Pisa.

———. 1983. Strutture sociali e politica romana in Italia nel II sec. a. C. In *Les "bourgeoisies" municipales italiennes aux IIe et Ier siècles av. J.C.*, 41–45. Paris and Naples.

———. 1985. Per un'interpretazione storica della centuriazione romana. *Ath.* 63:255–84.

———. 1989. Rome and Italy in the second century BC. In *CAH*. Vol. 8, *Rome and the Mediterranean to 133 BC*, edited by A. E. Astin, F. W. Walbank, M. W. Frederiksen, and R. M. Ogilvie, 197–243. 2d ed. Cambridge.

———. 1992. Storia e politica nei Gromatici. In *Die Römische Feldmeßkunst*, edited by O. Behrends and L. Capogrosso, 398–409. Göttingen.

———. 1994a. Rome and Italy: The social war. In *CAH*. Vol. 9, *The last age of the Roman republic 146–43 BC*, edited by A. Lintott, J. A. Crook, and E. Rawson, 104–28. 2d ed. Cambridge, New York, New Rochelle, Melbourne, and Sydney.

———. 1994b. *Italia Romana*. Como.

Gallant, T. 1991. *Risk and survival in ancient Greece*. Stanford, CA.

Galsterer, H. 1971. Die lex Osca tabulae Bantinae: Eine Bestandsaufnahme. *Chiron* 1:191–214.

———. 1976. *Herrschaft und Verwaltung im republikanischen Italien*. Munich.

Gargola, D. 1995. *Lands, laws, and gods: Magistrates and ceremony in the regulation of public lands in republican Rome*. Chapel Hill and London.

Garnsey, P. 1988. Mountain economies in southern Europe. In *Pastoral economies in classical antiquity*, edited by C. R. Whittaker, 196–209. Cambridge.

Garnsey, P., and G. Woolf. 1989. Patronage of the rural poor in the Roman world. In *Patronage in ancient society*, edited by A. Wallace-Hadrill, 153–70. London and New York.

Geertz, C. 1968. *The interpretation of cultures*. New York.

Gelzer, M. 1968. *Caesar: Politician and statesman*. Translated by P. Needham. 6th German ed. Cambridge, MA.

———. 1969. *The Roman nobility*. Translated by R. Seager. Oxford.

Glass, D. V., and D. E. C. Eversley, eds. 1965. *Population in history: Essays in historical demography*. London.

Göhler, J. 1939. *Rom und Italien*. Breslau.

Granet, J. 1990. La loi agraire et l'élevage. *Pallas* 36:125–54.

Greenidge, A. H. J. 1901. *The legal procedure of Cicero's time*. Oxford.

Grieve, L. J. 1985. The reform of the comitia centuriata. *Hist*. 34:278–304.

Griffin, M. 1973. The tribunate of C. Cornelius. *JRS* 63:196–213.

Gruen, E. 1968. Pompey and the Pisones. *Calif. Stud. Class. Ant*. 1:135–70.

———. 1974. *The last generation of the Roman republic*. Berkeley and Los Angeles.

———. 1992. *National identity in republican Rome*. Ithaca, NY.

Halstead, P. 1987. Traditional and rural economy in Mediterranean Europe: Plus ça change? *JHS* 107:77–87.

Hammond, N. 1989. *The Macedonian state*. Oxford.

Hantos, T. 1988. *Res publica constituta: Die Verfassung des Dictators Sulla*. Vol. 50, Hermes Einzelschriften. Stuttgart.

Hardy, E. G. 1924. The agrarian proposal of Rullus in 63. In *Some problems in Roman history: Ten essays bearing on the administrative and legislative work of Julius Caesar*, 68–98. Oxford.

Harmand, J. 1967. *L'armée et le soldat à Rome de 107 à 50 avant notre ère*. Paris.

Harris, W. V. 1971. *Rome in Etruria and Umbria*. Oxford.

———. 1972. Was Roman law imposed on the Italian allies? *Hist*. 22:638–45.

———. 1979. *War and imperialism in republican Rome, 327–70 BC*. Oxford.

———. 1989. *Ancient literacy*. Cambridge, MA.

Hayne, L. 1974. The politics of M'. Glabrio, cos. 67. *CP* 69:280–82.

Heikkilä, K. 1993. Lex non iure rogata: Senate and annulment of laws in the late Roman republic. In *Senatus populusque romanus: Studies in Roman republican legislation*, edited by J. Vaahtera. 117–42. Helsinki and Rome.

Hellegouarc'h, J. 1963. *Le vocabulaire latin des relations et des partis politiques sous le république*. Paris.

Hinard, F. 1983. La proscription de 82 et les Italiens. In *Les "bourgeoisies" municipales italiennes aux IIe et Ier siècles av. J.C.*, 325–31. Paris and Naples.

———. 1985. *Les proscriptions de la Rome républicaine*. Vol. 83, *Collection de l'École Française de Rome*. Rome.

Hinrichs, F. T. 1974. *Die Geschichte der gromatischen Institutionen: Untersuchungen zu Landverteilung, Landvermessung, Bodenverwaltung und Bodenrecht im römischen Reich*. Wiesbaden.

Hodge, A. T. 1992. *Roman aqueducts and water supply*. London.

Holden, P., and N. Purcell. 2000. *The corrupting sea: A study of Mediterranean history*. Oxford.

Hölkeskamp, K.-J. 1987. *Die Entstehung der Nobilität*. Stuttgart.

———. 1993. Conquest, competition, and consensus: Roman expansion in Italy and the rise of the nobilitas. *Hist*. 42:12–39.

Holloway, R. R. 1994. *The archaeology of early Rome and Latium*. London and New York.

Hopkins, K. 1978. *Conquerors and slaves*. Cambridge.

Hübner, W. 1992. Himmel und Erdvermessung. In *Die Römische Feldmeßkunst*, edited by O. Behrends and L. Capogrosso, 140–71. Göttingen.

Humbert, M. 1978. *Municipium et civitas sine suffragio: L'organisation de la conquête jusqu'à la guerre sociale*. Paris.

———. 1998. La normativité des plebiscites selon la tradition annalistique. In *Mélanges de droit romain et d'histoire ancienne: Hommage à la mémoire de André Magdelain*, edited by M. Humbert and Y. Thomas, 211–38. [Paris.]

Humbert, M., and Y. Thomas, eds. 1998. *Mélanges de droit romain et d'histoire ancienne: Hommage à la mémoire de André Magdelain*. [Paris.]

Humphrey, J. H., ed. 1991. *Literacy in the Roman world*. Vol. 3. JRA Supplementary Series. Ann Arbor, MI.

Hurlet, F. 1993. *La dictature de Sylla: Monarchie ou magistrature républicaine? Essai d'histoire constitutionnelle*. Vol. 30. Institut Historique Belge de Rome. Études de Philologie, d'Archéologie et d'Histoire Anciennes. Brussels and Rome.

Ilari, V. 1974. *Gli Italici nelle strutture militari romane*. Milan.

Isaac, Benjamin. 1992. *The limits of empire: The Roman army in the east*. Rev. ed. Oxford.

Jehne, M. 1993. Geheime Abstimmung und Bindungswesen in der römischen Republik. *HZ* 257:563–613.

———, ed. 1995. *Demokratie in Rom? Die Rolle des Volkes in der Politik der römischen Republik*. Vol. 96 of Historia Einzelschriften. Stuttgart.

Johannsen, K. 1971. Die lex agraria des Jahres 111 v. Chr. Ph.D. diss. Munich.

Jones, A. H. M. 1960. *Studies in Roman government and law*. Oxford.

Kaser, M. 1942. Typen der römischen Bodenrechte in der späteren Republik. *ZRG* 62:68–73.

———. 1955. *Das römische Privatrecht*. 2 vols. Munich.

———. 1966. *Das römische Zivilprozessrecht*. Munich.

Keaveney, A. 1987. *Rome and the unification of Italy*. London.

Keay, S., and N. Terrenato. 2001. *Italy and the West: Comparative issues in Romanization*. Oxford.

Kehoe, D. P. 1990. Pastoralism and agriculture. *JRA* 3:386–98.

Keppie, L. 1983. *Colonisation and veteran settlement in Italy, 47–14 BC*. London.

———. 1984. *The making of the Roman army: From republic to empire*. London.

Kiel, M. 1999. The Ottoman imperial registers: Central Greece and northern Bulgaria in the 15th–19th century: The demographic development of two areas compared. In *Reconstructing past population trends in Mediterranean Europe*, edited by J. Bintliff and K. Sbonias, 195–218. Oxford.

Kloppenburg, J. S. 1996. Collegia and thiasoi: Issues in function, taxonomy and membership. In *Voluntary associations in the Greco-Roman world*, edited by J. S. Kloppenburg and S. G. Wilson, 16–30. London and New York.

Kloppenburg, J. S., and S. G. Wilson, eds. 1996. *Voluntary associations in the Greco-Roman world*. London and New York.

Kromayer, J., and G. Veith. 1928. *Heerwesen und Kriegsführung der Griechen und Römer*. Munich.

Kunkel, W. 1962. *Untersuchungen zur Entwicklung des römischen Kriminalverfahrens in vorsullanischer Zeit*. Munich.

———. 1995. *Staatsordnung und Staatspraxis der römischen Republik*. 2 vols. Munich.

La Regina, A. 1970. Note sulla formazione dei centri urbani in area sabellica. In *Studi sulla città antica*, 191–207. Bologna.

Laffi, U. 1983. I senati locali nell'Italia repubblicana. In *Les "bourgeoisies" municipales italiennes aux II et Ier siècles av. J.-C.*, 59–74. Paris and Naples.

———. 1985. *Asculum*. 4 vols. Pisa.

Lanciani, R. 1967 [1897]. *The ruins and excavations of ancient Rome*. Boston and London.

Laslett, P. 1965. *The world we have lost*. London.

Laurence, R. 1999. *The roads of Roman Italy: Mobility and cultural change*. London and New York.

Lejeune M., and D. Briquel, eds. 1991. Lingue e scritture. In *Italia, omnium terrarum parens*, edited by C. Ampolo et al., 435–76. Milan.

Letta, C. 1972. *I Marsi e il Fucini nell'antichità*. Milan.

Linderski, J. 1986. The augural law. In *ANRW*, edited by H. Temporini, II 16.3: 2146–312.

Linderski, J., and A. Kaminska-Linderski. 1973. A. Gabinius A. f. Capito and the first voter in the legislative comitia tributa. *ZPE* 12:247–52.

Lintott, A. 1965. Trinundinum. *CQ* 59:281–85.

———.1968. *Violence in republican Rome*. Oxford.

———. 1972. Provocatio: From the struggle of the orders to the principate. In *ANRW*, edited by H. Temporini. I 2:226–67.

———. 1981. The *leges de repetundis* and associate measures under the republic. *ZRG* 98:162–212.

———. 1983. The so-called *tabula bembina* and the humanists. *Ath.* 61:201–14.

———. 1987. Democracy in the late republic. *ZRG* 117:34–52.

———. 1990. Electoral bribery in the Roman republic. *JRS* 80:1–16.

———. 1992. *Judicial reform and land reform in the Roman republic*. Cambridge.

———. 1993. *Imperium romanum: Politics and administration*. London and New York.

———. 1994. Political history, 146–95 BC. In *CAH*. Vol. 9, *The Last age of the Roman republic, 146–43 BC*, edited by J. A. Crook, A. Lintott, and E. Rawson. 2d ed. Cambridge, New York, New Rochelle, Melbourne, and Sydney.

———. 1999. *The constitution of the Roman republic*. Oxford.

Liou-Gille, B. 1996. Naissance de la ligue latine: Mythe et culte de fondation. *RBPhil* 74:73–97.

Livi-Bacci, M. 1992. *A concise history of world population*. Translated by C. Ipsen. Cambridge, MA, and Oxford.

Lloyd, J. A. 1991a. Farming the highlands: Samnium and Arcadia in the Hellenistic and early Roman empire. In *Roman landscapes: Archaeological survey in the Mediterranean region*, edited by G. Barker and J. A. Lloyd, 180–93. London.

———. 1991b. Forms of rural settlement in the early Roman empire. In *Roman landscapes: Archaeological survey in the Mediterranean region*, edited by G. Barker and J. A. Lloyd, 233–40. London.

Lo Cascio, E. 1994. The size of the Roman population: Beloch and the meaning of the Augustan census figures. *JRS* 84:23–40.

———. 1999. The population of Roman Italy in town and country. In *Reconstructing past population trends in Mediterranean Europe*, edited by J. Bintliff and K. Sbonias, 161–71. Oxford.

Lomas, K. 1993. *Rome and the western Greeks, 350–AD 200*. London and New York.

———. 1995. Urban elites and cultural definition: Romanization in southern Italy. In *Urban society in Roman Italy*, edited by T. Cornell and K. Lomas, 107–20. London.

Love, J. R. 1991. *Antiquity and capitalism: Max Weber and the sociological foundations of Roman civilization*. London and New York.

Lübtow, U. von. 1957. Catos leges venditiones et locationi dictae. *Eos* 48 (3): 227–441.

Luisi, A. 1995. La presenza dei Ligures Baebiani nel Sannio. In *Coercizione e mobilità umana nel mondo antico*, edited by M. Sordi, 203–14. Milan.

MacMullen, R. 1980. How many Romans voted? *Ath*. 53:454–57.

Magdelain, A. 1978. *La loi à Rome: Histoire d'un concept*. Paris.

Maine, H. 1970 [1861]. *Ancient law: Its connection with the early history of society and its relation to modern ideas*. Gloucester, MA.

Malcovati, H. 1967. *Oratorum romanorum fragmenta*. 3 vols. 3d ed. Turin.

Malone, C., and S. Stoddart, eds. 1985. *Papers in British archaeology IV: The Cambridge conference*. Oxford.

Mann, J. C. 1982. *Legionary recruitment and veteran settlement*. London.

Marshall, B. 1985. *A historical commentary on Asconius*. Columbia, MO.

Martin, J. 1970. Die Provokation in der klassischen und späten Republik. *Hermes* 98:72–96.

Mason, G. 1992. The agrarian role of coloniae maritimae, 338–241 BC. *Hist*. 41:75–87.

McDermott, W. C. 1972. Cicero's publication of his consular orations. *Philolo*. 116:277–84.

McDonnell, M. 1986. Legal language in Plautus. *AJP* 107:564–76.

Meier, C. 1980. *Res publica amissa: Eine Studie zu Verfassung und Geschichte der späten römischen Republik*. 2d ed. Wiesbaden.

Meiggs, R. 1973. *Roman Ostia*. 2d ed. Oxford.

Michels, A. K. 1967. *The calendar of the Roman republic*. Princeton.

Middleton, M. F., and R. Nimkoff. 1960. Types of family and types of economy. *AJS* 66:215–25.

Millar, F. G. B. 1984a. The constitution of the Roman republic. *JRS* 74:1–19.

———. 1984b. The political character of the classical Roman republic, 200–151 BC. *JRS* 74:1–19.

———. 1986. Politics, persuasion and the people before the social war. *JRS* 76:1–11.

———. 1995. Popular politics at Rome in the late republic. In *Leaders and masses in the Roman world*, edited by I. Malkin and Z. W. Rubinsohn, 91–114. Leiden, New York, and Köln.

———. 1998. *The crowd in Rome in the late republic*. Ann Arbor, MI.

Mingazzini, P. 1938. Il santuario della dea Marica alle foci del Garigliano. *Mon. Ant*. 37:693–957.

Misurare la terra: Centuriazione e coloni nel mondo romano. 1983–85. 4 vols. Modena.

Mitchell, R. E. 1990. *Patricians and plebeians: The origins of the Roman state*. Ithaca, NY.

Mommsen, T. 1844. *Die römischen tribus in administrativer Beziehung*. Altona.

———. 1887. *Römisches Staatsrecht. Handbuch der römischen Alterthümer*. Edited by J. Marquardt and T. Mommsen. 3 vols. 3d ed. Leipzig.

———. 1891. *History of Rome*. Translation of 4th German ed. 4 vols. New York.

———. [1903] 1965. *Gesammelte Schriften*. Vol. 1. Edited by T. Mommsen. Berlin.

Moore, D. C. 1966. Concession or cure: The sociological premises of the first reform act. *Historical Journal* 9:39–59.

______. 1976. *The politics of deference: A study of the mid-nineteenth century English political system*. Hassocks, NY.

Moreau, P. 1982. *Clodiana religio: Un procès politique en 61 av. J.-C.* Paris.
———. 1987. La lex Clodia sur le bannissement de Cicéron. *Ath.* 75:465–92.
———. 1988. Lex Iulia de sacerdotiis. *Ath.* 76 (n.s. 66): 365–69.
———. 1989. La rogatio des huit tribuns de 58 av. J.-C. et les clauses de sanctio régle-mentant l'abrogation des lois. *Ath.* 77 (n.s. 67): 151–78.
Morley, N. 1996. *Metropolis and hinterland: The city of Rome and the Italian economy, 200 BC–AD 200.* Cambridge.
———. 1997. Cities in context: Urban systems in Roman Italy. In *Roman urbanism: Beyond the consumer city,* edited by H. Parkins, 42–58. London and New York.
Mouritsen, Henrik. 1998. *Italian unification: A study in ancient and modern historiography.* London.
———. 2001. *Plebs and politics in the late Roman republic.* Cambridge.
Münzer, F. 1920. *Römische Adelsparteien und Adelsfamilien.* Stuttgart.
Neeve, P. W. de. 1984. *Colonus: Private farm tenancy in Roman Italy during the republic and the early principate.* Amsterdam.
———. 1988. The price of agricultural land in Roman Italy and the problem of eco-nomic rationalism. *Opus* 4:77–108.
Nicolet, C. 1966–74. *L'ordre équestre à l'époque républicaine (312–43 av. J.-C.).* 2 vols. Paris.
———. 1976a. *Le métier de citoyen dans la Rome républicaine.* Paris.
———. 1976b. *Tributum: Recherches sur la fiscalité directe sous la rébublique Romaine.* Bonn.
———. 1994. Economy and society, 133–43 BC. In *CAH.* Vol. 9, *The last age of the Roman republic, 146–43 BC,* edited by A. Lintott, J. A. Crook, and E. Rawson, 599–643. 2d ed. Cambridge, New York, New Rochelle, Melbourne, and Sydney.
———, ed. 1984. *Des ordres à Rome.* Paris.
Nippel, W. 1995. *Public order in ancient Rome.* Cambridge.
Niro, A. de. 1977. *Il culto d'Ercole tra I Sanniti Pentri e Frentani.* Rome.
Nissen, H. 1883–1902. *Italische Landeskunde.* 2 vols. Berlin.
North, J. A. 1976. Conservatism and change in Roman religion. *PBSR* 44:1–12.
———. 1989. Religion in republican Rome. In *CAH.* Vol. 7, part 2, *The Rise of Rome to 220 BC,* edited by F. W. Walbank, A. E. Astin, M. W. Frederiksen, and R. M. Ogilvie, 573–624. 2d ed. Cambridge.
———. 1990a. Democratic politics in republican Rome. *Past and Present* 126:3–21.
———. 1990b. Diviners and divination at Rome. In *Pagan priests: Religion and power in the ancient world,* edited by M. Beard and J. A. North, 51–71. Ithaca, NY.
———. 1995. Religion and rusticity. In *Urban society in Roman Italy,* edited by T. Cornell and K. Lomas, 135–50. London.
Oakley, S. P. 1995. *The hill forts of the Samnites.* Archaeological Monographs of the British School at Rome 10. London.
Paananen, U. 1993. Legislation in the comitia centuriata. In *Senatus populusque romanus: Studies in Roman republican legislation,* edited by J. Vaahtera, 9–73. Helsinki.
Pallottino, M. 1994. *A history of earliest Italy.* Ann Arbor, MI.
Palmer, R. E. A. 1974. *Roman religion and Roman empire: Five essays.* Philadelphia.
———. 1990. Cults of Hercules, Apollo Caelispex, and Fortuna in and around the Roman cattle market. *JRA* 3:234–44.

———. 1997. *Rome and Carthage at peace*. Vol. 113. Historia Einzelschriften. Wiesbaden.

Pandolfino, M., and A. L. Prosdocimi. 1990. *Alfabetari e insegnamento della scritture in Etruria e nell'Italia antica*. Firenze.

Parkin, T. 1992. *Demography and Roman society*. Baltimore and London.

———. 1999. Clearing away the cobwebs: A critical perspective on historical sources for Roman population history. In *Reconstructing past population trends in Mediterranean Europe*, edited by J. Bintliff and K. Sbonias, 153–60. Oxford

Pasquinucci, M. 1979. La transumante nell'Italia romana. In *Strutture agrarie e allevamento transumanza nell'Italia romana (III-I sec. a.c.)*, edited by M. Pasquinucci and E. Gabba, 79–182. Pisa.

Pasquinucci, M., and E. Gabba. 1979. *Strutture agrarie e allevamento transumante nell'-Italia Romana (III-I sec. a.c.)*. Pisa.

Paterson, J. 1999. Counting heads: An overview. In *Reconstructing past population trends in Mediterranean Europe*, edited by J. Bintliff and K. Sbonias, 259–61. Oxford.

Patterson, J. R. 1992. The city of Rome: From republic to empire. *JRS* 82:186–215.

———. 1993. Review of *L'ipogeo dei Vimini di Canosa (Adrias II)*, by E. M. de Julius, and six other books. *JRS* 83:189–93.

Pauly, A., G. Wissowa, and W. Kroll. *Real-Encyclopädie der klassischen Altertumswissenschaft*. Munich, 1894–1972.

Pellegrini, G. B. 1978. Toponimi ed etnici nelle lingue dell'Italia antica. In *PCIA*, edited by A. L. Prosdocimi and A. Marinetti, 6.1.80–127. Rome.

Penney, J. H. W. 1988. The languages of Italy. In *CAH*. Vol. 4, *Persia, Greece, and the western Mediterranean c. 525 to 479 BC*, edited by J. Boardman, N. G. L. Hammond, D. M. Lewis, and M. Ostwald, 720–38. 2d ed. Cambridge.

Perelli, L. 1982. *Il movimento popolare nell'ultimo secolo della repubblica*. Turin.

Perkins, P. 1999. Reconstructing the population history of the Albegna Valley and Ager Cosanus, Tuscany. In *Geographical information systems and landscape archaeology*, edited by M. Gillings, D. Mattingley, and J. van Dalen, 103–15. Oxford.

Peyre, C. 1979. *La cisalpine gauloise du IIIe au Ier siècle av. J.C.* Paris.

Pieri, G. 1968. *Histoire du cens jusqu'à la fin de la république Romaine*. Paris.

Pina Polo, F. 1996. *Contra arma verbis: Der redner vor dem Volk in der späten römischen Republik*. Stuttgart.

Piper, D. J. 1987. Latins and Roman citizenship in the Roman colonies. *Hist.* 36:38–50.

Pisani, V. 1978. Le lingue preromane d'Italia: Origini e fortune. In *PCIA*. edited by A. L. Prosdocimi and A. Marinetti, 6.1.15–77. Rome.

Platner, S., and T. Ashby. 1929. *A topographical dictionary of ancient Rome*. Oxford.

Poccetti, P. 1979. *Nuovi documenti italici*. Pisa.

Pontrandolfo Greco, A. 1982. *I Lucani: Etnografia e archeologia di una regione antica*. Milan.

Pospisil, L. 1971. *The anthropology of law: A comparative theory*. New York.

———. 1978. *The ethnology of law*. 2d ed. Menlo Park, CA.

Potter, T. W. 1979. *The changing landscape of south Etruria*. London.

Premerstein, A. von. 1901. Commentarii. In *PW*, 4:726.

Prosdocimi, A. L. 1989. La religioni degli Italici. In *Italia, omnium terrarum parens*, edited by C. Ampolo et al., 477–595. Milan.

Pugliese Carratelli, G. 1962. Santuari extramurani in Magna Graecia. *PP* 17:241–46.

Purcell, N. 1983. The apparitores: A study in social mobility. *PBSR* 51:125–73.
———. 1990. The creation of provincial landscape: The Roman impact on Cisalpine Gaul. In *The early Roman empire in the west*, edited by T. Blagg and M. Millett, 7–29. Oxford.
Putnam, M. C. J. 1967. Vortumnus. *AJA* 71:177–79.
Quilici-Gigli, S. 1982. Sistemi di cunicoli nel territorio tra Velletri e Cisterna. *Arch. Laz.* 5:112–23.
Rathbone, D. 1981. The development of agriculture in the "ager Cosanus" during the Roman republic: Problems of evidence and interpretation. *JRS* 71:10–23.
———. 1993. The census qualifications of the assidui and the prima classis. In *De agricultura: In memoriam P.W. de Neeve*, edited by H. Sancisi-Weerdenburg et al., 121–52. Amsterdam.
Rawson, E. 1971. The literary sources for the pre-Marian army. *PBSR* 39:13–31.
———. 1973a. The eastern clientelae of Clodius and the Claudii. *Hist.* 22:219–39.
———. 1973b. The interpretation of Cicero's *de legibus*. In *ANRW*, edited by H. Temporini, I 4:334–56.
———. 1985. *Intellectual life in the late Roman republic*. Baltimore.
———. 1991. *Roman culture and society: Collected papers*. Oxford.
Redford, A. 1964 [1926]. *Labour migration in England, 1800–1850*. 2d ed. Manchester.
Rich, J. 1976. *Declaring war in the Roman republic in the period of transmarine expansion*. Vol. 149 of Collection Latomus. Brussels.
Rich, J., and G. Shipley, eds. 1993. *War and society in the Roman world*. New York.
Richardson, J. S. 1980. The ownership of Italian land: Tiberius Gracchus and the Italians. *JRS* 70:1–11.
Richardson, L. 1992. *A new topographical dictionary of Rome*. Baltimore and London.
Rickman, G. 1971. *Roman granaries and store-buildings*. Cambridge.
Ridgway, D., and F. Ridgway, eds. 1979. *Italy before the Romans*. London and New York.
Riepl, W. 1913. *Das Nachrichtenwesen des Altertums, mit besonderem Rucksicht auf die Römer*. Leipzig and Berlin.
Riggsby, A. 1999. *Crime and community in Ciceronian Rome*. Austin, TX.
Rilinger, R. 1976. *Der Einfluss des Wahlleiters bei den römischen Konsulwahlen von 366 bis 50 v. Chr.* Munich.
La romanisation du Samnium aux IIe et Ier siècle av. J.C.: Actes du colloque organisé par le Centre Jean Bérard. 1991. Naples.
Rosafio, P. 1993. The emergence of tenancy and the precarium. In *De agricultura: In memoriam P.W. de Neeve*, edited by H. Sancisi-Weerdenburg et al., 164–76. Amsterdam.
Rotondi, G. 1966 [1912]. *Leges publicae populi romani*. Hildesheim.
Rubinsohn, Z. W., and I. Malkin, eds. 1995. *Leaders and masses in the Roman world: Studies in honor of Zvi Yavetz*. Leiden, New York, and Köln.
Ruoff-Väänänen, E. 1978. *Studies on the Italian fora*. Vol. 32. Historia Einzelschriften. Wiesbaden.
Ryberg, I. S. 1955. *Rites of the state religion in Roman art*. Vol. 2 of Papers and Monographs of the American Academy in Rome.
Salmon, E. T. 1967. *Samnium and the Samnites*. Cambridge.
———. 1969. *Roman colonization under the republic*. London.

———. 1982. *The making of Roman Italy*. London.

———. 1988. The Iron Age: The peoples of Italy. In *CAH*. Vol. 4, *Persia, Greece and the western Mediterranean c. 525 to 479 BC*, edited by J. Boardman et al., 676–719. 2d ed. Cambridge.

Sancisi-Weerdenburg, H., R. J. van der Speck, H. C. Teitler, and H. T. Wallinga, eds. 1993. *De agricultura: In memoriam P.W. de Neeve*. Amsterdam.

Sandberg, K. 1993. The concilium plebis as a legislative body. In *Senatus populusque romanus: Studies in Roman republican legislation*, edited by J. Vaahtera, 74–96. Helsinki.

Scheidel, W. 1996. *Measuring sex, age, and death in the Roman empire: Explorations in ancient demography*. *JRA* Supp. 21. Ann Arbor, MI.

Schiller, A. A. 1978. *Roman law: The mechanisms of its development*. New York, The Hague, and Paris.

Schneider, H. 1974. *Wirtschaft und Politik: Untersuchungen zur Geschichte der späten römischen Republik*. Erlangen.

Schulz, F. 1946. *History of Roman legal science*. Oxford.

Scullard, H. H. 1973. *Roman politics, 220–150 BC*. 2d ed. Oxford.

———. 1981. *Festivals and ceremonies of the Roman republic*. London.

Seager, R. 1994. Sulla. In *CAH*. Vol. 9, *The last age of the Roman republic, 146–43 BC*, edited by A. Lintott, J. A. Crook, and E. Rawson, 165–207. 2d ed. Cambridge, New York, New Rochelle, Melbourne, and Sydney.

Sereni, E. 1997 [1962]. *History of the Italian agricultural landscape*. Princeton.

Serrao, F. 1974. *Classi, partiti e legge nella repubblica romana*. Pisa.

Shackleton Bailey, D. R. 1965–70. *Cicero's letters to Atticus*. 7 vols. Cambridge.

Sherwin-White, A. N. 1972. The date of the lex repetundarum and its consequences. *JRS* 62:83–99.

———. 1973. *The Roman citizenship*. 2d ed. Oxford.

———. 1982. The lex repetundarum and the political ideas of Gaius Gracchus. *JRS* 72:18–31.

Skydsgaard, J. E. 1974. Transhumance in ancient Italy. *Analecta Romana Instituti Danici* 7:7–36.

Small, A., ed. 1992. *Gravinia: An Iron Age and Roman republican settlement on Botromagno, Gravina di Puglia, excavations 1965–74*. Vol. 1, *The Site*. Archaeological Monographs of the British School at Rome 5. London.

Smith, C. 1996. *Early Rome and Latium: Economy and society c. 1000–500 BC*. Oxford.

Solin, H. 1983. Lucani e romani nella valle del Tanagro. In *Les "bourgeoisies" municipales italiennes aux IIe et Ier siècles av. J.C.*, 411–14. Paris and Naples.

Spurr, M. S. 1986. *Arable cultivation in Roman Italy, c. 200 BC–c.AD 100*. London.

Stambaugh, J. E. 1988. *The ancient Roman city*. Baltimore.

Staveley, E. S. 1972. *Greek and Roman voting and elections*. London.

Steinby, E. M., ed. 1993–. *Lexicon topographicum urbis Romae*. 6 vols. Rome.

Stewart, R. 1995. Catiline and the crisis of 63–60 BC: The Italian perspective. *Latomus* 54:62–78.

Stouffer, S. A., et al. 1949–50. *The American soldier: Adjustment during army life*. Vol. 1. Princeton, NJ.

Studi sulla città antica: Atti del convegno di studi sulla città etrusca e italica preromana. 1970. Bologna.

Sumner, G. V. 1973. *The orators in Cicero's Brutus*. Toronto.

Suolahti, J. 1952. *Junior officers of the Roman army in the republican period*. Helsinki.

Syme, R. 1939. *The Roman revolution*. Oxford.

———. 1964. The historian Servilius Nonianus. *Hermes* 92:408–14.

Tagliamonte, G. 1997. *I Sanniti: Caudini, Irpini, Pentri, Carricini, Frentani*. Milan.

Talamo, P. 1987. L'Area aurunca nel quadro dell'Italia centromeridionale: Testimonianze archeologiche di età arcaica. *BARS* 384.

Tatum, W. J. 1999. *The patrician tribune: Publius Clodius Pulcher*. Chapel Hill and London.

Taylor, L. R. 1949. *Party politics in the age of Caesar*. Berkeley, Los.Angeles, and London.

———. 1951. On the chronology of Caesar's first consulship. *AJP* 62:254–68.

———. 1960. *The voting districts of the Roman republic*. Vol. 20 of Papers and Monographs of the American Academy in Rome. Rome.

———. 1962. Forerunners of the Gracchi. *JRS* 52:19–27.

———. 1966. *Roman voting assemblies from the Hannibalic war to the dictatorship of Caesar*. Ann Arbor, MI.

Thernstrom, S. 1973. *The other Bostonians*. Cambridge, MA.

Thomas, J. A. C. 1976. *Textbook of Roman law*. Amsterdam, New York, and Oxford.

Tibiletti, G. 1950. Ricerche di storia agraria romana. *Ath*. 28:183–206.

———. 1978. Considerazione sulle popolazioni dell'Italia preromana. In *PCIA*, edited by M. Pallotino et al., 7:15–49. Rome.

Torelli, M. 1989. Archaic Rome between Latium and Etruria. In *CAH*. Vol. 7, part 2, *The rise of Rome to 220 BC*, edited by F. W. Walbank, A. E. Astin, M. W. Frederiksen, and R. M. Ogilvie, 30–51. 2d ed. Cambridge, New York, Port Chester, Melbourne, and Sydney.

Toynbee, A. G. 1965. *Hannibal's legacy: The Hannibalic war's effects on Roman life*. 2 vols. Oxford.

Trapenard, C. 1908. *L'ager scripturarius: Contribution à l'histoire de la propriété collective*. Paris.

Ungern-Sternberg, J. von. 1970. *Untersuchungen zum spätrepublikanischen Notstandsrecht: Senatusconsultum ultimum und hostis-Erklärung*. Munich.

United Nations. Statistical Office. 1958. *Principles and recommendations for national population censuses*. Statistical papers. Series M, No. 27. New York.

Vaahtera, J., ed. 1993. *Senatus populusque romanus: Studies in Roman republican legislation*. Edited by H. Solin. Vol. 13. Acta Instituti Romani Finlandiae. Helsinki.

Vallat, J.-P. 1983. Ager publicus, colonie et territoire agraire en Campanie du nord à l'époque républicaine. In *Cadastres et espace rurale*, edited by M. Clavel-Lévêque, 187–98. Paris.

———. 2001. The romanization of Italy: Conclusions. In *Italy and the west: Comparative issues in romanization*, edited by S. Keay and N. Terrenato, 102–10. Oxford.

Vanderbroeck, P. J. J. 1987. *Popular leadership and collective behavior in the late Roman republic (ca. 80–50 BC)*. Amsterdam.

Vetter, E. 1953. *Handbuch der Italischen Dialekte*. Heidelberg.

Walker, D. S. 1967. *A geography of Italy*. 2d ed. London.

Wallace-Hadrill, A., ed. 1989. *Patronage in ancient society*. London and New York.

Waltzing, J.-P. 1895–1900. *Étude historique sur les corporations professionnelles chez les Romains*. 4 vols. Paris.

Watson, A. 1968. *The law of property in the later Roman republic*. Oxford.

———. 1970. Development of the praetor's edict. *JRS* 60:105–19.

Weber, M. 1891. *Die römische Agrargeschichte*. Stuttgart.

———. 1976. *The agrarian society of ancient civilizations*. Translated by R. I. Frank. London. Originally published as *Agrärverhältnisse im Altertum* in *Handwörterbuch der Staatswissenschaften*, 1.52–188, 3d ed., 1909.

White, K. D. 1973. Roman agricultural writers. In *ANRW*, edited by H. Temporini, I 4:439–97. Berlin and New York

Whittaker, C. R., ed. 1988. *Pastoral economies in classical antiquity*. Cambridge.

Wightman, E. 1981. The Lower Liri Valley: Problems, trends and peculiarities. In *Archaeology and Italian society*, edited by G. Barker and R. Hodges, 275–85. Oxford.

Willems, P. 1885. *Le sénat de la république romaine: Sa composition et ses attributions*. 2 vols. Louvain, Paris, and Berlin.

Williamson, C. 1984. Lawmaking in the comitia of republican Rome: The processes of drafting and disseminating, recording and retrieving laws and plebiscites. Ph.D. diss., University of London.

———. 1987. Monuments of bronze: Roman legal documents on bronze tablets. CA 6:160–83.

———. 1990. The Roman aristocracy and positive law. *CP* 85:266–76; 296–97.

———. 1995. The display of law and archival practice in Rome. In *Acta colloquii epigraphici latini*, edited by H. Solin, O. Salomies, and U.-M. Liertz. Helsinki.

Wilson, S. G. 1996. Voluntary associations: An overview. In *Voluntary associations in the Greco-Roman World*, edited by J. S. Kloppenburg and S. G. Wilson, 1–15. London and New York.

Wirzubski, C. 1950. *Libertas as a political idea at Rome*. Cambridge.

Wiseman, T. P. 1964. Viae Anniae. *PBSR* 32:21–37.

———. 1969a. The census in the first century BC. *JRS* 59:59–75.

———. 1969b. Viae Anniae again. *PBSR* 37:82–91.

———. 1970a. Roman republican road-building. *PBSR* 38:122–52.

———. 1970b. The definition of "eques Romanus" in the late republic and early empire. *Hist*. 19:67–83.

———. 1971. *New men in the Roman senate, 139 BC–AD 14*. Oxford.

———. 1983. Domi nobiles and the Roman cultural elite. In *Les "bourgeoisies" municipales Italiennes aux IIe et Ier siècles av. J.C.*, 299–308. Paris and Naples.

———. 1994. The senate and the populares, 69–60 BC. In CAH. Vol. 9, *The last age of the Roman republic, 146–43 BC*, edited by A. Lintott, J. A. Crook, and E. Rawson, 327–67. 2d ed. Cambridge.

Wonterghem, F. van. 1973. Le culte d'Hercule chez les Paeligni. *Ant. Class*. 42:36–48.

———. 1976. Archäologische Zeugnisse spätrepublikanischer Zeit aus dem Gebiet der Peligner. In *Hellenismus in Mittelitalien*, edited by P. Zanker. Göttingen.

Yakobsen, A. 1992. Petitio et largitio: Popular participation in the centuriate assembly of the late republic. *JRS* 82:32–52.

———. 1993. Dionysius of Halicarnassus on a democratic change in the centuriate assembly. *Scripta Classica Israelica* 12:139–55.

———. 1999. *Elections and electioneering in Rome*. Vol. 128. Historia Einzelschriften. Stuttgart.

Yavetz, Z. 1983. *Julius Caesar and his public image*. Ithaca, NY.

Zanker, P., ed. 1976. *Hellenismus in Mittelitalien*. Göttingen.

Zubrow, E., and J. Robinson. 1999. Chance and the human population: Population growth in the Mediterranean. In *Reconstructing past population trends in Mediterranean Europe*, edited by J. Bintliff and K. Sbonias, 133–44. Oxford.

Index